VOCE MEA

D. DIONYSIVS CARTHVSIEÑ
DOCTOR EXTATICVS.

BENEDIC
TVS DEVS
IN SECVIA

VOCE MEA

DENIS THE CARTHUSIAN

COMMENTARY
on the
DAVIDIC
Psalms

VOLUME IV
[PSALMS 76–100]

*Which are most learnedly explained, to the degree able,
in their multiple senses, namely* LITERAL, ALLEGORICAL,
TROPOLOGICAL, *&* ANAGOGICAL, *with nothing except
the most sound Scriptures of both Testaments.*

Translation & Introduction by
ANDREW M. GREENWELL

AROUCA
PRESS

Commentary in Latin taken from
Opera Omnia, Vol. 6
(Montreuil: Typis Cartusiae S. M. de Pratis 1898).
English Translation & Introduction © Andrew M. Greenwell
Copyright © Arouca Press 2023

ISBN: 978-1-99068-5-47-7 (pbk)
ISBN: 978-1-99068-5-50-7 (hardcover)

Arouca Press
PO Box 55003
Bridgeport PO
Waterloo, ON N2J3G0
Canada
www.aroucapress.com
Send inquiries to info@aroucapress.com

DEDICATION

To my children,
Elizabeth Grace, Mary Abigail, and Christopher Michael

Ecce haereditas Domini, filii; merces, fructus ventris.
Sicut sagittae in manu potentis, ita filii excussorum.
Beatus vir qui implevit desiderium suum ex ipsis:
non confundetur cum loquetur inimicis suis in porta.
— Psalm 126:3–5

And to my grandchildren,
Piper Feliz, Ryder James, Blaise Francisco, Zephyr
Amoreena, Roque Telemachus, Caio Augustus,
Fisher Invenio, Rainer Ignatius, and Jesse Radix.

Ecce sic benedicetur homo qui timet Dominum . . .
videas filio filorum tuorum.
— Psalm 127:4, 6

In the Psalms are expressed and interwoven joy and suffering, the longing for God, and the perception of our own unworthiness, happiness, and feeling of abandonment, trust in God and sorrowful loneliness, fullness of life and fear of death. The whole reality of the believer converges in these prayers.

—Pope Benedict XVI,
Audience, June 22, 2011

CONTENTS

ABBREVIATIONS

DS Heinrich Denziger, *Enchiridion Symbolorum Definitionum et Declarationum de Rebus Fidei et Morum* (*Compendium of Creeds, Definitions, and Déclarations on Matters of Faith and Morals*) (P. Hünerman, ed.) (Robert Fastiggi and Anne Englund Nash, eds., Eng. ed.) (43rd ed.) (San Francisco: Ignatius Press 2012).

PG *Patrologiae cursus completus. Series Graeca.* Ed. J.-P. Migne. Paris: Migne, 1857–1886.

PL *Patrologiae cursus completus. Series Latina.* Ed. J.-P. Migne. Paris: Migne, 1844–1864.

ST St. Thomas Aquinas, *Summa Theologiae* (corpusthomisticum.org)

CCC Catechism of the Catholic Church

INTRODUCTION
to
DENIS THE CARTHUSIAN'S
Commentary on the Psalms

PART 4
[PSALMS 76–100]

[A]nyone who does not know God, even though he may enter-
tain all kinds of hopes, is ultimately without hope, without the
great hope that sustains the whole of life. Man's great, true
hope which holds firm in spite of all disappointments can only
be God — God who has loved us and who continues to love
us "to the end," until all "is accomplished." Homo indiget Deo,
aliter sine spe manet.[1]

N THE INTRODUCTION TO VOLUME 1 TO THE
Commentary of the Davidic Psalms by Denis the Carthusian, I provided a general overview of the *Commentary's* qualities or characteristics
which distinguish it from its historical predecessors and successors. In
the Introduction to Volume 2, I addressed the issue of a fundamental
theological doctrine that underlies the entire commentarial project of
Denis, namely, that the human nature of Jesus, from the first moment
of his human existence, was graced with both infused knowledge and—
most importantly—with the beatific vision. Relying on this received and
settled doctrine, Denis believed that Jesus, in his human nature, from
the first instant of his human life, saw God face-to-face, and knew all
things, as St. Thomas Aquinas expressed it, "in the Word." It would
not be an exaggeration to say that this robust understanding of Jesus
Christ—an extension of Chalcedon—is the theological backbone of
Denis's *Commentary*. Lastly, in the Introduction to Volume 3, I discussed
the so-called *facientibus* principle, a generally accepted theological axiom

---

1   Benedict XVI, *Spe salvi*, 27, 23 ("Man needs God, otherwise, he remains without
hope.").

whose theological ancestry is lost to us, but one particularly popular during the *devotio moderna*. Denis adopted it in its Thomistic form, laundering it from any possible stain of Pelagianism or neo-Pelagianism, and it is found peppered throughout the *Commentary*.

In this introduction to Volume 4, however, I would like to address another principle which is also found peppered, though perhaps with less relish, throughout the *Commentary*. Unlike the *facientibus* principle, which was not of Dionysian origin, this principle appears to be one of Dionysian invention. The phrase I would like to dwell on in this introduction is: "the word of good hope," *verbum bonae spei*.[2] As far as I have been able to garner, this phraseology is unique to Denis. It is used on occasion in the *Commentary of the Psalms*,[3] but used sufficiently frequently for me to have noticed its recurrence. It is also found in his other scriptural commentaries.[4]

In addressing what Denis means by *word of good hope*, we should begin with the watershed distinction between the natural virtue of hope and the supernatural virtue of hope. Following St. Thomas Aquinas, Denis would have distinguished between *natural* hope (hope as an irascible passion) and the *supernatural* theological virtue of hope, a supernatural habit infused by God. As will be clear from the context when Denis uses the phrase *word of good hope*, he speaks of the supernatural theological virtue of hope.[5] We are not dealing with the natural appetitive power which seeks a future good which is difficult but possible to obtain, an appetitive power shared by animals to a

---

2   On occasion, Denis uses the plural: *verba bonae spei*, words of good hope.

3   *See* Commentary to Psalms in Volume 1 (*Beatus Vir*): 4:4, 5:8, 11:8, 15:11; Volume 2 (*Dominus Illuminatio Mea*): 29:13, 33:21; Volume 3 (*Quid Gloriaris*): Ps. 61:9; Volume 4 (*Voce Mea*); Ps. 91:11; Volume 5 (*Domine Exaudi*): 114:1 (as yet unpublished), and Volume 6 (*Nisi Dominus*): 138:18 (as yet unpublished). They will be referred to by Volume and page (if published at the time of this Introduction), otherwise by Article and Psalm and verse.

4   *See* Commentary to Gen. 24:7, Is. 64:5, Micah 7:7, 1 Macc. 3:22, and Rom. 14:4. It is also used in Denis's *Commentary* on the Prayer of Manasseh which is treated at the end of his *Commentary* on 2 Chronicles. References to these are to Doctoris Ecstatici D. Dionysii Cartusiani *Opera Omnia*, which will be referred as *Opera Dionysii Cartusiani*, followed by volume and page.

5   That is not to say that there are not analogies between the natural passion of hope and the theological virtue of hope. They are not entirely equivocal concepts. The passion of hope is an appetitive power which seeks a future good difficult, but possible, to obtain. ST IaIIae, q. 40, art. 1, co. & art. 2, co. As Garrigou-Lagrange notes, St. Thomas uses his "doctrine on the passion of hope . . . analogically in his study of the infused virtue of hope." Réginald Garrigou-Lagrange, *Reality: A Synthesis of Thomistic Thought* (London: Herder, 1950), ch. 46 (herein *Reality*).

degree,[6] and one that abounds even in young men and drunkards, as St. Thomas points out.[7]

No, while the hope Denis speaks of does involve youth and inebriation, it is not temporal youth and alcohol that spur it. Rather, the hope Denis has in mind involves God, the God whose altar we approach, and who gives joy to our spiritual youth, the God whom we command ourselves to hope in in the Psalm verse used at the foot of the altar. *Hope in God, spera in Deo*, we tell our wavering, fickle, needful souls. (Ps. 42:4, 6) It is the God that we approach with intoxication, but one of a whole different order: it is the sober inebriation of the Spirit, the *sobriam ebrietatem Spiritus*.

So the hope Denis deals with is of another order entirely. It is not "the greater and lesser hopes that keep us going day by day," naturally-based hopes which "are not enough without the great hope, which must surpass everything else."[8] When referring to the *word of good hope*, Denis is speaking of the "great hope," which "can only be God, who encompasses the whole of reality and who can bestow upon us what we, by ourselves, cannot attain."[9] It is a hope founded upon the *supernatural* theological virtue of hope. The hope Denis deals with pertains to God: it is given by God, it is preserved by God, its object is God, and it leads to God as its end. In the succinct formulation of St. Thomas Aquinas, this hope "attains God himself, on whose help it leans."[10] Its object is "in one way, eternal happiness, and in another way, the divine assistance."[11] With this initial understanding in mind, let us explore Denis's use of the term in his *Commentary on the Davidic Psalms*.

Urged by a prevenient hope in God, one already founded in at least incipient charity, the man with the *word of good hope* can say without presumption or superstition, *the Lord will hear me when I shall cry out to him.* (Ps. 4:4) "This," Denis tells us, "is the word of good hope which is born out of the love of God. For he who loves God, firmly hopes, and God will not deny to him any of those things that incline to true salvation." The *word of good hope*, then, "is the hope of attaining the grace of the Lord, by which we are made holy and by which we are glorified by him."[12] Clearly, the love of God — charity — is at the center of the *word*

---

6   ST IaIIae, q. 40, art. 3.
7   ST IaIIae, q. 40, art. 6.
8   *Spe salvi*, 31.
9   *Spe salvi*, 31.
10   ST IIaIIae, q. 17, art. 1, co.
11   ST IIaIIae, q. 17, art. 7, co.
12   Volume I, p. 88.

of good hope. Unquestionably, then, we are dealing with a supernatural virtue, and not a natural one.

Moreover, the *word of good hope* is found in the man who disdains the works of iniquity; therefore, he is already turned away from worldly things and turned to God. He lives a life with an *aversio a creatura* and a *conversio ad Deum*, a turning away from disordered love of the created order, and a conversion to God. This man is marching forward with an end in view and, even in the midst of suffering adversity and encountering adversaries (including himself), he is making progress. Yet during the course of this pilgrimage, he is not foolish enough to rely upon his own strength in his efforts at preserving or increasing this state of grace. Rather, in a spirit of prayer and humility, he must recognize his weakness and his absolute dependence upon the mercy and grace of God for any hope in persevering in this state and having any expectation of progress and reaching the heavenly fatherland. He seeks refuge *in the multitude of [God's] mercy,* for he knows there is no refuge in himself. (Ps. 5:8). And so he learns that "[a] first essential setting for learning hope is prayer."[13]

Seeking refuge in the multitude of God's mercy means that God will supply his grace, so that the Christian prays thus: *I will come into your house,* so that *I will worship towards your holy temple,* and I will do so *in [God's] fear.* (Ps. 5:8) This refuge of clemency, this house of mercy, this holy temple, is nothing other than Christ's mystical body, the Church, where alone the fullness of truth and of grace is found. The Christian seeks refuge and confesses the reason why he has the felt need to enter into the house of God: "so that I might be delivered from . . . sins and punishments, that I may persevere in your grace, and I may round out my life with a blessed end."[14] It is the hope of the Christian *in via,* who walks not in the counsel of the ungodly, stands not in the way of sinners, and sits not in the chair of pestilence; rather, his delight is in the law of the Lord.[15] A man in mortal sin, a man spiritually dead, a man outside the Church, cannot have the *word of good hope.* The necessary Dionysian concomitant to the Cyprian dogma *extra ecclesiam nulla spes salutis* is *extra ecclesiam nullum verbum bonae spei,* outside the Church there is no word of good hope. "This is the word of good hope," Denis concludes, "or so it can be understood by means of prayer."[16]

---

13   *Spe salvi,* 32.
14   Volume I, p. 103.
15   Ps. 1:1–2.
16   Volume I, p. 103.

Denis thus instructs us that the *word of good hope* necessarily implies a life of prayer, but not all prayer. The *word of good hope* is not to be found amidst hackneyed, rote, superficial, mindless, hurried prayers, abuses of prayer he constantly warns against in the *Commentary*, especially in his perorations at the conclusion of the commentary with each Psalm. The *word of good hope* is not found in the prayer of pagans who "heap up empty phrases," who "use . . . vain repetitions," who "keep on babbling," who are "verbose," and who hope vainly that they we will be heard thereby,[17] for all the gods of the Gentiles are devils.[18] The *word of good hope* is not found amidst the foul fog of the "double, double toil and trouble" of superstitious incantations and magical formulae.[19] The *word of good hope* is not found in the mesmerizing atheistic Buddhist chant or the pantheistic or panentheistic Hindu Om. The *word of good hope* is not found praying to the monomaniacal and lonely Allah of Islam, who neither loves paternally nor seeks filial love, but demands raw submission, an *obedientia nuda*, stripped of all reason, disdainful of any need for redemption, and ignorant of the virtue of charity. No. Among these prayers and among these people and among these gods the *word of good hope* is not to be found. "To come to know God—the true God—means to receive hope." For "God is the foundation of hope: not any god, but the God who has a human face," that is to say Jesus Christ, "and who has loved us to the end, each one of us and humanity in its entirety."[20]

So the *word of good hope* arises with intensive, sincere, yearning, personal prayers firmly anchored in trust in the true God, the God of Abraham, Isaac, and Jacob *per Christum Dominum nostrum*. In Christ and to Christ, the faithful prays: *You, O Lord, will preserve us: and keep us from this generation forever.* (Ps. 11:8) "And this is the word of good hope" says Denis, and it is "implicitly a *certain kind* of prayer," namely, one that has this tenor, this sentiment, this plea: "You, O Lord, will protect us, that is, out of the love and great trust that I place in you, O Lord, I hope that you will protect us: indeed, I pray this intently."[21]

Perhaps the centerpiece of the *word of good hope* is Psalm 15. This Psalm recognizes man's great need for God. He who prays this Psalm begs to be preserved from sin, and in hopes of such preservation puts his trust entirely in God. (Ps. 15:1). He recognizes his own nothingness

---

17   Matt. 6:7 (NRSVCE), (KJV), (NIV), (ABPE).
18   Ps. 95:5.
19   Macbeth, IV, sc. 1.
20   *Spe Salvi*, No. 3. 31.
21   Volume 1, p. 208.

before God: "For in you is the perfect and immense perfection of all good and all beautiful and desirable things," as Denis states. With full awareness of his nothingness before God, the faithful prays in this way with the *word of good hope*: "I hope in you, and I submit to you, God alone, for you are sufficient to yourself in yourself and by yourself, and you, who in no manner are in need of me, alone are able to save me."[22] The man with the *word of good hope* desires God to be his inheritance, seeks God above all created goods, strives constantly under the influence of grace to convert to and make progress towards him, and gives all honor and glory to him, to *set the Lord always* [in his] *sight*. (Ps. 15:8) He puts his trust in God, he seeks communion with the saints, and he avoids the conventicles of the men "who are vicious for blood."[23] He seeks the Lord as his inheritance, he blesses the Lord for the understanding he has received from him, and even for his correction. It is in this way that he learns from him the ways of eternal life, and so he rejoices in God and entrusts him with his eternal destiny. He rejoices in God, rests in hope, and trusts that he will be spared the horrors of hell, and enjoy the bliss of heaven. (Ps. 15:4–11) "All these," Denis says, "are *words of good hope*, and thus implicitly are the words to be used by all persons praying."[24]

Denis also warns us that the *word of good hope* is not to be found with the "incautiously presumptuous" man, something frequently found with the "newly-converted" or with those "not thinking sufficiently" of their own weakness and need for God.[25] Nor will it be found in the man who hubristically supposes either Pelagian self-sufficiency, Stoic fortitude or dispassion, or relies the availability of "a grace that comes cheap."[26] It is not found in the one who says in the abundance of his pride and folly, *I shall never be moved*. (Ps. 29:7) Rather, he must be a man "not troubled with an evil conscience," a contemplative man who strives to be holy, a grateful man, one "thankful to the Lord," eagerly looking toward eternity as his end, and desiring to "sing to the Lord his glory."[27] He is the man who says: *Domine Deus meus, in aeternum confitebor tibi. O Lord my God, I will give praise to your forever.* (Ps. 29:13) "[T]his is the word of good hope and the holy undertaking," Denis says.

---

22   Volume I, p. 252.

23   Volume I, p. 253.

24   Volume I, p. 253.

25   Volume 2, p. 65.

26   Joseph Cardinal Ratzinger, Mass *Pro Eligendo Romano Pontifice*, Homily, April 18, 2005.

27   Volume 2, p. 68.

This is a hope and it is entirely unlike that counterfeit double of hope "bursting forth," like puss from some hubristic boil, "from an abundance of presumption."[28]

The soul of the man with the *word of good hope* must confide in, and wait upon, the Lord as his helper and protector. He must trustingly hope and hopingly trust *in his holy name* (Ps. 33:21). And here particularly one must hope for hope; that is, the Christian must realize that hope is not something engendered by him, like an Indian rubbing two sticks can make a fire, but something that is given by God, like lightning from the sky, and which must be sought in prayer. "The fact that it comes to us a gift is actually part of hope."[29] *In his holy name we have trusted*, says the Psalm. "But this we can in no manner do," Denis explains, "unless the Lord himself gives us help. And this is the word of good hope and holy undertaking—not of presumption or out of trust in our own perfection."[30]

In his peroration following his tropological commentary on Psalm 60, Denis refers to the "words of good hope" of the Psalm by which "our pious resolution is inflamed."[31] The subject matter of Psalm 60 is a plea to God to be *attentive* to one's prayer. It is an invocation to God in *anguish* when confronted by enemies of salvation, and yet one firmly planted in *hope* and trust in God the *tower of strength*. It is a bold plea to God to scrutinize the sincerity of the one praying. It acknowledges the need to walk in conformity with the commandments of God, to *pay one's vows from day to day*, in full recognition of the need of God's grace to do so. It acknowledges the vital need for membership in the Church, the *tabernacle* of God to be protected *under the covert* of the *wings* of God, so as to become part of the *inheritance* of those *that fear* God's name. It looks towards the reward of the blessed in heaven where one my abide *forever in the sight of God*. (Ps. 60:1-9).[32]

Reliance upon the grace of God will allow the Christian not only to preserve his salvation, but also to flourish and make progress in the spiritual life. This is also the *word of good hope*. As Psalm 91:11 puts it: *my horn shall be exalted like that of a unicorn*. Denis comments on this verse by saying that "the empire of my reason, ruling over my sensuality and inclinations, is raised up by the confirmation of the grace of God, as a

---

28 Volume 2, p. 68.
29 *Spe salvi*, 31.
30 Volume 2, p. 131.
31 Volume 3, p. 200.
32 Volume 3, pp. 195-200.

unicorn is raised up by his horn: for this animal is most strong.... So my horn, that is, my fortitude or the dominion of my reason, is strengthened against all assaulting passions, temptations, and persecutions. For in the day of judgment, the horn of the soul will be so exalted in the elect that the flesh never will desire against the spirit, nor will anything hinder the act of reason.... And *though our outward man is corrupted, yet the inward man is renewed day by day* by the grace of God, according to the Apostle [Paul]. These things are the words of good hope, and not of unfounded presumption: because these things are said by the Church and by any just man out of the mind's ardent charity and a great trust in God."[33]

The Lord will hear the voice of my prayer, writes the Psalmist. (Ps. 114:1) "This is a word of good hope," Denis tells us. He explains why: "For we ought to hope in all things that God will not regard our prayers vain." But there is a caveat to this: this is true only "as long as we ask for that which we ought to seek; otherwise, that which James says befits us: *You ask, and receive not, because you ask amiss.* (James 4:3) Now such a petition neither truly nor properly is able to be called prayer, because prayer (according to the Damascene) is the petition to God for something befitting."[34] "In prayer," Pope Benedict XVI said, "we must learn what we can truly ask of God—what is worthy of God."[35]

Finally, in his *Commentary* on Psalm 138:18, Denis states: "*I rose up* by your grace from the death of sin, from depraved habits, from the sleep of slothfulness, *and I am still with you*, faithfully adhering to you by charity." "This," Denis tells us, "is the word of good hope." Yet as he says—consonant with the Council of Trent which was more than 100 years in the future—"[W]e are not able to know this with any certainty, but only conjecturally, unless by a special inspiration."[36] Yet, Denis would agree with Garrigou-Lagrange that "in the *chiaro oscuro* of life here below, grace, which is a participation of the Deity, tranquillizes the just man, and the inspirations of the Holy Spirit console him, strengthen his hope, and make his love more pure, disinterested, and strong, so that in the incertitude of salvation he has the ever-growing certitude of hope, which is a certitude of tendency toward salvation. The proper and formal object of infused hope is not, in fact, our own effort, but the infinite mercy of the 'God who aids us.'"[37]

---

33   Volume 4, p. 374.
34   Volume 5, Article XXIV (Psalm 114 :1) (yet unpublished).
35   *Spe salvi*, 33.
36   Volume 6, Article LV (Psalm 138:18) (yet unpublished).
37   *Reality*, ch. 11.

In fathoming more deeply the notion of the *word of good hope*, we can profitably turn to other mentions of the phrase in the Dionysian commentarial corpus. If we do so, we see the *word of good hope* among the patriarchs and fathers. For example, the *word of good hope* is found with "our father in faith,"[38] Abraham, who had been told that the promised land would be given to his seed, that God would send an angel before him, and that a son would be given Sarah his wife.[39] In his *Commentary on Genesis*, Denis points out that, as a result of his faith in the promises of future doings by God, Abraham "knew of the future," and this prophetic word was "the *word of good hope* in God." That is, we can find the *word of good hope* in the revelations and the promises of God who can neither deceive nor be deceived.[40] Faith and hope are so closely twinned, that they might be called cousins-german: as Pope Benedict observed in his Encyclical *Spe Salvi*, "in several passages" in the Scriptures "the words 'faith' and 'hope' seem interchangeable."[41] Indeed, sometimes "hope" is equivalent to "faith."

We also find the *word of good hope* with Judas Maccabeus, the man of leonine courage, in the midst of his military victories over Apollonius and Seron. The Jewish general trusted in God before he did soldier, chariot, and horse.[42] Unlike Napoleon, whom De Tocqueville described as being "as great as a man can be without virtue,"[43] Judas, a man of great virtue and faith, did not think that an army marches principally on its stomach. *For the success of war*, the Maccabean leader told his men, *is not in the multitude of the army*, or in quartermasters and their provisions, *but strength comes from heaven*. (1 Macc. 3:19). Fueled by this courage, and nourished by the virtue of fortitude and prophetic fervor, Judas Maccabeus promised his men: *And the Lord himself will overthrow the enemies before our face*. (1 Macc. 3:22) "This was a *word of good hope*," Denis observes in his commentary, for "indeed it was brought forth by divine inspiration."[44] And Lord delivers on his promises. We might think of this when we pray to God: *Benedictus Dominus Deus meus, qui docet manus meas ad praelium, et digitos meos ad bellum. Blessed be the Lord my God, who teaches my hands to fight and my fingers to war*. (Ps. 143:1)

---

38   Gal. 3:6.
39   Gen. 24:7.
40   *Opera Dionysii Cartusiani*, Vol. 1, p. 296.
41   *Spe salvi*, 2.
42   Cf. Ps. 20:7.
43   Hugh Brogan, *Alexis de Tocqueville: A Life* (New Haven: Yale, 2006), 404.
44   *Opera Dionysii Cartusiani*, Vol. 5, p. 282.

The *word of good hope* is that God will provide us the grace to overthrow the enemies of our salvation before our face.

The *word of good hope* is not only found with the wandering Aramean and the stalwart Maccabean general, but we also find the notion of the *word of good hope* with the prophets and the apostles, especially when they proclaim the Gospel of salvation. And this makes consummate sense since we who live in the evangelical dispensation know: *spe salvi facti sumus*, in hope we are saved (Rom. 8:24).

Isaiah states to the Lord: *Behold you are angry, and we have sinned; in them we have been always, and we shall be saved.* (Is. 64:5b) In light of this Isaian pericope, "We must," Denis insists, "always pray to the Lord that he might mercifully precede (*praeveniat*), take away the occasions of sin, and chastise us in a fatherly way. *In them*, in our sins, *we have been always*, when your grace has been withdrawn from us — indeed, we fall daily, and *if we say that we have no sin, we deceive ourselves.* (1 John 1:8). For *no one is clean from stain, not even the infant who has lived but one day.* (Job 14:4–5 LXX). *And we shall be saved* by your grace which anticipates our needs (*nos praevenientem*). This is the word of good hope."[45] God is the God of forecoming, of prevenience: he bests us, firsts us, he anticipates us. God's grace may be our rearguard; but is also our vanguard.

Something similar is found in Micah 7:7. That prophet proclaims: *But I will look towards the Lord, I will wait for God my Savior: my God will hear me.* Denis expounds on this: "But *I* Micah, *will look towards the Lord*, contemplating, loving, and venerating the most high God with the eye of the heart, and reflecting upon his mercy and his justice, just as is written in the Psalm, *My eyes are ever towards the Lord* (Ps. 24:15); and also *To you have I lifted up my eyes, who dwell in heaven.* (Ps. 122:1).... And *I will wait for God my Savior*, that is, I will hope in him in the present moment, and I will await patiently his mercy, and my trust shall not be broken by any adversity.... *And my God will hear me*, that is, he will hear my prayers. This is the word of good hope, by which the previously-mentioned fruits are grasped, and the confidence of our hope given to us."[46] The ear of God is most attuned, and the *word of good hope* is deafening as it were to God, when one prays to God as Savior.

This *word of good hope* mentioned in Isaiah and Micah, this *word of good hope* in the God who wishes all men to be saved,[47] the God who does not desire a sinner to die, but rather that he return to him from

---

45   *Opera Dionysii Cartusiani*, Vol. 8, p. 746.
46   *Opera Dionysii Cartusiani*, Vol. 10, p. 508.
47   1 Tim. 2:4.

his errant ways,[48] is also echoed in the second book of Chronicles. In Denis's *Commentary* of that book, he handles the beautiful apocryphal Prayer of Manasseh, what might be called the standard or epitome of all penitential prayers. At the end of *Commentary on Second Chronicles*, Denis observes: "Therefore so humbly and contritely, so fervently and attentively praying, [Manasseh] senses in himself, by the most gracious touch from the Holy Spirit, a certain hope of forgiveness, and so he trustingly adds: *For unworthy as I am, you will save me according to your great mercy*, which is infinitely greater than all our depravity and misery: and this is the word of good hope, not of careless assertion, for he is not yet certain that he worthy of love and of predestination."[49] While the mercy of God is gratuitous, and though we ought to approach the throne of grace with confidence (*cf.* Heb. 4:16), we must recognize that God does not operate as if he were a free vending machine. Mercy comes from the living God, the *Deus viventium*, not a *deus ex machina*.

Finally, we can turn to Denis's *Commentary* on St. Paul's letter to the Romans to help us see that the *word of good hope* can be found in the most unlikely situations. The Apostle Paul asks the Romans rhetorically: *Who are you that judges another man's servant? To his own lord he stands or falls. And he shall stand: for God is able to make him stand.* (Rom. 14:4). The *word of good hope* is what drives the chastisement of St. Paul. It is the *word of good hope*, Denis tells us, that allows the other man's servant to stand. It is because of the *word of good hope* that the man's servant "will be lifted upon in heart to God and will do rightly." This *word of good hope* is of such supernatural vigor, that it is as if St. Paul had said, "this you are able in piety to presume, that he would stand even if he is already seen fallen."[50] *For God is able to make him stand*, that is, to raise him up by grace from the fall of sin, so that—when it comes to salvation from sin—there is no room for despair. We ought to recall that God can make children of Abraham from stones.[51] And, as Curé d'Ars reminds us, contrition and salvation can come between the bridge and the water.

Gathering together the clues from the various mentions of the *word of good hope* in the Dionysian commentarial corpus, we might summarize as follows. The *word of good hope* refers to the supernatural virtue of hope, not the natural virtue. Once we enter the inner sanctum of

---

48 Ez. 18:23.
49 *Opera Dionysii Cartusiani*, Vol. 4, p. 278.
50 *Opera Dionysii Cartusiani*, Vol. 13, p. 104.
51 Matt. 3:9.

supernatural hope, however, we get into the distinction between a *spes formata caritatis*, a hope formed by charity, and a *spes informis cartitatis*, a hope not formed by charity. Is the *word of good hope*, a hope based upon a *spes informis* or one based upon a *spes formata*?[52]

In further investigating Denis's notion of a *word of good hope*, and whether we are dealing with a *spes formata* or a *spes informis*, we might turn to the *Summa Theologiae* of Alexander of Hales (*ca.* 1185–1245) and the *Summa Theologiae* of St. Thomas (1227–1274) for some guidance. For Alexander, the *spes informis* is hope that is not accompanied by the theological virtue of charity, a hope *quae non habet sociam charitatem*.[53] On the other hand, formed hope, as Alexander explains in his *Summa*, cannot be presumption, since it is founded upon charity; it is a hope that comes from grace and earns merit. In a way, it is already participating in eternity. On the other hand, the infused virtue of hope *can* exist without charity (if one has not sinned against hope — through presumption or despair), but in such case — like unformed faith — hope is dead.[54] It is a lifeless appendage of the theological virtue that avails a man little; a shadow of an infused virtue; a potentiality of virtue. It presupposes no sanctifying grace, but only a remnant of faith, a faith that is itself dead without charity. For without faith, there is absolutely no hope — formed or unformed — since hope relies upon faith.[55] After all, *faith is the substance of things to be hoped for*, and so hope has not object to hope in without faith giving it one. (Heb. 11:1)

Any reliance upon an unformed hope is presumption. A *spes informis*, a faith not accompanied by, conjoined by, partnered with charity, is not, in Denis's words, the *word of good hope*. Like a faith informed by charity, a *fides formata*, the *word of good hope* is accompanied by conversion, by works, by following the commandments, by prayer, by a serious commitment to make progress in the Christian life. And hope without these

---

52   "All theologians admit and the Church has defined that the state of mortal sin does not prevent the sinner from having 'uninformed' acts of faith and hope, which acts are personally supernatural and salutary, although not meritorious." *Reality*, ch. 41.

53   Alexander of Hales, *Summa Theologiae* (Venice: 1575), IIIa, q. 65, mm. 1–3, pp. 177–78.

54   *Cf.* James 2 :17. ST IIaIIae, q. 18, art. 3, ad 2. "Infused hope, like infused faith, can be lost only by a sin contrary to itself, *i.e.*, by a mortal sin either of despair or of presumption. But though it remains in the soul under mortal sin, it does not remain in a state of virtue, because the soul deprived of grace is not a connatural subject of virtue." *Reality*, ch. 50, art. 3.

55   As St. Thomas Aquinas says, "absolutely speaking, faith precedes hope." This is so because faith is what holds out the possibility of eternal life and of God that provides us aid to achieve it. ST IIIa, q. 17, art. 7, co.

works, a hope not animated by the love of God, is dead. We might paraphrase St. Augustine: *Sine caritate quippe spes potest quidem esse, sed non prodesse*, without charity hope can indeed exist, but it avails one nothing.[56] Therefore, a hope bereft of charity is an empty hope, a foolish hope, a cheap hope, a trinket of hope; in fine, foolish optimism. It is the theological equivalent of trying to clap with one hand. It is *having no hope of the promise, and without God in this world*. (Eph. 2:12) It is certainly not the *word of good hope* that Denis has in mind.

One reason why an unformed hope is not a *word of good hope* is that an unformed hope — a hope without sanctifying grace — cannot cast out fear of damnation: there is only judgment and justice and not mercy and grace. If the judgment of God "were merely justice, in the end it could bring only fear to us all."[57] But *perfect love casts out fear*, St. John tells us.[58] Therefore, an unformed hope — a hope not accompanied by charity, which is perfect love — is not hope in any live sense, since it is a hope that *cannot cast out fear*, and so it is a foolish, dead hope indeed. But graced with charity, the judgment of God is transformed and with it comes a formed hope, a *word of good hope*. "The judgment of God" becomes "hope, both because it is justice and because it is grace."[59]

Moreover, an unformed hope is one that may be found in inveterate sinners as long as they are *in via*, though it is nowhere to be found in the reprobate following their damnation or in the devil who is already damned.[60] Here we might turn towards the *Sentences* of Peter Lombard, which Alexander appeared to have done in discussing the virtue of hope. Peter Lombard sets forth the classical distinction between the three kinds of faith:

> For it is one thing to believe in God, another to believe in a God, and yet another to believe God. To believe God (*credere Deo*) is to believe that what he says is true, which the evil ones also do; and we believe also a man, but not in a man. To believe

---

56 *Cf.* St. Augustine, *De Trinitate*, XXV, 18 : *Sine caritate quippe fides potest quidem esse, sed non et prodesse*. ("Without charity faith can indeed exist, but it avails one nothing").

57 *Spe salvi*, 47.

58 1 John 4:18.

59 *Spe salvi*, 47.

60 ST IIaIIae, q. 18, art. 3, ad 2. Though "lifeless faith" can exist in the devils and damned souls (the reprobate), that is not true for hope. A "lifeless hope" does not exist among the damned because "hope is only about good things, future and concerning oneself."

in a God (*credere Deum*) is to believe that he is God, which
the evil ones also do. To believe in God (*credere in Deum*) is
to love by believing, to go to him by believing, to adhere to
him by believing and to be incorporated into his members.[61]

Analogizing from this three-fold distinction of faith, Alexander of
Hales finds a similar three-fold distinction in hope. There is *sperare Deo*,
sperare Deum, and *sperare in Deum*, to hope God, to hope in a God, and
to hope in God. Similar to unformed faith — which the evil man *in via*
can have — so to hope God and to hope in a God is unformed hope; in
a supernatural sense, these avail exactly nothing. On the other hand, to
hope in God — *sperare in Deum* — is, to adapt the words of the Lombard,
to love God by hoping, to go to God by hoping, to adhere to God by
hoping. This is equivalent to the Dionysian *word of good hope*.[62] Denis's
word of good hope, then, presupposes a supernatural love of God. It is a
formed hope, *spes formata*, a hope formed in charity, a hope "in which
one hopes from God because He loves and is loved."[63]

There is no better a way to nourish the *word of good hope* than by
praying the Psalms in the Spirit of Christ under the guidance of Denis
the Carthusian. The Psalms prayed in the spirit of Christ are calculated,
as it were, to lead and give increase to the *word of good hope*, that particular species of hope that is obtained as a gift of God by relying entirely
upon God, becoming a member of Christ's mystical body, frequenting
the Church's sacraments, placing great stock in the Lord's mercy, having
confidence in him and his promises, humbly entrusting one's life to him,
striving to please him by obeying his commandments, praying intently to
him in the prayers of confession, thanksgiving, and praise, and looking
toward the eternal felicity that God has promised to those who love
him.[64] It is my prayer, and the hope of my translating efforts, that my

---

61   *Sentences* III, dist. 23, ch. 4.
62   We should point out that while the damned souls and devils have unformed "faith"
without charity in eternal hell, this is not the case for hope. All hope entirely disap-
pears to the eternally damned. It is not mere poetics, but good theology, when Dante
had written over the gates of hell in his *Inferno*: *Lasciate ogni speranza, voi ch'entrate*,
"abandon all hope you who enter here." Canto 3, 9. This is so because the damned know
that there is no means to escape their fate and obtain happiness, therefore, happiness
is an unrealizable good, which extinguishes all hope. ST IIaIIae, q. 18, art. 3.
63   John J. Elmendorf, S. T. D., *Elements of Moral Theology Based on the Summa
Theologiae of St. Thomas Aquinas* (New York: James Pott & Co., 1892), 178.
64   In the words of Garrigou-Lagrange, the *word of good hope* would require in an
adult the admixture of the following virtues: faith, filial fear, love, contrition, firm
proposal of amendment of life, humility. *Reality*, chp. 49, art. 6.

readers might attain and maintain, through the words of Denis rendered into English, that *word of good hope* which should accompany us while on this pilgrim way and should allow us to hear those words we should all desire: *Well done, good and faithful servant ... Enter into the joy of your Lord.* (Matt. 25:23).

ACKNOWLEDGMENTS

As always, I want to thank Alex Barbas with Arouca Press for pursuing the endeavor of making Denis's Commentary on the Davidic Psalms available to the English-speaking audience. His hard work and dedication to this project has made this fourth volume possible. I again thank my wife Betsy, who has patiently endured the demands of this project. Again, I thank Cindi, my legal assistant, for her thankless task of proofreading this text. Finally, I appreciate the continued recommendations of Bishop Daniel Flores of Brownsville, Texas, of Deacon Keith Fournier of Tyler, Texas, Dom Hugh Knapman, OSB, of Douai Abbey, Dom Pius Mary Noonan, OSB, of Notre Dame Prior, Abbot Philip Anderson, OSB, of Clear Creek Abbey, and Dom Alcuin Reid, OSB, Prior of Monastère Saint-Benoît in Brignoles, France. *Gratias vobis ago.*

—Feast of St. James (MMXXII)

COMMENTARY
on the
DAVIDIC
Psalms

PART 4
[PSALMS 76–100]

Psalm 76

ARTICLE XLVII

EXPLANATION OF THE SEVENTY-SIXTH PSALM:
VOCE MEA AD DOMINUM CLAMAVI.
I CRIED TO THE LORD WITH MY VOICE.

76{77}[1] *Unto the end, for Idithun, a psalm of Asaph.*

In finem, pro Idithun. Psalmus Asaph.

THE PSALM NOW BEING ADDRESSED HAS THIS title before it: 76{77}[1] *In finem, pro Idithun. Psalmus Asaph; unto the end, for Idithun, a Psalm of Asaph.* Idithun is interpreted as meaning "one leaping over," but Asaph [is interpreted] as "congregation." So it is [to be understood] in this sense: *A Psalm of Asaph*, that is, this writing is for the congregation of the faithful, namely, for the Church, which coincides [with the congregation of the faithful], and directing us *unto the end*, who is Christ and who is eternal life, written and edited for Idithun, that is, for the perfect man, leaping over all transient, all vain, all transitory, created, and finite things, reckoning them and disdaining them as inconsiderable, and singularly and greatly desiring only divine, eternal, and heavenly things, or—better—the exceedingly simple God. This indeed is true, for Augustine himself confessed that he was unable to sense, to taste, or intellectually to relish the virtue and sense of this Psalm, until he attained the ability to leap over things in this way,[1] and counted, along with the Apostle, *all things as if dung* so that he might gain Christ.[2]

76{77}[2] *I cried to the Lord with my voice; to God with my voice, and he gave ear to me.*

Voce mea ad Dominum clamavi; voce mea ad Deum, et intendit mihi.

The Prophet [David], therefore, speaking in the person of a just man or the Church, says 76{77}[2] *Voce mea ad Dominum clamavi, I cried to the Lord with my voice*, that is, with a voice that is in harmony with my

---

1 E. N. Probably a reference to St. Augustine's own commentary on this Psalm.
2 Phil. 3:8.

heart, with an attentive voice, one that is my own and not alien. I cry out to the Lord, not with a loud sound, but rather with great affection: for man does not break forth in vocal cries unless it so happens out of a fervent desire. I cry out, therefore, praying ardently, not as if God stood a long distance away from me, or that my crying out will stir him up, since he exists everywhere, and he knows distinctly all things; but I cry out, so that God might see me doing what is in me to do, and taking note of the ardor of my effort and desire, he might attend to me quickly: in the manner that is written, *If you will beseech the Almighty, and if you will walk clean and upright, he will presently awake onto you.*[3] With my interior and exterior voice, I will cry out *ad Deum, to God,* invoking him alone, hoping in him and in nothing other than him, asking nothing from him but that which I need, and that which pertains to him: lest I do so uselessly, for God *intendit mihi, gave ear to me,* mercifully considering my prayers and hearing them. He shows, therefore, in me truly to be that which Scripture says: *Who has called upon him, and he despised him?*[4] And in the Gospel: *All things, whatsoever you ask when you pray, believe that you shall receive; and they shall come unto you.*[5] Moreover, in this verse and in the one following, the just man acknowledges the fruit of his prayers and the effort of his devotion, seeing that he provides to us confidence of being heard, and he incites and inflames us toward a holy manner of life and inmost exertions.

76{77}[3]   *In the day of my trouble I sought God, with my hands lifted up opposite him in the night, and I was not deceived. My soul refused to be comforted.*[6]

   In die tribulationis meae Deum exquisivi; manibus meis nocte contra eum, et non sum deceptus. Renuit consolari anima mea.

76{77}[3] *In die tribulationis meae, in the day of my trouble,* that is, in the time of adversity, persecution, or temptation, *Deum exquisivi, I sought God* as helper, and in an extraordinary way and with diligent effort I strove, *manibus meis, with my hands,* bodily extending them up toward the heavens, in the way that Jeremiah does in Lamentations, *Let us lift up our hearts with our hands to the Lord in the heavens.*[7] Or [alternatively], *with my hands,*

---

3   Job. 8:5b–6a.
4   Ecclus. 2:12b.
5   Mark 11:24.
6   E. N. For *contra,* I have put "opposite," replacing the Douay-Rheims's "to."
7   Lam. 3:41.

that is, with my good works, which draw their power from prayer: for he who does not cease doing good does not cease to pray. *Nocte, in the night*, that is, during the hours of the night; these are most befitting for prayer because of the cessation of external clamor and the freeing up of the exterior senses. For this reason, Isaiah said: *My soul has desired you in the night.*[8] And Jeremiah: *Arise, give praise in the night, in the beginning of the watches.*[9] Or [interpreted another way], *Night*, that is, the present life, which by comparison to the day of eternity and future life, it might be better called night rather than day. But in such a way I prayed *contra eum, opposite him*, that is, directing my eyes to the place that is beyond me or in a place opposite from me, the place in which God dwells, namely, in the empyrean heaven, which is opposite me because it is above, and I am down below. Or [alternatively], *opposite him*, that is, before him, placing myself in the presence of God, and praying as if in his presence — according to that which Elijah said, *As the Lord lives the God of Israel, in whose sight I stand.*[10] In this place where the Psalm here says *opposite him (contra eum)*, other translations have *before him (coram eum)*. *Et non sum deceptus, and I was not deceived*, that is, I have not been defrauded of the fulfillment of my hope, but I have experienced that which is written in the Gospel to be true: *Everyone that asks, receives; and he that seeks, finds; and to him that knocks, it shall be opened.*[11] Sacred Scripture fails nobody, but it is more possible that heaven and earth pass away, *than one tittle of the law to fall*, as the Savior said.[12] Since divine Scripture frequently promises God to be present to those who call upon him, it is well known to all that no one calling upon God can be deceived — if, however, he prays as should be prayed. Christ points out the manner in which prayer should be done: *We ought always to pray, and not to faint.*[13] And we ought to believe most certainly and hope this; and we ought to pray to God with this kind of assurance and faithful trust; and in so doing we will never be disappointed: for to the degree that we more faithfully entreat him, to that degree he will more readily and more generously hear us.[14]

---

8 Is. 26:9a.

9 Lam. 2:19a.

10 1 Kings 17:1a.

11 Matt. 7:8; Luke 11:10.

12 Luke 16:17; Matt. 5:18.

13 Luke 18:1b.

14 Cf. James 1:5–6: *But if any of you want wisdom, let him ask of God, who gives to all men abundantly, and upbraids not; and it shall be given him. But let him ask in faith, nothing wavering. For he that wavers is like a wave of the sea, which is moved and carried about by the wind.*

Consequently, [the Psalmist] sets forth a most wholesome example and perfect instruction, by which man is made worthy to obtain a divine hearing, consolation, and perpetual dwelling. *Renuit consolari anima mea, my soul refused to be comforted*, that is, in the present miserable age, full of affliction, in which I am troubled in many ways, losing temporal goods, weakening in body, falling into various temptations, lamenting over my and others' sins, and most of all because I advance in the good less than I desire — I fall often, I suffer the reduction of grace, I incur the falling away of consolation and fervor, and I cause my mind to be hard and barren. But even in the midst of such great misery I do not welcome the cheap consolations:[15] I value little in exulting in temporal things, I spurn human solace, empty words, scurrilous gestures, and — for the love of God above all other loves — I reject all adulterated joy, trusting and anticipating his return — to me and to my soul afflicted by, and languishing for, his love — with his most merciful consoling. Now this is a sign of a perfect and sincere love: to spurn all consolations contrary to the beloved, and to await patiently his return. Whence, in Hosea the beloved lover is told: *You shall wait for me many days: you shall not play the harlot, and you shall be no man's.*[16] And with the same Hosea also the Lord said: *My people shall long for my return.*[17] He who is like this can say what is stated in Ecclesiastes: *Laughter I counted error: and to mirth I said: Why are you vainly deceived?*[18] And so Solomon again acknowledges: *It is better to go to the house of mourning, than to the house of feasting: for in that we are put in mind of the end of all, and the living thinks what is to come.*[19] For one should have one's mind in the destination of all men, and one should live thinking about that which is in the future. Moreover, Christ says that placing consolations in riches, delights, honors, palaces, families and similar things of this world is folly: *Woe to you that are rich: for you have your consolation.*[20] And this pertains even more greatly to those in the religious or eremitical life to the extent they possess a more eminent love for the Godhead. For theirs is to love God alone.

---

15   Cf. Phil. 3:8: *Furthermore I count all things to be but loss for the excellent knowledge of Jesus Christ my Lord; for whom I have suffered the loss of all things, and count them but as dung, that I may gain Christ.*

16   Hosea 3:3.

17   Hosea 11:7.

18   Eccl. 2:2.

19   Eccl. 7:3.

20   Luke 6:24.

76{77}[4] *I remembered God, and was delighted, and was exercised,
and my spirit swooned away.*

*Memor fui Dei, et delectatus sum; et exercitatus sum, et defecit
spiritus meus.*

76{77}[4] *Memor fuit Dei,* I remembered God, reflecting upon his
goodness, recalling his benefits, and expecting his promises, *et delectatus sum, and was delighted,* with an intellectual delight from this kind
of reflection; *et exercitatus sum, and was exercised,* that is, I occupied
myself with the praises and the works of God: because charity is not
idle; *et defecit spiritus meus, and my spirit swooned away:* either because
it is not strong enough to be worthy to praise, sufficiently to know, fully
to love, and efficaciously to honor God; or because from a great and
ecstatic elevation or rapture in God, it is detached from the operation
of its exterior senses, and it is entirely absorbed in God, such as often
occurs to the most devoted children of the Lord Savior, to whom God
shows the riches of his glory.[21]

76{77}[5] *My eyes prevented the watches: I was troubled, and I spoke not.*

Anticipaverunt vigilias oculi mei; turbatus sum, et non sum locutus.

76{77}[5] *Anticipaverunt vigilias oculi mei, my eyes prevented the watches:*
that is, before the light arose, or before the time that others have risen, I
have arrived earlier so that I might pray, praise, and contemplate God in
the manner that Scripture puts it: *The just man will give his heart to resort
early to the Lord.*[22] A burning love — which is impatient with separation,
and always sighs for the union and the embrace of the Beloved — brings
this about in the loving servants of Christ. The fervid love of the blessed
Creator is does not know delayed efforts,[23] for regarding it is truly written: *Many waters cannot quench charity. The lamps thereof are fire and
flames.*[24] *Turbatus sum, I was troubled* by the consideration of my sins
by which I am interiorly stained, and of the snares or the dangers, by

---

21 Cf. Rom. 9:23: *That he might show the riches of his glory on the vessels of mercy,
which he has prepared unto glory.*
22 Ecclus. 39:6a.
23 E. N. This appears to be a reference to St. Ambrose's *Exposition on the Gospel of
Luke: Nescit tarda molimina Spiritus Sancti gratia,* "the grace of the Holy Spirit does
not know delayed efforts," *Exp. in Evang. Lucam,* II, 19, PL 15, 1560. Ambrose uses
this phrase to describe the haste with which Mary went to visit Elizabeth following
the visitation by the angel Gabriel.
24 Songs 8:7a, 6b.

which I am externally surrounded; *et non sum locutus, and I spoke not,* that is, by reason of confusion I dared not to open my mouth to the Lord, like that which is contained in the first book of Ezra: *My God I am confounded and ashamed to lift up my face to you: for our iniquities are multiplied over our heads, and our sins are grown up even unto heaven.*[25] Similarly, the three youths spoke within the furnace: *And now we cannot open our mouths: we are become a shame and reproach to your servants, and to them that worship you.*[26] But a man ought not to long persist or despair in such dread: for such things are said so as to emphasize the gravity of our misdeeds. Or [an alternative understanding is], *I spoke not,* excusing myself, or placing my sins upon others, or seeking human sustenance. Or [yet another interpretation], *I spoke not,* unfolding my secrets of my considerations to others; but I did that which was said by someone else, *My secret to myself, my secret to myself.*[27]

76{77}[6]   *I thought upon the days of old: and I had in my mind the eternal years.*

Cogitavi dies antiquos, et annos aeternos in mente habui.

76{77}[6] *Cogitavi dies antiquos, I thought upon the days of old,* that is, I recall the past events of old and the works of God at the beginning of the world, and during the course of the ages even up to the time this very instant, as Ecclesiasticus says, *Wise men will seek out the wisdom of all the ancients, and will be occupied in the prophets.*[28] But because I will find that all things which occur under the sun are subject to vanity,[29] therefore, *annos aeternos in mente habuit, I had in my mind the eternal years,* that is, I reflected in my heart the day when the elect will live with God, and the reprobate in Hell, and, in consideration of the state of the future age, the eternal joy in Heaven and of the perpetual torments in Hell, I had esteemed lightly all things which delight for a short time, and had patiently borne whatever

---

25   1 Ezra 9:6.

26   Dan. 3:33.

27   Is. 24:16. E. N. As St. John of the Cross said: *Calle lo que Dios le diere y acuérdese de aquel dicho de la esposa: Secretum meum mihi.* (Is. 24:16). San Juan de la Cruz, *Obras Completas* (Burgos: El Monte Carmelo, 1972), 144. "Keep quiet about those things that God may have granted you and remember that saying of the bride: *My secret for myself.*" So also St. Philip Neri in his sayings: "We ought not to publish or manifest to everyone the inspirations which God sends us, or the favors he grants us. *Secretum meum mihi! Secretum meum mihi!*" *If God be With Us: The Maxims of St. Philip Neri* (Herefordshire: Gracewing, 2004), 42. (ed., F. W. Faber)

28   Ecclus. 39:1.

29   Cf. Rom. 8:20a: *For the creature was made subject to vanity.*

temporarily burdened me. O how wholesome is such thinking! For if we weigh the length of these eternal years, we will consider the present life to be but a brief moment, however long it may be;[30] and so we are enkindled in this disdain [of this world and its attractions] and in the love of the future life. Indeed, even if you had lived from the time of our first parents until today, would not all this past time seem like only a moment, especially if it is compared to the eternal years of future life? We ought to consider, therefore, wholeheartedly and in our innermost heart, the brevity of this present life, the deceits of the joys of this world, and its state of infinite danger. Let us have topmost in the mind the eternal years that are opposed to this, contemplating the solace of the elect and the torments of the reprobate: and thinking of this, let us choose that which we judge to be more expedient, either now to rejoice with the world, and after a while to be tortured eternally with the reprobate in hell, or now to follow the footsteps of Christ, and but a short time later to possess the joys of heaven. Here, indeed, the most wise Solomon stated: *If a man live many years, and have rejoiced in them all, he must remember the darksome time, and the many days: which when they shall come, the things past shall be accused of vanity.*[31]

76{77}[7]   *And I meditated in the night with my own heart: and I was exercised and I swept my spirit.*

Et meditatus sum nocte cum corde meo, et exercitabar, et scopebam spiritum meum.

76{77}[8]   *Will God then cast off forever? Or will he never be more favorable again?*

Numquid in aeternum proiiciet Deus? Aut non apponet ut complacitior sit adhuc?

76{77}[9]   *Or will he cut off his mercy forever, from generation to generation?*

Aut in finem misericordiam suam abscindet, a generatione in generationem?

76{77}[10]   *Or will God forget to show mercy? Or will he in his anger shut up his mercies?*

Aut obliviscetur misereri Deus? Aut continebit in ira sua misericordias suas?

---

30   2 Cor. 4:17: *For that which is at present momentary and light of our tribulation, works for us above measure exceedingly an eternal weight of glory.*

31   Eccl. 11:8.

76{77}[7] *Et meditatus sum nocte cum corde meo, and I meditated in the night with my own heart*: that is, with my intellect I thought about things that were not vain, and frivolous, and illicit, but I reflected upon the law of the Lord, investigating and giving attention to the way by which to avoid the eternal years of misery and to gain the eternal years of the blessed in the heavenly fatherland; *et exercitabar, and I was exercised*, that is, I was mentally and earnestly preoccupied with this, *et scopebam spiritum meum, and I swept my spirit*, that is, I scrutinized my soul, I examined my conscience, and whatever was worthy of remorse, I rejected, I made clean, and I purposed to avoid.

But because God does not always hear man as quickly as he desires,[32] but, on the contrary, he permits him to be afflicted for a length of time, therefore, the voice of the just man — who confronting such a delay, and because of the gravity of the punishment and penalty, and from human weakness — complains and says: 76{77}[8] *Numquid in aeternum proiiciet Deus, will then God cast off forever* my prayers, not hearing them, and not bestowing upon me the desired grace? For this is the manner of speaking of the afflicted: where a short passage of time seems long, but a long passage of time [seems] eternal. Whence, the blessed Job says: *I cry to you, and you hear me not: I stand up, and you do not regard me.*[33] *Aut non apponet ut complacitior sit adhuc? Or will he never be more favorable again?* That is, will God always be cruel and unyielding to this degree, and is there no way to be able to placate him? This is said not in the sense of affirming it [to be true], but it is said so as to negate it, as [is clear] from that which follows: indeed, God not only deigns to be placated, but because of his ineffable clemency he also seeks occasions whereby he might be assuaged. For this reason, this is stated in Ezekiel: *I sought among them for a man that might set up a hedge, and stand in the gap before me in favor of the land, that I might not destroy it.*[34] And Job: *If there shall be an angel speaking for him, . . . God shall have mercy on him, and shall say, Deliver him . . . I have found wherein I may be merciful to him.*[35] 76{77}[9] *Aut in*

---

32 Cf. Prov. 1:28: *Then shall they call upon me, and I will not hear: they shall rise in the morning and shall not find me.* Micah 3:4: *Then shall they cry to the Lord, and he will not hear them: and he will hide his face from them at that time, as they have behaved wickedly in their devices.*

33 Job 30:20.

34 Ez. 22:30. *E. N.* As Denis explains in his *Commentary on Ezekiel*, the hedge is a "medium of hindrance of the divine vengeance," and the man standing in the gap is one who "might struggle to resist the threats and anger" of God, "hindering their effect." *Doctoris Ecstatici D. Dionysii Cartusiani, Opera Omnia*, Vol. 9 (Montreuil: 1900), 525.

35 Job 33:23a, 24b.

finem misericoridam suam abscindet, or will he cut off his mercy forever, not
providing help to us wayfarers crying out to him? Either, I say, he will cut
off his mercy, or he will not bestow the effect of his mercy, *a generatione
in generationem, from generation to generation,* that is, in the generation
and its successor generations, visiting upon them or avenging the sins of
the parents to posterity without ceasing.[36] **76{77}[10]** *Aut obliviscetur
miserere Deus, Or will God forget to show mercy,* [that is, will God,] whose
property is to be merciful, [forget to show mercy]? *Aut continebit in ira
sua misericordias suas, or will he in his anger shut up his mercies?* It is as
if he were implying, "No": because about this is written, *When you are
angry, you will remember mercy.*[37] Finally, some have employed these words
of truth and life them as occasions for falsity and death, saying that the
punishments of hell will at some time receive an end, even though it is
nevertheless manifestly clear that this present scripture speaks of God
in providing [mercy] to wayfarers and penitents.[38]

76{77}[11] *And I said, Now have I begun: this is the change of the right
hand of the most High.*

Et dixi: Nunc coepi; haec mutatio dexterae Excelsi?

76{77}[11] *Et dixi, Nunc coepi: haec mutatio dexterae Excelsi; and
I said, Now have I begun: this is the change of the right hand of the most
High.* The Hebrew original, and also the translation of Jerome according
to the Hebrew, is noted to say: *And I said, This is my feebleness:* that is,
according to the reason I have asserted, the preceding complaint is born
from the feebleness of human weakness. But our [Latin] translation is

---

36   E. N. Cf. Deut. 5:9: *I am the Lord your God, a jealous God, visiting the iniquity of
the fathers upon their children unto the third and fourth generation, to them that hate me.*
37   Hab. 3:2b.
38   E. N. Although rejected by the Church as formally heretical, DS 72, 76, 212,
342, 411, 443, 486, 574, 596, 630, 780, 801, 839, 4657, some in the past touted various
notions of universalism, wherein all would be saved in the end, and thus hell was not
eternal. Psalm 76:10 was one of their *dicta probanta* or "proof texts." Chief among
these universalists are Origen (*ca.* 184–*ca.* 253), Eusebius of Caesarea (260–340),
St. Gregory of Nyssa (*ca.* 335–*ca.* 395), St. Didymus of Alexandria (*ca.* 313–398),
and Evagrius Ponticus (345–399). Origen's theory was so extreme that it included
the Devil. Modernly, this thinking has found spokesmen in, for example, Hans Urs
von Balthasar (1905–1988) in his *Dare We Hope "That All Men Be Saved?"* (San
Francisco: Ignatius, 1988) (trans., David Kipp and Lothar Krauth), though such
moderns seek to avoid the Church's censures by various stratagems. The eternity of
the punishment of hell is *de fide.* Ludwig Ott, *Fundamentals of Catholic Dogma* (North
Carolina: TAN Books 1974), 481 (trans., Patrick Lynch, ed. James Canon Bastible).

explained in this manner: *And I said*, with the heart or with the mouth, *Now have I begun*, that is, now I have just begun to live spiritually, to understand wisely, and I have begun truly to know: understanding the vanity of this life, and the happiness of the future age; or I have begun to discern my prior manner of living, progress, and perfection as nothing, and with renewed purpose, with new fervor, with eager desire to embrace the paths of a better life, advancing in the way of spiritual progress, indeed, daily beginning as it were anew. For so did our illustrious father Arsenius teach.[39] For also the blessed Apostle [Paul] professed for our information: *Forgetting the things that are behind, and stretching forth myself to those that are in front.*[40] Christ also: *When*, he says, *you shall have done all these things that are commanded you, say: We are unprofitable servants; we have done that which we ought to do.* We ought not therefore glory in the merits of our prior life, nor should we estimate ourselves to be something; but every day let us conduct ourselves afresh and so fervently, as if we were commencing that day for the first time and as if we were on that day to die, attending to that which of the divine Apostle: *I do not count myself to have apprehended*, but I follow *if I may by any means apprehend.*[41]

But because this progress is not something within human power, but is the gift of the grace of God, so is added: *haec mutatio dexterae Excelsi*, this is the change of the right hand of the most High: that is, it is attributable to the kind help or the mercy of the sublime presence of God that I might be so changed from the darkness of ignorance to the splendor of knowledge, from vices into virtues, from carnal and animal things to spiritual ones. For *we are not sufficient to think anything of ourselves, as of ourselves: but our sufficiency is from God.*[42] Whence it is said by Jeremiah: *I know, O Lord, that the way of a man is not his: neither is it in a man to walk, and to direct his steps.*[43] For this reason, the Apostle [Paul] says: *It is God who works in you, both to will and to accomplish, according to his good will.*[44]

---

39   E. N. This is a reference to Abba Arsenius (360–449 AD): "Some demons were once standing near Abba Arsenius in his cell, and were troubling him. Then some brothers came, who usually ministered to him. And as they stood outside the cell, they heard him crying aloud to the Lord: 'Lord, do not leave me, though I have done nothing good in your sight. Grant me, Lord, according to your loving-kindness, at least the very beginning of a good life.'" *Western Asceticism* (Philadelphia: Westminster Press, 1968) (trans., Owen Chadwick), 156.

40   Phil. 3:13b.

41   *Cf.* Phil. 3:13, 12.

42   2 Cor. 3:5.

43   Jer. 10:23.

44   Phil 2:13.

But all that has just been said regarding that verse, *Will God then cast me off forever?* until this present verse [*i.e.,* from Ps. **76:8–76:11**] can be understood not only as expressing extended weakness [on the part of the person praying], but as consolatory words with a negative implication, namely, so that the words are taken altogether [are understood to mean] that God does not delay eternally, nor does he refuse to be placated, nor does he cut off his mercy, *etc.* And so by this the soul of the person praying is strengthened to pray perseveringly and trustingly, even while God delays for a long time.

76{77}[12] *I remembered the works of the Lord: for I will be mindful of your wonders from the beginning.*

Memor fui operum Domini, quia memor ero ab initio mirabilium tuorum.

76{77}[13] *And I will meditate on all your works: and will be employed in your inventions.*

Et meditabor in omnibus operibus tuis, et in adinventionibus tuis exercebor.

76{77}[12] *Memor fui operum Domini,* I remembered the works of the Lord, that is, of his grace and of his mercy which he bestowed, infused, and preserved in me: for the Apostle [Paul] said: *Neglect not the grace that is in you.*[45] This is also a sign of my remembering, *quia memor ero ab initio mirabilium tuorum,* for I will be mindful of your wonders from the beginning which you have done from the origin of the world in heaven, on earth, and in the sea. **76{77}[13]** *Et meditabor in omnibus operibus tuis,* and I will mediate on all your works, which I read or hear about in sacred Scripture, contemplating you, God, the Worker, from your works in the manner that the Apostle asserts, *The invisible things* of God *are clearly understood by the things that are made: his eternal power also, and divinity.*[46] And Wisdom: *By the greatness of the beauty, and of the creature, the Creator of them may be seen, so as to be known thereby.*[47]

Et in adinventionibus tuis, and ... *in your inventions,* that is, in these most secret mysteries of human redemption which you alone ineffably have thought about, decreeing the human race to be redeemed by the Incarnation, Passion, and Death of Christ, *excercebor,* I will be employed,

45 1 Tim. 4:14a.
46 Rom. 1:20.
47 Wis. 13:4.

wholeheartedly pondering these things in the way that Jeremiah speaks about, *I will be mindful and remember, and my soul shall languish within me;*[48] and, he adds, *These things I shall think over in my heart, therefore will I hope.*[49] For most truly, anyone who considers the things that have been devised (*adinvenisse*) and have been done or suffered for the human race has confidence in the Lord. Or [alternatively], *in your inventions,* that is, in your precepts and counsels which you have instituted for our salvation. For God is said to have devised [or invented] (*adinvenisse*), not indeed [in the sense] of inquiring or coming upon, but in a manner other than receiving.[50] For such a manner of speaking and such similar [manners of speaking] are to be understood in a negative sense. And this is the way with other Scripture [as for example in Hosea]: *He who made the stars; this is our God, and there shall no other be accounted of in comparison of him. He devised (adinvenit) all the way of knowledge.*[51] One ought also to consider that this is said of the Son of God. For later [in Hosea] it says: *Afterwards, he was seen upon earth and conversed with men.*[52] Since, therefore, the Son of God received from the Father all that he had and was, in what way is it said that he devised all the way of knowledge? [How is this said] especially since he clearly testified, *The Father loves the Son, and shows him all things which he himself does;*[53] and elsewhere, *I speak not of myself,*[54] *but as the Father has taught me?*[55] For these things are not said by Christ merely because of the assumed [human] nature, since Christ says of the Holy Spirit, *He shall not speak of himself, but what things soever he shall hear, he shall speak.*[56] So the answer to this is that the Son of God is said to have devised the way of all teaching because he did not receive it from anyone substantially

---

48   Lam. 3:20.
49   Lam. 3:21.
50   E. N. The Latin word *adinvenire* can mean "to come upon," "to discover," (such a sense is residual in the English word "inventory") but it can also mean "to invent," "to devise," "to contrive," "to create." Denis is clarifying that the word as used in this verse does not fall in the former line of meaning (which suggests "receiving" something passively), but in the latter line (which suggests an active contrivance or plan).
51   Baruch 3:35b–37a. E. N. I have departed from the Douay-Rheims's translation which translates *hic adinvenit omnem viam disciplinae* as "he *found out* all the way of knowledge." Denis understands the word *adinvenit* in the sense of "devised," "conceived," or "originated."
52   Baruch 3:38.
53   John 5:20a.
54   John 14:10b.
55   John 8:28b.
56   John 6:13b.

distinct from him: indeed, he and the Father are one wisdom, and the one principle of all created wisdom: for of the Son is written, *The Word of God on high is the fountain of wisdom.*[57]

76{77}[14] *Your way, O God, is in the holy place: who is the great God like our God?*

Deus, in sancto via tua: quis Deus magnus sicut Deus noster?

76{77}[15] *You are the God that does wonders. You have made your power known among the nations:*

Tu es Deus qui facis mirabilia: notam fecisti in populis virtutem tuam.

76{77}[16] *With your arm you have redeemed your people the children of Jacob and of Joseph:*

Redemisti in brachio tuo populum tuum, filios Iacob et Ioseph.

76{77}[17] *The waters saw you, O God, the waters saw you: and they were afraid, and the depths were troubled:*

Viderunt te aquae, Deus; viderunt te aquae, et timuerunt; et turbatae sunt abyssi.

76{77}[14] *Deus, in sancto via tua;* your way, O God, is in the holy place: that is, in Christ, the Saint of Saints, is [to be found] the way of worshiping you: because he is the teacher, exemplar, and cause of all virtue and perfection; and he who follows him *walks not in darkness,*[58] but he *shall go in* by faith and contemplation, and *he shall go out* by deeds.[59] He also *is the way, the truth, and the life.*[60] Or [alternatively] thus: *God, in the holy place,* that is in every pure heart is *your way,* that is, [God is to be found in] the observation of your commandments. Or [yet another way of understanding this], *Your way . . . is in the holy place,* that is, your way, namely, in the divine law, is what true holiness consists in, as Daniel commemorates: *Blessed are you, O Lord, . . . for you are just in all . . . and your ways are right, and all your judgments are true.*[61] *Quis Deus magnus,*

---

57 Ecclus. 1:5a. E. N. In other words, God the Son did not "discover" the knowledge of the Father, but in fact eternally was himself—with the Father and the Holy Spirit—the "deviser," "creator," or "originator" of that knowledge.

58 John 8:12b.

59 John 10:9: *I am the door. By me, if any man enter in, he shall be saved: and he shall go in, and go out, and shall find pastures.*

60 John 14:6.

61 Dan. 3:26a, 27.

who is the great God, [great] in all nobility, wisdom, beauty, majesty, blessedness, holiness, and sweetness, *sicut Deus noster, like our God*, who is three
in Persons, and one in essence? Indeed, no one, because God sublime
and blessed incomparably or infinitely exceeds all other things. For this
reason, the prophet Isaiah asked: *To whom then have you likened God?
Or what image will you make for him?*[62] 76{77}[15] *Tu es Deus qui facis,
you are the God that does* by your own power *mirabilia, wonders*, that is,
supernatural works: of whom in the book of Job is said, *Who does great
things and unsearchable and wonderful things without number.*[63]

  *Notam fecisti in populis virtutem tuam; you have made your power
known*: that is, in Pharaoh and in his people you have demonstrated
your power; indeed, you have made your power known to the people of
the whole earth to whom the report of the defeat of the Egyptians has
reached. Whence God said to Pharaoh: *Therefore have I raised you, that I
may show my power in you, and my name may be spoken of throughout all
the earth.*[64] Here, as is well known, Jethro, who was related to Moses,[65]
hearing of the defeat of the Egyptians, said: *Now I know that the Lord
is great above all gods.*[66] 76{77}[16] *Redemisti in brachio tuo, with your
arm you have redeemed*, that is, in the strength of your arm you also have
lead from the land of the Egyptians *populum tuum, filios Iacob et Ioseph;
your people, the children of Jacob and Joseph*, that is, both those who were
born of these men, who together with Jacob had gone down into Egypt
from the land of Canaan, as well as those that Joseph had brought forth
in the land of Egypt, namely from Ephraim and Manasseh.[67] 76{77}[17]
Viderunt te aquae, Deus; the waters saw you, O God: that is, the Red Sea
so obeyed you in its division and in its drying up as if it had been of an
intellectual nature and had recognized your authority.[68] For all things
are obedient to the divine power by an innate obediential potency in all
created nature.[69] Then this sentence is repeated so as to confirm this:

---

62 Is. 40:18.
63 Job. 5:9.
64 Ex. 9:16.
65 E. N. Moses married Zipporah, the daughter of Jethro; hence, Jethro was Moses's
father-in-law.
66 Ex. 18:11.
67 E. N. Ephraim and Manasseh were children of Joseph born in Egypt. *See* Gen.
41:50–52; 48:5.
68 Ex. 14:21–22.
69 E. N. The concept of obediential potency refers to the aptitude in created nature
to receive either a supernatural gift (*e.g.*, man has an obediential potency to receive
supernatural grace) or to receive a supernatural effect (*e.g.*, a miracle). It is the latter
obediential potency that Denis has in mind. St. Thomas explains: "For water or earth

viderunt te aquae, the waters saw you, [the waters] of the Red Sea [speak of you], *et timuerunt, and they were afraid,* that is, [the waters] behaved in the manner of one who is afraid, fleeing from the banks and holding themselves there in the manner of a wall; *et turbatae sunt abyssi, and the depths were troubled,* that is, both parts of the Red Sea, those parts opposite of each other, or better those parts on either side — against the course of nature — did not flow toward that lower place where the children of Israel crossed over, as is related in Exodus: But the children of Israel marched through the midst of the sea upon dry land, and the waters were to them as a wall on the right hand and on the left.

76{77}[18] *Great was the noise of the waters: the clouds sent out a sound. For your arrows pass:*

Multitudo sonitus aquarum; vocem dederunt nubes. Etenim sagittae tuae transeunt;

76{77}[19] *The voice of your thunder in a wheel. Your lightnings enlightened the world: the earth shook and trembled.*

Vox tonitrui tui in rota. Illuxerunt coruscationes tuae orbi terrae; commota est, et contremuit terra;

76{77}[18] *Multitudo sonitus aquarum, great was the noise of the waters:* that is, a great sound or din was in the waters of the Red Sea because with enormous crashing and fury the waters of the Red Sea returned to their former place over the Egyptians, and they carried the Egyptians away in the depths;[70] *vocem dederunt nubes, the clouds sent out a sound,* that is, God caused to proceed from the column of fire and of cloud[71] lighting and thunder against the Egyptians. *Et enim sagittae tuae transeunt, for your arrows pass:* that is, your punishments against the Egyptians succeeded, for you overthrew their chariots and horsemen; 76{77}[19] *vox tonitrui, the voice of your thunder,* that is, the sound of that thundering was *in rota, in a wheel,* that is, had a similarity to a wheel because as noise of a quickly moving wheel is great, so was the voice of your thundering emanating from the earlier-mentioned cloud. *Illuxerunt coruscationes tuae orbi terrae, your lightnings enlightened the*

[as well as any created nature] . . . can become something else by virtue of a super-natural agent that it cannot become by the power of a natural agent; and according to this we say that in every creature there is an obediential potency, since every creature obeys God in receiving whatever God wills." *De virtutibus,* q. 1, a. 10, ad 13.

70 Ex. 14:27, 25.

71 Ex. 14:24.

world: that is, in the manner that is written, you made your lightning flash in the land of Egypt: *The Lord sent thunder and hail, and lightning running along the ground.*[72] Or [alternatively]: *Your lightnings enlightened the world*, that is, those lightnings that occurred in Egypt were notice to all men that were to come. *Commota est et contremuit terra, the earth shook and trembled*: that is, the Egyptians were moved by such prodigies, some towards admiration, others towards obstinacy, but some to the faith and worship of the one God, *as a mixed multitude without number went up at the same time with the children of Israel out of Egypt*, as it states in Exodus.[73] The earth also trembled, that is, the Egyptians were terrified at from those miracles. Or [alternatively], the whole *earth*, that is, all mankind, to whom would come the news of the marvelous works of God in Egypt *shook and trembled* in the manner just stated.

76{77}[20] *Your way is in the sea, and your paths in many waters: and your footsteps shall not be known.*

In mari via tua, et semitae tuae in aquis multis, et vestigia tua non cognoscentur.

76{77}[21] *You have conducted your people like sheep, by the hand of Moses and Aaron.*

Deduxisti sicut oves populum tuum, in manu Moysi et Aaron.

76{77}[20] *In mari via tua, your way is in the sea*, for you prepared your people by the way of the Red Sea; *et semitae tuae, and your paths*, that is, the way by which you lead the children of Israel were *in aquis multis, in many waters*, that is, in the midst of the waters of the Red Sea, or between the sections of that sea, for the waters were solid on either side.[74] *Et vestigia tua non cognoscentur, and your footsteps shall not be known*: that is, since your people passed over [the Red Sea], no signs appeared of your steps or path; for the sea immediately returned to its proper place and it covered them up within itself. And in a similar sense the book of Wisdom says: *All those things are passed away like a shadow, . . . and as a ship that passes through the waves: whereof when it is gone by, the trace cannot be found, nor the path of its keel in the waters.*[75] 76{77}[21] *Deduxisti sicut oves populum tuum, you have conducted your people like sheep*, that is, the children of Israel through the desert, in which

---

72   Ex. 12:28. *E. N.* This was in response to Moses stretching his rod towards heaven.
73   Ex. 12:38.
74   Ex. 14:29.
75   Wis. 5:9a, 10.

you fed them, protected them, and took care of them, in the manner that a shepherd feeds and protects his sheep: and this you did *in manu Moysis et Aaron, by the hand of Moses and Aaron,* that is, you led your people by the hand and the ministry of Moses and of Aaron, your first and highest priest among the Jewish people.

SPIRITUAL OR MYSTICAL EXPOSITION

76{77}[15]   *You are the God that does wonders. You have made your power known among the nations:*

Tu es Deus qui facis mirabilia: notam fecisti in populis virtutem tuam.

76{77}[16]   *With your arm you have redeemed your people the children of Jacob and of Joseph:*

Redemisti in brachio tuo populum tuum, filios Iacob et Ioseph.

76{77}[17]   *The waters saw you, O God, the waters saw you: and they were afraid, and the depths were troubled:*

Viderunt te aquae, Deus; viderunt te aquae, et timuerunt; et turbatae sunt abyssi.

Now this part is expounded spiritually or mystically in this fashion: 76{77}[15] ... *Notam fecisti,* you have made known, O God, the Father, *in populis,* among the nations of the whole world *virtutem tuam, your power,* that is, Christ, who is power of God and *the wisdom of God:*[76] for you have enlightened men by sending your Son into the world by the Incarnation, and then ultimately converting the whole world to the knowledge of Christ through the holy Apostles. 76{77}[16] *Redemisti in brachio tuo populum tuum, with your arm you have redeemed your people:* that is, in Christ by whom you worked all things and who is called your power,[77] you have delivered all the elect from the punishment of Hell and the death of sin: indeed, *filios Iacob, the children of Jacob,* that is, the Jews, who followed the faith and deeds of Jacob, *et Ioseph, and Joseph,* who is interpreted as [meaning] increase, that is, the people of the Gentiles, from which the Church has increased. 76{77}[17] *Viderunt te aquae, Deus, viderunt te aquae; the waters saw you, O God, the waters saw you:* that is, the people converted to the faith, both from the Gentiles as well as from the Jews, considered you and acknowledged you with the eye of

---

76   1 Cor. 1:24b.
77   *Ibid.*

contemplation or of faith. For the many waters are many people.[78] *Et timuerunt, and they were afraid,* they having already brought to the faith by your justice, [were afraid] of your majesty, the punishments of Hell, and the adversities of this world; *et turbatae sunt abyssi, and the depths were troubled:* that is, human hearts were moved by the preaching of the Gospel, some to becoming hardened, others to penance. The human heart is said to be an abyss, that is, insofar as it is inscrutable and profound, so that it is known only by God. For this reason it is written elsewhere: *The heart is perverse above all things, and unsearchable, who can know it? I am the Lord who searches the heart and proves the reins.*[79]

76{77}[18] *Great was the noise of the waters: the clouds sent out a sound. For your arrows pass:*

Multitudo sonitus aquarum; vocem dederunt nubes. Etenim sagittae tuae transeunt;

76{77}[19] *The voice of your thunder in a wheel. Your lightnings enlightened the world: the earth shook and trembled.*

Vox tonitrui tui in rota. Illuxerunt coruscationes tuae orbi terrae; commota est, et contremuit terra;

76{77}[18] *Multitudo sonitus aquarum, great was the noise of the waters:* that is, the voice of the people converted to the Catholic faith was various. For some blessed God with hymns and confession, others lamented their sins by prayers and tears, others informed other persons by preaching holy doctrines. But this was all done because *vocem dederunt nubes, the clouds sent out a sound,* that is, because the Apostles by their preaching led them to such holy exertions. Now the Apostles are called clouds according to this in Isaiah: *Who are these, that fly as clouds?*[80] *Etenim sagittae tuae transeunt, for your arrows pass:* that is, the most acute words of the Holy Spirit fasten in the heart of the elect by the mouth of holy preachers. For they that are of God receive the words of God.[81] **76{77} [19]** *Vox tonitrui tui in rota, the voice of your thunder in a wheel:* that is, the voices of your thunder, namely, the sermons of the Apostles, proceeded

---

78   *Cf.* Rev. 17:1, 15: *The waters which you saw . . . are peoples, and nations, and tongues.*
79   E. N. For "reins" meaning the inmost part of man, *see* footnote 7- 10 in Volume 1 (*Beatus Vir*).
80   E. N. As Denis explains in Article XII (Psalm 56:11), the Apostles are "called clouds because from them, like from clouds, God thunders commandments, flashes like lightning signs, and rains down the saving message."
81   *Cf.* John 8:47a: *He that is of God, hears the words of God.*

throughout all the earth.[82] The Apostles are called thunder because of the most eminent height of their preaching. Whence also we read that Christ in the Gospel called John and James the sons of thunder.[83] *Illuxerunt coruscationes tuae orbi terrae; your lightnings enlightened the world*: that is, the virtues and graces and miracles which you bestowed upon your Apostles and future saints are manifest to all men, you Lord *conforming the word with signs that followed.*[84] *Commota est et contremuit terra, the earth shook and trembled*: that is, the inhabitants of the earth, through the preaching and the prodigies of the Apostles and of other apostolic men, were moved in diverse ways, and they were made to tremble, namely toward admiration or penance, or even to persecution and also blasphemy.

76{77}[20] *Your way is in the sea, and your paths in many waters: and your footsteps shall not be known.*

In mari via tua, et semitae tuae in aquis multis, et vestigia tua non cognoscentur.

76{77}[21] *You have conducted your people like sheep, by the hand of Moses and Aaron.*

Deduxisti sicut oves populum tuum, in manu Moysi et Aaron.

76{77}[20] *In mari via tua, your way is in the sea*, that is, among the Gentile people the evangelical law was preached; *et semitae tuae, and your paths*, that is, your precepts and counsels, *in aquis multis, in many waters*, that is, were manifested, received, and performed in many nations. *Et vestigia tua, and your footsteps*, O Christ, that is, your works and your examples, *non cognoscentur, shall not be known* by the people to whom you were specially sent, namely by the unbelieving Jews,[85] who ascribed your works to Beelzebub.[86] Or [another way of viewing this]: *Your footsteps shall not be known*, that is, the hidden impressions and the marvelous effects which you employ throughout all the world no wayfaring man can thoroughly scrutinize. Whence it was said to Job: *Peradventure will you comprehend the steps of God, and will you find out the Almighty perfectly?*[87]

---

82 Cf. Ps. 18:5: *Their sound has gone forth into all the earth: and their words unto the ends of the world*. See Volume 1, Article XLV (Psalm 18:5).

83 Mark 3:17.

84 Mark 16:20b.

85 Matt. 15:24.

86 Matt. 12:24. E. N. Beelzebub ("Lord of the Flies") is another name for Satan. See 2 Kings 1:2–3, 6, 16; Mark 3:22; Matt. 10:25, 12:24, 27; Luke 11:15, 18–19.

87 Job 11:7.

76{77}[21] *Deduxisti, you have conducted,* O God, O Trinity, *sicut oves populum tuum, your people like sheep,* namely, the Christians, in the way of this exile to the heavenly fatherland of eternal happiness, *in manu Moysis et Aaron, by the hand of Moses and Aaron,* that is, in the virtue and grace of Christ, prefigured by Moses and Aaron, for Christ is our leader (*dux*) and our priest. Whence of him is stated in Daniel: *From the going forth of the word, to build up Jerusalem again, unto Christ the prince (ducem), etc.*[88] And Zechariah says: *He shall be a priest upon his throne.*[89] And the Apostle: Christ, *for that he continues forever, has an everlasting priesthood.*[90]

See we have heard this meaningful, doctrinal Psalm, which includes all the teaching of the entire spiritual journey: in which man, first of all, acknowledges himself leaping [or passing through this world], spurning the things of this world, regarding with most ardent longing God alone, so that having proclaimed his great affection to the Lord, and wholeheartedly having prevailed upon him in tribulation, not having wanted to admit any vile, carnal, or unworthy consolation, but having been remembered by God, and by this he is mentally delighted. In addition, he asserts himself to have anticipated the watches by reason of praying and praising the Lord, to have considered also the eternal years, and to have scrutinized most diligently his own conscience. And so it becomes clear how immeasurable the mercy of the Creator is; and after this he praises and greatly exalts God, he brings to mind his marvelous doings, and he recalls his benefits. All, therefore, should endeavor to sing the fiery words of so great a Psalm with fervent mind, to implement the teachings of such a doctrinal Psalm, to spurn all earthly things with heavenly love, to seek true solace only in the Savior, to be mindful of God in all distress, and to repulse from the joy of contemplation all inordinate sadness.

---

88   Dan. 9:25a.
89   Zech. 6:13b.
90   Heb. 7:24. *E. N.* On the authorship of Hebrews and Denis, *see* footnote 8-34 in Volume I (*Beatus Vir*).

PRAYER

O GOD OF INEFFABLE KINDNESS, MERCIFUL unto thousands,[91] though angry because of our sins, do not in the end cut off your mercy from us: do not forget our misery, but through your tender mercy bid us to be counted among those eternally saved.

Ineffabilis pietatis Deus, misericors in millibus, non in finem iratus pro peccatis nostris misericordiam tuam abscindas a nobis: non obliviscaris misereri nostri; sed tua miseratione iube nos aeterne salvationi annumerari.

---

91   E. N. Cf. Ex. 20:6: *Showing mercy unto thousands to them that love me and keep my commandments.*

Psalm 77

ARTICLE XLVIII

ELUCIDATION OF THE SEVENTY-SEVENTH PSALM: ATTENDITE, POPULE MEUS, LEGEM MEAM. ATTEND, O MY PEOPLE, TO MY LAW.

77{78}[1] *Understanding for Asaph. Attend, O my people, to my law: incline your ears to the words of my mouth.*

Intellectus Asaph. Attendite, popule meus, legem meam; inclinate aurem vestram in verba oris mei.

THIS LONG PSALM IS INSCRIBED WITH THIS short title: 77{78}[1] *Intellectus Asaph. Understanding for Asaph.* That is, this present Psalm is given to us to understand how those things that God said and did for his people in the Old Testament are to be received. *For all these things happened to them in figure:*[1] and they *were written for our learning.*[2] For when the title of the Psalm says, *understanding for Asaph*, we are admonished by this not simply or only to receive this historically, but to elucidate it mystically, especially since in the second verse it says, *I will open my mouth in parables.* Now parabolic expressions are not to be examined superficially, but rather [are to be examined] with great diligence. Indeed, the evangelist Matthew asserts this verse of the Psalm as predictive of Christ: *All these things* (he says) *were done that it might be fulfilled* that which was written, *I will open my mouth in parables, I will utter things hidden from the foundation of the world:*[3] which, in this Psalm, is so expressed in other words, *I will utter propositions from the beginning.*[4] Here, St. Jerome infers that the evangelist Matthew understood this in the person of Christ. The Prophet, that is, the author of the present Psalm—whether it be David or Asaph—says the two first verses of this Psalm which serve as a sort of preface or prologue which precede what follows, in the person of Christ. But that which follows, we see literally to be said of the people of the Old Testament, namely,

---

1 1 Cor. 10:11a.
2 *Cf.* Rom. 15:4a: *For what things soever were written, were written for our learning.*
3 Matt. 13:34a, 35.
4 E. N. In other words, there is a variance between the words used in the Gospel of Matthew and the words used in the Psalm.

of the miracles of God regarding that people, once peculiar to him;[5] but also of the ingratitude of this people and their fitting punishment, and the choice of David and his posterity as their king,[6] all of which can be spiritually exposited of the Christian people, as is, to some extent, touched upon below.

The Prophet, therefore, wanting to make the people to whom he speaks teachable, good-willed, and attentive, begins in this way, speaking (as I said) not in his own person, but in Christ's person, who also has spoken through the mouth of all the Prophets:[7] *Attendite, popule meus; attend, O my people* chosen by me to faith and to divine worship, *legem meam, to my law,* that is, the ten laws of moral precepts, which in the Old Testament and the New are the same, which were first made known to Moses on Mount Sinai by God,[8] and which were approved by Christ in the Gospel. *Inclinate aurem vestram, incline your ears,* both those of the body as well as those of the heart, *in verba oris mei, to the words of my mouth,* that is, to the words of sacred Scripture and the divine preaching, reverently paying attention to them and faithfully observing them.

77{78}[2]   *I will open my mouth in parables: I will utter propositions from the beginning.*

   Aperiam in parabolis os meum; loquar propositiones ab initio.

77{78}[3]   *How great things have we heard and known, and our fathers have told us.*

   Quanta audivimus et cognovimus ea, et patres nostri narraverunt nobis.

77{78}[4]   *They have not been hidden from their children, in another generation. Declaring the praises of the Lord, and his powers, and his wonders which he has done.*

   Non sunt occultata a filiis eorum in generatione altera, narrantes laudes Domini et virtutes eius, et mirabilia eius quae fecit.

77{78}[2] *Aperiam in parabolis os meum, I will open my mouth in parables.* This is literally true of Christ, for which reason in the Gospel

---

5   Deut. 7:6: *Because you are a holy people to the Lord your God. The Lord your God has chosen you, to be his peculiar people of all peoples that are upon the earth.*
6   1 Sam. 16:13.
7   Luke 1:70: *As he spoke by the mouth of his holy prophets, who are from the beginning.* (Song of Zechariah).
8   Ex. chp. 34.

it is said, *Without parables he did not speak to them.*[9] And he said to his disciples: *To you it is given to know the mystery of the kingdom of God: but to them that are without, all things are done in parables.*[10] Now they are called parables because of a certain resemblance between the things that are treated and the things with which they are compared, since what is asserted of the former, is understood to apply to the latter. *Loquar propositiones ab initio, I will utter propositions from the beginning.* As has already been made clear, Matthew asserts this: *I will utter things hidden from the foundation of the world.*[11] Now commonly those explaining [this Psalm] say that the words *from the beginning (ab initio)* as our translation puts it, is not referring to the beginning of the world, but to the beginning of the leading of the Israelites out of Egypt. But, because the Evangelist [Matthew] filled with the Holy Spirit asserts, *from the foundation of the world (a constitutione mundi)*, it seems that in this Psalm, at least implicitly and in general, the marvels of God executed at the beginning of the world are recalled: because in that [verse] which follows — *How great things have we heard and known, and our fathers have told us* — not only can be fittingly understood to the works of God done from the time of Moses and and reported to posterity by the fathers contemporaneous with him or after him, but above all we can understand this as referring to the marvels of God done from the beginning of the world, such as was the flood, the submersion [by fire] of the Pentapolis, namely, Sodom, Gomorrah, Admah, Zeboim, and Zoar,[12] and such other similar things, which Abraham, Melchizedek, Lot, and various others of the old Patriarchs narrated to their posterity, and indirectly also to the children of Israel. But such hidden things Christ in the Gospels sets forth, as a studious reader would agree. For he makes mention of Noah and the flood,[13] the submersion [by fire] of Sodom,[14] and of the beginning and the institution of matrimony.[15] But some explain where it now says — *I will open my mouth in parables, etc.* — as applying to the author of the present Psalm, so that it reads in this sense: *I will open my mouth,* that is, I will narrate the sayings and the facts of the Old Testament, which are figures of those things in the New Testament. *I will utter propositions,*

---

9 Matt. 13:34b.

10 Mark 4:11.

11 Matt. 13:35b.

12 E. N. Wis. 10:6: *She delivered the just man who fled from the wicked that were perishing, when the fire came down upon Pentapolis.*

13 Luke 17:26–27; Matt. 24:37–39.

14 Luke 17:28–29.

15 Matt. 19:4–9.

that is, utterances or disputed questions, which the Greeks call *problemata*, but the Hebrews *enigmata: things hidden*, I say, speaking of things which pertained from the beginning of the liberation of Israel from Egypt.

Then the author of the Psalm, speaking in the person of the Israelite people, adds: 77{78}[3] *Quanta, how great* the marvelous works and magnificent benefits of God, *audivimus et cognovimus ea, we have heard and known*, that is, we have perceived, understanding with the ears of the heart, *et patres nostri, and our fathers*, namely, Moses, Joshua, and similar holy fathers, *narraverunt nobis, have told us* mediately, and through the books which they produced and delivered to us. 77{78}[4] *Non sunt occultata, they have not been hidden* those works of God accomplished in Egypt, in the Red Sea, in the desert, and in the land of Canaan, *a filiis eorum, from their children*, that is, from those who have followed the faith and deeds of their fathers, not forgetting the benefits of the most-high God. Yet they were not made known to all their children, for it is written in the book of Judges: *There arose others that knew not the Lord, and the works which he had done for Israel.*[16] For such persons were only children according to the flesh, not according to the imitation of faith. They have not, therefore, been hidden from their children *in generatione altera, in another generation*, that is, to those children who were in the succeeding generation, for the memory of the things done was made known to those who came after them. Now what it was that the fathers related to their children follows: *Narrantes laudes Domini, declaring the praises of the Lord*, that is, his laudable works, and the words that contain the divine praises, *et virtutes eius, and his powers*, that is, the might of God which struck the Egyptians with ten principal plagues, *et mirabilia eius quae fecit, and his wonders which he has done*, dividing the Red Sea, and drowning the Egyptians.

77{78}[5] *And he set up a testimony in Jacob: and made a law in Israel. How great things he commanded our fathers, that they should make the same known to their children:*

Et suscitavit testimonium in Iacob, et legem posuit in Israel, quanta mandavit patribus nostris nota facere ea filiis suis.

77{78}[6] *That another generation might know them. The children that should be born and should rise up, and declare them to their children.*

---

16   Judges 2:10b.

Ut cognoscat generatio altera; filii qui nascentur et exsurgent, et narrabunt filiis suis.

77{78}[7] That they may put their hope in God and may not forget the works of God: and may seek his commandments.

Ut ponant in Deo spem suam, et non obliviscantur operum Dei, et mandata eius exquirant.

77{78}[5] *Et suscitavit testimonium in Iacob, and he set up a testimony in Jacob,* that is, he conferred a covenant to certain of the Jews born of Jacob; *et legem posuit in Israel, and made a law in Israel:* He gave the law through Moses, and he wrote this law on stone tablets so that it might be preserved and it might serve as testimony of the divine pronouncement and heavenly legislations to the posterity [of the faithful], and also so that it might be a testimony to the perverse of their condemnation, as Moses often attests in the book of Deuteronomy. For this reason the Lord commanded the Deuteronomic law to be written down, and the tablets of the testament to be preserved in the tabernacle.[17] The testimony and the law are the same thing, in the way that Jacob and Israel are the same thing; but they differ in condition. Of course, it is called law because it commands, restrains, and binds: it commands, I say, that which ought to be done and that which ought to be avoided; it restrains from evil by prohibitions and punishments; it binds the soul under God by legal observations. But it is called testimony because it both approves and convicts.

Quanta, *how great things,* that is, with how many and how great deeds and words, *mandavit patribus nostris, he commanded our fathers* as he led them out of Egypt, *nota facere ea filiis suis, that they should make the same known to their children,* relating or writing that which they had witnessed, 77{78}[6] *ut cognoscat generatio altera, that another generation might know them,* that is, that all generations succeeding them [might know them]. Filii qui nascentur, *the children that should be born* [physically] from the womb, *et exsurgent, and should rise up* to the perfection of age, of strength, and of reason, will *narrabunt filiis suis, declare them to their children.* This was often fulfilled by the Jewish people. And so they made known this to their children, since they taught them to trust in God: and so there follows: 77{78}[7] *Ut ponant, that they may put,* [that is, that their] children [may put] *in Deo spem suam, their hope in God,* not in their own strength or in any creature, *et non obliviscantur*

---

17 Deut. 31:10–13, 26.

operum Dei, and may not forget the works of God which he had performed, saving their fathers, and killing the unbelievers, *et mandata eius exquirant, and may seek his commandments,* that is, they may desire carefully and diligently to know them, so that they might fulfill them.

77{78}[8]   *That they may not become like their fathers, a perverse and exasperating generation. A generation that set not their heart aright: and whose spirit was not faithful to God.*

Ne fiant, sicut patres eorum, generatio prava et exasperans; generatio quae non direxit cor suum, et non est creditus cum Deo spiritus eius.

77{78}[8] *Ne fiant sicut patres eorum, that they may not become like their fathers,* led out of Egypt, who were *generatio prava, a perverse . . . generation,* that is, disobedient, *et exasperans, and exasperating,* that is, rousing the divine justice and vengeance. Whence also Moses said to this generation: *I know your obstinacy, and your most stiff neck; while I am yet living, and going in with you, you have always been rebellious against the Lord.*[18] For in large part they were evil: and for this reason, they were cast off into the desert.[19] *Generatio quae non direxit cor suum, a generation that set not their heart aright,* that is, which did not seek the Lord God with a perfect, and true, and sincere heart. For this reason, Moses said to them: *You have seen all the things that the Lord did before you . . . And the Lord has not given you a heart to understand . . . unto this present day.*[20] *Et non est creditus cum Deo spiritus eius, and whose spirit was not faithful to God:* that is, the spirit or the soul of this people was not joined unto God by faith, because they did not believe in the divine promises. Whence, other translations are more clear, saying: *And their spirit did not believe God.*[21] And this is to be referred not to all the Israelite people, but only to the perverse who were among them, according to the rule introduced in the beginning part of this Commentary, which says, that at times sacred Scripture speaks in mixed terms of the body of the Lord as a mixture of good and evil: wherein it must be considered what is fitting to refer

---

18   Deut. 31:27.

19   Num. 14:29: *In the wilderness shall your carcasses lie. All you that were numbered from twenty years old and upward, and have murmured against me.* Ps. 105:26: *And he lifted up his hand over them: to overthrow them in the desert.*

20   Deut. 29:2a, 4.

21   E. N. *Et non credidit Deo spiritus eius.* This appears to be St. Jerome's translation from the Hebrew.

to whom. For sometimes the entire congregation is praised because of some of the good men contained in it; conversely it is also reproached because of some of the evil men contained in it, as it now is.[22]

77{78}[9]   *The sons of Ephraim who bend and shoot with the bow: they have turned back in the day of battle.*

Filii Ephrem, intendentes et mittentes arcum, conversi sunt in die belli.

77{78}[10] *They kept not the covenant of God: and in his law they would not walk.*

Non custodierunt testamentum Dei, et in lege eius noluerunt ambulare.

77{78}[9] *Filii Ephrem,* that is, some born of the progeny of Ephraim, the son of Joseph,[23] *intendentes et mittentes arcum, who bend and shoot the bow,* that is, those stretching the bow and discharging arrows from the bow, *conversi sunt in die belli, have turned back in the day of battle,* that is, taking flight, they turned around and fled in the day when against the precept of Moses they ascended unto the mountain to battle against the Amalekites and the Amorites, as is written in the book of Numbers.[24] For from the beginning the sons of Ephraim were presumptuous and ambitious, because their father, namely, Joseph, was lord over his brothers; and because Jacob preferred Ephraim, the second born, to the first-born of Joseph, who was Manasseh;[25] and because Joshua, the minister of Moses chosen from many [other tribes], exalted the Ephraimites.[26] Whence, their self-exaltation is often exposed in the book of Judges; and so the Prophet in this Psalm singularly inveighs against the sons of Ephraim, showing that they were not chosen for the dignity of kingship, but rather the tribe of Judah was. 77{78}[10] *Non custodierunt testamentum Dei, they kept not the covenant of God:* for they transgressed the commands

---

22   E. N. This is a reference to the rules of Tyconius, one of which (the second) addresses how statements regarding the Mystical Body of Christ, and by analogy the Synagogue or the Jewish people, should be construed, since the Mystical Body of Christ contains both wheat and tares. *See* Volume I, Article IV and footnote P-91.

23   Gen. 41:52.

24   Num. 14:40–45.

25   Gen. 48:14, 17–20.

26   E. N. Hosea, was the son of Nun, of the tribe of Ephraim (Num. 13:9); but Moses called him Joshua (Num. 13:17): "And [Moses] called Hosea, the son of Nun, Joshua."

of God given through Moses, proceeding to battle as was just now mentioned; *et in lege eius noluerunt ambulare, and in his law they would not
walk,* that is, they disdained to fulfill the divine precepts.

77{78}[11]   *And they forgot his benefits, and his wonders that he had
shown them.*

Et obliti sunt benefactorum eius, et mirabilium eius quae
ostendit eis.

77{78}[11] *Et obliti sunt benefactorum eius, and they forgot his benefits:* that is, the children of Israel in general — and not only the sons of
Ephraim or Ephrem, which is the same — were ungrateful to God for
his benefits, either by utterly not recalling or not giving thanks, and
thus neither loving nor revering their benefactor. So also they forgot
mirabilium eius quae ostendit eis, the wonders that he had shown them in
the land of Egypt, saying among themselves: *Let us appoint a captain,
and let us return into Egypt.*[27]

77{78}[12]   *Wonderful things did he do in the sight of their fathers, in
the land of Egypt, in the field of Tanis.*

Coram patribus eorum fecit mirabilia in terra Aegypti, in
campo Taneos.

77{78}[13]   *He divided the sea and brought them through: and he made
the waters to stand as in a vessel.*

Interrupit mare, et perduxit eos; et statuit aquas quasi in utre.

77{78}[14]   *And he conducted them with a cloud by day: and all the
night with a light of fire.*

Et deduxit eos in nube diei, et tota nocte in illuminatione ignis.

77{78}[12] *Coram patribus eorum fecit mirabilia in terra Aegypti, wonderful things did he do in the sight of their fathers in the land of Egypt:* as
is set forth in the book of Exodus.[28] And this God did in a very great
way *in campo Taneos, in the field of Tanis,* that is, in the plains of that
city. For Tanis was a royal city in which the king was accustomed to live
along with his counselors. For this reason, we find written in Isaiah: *The
princes of Tanis are become fools, the wise counselors of Pharaoh have given*

---

27   Num. 14:4.
28   Ex. chps. 7–14.

foolish counsel.[29] This is said because the king and his counselors, who were the main causes of all the sins and the afflictions of Egypt, were accustomed to dwell in that royal city; so is it apparently true that this city was more heavily scourged than the others. And here, as has already been mentioned, God in a special way performed marvels in the location or the plains of this city.[30] **77{78}[13]** *Interrupit mare,* he divided the sea, the Red Sea, dividing it, *et perduxit eos,* and brought them through with dry feet through the sea's bed; *et statuit aquas,* and he made the waters stand, and so divided the Red Sea *quasi in utre,* as in a vessel, that is, he so affixed the waters in their place that they did not flow, as if they were collected in a vase. **77{78}[14]** *Et deduxit eos,* and he conducted them, namely, the children of Israel out of Egypt, and through the Red Sea and the desert, *in nube diei, with a cloud by day,* that is, with a column of cloud visible in the day, *et tota nocte, and all the night,* that is, during all the nights that they travelled, *in illuminatione ignis, with a light of fire,* that is, with a column of fire showing the way in the dark of night. For in the manner they travelled by day under the cloud, protected thereby from the heat of the sun, so at night they followed the lead of the fire; never did the column of cloud or fire fail them until they entered into the land of promise; nor did they set forth by day or night unless the column of cloud or fire first changed place, moving away from the tabernacle: all of which is frequently described by Moses in Exodus and Numbers.[31]

77{78}[15] *He struck the rock in the wilderness: and gave them to drink, as out of the great deep.*

Interrupit petram in eremo, et adaquavit eos velut in abysso multa.

77{78}[16] *He brought forth water out of the rock: and made streams run down as rivers.*

Et eduxit aquam de petra, et deduxit tamquam flumina aquas.

77{78}[15] *Interrupit petram in eremo,* he struck the rock in the wilderness. Twice do we read that almighty God brought forth water from a rock for the children of Israel: once, namely, from the rock at Horeb, of

---

29 Is. 19:11a.
30 E. N. The city of Tanis (in Greek) or Zoan (צוֹעַן in Hebrew) was for a time the capital of Egypt. Located in lower Egypt, in the delta of the Nile River, it is the place not only where Moses was discovered among the reeds, but also where he performed the various signs and marvels before Pharaoh to persuade him to let his people go.
31 Ex. chps. 13–14; Num. chps. 10–12.

which bringing forth this verse speaks, and which we find fully described in Exodus.[32] The second time, when Moses struck the stone twice, and *there came forth water in great abundance, so that the people and their cattle drank*, of which bringing forth the book of Numbers relates.[33] These were different instances of bringing forth [water from the rock] because the first was before the giving of the law, and the second after it. Therefore, it says: *He struck the rock in the wilderness*, that is, he caused a certain cavity or division in it, as if it had been split, and from the rock so split came forth waters; *et adaquavit eos, and gave them to drink*, that is, they drank the water, *velut in abysso multa, as out of the great deep*, that is, so abundantly, and as if it were like a great sea from which water could be drawn as one pleased. For since there were six hundred thousand men in the army of the Hebrews, besides women and children, those, namely, that had not yet attained twenty years of age, and also not including a mixed multitude of Egyptians without number,[34] it follows that a great flow of water flowed from the rock from which they all drank. 77{78}[16] *Et eduxit aquam de petra, and he brought forth water out of a rock*, when Moses struck twice the rock or stone, as has already been stated; *et deduxit, and . . . made run down* out of that rock, *tanquam flumina aquas, streams . . . as rivers*, that is, waters flowing so copiously as if they were a river.

77{78}[17]   *And they added yet more sin against him: they provoked the most High to wrath in the place without water.*

Et apposuerunt adhuc peccare ei; in iram excitaverunt Excelsum in inaquoso.

77{78}[18]   *And they tempted God in their hearts, by asking meat for their desires.*

Et tentaverunt Deum in cordibus suis, ut peterent escas animabus suis.

77{78}[17] *Et apposuerunt adhuc peccare ei, and they added yet more sin against him*: that is, they were ungrateful for so many of the Creator's benefits, and they returned evil for good, and to the prior wicked deeds they added new sins: for ingratitude is also a great sin; *in iram excitaverunt Excelsum, they provoked the most High to wrath*: that is, by their sins

---

32   Ex. 17:6: *Behold I will stand there before you, upon the rock Horeb: and you shall strike the rock, and water shall come out of it that the people may drink. Moses did so before the ancients of Israel.*

33   Num. 20:11.

34   E. N. Ex. 12:37–38.

they provoked the most sublime God to the likeness of wrath, or to the effect of anger, namely, to the just avenging and the infliction of great punishments; and this, *in inaquoso, in the place without water,* that is, in the desert, in which there is naturally a lack a dearth of water. 77{78} [18] *Et tentaverunt Deum in cordibus suis, and they tempted God in their hearts:* that is, with the intention and premeditation of heart, they desired to test the providence of God, namely, whether God would take care of them by providing them the necessities to live. And so it continues: *ut peterent escas animabus suis, by asking meat for their desires,* that is, nourishment supportive of life. But we read that twice they asked for food in this manner. Once before the giving of the law, when they said to Moses: *Why have you brought us into this desert, that you might destroy all the multitude with famine?*[35] And then the Lord began to rain down manna. The second time they asked that meat might be given them, saying: *Our soul is dry, our eyes behold nothing else but manna,*[36] as is written in the book of Numbers.

77{78}[19]   *And they spoke ill of God: they said: Can God furnish a table in the wilderness?*

Et male locuti sunt de Deo; dixerunt: Numquid poterit Deus parare mensam in deserto?

77{78}[20]   *Because he struck the rock, and the waters gushed out, and the streams overflowed. Can he also give bread, or provide a table for his people?*

Quoniam percussit petram, et fluxerunt aquae, et torrentes inundaverunt. Numquid et panem poterit dare, aut parare mensam populo suo?

77{78}[19] *Et male, and . . . ill,* namely, unfaithfully and perversely, *locuti sunt de Deo, dixerunt; they spoke . . . of God; they said* that which follows: *Numquid poterit Deus parare mensam in deserto, Can God furnish a table in the wilderness?* That is, [can he furnish us] a rich and delicious meal? This they said not assertively, but doubtfully; and yet, they declared that God was able to do this.[37] 77{78}[20] *Quoniam*

---

35   Ex. 16:3.
36   Num. 11:6.
37   E. N. The evil here is not doubting that God had the power to provide them bread, for they had witnessed God's ability to bring water out of a rock. The evil is doubting that God would do so in this particular instance, or in the manner that the murmurers desired.

perxussit petram, et fluxerunt aquae; because he struck the rock, and the waters gushed out, that is, from that place the abundant waters came forth: as had become apparent to them. Since it was so, therefore, *Numquid et panem poterit dare? Can he also give bread?* By bread (according to some [commentators]) manna is not to be understood, because God had given this sort of bread before the bringing forth of the water; but by bread here is understood any kind of luxurious bread that was desirable to them. Indeed, with the word of bread (*panis*) Scripture customarily designates any kind of food. Whence we find with respect to Saul, that the whole day *he had eaten no bread;*[38] and of Ezra, who *ate no bread, nor did he drink water,*[39] that is, he did not taste anything. And we read that Elisha told the king of Israel that he should place bread (*panem*) and water before the army of the king of Syria,[40] which Elisha miraculously led away. And then what follows occurred: *A great provision of meats (ciborum) was set before them.*[41] So therefore also now by bread we are to understand that they meant delicious food: and so it adds, *aut parare mensam populo suo? Or provide a table for his people?* Here, by table is understood that they wanted a rich meal, especially since in the Hebrew and in the translation of Jerome according to the Hebrew we read: *Is God among us or not?*[42] And so about this most faithless temptation of theirs is written in Numbers: *They burned with desire of the flesh, and they said: Who shall give us flesh to eat? ... The cucumbers come into our mind, and the melons, and the leeks, and* other things, which we had eaten in Egypt.[43]

77{78}[21] *Therefore the Lord heard, and was angry: and a fire was kindled against Jacob, and wrath came up against Israel.*

Ideo audivit Dominus et distulit; et ignis accensus est in Iacob, et ira ascendit in Israel.

77{78}[21] *Ideo, therefore,* that is, from the fact that they said this from their unfaithfulness, lacking the certainty that the Lord was able to fulfill their desires, *audivit Dominus, the Lord heard* their petition, not because they deserved it, but so that he might reveal his omnipotence;

---

38   1 Sam. 28:20b.
39   1 Esdras 10:6b.
40   2 Kings 6:22.
41   2 Kings 6:23.
42   Ex. 17:7b.
43   Num. 11:4b, 5.

et distulit, and was angry, that is, he did not immediately take vengeance against their sin, but he delayed the due punishment, so that he might inflict it after a suitable time; but first he would exhibit his power [to provide them with bread]. *Et ignis, and a fire,* that is, the vehement fury or the great vindication, *accensus est in Iacob, was kindled against Jacob,* that is, justly inflicted to the posterity of Jacob, namely, the children of Israel. This is clearly stated in what follows: *et ira, and wrath of* God, that is, the vengeance of divine justice, *ascendit in Israel, came up against Israel,* that is, against the Israelite people, born of the seed of Jacob, who are called Israel. This verse is commonly explained in this way [by commentators]. But because in the book of Numbers it clearly states — *There arose a murmuring of the people ... as it were repining at their fatigue. And when the Lord heard it he was angry. And the fire of the Lord being kindled against them, devoured them that were at the uttermost part of the camp*[44] — it is certain that a material fire is meant; and so this verse can be explained in reference to that fire. It does not matter that the kindling of this fire preceded this temptation, because in divine Scripture, events are not always described in the order that they took place; but they are said sometimes stated by anticipation, sometimes by recapitulation, sometimes as a supplementation. This [sort of chronological license] occurs most often in those books of poetic genre, such as the book of Psalms.

77{78}[22] *Because they believed not in God: and trusted not in his salvation.*

Quia non crediderunt in Deo, nec speraverunt in salutari eius.

Therefore, God punished them so, 77{78}[22] *Quia non crediderunt in Deo, because they believed not in God,* who promised them that he would lead them into the land of Canaan. For they said, as is contained in the book of Numbers: *Would that ... we may die ... and that the Lord may not bring us into this land, lest we fall by the sword, and our wives and children.*[45] Whence the Lord said to Moses: *How long will this wicked* multitude *not believe in me?*[46] *Nec speraverunt in salutari eius, and they trusted not in his salvation,* that is, the salubrious help of God that God had promised them through Moses, saying: *The Lord will fight for you.*[47]

---

44   Num. 11:1.
45   Num. 14:3.
46   Num. 14:11.
47   Ex. 14:14a.

77{78}[23] *And he had commanded the clouds from above, and had opened the doors of heaven.*

Et mandavit nubibus desuper, et ianuas caeli aperuit.

77{78}[24] *And he had rained down upon them mana to eat, and had given them the bread of heaven.*

Et pluit illis manna ad manducandum, et panem caeli dedit eis.

77{78}[25] *Man ate the bread of angels: he sent them provisions in abundance.*

Panem angelorum manducavit homo; cibaria misit eis in abundantia.

77{78}[23] *Et mandavit nubibus desuper,* and he had commanded the clouds from above: that is, by divine power manna was made to descend as from the atmosphere wherein the clouds are produced. For God is said to command irrational and inanimate things when they suffer or do something from the will of divine rule. For this reason, the Lord said to Elijah: *I have commanded the ravens to feed you there.*[48] *Et ianuas caeli aperuit,* and had opened the doors of heaven, that is, he caused to be made in the heavenly atmosphere means by which manna descended. 77{78}[24] *Et pluit illis manna ad manducandum, et panem caeli;* and he had rained down upon them manna to eat, and . . . the bread of heaven, that is, [bread] formed in the heavenly atmosphere by the ministry of the angels, *dedit eis,* he had given them to feed upon. Therefore, there is added: 77{78}[24] *Panem angelorum,* the bread of angels, that is, by the angelic ministry produced and made to descend (and not that the holy angels fed on it, for they do not use bodily food, as is stated in the book of Tobit);[49] *manducavit homo,* man ate, every man in the army of the Hebrews; *cibaria misit eis in abundantia,* he sent them provisions in abundance, that is, even unto satiety. It seems to follow from those words stated above — *Can he also give bread?* — that they can be understood as referring to the manna, for God is said to have heard their petition, and then to have given them manna or heavenly bread. Of this bread or manna that descended together with the dewfall the book of Exodus says this: *In the morning, a dew lay round about the camp, . . . and it appeared in the wilderness small, and as it were beaten with a pestle, like unto the hoar frost on the ground; and the children of Israel called it Manhu, that is, What is*

---

48 1 Kings 17:4b.
49 Tob. 12:19: E. N. The archangel Raphael says, *I seemed indeed to eat and to drink with you: but I use an invisible meat and drink, which cannot be seen by men.*

it? It was like coriander seed white, and the taste thereof like to flour with honey.[50] For this reason also it is written elsewhere: *With the food of angels you did feed your people, and gave them bread from heaven,... having in it all that is delicious, and the sweetness of every taste:... serving every man's will, it was turned to what every man liked.*[51]

77{78}[26]   *He removed the south wind from heaven: and by his power brought in the southwest wind.*

Transtulit austrum de caelo, et induxit in virtute sua africum.

77{78}[27]   *And he rained upon them flesh as dust: and feathered fowls like the sand of the sea.*

Et pluit super eos sicut pulverem carnes, et sicut arenam maris volatilia pennata.

77{78}[28]   *And they fell in the midst of their camp, round about their pavilions.*

Et ceciderunt in medio castrorum eorum, circa tabernacula eorum.

77{78}[26] *Transtulit austrum de caelo, he removed the south wind from heaven,* that is, God caused the southern or meridional wind to cease in the atmosphere, *et induxit in virtute sua africum, and by his power brought in the southwest wind,* that is, with his power he caused to blow the western wind, laterally against the southern wind. For the wind blew in between the south and the west. And so this wind was led to blow from the southwest, since a multitude of quail lived in those parts, and with the impulse it was driven over the sea to the children of Israel, as it states in the book of Numbers: *And a wind going out from the Lord, taking quails up beyond the sea brought them, and cast them into the camp.*[52] And so it continues: 77{78}[27] *Et pluit super eos sicut pulverem carnes, and he rained upon them flesh as dust,* not dead flesh, but live flesh, of which it states, *et sicut arenam maris volatilia pennata, and feathered fowls like the sand of the sea.* For the quail were birds that flew close to the earth, *two cubits high above the ground.*[53] Now God rained these animals, that is, he sent them from the air in the manner of rain so copiously that they were as the sands of the sea according to that which Moses said:

---

50   Ex. 16:13–15, 31.
51   Wis. 16:20–21.
52   Num. 11:31a.
53   *Ibid.*

A wind brought quails into the camp, *for the space of one day's journey,* *on every side of the camp round about.*[54] 77{78}[28] *Et ceciderunt,* and *they fell* these animals did *in medio castrorum eorum, in the midst of their camp,* that is, within or near the camp or tents of the children of Israel, namely, *circa tabernacula eorum, round about their pavilions* or canopies, so that they were able to be captured without effort. Whence it says in Numbers: *The people therefore rising up all that day, and night, and the next day, gathered together a multitude of quails,* . . . *and they dried them round about the camp.*[55]

77{78}[29] *So they did eat, and were filled exceedingly, and he gave them*
          their desire:

          Et manducaverunt, et saturati sunt nimis; et desiderium eorum
          attulit eis:

77{78}[30] *They were not defrauded of that which they craved. As yet*
          their meat was in their mouth.

          Non sunt fraudati a desiderio suo. Adhuc escae eorum erant
          in ore ipsorum.

77{78}[31] *And the wrath of God came upon them. And he slew the fat*
          ones among them, and obstructed the chosen men of Israel.[56]

          Et ira Dei ascendit super eos; et occidit pingues eorum, et
          electos Israel impedivit.

  77{78}[29] *Et manducaverunt, so they did eat,* the children of Israel [ate] these meats, *et saturati sunt nimis, and were filled exceedingly,* even to the point of discomfort[57] and loathsomeness, *et desiderium eorum atulit eis, and he gave them their desire,* that is, he bestowed upon them the thing that they desired; 77{78}[30] *non sunt fraudati a desiderio suo, they were not defrauded of that which they craved,* that is, they were not deprived from obtaining the thing they desired, because they obtained an abundance of meats. All of this is most clearly brought out in the book of Numbers, in this fashion: *You shall say to the people, tomorrow you shall eat flesh, and you shall eat not for one day, nor two, nor five,* . . . *but even for a month of days, till it come out at your nostrils, and become loathsome*

---

54 *Ibid.*
55 Num. 11:32.
56 E. N. I have departed from the Douay Rheims's translation of *impedivit* as "brought down," and replaced it with "obstructed."
57 E. N. Literally *ad collum,* up to their necks.

to you.[58] *Adhuc escae eorum, as yet their meat,* namely, these meats, *erant in ore ipsorum,* were in their mouth, 77{78}[31] *et ira Dei, and the wrath of God,* namely, the vengeance which was to follow, *ascendit super eos, came upon them.* For *occidit pingues eorum, he slew the fat ones amongst them,* that is, those abounding in riches, the proud, the carnally inclined; *et electos Israel impedivit, and obstructed the chosen men of Israel.* This can be understood in two ways. The first is in this way: *the elect of Israel,* that is, he hindered the good and just Jews so that their exhortations and prayers would be unable to profit the reprobate in any way: for the elect are not heard [in their prayers] for the reprobate because of the weight of the latter's condemned vices. The second is in this way: *the elect of Israel,* that is, those among the people who were critical were hindered from entering the land of promise. And this is what is said in Numbers: *As yet the flesh was between their teeth, neither had that kind of meat failed: when behold the wrath of the Lord being provoked against the people, struck them with an exceeding great plague. And that place was called, the graves of concupiscence: for there they buried the people that had desired the meats.*[59]

77{78}[32]   *In all these things they sinned still: and they believed not for his wondrous works.*

In omnibus his peccaverunt adhuc, et non crediderunt in mirabilibus eius.

77{78}[33]   *And their days were consumed in vanity, and their years in haste.*

Et defecerunt in vanitate dies eorum, et anni eorum cum festinatione.

77{78}[32] *In omnibus his,* in all these things that have been mentioned they failed to atone for, but they persisted in their perversities, *peccaverunt adhuc, they sinned still,* namely, by then desiring to return to Egypt after the return of the spies [sent to survey the land of Canaan];[60] *et*

---

58   Num. 11:16, 18–20.
59   Num. 11:33–34. I have departed from the Douay-Rheims which uses "lust" to translate *concupiscentiae* and "lusted" to translate *desideraverat*; I have translated these words as "concupiscence" and "desired," respectively. While the Latin term for lust (*luxuriae*) can refer to the disordered desire for food, the modern connotation of lust generally limits it to sexual desire, which is clearly not the context here. In Hebrew, the word קִבְרוֹת הַתַּאֲוָה (Qibroth-hattaavah), "graves of desire," is translated in the Latin by *sepulcra concupiscentiae.*
60   Num. 14:3–4. E. N. The twelve spies were sent out by Moses. See Num. 13:3–28. Though the land flowed "with milk and honey," it was inhabited by walled cities and

non crediderunt in mirabilibus eius, and they believed not for his wondrous works: that is, because of the strength of the people, of the cities, and of the walls of that land, they were unwilling to believe that God would be able to lead them safely into the land of Canaan by recalling the first marvels which God did before them in Egypt, in the Red Sea, in the desert: indeed, they wanted to stone Caleb and Joshua because they said that it was possible for God to fulfill his word and destroy the Canaanites.[61] 77{78}[33] *Et defecerunt in vanitate dies eorum, and their days were consumed in vanity*, that is, because of their sins their days were worthless; *et anni eorum cum festinatione, and their years in haste were lost*, that is, were quickly spent, and they died and suffered ruin in the desert: because all those who were numbered among them and murmured died within the forty years that they were in the desert, and they were unable to enter into the promised land.[62] Many of them were also killed with a quick death by fiery serpents,[63] and at the insurrection of Korah,[64] and because of the sin of Peor.[65]

77{78}[34] *When he slew them, then they sought him: and they returned, and came to him early in the morning.*

Cum occideret eos, quaerebant eum et revertebantur, et diluculo veniebant ad eum.

77{78}[35] *And they remembered that God was their helper: and the most high God their redeemer.*

Et rememorati sunt quia Deus adiutor est eorum, et Deus excelsus redemptor eorum est.

---

strong leaders and inhabitants, and this soured the Israelites, causing them to murmur and engendering their desire to return to Egypt. Num. 13:29–34.

61 Num. 14:6–10.

62 Num. 26:64–65. E. N. "As long as we are in a state of grace, Christ is within us, ... [a]nd what great value our works have when they are presented to the Father as having been performed with Christ! But without this union, our works are worthless, as Christ has taught (John 15:5)." Antonio Royo Marín, O. P., *The Theology of Christian Perfection* (Eugene, OR: Wipf & Stock 2011), 209. (trans., Jordan Aumann, O. P.).

63 Num. 21:6. *Wherefore the Lord sent among the people fiery serpents, which bit them and killed many of them.*

64 Num. chp. 16. E. N. Korah, a member of the tribe of Levi, rebelled against Moses and Aaron; as punishment, he was swallowed by the earth.

65 Num. chp. 25. E. N. The Israelites consorted with the Moabite women who introduced them to the worship of the Moabite gods, including sacrifice to *Baal Peor*. For their apostasy, the leaders of these apostates were hung and the apostates ordered killed, resulting in death of twenty-four thousand Israelites.

77{78}[36] *And they loved him with their mouth: and with their tongue they lied unto him.*

Et dilexerunt eum in ore suo, et lingua sua mentiti sunt ei.

77{78}[37] *But their heart was not right with him: nor were they counted faithful in his covenant.*

Cor autem eorum non erat rectum cum eo, nec fideles habiti sunt in testamento eius.

77{78}[34] *Cum occideret eos, quaerebant eum, et revertebantur; when he slew them, then they sought him, and they returned:* not that the same number were slain and returned; but according to that rule set forth at the beginning [of this Commentary], Scripture here speaks about separate things that pertain to the same people, as if they were the same subject.[66] And so, since God killed certain apostates, others were terrified that they might not suffer the same torment: and so they sought him, that is, they invoked the mercy of God seeking indulgence, and they returned to God through repentance. *Et diluculo, and early in the morning,* that is, quickly out of fear of great punishment, *veniebant ad eum, they came to him,* not in terms of the stepping of feet or the distance of space, but by change of the mind and repentance of the heart. 77{78}[35] *Et rememorate sunt, and they remembered* by considering the former marvels of God, and the death of those who had not so considered them, *quia Deus adiutor est eorum, that God was their helper* in all good, as he was their helper in Egypt and against Amalek,[67] *et Deus excelsus redemptor eorum est, and the most high God is their redeemer,* delivering them from all danger, as he had delivered them from the hand of Pharaoh and his army. 77{78}[36] *Et dilexerunt eum in ore suo, and they loved him with their mouth,* that is, with the words of prayer they pretended to love God, *et lingua sua mentiti sunt ei, and with their tongue they lied unto him,* that is, their words were false, and they were not uttered with a sincere heart. 77{78}[37] *Cor autem eorum non erat rectum cum eo, but their heart was not right with him,* that is, it did not please God, for it was not just or true; *nec fideles habiti sunt*

---

66 E. N. This is a reference to the fourth rule of Tyconius, which relates to the breadth or reach of certain words. *See* Volume 1 (Article IV), p. 17 and footnote P-99. In this case, the third person plural person (they/them) refers to different subgroups of the Israelites, the first of those being the Israelites who were slain, the second being those Israelites who survived and who turned to God and returned to him.
67 Ex. chps. 4 and 17. E. N. Joshua defeats the Amalekites at the battle in Rephidim while Moses watches from a height nearby. So long as Moses had his arms raised, Israel prevailed by divine aid.

in testamento eius, nor were they counted faithful in his covenant, that is, they did not faithfully comply with the divine law by keeping its precepts.

77{78}[38]   *But he is merciful and will forgive their sins: and will not destroy them. And many a time did he turn away his anger: and did not kindle all his wrath.*

Ipse autem est misericors, et propitius fiet peccatis eorum et non disperdet eos. Et abundavit ut averteret iram suam, et non accendit omnem iram suam.

77{78}[39]   *And he remembered that they are flesh: a wind that goes and returns not.*

Et recordatus est quia caro sunt, spiritus vadens et non rediens.

77{78}[38] *Ipse autem, but he* God *est misericors, et propitius fiet peccatis eorum, is merciful and will forgive their sins,* by not wholly destroying their posterity, and by punishing them less than they deserve; *et non disperdet eos, and will not destroy them,* that is, he will not wholly destroy them, but some he will keep safe during their lifetime and will grant concessions to their posterity. *Et abundavit ut averteret iram suam, and many a time did he turn away his anger,* that is, he was abundantly ready at times to pull back on the starting of punishment, to spare the people, and to accept the prayers of Moses and the sacrifices of Aaron for sins; *et non accendit omnem iram suam, and did not kindle his wrath,* that is, he did not scourge them as much as they deserved. 77{78}[39] *Et recordatus est, and he remembered,* that is, he held himself out like one who had remembered, mercifully pardoning, *quia caro sunt, spiritus vadens et non redidens; that they are flesh: a spirit that goes and returns not.* Here is put a part for the whole, calling men flesh, and then [calling them] a spirit that goes and returns not. So that this verse is [to be understood] in this sense: *He remembered that they are flesh,* that is, God kindly considers that they were embodied creatures and weak, and that they had proclivities to evildoing; *he remembered* also that the spirit goes and returns not, that is, that the souls of men are very unsound, so that they move from one disposition to another, wandering, unstable, and finally they go from this mortal body to an unknown region, not to return to their former state through natural power. But as result of "remembrance" God is easily led to be merciful to us. Whence also he himself elsewhere asserts: *I will no more curse the earth for the sake of man: for the imagination and thought of man's heart are prone to evil from* his youth.[68] For which reason, Ezra says to the Lord: *But what is man, that you are angry with him? Or what is a corruptible race, that you are so bitter against it?*[69]

77{78}[40]   *How often did they provoke him in the desert: and move him to wrath in the place without water?*

Quoties exacerbaverunt eum in deserto, in iram concitaverunt eum in inaquoso?

77{78}[41]   *And they turned back and tempted God: and grieved the Holy One of Israel.*

Et conversi sunt, et tentaverunt Deum, et sanctum Israel exacerbaverunt.

77{78}[42]   *They remembered not his hand, in the day that he redeemed them from the hand of him that afflicted them.*

Non sunt recordati manus eius, die qua redemit eos de manu tribulantis.

77{78}[43]   *How he wrought his signs in Egypt, and his wonders in the field of Tanis.*

Sicut posuit in Aegypto signa sua, et prodigia sua in campo Taneos.

Consequently, God shows the enormity of the sin of this people because of the multitude and the recurrence of their transgressions. 77{78}[40] *Quoties exacerbaverunt eum in deserto, in iram concitaverunt eum in inaquoso? How often did they provoke him in the desert: and move him to wrath in the place without water?* It is as if he were saying, "Many times." Whence the Lord said to Moses: *They have tempted me now ten times.*[70] Now in what way the most sweet and unchangeable God is said to be provoked and roused to anger has already been often addressed.[71] 77{78} [41] *Et conversi sunt,* and they turned back to themselves, so that they might follow their own will and turn from God, *et tentaverunt Deum, and tempted God:* as has now often been stated; *et Sanctum Israel, and the Holy One of Israel,* that is, God, the sanctifier of all the true Israelites, *exacerbaverunt, they grieved:* so that he — who in himself is naturally,

---

68   Gen. 8:21.
69   2 Ezra 13:34. E. N. This is an apocryphal book sometimes called 4 Esdras. It is included in some versions of the Vulgate as an appendix.
70   Num. 14:22b.
71   E. N. E.g., Volume 1, Article XX (Psalm 5:7), Volume 3, Article XLI (Psalm 73:1).

eternally, and invariably goodly, gentle, and kind—was made austere, bitter, and hard towards them, by reason of effect or vengeance because of their sins. 77{78}[42] *Non sunt recordati, they remembered not,* [that is,] these ingrates [did not keep in mind,] *manus eius, his hand,* that is, the divine exhibitions of power and operation they had witnessed, *die qua redemit eos de manu tribulantis, in the day that he redeemed them from the hand of him that afflicted them,* that is, from the rule and oppression of the king of Egypt. 77{78}[43] *Sicut, how,* that is, in what manner and in what way, God *posuit in Aegypto signa sua, wrought his signs in Egypt,* that is the ten plagues: according to that which Exodus says, *I will strike Egypt with all my wonders;*[72] *et prodigia sua in campo Taneos, and his wonders in the fields of Tanis,* and how this ought to be understood has been satisfactorily and comprehensively addressed just a short time ago.[73]

77{78}[44]   *And he turned their rivers into blood, and their showers that they might not drink.*

Et convertit in sanguinem flumina eorum, et imbres eorum, ne biberent.

77{78}[45]   *He sent among them diverse sores of flies, which devoured them: and frogs which destroyed them.*

Misit in eos coenomyiam, et comedit eos, et ranam, et disperdidit eos.

Then [the Psalm] touches upon these prodigies with specificity. 77{78} [44] *Et convertit in sanguinem flumina eorum,* and he turned their rivers into blood, namely, [the rivers] of the Egyptians, *et imbres eorum,* and their showers, that is, their cisterns or sources of water springing from rain, *ne biberent,* that they might not drink. In the manner that is stated in Exodus, the first plague in Egypt was that all the waters of Egypt changed to blood when Moses held out his staff upon the rivers of Egypt;[74] and everywhere the Egyptians searched for water they found blood, and they were unable to drink the waters of the rivers because of their aversion to its taste. 77{78}[45] *Misit in eos,* he sent among them, God, namely [sent] to the Egyptians, *coenomyiam, diverse sores of flies,* that is, flesh-biting flies—for coenomyiam [the word used here] comes from κυνός (kynos), which is "of a dog," and μυῖα (myia), which means a fly; or all kinds of

72   Ex. 3:20a.
73   In verse 77:12.
74   Ex. 7:19–24.

flies; *et comedit eos, which devoured them*: that is, these flies stung and bit them; *et ranam, et disperdidit eos; and frogs which destroyed them.* Now in this verse, the singular is sued for the plural, for by fly and frog is understood a multitude of flies and frogs.[75] The sending of the flies was the fourth plague of Egypt, since the Lord said to Pharaoh: *I will send in upon you, and upon your servants, and upon your houses all kind of flies.*[76] And elsewhere it says, *There came the very grievous fly* (that is, a multitude of flies) *into the houses of Pharaoh and of his servants, and into all the land of Egypt: and the land was corrupted by this kind of flies.*[77] Now, the sending of frogs was the second plague of Egypt. Of this is written in Exodus: *The Lord said to Pharaoh: Behold I will strike all your coasts with frogs, and the river shall bring forth an abundance of frogs: which shall come up, and enter into your house, and your bedchamber, and upon your bed, and in the houses of your servants, and to your people, and into your ovens, and into the remains of your meats.*[78]

77{78}[46]   *And he gave up their fruits to the blast, and their labors to the locust.*

         Et dedit aerugini fructus eorum, et labores eorum locustae.

77{78}[47]   *And he destroyed their vineyards with hail, and their mulberry trees with hoarfrost.*

         Et occidit in grandine vineas eorum, et moros eorum in pruina.

77{78}[48]   *And he gave up their cattle to the hail, and their stock to the fire.*

         Et tradidit grandini iumenta eorum, et possessionem eorum igni.

77{78}[46] *Et dedit aerugini, and he gave up . . . to the blast*, that is, to the scorching wind, destroying the cornfields; or, to blight, that is, to noxious winds, or fungus; *fructus eorum, their fruits*, that is, the grains of the earth, to their destruction. Just like the plague of hoarfrost which

---

75   E. N. The translators of the Douay-Rheims have already taken into consideration this. Translated literally, the Latin would read: "He sent among them the fly and it devoured them, and the frog, and it destroyed them." I have kept the original plural translation here.

76   Ex. 8:21a.

77   Ex. 8:24. E. N. I have changed the plural "swarm of flies" in the Douay-Rheims (which translates the singular word *musca* (fly) so that Denis's parenthetical explanation the word "fly" means a "multitude of flies" makes sense.

78   Ex. 8:2b–3.

is mentioned at the end of the next verse, this plague is not written about in Exodus: for in Exodus there is only recounted the principal and notable plagues. *Et labores eorum, and their labors,* that is the fruits of the Egyptians, the products of their labor, God gave *locustae, to the locust,* that is, to be devoured by the multitude of locusts. The Lord said this to Pharaoh: *Behold I will bring in tomorrow the locust into your coasts, which will cover the face of the earth that nothing thereof may appear.*[79] 77{78}[47] *Et occidit in grandine, and he destroyed . . . with hail,* that is, by means of large hailstones, *vineas eorum, their vineyards.* This was the seventh plague of Egypt. Of this [plague] Moses states that a great hail fell upon the land of Egypt; and men and beasts upon whom the hail fell were killed; and it also struck *every herb of the field, and broke every tree of the country.*[80] *Et moros eorum, and their mulberry trees* God destroyed *in pruina, with hoarfrost,* that is, in a freezing and night-time frost, or with noxious liquid of decay. 77{78}[48] *Et tradidit grandini iumenta eorum, and he gave up their cattle to the hail:* for the hailstones killed all the brute animals found in the fields; it gave *possessionem eorum, their stock,* namely, [the stock] of the Egyptians, *igni, to the fire* so as to be consumed: for as it says in Exodus, *The hail and fire mixed with it drove on together.*[81]

77{78}[49]   And he sent upon them the wrath of his indignation: indignation and wrath and trouble, which he sent by evil angels.

Misit in eos iram indignationis suae, indignationem, et iram, et tribulationem, immissiones per angelos malos.

77{78}[50]   He made a way for a path to his anger: he spared not their souls from death, and their cattle he shut up in death.

Viam fecit semitae irae suae, non pepercit a morte animabus eorum, et iumenta eorum in morte conclusit.

77{78}[49] *Misit in eos iram indignationis suae, and he sent upon them the wrath of his indignation,* that is, the vindication of his avenging justice, namely, *indignationem, indignation,* that is, the effect of his contempt, which he imposed for their unworthy deeds, *et iram, and wrath,* that is, the vengeance from his justice, *et tribulationem, and trouble* of many kinds, here not expressly stated; *immisiones, that which he sent* also *by evil angels,* that is, God allowed utterly bad thoughts, hardness, and

---

79   Ex. 10:4b–5a.
80   Ex. 9:23–25.
81   Ex. 9:24a.

obstinacy to enter into the hearts of the Egyptians by the suggestions or workings of the devils. For the evil of punishment is effectively from God, but the evil of fault is only permissively [from God]:[82] for the prophet Amos says with respect to the evil of punishment: *Shall there be evil in a city, which the Lord has not done?*[83] 77{78}[50] *Viam fecit semitae irae suae, he made a way for a path to his anger*: that is, he sent the plagues of his anger against the Egyptians, not against the Hebrews; and so the devastating angel was made to come down to the land of Ramses wherein the Jews dwelt.[84] Whence the Lord said to Pharaoh: *I will put a division between my people and your people.*[85] *Non pepercit a morte animarum eorum, he spared not their souls from death*: that is, without mercy God killed Egyptians, both great and small. *Et iumenta eorum in morte conclusit, and their cattle he shut up in death*, that is, he killed. And this was the fifth plague of Egypt. Of this the Lord said to Pharaoh: *Behold my hand shall be upon your fields, and a very grievous murrain upon your horses, and asses, and camels, and oxen, and sheep.*[86] And all the domesticated beasts of the Egyptians, namely, those of the field, died by pestilence.[87]

82　E. N. The most holy God does not affirmatively will moral evil, either as an end or a means. Moral evil occurs permissively only, and is attributable to our own evil wills or the evil wills of the devils, which are allowed their day by God for some greater good. "In the final end," Ludwig Ott says, "moral evil will serve the supreme aim of the world, the glorification of God, in as much as it reveals His mercy in forgiving and His justice in punishing." Ludwig Ott, *Fundamentals of Catholic Dogma* (Fort Collins, CO: Roman Catholic Books, undated), 46. In the exercise of his inscrutable providence, God both permissively (and, on occasion, effectively) imposes physical evil (as distinguished from moral evil), including the evil of punishment or natural evil (suffering) for reasons of the greater good: *e.g.*, to satisfy justice, to prevent a greater evil, to allow for the exercise of charity, or to prompt the conversion of the sinner. "In a marvelous and ineffable way," St. Augustine observes, "even that which is done in opposition to his will is done in accordance with his will, for it would not be done, if he did not permit it — and, of course, his permission is not unwilling, but willing — nor, being good, would he permit evil to be done, unless he in an omnipotent way is able to bring good even out of evil." St. Augustine, *Enchiridion*, 26, 100, PL 40, 279.

83　Amos 3:6b.

84　E. N. Denis is evidently referring to Ramses II (*ca.* 1304–1246 BC), the Pharaoh of Egypt.

85　Ex. 8:23.

86　E. N. Murrain is a term meaning a pestilence or plague affecting domesticated animals, including such things as anthrax, foot-and-mouth disease. The term comes from Anglo-French *moryn*, which comes from Old French *mourir* ("to die"), which in turn comes from the Latin *mori*, to die.

87　Ex. 9:6.

77{78}[51] *And he killed all the firstborn in the land of Egypt: the first-fruits of all their labor in the tabernacles of Ham.*

> *Et percussit omne primogenitum in terra Aegypti, primitias omnis laboris eorum in tabernaculis Cham.*

77{78}[51] *Et percussit omne primogenitum, and he killed all the firstborn,* both men and beast, *in terra Aegypti:* and this was the tenth plague of Egypt, as is stated in Exodus.[88] God killed also *primitias omnis laboris eorum, the firstfruits of all their labor,* that is, the first and most preferable fruits of the land of Egypt, namely, grain and so forth, *in tabernaculis Cham, in the tabernacles of Ham,* that is, in the place of the Egyptians where the progeny of Ham, the son of Noah, was born. Indeed, Mizraim, as is stated in Genesis, was the son of Ham, and from this Mizraim, the name of Egypt was taken, for [that tribe] had dominance within it.[89]

77{78}[52] *And he took away his own people as sheep: and guided them in the wilderness like a flock.*

> *Et abstulit sicut oves populum suum, et perduxit eos tamquam gregem in deserto.*

77{78}[53] *And he brought them out in hope, and they feared not: and the sea overwhelmed their enemies.*

> *Et deduxit eos in spe, et non timuerunt, et inimicos eorum operuit mare.*

And so after describing the plagues of Egypt, the liberation of the Hebrews is recited. 77{78}[52] *Et abstulit sicut oves populum suum, and he took away his own people as sheep:* that is, in the manner that a good shepherd delivers his sheep from the depredations of wolves, so God took away the children of Israel from the reprobate and evil Egyptians; *et perduxit eos tanquam gregem in deserto, and he guided them in the wilderness like a flock:* for he provided for them a good pastor and leader, namely, Moses, and food and drink. 77{78}[53] *Et deduxit eos in spe, and he brought them out in hope,* promising that he would lead them to the land flowing with milk and honey;[90] *et non timuerunt, and they*

---

88   Ex. chp. 13.
89   Gen. 10:6. *E. N.* Mizraim is the Hebrew name for the land of Egypt. Denis is saying that because of the dominant nature of the tribe of Mizraim, son of Ham, the land of Egypt was called Mizraim by the Hebrews.
90   Ex. 3:8, 17.

feared not at the time, for they followed Moses through the middle of the Red Sea;[91] *et inimicos eorum operuit mare, and the sea overwhelmed their enemies,* namely, the Pharaoh and all his army.

77{78}[54]   *And he brought them into the mountain of his sanctuary: the mountain which his right hand had purchased. And he cast out the Gentiles before them: and by lot divided to them their land by a line of distribution.*

Et induxit eos in montem sanctificationis suae, montem quem acquisivit dextera eius; et eiecit a facie eorum gentes, et sorte divisit eis terram in funiculo distributionis.

77{78}[55]   *And he made the tribes of Israel to dwell in their tabernacles.*

Et habitare fecit in tabernaculis eorum tribus Israel.

77{78}[54] *Et induxit eos in montem sanctificationis suae,* and he brought them out into the mountain of his sanctuary, that is, into Jerusalem and Mount Sion, upon which after some time was built the temple. He brought them into — referring not to them who were numbered among those who left Egypt (other than Caleb and Joshua), but their children — according to that which the Lord said: *All those that . . . murmured against me shall not enter into the land, which I lifted up my hand to make you dwell therein, except Caleb, the son of Jephunneh, and Joshua, son of Nun.*[92] Therefore, he led them into the mountain of his sanctuary, *montem quem acquisivit dextera eius, the mountain which his right hand purchased,* that is, [the mountain] which God, whose are all things, took away from the hand of the unworthy and gave to his own people. For this reason, it adds: *Et eiecit a facie eorum gentes, and he cast out the Gentiles before them,* that is, he expelled the Gentiles that were inhabiting the land of promise from the sight of the Israelites, killing them, putting them to flight, or subjecting them to his people, as is clear of the Gibeonites and other Canaanites, who through tribute remain among the children of Israel, as is memorialized in the book of Joshua.[93] *Et sorte divisit eis terram in funiculo distributionis, and by lot divided to them their land by a line of distribution,* through the hand of the priest Eleazar, and Joshua, and the princes of the tribes of Israel,[94] who at the command of the Lord

---

91   Ex. 14:22.
92   Num. 14:29–30.
93   Joshua 9:27.
94   Num. 19:51.

divided the land of Canaan among the nine tribes, and half the tribe of Manassas, giving more to the larger and less to the smaller [tribes]. This division is fully addressed in the book of Joshua.[95] Now the tribes of Ruben and Gad, and half the tribe of Manassas had earlier received their division of possession beyond the Jordan.[96] But the tribe of Levi did not have possessions, except a place to dwell and livestock so as to eat; but the God of Israel was their inheritance.[97] **77{78}[55]** *Et habitare fecit in tabernaculis eorum, and he made . . . to dwell in their tabernacles,* that is, in the cities and villages of the Canaanites, *tribus Israel, the tribes of Israel.*

77{78}[56]   *Yet they tempted and provoked the most high God: and they kept not his testimonies.*

Et tentaverunt, et exacerbaverunt Deum excelsum, et testimonia eius non custodierunt.

77{78}[57]   *And they turned away and kept not the covenant: even like their fathers they were turned aside as a crooked bow.*

Et averterunt se, et non servaverunt pactum, quemadmodum patres eorum, conversi sunt in arcum pravum.

Following this, the sins of the children of Israel committed in the land of promise are stated. **77{78}[56]** *Et tentaverunt, yet they tempted* God, the faithful and true one, doubting of his power, *et exacerbaverunt Deum excelsum, and they provoked the most high God:* in the sense previously explained; *et testimonia eius non custodierunt, and they kept not his testimonies.* Two are the parts of the divine law, namely, the testimonies and the precepts. The testimonies pertain to those things which are to be believed (*credenda*), the precepts to those things that are to be done and not to be done (*operanda aut omittenda*). They thus tempted God by their infidelity, which consisted in the fact that they did not hold, and firmly and inviolably believe, those testimonies, that is, the assertions of sacred Scripture inspired by God. **77{78}[57]** *Et averterunt se, and they turned away* from God and his rule, *et non servaverunt pactum, and they kept not the covenant* that they had entered into with God, when they had said, as it states in Exodus: *All things that the Lord has spoken we will do, we will be obedient.*[98] *Sicut patres eorum, like their fathers* who

---

95   Joshua chps. 13–19.
96   Num. 32:33–42.
97   Joshua 13:33.
98   Ex. 24:7b.

were murmurers,[99] rebellious against God, and adorers of the calf,[100] *conversi sunt in arcum pravum, they were turned aside as a crooked bow,* that is, they were made similar to a bad bow: because as a misshapen bow shoots forth arrows that are not injurious, so from their mouths proceed words that bring death; and again, because as the misshapen bow that is stretched quickly slackens and yields, so they are easily turned from their good intention and the divine worship, and give way into iniquity.

77{78}[58] *They provoked him to anger on their hills: and moved him to jealousy with their graven things.*

In iram concitaverunt eum in collibus suis, et in sculptilibus suis ad aemulationem eum provocaverunt.

77{78}[58] *In iram concitaverunt eum in collibus suis, they provoked him to anger on their hills,* sacrificing on high: which was unlawful. Now we ought to keep in mind that when the ark of the Lord did not have a fixed and stable place of abode, namely — before it was placed in Shiloh, and after the destruction of Shiloh even up until the construction of the temple of Solomon — it was lawful for the Jews to offer oblations and votive sacrifices elsewhere than where the ark was; but when it was in Shiloh or the temple of Solomon, doing this was not lawful. Because the Hebrews had entered into the land of promise, they offered sacrifice to God in high places or hills, even at the time when the ark was in Shiloh or the temple of Solomon, so here it is said — *they provoked him to anger on their hills.*[101] Also to be considered is that, by divine dispensation, it was lawful at the prior time [before the ark had a fixed place at Shiloh or the Solomonic temple] to offer sacrifice elsewhere than the place of the ark, in the manner that we read in the first book of Kings where Elijah presented sacrifice on Mount Carmel.[102] By this one knows how to explain that Solomon is said to have offered sacrifice in the heights

---

99   E. N. "If there be — God forbid — among you any one that is a whisperer, or double-tongued, a murmurer, or contumacious, or impatient of discipline, or restless or a wanderer, and who without shame eats the bread of idleness, even if he be present in body, my soul would be far away from him, because he would have made himself — by manner of life, not by space — far from God." St. Bernard of Clairvaux, Letter 143, 2, PL 182, 299.

100   Ex. 32:4, 6.

101   E. N. In other words, the Psalm was written during the time when it was lawful only to offer sacrifices and votive offerings in Shiloh or at the temple built by Solomon.

102   1 Kings 18:30–38.

of Gibeon;[103] and also Samuel offered sacrifice in the heights, as one reads in the book of Samuel that he frequently offered sacrifice in the high places for sins imputed to the people.[104] *Et sculptilibus suis, and with their graven things,* that is, adoring idols, *ad aemulationem, to jealousy,* that is, indignation, *eum provocaverunt, they moved him.*

77{78}[59] *God heard, and despised them, and he reduced Israel exceedingly as it were to nothing.*

Audivit Deus, et sprevit, et ad nihilum redegit valde Israel.

77{78}[60] *And he put away the tabernacle of Shiloh, his tabernacle where he dwelt among men.*

Et repulit tabernaculum Silo, tabernaculum suum, ubi habitavit in hominibus.

77{78}[59] *Audivit Deus, God heard,* that is, he knew in his mind this their sin; *et sprevit, and despised* both them and their faults, because as it says in the book of Wisdom, *The wicked and his wickedness are hateful alike.*[105] Here also they did not have the ability to correct, according to that of the most wise Solomon: *Consider the works of God, that no man can correct whom he has despised.*[106] *Et ad nihilum redegit valde Israel, and he reduced Israel exceedingly as it were to nothing.* For spiritually he reduced them to nothing, because he withdrew from them all being of charity and grace; also corporally he rendered them to nothing, handing over the iniquitous to the powers of their enemies, as it made clear in the book of Samuel and Judges.[107] 77{78}[60] *Et repulit tabernaculum Silo, and he put away the tabernacle of Shiloh:* that is, he destroyed the structure wherein the ark was placed, and he allowed the ark to be captured.[108] He therefore put away the tabernacle of Shiloh, or rather the occupants of their tabernacle, for God did not choose the place because of the people, but because of the people chose the place. Similarly, not because of the place did the Lord put away the people, but because of the people the Lord put away the place. *Tabernaculum suum, his tabernacle,* I say, *ubi, where,* that is, in which, *habitavit in hominibus, he dwelt among men,* that is, around men. For God dwells in the hearts of good men by grace; and as long as he remains in those men, he

---

103 1 Kings 3:4.
104 1 Sam. 7:9.
105 Wis. 14:9.
106 Eccl. 7:14.
107 Judges 2:14.
108 1 Sam. 4:11.

is resolved also to dwell in their tabernacles, and most of all in the sacred sacrifice. For this reason, Scripture says: *Behold the tabernacle of God with men, and he will dwell with them.*[109] And Moses said: *The Lord your God walks in the midst of your camp.*[110] And the Lord himself through Moses: *I am he who dwells, he said, among the children of Israel.*[111]

77{78}[61]   *And he delivered their strength into captivity: and their beauty into the hands of the enemy.*

Et tradidit in captivitatem virtutem eorum, et pulchritudinem eorum in manus inimici.

77{78}[62]   *And he shut up his people under the sword: and he despised his inheritance.*

Et conclusit in gladio populum suum, et haereditatem suam sprevit.

77{78}[63]   *Fire consumed their young men: and their maidens were not lamented.*

Iuvenes eorum comedit ignis, et virgines eorum non sunt lamentatae.

77{78}[64]   *Their priests fell by the sword: and their widows did not mourn.*

Sacerdotes eorum in gladio ceciderunt, et viduae eorum non plorabantur.

77{78}[61] *Et tradidit,* and he delivered, the Lord [delivered], *in captivitatem,* into captivity of the Philistines, who are also known otherwise as Palestinians or Allophyli,[112] *virtutem eorum,* their strength, that is, the power of the children of Israel, by which one can understand the strength of their army or their courage; or that ark, whose presence and power habitually allowed them to prevail in battle;[113] *et puchritudinem eorum, and their beauty,* that is, beautiful persons or the ark with its beauty and glory, *in manus inimici, in the hands of the enemy,* namely, the Philistine people. 77{78}[62] *Et conclusit in gladio populum suum, and he shut up his people under the sword,* that is, by the arms and wars of the Philistines

---

109   Rev. 21:3a.
110   Deut. 23:14a.
111   Num. 35:34b; *Cf.* Ez. 43:7.
112   E. N. The word *Allophyli* is a Greek term (ἀλλόφυλοι) meaning alien or stranger; however, it is often used in Scripture (the Septuagint, or Greek translation of the Old Testament) to refer to the Philistines.
113   1 Sam. 4:3 *et seq.*

he allowed the children of Israel to be killed; *et hereditatem suam sprevit, and he despised his inheritance,* that is, he did not protect his people whom he had chosen and cherished. But these outcasts are not said to be the people or the inheritance of God except by being called that or in name only, in the manner that the Savior in the Gospel speaks of the Jews, *But the children of the kingdom shall be cast out into the exterior darkness.*[114] 77{78}[63] *Ignis, fire,* that is, the great assault and powerful furor of the Philistines, *comedit, consumed,* that is, devoured and destroyed, *iuvenes eorum, their young men,* namely, [the young men] of the Jews; *et virgines eorum non sunt lamentatae, and their maidens were not lamented:* because each [of the soldiers] was so concerned for his own escape, that he was not able to concern himself with lamenting for others. 77{78} [64] *Sacerdotes eorum, their priests,* namely, the sons of Eli, Hophni, and Phinehas,[115] *in gladio by the sword* of the Philistines *ceciderunt, fell* and were killed; *et viduae eorum non plorabantur, and their widows did not mourn,* for the same reason pointed out with respect to the virgins. For the wife of Phinehas, hearing the report of the death of her husband, thereupon bowed herself down, and she died in that childbirth, and was not able to lament because of that confusion.[116]

77{78}[65]   *And the Lord was awaked as one out of sleep, and like a mighty man that has been surfeited with wine.*

Et excitatus est tamquam dormiens Dominus, tamquam potens crapulatus a vino.

77{78}[66]   *And he smote his enemies on the hinder parts: he put them to an everlasting reproach.*

Et percussit inimicos suos in posteriora, opprobrium sempiternum dedit illis.

---

114   Matt. 8:12. E. N. What was true for the circumcised Jew is true for the baptized Christian, we can end up being a Christian "in name" only: "[I]n Baptism a special mark [an indelible character] is stamped on the person baptized ... and the mark will never be erased. If you are baptized, you are marked indelibly; you are God's man forever, and even if you should have the terrible misfortune of being damned in hell, the mark of God received in your Baptism will be just as prominent on your soul as if you were face to face with Christ. Hell rejoices when one of God's sealed packages is lost." Francis X. Doyle, S. J., *The Wonderful Sacraments* (London: Burns Oats and Washbourne, Ltd., 1924), 57–58.

115   1 Sam. 4:11.

116   1 Sam. 4:19–22. E. N. The unnamed wife of Phinehas died during childbirth calling her son Ichabod, which means "the glory has departed from Israel, because the ark of God was taken."

Thereafter the reconciliation of God with his people and his indignation against their adversaries is described. 77{78}[65] *Et excitatus est tamquam dormiens Dominus, tamquam potens crapulatus a vino; and the Lord was awakened as one out of sleep, and like a mighty man that has been surfeited with wine.* In the manner that a man sleeping and drunk with wine does not use his own strength and is unable to engage in battle, but once awakened from sleep and returned to sobriety can manifest his strength, and fight strongly, and overthrow his enemies, so almighty God when he was angered with his people and did not help them, acted as if he was sleeping, and drunk or inebriated with wine, in appearing not to attend to the affliction of his people and the capture of the ark of the covenant; but when he began to destroy, kill, and devastate the Philistines through Samuel, Saul, and David, it seemed as if he was awakened from sleep and returned to the use of reason from being drunk. 77{78}[66] *Et percussit inimicos suos, and he smote his enemies* the Philistines *in posteriora, on their hinder parts,* that is, in the hidden parts of their buttocks, where mice gnawed on their rectal outgrowths, and they became putrid;[117] *opprobrium sempiternum dedit illis, he put them to an everlasting reproach:* for the memory of such great a confusion in the present life shall never be forgotten, and for their sin they will also be tormented in hell without end.

77{78}[67]   *And he rejected the tabernacle of Joseph: and chose not the tribe of Ephraim.*

Et repulit tabernaculum Ioseph, et tribum Ephraim non elegit.

Then is expressed the fact that only the tribe of Judah was chosen for the royal dignity. 77{78}[67] *Et repulit, and he rejected,* God [rejected] *tabernaculum, the tabernacle,* that is, the family, *Ioseph, of Joseph;* or, the Tabernacle of Joseph, that is, the place in the city of Shiloh which is called the tabernacle of Joseph, because in the division of land it was given to the tribe of Ephraim, the son of Joseph, and the ark was placed in the tabernacle in Shiloh by Joshua the Ephraimite,[118] which is fully recited in the first book of Samuel. *Et tribum Ephraim non elegit, and he chose not the tribe of Ephraim* to rule. For although God conferred upon Jeroboam, the son of Nebat of the tribe of Ephraim, [leadership over] the

---

117   1 Sam. 5:6, 9. E. N. 1 Sam. 5:9 states that the Philistines had "emerods [hemorrhoids] in their secret parts." Because the Philistines were overcome with mice, 1 Sam. 5:6, some posit that the Philistines may have suffered something like the bubonic plague.
118   Joshua 18:1.

ten tribes of Israel,[119] yet he was not also chosen to persevere in royal authority through his posterity, just as Saul from the tribe of Benjamin was not;[120] but both assumed [their power] for a limited period of time. And the Psalm declares that the tribe of Judah was chosen to reign, rightly excluding the tribe of Joseph, that is, of Ephraim and Manassas, and especially the tribe of Ephraim. First, because Joseph was holier than his brothers who had unjustly sold him.[121] Second, because he was more sublime than they, namely, as a ruler in Egypt.[122] Third, because firstborn rights were given to him, according to this: *Ruben was the firstborn of Israel, . . . but forasmuch as he defiled his father's bed, his first birthright was given to the sons of Joseph,*[123] and this was done by the patriarch Jacob. And so the progeny of Joseph seemed to be the closest to the royal authority next, especially the tribe of Ephraim, because as it is stated in Genesis, Jacob *set Ephraim before Manassas.*[124]

77{78}[68]   But he chose the tribe of Judah, mount Sion which he loved.
              Sed elegit tribum Iuda, montem Sion, quem dilexit.

77{78}[69]   And he built his sanctuary as of unicorns, in the land which he founded forever.

              Et aedificavit sicut unicornium sanctificium suum, in terra quam fundavit in saecula.

77{78}[68] *Sed elegit tribum Iuda,* but he chose the tribe of Judah to the scepter and royal power. Whence also Jacob predicted: *The scepter shall not be taken away from Judah, nor a ruler from his thigh, till he come that is to be sent.*[125] *Montem Sion quem dilexit,* mount Sion which he loved: for God is said to have chosen this mount so that he might have in it his dwelling: because *David built upon it an altar, and after that Solomon the temple.*[126] 77{78}[69] *Et aedificavit sicut unicornium sanctificium suum,* and he built his sanctuary as of unicorns: that is, God caused to be built his holy temple upon this mount, *as of unicorns.* This can be received in two ways. The first is thus: *As of unicorns,* that is, of the Jews, who are

---

119   1 Kings 11:31.
120   1 Sam. 9:1, 17.
121   Gen. 37:28.
122   Gen. 41:41.
123   1 Chr. 5:1.
124   Gen. 48:20b.
125   Gen. 49:10.
126   1 Chr. 21:26; 2 Chr. 3:1.

called unicorns by similarity, because as the animal that is called a unicorn has only one horn in front, so they had only one worship and faith of the one God. *He built*, therefore, *his sanctuary as of unicorns*, that is, as it was befitting to build the temple of the Jews of the worship of the one true God. The second is thus: *as of unicorns*, that is, as one would build a dwelling of animals which are called unicorns or rhinoceroses: because as this animal prohibits all other brute animals from entering into its tabernacle, so God prohibits foreigners from entering the temple. Here also Balaam compares God to a rhinoceros, saying: *God has brought Israel out of Egypt, whose strength is like to the rhinoceros.*[127] *In terra quam fundavit in saecula, in the land which he founded forever*: that is, God caused his temple to be built in the land of promise, which he consecrated to his perpetual worship, as much as was in him.

77{78}[70] *And he chose his servant David, and took him from the flocks of sheep: he brought him from following the ewes great with young,*

Et elegit David, servum suum, et sustulit eum de gregibus ovium; de post foetantes accepit eum,

77{78}[71] *To feed Jacob his servant, and Israel his inheritance.*

Pascere Iacob, servum suum, et Israel, haereditatem suam.

77{78}[72] *And he fed them in the innocence of his heart: and conducted them by the skillfulness of his hands.*

Et pavit eos in innocentia cordis sui, et in intellectibus manuum suarum deduxit eos.

77{78}[70] *Et elegit David servum suum*, and he chose his servant David to reign in a stable fashion, *et sustulit eum de gregibus ovium*, and he took *him from the flocks of sheep*, that is, he took him away from the sheep of his father which he fed; *et post foetantes*, and *from following the ewes great with young*, that is, after the ewes bore their young or had their offspring, *accepti eum*, he brought him to the glory of kingly reign; 77{78}[71] *Pascere Iacob servum suum, et Israel hereditatem suam; to feed Jacob his servant, and Israel his inheritance*, that is, to rule well and worthily in spiritual things and temporal things the people of the Hebrews, born of Jacob, who also is called Israel.[128] 77{78}[72] *Et pavit eos*, and *he fed them*, David [fed them] in this way, *in innocentia cordis sui, in the innocence of his heart*, that

---

127 Num. 23:22.
128 Gen. 32:28.

is, with a pure and simple intention; *et in intellectibus manuum suarum,* and ... *by the skillfulness of his hands,* that is, in the prudence of his deeds, *deduxit eos,* he conducted *them* to their destined end and true peace.

ARTICLE XLIX

MYSTICAL EXPOSITION OF THE SAME SEVENTY-SEVENTH PSALM.

77{78}[1] ... *Attend, O my people, to my law: incline your ears to the words of my mouth.*

> ... *Attendite, popule meus, legem meam; inclinate aurem vestram in verba oris mei.*

77{78}[2] *I will open my mouth in parables: I will utter propositions from the beginning.*

> *Aperiam in parabolis os meum; loquar propositiones ab initio.*

IN THE MANNER THAT DAVID STOOD AS A figure of Christ, so the Synagogue was the figure of the Church; and the reign and people of David was a type of the reign of Christ and the Christian people. Expounding this Psalm, therefore, of Christ and the Christian people, our Savior and Lord Jesus Christ first excites us to the most attentive awareness of command, and he says: 77{78}[1] *Attendite, attend* with the entire exertion of the mind, *popule meus, O my people,* that is, the Christian people, freed by my Blood, and called Christian on account of me, the Christ,[129] *legem meam, to my law,* the evangelical [law]; *inclinate aurem vestram in verba oris mei, incline your ears to the words of my mouth,* that is, reverently receive and humbly implement the teachings of the New Testament, which I taught with my own mouth. 77{78}[2] *Aperiam in parabolis os meum, etc. I will open my mouth in parables, etc.* The way that this is to be explained relative to Christ has been clearly elucidated in the prior article.

77{78}[3] *How great things have we heard and known, and our fathers have told us.*

> *Quanta audivimus et cognovimus ea, et patres nostri narra-verunt nobis.*

---

129 Acts 11:26.

77{78}[4] *They have not been hidden from their children, in another generation. Declaring the praises of the Lord, and his powers, and his wonders which he has done.*

Non sunt occultata a filiis eorum in generatione altera, narrantes laudes Domini et virtutes eius, et mirabilia eius quae fecit.

The voice of the Church is what follows.[130] 77{78}[3] *Quanta audivimus,* how great things have we heard in the miracles of Christ, which he performed in the world, and which are said and written of him, and performed by his disciples by believing in his name; *et cognovimus ea, and we have known them* by a most certain faith. And because *faith comes by hearing,*[131] according to the Apostle [Paul], so is added: *et patres nostri, and our fathers,* the Evangelists and the Apostles, *narraverunt nobis, have told us:* for they preached the works of Christ throughout the entire world,[132] and they reduced them for us in writing so they would be forever remembered and for our instruction. 77{78}[4] *Non sunt occultata a filiis eroum, they have not been hidden from their children,* [their] spiritual [children], namely, the good Christians, who because they are of God, avidly hear the word of God,[133] *in generatione altera, in another generation,* that is, in the Christian people, imitating the paths of the early Christian faithful. *Narrantes, declaring,* our fathers [declaring, that is,] *laudes Domini, the praises of the Lord,* that is, the proclamation of Christ, witnessing that he is the only-Begotten Son of God the Father, consubstantial with the eternal Father, coeternal, and coequal, truly incarnate, and that he suffered for the salvation of the world, and was appointed judge of all;[134] *et virtutes eius, and his powers,* that is, his divine omnipotence, and his human powers, to which were given all power in heaven and on earth.[135] Or [alternatively], *his powers,* that is, the most perfect

---

130   E. N. The voice of the Church (*vox Ecclesiae*) as distinguished from the voice of Christ (*vox Christi*).

131   Rom. 10:17.

132   Mark 16:15, 20.

133   Cf. John 8:47: *He that is of God, hears the words of God. Therefore, you hear them not, because you are not of God.*

134   Acts 10:42: *And he commanded us to preach to the people, and to testify that it is he who was appointed by God, to be judge of the living and of the dead.*

135   Matt. 28:18. E. N. "Christ himself.... solemnly proclaimed that all power was given him in heaven and on earth. These words can only be taken to indicate the greatness of his power, the infinite extent of his kingdom.... If to Christ our Lord is given all power in heaven and on earth ... it must be clear that not one of our faculties is exempt from his empire. He must reign in our minds, which should assent with perfect submission and firm belief to revealed truths and to the doctrines

holiness of his manner of living, namely, his charity, meekness, humility, and patience. *Et mirabilia eius quae fecit, and his wonders which he has done,* raising three people from the dead,[136] giving sight to those born blind,[137] making known the secrets of the heart. Yet not all marvels of Christ were written down, as is written: *There are also many other things which Jesus did; which, if they were written every one, the world itself, I think, would not be able to contain the books that should be written.*[138]

77{78}[5] *And he set up a testimony in Jacob: and made a law in Israel. How great things he commanded our fathers, that they should make the same known to their children:*

> *Et suscitavit testimonium in Iacob, et legem posuit in Israel, quanta mandavit patribus nostris nota facere ea filiis suis.*

77{78}[6] *That another generation might know them. The children that should be born and should rise up and declare them to their children.*

> *Ut cognoscat generatio altera; filii qui nascentur et exsurgent, et narrabunt filiis suis.*

77{78}[7] *That they may put their hope in God and may not forget the works of God: and may seek his commandments.*

> *Ut ponant in Deo spem suam, et non obliviscantur operum Dei, et mandata eius exquirant.*

77{78}[8] *That they may not become like their fathers . . . .*[139]

> *Ne fiant, sicut patres eorum . . . .*

77{78}[5] *Et suscitavit testimonium, and he set up testimony,* that is, Christ [set up] the New Testament, and those things which are to be believed, *in Iacob, in Jacob,* that is, by the people of the Christian faithful,

---

of Christ. He must reign in our wills, which should obey the laws and precepts of God. He must reign in our hearts, which should spurn natural desires and love God above all things, and cleave to him alone. He must reign in our bodies and in our members, which should serve as instruments for the interior sanctification of our souls, or to use the words of the Apostle Paul, as instruments of justice unto God." Pope Pius XI, *Quas Primas,* 11, 33 (quoting Rom. 6:13).

136   Matt. 9:25 (the daughter of Jairus); Luke 7:14–15 (the son of the widow of Nain); John 11:43–44 (Lazarus)

137   John 9:6–7.

138   John 21:25.

139   E. N. Denis does not address the remainder of this verse in his part of the Commentary.

wrestling against vices, and supplanting the same; *et legem, and a law* of life and grace, *posuit in Israel, he made . . . in Israel,* that is, in the Holy Catholic Church, spiritually contemplating God.[140]

Quanta mandavit patribus nostris, nota facere ea filiis suis, how great things he commanded our fathers, that they should be made known to their children, that is, Christ instructed many sound things to his Apostles and some of his disciples in order that they might make them manifest to those whom they would spiritually beget in Christ: as the Apostle says to the Galatians, *My little children, of whom I am in labor again, until Christ be formed in you;*[141] 77{78}[6] *ut cognoscat generatio altera, that another generation might know them,* that is, all posterity. *Filii qui nascentur, the children that should be born,* that is, those spiritually reborn by water and the Holy Spirit,[142] *et exsurgent, and should rise up* from the sleep of sin[143] to the vigilance of the custody of the heart,[144] and from worldly things to heavenly love, *et narrabunt filiis suis, and declare them to their children* to be truly Christians, that they might know and fulfill the divine precepts. The holy Apostle [Paul] exhorts us to this announcement [of the Gospel] saying: *Be filled with the Holy Spirit, speaking to yourselves in psalms, and hymns, and spiritual canticles.*[145] And again: *Fathers, provoke not your children to anger; but bring them up in the discipline and correction of the Lord.*[146] 77{78}[7] *Ut ponant in Deo spem suam, that they may put their hope in God,* that is, that they may have trust

---

140   E. N. Denis expressly speaks of the *credenda,* the things to be believed by divine faith (*de fide credenda*) because formally revealed by God; these are found expressly either in the Word of God (including Tradition) or implicitly there, but expressly declared in a solemn, extraordinary definition of the Pope, or the Church in council (extraordinary Magisterium), or as a result of the ordinary and universal Magisterium. These require the assent of theological faith. Denis also appears to include the so-called *tenenda,* the things to be definitively held (*de fide tenenda*) by reason of the authority of the Magisterial teaching of the Church on faith and morals, though they may not have been (or not yet recognized as being) formally revealed. These also, if solemnly taught, must be accepted (or "held") by the firm and definite assent of ecclesiastical faith. Beyond these are those teachings that require a religious submission of will and intellect. See Congregation for the Doctrine of the Faith, *Doctrinal Commentary on the Concluding Formula of the Professio fidei,* June 29, 1998.

141   Gal. 4:19.

142   John 3:5.

143   E. N. On the "sleep of sin," see Volume 3, Article XLVI (Psalm 75:6).

144   E. N. Jesus Christ "urges us to vigilance of the heart in communion with his own. Vigilance is 'custody of the heart,' and Jesus prayed for us to the Father: 'Keep them in your name.' The Holy Spirit constantly seeks to awaken us to keep watch." CCC § 2849 (quoting John 17:11 and citing to Mark 13:9, 23, 33–37; 14:38; Luke 12:35–40; 1 Cor. 16:13; 1 Col. 4:2; 1 Thess. 5:6 and 1 Pet. 5:8).

145   Eph. 18b–19a.

146   Eph. 6:4.

to be saved by the merits of Christ, not be ignorant (God forbid) of the justice of God,[147] and, if they are not operating under the justice of God, that they may seek to be established in it; *et non obliviscantur operum Dei, and they may not forget the works of God*, but that we may unceasingly recall the works of Christ, because all his actions are for our instruction.[148] Whence the Apostle [Paul] admonishes: *Think diligently upon him that endured such opposition from sinners against himself.*[149] And Peter: *Christ also suffered for us, leaving you an example that you should follow his steps.*[150] For he who with all his heart recalls the works of Christ finds the example of complete perfection, and he will not easily be able to fall or to be lost. *Et mandata eius exquirant, and may they seek his commandments.* This is what Christ said to his Apostles: *Going . . . teach all nations, . . . teaching them to observe all things whatsoever I have commanded you.*[151] For nobody can be saved without keeping the commandments. For this reason, John says: *He who says that he knows him, and keeps not his commandments, is a liar.*[152] 77{78}[8] *Ne fiant sicut patres eorum, that they may not become like their fathers* carnal.[153]

77{78}[9] *The sons of Ephraim who bend and shoot with the bow: they have turned back in the day of battle.*

---

147 Rom. 10:3a. E. N. This is not referring to the justice of God (as in judgment), but to the justice of God (as in justification), *i.e.*, being ignorant of sanctifying grace, that is, not being in the state of justifying grace (*in gratiam iustificantem*), and thus being in a state of mortal sin and living on the shards of presumption instead of the sound vessel of hope.

148 E. N. This is a fundamental axiom, probably stemming from Cassiodorus: *Omnis Christi actio nostra est instructio*, all the actions of Christ are for our instruction. St. Thomas Aquinas refers to it more than a dozen times in the *Summa Theologiae*, e.g., "The Lord by his manner of living (*conversatione*) gave the example of perfection in everything that pertains in itself to salvation." ST IIIa, q. 40, art. 2, ad 1. "The action of Christ was our instruction." ST IIIa, q. 40, art. 1, ad 3. See generally Richard Schenk, "*Omnis Christi actio nostra est instructio*, The Deeds and Sayings of Jesus as Revelation in the View of Thomas Aquinas," Léon Elders, ed., *La doctrine de la revelation divine de saint Thomas d'Aquin*, Studi Tomistici 37 (Rome: Libreria Editrice Vaticana, 1990), 104–31.

149 Heb. 12:3a.

150 1 Pet. 2:21.

151 Matt. 28:19a, 20a.

152 1 John 2:4.

153 E. N. "At whatever time, therefore, such men have begun to be in this life, so that though during the course of time they have been imbued by the divine sacraments, yet they still have a taste for carnal things, and if they hope or desire either in this life or after this life for carnal things from God, they remain brute animals." St. Augustine, On Baptism (*De Baptismo*), I, 15, PL 43, 122.

Filii Ephrem, intendentes et mittentes arcum, conversi sunt in die belli.

77{78}[10] They kept not the covenant of God: and in his law they would not walk.

Non custodierunt testamentum Dei, et in lege eius noluerunt ambulare.

77{78}[9] *Filii Ephrem,* the sons of Ephraim, that is the evil and reprobate Christians, who are many, and are placed as practicing with the elect: for Ephraim is interpreted as meaning bearing fruit; *intendentes et mittentes arcum, who bend and shoot with the bow* of their mouth, that is, speaking beautiful things and promising of many things, but doing filthy works and not fulfilling promises; *conversi sunt, they have turned back* to themselves and their vicious life, *in die belli, in the day of battle,* that is, during the time of adversity inflicted upon them by the world, the flesh, or the devil. For as the Savior said, *These have no roots; for they believe for a while, and in time of temptation, they fall away.*[154] Indeed, *that of the true proverb* that Peter recalls to mind *has happened to them,* namely: *The dog is returned to his vomit: and, The sow that was washed, to her wallowing in the mire.*[155] For this reason, Christ says again: *Why call you me, Lord, Lord; and do not the things which I say?*[156] 77{78}[10] *Non custodierunt testamentum Dei, they kept not the covenant of God,* saying *they know God: and in their works deny him;*[157] *et in lege eius,* and in his law, [his] evangelical [law], *noluerunt ambulare, they would not walk:* and so they sinned out of a certain malice, and purposefully, not from weakness, or from ignorance, which is damnable, as Peter teaches: *It had been better for them not to have known the way of justice, than after they have known it, to turn back.*[158] For the servant knowing the will of his Lord, and not doing it, *shall be beaten with many stripes.*[159]

77{78}[11] And they forgot his benefits, and his wonders that he had shown them.

Et obliti sunt benefactorum eius, et mirabilium eius quae ostendit eis.

---

154 Like 8:13; *cf.* Matt. 13:21.
155 2 Pet. 2:22 (*cf.* Prov. 26:11).
156 Luke 6:46.
157 Titus 1:16a.
158 2 Pet. 2:21.
159 Luke 12:47.

77{78}[11] *Et obliti sunt benefactorum eius, and they forgot his benefits:* that is, evil Christians delivered into oblivion the benefits of Christ, who became incarnate, conversed [with men] in the world,[160] and hung upon the wood [of the Cross] for them; he who loved them so much, that he laid down his life for them,[161] and left as a provision for the journey his most salvific Body and Blood, the most excellent perpetual memorial of his most bitter Passion and love. In this way are the benefits of Christ forgotten: whoever does not love him, or makes room for the vanities of the world, or services the disordered desires of his flesh. For he who suffers with Christ, carrying upon his own cross of his sufferings, daily imitating [Christ], and daily dying to himself in the work of penance, such a one truly is mindful of the benefits of his Lord. For a naked and superficial recollection does not supply a true and thankful memory; but it is necessary to have a certain affectionate recollection and the exhibition of works. Forgotten also are *mirabilium eius, his wonders,* namely, of Christ, *quae ostendit eis, that he had shown them* by preaching of his servants and the instruction of sacred Scripture, or by inspiration and illumination of the Holy Spirit. For the marvels of Christ were that *he went about doing good,*[162] healing all manner of sickness and every infirmity among the people, according to that testified to by the Evangelist,[163] and all oppressed by the devil, as Peter adds.[164] For those that he healed in body, he justified in soul. Those who forget *his wonders* are therefore those who do not hurry towards Christ, the most merciful, most prudent, most powerful physician, who do not lay bare the wounds of their soul to him, plead for the fountain of all salvation and grace, for the oil of goodness and the river of grace, especially since he proclaims: *Come to me, all you that labor, and are burdened, and I will refresh you;*[165] and elsewhere, *He that comes to me, I will not cast out.*[166]

77{78}[12]   Wonderful things did he do in the sight of their fathers, in the land of Egypt, in the field of Tanis.

Coram patribus eorum fecit mirabilia in terra Aegypti, in campo Taneos.

---

160   Cf. Baruch 3:38: *Afterwards he was seen upon earth, and conversed with men.*
161   John 10:15.
162   Acts 10:38.
163   Matt. 4:23.
164   Acts 10:38.
165   Matt. 11:28.
166   John 6:37b.

77{78}[12] *Coram patribus eorum, in the sight of their fathers,* that is, in the presence of the Apostles and his disciples, who are the fathers of all Christians, *fecit, did he do,* [that is,] Christ [did] *mirabilia in terra Aegypti, wonderful things . . . in the land of Egypt,* that is, in this world. For Egypt is interpreted as meaning darkness or tribulation: and so by it is understood this good-for-nothing age and *the whole world* which *is seated in wickedness,*[167] in which the elect are in many ways troubled. *In campo Taneos, in the field of Tanis,* that is, in the plain of the commandment of humility: for Christ also said, *As the Father has given me commandment, so do I.*[168] Not, however, that he did something in a boastful manner, in the manner that he himself says again: *I receive glory not from men.*[169] For Christ proposed to us a precept of humility, saying, *Learn of me, because I am meek, and humble of heart.*[170] And since Tanis is interpreted as the commandment to be humble, it is right to designate the field of Tanis as the plain of the commandment of humility. We ought therefore always to learn and to follow humility especially from Christ.

77{78}[13] *He divided the sea and brought them through: and he made the waters to stand as in a vessel.*

> *Interrupit mare, et perduxit eos; et statuit aquas quasi in utre.*

77{78}[14] *And he conducted them with a cloud by day: and all the night with a light of fire.*

> *Et deduxit eos in nube diei, et tota nocte in illuminatione ignis.*

77{78}[13] *Interrupit mare et perduxit eos, he divided the sea and brought them through.* By sea (as has been often said) one can understand the Gentiles, with specific reference to the bitterness of [their] vices. Whence, Paul exclaims to the converted Gentiles: *Let all bitterness, and anger, and indignation, and clamor . . . be put away from you.*[171] One can also designate by the sea the multitude of tribulations, such as Jeremiah says in Lamentations: *Great as the sea is your destruction.*[172] Now in both ways Christ disrupted the sea and led our fathers the Apostles and their followers through it. For he led them through the sea of Gentiles, converting pagans to the faith and sundering nations, destroying the rites of heathens, and crushing the sins

---

167 1 John 5:19.
168 John 14:31b.
169 John 5:41.
170 Matt. 11:29.
171 Eph. 4:31.
172 Lam. 2:13b.

and the idols of the pagans. He led them moreover through various tribulations and from all of them he delivered them, in the manner that Paul attests to: *Blessed be the God . . . who comforts us in all our tribulation.*[173] *Et statuit aquas quasi in utre, and he made the waters to stand as in a vessel:* for the Gentiles converted to the faith were made firm with the fear of God, and by the yoke of the divine precepts they were restrained from the flow of desire; for the tribulations were made to cease, as if they were held still in a vessel. 77{78}[14] *Et deduxit eos, and he conducted them,* namely, all of Christ's faithful who desired to live in a godly manner in Christ and who suffered persecution,[174] *in nube diei, with a cloud by day,* that is, with the refreshment of divine consolation, and under the dew and raindrops of his grace; *et tota nocte, and all the night,* that is, in all adversity and assaults, *in illuminatione ignis, with a light of fire,* that is, in the splendor of the wisdom of the Holy Spirit, and with the interior rays of the illumination of Christ, who is most close to those who are afflicted.

77{78}[15]   He struck the rock in the wilderness: and gave them to drink, as out of the great deep.

Interrupit petram in eremo, et adaquavit eos velut in abysso multa.

77{78}[16]   He brought forth water out of the rock: and made streams run down as rivers.

Et eduxit aquam de petra, et deduxit tamquam flumina aquas.

God, the Father, 77{78}[15] *interrupit, struck,* that is, he allowed to be perforated and broken, *petram, the rock,* that is, Christ,[175] or his side,[176] *in eremo, in the wilderness* of this world, or on the Cross, destitute of all human consolation. For this reason Christ cried out: *My God, my God, why have you forsaken me?*[177] In the wounds of the rock, we are kept safe from all enemy attacks, and indeed from the wrath of God.[178] For this reason [Scripture] states: *Enter into the rock, hide in the pit from the face of the fear of the Lord.*[179] *Et adaquavit eos velut in abysso multa,*

---

173   2 Cor. 1:3a, 4a.

174   *Cf.* 2 Tim. 3:12: *And all that will live godly in Christ Jesus, shall suffer persecution.*

175   1 Cor. 10:4: *And all drank the same spiritual drink; and they drank of the spiritual rock that followed them, and the rock was Christ.*

176   John 19:34: *But one of the soldiers with a spear opened his side, and immediately there came out blood and water.*

177   Matt. 27:46b.

178   *E. N. Intra tua vulnera, absconde me,* "within your wounds, hide me," as the *Anima Christi* expresses this.

179   Is. 2:10.

and he gave them to drink as out of a great deep: that is, God, through
the merits of the Blood of Christ, abundantly gives Christians to drink
from the water of saving grace and of the gifts of the Holy Spirit, and
so Christ says: *If any man thirst, let him come to me, and drink. He
that believes in me, as the Scripture says, out of his belly shall flow rivers
of living water.*[180] 77{78}[16] *Et eduxit aquam de petra*, and he brought
forth water out of the rock: for from the side of Christ perforated by the
lance flowed out blood and water;[181] *et deduxit tamquam flumina aquas,*
and made streams run down as rivers: that is, God the Trinity made
flow abundant gifts of graces from Christ our head into his members
(that is, into us):[182] for, as John said, *Of his fulness we all have received,
and grace for grace.*[183] The Apostle [Paul] also said to Titus: *According
to his mercy, he saved us, by the laver of regeneration, and renovation of
the Holy Spirit, whom he has poured forth upon us abundantly, through
Jesus Christ.*[184] Of this water, the Lord said through Ezekiel: *I will pour
upon you clean water, and you shall be cleansed from all your filthiness.*[185]

77{78}[17]   *And they added yet more sin against him: they provoked the
most High to wrath in the place without water.*

*Et apposuerunt adhuc peccare ei; in iram excitaverunt Excel-
sum in inaquoso.*

77{78}[18]   *And they tempted God in their hearts, by asking meat for
their desires.*

*Et tentaverunt Deum in cordibus suis, ut peterent escas ani-
mabus suis.*

---

180   John 7:37b–38.
181   John 19:34.
182   E. N. Denis refers to the "capital grace" or the "grace of headship" of Christ,
which is the "constitutive element of the Church." "Three points about Christ's capital
grace deserve particular emphasis: First, as Head, Christ himself remains preeminent
among the members; second, Christ's ability to impart grace to the other members
ultimately derives from his divinity; finally, the specific identity of human natures
in the Incarnate Word and in each member of the human race provide a ground to
explain the joining of member to Head. Because Christ shares in a common nature
with all the members of the human race—that is, he possesses the same kind of
human nature that we possess—he is able to communicate to us his divine benefits."
Romanus Cessario, O. P., *Christian Faith & the Theological Life* (Washington, DC:
Catholic University of America Press,1996), 22. See also ST IIIa, q. 8; *see also* St.
Thomas Aquinas's *Commentary on the Letter to the Ephesians,* I, 8.
183   John 1:16.
184   Tit. 3:5b–6.
185   Ez. 36:25a.

77{78}[**17**] *Et apposuerunt adhuc peccare ei, and they added yet more sin against him.* So many Christians multiply offenses [against God] (Alas! The anguish of it!) after the grace of Baptism and all the other blessings of Christ that are acts of grace. *In iram excitaverunt Excelsum, they provoked the most High to wrath,* that is, Christ the power of God,[186] *in inaquoso, in the place without water,* that is, in their arid and unfruitful heart, deprived of all the water of heavenly grace. 77{78}[**17**] *Et tentaverunt Deum in cordibus suis, ut peterent escas animabus suis; and they tempted God in their hearts, by asking meat for their desires.* This has in mind those persons who are excessively solicitous [of material goods], who do not believe in the promises of Christ, of whom is said: *Seek you therefore first the kingdom of God, and his justice, and all these things shall be added unto you;*[187] and again: *Be not solicitous therefore, saying, What shall we eat: or what shall we drink, or wherewith shall we be clothed? For after all these things do the heathens seek. For your Father knows that you have need of all these things.*[188] To those who are excessively solicitous for amassing temporal goods and are restless, Paul, who also calls avarice the *service of idols,*[189] says: *Having food, and wherewith to be covered, with these we are content.*[190]

77{78}[**21**]   *Therefore the Lord heard and was angry: and a fire was kindled against Jacob, and wrath came up against Israel.*[191]

Ideo audivit Dominus et distulit; et ignis accensus est in Iacob, et ira ascendit in Israel.

77{78}[**22**]   *Because they believed not in God: and trusted not in his salvation.*

Quia non crediderunt in Deo, nec speraverunt in salutari eius.

77{78}[**21**] *Ideo audivit Dominus Iesus, therefore the Lord Jesus heard* these sins of the Christians, *et distulit, and was angry,* not, however, immediately taking vengeance, but waiting in long-suffering, in the manner that is written in Ecclesiasticus: *The most High is a patient rewarder.*[192] And Peter says: The Lord *patiently deals for our sake not willing that anyone should perish, but that all should return to penance.*[193]

---

186   *E. N.* 1 Cor. 1:24b.
187   Matt. 6:33.
188   Matt. 6:31–32.
189   Col. 3:5: *Mortify therefore . . . covetousness, which is the service of idols.*
190   1 Tim. 6:8.
191   *E. N.* Denis skips over verses 19 and 20.
192   Ecclus. 5:4b.
193   2 Pet. 3:9.

But the patience of God most notably appears during the time of the New Law; for as the Philosophers knew the majesty of God, and the Jews his justice, so the Christians know the mercy of the Creator. For this reason, the Apostle [Paul] asserts: *The goodness and kindness of God our Savior appeared.*[194] *Et ignis, and a fire* of the wrath of Christ, namely, his vengeance, *accensus est in Iacob, was kindled against Jacob*, that is, against the Christian Church, for the longer Christ waits patiently for them, the more horribly will he punish those who do not return or repent; *et ira, and the wrath* of God *ascendit in Israel, came up against Israel*: for the Church of Christ is often in various ways oppressed because of its sins. Even now it is oppressed by the Saracens,[195] heretics, and tyrants in the manner that in times past the Synagogue was by the Canaanites, the Philistines, the Ammonites, and the Moabites. 77{78}[22] *Quia non crediderunt in Deo, because they believed not in God*, that is, in the one God, by complying with his commandments; *nec speraverunt in salutari eius, and trusted not in his salvation*, that is, in Christ; but rather they trusted in their falsehoods, or in their own merits or virtues.

77{78}[23]   *And he had commanded the clouds from above, and had opened the doors of heaven.*

Et mandavit nubibus desuper, et ianuas caeli aperuit.

77{78}[24]   *And had rained down manna upon them to eat, and had given them the bread of heaven.*

Et pluit illis manna ad manducandum, et panem caeli dedit eis.

77{78}[25]   *Man ate the bread of angels: he sent them provisions in abundance.*

Panem angelorum manducavit homo; cibaria misit eis in abundantia.

77{78}[23] *Et mandavit nubibus desuper, and he had commanded the clouds from above*. According to Dionysius [the Areopagite], by clouds we are able to understand the holy angels;[196] and also the Apostles, of whom Isaiah

---

194   Titus 3:4.
195   E. N. In the Middle Ages, the term Saracen was equivalent to the term Muslim. Though the etymology of the word is not certain and a matter of controversy, it may derive from Arabic sariq (سارق) [plural sariqin (سارقين)], which means thief, marauder, or plunderer. Sophia Rose Arjana, *Muslims in the Western Imagination* (Oxford: Oxford University Press, 2015), 91.
196   E. N. On the angels and apostles as "clouds," *see* Volume 3, Article XXXII (Psalm 67:35) and footnote 67-175.

asks: *Who are these, that fly as clouds?*[197] Since the glorious Incarnation of Christ was announced to the Virgin by the ministry of the archangel Gabriel,[198] and the nativity of Christ after it occurred was announced to the shepherds also by the ministry of angels,[199] the prophets were then also illuminated to prophecy of the future incarnation of Christ by the ministry of the angels; and so, God is said here [in this verse] to command the clouds of heaven from above, that is, the holy angels, namely, so that they display reverence regarding the descent of Christ into the world. Moreover, the Apostles preached throughout the world the fulfillment of the Incarnation of Christ, and he commanded the Apostles to devote themselves to the glorification of Christ in the hearts of men in servitude [of ignorance and sin], according to Peter: *He commanded us to preach to the people, and to testify that it is he who was appointed by God, to be judge of the living and of the dead.*[200] God, therefore, commanded both clouds. *Et ianuas caeli*, and the doors of heaven, that is, the mouths of the Apostles, *aperuit*, he had opened so that they might preach the Gospel of Christ. For Christ also told them: *I will give you a mouth and wisdom.*[201] Or [alternatively], the doors of heaven of the empyreal heaven he opened,[202] to the extent that from it he sent angels to us.

77{78}[24]   *And had rained down manna upon them to eat, and had given them the bread of heaven.*

Et pluit illis manna ad manducandum, et panem caeli dedit eis.

77{78}[25]   *Man ate the bread of angels: he sent them provisions in abundance.*

Panem angelorum manducavit homo; cibaria misit eis in abundantia.

77{78}[24] *Et*, and so *pluit illis manna ad manducandum, he rained down manna upon them to eat,* that is, in this way he sent Christ into the world, and announced him to the Gentiles, so that they might believe in him and eat his Body in the Sacrament [of the Eucharist]. Whence, Isaiah states: *Drop down dew, you heavens, from above, and let the clouds rain the just.*[203] For Christ is the true manna, whose figure was that manna given

---

197   Is. 60:8a.
198   Luke 1:31.
199   Luke 2:10–11.
200   Acts 10:42.
201   Luke 21:15a.
202   E. N. On the empyreal or empyrean heaven, *see* footnote 19-11.
203   Is. 45:8a.

to the fathers.[204] *Et panem caeli dedit eis, and had given them the bread of heaven,* that is, the Body of Christ bestowed to the Christians as the most saving bread of the soul, according to that which Christ asserts: *Moses gave you not bread from heaven, but my Father gives you the true bread from heaven;*[205] and again, *I am the living bread which came down from heaven.*[206] 77{78}[25] *Panem angelorum, the bread of angels,* that is, Christ under the form of the Sacrament of the Altar, *manducavit homo, man ate,* [that is to say,] any of the Christian chosen,[207] sacramentally or spiritually,[208] or in both ways. For Christ, who is the refreshment of all the blessed in heaven, is also our food on earth, as he himself attested: *He that eats my flesh . . . abides in me, and I in him.*[209] And it is necessary for all believers to eat this Bread in one of these mentioned ways, as he himself affirms: *Except you eat the Flesh of the Son of man, and drink my Blood, you shall not have life in you.*[210] God the Father *cibaria misit, sent*

---

204 Ex. 16:14–15.

205 John 6:32.

206 John 6:51.

207 E. N. Denis uses term *electus* ("elect" or "chosen") in a corporate sense, that is, as it is used in the notion of a "chosen people," in reference to the Christian people as a whole, as the "people of God." It has no reference to whether the individual is one of the "elect" in the senses of "predestined," *i.e.,* one who will enjoy heaven. To avoid confusion, I have used the term "chosen" here and elsewhere where this term appears.

208 E. N. When unable to take the Eucharist sacramentally because of some physical or other impediment (*e.g.,* one has not kept the fast), one can partake in a spiritual communion. With respect to spiritual communion, St. Alphonsus Liguori states: "A spiritual communion, according to St. Thomas, consists in an ardent desire to receive Jesus in the Most Holy Sacrament, and in lovingly embracing Him as if we had actually received Him." St. Alphonsus Liguori, *Visits to the Most Holy Sacrament* (London: Burns & Lambert, 1855), 15 (trans. R. A. Coffin, C.SS. R.). See ST IIIa, q. 80, arts. 1–2. "To eat Christ spiritually is as he is under the species of this Sacrament, inasmuch, namely, someone believes in Christ with desire to consume this Sacrament. And this is not only to eat Christ spiritually, but likewise to eat spiritually this sacrament." ST IIIa, q. 80, art. 2, c. Importantly, to partake in an authentic spiritual communion, one must be in a state of grace; that is, one cannot be in a state of mortal sin or under some moral or canonical impediment to receiving the Sacrament. This is made clear by the Council of Trent (Session 13, chapter 8), which requires for a spiritual communion (as well as a sacramental *and* spiritual communion) "a lively faith which works by love," *fide viva, quae per dilectionem operatur,* which is equivalent to being in a state of sanctifying grace.

209 John 6:58.

210 John 6:54. E. N. As St. Thomas makes clear, when the bread through consecration becomes the sacramental Body of Christ, the precious Blood is there by concomitance. Likewise, when wine is transubstantiated to the precious Blood sacramentally, the Body is there by concomitance. *Quodlibet* VII, q. 4 a. 1 co. Hence, he who takes communion only under the species of the bread alone consumes both

them provisions, namely to the Christians, *in abundantia*, in abundance: for all Christians who so desire are able to obtain refreshment from this heavenly bread, yet they are not able to exhaust it or diminish it.[211]

77{78}[26]   *He removed the south wind from heaven: and by his power brought in the southwest wind.*

Transtulit austrum de caelo, et induxit in virtute sua africum.

77{78}[27]   *And he rained upon them meats as dust: and feathered fowls like the sand of the sea.*[212]

Et pluit super eos sicut pulverem carnes, et sicut arenam maris volatilia pennata.

77{78}[28]   *And they fell in the midst of their camp, round about their pavilions.*

Et ceciderunt in medio castrorum eorum, circa tabernacula eorum.

77{78}[26]   *Transtulit Austrum de caelo*, *he removed the south wind from heaven*: that is, the preachers of the angelic manner of living sent throughout all the world, blowing the divine word over every heart that is open to hearing it; *et induxit*, *and he brought in*, [that is,] God, the Trinity [brought in], *in virtute sua*, *by his power*, divine and particular to him, *Africum*, *the southwest wind*, that is, the preachers preaching more downward doctrines. For the *Auster* is a wind from the south; but the *Africus* is a westward wind, and it is cross-wise with respect to the south.[213] Therefore by south wind is designated the preachers of sublime things, in the matter that the Apostle [Paul] says, *We speak wisdom among the perfect;*[214] but by southwest, the preachers of humble things [is meant], of which the same person says, *I judged not myself to*

---

the Body (and by concomitance) the Blood, fully fulfilling the precept of Christ. DS 1199, 1731 (Council of Trent).

211   E. N. "For as often as you ... [worthily] receive the Body of Christ, so often do you go over the work of your redemption and are made participant of all the merits of Christ. For the love (*caritas*) of Christ is never diminished and the greatness of his propitiation is never exhausted." Thomas á Kempis, *The Imitation of Christ*, IV, 2, 6.

212   E. N. I have changed the Douay-Rheims's "flesh" to "meats" for the Latin *carnes*. The Latin is plural, and Denis in his *Commentary* explains why this is so.

213   E. N. In the ancient Mediterranean world the winds were divided into the points of the compass. For the cardinal directions, the winds were: *Septentrio* (North), *Auster* (South), *Favonius* (West), and *Eurus* (East). The wind known as *Africus* was from the Southwest.

214   1 Cor. 2:6a.

know anything among you, but Jesus Christ and him crucified.[215] 77{78}
[27] *Et pluit super eos,* and he rained upon them, that is, upon all that
converted to the Catholic Faith, *sicut pulverem,* as dust, that is, exceedingly abundantly, *carnes, meats,* that is, the Body of Christ: which though
one and the same in all consecrated hosts, yet because of the multitude
of matter or bread which is converted into him, is said to be *meats;* or
[alternatively, the plural is used] because of the parts [of his Body]:
whence the Psalmist says, *Pierce my meats (carnes) with your fear: for I
am afraid of your judgments.*[216] That the Body of Christ is the flesh and
food that refreshes the faithful, he himself speaks of it, saying: *My flesh
is meat indeed: and my blood is drink indeed.*[217]

So God rains over Christians *sicut arenam maris, like the sand of the sea,*
that is, in an uncountable multitude, and *volatilia pennata, and feathered
fowls,* that is, contemplative men, the friends of God of which a Psalm
below states, *I will number them, and they shall be multiplied above the
sand.*[218] God rained upon his Church these sorts of men, so that they
might water or make fruitful the people with the rain of heavenly words
and be pastors of others. It is also possible to understand *feathered fowls*
to mean the holy angels: because God sends a particular angel to keep
and protect each Christian;[219] indeed, according to the Apostle, *All are
ministering spirits, sent to minister for them, who receive the inheritance of
salvation.*[220] God sends these in great abundance and more frequently

---

215 1 Cor. 2:2. E. N. This intermingling of the sublime and the humble, which
is at the heart of the Christian message, and which Denis sees in the blending of
the south and southwest winds in this Psalm, and which is personified in St. Paul's
sublime doctrine humbly delivered is wonderfully captured in St. Francis of Assisi's
reflections on the Eucharist: *O humilitas sublimis! O sublimitas humilis! quod Dominus
universitatis, Deus et Dei Filius, sic se humiliat, ut pro nostra salute sub modica panis
formula se abscondat! Videte, fratres, humilitatem Dei et effundite coram illo corda
vestra; humiliamini et vos, ut exaltemini ab eo.* "O sublime humility! O humble sublimity! That the Lord of the universe, God and the Son of God, should so humble
himself that for our salvation he hides himself under the form of humble bread!
See, O brothers, the humility of God and pour out your hearts before him, and
humble also yourselves, so that you may be exalted by him." *Opuscula Sancti Patris
Francisci Assisiensis* (Grottaferrata: Editiones Collegii S. Bonaventurae, 1978), 144.
(ed., Cajetan Esser, O. F. M.).
216 Ps. 118:120. E. N. Again, the Douay-Rheims has the singular "flesh" for plural
carnes; I have modified the translation so that it is in keeping with Denis's argument.
217 John 6:56.
218 Ps. 118:18. E. N. On contemplation being the "feather of the soul," *penna animae,*
see Volume 1, footnote 17-31.
219 E. N. On guardian angels, *see* also footnotes 33-42 (Volume 2), 66-13, and
69-20 (Volume 3).
220 Heb. 1:14.

during the time of the law of Christ than he did during the law of Moses. 77{78}[28] *Et ceciderunt, and they fell,* that is, the pastors and holy angels just mentioned descended, *in medio castrorum eorum, in the midst of their camp,* that is, of the faithful of the Church, *circa tabernacula eorum, round about their pavilions,* that is, around cities, villages, indeed around the bodies of Christians persons. For the angels guard the bodies of men from many injuries and dangers. Whence, in the Act of the Apostles, the angel of God first leads all the Apostles from the enclosure of prison, and later delivered Peter.[221] And so we read in the Gospel that Christ send his disciples two-by-two to *into every city and place where he himself was to come.*[222]

77{78}[29]   *So they did eat, and were filled exceedingly, and he gave them their desire:*

   Et manducaverunt, et saturati sunt nimis; et desiderium eorum attulit eis:

77{78}[29] *Et manducaverunt, so they did eat,* [that is, so] the Christian chosen [did eat] the Body of their Lord, as he commanded, when he said: *Do this in commemoration of me;*[223] *et saturati sunt nimis, and were filled exceedingly,* that is, they were interiorly filled with the grace of the Holy Spirit and spiritually fattened, according to that which Christ said: *He that eats my flesh, and drinks my Blood, abides in me, and I in him;*[224] and again, *He that eats this bread, shall live forever.*[225] *Et desiderium eorum attulit eis, and he gave them their desire,* hearing their prayers.

77{78}[30]   *They were not defrauded of that which they craved. As yet their meat was in their mouth.*

   Non sunt fraudati a desiderio suo. Adhuc escae eorum erant in ore ipsorum.

77{78}[31]   *And the wrath of God came upon them. And he slew the fat ones amongst them, and obstructed the chosen men of Israel.*

   Et ira Dei ascendit super eos; et occidit pingues eorum, et electos Israel impedivit.

---

221   Acts 5:19; 12:7–10.
222   Luke 10:1.
223   Luke 22:19b.
224   John 6:57.
225   John 6:59b.

77{78}[30] *Adhuc escae erant in ore ipsorum, as yet their meat was in their mouth,*[226] not of those chosen, but those [among them] who unworthily eat, 77{78}[31] *et ira Dei ascendit super eos, and the wrath of God came upon them:* because Satan entered into them, as it did the traitor Judas,[227] for the Apostle [Paul] said of this: *Whosoever shall eat this bread, or drink the chalice of the Lord unworthily, shall be guilty of the Body and of the Blood of the Lord.*[228] *Et occidit, and he slew,* God, [that is, slew], *pingues eorum, the fat ones:* that is, he spiritually killed those who carnally consumed Christ, withdrawing charity and grace from them. For as the Apostle says, *He that eats and drinks unworthily, eats and drinks judgment to himself, not discerning the Body of the Lord,*[229] that is, not spiritually perceiving it [to be truly the Body of Christ] or not consuming it reverently or faithfully, but merely as one would other food. *Et electos Israel, and the chosen men of Israel,* that is, they who are seen to be great in the Church, *impedivit, he obstructed* from the entering into the kingdom of heaven because of the sin of unworthy communions. For in sacred Scripture the chosen are not always said to be predestined to eternal life, because Christ in the Gospel tells the Apostles: *Have not I chosen you twelve; and one of you is a devil?*[230] And elsewhere we have it said that Saul was a man chosen [by God], yet whom many of the Saints say is damned.[231]

77{78}[32] *In all these things they sinned still: and they believed not for his wondrous works.*

In omnibus his peccaverunt adhuc, et non crediderunt in mirabilibus eius.

---

226 E. N. Denis skips over the first half of verse 29.

227 John 13:27.

228 1 Cor. 11:27.

229 1 Cor. 11:29.

230 John 6:71.

231 Cf. 1 Sam. 9:2: *He [Benjamin] had a son whose name was Saul, a choice and goodly man, and there was not among the children of Israel a goodlier person than he: from his shoulders and upward he appeared above all the people.* E. N. In his *Purgatorio,* Dante has King Saul depicted on a bas relief as one of several examples of the sin of pride, emphasizing his suicide. *O Saùl come in su la propria spada quivi pareve morto in Gelboè,* "O Saul, how in your own sword, you appeared dead in Gilboa." Dante, *Purgatorio,* XII, 40–41. King Saul is only one of three people in the Bible who committed suicide (1 Sam. 31:1–6), the others being Ahitophel (2 Sam. 17:23), and Judas (Matt. 27:5). The common opinion that Saul is numbered among the damned is based upon a reading of 1 Sam. 7:15, which refers to Saul in reference to Solomon: "But my mercy I will not take from him [Solomon], as I took it from Saul, whom I removed from before my face."

77{78}[33]   *And their days were consumed in vanity, and their years in haste.*

Et defecerunt in vanitate dies eorum, et anni eorum cum festinatione.

77{78}[34]   *When he slew them, then they sought him: and they returned, and came to him early in the morning.*

Cum occideret eos, quaerebant eum et revertebantur, et diluculo veniebant ad eum.

77{78}[35]   *And they remembered that God was their helper: and the most high God their redeemer.*

Et rememorati sunt quia Deus adiutor est eorum, et Deus excelsus redemptor eorum est.

77{78}[36]   *And they loved him with their mouth: and with their tongue they lied unto him.*

Et dilexerunt eum in ore suo, et lingua sua mentiti sunt ei.

77{78}[32] *In omnibus his peccaverunt adhuc, in all these things they sinned still*: that is, notwithstanding the many benefits of Christ, the ungrateful Christians offended Christ.[232] 77{78}[33] *Et defecerunt in vanitate dies eorum, and their days were consumed in vanity*, that is, they descended through [life] without fruit and merit;[233] *et anni eorum cum festinatione, and their days were consumed in vanity*: for as is contained in the book of Job, the godless man, *before his days be full he shall perish.*[234] And again Scripture attests with respect to sinners: that they were all *taken away before their time.*[235] Whence of these it is predicted: *We being born, forthwith ceased to be, and ... are consumed in our wickedness.*[236] 77{78}[34] *Cum occideret eos, quaerebant eum et revertebantur; when he slew them, then they sought him.* For many of the perverse, who during the time of security spurn conversion, convert to the Lord when they observe perishing those who are similar to them, and

---

232 E. N. Denis does not address the second half of this verse in the *Commentary*.
233 E. N. This fruitless and meritless descent brings to mind that truth stated by Virgil in his *Aeneid: Facilis descensus Averno; noctes atque dies patet atri ianua Ditis; sed revocare gradum superasque evadere ad auras, hoc opus, hic labor est.* "The path to hell [literally, Avernus, a volcano near Cuma, Italy, a symbol of the entry into hell] is easy: black Dis's door [Dis was the Roman god of the underworld] is open night and day: but to retrace your steps, and go out to the air above, that is work, that is the task." Virgil, *Aeneid* (Poetry in Translation: 2002), VI, 127–29. (trans., A. S. Kline).
234 Job. 15:32a.
235 Job 22:16a.
236 Wis. 5:13.

they consider that they are imminently threatened with the same scourges. And then they begin to be mindful 77{78}[35] *Deus adiutor est eorum, that God was their helper.*[237] But because customarily this repentance chiefly proceeds from human fear rather than divine love, so there is immediately added regarding it: 77{78}[36] *Et dilexerunt eum in ore suo, and they loved him with their mouth,* saying, Lord, Lord;[238] *et lingua sua mentiti sunt, and with their tongue they lied to him,* for they did not back away from evil out of reverence for him.

77{78}[38]   *But he is merciful and will forgive their sins: and will not destroy them. And many a time did he turn away his anger: and did not kindle all his wrath.*[239]

   Ipse autem est misericors, et propitius fiet peccatis eorum et non disperdet eos. Et abundavit ut averteret iram suam, et non accendit omnem iram suam.

   77{78}[38] *Ipse autem,* but he, Christ, *est misericors,* is merciful from his natural attributes, *et propitius fiet peccatis eorum,* and will forgive their sins, provided they convert, and worthily do penance; *et non disperdet eos,* and will not destroy them from the company of the elect, nor will he deny them grace in the present or glory in the future: for he himself says, there is joy among the angels of God *upon one sinner that does penance;*[240] and elsewhere, *I am not come to call the just, but sinners.*[241] *Et abundavit,* and many a time Christ in whom there is the riches of his mercy, *ut averteret iram suam,* did he turn away his anger from his Church, most mercifully exercising forbearance. For *while we were still enemies, he died for us;*[242] and he will not allow anyone to be lost to the extent it is in his power. *Et non accendit,* and he did not kindle against us *omnem iram suam,* all his wrath, that is, the rigor of his justice, but pours out over us abundantly his mercy.

77{78}[40]   *How often did they provoke him in the desert: and move him to wrath in the place without water?*[243]

---

237   E. N. Denis skips the first and last parts of verse 35, focusing on the middle of the verse only.

238   Matt. 7:21.

239   Denis skips verse 37.

240   Luke 15:7a.

241   Matt. 9:13b.

242   Rom. 5:8a, 9a.

243   E. N. Denis skips over verse 39.

*Quoties exacerbaverunt eum in deserto, in iram concitaverunt
eum in inaquoso?*

77{78}[41]   And they turned back and tempted God: and grieved the
Holy One of Israel.

*Et conversi sunt, et tentaverunt Deum, et sanctum Israel
exacerbaverunt.*

77{78}[42]   They remembered not his hand, in the day that he redeemed
them from the hand of him that afflicted them.

*Non sunt recordati manus eius, die qua redemit eos de manu
tribulantis.*

77{78}[43]   How he wrought his signs in Egypt, and his wonders in the
field of Tanis.

Sicut posuit in Aegypto signa sua, et prodigia sua in campo Taneos.

But how great is the ingratitude of certain Christians! For 77{78}[40]
quoties, how often, that is, how frequently — it is as if it were saying, very
often — *exacerbaverunt eum, did they provoke him,* namely the most merciful, most sweet, and most meek Savior, *in deserto, in the desert,* that is, in
this world so parched and unfruitful, so forsaken of good and full of evil!
And how often *in iram concitaverunt eum in inaquoso, did they move him to
wrath in the place without water,* namely, in their soul, hardened and dry, so
destitute of the water of grace! 77{78}[41] *Et conversi sunt, and they turned
back,* after Baptism and Penance, to their former worldly manner of living;
et tentaverunt Deum, and they tempted God, seeking to contend with his
power, providence, and knowledge, as if entertaining doubts whether God
had power over all things, had providence over everything, and whether he
knew all things. 77{78}[42][244] *Non sunt recordati, they remembered not,* the
ungrateful Christians [remembered not], *manus eius, his hand,* that his, the
kindly rendering of aid of Jesus Christ, who aided them, *die quae redemit
eos de manu tribulantis, in the day that he redeemed them from that hand of
him that afflicted them,* that is, from the power of the devil, the slavery to sin,
and eternal death. Christ accomplished this on Good Friday, the day before
the Passover, when he, *the just for the unjust,* suffered so *that he might offer
us to God, being put to death indeed in the flesh, but enlivened in the spirit.*[245]
77{78}[43] *Sicut posuit in Aegypto, how he wrought . . . in Egypt,* that is in
this world enveloped by vice, *signa sua, his signs:* because while he hung

---

244   E. N. Denis skips the remainder of verse 77:41.
245   1 Pet. 3:18.

on the Cross, the sun became darkened,[246] during a time of opposition, by a supposition of the moon under the sun:[247] this was a most marvelous thing, as the great Dionysius [the Areopagite] beautifully describes in his epistle to Polycarp.[248] But also the earth then was shaken,[249] and many of the dead rose again from the grace, not in the day of the Passion, but of the Resurrection.[250]

77{78}[44] *And he turned their rivers into blood, and their showers that they might not drink.*

Et convertit in sanguinem flumina eorum, et imbres eorum, ne biberent.

77{78}[45] *He sent among them diverse sores of flies, which devoured them: and frogs which destroyed them.*

Misit in eos coenomyiam, et comedit eos, et ranam, et disperdidit eos.

Then it touches upon these prodigies in a specific manner. 77{78} [44] *Et convertit in sanguinem flumina eorum*, and he turned their rivers into blood. The ten plagues which befell the Egyptians in a bodily way, have in a spiritual way fallen upon the perverse faithful. For they turned their rivers into blood when their wisdom turned to carnal things, and spiritual realities were overcome by their fleshly concerns: because, as the Apostle [Paul] said, *The sensual man perceives not these things that are of the Spirit of God.*[251] 77{78}[45][252] *Misit*, he sent, and Christ sends daily,

---

246   Matt. 27:45.

247   E. N. Meaning a solar eclipse, where the moon's orbit gets between the earth and the sun, thus casting its shadow upon the earth.

248   E. N. "At the time the two of us [Dionysius and Apollophanes] were in Heliopolis and we both witnessed the extraordinary phenomenon of the moon hiding the sun at a time that was out of season for their coming together, and from the night hour until evening, it was supernaturally positioned in the middle of the sun. And . . . . [w]e saw the moon begin to hide the sun from the east, travel across to the other side of the sun, and return to its path so that the hiding and he restoration of the light did not take place in the same direction but rather in diametrically opposite directions. Those were the amazing things which happened at that time, possible only to Christ the cause of all, 'who does great and marvelous things without number.'" Pseudo-Dionysius: The Complete Works (New York: Paulist Press, 1987) 268–69 (trans., Colm Luibheid)

249   Matt. 45:51.

250   Matt. 45:52–53.

251   1 Cor. 2:14a.

252   E. N. Denis skips the latter part of verse 44.

not effectively, but permissively, *in eos, among them,* that is, among the ungrateful Christians, *coenomyiam, diverse sores of flies,* that is, dog-like manners (*mores caninos*), namely, the rabies of anger, the fury of impatience, irreverence to parents and to prelates,[253] *et comedit eos, which devoured them,* that is, their twistedness immediately annihilated them spiritually; *et ranam, and frogs,* that is, the failure to keep custody of the tongue, and the most impudent and garrulous loquacity,[254] *disperdidit eos, destroyed them,* that is, in various ways, the sin of loquacity caused their souls to be lost. Whence Solomon said: *Have you seen a man hasty to speak? Folly is rather to be looked for, than his amendment.*[255] And James: *The tongue constitutes a world of iniquity.*[256] Hence, in Ecclesiasticus also is written: *He that uses many words shall hurt his own soul.*[257] *Let every man, therefore, be swift to hear, but slow to speak, and slow to anger.*[258]

77{78}[46] And he gave up their fruits to the blast, and their labors to the locust.

Et dedit aerugini fructus eorum, et labores eorum locustae.

77{78}[47] And he destroyed their vineyards with hail, and their mulberry trees with hoarfrost.

Et occidit in grandine vineas eorum, et moros eorum in pruina.

77{78}[46] *Et dedit aerugini fructus eorum, and he gave up their fruits to the blast.* By "the blast" (*aeruginem*), which is a wind or breeze that is hiddenly noxious and blighting of fruit, is meant hidden arrogance of the heart: by this all the fruits of good works are destroyed, because by itself pride destroys all things it accompanies. One ought not to marvel at this because *God resists the proud;*[259] and this is certain because it is neither safe nor easy to fight against God. *Et labores eorum locustae, and their labors to the locust:* that is, God permits the laborious efforts and the good works done before by those who are ungrateful and by those who return to their

---

253   E. N. This interpretation is commonplace, and is found, for example, in St. Augustine and Cassiodorus. It stems from interpreting the word flies. As the Gloss of Anselm of Laon (†1117 AD) succinctly states: *Cynomia. Canini mores sunt.* "The flies are dog-like manners." PL 113, 971.
254   E. N. Again, this is a common interpretation. Anselm of Laon's Gloss states: *Rana. Loquax vanitas.* "Frog. Loquacious vanity." PL 113, 971.
255   Prov. 29:20.
256   James 3:6a.
257   Ecclus. 20:8a.
258   James 1:19.
259   James 4:6b; 1 Pet. 5:5b.

sinful lives to be emptied from reward by the vice of detraction: for the person who is ungrateful to God habitually falls into the vice of detraction,[260] which is a greatly abominable thing according to Ecclesiastes, *If a serpent bite in silence, he is nothing better that he who backbites secretly.*[261] 77{78}[47] *Et occidit in grandine, and he destroyed . . . with hail,* that is, by the iniquity of those violently oppressing others, such as by tyrannical power, *vineas eorum, their vineyards,* that is, their souls: for so long as those ungrateful to God and those who are arrogant oppress and bring grief to others, they kill themselves internally and they ruin themselves spiritually with their own sword; *et moros eorum, and their mulberry trees,* that is, God kills, that is, he allows to be killed, their former good works which were, inflamed with the fire of charity, *in pruina, with hoarfrost,* that is, with the nighttime chill of the mind, namely, with rancor and hate, which is the coldness or freezing of the spirit, just as love is fire and the melting of it. For he who is led to the interior coldness of hate and is in the thrall of various vices, after having received charity, is justly deprived of the reward for the prior works done in charity.[262] For this reason, the Savior said: *Iniquity has abounded, and the charity of many shall grow cold.*[263] Regarding this contact with the cold, John, or rather Christ through John, says: *I have something against you, because you have left your first charity. Be mindful therefore from whence you are fallen, and do penance.*[264]

77{78}[48]   *And he gave up their cattle to the hail, and their stock to the fire.*

Et tradidit grandini iumenta eorum, et possessionem eorum igni.

77{78}[48]   *Et tradidit grandini, and he gave up . . . to the hail,* that is, to the iniquitous men previously referred to, *iumenta eorum, their cattle,* that is, their sensitive powers, both cognitive as well as appetitive, namely, the exterior and interior senses, and also the concupiscible and irascible appetite. For while a sinner ungrateful to God seeks with full eagerness the way to oppress, injure, or prevail over others, he is delivered over to the previously-mentioned power of hail, because through these efforts, he seeks and is preoccupied with how he might bring about his perverse

---

260   E. N. Detraction is the disclosure, "without objectively valid reason," of "another's faults and failings to persons who did not know" of them. CCC § 2477.

261   Eccl. 10:11.

262   E. N. All merit obtained by good works performed while in a state of grace is lost when the soul is in mortal sin. For more on this, *see* footnote Volume 1, footnote 6-13.

263   Matt. 24:12.

264   Rev. 2:4-5a.

purpose. *Et possessionem eorum, and their stock,* that is, their state and perfections, or the interior riches of the mind of these men, God gives *ignis, to the fire,* that is, to the heat of avarice: for so long as one turns toward the desire of worldly and empty things, he falls away from the love of spiritual goods; and so the fire of avarice in such a person devastates and destroys whatever perfection had inhered in him before. Whence also Paul writes to Timothy: *For they that will become rich, fall into temptation, and into the snare of the devil.*[265] And Ecclesiasticus: *There is not a more wicked thing than to love money. For such a one* (namely, an avaricious man) *sets even his own soul to sale.*[266]

77{78}[50]   *He made a way for a path to his anger: he spared not their souls from death, and their cattle he shut up in death.*[267]

Viam fecit semitae irae suae, non pepercit a morte animabus eorum, et iumenta eorum in morte conclusit.

77{78}[50] *Viam fecit, he made a way,* God [made a way], *semitae irae suae, for a path to his anger,* that is, for the outpouring of his vindication. For as long he abandons the sinner to his error, he makes a way for a path to his anger, for he does not take up the impediments to incurring the punishment of divine justice. God does this in the vessels of ire, which have become contumacious, namely, in the reprobate, which God justly abandons to their own devices, for he purposes to exhibit in them the severity of his justice. The Apostle [Paul] teaches about this in a most complete way.[268] *Non pepercit a morte animarum eorum, he spared not their souls from death:* because God immediately withdraws charity, which is the life of the soul, from all men who sin mortally. *Et iumenta eorum, and their cattle,* that is, their carnal affections and their works of the flesh, God *in morte conclusit, he shut up in death,* that is, he damns to eternal death: for the Apostle attests, *They who do such things shall not obtain the kingdom of God;*[269] and again, *For if you live according to the flesh* (he says), *you shall die.*[270]

----

265   1 Tim. 6:9a.

266   Ecclus. 10:10a.

267   E. N. Denis skips over verse 49.

268   Rom. 9:21–23: *Has not the potter power over the clay, of the same lump, to make one vessel unto honor, and another unto dishonor? What if God, willing to show his wrath, and to make his power known, endured with much patience vessels of wrath, fitted for destruction, that he might show the riches of his glory on the vessels of mercy, which he has prepared unto glory?*

269   Gal. 10:21b.

270   Rom. 8:13a.

77{78}[51] *And he killed all the firstborn in the land of Egypt: the first-fruits of all their labor in the tabernacles of Ham.*

Et percussit omne primogenitum in terra Aegypti, primitias omnis laboris eorum in tabernaculis Cham.

77{78}[51] *Et percussit omne primogenitum in terra Aegypti, and he killed all the firstborn in the land of Egypt*: that is, God kills the formed faith, to the degree it was formed, in all the hearts adhering to the darkness of this world (although an informed faith may persevere in them).[271] For a formed faith is the first-born in us, that is, it is the first gift of God, and the principle of all meritorious works, according to that in Habakkuk: *Behold, he that is unbelieving, his soul shall not be right in himself: but the just shall live in his faith.*[272] And Isaiah: *He that is unfaithful deals unfaithfully.*[273] *Primitias omnis laboris eorum, the firstfruits of all their labor,* that is, God kills in the manner just stated the interior ardors of holy charity in the ungrateful and in those returning back to their former life, from which [charity] proceeds all the work that is pleasing to God and that is meritorious, *in tabernaculis Cham, in the tabernacles of Ham,* that is, in worldly men or the devils, who *are wise to do evil, but to do good they have no knowledge.*[274] For the name "Ham" is understood to mean shrewd. And as Christ attested, *The children of this world are wiser in their generation than the children of light.*[275]

77{78}[52] *And he took away his own people as sheep: and guided them in the wilderness like a flock.*

Et abstulit sicut oves populum suum, et perduxit eos tamquam gregem in deserto.

77{78}[53] *And he brought them out in hope, and they feared not: and the sea overwhelmed their enemies.*

---

271   E. N. A soul is justified only if it is in the state of sanctifying grace, that is, only if it has a *faith formed in charity,* a *fides formata caritate.* Gal. 5:6. While faith is a necessary requirement of salvation, Eph. 2:8; Rom. 3:28, faith alone (*fides informis*) is not sufficient without the theological virtue of charity. For even devils believe. James 2:19. "Faith without charity does not prove useful [to lead to the Kingdom of God]. Without charity, indeed, faith can exist, but not also with profit." St. Augustine, *De Trinitate,* XV, 18, 32, PL 42, 1083. "For faith without hope and charity neither units a man perfectly with Christ nor makes him a living member of his body." DS 1531 (Council of Trent).

272   Hab. 2:4.

273   Is. 21:2a.

274   Jer. 4:22b.

275   Luke 16:8b.

Et deduxit eos in spe, et non timuerunt, et inimicos eorum
operuit mare.

77{78}[52] *Et abstulit,* and he took away, Christ [took away] *sicut*
oves populum, his own people as sheep, that is, the elect from the power
of the devil, from a worldly manner of living, from the society of the
reprobate in the way he said through Hosea: *I will deliver them out of*
the hand of death. I will redeem them from death.[276] And it is written
elsewhere about the elect: *You are not of the world, but I have chosen*
you out of the world.[277] The Savior says this of every man he infuses
with the grace of conversion. *Et perduxit eos tamquam gregem in deserto,*
and he guided them in the wilderness like a flock, that is, in the present
exile, shepherding them with graces and virtues. That is why he says
of himself: *I am the good shepherd; and I know mine, and mine know*
me, . . . and I give them life everlasting.[278] He feeds them also with the
most worthy food, namely, his most precious Body and Blood in the
Sacrament. 77{78}[53] *Et deduxit eos in spe,* and he brought them out
in hope of future felicity, *et non timuerunt,* and they feared not with an
inordinate fear the times of suffering or the temptations of the devils
because they heard that which the Savior said to them: *In the world you*
shall have distress: but have confidence, I have overcome the world.[279] And
elsewhere: *Let not your heart be troubled, nor let it be afraid;*[280] and *Fear*
not them that kill the body.[281] *Et inimicos eorum,* and their enemies, that
is, the persecutors of the just, *operuit mare,* the sea overwhelmed, that is,
[they were overwhelmed by] their own iniquity or infernal damnation,
or the tumult of the employments of a worldly life.

77{78}[54] *And he brought them into the mountain of his sanctuary: the*
mountain which his right hand had purchased. And he cast
out the Gentiles before them: and by lot divided to them their
land by a line of distribution.

Et induxit eos in montem sanctificationis suae, montem quem
acquisivit dextera eius; et eiecit a facie eorum gentes, et sorte
divisit eis terram in funiculo distributionis.

---

276   Hosea 13:14a.
277   John 15:19b.
278   John 10:14, 28a.
279   John 16:33b.
280   John 14:27b.
281   Matt. 10:28a.

77{78}[55]   *And he made the tribes of Israel to dwell in their tabernacles.*
Et habitare fecit in tabernaculis eorum tribus Israel.

77{78}[56]   *Yet they tempted and provoked the most high God: and they kept not his testimonies.*

Et tentaverunt, et exacerbaverunt Deum excelsum, et testimonia eius non custodierunt.

77{78}[58]   *They provoked him to anger on their hills: and moved him to jealousy with their graven things.*[282]

In iram concitaverunt eum in collibus suis, et in sculptilibus suis ad aemulationem eum provocaverunt.

77{78}[54] *Et induxit eos in montem sanctificationis suae,* and he brought them out into the mountain of his sanctuary, that is, in obedience to holy Mother Church, which is the Kingdom of Christ, reigning in her through faith.[283] And so the Apostle [Paul] says: *We give thanks to God, and the Father. . . . who has translated us into the kingdom of the Son of his love.*[284] *Montem quem acquisivit dextera eius,* the mountain which his right had had purchased, namely, [purchased] by Christ stretching out and being transfixed upon the Cross for us. For Christ purchased the Church not *with corruptible things as gold or silver, . . . but with his precious Blood,* according to that which was said by the Apostle [Paul]: *Christ was offered once to exhaust the sins of many.*[285] Also, in the Acts of the Apostles, Paul speaking openly and exhorting pastors, said: *Take heed to yourselves, and to the whole flock, wherein the Holy Spirit has placed you bishops, to rule the Church of God, which he has purchased with his own Blood.*[286] *Et eiecit a*

---

282   E. N. Denis skips verse 57 in this Article.
283   E. N. "The meaning of the expressions *kingdom of heaven, kingdom of God,* and *kingdom of Christ* in Sacred Scripture and the Fathers of the Church, as well as in the documents of the Magisterium, is not always exactly the same, nor is their relationship to the Church, which is a mystery that cannot be totally contained by a human concept. Therefore, there can be various theological explanations of these terms. However, none of these possible explanations can deny or empty in any way the intimate connection between Christ, the kingdom, and the Church. In fact, the kingdom of God which we know from revelation, 'cannot be detached either from Christ or from the Church. . . . If the kingdom is separated from Jesus, it is no longer the kingdom of God which he revealed. . . . Likewise, one may not separate the kingdom from the Church. . . . [W]hile remaining distinct from Christ and the kingdom, the Church is indissolubly united to both.'" Congregation for the Doctrine of the Faith, *Dominus Iesus,* 18 (quoting Pope St. John Paul II, *Redemptoris missio,* 18).
284   Col. 1:3a, 13b.
285   Heb. 9:28a.
286   Acts 20:28.

facie eorum gentes, and he cast out the Gentiles before them. This was literally fulfilled in the Christians, because all over the world, where in times past the Gentiles dwelled, Christians, who now dwell there, quickly occupied: and this certainly occurred through divine power by many miracles, by which idolatry was eradicated and the Catholic faith made public. *Et sorte divisit eis terram in funiculo distributionis, and by lot divided to them their land by a line of distribution.* By the word "lot," Dionysius [the Areopagite] sometimes will understand a certain splendor or ordination of the Holy Spirit. Because, therefore, the Apostles, according to the promptings of the Holy Spirit, divided the world between them, each one departing to that lot or part that was deputed to them, such as John to Asia, Peter to Italy, Andrew to Achaia, Thomas to India, etc.,[287] so God divided the earth among them by a line of distribution. Whence also Paul acknowledged: *We will not glory beyond our measure; but according to the measure of the rule, which God has measured to us, a measure to reach even unto you.*[288] 77{78}[55] *Et habitare fecit, and he made . . . to dwell,* God [made to dwell], *in tabernaculis eorum, in their tabernacles,* that is, in the place, lands, and cities of the pagans, *tribus Israel, the tribes of Israel,* that is, the Christian people, who are children of the Patriarchs, not in the flesh, but in the spirit.[289] 77{78}[56] *Et tentaverunt et exacerbaverunt Deum excelsum, yet they tempted and provoked the most high God:* in the manner that that has been often explained here. 77{78}[58] *In iram concitaverunt eum in collibus suis, they provoked him to anger on their hills,* that is, in the swelling of their pride, transferring unto themselves the honor of God, who alone is due all honor and glory,[290] seeking to be set above others, to have dominion, and to be honored. To people such as this Christ says: *How can you believe, who receive glory one from another: and the glory which is from God alone, you do not seek?*[291] *Et in sculptilibus suis, and with their graven images,* that is, with their idols, or with the phantoms of their imaginations, and with

---

287   E. N. This is a reference to the so-called *sortes apostolorum* or *divisio apostolorum*, where the Apostles divided the known world among them by lot so as to assign responsibilities to the various apostles to spread the Gospel, and, if need be, suffer martyrdom there. The event is briefly mentioned in Eusebius's *Ecclesiastical History* (Book III, 1).

288   2 Cor. 10:13. E. N. Denis is suggesting that St. Paul is acknowledging here that he has been assigned a certain boundary or measure which includes the Corinthians.

289   E. N. *Nous sommes spirituellement des sémites.* "Spiritually, we are Semites," Pope Pius XI is reputed to have said to some Belgian pilgrims on September 6, 1938. *La Documentation catholique* 39, No. 885 (December 5, 1938), col. 1460.

290   Cf. 1 Tim. 1:17: *Now to the king of ages, immortal, invisible, the only God, be honor and glory for ever and ever. Amen.*

291   John 5:44.

the vain recollection of their images, *ad aemulationem, to jealousy*, that is, to indignation, *eum provocaverunt, they moved him*, thinking perverse thoughts, and clinging to the recollections of vile things, and, as a result of these things, unmindful of godly things, and offending thereby God the Judge: of whom he says through Micah, *Woe to you that devise that which is unprofitable;*[292] and similarly through Isaiah, *Take away the evil of your devices from my eyes.*[293] For of such people, Zechariah says: *They made their heart as the adamant stone,*[294] *lest they should hear the law.*[295]

77{78}[59] *God heard, and despised them, and he reduced Israel exceedingly as it were to nothing.*

Audivit Deus, et sprevit, et ad nihilum redegit valde Israel.

77{78}[60] *And he put away the tabernacle of Shiloh, his tabernacle where he dwelt among men.*

Et repulit tabernaculum Silo, tabernaculum suum, ubi habitavit in hominibus.

77{78}[59] *Audivit Deus, God heard*, that is, he knew all these sins of the people, in the manner as he acknowledged by Amos: *I know your manifold crimes;*[296] *et sprevit, and he despised them* both the doers and the deeds as it says in a Psalm below: *You have despised all them that fall off from your judgments;*[297] *et ad nihilum redebit valde Israel, and he reduced Israel exceedingly as it were to nothing*, that is, the faithful people, despoiling them of all the virtue and grace of the Holy Spirit because of the sin they committed. **77{78}[60]** *Et repulit tabernaculum Silo, and he put away the tabernacle of Shiloh*: by which one can understand the Church, which God frequently permits to be devasted by tyrants and godless men, because they have abandoned the law of Christ. By this can also be understood our body, in which God deigns to dwell, as the Apostle says: *Glorify and bear God in your body;*[298] and again: *know you not that your bodies are the temple of the Holy Spirit?*[299] God spurns this tabernacle when he deserts the soul, offended by it because of fleshly

---

292   Micah 2:1a.
293   Is. 1:16a.
294   E. N. The adamant stone (Latin: *adamas*) refers a stone of extremely hard metal.
295   Zech. 7:12a.
296   Amos 5:12a.
297   Ps. 118:118.
298   1 Cor. 6:20b.
299   1 Cor. 6:19a.

life. Whence the Lord said long ago: *My spirit shall not remain in man forever, because he is flesh.*[300]

77{78}[61] *And he delivered their strength into captivity: and their beauty into the hands of the enemy.*

Et tradidit in captivitatem virtutem eorum, et pulchritudinem eorum in manus inimici.

77{78}[62] *And he shut up his people under the sword: and he despised his inheritance.*

Et conclusit in gladio populum suum, et haereditatem suam sprevit.

77{78}[61] *Et tradidit in captivitatem virtutem eorum, and he delivered their strength into captivity,* that is, he permitted them to be overcome by the tempter and their perfection to be extinguished. For the proud are confident in themselves and ungrateful, and, not ascribing all their good to God, they are unworthy of divine protection, and so they are overcome by demons. *Et pulchritudinem eorum in manus inimici, and their beauty into the hands of the enemy:* that is, he permits the interior splendor of the ornament of grace in men who are ungrateful to him to be darkened and to be done away with by the suggestions and the attacks of the flesh, the world, or the devil. For the Savior in the Gospel says about the ungrateful: *But from him that has not, that also which he seems to have shall be taken away.*[301] They are thus held captive, according to that which is witnessed by Peter: The iniquitous, *are the slaves of corruption: for by that by which a man is overcome, of the same also he is the slave.*[302] 77{78}[62] *Et conclusit in gladio, and he shut up ... under the sword* the unfaithful of *populum suum, his people,* the Christian [people], whom the Saracens in the Holy Land have often put to death and expulsed. One can also understand by the word "sword" the attack of the tempter, or the perversity of the soul which kills itself, indeed, all men spiritually killed with the sword of illicit consent.[303] *Et hereditatem suam sprevit, and he despised his inheritance:* that is, he did not protect

---

300   Gen. 6:3a.

301   Matt. 25:29b.

302   2 Pet. 2:19.

303   *E. N. See* St. Thomas Aquinas's *De Veritate:* "[I]f the external pleasure is given to be mortally sinful, then the interior pleasure also is considered in itself and absolutely of the genus of mortal sin.... Hence, we concede absolutely that consent in the pleasure ... of any ... mortal sin is a mortal sin." q. 15, art. 4, co.

from the infidel nor call back from their fault the Christian people, who should deservedly be the favored inheritance of God, since they were purchased by his Blood.

77{78}[63] *Fire consumed their young men: and their maidens were not lamented.*

Iuvenes eorum comedit ignis, et virgines eorum non sunt lamentatae.

77{78}[64] *Their priests fell by the sword: and their widows did not mourn.*

Sacerdotes eorum in gladio ceciderunt, et viduae eorum non plorabantur.

77{78}[63] *Iuvenes eorum comedit ignis,* fire consumed their young men with the concupiscence of the flesh: as Hosea said, *The spirit of fornication has deceived them;*[304] *et virgine eorum,* and their maidens vain and foolish *non sunt lamentatae,* were not lamented: because there is no one who deplores their vanity from the compassion of fraternal charity, but they praise these sinning women *in the vanity of their souls.*[305] 77{78}[64] *Sacerdotes eorum in gladio ceciderunt,* their priests fell by the sword. The spiritual sword, according to the Apostle, is the word of God.[306] And so [this verse] is understood in this sense: The priests of the Christians are internally felled by the preaching of their own mouth. For so long as they teach that which they do not themselves do, they sin mortally: and so they condemn themselves and they spiritually kill themselves. Hence the Apostle [Paul] said: *For wherein you judge another, you condemn yourself. For you do the same things.*[307] And Job said: *Your own mouth shall condemn you, and not I: and your own lips shall answer you.*[308] *Et viduae eorum non plorabantur,* and their widows did not mourn: as the Apostle said, *The widow that lives in pleasures is dead while she is living.*[309] The widows, therefore, do not mourn, since they do not deplore carnal delights by pious affection of compassion.

---

304 Hosea 4:12b.
305 Ps. 10:3 (according to the Hebrew).
306 *Cf.* Eph. 6:17b.
307 Rom. 2:1b.
308 Job 15:6.
309 1 Tim. 5:6.

77{78}[66] *And he smote his enemies on the hinder parts: he put them to an everlasting reproach.*[310]

> *Et percussit inimicos suos in posteriora, opprobrium sempiternum dedit illis.*

77{78}[66] *Et percussit inimicos suos in posteriora, and he smote his enemies on the hinder parts,* that is, he damned them with the extreme and final punishment, in the manner that the Lord said about some people through Jeremiah: *I will bring an everlasting reproach upon you, and a perpetual shame which shall never be forgotten.*[311] And so it now adds, *opprobrium sempiternum dedit illis, he put them to an everlasting reproach,* hurling them into the pit of the prison of hell. For this reason the Lord says in Jeremiah: *I will deliver* those who did not hear my word *to vexation and . . . to be a curse,* and to confusion, and in hissing, and in reproach.[312]

77{78}[67] *And he rejected the tabernacle of Joseph: and chose not the tribe of Ephraim.*

> *Et repulit tabernaculum Ioseph, et tribum Ephraim non elegit.*

77{78}[68] *But he chose the tribe of Judah, mount Sion which he loved.*

> *Sed elegit tribum Iuda, montem Sion, quem dilexit.*

77{78}[69] *And he built his sanctuary as of unicorns, in the land which he founded forever.*

> *Et aedificavit sicut unicornium sanctificium suum, in terra quam fundavit in saecula.*

Consequently, the Prophet addresses the people truly belonging to the kingdom of Christ 77{78}[67] *Et repulit,* and he rejected, God [rejected], *tabernaclum,* the tabernacle, that is the posterity, the home, the family, *Ioseph, of Joseph,* that is, the people of the Jews, establishing themselves finally and sufficiently in the Law, regarding themselves to be able to be saved by the Law without the grace of Christ. With good reason the people of the Jews are signified by Joseph. First, because Joseph by his holiness and his dominion stood out from the patriarchs that were his brothers. Second, because Joseph is interpreted to mean "increase": and so the Jews are designated by him who were promised the increase in

---

310 E. N. Denis skips verse 65 in this article.
311 Jer. 23:40.
312 Jer. 24:9.

temporal goods. *Et tribum Ephraim non elegit, and he chose not the tribe of Ephraim.* Ephraim is understood as meaning "fruitful" or "the bearing of fruit": by which is signified also the same people who are meant by Joseph, to the extent they regarded with longing the fruitful land. 77{78} [68] *Sed elegit tribum Iuda, but he chose the tribe of Judah,* that is, the Christian people, putting their trust in the Lord with devotion and purity because of heavenly and divine goods, namely, *montem Sion, mount Sion,* that is, the Church militant, *quem dilexit, which he loved* as that stated by the Apostle: *Christ loved the Church, and delivered himself up for it, that it might be sanctified.*[313] 77{78}[69] *Et aedificavit sicut unicornium, and he built . . . as of unicorns,* that is, so as to build a fitting home of Christ's faithful, worshipping the one true God, *sanctificium suum, his sanctuary,* that is, the Church militant or the Christian people: whom he built, making for himself in our hearts a fitting dwelling place by faith and the grace of the Holy Spirit. Indeed, of this construction Christ says through Amos: *I will raise up the tabernacle of David, that is fallen: and I will close up the breaches of the walls thereof.*[314] God raises this sanctuary *in terra quam fundavit in saecula, in the land which he founded forever,* that is, in the whole world, as he stated in Malachi: *From the rising of the sun even to the going down, my name is great among the Gentiles, and in every place there is sacrifice, and there is offered to my name a clean oblation,*[315] namely, the Sacrament of the Altar. And this land is founded in this age, because, as Ecclesiastes says, *the earth stands forever.*[316]

77{78}[70]   *And he chose his servant David, and took him from the flocks of sheep: he brought him from following the ewes great with young,*

Et elegit David, servum suum, et sustulit eum de gregibus ovium; de post foetantes accepit eum,

77{78}[70] *Et elegit, and he chose,* God, the Trinity, [chose] *David servum suum, his servant David,* that is, the man Christ, who insofar as he was man was the servant of God and his elect, in the manner that the Lord said through Isaiah: *Behold my servant, I will uphold him: my elect, my soul delights in him.*[317] This the evangelist Matthew asserts was said

---

313   Eph. 5:25–26.
314   Amos 9:11.
315   Mal. 1:11.
316   Eccl. 1:4b.
317   Is. 42:1a.

of Christ.[318] God therefore chose Christ so that he might be the head and prince of the universal Church, the leader, the pastor, the judge, and the Lord of all the elect. For this reason, the Lord said: *I will save my flock, . . . and I will set up one shepherd over them, and he shall feed them, even my servant David,* that is Christ, as all explain [this verse].[319] *Et sustulit eum,* and he took him, namely, God the Trinity [took] Christ, *de gregibus ovium, from the flocks of sheep,* that is, he exalted and glorified him before all the elect, in the manner the Bride sings: *My beloved is white and ruddy, chosen out of thousands.*[320] *De post foetantes accepit eum, he brought him from following the ewes great with young:* that is, after he made fruitful, redeemed, and confirmed his sheep in this world, the Father received him in heaven at his right hand. For this reason, Christ said to the Father: *I have finished the work which you gave me to do . . . and now I come to you.*[321] Or [alternatively], *he brought him from following the ewes great with young,* because Christ was first sent to the lost sheep of the house of Israel,[322] which once accomplished as far as the elect, he sent his disciples throughout the whole world to the sheep gathered together from the Gentiles, as he himself said: *Other sheep I have that are not of this fold, them also must I bring.*[323]

77{78}[71]   *To feed Jacob his servant, and Israel his inheritance.*

   Pascere Iacob, servum suum, et Israel, haereditatem suam.

77{78}[72]   *And he fed them in the innocence of his heart: and conducted them by the skillfulness of his hands.*

   Et pavit eos in innocentia cordis sui, et in intellectibus manuum suarum deduxit eos.

Now God accepted Christ, 77{78}[71] *pascere, to feed,* that is, that he may cause to be fed, *Iacob servum suum, Jacob his servant,* that is, the Christian people who despise vices; *et Israel hereditatem suam, and Israel his inheritance,* that is, the same people contemplating spiritual things, and chosen for eternal life. 77{78}[7q] *Et pavit eos, and he fed them,* Christ while living bodily in the world [fed them] with knowledge and

---

318   Matt. 12:17–18.
319   Ez. 34:22a, 23a.
320   Songs 5:10.
321   John 12:4b, 13a.
322   Matt. 15:24.
323   John 10:16a.

doctrine: and this, *in innocentia cordis sui, in the innocence of his heart,* because he did nothing iniquitous, nor was there deceit in his mouth, as we read in Isaiah.[324] *Et in intellectibus manuum suarum deduxit eos, and conducted them by the skillfulness of hands.* Indeed, he is the virtue and wisdom of the Father, which he said of himself to his disciples: *You call me Master, and Lord; and you say well, for so I am.*[325] And again: *For one is your master; and all you are brethren.*[326] Christ therefore led his sheep in the skillfulness of his hands, that is, in doctrine and holiness, because he *began to do and to teach.*[327] Now, Christ leads and feeds his sheep by himself, through his vicars, the prelates and preachers of the Church, and by the holy angels. For grace flows from him alone; but the angels dispose us to it and enlighten us: something which men also are able to do, in the way Paul states to the Corinthians: *I have planted, Apollo watered, but God gave the increase.*[328]

See we have heard this lengthy Psalm which is plain on its surface, but full of mystery in its interior meaning, and which is useful clearly to understand, because it includes in an abridged manner those things addressed in a lengthy way in the various books of Moses. The rest of the matters in this Psalm, omitted at this time, are explained in the previous article, are clear in every way, or can be easily to be understood.

---

324 Is. 53:9. *See also* 1 Pet. 2:22.

325 John 13:13.

326 Matt. 23:8.

327 E. N. So, in following Christ, we must do rightly and believe rightly. "It is useless to play off orthopraxis [*rectus vitae usus*, "a right use of life"] against orthodoxy [*rectam doctrinam*, "right teaching"]: For the Christian religion comprehends and wraps both together in a most tight bond, so that certain and well-thought-out convictions lead to courageous and upright action" St. John Paul II, *Catechesi Tradendae*, 22, AAS LXXI, 1296 (1979).

328 1 Cor. 3:6.

PRAYER

GOD, WHO ARE MERCIFUL UPON ALL things, out of your paternal kindness do not cease to help the fallen to return to you; remember, we beseech you, that we are flesh, and be indulgent so that you may avert your anger, and may not kindle against us all your wrath; but mitigate it, and bountifully give to us your unfailing grace.

Deus, qui omnium misereris, et lapsos ad te redeuntes paterna
pietate suscipere non desinis: recordare, quaesumus, quia
caro sumus, et abunda ut avertas iram, et non
accendas contra nos omnem iram tuam;
sed mitiga eam, et largire nobis
indeficientem gratiam tuam.

Psalm 78

ARTICLE L

78{79}[1]   *A Psalm for Asaph. O God, the heathens are come into your inheritance, they have defiled your holy temple: they have made Jerusalem as a place to keep fruit.*

Psalmus Asaph. Deus, venerunt gentes in haereditatem tuam; polluerunt templum sanctum tuum; posuerunt Ierusalem in pomorum custodiam.

HE SENSE OF THE TITLE OF THE PSALM NOW addressed, namely, 78{79}[1] *Psalmus Asaph, a Psalm for Asaph,* is clear from what has been said before. We should keep in mind that, of the three times we read that the Jews had been exiled [from the temple], this is speaking of the most famous and weighty of such exiles: for the first was by the Chaldeans, the second by the king Antiochus,[1] and the third by the Romans. But that this Psalm is not written about the Jews' exile caused by the Romans, Augustine satisfactorily explains in his exposition of this Psalm. For what is contained in the second verse of this Psalm does not correspond to such a view, namely [the verse], *They have given the dead bodies of your servants to be meat for the fowls of the air, the flesh of your saints for the beasts of the earth.* For the Jews killed by the Romans were unbelievers, obstinate, and reprobate.[2] Cassiodorus, therefore, and Hugo[3] expound upon this Psalm as being of the oppression of the Jews introduced by Antiochus. But Nicolas of Lyra

---

1   E. N. A reference to the Hellenistic King Antiochus IV Epiphanes (*ca.* 215–*ca.* 164 BC).

2   E. N. The argument is that since the Jews are described as "servants" of God in verse 2, it clearly did not comprehend the Jews during the Roman siege, since they, as a body and through their leadership, had rejected the Christ. Accordingly, it must refer to one of the two earlier sieges.

3   E. N. Probably Hugh of St. Cher (1200–1263 AD), who states this in his exposition of this Psalm. Hugonis de Sancto Charo, *Opera Omnia* (Venice: Pezzana, 1703), Vol. II, 208

does not agree with this because of that which is contained in the first verse of this Psalm—*they have made Jerusalem as a place to keep fruit*, in which place the Hebrew has in truth, *they have made Jerusalem a heap*; also Jerome translates it, *they have made Jerusalem a heap of stones*. This appears to indicate the destruction of the city and the temple, which was something not seen at the time of Antiochus; but he polluted the temple, placing in it an abominable idol.[4] But this objection is easily addressed. For the city and the temple are said to be destroyed [in the Psalm], either because of the killing of the people and priests, or because of a destruction of some part of the city of Jerusalem, which during the time of Antiochus was greatly embattled and partially destroyed, as is made clear in the book of Maccabees. For in the divine Scriptures inhabitants are often described as dwellings, and, additionally, the whole is described by a part.[5] To understand this Psalm literally as only applying to the levelling of Jerusalem and the destruction of the city and the temple as occurred during the time of the Chaldeans is therefore unwarranted. It seems also to me that it can aptly be understood literally as applying to both of those devastations, because it can easily be applied literally to both; and whether as to one or to the other we are able to believe that it was revealed to divine Prophet, and through this, he prophesied at the same time of both. For the foretelling in the present Psalm as to one [of the historical events] can reasonable be said as prophesying of the other [historical event].

The prophet [David] therefore says in the person of the congregation of the faithful: *Deus, venerunt gentes; O God, the heathens are come*, namely, the Babylonians and Antiochus with his entourage, *in hereditatem tuam, into your inheritance*, that is, into Judea, which was the land chosen for the divine worship, and the children of Israel specially and by inheritance devoted to God. Or [alternatively], *into your inheritance*, that is, into the people of the Jews. Whence the Lord says by Isaiah: *Blessed be my people of Egypt, and the work of my hands to the Assyrian: but Israel is my inheritance*.[6] For the Chaldeans polluted and destroyed the temple built by Solomon;[7] but Antiochus with his followers, polluted the temple of Zerubbabel which was built by the people returning from the Babylonian

---

4   1 Macc. 1:57. E. N. This verse indicates that Antiochus placed an idol in the temple, which suggests it was not destroyed.
5   E. N. Denis is referring to the custom in Scripture to use synecdoche, where a part of something is used to refer to the whole, e.g., "soul" for "man."
6   Is. 19:25.
7   2 Kings 25:9.

captivity.[8] Now it is said that the temple was polluted because they did
in it those things which were prohibited by the Law: placing idols in it
and allowing Gentiles to enter into it. Whence Jeremiah says: *She has
seen the Gentiles enter into her sanctuary of whom you gave commandment
that they should not enter into your church.*[9] Of this pollution of the
temple the first book of Maccabees writes about: *Antiochus took away
the golden altar, . . . and all the vessels thereof, . . . and he broke them all in
pieces.*[10] And again: *King Antiochus set up the abominable idol of desolation
upon the altar of God:*[11] indeed (as it says elsewhere) he placed a statue
of Jupiter in the temple.[12]

Posuerunt Ierusalem, they have made Jerusalem, that is, their homes
and the temple, *in pomorum custodiam, as a place to keep fruit,* that is,
they were regarded as worthless, like a small storehouse in which one
keeps fruit. Or [alternatively], *as a place to keep fruit:* because like the
keeping of fruit, that is, a house in which fruit is kept is abandoned and
demolished when the fruits are removed, so they destroyed the city of
Jerusalem and caused it to be abandoned by its proper inhabitants. For
this reason we read in the first book of Maccabees: *The king sent the
chief collector . . . and he took the spoils of the city, and burnt it with fire, and
threw down the houses thereof, and the walls thereof round about.*[13] From
this it is clear that the objection of Nicolas [of Lyra] who was mentioned above [that this Psalm could not refer to the siege of Jerusalem by
Antiochus] is of no account. And again Scripture says of this previously
mentioned place: *The inhabitants of Jerusalem fled away by reason of them,
and the city was made the habitation of strangers.*[14] Whence also Isaiah:
*The daughter of Sion shall be left as a covert in a vineyard, and as a lodge
in a garden of cucumbers.*[15]

---

8   1 Macc. 1:57.

9   Lam. 1:10.

10   1 Macc. 1:23.

11   1 Macc. 1:57a.

12   2 Macc. 6:2.

13   2 Macc. 1:30a, 33.

14   1 Macc. 1:40a.

15   Is. 1:8. E. N. In his *Commentary on Isaiah,* Denis explains: "*as a covert in a
vineyard,* that is, as a small shed next to a vineyard is abandoned when the grapes
are done being picked, for such sheds are called places of shade. *And as a lodge in
a garden of cucumbers,* that is, as an abandoned home, or small hut, built where
cucumbers are grown. For such shacks are to made to avoid the heat of the sun."
Doctoris Ecstatici D. Dionysii Cartusiani, *Opera Omnia,* Vol. 8 (Montreuil: 1899), 324.

78{79}[2]   *They have given the dead bodies of your servants to be meat for the fowls of the air: the flesh of your saints for the beasts of the earth.*

Posuerunt morticina servorum tuorum escas volatilibus caeli, carnes sanctorum tuorum bestiis terrae.

78{79}[3]   *They have poured out their blood as water, round about Jerusalem and there was none to bury them.*

Effuderunt sanguinem eorum tamquam aquam in circuitu Ierusalem, et non erat qui sepeliret.

78{79}[4]   *We are become a reproach to our neighbors: a scorn and derision to them that are round about us.*

Facti sumus opprobrium vicinis nostris, subsannatio et illusio his qui in circuitu nostro sunt.

78{79}[2] *Posuerunt morticina servorum tuorum,* they have given the dead bodies of your servants, that is, the bodies of the Jews that were slain, *escas volatilibus caeli; carnes sanctorum tuorum;* to be meat for the fowls of the air: the flesh of your saints, that is, they gave the cadavers of the better and more perfect of your servants as meat *bestiis terrae, for the beasts of the earth:* for they did not bury them, but they threw them out to be devoured by the birds of the air and the beasts of the earth. For this reason, Jeremiah says regarding the valley of the son of Hinnom: *It shall no more be called . . . the valley of the son of Hinnom, but the valley of slaughter.*[16] 78{79}[3] *Effuderunt sanguinem eorum tamquam aquam in circuitu Ierusalem, et non erat qui sepeliret;* they have poured out their blood as water, round about Jerusalem, and there was none to bury them. On account of this, the first book of Maccabees contains: *They shed innocent blood round about the sanctuary.*[17] And because of the number of the dead bodies, there was no one who could bury the dead. For according to the second book of Maccabees, *there were slain in the space of three whole days eighty thousand by Antiochus.*[18] 78{79}[4] *Facti sumus opprobrium vicinis nostris,* we are become a reproach to our neighbors: which is more clearly stated in what follows: *subsannatio et illusio his, qui in circuitu nostro sunt;* a scorn and derision to them that

---

16   Jer. 7:32. E. N. This valley outside the Jerusalem city walls was the city dump, and former site of child sacrifice. It was called the valley of Hinnom's son (*Gei ben Hinnom*), but it became known as valley of slaughter (*Gei Hinnom*) which we know as Gehenna.
17   1 Macc. 1:39.
18   2 Macc. 5:14.

are round about us. For the Gentiles remaining around the Jews, namely, the Ammonites, the Moabites, the Idumeans, the Philistines, *etc.* were accustomed commonly to glory when the children of Israel came upon any adversity: in those times they derided them and scorned them. And so Nehemiah asserts: *Hear us, our God, for we are despised.*[19] And also in the book of Maccabees, we read: *The sanctuary of Jerusalem was desolate like a wilderness; her festival days were turned into mourning, her sabbaths into reproach, her honors were brought to nothing. Her dishonor was increased according to her glory.*[20]

78{79}[5] *How long, O Lord, will you be angry forever? Shall your zeal be kindled like a fire?*

Usquequo, Domine, irasceris in finem? Accendetur velut ignis zelus tuus?

78{79}[6] *Pour out your wrath upon the nations that have not known you: and upon the kingdoms that have not called upon your name.*

Effunde iram tuam in gentes quae te non noverunt, et in regna quae nomen tuum non invocaverunt.

78{79}[7] *Because they have devoured Jacob; and have laid waste his place.*

Quia comederunt Iacob, et locum eius desolaverunt.

The voice of the people so afflicted then follows [in this Psalm], with great lamentation and querulousness crying out to the Lord **78{79} [5]** *Usquequo, Domine, irasceris in finem? How long, O Lord, will you be angry forever?* That is, how long will you take vengeance upon our sins and permit us to be laid waste so greatly? It is as if the people were saying, "Be not angry with your people any longer." *Accendetur velut ignis zelus tuus? Shall your zeal be kindled like a fire?* That is, how long will your indignation so furiously avenge itself upon us, handing us over into the powers of cruel men? **78{79}[6]** *Effunde iram tuam in gentes quae te non noverunt, pour out your wrath upon the nations that have not known you:* that is, mercifully withdraw [your vengeance] from us, who are your worshippers, who know you by faith, and distribute it against the aforementioned idolatrous and ignorant men; *et in regna, and upon*

---

19   Neh. 4:4a.
20   1 Macc. 1:41–42a.

the kingdoms of the Chaldeans, and upon those that were governed by Antiochus, *quae nomen tuum non invocaverunt, that have not called upon your name,* but have worshipped false gods. 78{79}[7] *Quia comederunt Iacob, because they have devoured Jacob:* that is, they have consumed with the mouth of the sword, or by some other form of death, the people born from the patriarch Jacob, your beloved child, in the manner that a man eating consumes meat. Hence, the prophet Jeremiah said: *First . . . Assyria devoured him: and last this Nebuchadnezzar . . . has broken his bones.*[21] *Et locum eius desolaverunt, and they have laid waste his place:* because they destroyed the city of Judah, or the people that fled from it. According to what is written in the first book of Maccabees: *Mattathias cried out in the city with a loud voice, saying: Everyone that has zeal for the law, and maintains the testament, let him follow me. So he, and his sons fled into the mountains, and left all that they had in the city.*[22] Now punishment of the adversaries is prayed for in this verse, not out of hate, but from the zeal of justice, or out of charity, so that they may be corrected in the present, and may be prohibited from doing more evil, so that they may not add sins upon sins, and thereafter be more heavily condemned.[23]

78{79}[8]   *Remember not our former iniquities: let your mercies speedily prevent us, for we are become exceeding poor.*

Ne memineris iniquitatum nostrarum antiquarum; cito anticipent nos misericordiae tuae, quia pauperes facti sumus nimis.

78{79}[8] *Ne memineris iniquitatum nostrarum antiquarum,* remember not our former iniquities, which we and our fathers have many times perpetrated. Although his knowledge perseveres eternally invariable, God is said to remember our iniquities while he is avenging them upon us; but when he is merciful, he is asserted to have forgotten them. *Cito anticipent nos misericordiae tuae, let your mercies speedily prevent us,*[24] that is, let the effect of your eternal mercy prevent us, lest we come upon your judgment; and let not the effects of your justice preoccupy us, wreaking upon us that which we deserve. Now this we pray, *quia pauperes facti sumus nimis, for*

---

21   Jer. 1:17b.

22   1 Macc. 2:27-28.

23   *Cf.* Ecclus. 3:29: *A wicked heart shall be laden with sorrows, and the sinner will add sin to sin.*

24   E. N. "Prevent," used here used to translate *anticipent,* "let them anticipate." As used here, prevent means to come before or to anticipate, *"prae venire."* It is used in this manner in, *e.g.,* prevenient grace (grace before the act) or in preventative medicine (medicine before illness).

we are become exceedingly poor, because we have been despoiled of temple and possessions and cities. Also, we are spiritually poor as is ascertainable by our vices. For by our sinning we have lost grace and the supply of spiritual goods. For sin is spiritual poverty and the cause of misery, according to that said by Solomon: *Sin makes nations miserable.*[25] And also Ecclesiastes: *He that shall offend in one, shall lose many good things.*[26] Therefore, they are ignorant of the weakness of their own mind and are spiritually blind because they lack grace, as it says in Revelation: *You say, Because I am rich ... and know not that you are wretched, and miserable, and poor, and blind, and naked.*[27] About this excessive poverty, Mattathias says: *Behold our sanctuary, and our beauty, and our glory is laid waste.*[28]

Oh how great is the virtue of this verse, and of the two verses that follow! For truly its power transcends every observation of man, and the tongue lacks in the utterance of its praises. But also how good is it to acknowledge one's own poverty, as we so unceasingly proclaim in the Lord's prayer, *Give us this day our daily bread!*[29] The virtues of these verses are marvelous; and it is most wholesome to proclaim these sacred verses with mental affection, great attention, and heartfelt relish: for it is more likely that heaven and earth should be made to perish than that such a prayer be found inefficacious.

78{79}[9] *Help us, O God, our Savior: and for the glory of your name, O Lord, deliver us: and forgive us our sins for your name's sake:*

Adiuva nos, Deus, salutaris noster; et propter gloriam nominis tui, Domine, libera nos, et propitius esto peccatis nostris, propter nomen tuum.

78{79}[9] *Adiuva nos, Deus salutaris noster; help us, O God, our Savior,* that is, our Savior and the cause of our salvation. For you said, *Without me you can do nothing;*[30] we are not sufficient to think anything of ourselves, as of ourselves: but our sufficiency is from you.*[31] And so help us, strengthen-

---

25 Prov. 14:34.

26 Eccl. 9:18b.

27 Rev. 3:17.

28 1 Macc. 2:12a. *E. N.* Mattathias is, of course, referring to the temple itself; however, keeping in mind that we are the Lord's temple, Denis is using it in this context to refer to the destruction of sanctifying grace and the presence of God in our souls which is caused by mortal sin.

29 Luke 11:3.

30 John 15:5.

31 2 Cor. 3:5.

ing our nature through grace, giving us patience in adversity, victory over temptation, and rescuing us from persecution. For our aid, send to us also those heavenly citizens, the holy angels; and, by the prayers and the merits of all those who please you—and not by what [the merits] our own life might obtain—grant that our prayer may be found deserving to our benefit. *Et propter gloriam nominis tui, Domine, libera nos; and for the glory of your name, O Lord, deliver us*: that is, because of and to this end deliver us from all tribulations, and all sins, and all dangers, so that your mercy may be glorified in us in all things, and your mercy might be proclaimed, and for this reason be praised and honored by all. This is a most properly ordered plea. For since we ought to call upon God for our own delivery and blessedness, so ought we to refer the honor of our redemption to God, and to pray to God that he may hear us for his sake and the honor of his name. For regarding this Solomon said: *The Lord has made all things for himself.*[32] We honor God by praying in this manner, and so we deserve to be heard and honored by him, in the manner that he himself attests: *Whosoever shall glorify me, him will I glorify.*[33] For God is glorious and holy, and he created all the elect to his praise and glory, according to that which he elsewhere asserts: *Every one that calls upon my name, I have created him for my glory.*[34] Therefore, with complete affection and sincere intention we should always refer to the honor and glory of God whatever we claim for ourselves or for others; we should never reflect self-love upon ourselves, nor should we glory in ourselves by a most foolish vanity.[35]

---

32   Prov. 16:4a. *E. N.* "Scripture and Tradition never cease to teach and celebrate this fundamental truth: 'The world was made for the glory of God.' St. Bonaventure explains that God created all things 'not to increase his glory, but to show it forth and to communicate it,' for God has no other reason for creating than his love and goodness: 'Creatures came into existence when the key of love opened his hand.'.... The glory of God consists in the realization of this manifestation and communication of his goodness, for which the world was created. God made us 'to be his sons through Jesus Christ, according to the purpose of his will, to the praise of his glorious grace,' for 'the glory of God is man fully alive.'.... The ultimate purpose of creation is that God 'who is the creator of all things may at last become 'all in all,' thus simultaneously assuring his own glory and our beatitude.'" CCC §§ 293–94 (footnotes omitted).

33   1 Sam. 2:30b.

34   Is. 43:7.

35   *E. N.* "In determining the end of creation, we must carefully distinguish the extrinsic glory of God from the happiness of man. The former constitutes the principal end, the latter the secondary end of creation. God consequently orders all things for the attainment of His chief end, His glory, by the manifestations of His attributes and perfections. The just, acting in conformity with this divine purpose and fulfilling God's holy will, secure to themselves heavenly happiness, their second end, and proclaim God's mercy and goodness for all eternity.... The two ends, the glory of

Et propitius esto peccatis nostris, and forgive us our sins, mitigating the punishment, and fully forgiving the fault, *propter nomen tuum, for your name's sake,* that is, for your own sake, and your own goodness, for you said: *It is not for your sake that I will do this, let it be known to you, but for my holy name's sake.*[36]

78{79}[10] *Lest they should say among the Gentiles: Where is their God? And let him be made known among the nations before our eyes, by revenging the blood of your servants, which has been shed:*

Ne forte dicant in gentibus: Ubi est Deus eorum? Et innotescat in nationibus coram oculis nostris ultio sanguinis servorum tuorum qui effusus est.

And this do, O Lord God, 78{79}[10] *Ne forte dicant in gentibus, lest they should say among the Gentiles,* that is, among the Gentiles and the unwise: *Ubi est Deus eorum, Where is their God?* That is, it now appears that their God is not able to save them, or he regards with disdain their worship. Therefore, O Lord, do not inflict such great injury to yourself, but hear us, as you said through Isaiah: *For my own sake, for my own sake will I do it, that I may not be blasphemed.*[37] *Et innotescat in nationibus, and let him be made known among the nations,* that is, among the Gentiles previously mentioned, *coram oculis nostris, before our eyes,* that is, so apparent that it is obvious to us, *ultio sanguinis servorum tuorum, qui effusus est, by revenging the blood of your servants, which has been shed:* that is, avenge against these Pagans the shedding of the innocent blood of our people. The Prophet [David] prays in the person of the Jewish people for vengeance of the killings done in Jerusalem and Judea. Whence in the second book of Maccabees, these people pray: *Punish them that oppress us, and that treat us injuriously with pride.*[38] Moses also said before that God would do this: *He will revenge the blood,* he said, *of his saints, and will render vengeance to their enemies.*[39]

God and the happiness of man, are so intimately connected that if man seeks the former, he will infallibly secure the attainment of the latter. On the contrary, his neglect of the former will necessarily entail the loss of the latter. Joseph C. Sasia, S. J., *The Future Life* (New York: Benziger Brothers, 1918), 450–51.

36 Ez. 36:22, 32. E. N. Denis is quite free in blending portions of these two verses in Ezechiel towards his needs.

37 Is. 48:11.

38 Macc. 1:28.

39 Deut. 32:43. E. N. Instead of the Sixto-Clementine's *servorum suorum* (his servants), Denis states *sanctorum suorum* (his saints).

78{79}[11] *Let the sighing of the prisoners come in before you. According to the greatness of your arm, take possession of the children of them that have been put to death.*

Introeat in conspectu tuo gemitus compeditorum; secundum magnitudinem brachii tui posside filios mortificatorum.

78{79}[12] *And render to our neighbors sevenfold in their bosom: the reproach wherewith they have reproached you, O Lord.*

Et redde vicinis nostris septuplum in sinu eorum; improperium ipsorum quod exprobraverunt tibi, Domine.

78{79}[11] *Introeat in conspectu tuo gemitus compeditorum, let the sighing of the prisoners come in before you:* that is, kindly hear the sighs of your captives, and deliver them from captivity. For many of the Jews were captured to be servants to Antiochus and the Chaldeans. *Secundum magnitudinem brachii tui, according to the greatness of your arm,* that is, according to your great power, *posside filios mortificatorum, take possession of the children of them that have been put to death,* that is, [take possession of] us, whose fathers have been killed by these Gentiles, so that you might protect and preserve us as one's own possession is preserved by an heir. 78{79}[12] *Et redde vicinis nostris, and render to our neighbors* of whom is stated above — *We are become a reproach to our neighbors;*[40] *septuplum, sevenfold,* that is, by perfect vindication; for the number seven designates perfection;[41] *in sinum eorum, in their bosom:* that is, so greatly evidently and infallibly does punishment fall upon them and is received by them, that they are not able to avoid it, just as a man infallibly receives a blow that is flung against his chest. For this kind of thing is not shrugged off. *Improperium ipsorum, their reproach,* that is, the punishment for such insult, *quod exprobraverunt tibi, Domine; wherewith they have reproached you, Lord,* saying about us: *Where is their God?*[42]

78{79}[13] *But we your people, and the sheep of your pasture, will give thanks to you forever. We will show forth your praise, unto generation and generation.*

---

40 Verse 4.
41 E. N. From the book of Genesis (seven days), to the seven gifts of the Holy Spirit, to the book of Revelation (seven seals), to the Seven Sacraments, the number seven is highly significant in Scripture and Tradition. It is a number that is perceived as designating perfection. "Scripture commends, and the Church knows," says St. Augustine in his study of the book of Genesis, "this number seven is in some way dedicated to the Holy Spirit." *De Gen. ad litt.,* V, 5, 15, PL 34, 326.
42 Ps. 113:10.

Nos autem populus tuus, et oves pascuae tuae, confitebimur tibi in saeculum; in generationem et generationem annuntiabimus laudem tuam.

78{79}[13] *Nos autem populus tuus,* but we your people, [your] particular [people], *et oves pascuae tuae,* and the sheep of your pasture, of which elsewhere you have said, *I will feed my sheep, I will save my flock, I will feed them in the mountains of Israel;*[43] *confitebimur tibi in saeculum,* we will give thanks to you forever, that is, we have praised you continually and perseveringly, giving thanks to you in song for our deliverance. *In generationem et generationem annuntiabimus laudem tuam; we will show forth your praise, unto generation and generation,* that is, in that certain generation in which we live, we ourselves shall praise you; and in the generations in the future, we will praise you through our children or through those who practice our faith, to whom we have bequeathed the matter for praising you at the time you showed to us your benefits, which we have made known by word and in writing.

ARTICLE LI

TROPOLOGICAL EXPLANATION
OF THE SAME SEVENTH-EIGHTH PSALM.

78{79}[1] *A Psalm for Asaph. O God, the heathens are come into your inheritance, they have defiled your holy temple: they have made Jerusalem as a place to keep fruit.*

Psalmus Asaph. Deus, venerunt gentes in haereditatem tuam; polluerunt templum sanctum tuum; posuerunt Ierusalem in pomorum custodiam.

Moreover, the Church of Christ and any individual Christian can rightly sing, and ought to sing, this Psalm with a sorrowful voice because of the loss of the Holy Lands, especially because that Holy City of Jerusalem, where Christ was buried, along with the most venerated and holy sepulcher of Christ, is given over to the hands of the Saracens, and has for some time been possessed by them.[44] And this Psalm can be applied to

---

43   Ez. 34:15a, 22a, 13b.
44   E. N. The history of the Muslim occupation of Jerusalem is complex, but briefly it was captured from Christian hands in 638 AD by the Muslim forces of Caliph Umar. It continued under Muslim rule until recaptured by the Crusaders in 1099.

this situation in this way: 78{79}[1] *Deus,* O God, the only-Begotten of God, Jesus Christ, who are true God and eternal life, *venerunt gentes, the heathens are come,* namely, the Saracens or those following the law of the pagan Muhammad,[45] *in hereditatem tuam, into your inheritance,* that is, into the city of Jerusalem rebuilt by the Emperor Aelius,[46] or into the population of Christian faithful in that city, which is your inheritance. *Polluerunt templum sanctum tuum, they have defiled your holy temple,* that is, the church which contains your sepulcher, because they handled this temple irreverently, as they would not permit the worship of Christ to be done within it. *Posuerunt Ierusalem in pomorum custodiam, they have made Jerusalem as a place to keep fruit,* killing within it, or expelling from it, all Christians.

78{79}[2] *They have given the dead bodies of your servants to be meat for the fowls of the air: the flesh of your saints for the beasts of the earth.*

> *Posuerunt morticina servorum tuorum escas volatilibus caeli, carnes sanctorum tuorum bestiis terrae.*

78{79}[3] *They have poured out their blood as water, round about Jerusalem and there was none to bury them.*

> *Effuderunt sanguinem eorum tamquam aquam in circuitu Jerusalem, et non erat qui sepeliret.*

78{79}[4] *We are become a reproach to our neighbors: a scorn and derision to them that are round about us.*

> *Facti sumus opprobrium vicinis nostris, subsannatio et illusio his qui in circuitu nostro sunt.*

The city was recaptured again by the Muslims led by Saladin in 1187. Jerusalem was again recaptured by Christian forces in 1229, but shortly thereafter it was regained by the Muslim Khwarezmians. At the time Denis wrote this *Commentary* Jerusalem was still in Muslim hands. Since the first Muslim capture, however, the keys to the Church of the Holy Sepulcher have been in Muslim hands (with the keys in the possession of the Nuseibeh and later also Joudeh clans) even to the present.

45 E. N. It was common to refer to Islam either as a form of paganism or as a Christian heresy. Peter the Venerable in his *Summa Totius Haeresis Saracenorum* was indecisive: "I cannot clearly decide . . . whether the Mohammedan error must be called a heresy and its followers heretics, or whether they are to be called pagans." Kritzeck, *Peter the Venerable and Islam* (Princeton: Princeton University Press, 1964), 143.

46 E. N. A reference to Emperor Hadrian (Publius Aelius Hadrianus, emperor 76–138 AD) who rebuilt the city of Jerusalem after it had been razed by Titus in 70 AD.

And of the many Christians killed in it [Jerusalem] and in the Holy Land, the following verse speaks regarding the cadavers. 78{79}[2] *Posuerunt morticina [servorum tuorum escas volatilibus caeli, carnes sanctorum tuorum bestiis terrae]*; they have given the dead bodies [of your servants to be meat for the fowls of the air: the flesh of your saints for the beasts of the earth],[47] in the sense already discussed. 78{79}[3] *Effuderunt sanguinem eorum,* they have poured out their blood, namely the Saracens [poured out the blood] of the Christians, *tanquam aquam, as water,* that is, very abundantly, *in circuitu Ierusalem, round about Jerusalem,* and in the cities that lying around it. This — Alas! — was done very frequently, in the manner that is attested to in the Chronicles [of the Crusades]. 78{79}[4][48] *Facti sumus opprobrium vicinis nostris, we are become a reproach to our neighbors.* For all the lands situated around the Holy Land, namely, [the lands] of the Philistine, the Ammonite, the Moabite, *etc.* and which are subject to the law of Muhammad spurn us, and jeer at us, that the Holy Land and Christ's sepulcher is subject to their power.

78{79}[6]   *Pour out your wrath upon the nations that have not known you: and upon the kingdoms that have not called upon your name.*[49]

   Effunde iram tuam in gentes quae te non noverunt, et in regna quae nomen tuum non invocaverunt.

78{79}[7]   *Because they have devoured Jacob; and have laid waste his place.*

   Quia comederunt Iacob, et locum eius desolaverunt.

78{79}[6] *Effunde iram tuam in gentes, pour out your wrath upon the nations,* namely, upon the Saracens, *quae te non noverunt, that have not known you* by faith and worship, but they serve the rite of a most unclean man, and keep a most fruitless law, *et in regna, and in the kingdoms* of the Saracens, *quae nomen tuum non invocaverunt, that have not called upon your name,* for they do not hope in you, but in all difficulties they invoke Muhammad. The Church therefore in this place prays for the recovery of the Holy Lands and the expulsion of those peoples from that place. 78{79}[7] *Quia comederunt Iacob, because they have devoured Jacob,* that is, the Christian people following the faith and the simplicity of

---

47   E. N. The parts in brackets replaces Denis's "etc."
48   E. N. Denis skips the remainder of verse 3.
49   E. N. Denis skips verse 5 entirely.

the patriarch Jacob, *et locum eius*, *and his place*, that is, the cities of the Holy Lands and the city of Jerusalem, *desolaverunt, they have laid waste*, that is, they have forced out the Christian inhabitants of that place, and they have filled the holy place with pagan men.

But the Christians deserve such great misery because of the wickedness of their lives, especially in that part of the Holy Land which is inhabited by Christians still dwelling in peace, since the Christians live in most wicked ways there. For this reason, the Church prays in this way for the mercy of so many and such habitual sinners, so that in attaining remission [of such sins], the land of Jerusalem may be repossessed, and may lead to the heavenly Jerusalem.[50]

ANOTHER EXPOSITION

ND SO MORE GENERALLY, ALL THIS CAN BE explained in this way: **78{79}[1]** *O God, the heathens are come*, that is, the infidels or those living an unfaithful life, *into your inheritance*, that is, into your chosen people and Christ's faithful, in the way wolves are accustomed to attack sheep and to scatter them. For Christ says to those who are chosen: *Behold, I send you as lambs among wolves;*[51] and, *In the world you shall have distress.*[52] They have defiled your holy temple because they have destroyed and dishonored the Church in many ways, and have committed nefarious deeds in it, and not only the pagans, but also heretics, most especially the Arians. *They have made Jerusalem*, that is the Church militant, in which there is the vision of peace, and the place of internal quiet, *as a place to keep fruit*, throwing out of it the ministers of the altar and crushing them.

Now the verses that follow can be fittingly expounded in a literal sense to refer to the bodies of many martyrs: indeed, sometimes the anger of the persecutors is so savage, that the buried bodies of the martyrs are dug up, burnt, scattered, or thrown out to be devoured by the birds of the air or the beasts of the earth. **78{79}[3]** *They have poured out*, the tyrants and their attendants [have poured out], *their blood*, namely, that of the martyrs, *as water, round about Jerusalem*, that is, throughout all the parts of the Church, since the Christian faith flourishes throughout the whole world. For the Church is spread throughout the whole world; and often the Roman emperors ordered and decreed that all Christians should be

---

50   E. N. Denis does not address the remaining verses in this section.
51   Luke 10:3.
52   John 16:33a.

massacred wheresoever they might be found, in order that the name and the memory of Christ might be forgotten. *And there was none to bury those killed.* For this was frequently prohibited under pain of death lest any man presume to bury the martyred Christians. **78{79}[4]** *We are become a reproach to our neighbors, etc.* In the sense already explained, the Church or every member of the faithful says this in the person of Christians dwelling next to or among pagans, heretics, or persecutors, who often mock Christians, especially when they prevail over them in wars.

78{79}[6] *Pour out your wrath upon the nations, etc.* Loving its enemies, the Church prays for the punishment and the degradation of its enemies in the present age, lest they perish in the future. **78{79}[10]** *And let him be made known among the nations before our eyes, by revenging the blood of your servants which has been shed.* The Church prays for the revenge of the blood of martyrs in the way that is contained in Revelation: *The souls of them that were slain . . . cried out with a loud voice: How long, O Lord, holy and true, do you not judge and revenge our blood on them that dwell on the earth?*[53] Whence also Christ in the Gospel said: *Will not God revenge his elect who cry to him day and night? . . . I say to you, that he will quickly revenge them.*[54]

78{79}[11] *Let . . . come in before you,* that is, may you hear, *the sighing of the prisoners* who for justice's sake were bodily bound and jailed, or bound together only with bonds of divine and fraternal love, so that they might faithfully pray for their enemies or persecutors, so that they may be said to bind and prohibit you, almighty God, as you yourself told Moses: *I see that this people,* that is, the children of Israel, *are stiffnecked; let me alone, that my wrath my be kindled against them, and that I might destroy them.*[55] But what did holy Moses do? He did not acquiesce to you, but rather he grabbed a hold of you, saying: *Either forgive this people this trespass, or if you do not, strike me out of the book you have written.*[56] Happily, O Lord, you are bound in this way with the bonds of holy love. For you are love, and nothing binds you except him whose mind you inflame so vehemently. Or, *the sighing of the prisoners,* that is, [the sighing] of your mortal servants with their many needs of human corruptibility and the chains of this present misery, and of those caught miserably by their daily falls, and of those sighing in their bodily prisons and crying out with Paul: *Unhappy man that I am, who*

---

53 Rev. 6:9a, 10.
54 Luke 18:7a, 8a.
55 Ex. 32:9–10.
56 Ex. 32:31–32.

shall deliver me from the body of this death?[57] And again: *I desire to be dissolved, and to be with Christ.*[58]

According to the greatness of your arm, take possession of, by the unceasing guarding and multiplication of grace, *the children of them that have been put to death,* that is, all of us who are spiritual children of the Apostles and of the martyrs and of the rest of the Saints, of those put to death in body for your name, or of those afflicted daily, and of a life unceasingly mortified by labors of penance and spiritual exercises, in the manner the Apostle stated: *Always bearing about in our body the mortification of Jesus, . . . that the life also of Jesus may be manifest in our mortal flesh.*[59]

Finally, the voice of the Church is again introduced, returning thanks to the Lord for his benefits: **78{79}[13]** *But we your people,* called Christians because of you, Christ,[60] delivered by your Blood, *a chosen generation, a kingly priesthood, a holy nation, a purchased people,*[61] who *have made us to our God a kingdom and priests;*[62] *and the sheep of your pasture,* that is, we who are recipients of your Sacraments are given the water of wisdom by you, are fed by the Bread of life, are strengthened and made to grow by your grace, subsist under your governance, and strain ahead to the blessed end; *we will give thanks to your forever.* The remainder [of the meaning of this Psalm] is clearly conspicuous from the preceding explanation.

It is fitting to elicit this Psalm daily with a mind most affectionate for the recovery of the Holy Lands, for to pray for such a pious intention is also truly a holy thing and to God most pleasing. And if we are not heard in this [particular intention], yet God approves of our desire, and will provide most abundant mercy in other ways.

---

57   Rom. 7:24.

58   Phil. 1:23. E. N. Denis uses the Latin locution *cupio dissolvi* ("I desire to be dissolved), the popular transcription of this verse, rather than the Vulgate's *desiderium habens dissolvi* ("having a desire to be dissolved").

59   2 Cor. 4:10a, 11b.

60   Acts 11:26.

61   1 Pet. 2:9.

62   Rev. 5:10.

PRAYER

E BESEECH YOU, O LORD, GRACIOUSLY
regard our prayers, and for the sake of your laudable and
glorious name, be not mindful of our past iniquities, so that through
your excellence, we may be delivered from all offenses, and may
continually keep vigilant with works of justice.

Preces nostras, quaesumus, Domine, placatus intende, ne memineris
iniquitatum nostrarum antiquarum propter nomen
tuum laudabile et gloriosum: ut te praestante,
ab omnibus liberi offensis, iugiter operibus
invigilemus aequitatis.

Psalm 79

ARTICLE LII

LITERAL EXPOSITION OF THE SEVENTY-NINTH PSALM:
QUI REGIS ISRAEL, INTENDE.
GIVE EAR, YOU THAT RULE ISRAEL.

79{80}[1] *Unto the end, for them that shall be changed. A testimony for Asaph, for the Assyrians.*[1]

In finem, pro his qui commutabuntur. Testimonium Asaph pro Assyriis.

THIS PSALM NOW BEING DISCUSSED HAS THIS title: **79{80}[1]** *In finem, pro his qui commutabuntur. Testimonium Asaph pro Assyriis. Unto the end, for them that shall be changed. A testimony for Asaph, for the Assyrians:* that is, the present Psalm, directing us to Christ who is the end of the precepts and the Law, is the *testimony for Asaph*, that is, the congregation of the faithful, receiving faithfully the Incarnation of Christ; and it is written *for them that shall be changed*, that is, to the instruction and for the utility of those who turn to the Lord with their whole heart, namely, *for the Assyrians*, that is, those rightly directing their lives before God. For the word Assyrians is interpreted to mean being directed. For in this place one is not to assume the name Assyrians refers to that people of which Jeremiah asserts in the Lamentations: *We have given our hand to Egypt, and to the Assyrians,*[2] about which is found in the book of Kings.[3]

According to Catholic teachers, this Psalm, therefore, is written literally of the first coming of Christ, namely of the Incarnation of the Savior. For the Incarnation of Christ was the salvation of the whole world, or of all the elect of the world who ever have been, are, or will be. Also, one is the Church of all the faithful, namely of all those who were before the Law, under the Law, and are under the time of grace.[4] Now this

---

1 E. N. Denis's reading departs from the Sixto-Clementine Vulgate.
2 Lam. 5:6a.
3 2 Kings chp. 17.
4 St. Augustine distinguishes these dispensations in relation to the effect they have upon us (*quoad nos*), and to these three he adds a fourth, an eschatological dispensation: "Let us distinguish these four stages of man: before the Law (*ante legem*), under

Church is designated by the name vine, because God cultivates it, makes it fruitful, and rules it. But because at the time of the Law of Moses almost all turned toward idolatry, so during that time the vine of the Lord was called the Synagogue, or the congregation of the Jews. Now during the time of the evangelical law, by the term vine of the Lord we understand the Church of Christians, because, in the way the Savior said, outside of the Church of Christ no one can be saved: *If anyone abide not in me, he shall be cast forth as a branch, and shall wither.*[5] The saints of the Old Testament, greatly desiring the Incarnation of Christ, prayed that God, who had visited often by holy angels and virtuous men, would himself deign to visit, appearing in the flesh. Indeed, they dared to desire this because God had promised this to them, in the way we see attested in Isaiah: *Therefore my people shall know my name in that day: for I myself that spoke, behold I am here.*[6] Whence also the most blessed Isaiah elsewhere prophesied: *The Lord our judge, the Lord our lawgiver, the Lord our king: he will come and save us.*[7] Also in Zechariah: *Sing praise, and rejoice, O daughter of Sion: for behold I come, and I will dwell in the midst of you.*[8]

79{80}[2]   *Give ear, O you that rule Israel: you that lead Joseph like a sheep. You that sit upon the cherubim, shine forth.*

Qui regis Israel, intende; qui deducis velut ovem Ioseph. Qui sedes super cherubim, manifestare.

79{80}[3]   *Before Ephraim, Benjamin, and Manassas. Stir up your might, and come to save us.*

Coram Ephraim, Beniamin, et Manasse. Excita potentiam tuam, et veni, ut salvos facias nos.

And so the two first verses pertain to the Church of God which existed during the time of the written Law, but which also can be allegorically expounded of the Church of God which exists during the time

---

the Law (*sub lege*), under grace (*sub gratia*), and in peace (*in pace*). Before the law we follow the concupiscence of the flesh, under the law we are drawn by it, under grace we neither follow nor are drawn by it, and in peace there is no concupiscence of the flesh." *Ex. prop. Rom.* 12, PL 35, 2065; *see also De Div. Quaes.*, 66, 3, PL 40, 62.

5   John 15:6a.

6   Is. 52:6.

7   Is. 33:22. E. N. Denis's verse departs from the Sixto-Clementine Vulgate, which does not have the verb *veniet*, "he will come."

8   Zech. 2:10.

of grace. And so it therefore says: **79{80}[2]** *Qui regis Israel, O you that rule* Israel, that is, you, God, who governed the patriarch Jacob, and the people who were born of *him, intende, give* ear, that is, mercifully look upon the prayers and the desires of your people, *qui deducis velut ovem Ioseph, you who lead Joseph like a sheep*, that is, you who kept Joseph in his innocence and candidness, as a chosen lamb belonging to your sheepfold;[9] or [we can understand it] thus: *you who lead Joseph*, that is, you who lead the people of Israel figured by Joseph, because he was the most excellent among his brothers, and he saved them during the time of famine.[10] God led this people through the desert, preceding them in a column of cloud by day, and in a column of fire by night;[11] or rather, by a holy angel, who moved the column of cloud and of fire. Whence the Lord said to Moses: *Behold I will send my angel, who shall go before you, and keep you in your journey, and bring you into the place that I have prepared.*[12] For in the Scriptures, we can understand the names Jacob or Israel to be either the person who was the son of Isaac, who is called Jacob and Israel, [or the people arising from the seed of Jacob].[13] Similarly also by the name Joseph, we sometimes understand the son of Jacob, who is called Joseph; but other times the people originating from the seed of Joseph;[14] but sometimes also the entire Israelite people.

Qui sedes super cherubim, you that sit upon the cherubim, that is, you who most eminently exceed all the heights of created knowledge, and dwell among those angels and spirits called the cherubim, illuminating them most excellently, *manifestare, shine forth*, that is, evidently show yourself to us, descending down toward us, and appearing to us visibly: *shine forth*, I say, **79{80}[3]** *coram Ephraim, Beniamin, et Manasse; before Ephraim, Benjamin, and Manassas*, that is, before all the faithful people who are signified by these tribes. For by Ephraim, which is interpreted as meaning fruitful, we understand those who produce worthy fruits of penance and holy deeds;[15] also by Benjamin, which means son of the right hand, are understood those who strongly and joyfully cling to God by the works of justice; and by Manassas, which means forgetfulness, is designated those who are forgetful of all earthly and carnal things because

---

9   Gen. 37:2 *et seq.*
10 Gen. 45:5.
11 Ex. 13:21.
12 Ex. 23:20.
13 Gen. 25:25; 32:28. *E. N.* The brackets are in the original, presumably added by the editor to complete the sentence.
14 Gen. 30:24.
15 *Cf.* Matt. 3:8: *Bring forth therefore fruit worthy of penance.*

of divine love. Now those persons who are of this kind are worthy and fitting to appear before God. And such men indeed existed among the ancient fathers, who eagerly wished for the coming of Christ. For they knew because they saw with blessed eyes. And of such men, Christ said to his disciples: *Many kings and prophets desired to see that which you see, and to hear the things which you hear.*[16]

Allegorically,[17] by Israel is designated the Church, looking attentively to God by faith, which God in a special way rules, directing it to eternal life, in the manner that he formerly specially ruled the Synagogue as his peculiar people. Also, by Joseph, which is interpreted as meaning an increase, is understood the faithful converted to Christ from the Gentile people and the increase in the Church obtained from the Jews: for these two peoples were unified by Christ the cornerstone as if they were two walls,[18] and they constituted one Church. Now God leads this people exiled in this world by the way of his commandments, illuminating them by the evangelical and apostolic doctrine, by hidden inspirations, and by the teaching of others. Whence, we have in Isaiah: *Thus says the Lord your Redeemer, the Holy One of Israel: I am the Lord your God that teach you profitable things, that governs you in the way that you walk.*[19]

But because it is not sufficient to invoke most ardently the presence of the beloved merely once or twice, so he asks yet again for that which he had asked for before, namely, the coming of Christ, saying: *Excita, stir up,* you, O Lord God, the Only-Begotten of God, *potentiam tuam, your power,* which appears as if you had been asleep, since you do not deliver your chosen ones, especially while you have forsaken the holy fathers in the lower limbo, and you have allowed the entire world to be seduced completely by idolatry and various errors, and to be miserably subjugated by diabolical domination. Stir up, therefore, that is, stretch yourself forth in action, show your power by which you are able to bind the strong man

---

16   Luke 10:24; *cf.* Matt. 13:17.

17   *E. N.* The text has *moraliter,* "morally," but the editor notes that this is in error, and Denis probably intended to say, "allegorically," since what follows is not a tropological analysis, but an allegorical one.

18   *E. N.* Eph. 2:19–22. The image of the Jewish wall and the Gentile wall joined by Christ, the cornerstone, is Augustinian in origin. See Sermon 137, 6, PL 38, 757. "Did not Christ come to found the Church, to separate those Jews believing rightly, hoping rightly, and loving rightly as wheat from chaff, and to make one wall of circumcision, to which would be adjoined another wall from the uncircumcised Gentiles, he himself being the cornerstone to which these two walls coming from different places would be joined."

19   Is. 48:17.

(that is, the devil), and to snatch away his vessels, that is, to save sinners; *et veni, and come,* not through a legate, but in your very person through the assumption of flesh *ut salvos facias nos, and come to save us* from the guilt of original sin, indeed from all mortal and venial sin, and from the power of the devil. For this is the reason Christ came, in the manner that John says: *For this purpose, the Son of God appeared, that he might destroy the works of the devil.*[20] Any one of us is able to pray this daily for himself, namely, that the Lord descend upon him by the infusion of grace or by a spiritual coming, as the Savior speaking of the God the Father said, *We will come to him, and will make our abode with him.*[21]

79{80}[4] *Convert us, O God: and show us your face, and we shall be saved.*

Deus converte nos, et ostende faciem tuam, et salvi erimus.

79{80}[4] *Deus, converte nos; convert us, O God,* that is, prepare our hearts for your coming, divert us from transitory and vain things, and make us to adhere to the unchanging good; *et ostende faciem tuam, and show us your face,* that is, manifest yourself to us, appearing in a visible form. Or [we can understand it thus], *show us your face,* that is, look upon us in a conciliatory way, and be not indignant against us your servants. Or [yet another way], *show us your face* after this life, so that we might see you in the heavenly homeland *face to face,*[22] that is, as you are, by sight: in the manner that John says in his first epistle: *We are now the sons of God; and it has not yet appeared what we shall be. We know, that, when he shall appear, we shall be like to him: because we shall see him as he is.*[23] And so show unto us your face immediately after we have left the body, that is, [show us] your essence, so that we might be like the angels of God, of whom it is written: *Their angels in heaven always see the face of my Father [who is in heaven].*[24] Moses desired to see this face, saying: *If therefore I have found favor in your sight, show me your face.*[25] Now if you shall do this, O Lord, *salvi erimus, we shall be saved,* in the present life from fault, and in the future from punishments; and we shall be saved, that is, blessed, now in hope and inchoatively, but afterwards in reality and completely.

---

20   1 John 3:8b.
21   John 14:23b.
22   1 Cor. 13:12.
23   1 John 3:2.
24   Matt. 18:10b. *E. N.* The words in brackets replace Denis's "etc."
25   Ex. 33:13a.

79{80}[5]   O Lord God of powers,[26] *how long will you be angry against
the prayer of your servant?*

*Domine Deus virtutum, quousque irasceris super orationem
servi tui?*

79{80}[6]   *How long will you feed us with the bread of tears: and give
us for our drink tears in measure?*

*Cibabis nos pane lacrimarum, et potum dabis nobis in lacrimis
in mensura?*

79{80}[5] *Domine, Deus virtutum;* O Lord, God of powers, that is,
giver and preserver of all powers, without whom all created nature has
no power. Or [we can understand it thus], *God of powers,* that is, of the
holy angels, whom everyone says are customarily called powers (*virtutes*),[27]
and of which Christ asserts, *For the powers (virtutes) of heaven shall be
moved.*[28] *Quousque irasceris super orationem servi tui? How long will you be
angry against the prayer of your servant?* That is, how long will you repel
the prayers of your servant and delay in hearing it? And how long also
79{80}[6] *cibabis nos pane lacrimarum, will you feed us with the bread of
tears,* that is, [how long] will you fill us, or will you allow us to be filled,
with sorrows and the hardships, as one is filled with food? *Et,* and how
long *potum dabis nobis in lacrimis, will you give us for our drink tears,* that
is, [how long] will you fill us with the drink of tears (in the manner as
was just addressed with bread), *in mensura,* in measure of your justice,
that is, as greatly as we deserve, namely, according to the demands of our
fault, and not mitigating our torments? [This is done] in the manner
as attested, *As much as she has glorified herself, and lived in delicacies, so
much torment and sorrow give to her.*[29] Or [alternatively], *in measure,* that
is according to our possibilities, namely, as much as you know we are
able to bear. For you do not permit us to be tempted beyond that which

---

26   E. N. I have departed from the Douay-Rheims, which translates the Latin
virtutum as "hosts," with reference to the angelic hosts or powers, rather than the
more generic "powers." Although this is one construction that Denis gives in the
Commentary, he also construes this verse as a reference to the causal role of God
as First Cause of all secondary, created causes. Therefore I used the more general
term "powers."

27   E. N. Denis maintains that the Latin word *virtutes* in Scripture frequently
refers to angels generically, in addition to it being the name for one of the nine
choirs of angels.

28   Luke 21:26b.

29   Rev. 18:7a. Revelation refers to Babylon, the figure of a disobedient, rebellious,
and idolatrous soul.

we are able to bear, but with the temptation you make provision that we are able to bear it.[30] Now there is a certain kind of bread and drink of tears that is strongly desirable and wholesome, as are the tears that proceed from the repentance of sins, or out the desire of the heavenly kingdom arising out of divine charity, or from the love of neighbor, or from compassion of their weaknesses: and this bread truly restores the soul, obtains mercy, and acquires grace.

79{80}[7]   *You have made us to be a contradiction to our neighbors: and our enemies have scoffed at us.*

Posuisti nos in contradictionem vicinis nostris, et inimici nostri subsannaverunt nos.

79{80}[7] *Posuisti nos in contradictionem vicinis nostris, you have made us to be a contradiction to our neighbors*: that is, you have permitted such great disgrace and misery to come and to fall upon us, that our enemies, those nations neighboring us, daringly speak against us; *et inimici nostri subsannaverunt nos, and our enemies have scoffed at us,* as if we have worshipped God in vain. The Synagogue was reproved and scoffed at by the Babylonians in this way during the time of the transmigration, and by the Samaritans after their return to the land of Judaea, according to that which we often encounter in the book of Nehemiah: *And it came to pass*, it says, *that when Sanballat heard that we were building the wall, he was angry, and . . . he scoffed at the Jews.*[31] But also *Tobias [the Ammonite] his neighbor said: Let them build: if a fox go up, he will leap over their wall.*[32] The early Church of Christ also suffered much from many reproving voices: first by the Jews, as is clear in the Acts of the Apostles;[33] thereafter, in all the world by the Pagans, as is written in the legends of the Saints. Jeremiah prays for the removal of this reproof and scoffing: *Give us not to be a reproach, for your name's sake, and do not disgrace us.*[34] But Paul — to whom the Athenian philosophers said: *What is it, that this word sower would say?* — did not fear this reproof and scoffing. He seemed [to them] to be the announcer of new gods.[35] Nevertheless, in this matter, the perfect man can pray to God that the scoffing and reproof be removed for two

---

30   *Cf.* 1 Cor. 10:13.
31   Neh. 4:1.
32   Neh. 4:3.
33   Acts chp. 4 *et seq.*
34   Jer. 14:21a.
35   Acts 17:18a.

reasons. First, because of the danger to the weak, lest they be overcome by the adversity. Second, for reasons of charity of our adversaries, for whose errors we ought to feel, for charity's sake, great pain, lest they perish: and in this manner we can desire that they cease in persecuting us, lest they offend God and incur damnation.

79{80}[8] *O God of powers, convert us: and show your face, and we shall be saved.*

> *Deus virtutum, converte nos, et ostende faciem tuam, et salvi erimus.*

79{80}[8] *O God of powers, convert us.* For, in the way stated by Jeremiah, without your prevenient grace we do not have the power to convert: *Convert us, O Lord, to you, and we shall be converted.*[36] Whence also Jeremiah again entreats: *Convert me, and I shall be converted. . . . For after you did convert me, I did penance.*[37] From this it is most clear that our salvation or beatitude consists in the manifestation or the vision of the divine countenance, namely, in an act of the intellect.[38] Whence the Savior said: *Now this is eternal life: That they may know you, the only true God, and Jesus Christ, whom you have sent.*[39] And so Christ promised the manifestation of his countenance as a reward, saying: *He that loves me, shall be loved of my Father: and I will love him, and will manifest myself to him.*[40] For this reason St. Augustine said, *The vision is the whole reward.*[41] Beatitude is not, therefore (as some say), essentially situated in the act of will.[42]

79{80}[9] *You have brought a vineyard out of Egypt: you have cast out the Gentiles and planted it.*

> *Vineam de Aegypto transtulisti, et eiecisti gentes, et plantasti eam.*

---

36 Lam. 5:21a.
37 Jer. 31:18b–19a.
38 E. N. See ST Ia, q. 26, art. 2, ad 2 (beatitude is to be found in an act of the intellect).
39 John 17:3.
40 John 14:21b.
41 E. N. *Visio . . . est tota merces.* The notion that the vision or knowledge of God is the whole reward of beatitude is quite frequent in St. Augustine. *E.g., Enarr. in Psalmos* (Ps. 90, 13), PL 37, 1170 (*tota merces nostra visio est*). Sermon 49, 3 (*Videbimus eum sicuti est, ipsa merces est*), PL 49, 322; *De Trinitate* I, 17 (*Contemplatio quippe merces est fidei*) PL 42, 832; *In Evang. Ioann. Tract.,* 29, 6 (*Intellectus enim merces est fidei*), PL 35, 1630.
42 E. N. ST IaIae, q. 3, art. 4, co. Thomas Aquinas rejects the notion that beatitude is essentially an act of the will.

79{80}[9] *Vineam de Aegypto transutlisti, you have brought a vineyard out of Egypt*: that is, you have led the Synagogue or the Jewish people out from the land of the Egyptians, and as a farmer might do, you transplanted them to another land, namely, to the land of promise. The Synagogue is called a vine because God diligently cultivates it, trims it, and makes it fruitful, and *he brought it into the cellar of wine*,[43] as it states in the Song of Songs. For this reason, Isaiah asserts: *The vineyard of the Lord of hosts is the house of Israel: and the man of Juda, his pleasant plant*.[44] *Eiecisti gentes, you have cast out the gentiles*, [that is,] the Canaanite people from the land of promise, *et plantasti eam, and planted it*, that is, you have firmly placed the Jewish people in that land, and you have caused them to dwell there without any fear.

79{80}[10] *You were the guide of its journey in its sight: you planted the roots thereof, and it filled the land.*

Dux itineris fuisti in conspectu eius; plantasti radices eius, et implevit terram.

79{80}[10] *Dux itineris fuisti in conspectu eius, you were the guide of its journey in its sight*, that is, you led the Hebrew people in the way from Egypt even unto their land of promise, going before them by a holy angel and a column of fire and of cloud:[45] just as was fully stated but a moment ago;[46] *et plantasti radices eius, and you planted the roots thereof*, that is, you strongly confirmed the souls of the progenitors or fathers, the leaders and princes of this people, and stably placed them in the aforementioned land; *et implevit terram, and it filled the land*, that is, this people were multiplied far and wide, and were diffused throughout all the promised land. For how many were the multitude of this people during the time of David is written in the first book of Chronicles: *Joab gave the number of people to David; and all the number was found to be eleven hundred thousand men . . . ; and of Juda four hundred and seventy thousand . . . . But Levi and Benjamin he did not number for Joab unwillingly executed the king's orders.*[47] See how this people filled the land: for when they departed from the land of Egypt, when they were first numbered by Moses, there were only around six hundred thousand, and by the time of David they were possibly three times as much.

---

43 Songs 2:4.
44 Is. 5:7a.
45 Ex. 13:21.
46 Ps. 79:2.
47 1 Chr. 21:5–6.

79{80}[11] *The shadow of it covered the hills: and the branches thereof the cedars of God.*

Operuit montes umbra eius, et arbusta eius cedros Dei.

79{80}[11] *Operuit montes umbra eius, the shadow of it covered the hills:* that is, this vine grew so high that it covered the mountains with shade: for so exalted were the persons born from this people, namely, the kings, the prophets, nazarites,[48] priests, and judges: whose *umbra, shadow,* that is, the grace conceded to them in this life (which grace is a shadow of the grace which is possessed in the heavenly fatherland), *operuit, covered,* that is, greatly transcended and exceeded, *montes, the hills,* that is, the exalted persons of other nations and all of the Gentiles. Whence Moses: *There is no other nation so great,* he said, *that has gods so nigh to them, as our God is present to all our petitions.*[49] And again: *What other nation is there so renowned that has ceremonies, and just judgments, and all the law as does the people of Israel?*[50] By shadow one can also understand the ceremonies of the old Law, which were obscure figures, not evidently the similitude of future goods, for according to the Apostle, *the law having a shadow of the good things to come,* [did] *not* [have] *the very image of the things.*[51] For in the manner that Dionysius [the Areopagite] teaches, the position of the Christian religion is midway between the state of the Old Testament and state of those blessed in the heavenly fatherland; and so those things that are carried out in the New Testament are evident similitudes of the future and heavenly goods, that is, of the state of those in the heavenly fatherland and those things that are carried out there; but those things that were done in the Old Testament were remote and obscure figures of future goods. So that [this verse] is [to be understood] in this sense: *The shadow of it covered the hills:* that is, the law of the ceremonial precepts and the figures of the Old Testament covered our understanding, that is, it imparted obscure and enigmatic things, *the hills,* that is, the prophets, who because of the excellence of their grace are called hills. For they spoke obscurely and, as it were, in the shadows. *Et arbusta eius cedros Dei, and the branches thereof are the cedars of God.* Branches habitually sprout forth from the tree, by which in this verse we understand the increase or the outgrowth of the vine,

---

48   E. N. A nazarite (the word comes from Hebrew nazir, meaning "consecrated" or "separated," was an Israelite that was consecrated to the service of God, and who took vows to abstain from alcohol, let his hair grow, and avoid ritual defilement. *See* Numb. 6:1–21. Both Samuel (1 Sam. 1:11) and Samson (Judges 13:5) were nazarites.
49   Deut. 4:7.
50   Deut. 4:8.
51   Heb. 10:1.

namely, the generations of the children of the Patriarchs and the fathers, whose adoption by grace and dignity of rule was so great, as the *cedars of God*, that is, they the greatly surpassed excellent persons. For from the Patriarchs and the people brought out of Egypt were born very holy and great kings, prophets, priests, and many other highly graced men.

But he who wants to interpret this vine in an absolute literal way, here also can explain this verse bodily in this way. *The shadow of it covered the hills*: that is, the buildings, towers, homes, and walls of the Jewish people were built so high that the hills of the land of Israel, which is very mountainous, were deprived of the rays of the sun because of them. And closely around Jerusalem there were hills, which certainly at times sustained shade from the eastern sun, from one side of the city because of the height of its edifices. Whence it is said of Jehoshaphat, that he built in Jerusalem houses akin to tall towers.[52] *And the branches thereof,* that is, the huts left next to the buildings, or the growths of the trees, covered because of their height the *cedars of God*, that is, the cedars of the land of promise which are called the cedars of God because they were cedars of the divinely chosen land.

79{80}[12] *It stretched forth its branches unto the sea, and its boughs unto the river.*

Extendit palmites suos usque ad mare, et usque ad flumen propagines eius.

The described height of this vine along with its breadth is described in that which follows: **79{80}[12]** *Extendit palmites suos usque ad mare, it stretched forth its branches unto the sea*: that is, the vine or the people of the Jews bore children whose dwelling places extended even unto the Mediterranean sea: *propagines, its boughs,* that is, their generations, extended *usque ad flumen, even... unto the river,* the great Euphrates: and so the children of Israel possessed all the land promised to them, and they were multiplied in it from one end even unto the other end.

79{80}[13] *Why have you broken down the hedge thereof, so that all they who pass by the way do pluck it?*

Ut quid destruxisti maceriam eius, et vindemiant eam omnes qui praetergrediuntur viam?

---

52   2 Chr. 17:12: *And Jehoshaphat grew and became exceeding great: and he built in Juda houses like towers, and walled cities.*

79{80}[14] *The boar out of the wood has laid it waste: and a singular wild beast has devoured it.*

Exterminavit eam aper de silva, et singularis ferus depastus est eam.

Since, therefore, O Lord, you in times past bestowed such good things upon this vine, **79{80}[13]** *Ut quid,* why after a time *destruxisti,* have you broken, that is, removed, *maceriam eius,* the hedge thereof, that is, the fences, walls, or protections, withdrawing from it your aid and angelic defense? In doing so it fell into idolatry and many other wicked deeds, and deserved that which followed: *et vindemiant eam,* so that they do pluck it, that is, they devastate, trample upon, and destroy it *eam omnes qui praetergrediuntur viam,* all they who pass by the way, that is, all the Gentile nations around it and those remaining more distant. Moreover, that this is the means of destruction which is indicated by the breaking down of the vineyard's hedge is predicted by Isaiah: *I will show you,* he says, *what I will do to my vineyard. I will take away the hedge thereof, and it shall be wasted: I will break down the wall thereof, and it shall be trodden down.*[53] Also what will be done is expressed by Jeremiah: *Many pastors have destroyed my vineyard.*[54] Whence also the first book of Maccabees brings this up: *What nation has not inherited her kingdom, and gotten of her spoils?*[55] **79{80}[14]** *Exterminavit eam aper de silva, et singularis ferus depastus est eam;* the boar of the wood has laid it waste, and a singular wild beast has devoured it. Some, following Cassiodorus, understand by the term boar Vespasian; but by the singular wild beast, [they understand] his son, Titus: but this does not seem right. For the people of the Jews during the time of their devastation caused by Vespasian and Titus were by no means the vine of the Lord: God did not cultivate them by grace, nor did they worship God by faith. Rather they were the people then, as they are also now, entirely unfaithful and reprobate; and they had that truth in them which John states in Revelation, *They say they are Jews and are not, but are the synagogue of Satan.*[56] It is more fitting, therefore, to understand by the terms boar and singular beast the same one tyrant, whether he be called Nebuchadnezzar or Antiochus. For both of them laid waste these people, that is, placed them outside their boundaries, destroying their buildings, and transplanting those dwelling

---

53 Is. 5:5.
54 Jer. 12:10a.
55 1 Macc. 2:10.
56 Rev. 2:9b.

in them or causing them to flee, as we read of Judas Maccabaeus and his brothers, who dwelt among the wild beasts in the desert places.[57] And this singular wild beast devoured this vineyard, terribly demolishing this people. But the Jews in their obdurate perfidy understand by the boar and singular wild beast either Titus or Vespasian.[58]

But this which is said of the Synagogue under the name of vineyard can be mystically understood as pertaining of the Church of Christ in this way: *A vineyard*, that is, the militant Church or the Christian people, *you have brought out of Egypt*, that is, you have brought out from the gloom of this world into the reign of Christ, so that Christians might be your *heirs, and joint heirs with Christ.*[59] For this reason, the Apostle says: God delivered us *from this present wicked world,*[60] *and has translated us into the kingdom of the Son of his love.*[61] *You have cast out the Gentiles,* that is, you changed the Gentiles into something better, converting them unto the Faith, and those unwilling to be converted you have caused to be forsaken; *and planted it,* that is, you have caused the Christian people to inhabit in those places and lands where pagans at one time dwelt; or [alternatively], *you have planted* it, [that is, the Christian people,] in Christ through [the theological virtues of] faith and charity. *You were the guide of its journey in its sight:* for you conducted the Apostles throughout all the world, and you led all the elect by grace to yourself, the Ultimate End of all things, in the manner that you bore witness: *I am the Way, the Truth, and the Life. No one comes to the Father but by me.*[62] And again: *I will not leave you orphans;*[63] *I go away, and I come unto you.*[64] And *you planted the roots thereof:* that is, the first princes of the Church, the spiritual progenitors of others, namely, the Apostles and their distinguished followers — as were Dionysius, Polycarp, Ignatius — you firmly strengthened in Christ, so that they might bring forth Christ in others, as branches sprout forth from a vine. For Christ also said: *I am the true vine . . . you are the*

---

57 Cf. 2 Macc. 5:27.

58 E. N. Denis is saying that the Jews interpret this verse wrongly to refer to Titus or Vespasian instead of Antiochus or Nebuchadnezzar because they do not recognize the fact that at the time of Judea's destruction by the Romans in 70 AD, they had lost their position as the Lord's vineyard, it having been transferred to the Church of the Lord upon its founding by Jesus, whom they rejected as Lord and Messiah.

59 Rom. 8:17a.

60 Gal. 1:4b.

61 Col. 1:13b.

62 John 14:6.

63 John 14:18.

64 John 14:28a.

branches.[65] *And it filled the land*: for the Church has spread all over the earth. Whence is written in Isaiah: *Israel shall blossom and bud, and they shall fill the face of the world with seed.*[66] This cannot be explained as the carnal generation and multiplication of the Jews, but [it can be explained as referring to] the spiritual generation of the Apostles, coming out of the people of Israel, and the multiplication of the faithful, who are the seed of the Apostles. *The shadow of it covered the hills*: that is, the election of the Christians exceeded the height of all given graces. For surely the Apostles were placed in front of the Prophets and the Church in front of the Synagogue. *And the branches thereof, the cedars of God*: because more grace has been poured forth as a whole upon the Christian people than formerly upon the exalted men of God. *It*, the Church, *stretched forth its branches*, that is, its children, *unto the sea*, the western as well as the eastern sea, as is stated of Christ elsewhere: *His power shall be from sea to sea.*[67] *And . . . unto the river*, that is, the fountain of Baptism, extends *its boughs*: because the Church begets however many are dipped in the waters of Baptism, as the Savior commanded the Apostles: *Teach all nations; baptizing them in the name of the Father, and of the Son, and of the Holy Spirit.*[68] For this reason it is written that Peter said to those brought to Christ by the exhortations of his preaching: *Be baptized every one of you in the name of Jesus Christ, for the remission of your sins.*[69] *Why have you broken down the hedge thereof?* That is, why have you permitted the Church to be forsaken by the withdrawal of your aid from it,? So that *they . . . do pluck at it*, that is, they despoil her of her spiritual goods, *all they who pass by the way*, that is, all those who transgress the paths of your commandments, namely, demons and perverse men. *The boar out of the wood has laid it waste*, that is, Muhammad, the lawgiver of the Saracens, whose people overthrew the Church in Jerusalem. *And a singular wild beast has devoured it.* By this singular beast can be understood Muhammad, or any other cruel tyrant or heresiarch.

79{80}[15] *Turn again, O God of power, look down from heaven, and see, and visit this vineyard:*

Deus virtutum, convertere, respice de caelo, et vide, et visita vineam istam.

---

65   John 15:1a, 5a.
66   Is. 27:6.
67   Zech. 9:10b.
68   Matt. 28:19.
69   Acts 2:38.

79{80}[16] *And perfect the same which your right hand has planted: and upon the son of man whom you have confirmed for yourself.*

Et perfice eam quam plantavit dextera tua, et super filium hominis quem confirmasti tibi.

79{80}[15] *Deus virtutum, convertere; turn again,* O God of power, that is, mercifully turn yourself toward us, in the manner that is stated: *Turn to me, says the Lord of hosts: and I will turn to you.*[70] *Respice de caelo, look down from heaven,* with the eyes of your immense kindness, *et vide, and see* our indigence; *et visita, and visit* in your own person *vineam ista, this vineyard,* that is, your Church; visit also daily the human heart by the infusion of grace and by the increase of spiritual goods. **79{80}[16]** *Et perfice eam, and perfect the same,* namely, the Church, giving it spiritual perfection and evangelical counsels, by which the precepts are perfected; *quam plantavit, which . . . are planted,* in faith and individual charity, *dextera tua, by your right hand,* that is, your mercy or your benign power. For Christ established his Church on earth. But in a unique sense look *super filium hominis, upon the Son of Man,* that is, Christ, who often calls himself the Son of Man in the Gospel,[71] and whose type, Ezekiel, was frequently called the son of man;[72] *quem, whom* [referring to] Christ [whom], *confirmasti tibi, you have confirmed for yourself,* that is, you have conjoined inseparably to your divinity, both as to a personal union and as to a fruitful union. And so Christ the man was not able to sin, nor was he in any manner to become separate from God, for even during the three days of his death, his body and his soul remained united to the Word. Or [we can understand it thus], *upon the son,* your beloved Son, the Lord Jesus, whom you *confirmed for yourself,* that is, whom you firmly attested to be your Son, confirming him for yourself before men, saying to them both in his baptism as well as in the holy mount [Tabor], *This is my beloved Son, in whom I am well pleased.*[73]

---

70   Zech. 1:3b.

71   Matt. 8:20 and elsewhere.

72   Ez. 2:1, 3, *etc.* E. N. Because Ezekiel is referred to as the "son of man" almost ninety times in the book of Ezechiel, he has been considered commonly to be a figure or type of Christ who also called himself the Son of Man. "No other prophet, I mean of the major prophets," St. Jerome observes, "is called 'son of man,'" and the title is "given strictly to Ezekiel," thus making him a type of Christ. *Homilies of St. Jerome: 60–96* (Washington, DC: CUA Press, 1966), 130 (trans., Marie Liguori Ewald, I. H. M.).

73   Matt. 3:17; 17:5.

79{80}[17] *Things set on fire and dug down shall perish at the rebuke of your countenance.*

Incensa igni et suffossa, ab increpatione vultus tui peribunt.

But if you do this, **79{80}[17]** *Incensa igni, things set on fire,* that is, sins committed from the fire of concupiscence or the flames of disordered loves, *et suffossa, and dug down,* that is, sins from evil, oppressive, and humiliating fear, *ab increpatione vultus tui peribunt, shall perish at the rebuke of your countenance,* that is, shall cease in the repentant sinner through the rebuke of your gaze, when you paternally reprove men, and — correcting them — you look upon them, illuminate them, and convert them. But those who persevere in vice perish in their sins, that is, they are eternally condemned by the rebuke of your countenance, that is, by the strictness of your justice, when you shall say to sinners: *Depart from me, you cursed, into everlasting fire.*[74] But knowing that as all good and meritorious work comes from a good love or a good fear, so all evil works are born either from evil love or evil fear. But fear is reducible to love, as its cause and root: for we do not fear except that we love its opposite. And so all good works proceed in their origin from divine love: for without charity nothing is meritorious. So also all evil [works] are born out of disordered love.[75]

79{80}[18] *Let your hand be upon the man of your right hand: and upon the son of man whom you have confirmed for yourself.*

Fiat manus tua super virum dexterae tuae, et super filium hominis quem confirmasti tibi.

79{80}[19] *And we depart not from you, you shall quicken us: and we will call upon your name.*

Et non discedimus a te; vivificabis nos, et nomen tuum invocabimus.

79{80}[18] *Fiat manus tua, let your hand be,* that is, [let] the power of your divinity, O God the Father, [be] *super virum dexterae tuae, upon the man of your right hand,* that is, upon the man Christ, so that his humanity may cooperate with your divinity in all things, and that our final salvation might be achieved through it,[76] in accordance with that which Christ

---

74   Matt. 25:41.

75   E. N. For the role of fear, love, and the doing of good and of evil, *see* ST IIaIIae, q. 19, arts. 1–8.

76   E. N. Denis here is making reference to the instrumental aspect of the humanity of Christ.

himself said: *The Father who abides in me, he does all the works;*[77] *et super filium hominis,* and upon the son of man, that is, Christ, the son of the Virgin Mother of God, *quem confirmasti tibi, whom you have confirmed for yourself.* In terms of explaining this, the latter part [of the verse] explains the former part. And so Christ is said to be a man at the right hand of God: first of all because, as is written, God's favor, love, grace, and mercy, and the happy presence[78] fully prevented, filled, and blessed his humanity in every way:[79] *We saw his glory, the glory as it were of the only begotten of the Father, full of grace and truth.*[80] Secondly, because he was equal to the Father according to his divinity, which equality is indicated by the name "of your right hand." Third, because he sits at the right hand of God the Father, according to this: *The Lord Jesus . . . was taken up into heaven, and sits on the right hand of God.*[81] **79{80}[19]** *Et non discedimus a te,* and we depart not from you, that is, we do not cease to cry out to you, and to invoke the presence of Christ: and so I confidently say, that *vivificabis nos, you shall quicken us,* by the merits of the Incarnation and Passion of our Lord and Savior, with the life of grace in the present, and the life of glory in the future. For you said to your own through Isaiah: *I am the Lord, for they shall not be confounded that wait for him.*[82] *Et nomen tuum invocabimus,* and we will call upon your name, until at length we obtain eternal beatitude. Not, however, that we forsake God if he delays in hearing us but, that we say with Job: *Although he should kill me, I will trust in him.*[83]

79{80}[20] *O Lord God of power, convert us: and show your face, and we shall be saved.*

Domine Deus virtutum, converte nos, et ostende faciem tuam, et salvi erimus.

79{80}[20] *Domine, Deus virtutum, converte nos, etc. O Lord God of power, convert us, etc.* See now how in this verse [God of power] is repeated three times: because our salvation consists in the vision of the

---

77 John 14:10b.
78 E. N. By "happy presence," *felix presentia,* Denis means the beatific vision.
79 E. N. By "prevented," *praevenit,* Denis means, preceded, anticipated, or coming before, so that there was never a time where Christ's sacred humanity lacked the gifts. The gifts were prevenient: they were there ready to join the human nature upon its creation.
80 John 1:14b.
81 Mark 16:19.
82 Is. 49:23b.
83 Job 13:15a.

most-high Trinity, but also to indicate the fervor of one's affections, and the utility, sweetness, and power of this verse. For this verse is chock full of admirable power, because it asks for that which is required for our salvation, and it also does it in the order it should be asked for. For first we turn back to God, for from him arises the principle of every good, and thereafter we become illumined by the divinity, and by this means our salvation is brought about.

The greatness, power, dignity, and sentiment of this verse cannot be adequately explained. For by that which is said—*O Lord, God of power*—one touches the divine majesty which is the fountainlike origin of all power; and our soul is aroused toward a reverential fear over such a powerful Lord, of which is written in Jeremiah: *You are great, and great is your name in might. Who shall fear you, O king of nations?*[84] Also, by that which is added—*convert us*—we acknowledge that all our perfection and salvation—its beginning, its pursuit, and its completion—depends upon God,[85] inasmuch as the beginnings of our conversion stem from the largesse of God. This Solomon implies when he prays thus: *The Lord our God be with us . . .* and *may he incline our hearts to himself, that we may walk in all his ways.*[86] That the pursuit or continuation in the good is also the gift of the most High is professed by David elsewhere, *O Lord God . . . keep forever this will . . . and let this mind remain always for the worship of you.*[87]

Now by the verse which follows—*et ostende faciem tuam, and show your face*—the divine love ought to be enkindled in us, and, by a kind of merit, the incomparable flame of love ought ardently to blaze. For what else is so good, loveable, sweet, beautiful, wholesome, pleasant, and noble as seeing the face of God? O beautiful face, O immense beauty, or infinite happiness! The sight of the face of our Creator is promised us: but who is worthy to see this except for one whose soul is purified from all uncleanliness? For this reason, *Blessed are the pure of heart, for they shall see God.*[88] Take heed: if we love God, let us say with great affection, *Show your face:* and that much more affectionately the more frequently we do so. For it does not behoove us, from frequent repetition and long-lasting habit, to lose our initial attentiveness and become

---

84   Jer. 10:6b–7a.
85   *E. N.* Latin: *inchoative, prosecutive, et completive,* literally, inchoatively, prosecutively, and completively: at the beginning, during the middle, and at the end.
86   1 Kings 8:57a, 58a.
87   1 Chr. 29:18.
88   Matt. 5:8.

lukewarm in, or turn away from, the good. For he who does not undertake the work of God negligently,[89] but discharges it reverently, grows daily in grace; and so from day to day he more perfectly fulfils his submission to God. Unceasingly, therefore, ought we to beg that the Lord might show his face to us, now, of course, by the illumination of faith and the splendor of grace, every day with a purer contemplation, yet in the future by sight and the light of glory. For the more clearly and joyfully we will see the face of God in our present exile and in the future age the more we now with greater affection utter this verse, which truly superabounds with immeasurable sweetness.

But also the entire psalm is exceedingly magnificent; and it is clear about this: how with most vehement desire the saints of old desired the coming of the holy Christ: and it is to our great disgrace if—the Incarnation having already occurred—we embrace it with lesser fervor of delight than they who desired it in the future.

PRAYER

GOD, FATHER OF POWER, IN THE SIGHT of your people, redeemed by the Blood of your Son, be a gracious guide of the right way, so that with the roots of Christian profession strongly planted by you, we may attain the land of eternal promise.

Deus, Pater virtutum, esto propitius dux itineris recti in conspectu populi, Filii tui sanguine redempti: ut forti a te plantata radice christianae professionis, impleat terram aeternae repromissionis.

---

89   *Cf.* Jer. 48:10a: *Cursed be he that does the work of the Lord deceitfully.*

Psalm 80

ARTICLE LIII

LITERAL EXPOSITION OF THE EIGHTIETH PSALM:
EXSULTATE DEO ADIUTORI NOSTRO.
REJOICE TO GOD OUR HELPER.

80{81}[1] *Unto the end, for the wine presses, the fifth day of the week, a Psalm for Asaph.*

In finem, pro torcularibus, quinta sabbati, psalmus ispsi Asaph.

THE TITLE OF THIS PSALM HAS ALREADY been looked at: 80{81}[1] *In finem, pro torcularibus, quinta sabbati, psalmus ipsi Asaph; unto the end, for the wine presses, the fifth day of the week, a Psalm for Asaph.* It appears that this title pertains more to the mystical rather than the literal explanation of this present Psalm, especially since there are many words in it which are not found in the Hebrew [texts]. And so in the explanation which follows, where this Psalm is spiritually explained, the aforesaid title will be explained correspondingly. Besides, Jerome, in his translation according to the Hebrew text, puts forth as a title: *To the victory, in the winepress, Asaph.* By this we have the knowledge that this Psalm was especially sung in the Feast of Trumpets,[1] which was in the first day of September, around that time that is customarily the end of the grape harvest in the land of promise, since it is then warm. And so they went to make offerings of sacrifice in the temple during that time. And therefore, this Psalm has received the title from the winepresses, since they squeeze out the wine, for by an act of thanksgiving is given to God for the fruit collected that year.

80{81}[2] *Rejoice to God our helper: sing aloud to the God of Jacob.*

Exsultate Deo adiutori nostro, iubilate Deo Iacob.

---

1 E. N. The "Feast of the Trumpets" is commonly known as "Rosh Hashanah," is the "Head of the Year," *i.e.,* the Jewish New Year and the feast which commemorates the creation of the world. Traditionally, the *shofar,* or ram's horn, is blown to summon the Jewish to religious services.

80{81}[3]   *Take a Psalm, and bring here the timbrel: the pleasant psaltery
with the harp.*

*Sumite psalmum, et date tympanum; psalterium iucundum,
cum cithara.*

And therefore it says: **80{81}[2]** *Exsultate Deo adiutori nostri, rejoice to
God our helper*: that is, to the glory and honor and praise of God, who
helps us in every way by his grace, rejoice in him wholeheartedly and
with great vehemence, so that out of an abundance of interior joy, there
may erupt outwardly signs of that interior rejoicing. For it is said that
exultation (*exultatio*) is, as it were, a leaping outside of one's self (*extra se
saltatio*),[2] namely, since from the fullness of interior joy are manifest external indications of it. *Iubilate Deo Iacob, sing aloud to the God of Jacob*, that
is, rejoice ineffably from within, and sing to God externally with a most
affectionate praise. For jubilation is the happiness of the soul, which by
reason of its surpassing vehemence cannot be fully explained, yet neither
can one be completely silent about it. But the God of all is in a special
way called the God of Jacob, because of the most excellent grace bestowed
upon him. Whence Scripture says of God: He gave *the way of knowledge,
and gave it to Jacob his servant*.[3] **80{81}[3]** *Sumite psalmum, take a Psalm,*
so that with it you might devoutly sing to God, *et date tympanum, and
bring here the timbrel*: that is, praise God not only with the voice, but also
with musical instruments, and with voices sing along with the sounds of
the timbrel. For the Hebrews were accustomed to sing the Psalms with
musical instruments, such as now the Church sings with the organ. And
so bring *psalterium iucundum cum cithara, the pleasant psaltery with the harp*,
praising God with such instruments: in the manner that David instituted.[4]

80{81}[4]   *Blow upon the trumpet on the new moon, on the noted day
of your solemnity,*

Buccinate in neomenia tuba, in insigni die solemnitatis vestrae.

80{81}[5]   *For it is a commandment in Israel, and a judgment to the
God of Jacob.*

Quia praeceptum in Israel est, et iudicium Deo Iacob.

---

2   E. N. Denis suggests that the etymology for the word exultation comes from
the combination of the words *extra se saltatio*, jumping or dancing outside of one's
self, a sort of "leaping for joy."
3   Baruch 3:37.
4   1 Chr. 13:8: *And David and all Israel played before God with all their might with
hymns, and with harps, and with psalteries, and with timbrels, and with cymbals, and with trumpets.*

80{81}[4] *Buccinate in neomenia, blow... on the new moon,* that is, in when the moon is entirely dark, *tuba, upon the trumpet,* formed to give a signal, because Moses ordered a trumpet for this.[5] Now the Jews held a feast at every new moon to memorialize the divine governance.[6] But in the new moon of the seventh month the Feast of the Trumpets generally occurred, and it was in memory of the redemption of Isaac from his sacrifice, as we read about in Leviticus,[7] and with the Hebrews this feast was particularly solemn. And so [the Psalm verse] adds: *in insigni die solemnitatis vestrae, on the noted day of your solemnity,* that is, in the solemn Feast of the Trumpets. Now why they ought to do this is disclosed: 80{81}[5] *Quia praeceptum in Israel est, for it is a commandment in Israel,* because the Lord ordered this to be done among the Iraelite people, as is contained in the book of Numbers.[8] *Et iudicium Deo Iacob, and a judgment to the God of Jacob*: that is, this commandment is by the God of Jacob, who dictated it justly. Or [one can interpret it] thus: *a judgment to the God of Jacob,* the judgment of damnation will be of Jacob, that is, the people born from Jacob, by the just God of all men, if these people fail to fulfill this precept.

80{81}[6] *He ordained it for a testimony in Joseph, when he came out of the land of Egypt: he heard a tongue which he knew not.*

Testimonium in Ioseph posuit illud, cum exiret de terra Aegypti; linguam quam non noverat audivit.

80{81}[7] *He removed his back from the burdens: his hands had served in baskets.*

Divertit ab oneribus dorsum eius; manus eius in cophino servierunt.

80{81}[6] *Testimonium in Ioseph posuit illud, he ordained it for a testimony in Joseph*: that is, God declared this precept with the attestation

---

5 Num. 10:2: *Make two trumpets of beaten silver, wherewith you may call together the multitude when the camp is to be removed.*
6 E. N. The new moon of every month is celebrated as a minor feast, the so-called "Rosh Hodesh," or "Head of the Month."
7 Lev. 23:24: *Say to the children of Israel: The seventh month, on the first day of the month, you shall keep a sabbath, a memorial, with the sound of trumpets, and it shall be called holy.*
8 Num. 29:1: *The first day also of the seventh month shall be venerable and holy unto you; you shall do no servile work therein, because it is the day of the sounding and of trumpets.*

of the testimony of Joseph, that is, the Jewish people figured by Joseph, because Jacob bestowed the first-born status upon him,[9] and he was more holy and of higher estate that his other brothers.[10] *Cum exiret, when he came out,* [when] Joseph, that is, the Jewish people, [came out], *de terra Aegypti, of the land of Egypt* by the hand of Moses. *Linguam quam non noverat audivit, he heard a tongue which he knew not,* that is, he took on the divine law given by God through Moses, which he had not known before. This is said [for one of two reasons]. [First,] either because the Jewish people heard God when they approached mount Sinai, or more likely because the angel of God spoke to them from the middle of the fire,[11] for which reason they — being terrified — said to Moses: *Let not the Lord speak to us, lest we die; you speak to us.*[12] For this reason Moses said: *Behold the Lord our God has shown us his majesty . . . and we have proved this day that God speaking with man, man has lived; we have heard his voice out of the midst of the fire.*[13] Or [second,] that which is said — *he heard a tongue which he knew not* — could possibly refer to the fact that the children of Israel who were born and educated in Egypt did not know the languages they heard when they came upon the lands of the Amorites, the Midianites, the Moabites, and the Edomites, *etc.* 80{81}[7] *Diverti ab oneribus dorsum eius, he removed his back from the burdens:* that is, God delivered by deportation the Jewish people from the burdens which they carried in the land of Egypt under the rule of the Pharaoh, building for them cities of tabernacles, as is made known in Exodus;[14] *manus eius in cophino servierunt, his hands had served in baskets.* For the children of Israel gathered together and carried away in baskets bricks or whatever other things were necessary to building.

---

9 1 Chr. 5:1: *Now the sons of Ruben the firstborn of Israel, for he was his firstborn: but forasmuch as he defiled his father's bed, his first birthright was given to the sons of Joseph the son of Israel, and he was not accounted for the firstborn.*

10 E. N. The commentary in this section will be confusing because the masculine singular pronoun "he" (*eius*) referring to Joseph, refers to an individual as well as a people, which in Latin normally takes a neuter singular personal pronoun "it," but which is the same as the masculine (*eius*), but in English "people" is ordinarily referred by a plural personal pronoun "they." The third person singular is also used to refer to God. There simply is no way to ameliorate the issue, except to warn the reader that "he," "it," "they" all have the same referent: Joseph as the Jewish people.

11 E. N. Cf. Ex. 14:19; Ex. 23:20–16.

12 Ex. 20:19. E. N. Denis reverses order of the verse from: *You to us, and we will hear: let not the Lord speak to us, lest we die.*

13 Deut. 5:24. E. N. Denis also takes liberty with the arrangement of this verse.

14 Ex. 1:11.

80{81}[8] *You called upon me in affliction, and I delivered you: I heard
you in the secret place of tempest: I proved you at the waters
of contradiction.*

*In tribulatione invocasti me, et liberavi te. Exaudivi te in
abscondito tempestatis; probavi te apud aquam contradictionis.*

And now the Prophet [David] changes person, and speaks in the person
of God, stating 80{81}[8] *In tribulatione invocasti me, you called upon
me in affliction,* that is, O Jewish people, you cried out to me for your
delivery when you were in Egypt afflicted by virtue of your labors and
the Egyptian people, resulting in the bitterness of your life;[15] *et liberavi
te, and I delivered you* by a strong hand and great signs. For this the Lord
said to Moses: *The cry of the children of Israel is come unto me, . . . and I
am come down to deliver them.*[16] *Exaudivi te in abscondito tempestatis, I
have heard you in the secret place of tempest,* that is, in the hidden affliction
of your heart, when you sighed to me groaning, not daring directly to
invoke or to complain to me because of fear of the Egyptians; *provabi
te apud aquam contradictionis, I proved you at the waters of contradiction,*
that is, I showed your ingratitude and perversity at that place. Whence
in the book of Numbers we read: *This is the water of contradiction, where
the children of Israel strove with words against the Lord.*[17] This can also
refer in a special way to Moses and Aaron, who offended God at this
place because of their disbelief, for which reason they were prohibited
from entering the promised land, the Lord saying to them: *Because you
have not believed me, to sanctify me before the children of Israel, you shall
not bring these people into the land, which I will give them.*[18]

80{81}[9] *Hear, O my people, and I will testify to you: O Israel, if you
will hearken to me,*

Audi, populus meus, et contestabor te: Israel, si audieris me,

80{81}[10] *There shall be no new god in you: neither shall you adore a
strange god.*

Non erit in te deus recens, neque adorabis deum alienum.

---

15 Ex. 2:23.
16 Ex. 3:9a, 8a.
17 Num. 20:13. The "waters of contradiction" are known also as the "waters of
Meribah." *See* footnote 73–35
18 Num. 20:12.

80{81}[11] *For I am the Lord your God, who brought you out of the land of Egypt: open your mouth wide, and I will fill it.*

Ego enim sum Dominus Deus tuus, qui eduxi te de terra Aegypti. Dilata os tuum, et implebo illud.

80{81}[9] *Audi, populus meus;* hear, O my people, [my] peculiar [people], the word of my Law with the ears of your heart and body, *et contestabor te, and I will testify to you,* that is, I will testify of my words, and of your works: according to this, *I am the judge and the witness, says the Lord.*[19] *Israel,* that is, the Israelite people, *si audieris me, if you will hearken to me,* that is, if you will fulfill the precepts of my Law, 80{81}[10] *non erit in te deus recens, there shall be no new god in you,* whom you worship: for you will not turn towards anything temporal or created as your god; *neque adorabis deum alienum, neither shall you adore a strange god,* but [you shall adore] me, the one, true, and eternal God.[20] 80{81}[11] *Ego enim sum Dominus Deus tuus, qui eduxi te de terra Aegypti; for I am the Lord your God, who brought you out of the land of Egypt,* and even now I am still ready to give many benefits. For *dilata os tuum, open your mouth wide,* that is, open your desire so as to receive, and your bodily mouth so as to request, *et implebo illud, and I will fill it* with my grace, giving to you that which you ask for.

80{81}[12] *But my people heard not my voice: and Israel hearkened not to me.*

Et non audivit populus meus vocem meam, et Israel non intendit mihi.

80{81}[13] *So I let them go according to the desires of their heart: they shall walk in their own inventions.*

Et dimisi eos secundum desideria cordis eorum; ibunt in adinventionibus suis.

Following this, the people exhibited ingratitude. 80{81}[12] *Et non audivit populus meus, but my people heard not* with the ears of the heart *vocem meam, my voice,* that is, the words of my precepts; *et Israel non intendit mihi, and Israel hearkened not to me,* that is, it did not advert to nor give any regard to me. But it appears marvelous that God called a

---

19 Jer. 29:23. E. N. "For the Lord is our judge, the Lord is our lawgiver, the Lord is our king: he will save us." Is. 33:22.
20 Ex. 20:3, 2.

rebellious and disobedient people *his* people, especially when he said of such people through the prophet Hosea: *You are not my people, and* I am not your God.[21] To respond to this: it is frequently said, as it is even today, that the people of the Jews are called the people of God (even if [strictly] false) to the extent that they were called by God out of all other nations, and he honored them with many benefits. And so the Lord said through Jeremiah: *As the girdle sticks close to the loins of a man, so have I brought close to me all of the house of Israel . . . that they might be my people, and for a name, and for a praise, and for a glory: but they would not hear.*[22] And so also are they called beloved by God according to that which the Lord says to them: *What is the meaning that my beloved has wrought much wickedness in my house?*[23] Not that they truly and finally were beloved by God, of whom is said [in a Psalm] above, *You hate all the workers of iniquity;*[24] but they are called beloved in so far as the benefits displayed to them by God in the present. But immediately added [to the verse] are the heavy punishments arising from their ingratitude: 80{81}[13] *Et dimisi eos secundum desideria cordis eorum, so I let them go according to the desires of their heart:* that is, I withdrew my grace; and this grace, once it was removed, meant they were not preserved from fault; rather, they followed their disordered desires, and they adhered to their own thoughts and inclinations. For this reason is added: *ibunt in adinventionibus suis, they shall walk in their inventions,* that is, they will live and will perdure in their errors and the vices thought up by them.

80{81}[14] *If my people had heard me: if Israel had walked in my ways: Si populus meus audisset me, Israel si in viis meis ambulasset,*

80{81}[15] *Perhaps for nothing I have humbled their enemies and laid my hand on them that troubled them.*[25]

Pro nihilo forsitan inimicos eorum humiliassem, et super tribulantes eos misissem manum meam.

80{81}[14] *Si populus meus audisset me, if my people had heard me,* that is, my Law, *Israel si in viis meis, if Israel . . . in my ways,* that is, in

---

21 Hosea 1:9b.
22 Jer. 13:11.
23 Jer. 11:15a.
24 Ps. 5:7a.
25 E. N. I have departed from the Douay-Rheims, exchanging "I should soon" with "perhaps for nothing" to translate *pro nihilo forsitan.* It is more literal and fits in more conveniently with Denis's *Commentary.*

the observance of my commandments, *ambulasset, had walked;* 80{81} [15] *Pro nihilo, for nothing,* that is, as if for nothing or freely,[26] *forsitan, perhaps,* that is, certainly,[27] in the way that they themselves persevered in my ways, *inimicos eorum humiliassem, I have humbled their enemies,* that is, I have destroyed the seven peoples of the land of promise[28] and the rest of the nations that were their enemies, and I have subjugated their power, as I often promised through Moses; *et super tribulantes eos, and . . . on them that troubled them,* that is, on their persecutors, *misissem manum meam, I have laid my hand,* that is, I have extended my power and the vengeance of my justice.

80{81}[16]   *The enemies of the Lord have lied to him: and their time shall be forever.*

Inimici Domini mentiti sunt ei, et erit tempus eorum in saecula.

80{81}[17]   *And he fed them with the fat of wheat, and filled them with honey out of the rock.*

Et cibavit eos ex adipe frumenti, et de petra melle saturavit eos.

80{81}[16] *Inimici Domini, the enemies of the Lord,* that is, the ungrateful Jews: of whom Moses said, *Listen, you rebellious and incredulous* people; *mentiti sunt ei, have lied to him,* that is, [they have lied to God] to their own injury, because they did not fulfill that which they had promised when they said, *All things that the Lord has spoken we will do.*[29] For a short time thereafter they adored the golden calf. *Et erit tempus eorum in saecula, and their time shall be forever:* that is, their condemnation and punishment will last for eternity, because they will be tormented without end in hell. Whence, the Lord said to Moses: *I in the day of revenge will*

---

26   E. N. Denis does not explain what "for nothing" means, but it suggests that the *motive* of the Jews to observe the commandments of God should not be contingent upon God humbling their enemies. There should be no *quid pro quo.* In other words, the Jews (like Christians) should obey the commandments "for nothing," for no reward, simply and completely out of obedient love.

27   E. N. Denis is not equating *forsitan* (perhaps) with *certitudinaliter* (certainty), but rather is saying that the humbling of the enemies is certainly tied to the perseverance of his people, and that it is only as certain as that perseverance. The fickle people's failure to persevere in God's law — and not God's immutable constancy — is what adds the element of uncertainty, resulting in the victory of the Lord's enemies over his people.

28   Ex. 3:8, 13:5, 23:23, 33:2 and elsewhere. These are the so-called seven nations, sometimes collectively or generically called the Canaanites, though composed of seven different tribes (Canaanites, Hittites, Amorites, Perezzites, Hivites, Jebusites, and the Girgashites).

29   Ex. 24:7b.

visit this sin also of theirs.[30] **80{81}[17]** *Et cibavit eos, and he fed them,* that is, notwithstanding the previously-mentioned ingratitude of the Jews, God fed them *ex adipe frumenti, with the fat of wheat,* namely, the heavenly bread or manna,[31] which indeed was sweet and as if it was made from flour and fat. Or [alternatively] thus: *he fed them with the fat of wheat:* because after they entered the land of promise that was abundant with wheat, he fed them with bread made from wheat flour.[32] *Et de petra melle saturavit eos, and filled them with honey out of the rock,* that is, with honey emanating from rock. For the land of promise was said to flow with milk and honey, since the bees in the cliffs of the land of promise made honey, and so honey was said to be amply and copiously produced from the rocky places.

ARTICLE LIV

TROPOLOGICAL OR MORAL EXPLANATION
OF THE SAME EIGHTIETH PSALM.

80{81}[1] *Unto the end, for the wine presses, the fifth day of the week, a Psalm for Asaph.*

In finem, pro torcularibus, quinta sabbati, psalmus ispsi Asaph.

OLLOWING A SPIRITUAL UNDERSTANDING, the title of this Psalm mentioned at the beginning of the prior exposition, is explained in this manner: **80{81}[1]** This *Psalmus, Psalm,* directs us *in finem, unto the end* who is Christ, was set forth and sung *ipsi Asaph, for Asaph,* that is, for the congregation of the faithful which is designated by Asaph; and he created this Psalm *pro torcularibus, for the wine presses,* that is, about those tribulations or the pressing down of tribulations upon the afflicted Church by which evil men are separated from good men: which separation is designated by the words *quinta sabbati, the fifth day from the sabbath,* that is, the fifth day of the week, in which the fish and birds were brought forth from the water; and the fish remained in the water, but the birds ascended up toward the air. By this is prefigured what will be contained in the Church of Christ. For all Christians are spiritually produced and reborn in the fount of Baptism;

---

30 Ex. 32:34b.
31 Ex. 16:15, 31.
32 Joshua 5:11.

but some of them remain upon the earth adhering to transitory things, the rest fly upward on high loving heavenly things.

80{81}[2] *Rejoice to God our helper: sing aloud to the God of Jacob.*

Exsultate Deo adiutori nostro, iubilate Deo Iacob.

And so, O all of the congregation of the children of the Church, 80{81}[2] *Exsultate Deo adiutori nostro, rejoice to God our helper,* namely, [rejoice in] the most high Trinity, the one God, *iubilate Deo Iacob, sing aloud to the God of Jacob,* that is, the supplanter of vices.[33] For by Jacob, which is interpreted as meaning supplanter, is understood those that are tramplers of vices. This verse overflows with spiritual joyousness, since it is a most joyful exhortation and most wholesome admonition—in short, it is an angelic doctrine. For what else is so heavenly, angelic, deiform, and splendid as to exult in God and to take joy in the Lord, rejoicing together in the infinite perfection of the Creator, the infinite beatitude of the Godhead, the infinite joyfulness of the most eminently glorious Trinity? This, of course, is the most excellent exercise of the highest virtue, namely, divine charity, something which cannot be more sublime in this world.[34] For the more we rejoice with a sincere heart in the dignity and glory of our Lord God, the more we acknowledge more ardently to love him; for we exist more nobly and godlike where we love God more earnestly, because divine love, that is, the actual delight of the most blessed Godhead, is the highest nobility of the created mind.

80{81}[3] *Take a Psalm, and bring here the timbrel: the pleasant psaltery with the harp.*

Sumite psalmum, et date tympanum; psalterium iucundum, cum cithara.

80{81}[3] *Sumite psalmum, take a Psalm,* that is, receive a good work by the grace of God: for no act is possible without the power of God, because (as the Apostle says) he it is who works in us *both to will and to accomplish, according to his good will.*[35] About which Isaiah says: *Lord, you*

---

33 *E. N. See* footnote 21-112. The name "Jacob" is interpreted as supplanter because he supplanted his brother Esau by obtaining the latter's birthright for a mess of pottage and by obtaining his blessing by trick. Gen. 27:26.

34 *E. N.* That is, the most sublime state a human soul can enjoy in this life is to be in a state of sanctifying grace, *i.e.,* to be in a state of faith formed by charity.

35 Phil. 2:13. *E. N.* Denis appears to be referring to the doctrine of divine concurrence,

will give us peace: for you have wrought all our works for us.[36] Whence also Jesus says to his disciples: *As the branch cannot bear fruit of itself, unless it abide in the vine, so neither can you, unless you abide in me.*[37] *Et date tympanum, and bring here the timbrel,* that is, render a sweet sound, one pleasing to the ear of God: which, of course, is not properly speaking referring to a sensible or exterior sound, but an intellectual one, namely, the mortification of the flesh and holy chastity, which also is a good odor. For in the way that a timbrel, that is, hide is stretched over wood, does not sound sweetly unless it is struck, so flesh wearied and weakened with the penitential punishments of scourges pleases the Lord, and the performing of such works sounds before the most High. Take also *psalterium iucundum cum cithara, the pleasant psaltery with the harp.* The psaltery which has its soundbox on top and ten strings stands for the Decalogue of the law given by God. But the harp has six strings, and its soundbox is on the bottom, and its stands for the six works of mercy.[38] Therefore [it should be understood] in this sense: Take *the pleasant psaltery with the harp,* that is, fulfill the precepts of the divine law, making yourself open to heavenly things: but with a harp, namely simultaneously exercise yourself in the works of mercy, because you ought not to be so attentive to heavenly things that you neglect to provide aid to your neighbors in need.

80{81}[4] *Blow upon the trumpet on the new moon, on the noted day of your solemnity,*

  Buccinate in neomenia tuba, in insigni die solemnitatis vestrae.

80{81}[5] *For it is a commandment in Israel, and a judgment to the God of Jacob.*

  Quia praeceptum in Israel est, et iudicium Deo Iacob.

---

which has both a natural component (*concursus naturalis*) and a supernatural component (*concursus supernaturalis*), with a clear emphasis on the latter. Because our good works are not meritorious unless done in God's grace, we can be said to *"receive our good works* by the grace of God."

36 Is. 25:12.

37 John 15:4.

38 E. N. The biblical pericope that provides the "six works of mercy" is Matthew 25:31–46 (feeding the hungry, giving drink to the thirsty, sheltering the homeless, clothing the naked, and visiting the sick and imprisoned). However, in the Middle Ages a seventh work of mercy, "burying the dead," was added, which is based upon the book of Tobit (Tobit 1:16–17). Sometimes redeeming those in prison was also added. However, the list has been standardized to for centuries as the "seven works of mercy." See CCC § 2447.

80{81}[4] *Buccinate, blow,* O Christian faithful, that is, by a public proclamation of God, boldly and with loving sound, [publicly proclaim] your sinfulness and the example of your neighbors, so that you might praise God, disparage yourselves, and might warn your neighbors; *in neomenia, on the new moon,* that is, at the start of your illumination by the Sun of Justice, namely, *in insigni die solemnitatis [interioris] vestrae, on the noted day of your* internal *solemnity,* when, namely, the Holy Spirit comes to you, and makes his abode in you:[39] for then you must freely communicate to others the grace that has been given to you. So, then, blow *tuba, the trumpet,* that is, the word of God: 80{81}[5] *quia praeceptum in Israel est, for it is a commandment in Israel,* that is, it is the divine command to the Church of Christians who have caught sight of God by faith to do just that. For Christ in the Gospel condemns that servant who hides the talents given to him.[40] And Paul wishes that we not seek those things that are our own, but those things which are another's.[41] For this reason in Ecclesiasticus is written: *Wisdom that is hid, and treasure that is not seen: what profit is there in them both?*[42] And so that most excellent prince of the apostolic order, manifestly and clearly speaking, says: *Every man as he has received grace, [should be] ministering the same one to another: as good stewards of the manifold grace of God.*[43]

80{81}[6]   *He ordained it for a testimony in Joseph, when he came out of the land of Egypt: he heard a tongue which he knew not.*

Testimonium in Ioseph posuit illud, cum exiret de terra Aegypti; linguam quam non noverat audivit.

80{81}[7]   *He removed his back from the burdens: his hands had served in baskets.*

Divertit ab oneribus dorsum eius; manus eius in cophino servierunt.

80{81}[6] *Testimonium in Ioseph posuit illud, he ordained it for a testimony in Joseph,* that is, in the people converted from the Gentiles to Christ and added to the Church. For Joseph is interpreted to mean "increase"; and so by that name is designated the increases from the

---

39   *Cf.* John 14:23b: *If any one love me, he will keep my word, and my Father will love him, and we will come to him, and will make our abode with him.*

40   Matt. 25:24–30.

41   *Cf.* 1 Cor. 10:24: *Let no man seek his own, but that which is another's.*

42   Ecclus. 20:32; see also Ecclus. 41:17b.

43   1 Pet. 4:10.

Gentiles engendered by faith in Christ: and God attested to this aforesaid precept, as is clear from the aforementioned authorities.[44] *Cum exiret de terra Aegypti, when he came out of the land of Egypt,* that is, when the Gentiles believing in Christ left their former darkness, vices, and ignorance. *Linguam quam non noverat, audivit; he heard a tongue which he knew not,* that is, then they began to hear the evangelical proclamation and the apostolic teaching, which they had not known before. For this reason the Athenians stated to Paul: We want to know what this new doctrine stated by you is. *For you bring in certain new things to our ears.*[45] Also, at the time this people from Egypt left Egypt God **80{81}** **[7]** *divertit ab oneribus dorsum eius, removed his back from the burdens,* that is, [God relieved the converted Gentiles] from the burden of their vices, from their slavery to sin, from the yoke of the world, the flesh, and the devil. For Christ cried out to such people: *Come to me, all you that labor, and are burdened, and I will refresh you.*[46] *Manus eius, his hands,* that is, the acts of this people before they converted to God, *in cophino, in baskets,* that is, in vessels of uncleanness and of sordid vices, *sevierunt, they served* the law of sin, indeed, [they served] sin and the devil. For while a sinner remains immersed in his vices, he has the hand of his works in a vessel of sin, that is, in some disordered activity, or in a perverse will, in which fault is founded.[47]

---

44   E. N. This section suffers from the same problem discussed in footnote 80-10. The commentary in this section will be confusing because the masculine singular pronoun "he" (*eius*) referring to Joseph, refers to an individual as well as the converted Gentiles, which in English would be referred by a plural personal pronoun "they." The third person singular is also used to refer to God. There simply is no way to ameliorate the issue, except to warn the reader that "he," "it," "they" all have the same referent: Joseph as the converted Gentiles.

45   Acts 17:19–20.

46   Matt. 11:28.

47   E. N. Denis is referring to two of the three so-called fonts or sources of morality (*fontes moralitatis*), which are the factors that together combine to define the goodness (or evil) of a moral act. A fundamental moral principle is that all three fonts must be good, and a defect in, or absence of, one or more of the fonts vitiates the act and makes it evil, regardless of the goodness of the others. Thus the axiom: *bonum ex integra causa, malum ex quocumque defectu*: an act is good if all three fonts are good, but the absence of, or evil in, any one of them makes the act evil. "The morality of human acts depends on three sources: the object [or the end] chosen, either a true or apparent good; the intention [purpose, or motive] of the subject who acts, that is, the purpose for which the subject performs the act; and the circumstances of the act, which include its consequences." "An act is morally good when it assumes simultaneously the goodness of the object, of the end, and of the circumstances." *Compendium of the Catechism* §§ 367, 358; *see also* CCC §§ 1749–60.

80{81}[8] *You called upon me in affliction, and I delivered you: I heard*
you in the secret place of tempest: I proved you at the waters
of contradiction.

In tribulatione invocasti me, et liberavi te. Exaudivi te in
abscondito tempestatis; probavi te apud aquam contradictionis.

And so Christ says to the Church, and to any one of the devout:
80{81}[8] *In tribulatione, in affliction,* that is, in persecution, temptation,
or any other distress, *invocasti me, you have called upon me:* which is
the most secure and most salubrious remedy. And so whenever we are
afflicted, whether by a demon, or whether by evil men, or whether by
our own passions, we ought to invoke God with all trust and constancy,
and in this way we will be made secure: for we will be heard, as it states
subsequently. *Et liberavi te; exaudivi te in abscondito tempestatis; and I*
delivered you, I heard you in the secret place of tempest, at the time of
diabolical suggestion or deepest afflictions, when you were unable to take
refuge with anyone else. And so this ought to be the utmost and only
consolation to everyone that is afflicted, since it is most certain that God
is especially at hand to those who are afflicted, because he is prompt to
render them aid, as is said in a Psalm above: *The Lord is nigh unto them*
that are of a contrite heart.[48] And this is also attested in a later Psalm:
I [God] am with him in tribulation.[49] Therefore, perfect men rejoice in
tribulations, and because of God's presence they gladly proceed through
them, but they pray to God for patience and fortitude of soul. *Probavi*
te apud aquam contradictionis, I proved you at the waters of contradiction,
that is, during whatever adversity and opposition is resisted by doing
good against the enemies of your salvation, namely, the world, the flesh,
and the devil. For the adversity and opposition which man suffers by
those things which endeavor to prevent him from doing good works
while he is in the way of God reveal whether man truly and faithfully
adheres to God. Whence Moses said: *The way . . . the Lord your God*
has brought you . . . to afflict you and to prove you, and that the things that
were in your heart might be made known, whether you would keep his com-
mandments or no.[50] And this is the reason why God allows his servants
to suffer such impediments, namely, so that they might be proved, and
they might know whether they sincerely seek justice, and they might
acquire a greater degree of grace, and they might show an example to

---

48   Ps. 33:19a.
49   Ps. 90:15a.
50   Deut. 8:2.

others. For this reason, it is written: *As gold in the furnace the Lord has proved the elect, and as a victim of a holocaust he has received them.*[51]

80{81}[9] *Hear, O my people, and I will testify to you: O Israel, if you will hearken to me,*

    Audi, populus meus, et contestabor te: Israel, si audieris me,

80{81}[10] *There shall be no new god in you: neither shall you adore a strange god.*

    Non erit in te deus recens, neque adorabis deum alienum.

80{81}[11] *For I am the Lord your God, who brought you out of the land of Egypt: open your mouth wide, and I will fill it.*

    Ego enim sum Dominus Deus tuus, qui eduxi te de terra Aegypti. Dilata os tuum, et implebo illud.

80{81}[9] *Audi, populus meus; hear, O my people,* who were called Christian by me; who also may be said to be Israel, looking attentively upon God with faith. You therefore *si audieris me, if you will hearken to me,*[52] fulfilling my precepts, so that you love God with all your soul, all your heart, and all your strength,[53] **80{81}[10]** *non erit in te deus recens, there shall be no new god in you,* that is, you will not forsake me, nor will you adhere to anything else more than me. You will not serve a creature more than your Creator;[54] you will not love gluttony of the belly, lust of the flesh, honor of the world, temporal goods or money more than me, the highest and immutable good. For he who abandons chastity and serves pleasure takes up a new god: because the god of lust is his beloved, and the god of gluttony is his belly; [and the god] of avarice is money. For that thing that someone thinks about most often is that which he loves and serves, and this proves to be his god. **80{81}[11]** *Ego enim, for I* the Only-Begotten of God who became incarnate for you, *sum Dominus Deus tuus, qui eduxi te de terra Aegypti; am the Lord your God, who brought you out of the land of Egypt,* that is, *from this present wicked world,*[55] namely, out of the gloom of fault and the

---

51 Wis. 3:6.

52 E. N. Denis skips over the center of this verse — "and I will testify to you" without comment.

53 Deut. 6:5.

54 Cf. Rom. 1:25: *The perverse, who changed the truth of God into a lie; and worshipped and served the creature rather than the Creator, who is blessed forever. Amen.*

55 Gal. 1:4a.

darkness of ignorance, by the merits of my death and the price of my Blood, by the baptismal grace, by infused virtues, and by the manifold illumination of the Holy Spirit.

Dilata os tuum, et implebo illud; open your mouth wide, and I will fill it, that is, I will dispose you to grace, and you will receive it. Beg for my mercy, and I will give you my mercy; invite me to be a guest in your heart, and I will enter into it. For *I stand at the gate and knock.*[56] Pray for enlightenment within, and I will give you the brightness of wisdom, in the manner that my Apostle assures, saying: *If any of you want wisdom, let him ask of God, . . . and it shall be given him. But let him ask in faith, nothing wavering.*[57] At the very minimum, he will receive that wisdom which is the gift of the Holy Spirit,[58] which is allotted to everyone who has sanctifying grace.[59] And so, *open your mouth wide,* that is, open your heart and remove any impediment, and *I will fill it,* my hand is not shortened so that it has not the power to save.[60]

80{81}[12]   *But my people heard not my voice: and Israel hearkened not to me.*

Et non audivit populus meus vocem meam, et Israel non intendit mihi.

80{81}[13]   *So I let them go according to the desires of their heart: they shall walk in their own inventions.*

Et dimisi eos secundum desideria cordis eorum; ibunt in adinventionibus suis.

80{81}[12] *Et non audivit populus meus,* but *my people heard not,* [that is, my people] who are only in name Christian, or [are Christian] by faith, but not through charity; who say *that they know God* yet *in their works deny him;*[61] *vocem meam, my voice,* that is, the precepts and the exhortations of Sacred Scripture. For the reprobate are called the people of Christ in such a fashion, in the manner that he himself says about some in the Gospel: *Friend, how came you in here not having a wedding*

---

56   Rev. 3:20a.
57   James 1:5–6a.
58   Is. 11:2.
59   E. N. Literally, *gratiam gratum facientem,* the grace the makes one pleasing or ingratiates us to God; in this context meaning sanctifying grace.
60   *Cf.* Is. 59:1a.
61   Titus 1:16a.

garment?[62] And as he said regarding some others: *He came unto his own, and his own received him not.*[63] And so, 80{81}[13] *et dimisi eos secundum desideria cordis eorum,* so *I let them go according to the desires of their heart.* This is the greatest vengeance of God, when he abandons men to themselves on the grounds of their sins. For this is as evil [a condition] as it is a good [condition] to be preserved by God, to be filially corrected in the present life, and to be kept from vice. Whence to prosper now in all things at one's pleasure, to be left by God to one's own desires, and not to be chastised like his adopted children is a most certain sign of divine reprobation and future damnation. For the Lord says: *Such as I love, I rebuke and chastise.*[64] And also the Apostle says to the Hebrews: *What son is there, whom the father does not correct? But if you be without chastisement, whereof all are made partakers, then are you bastards, and not sons*[65] And this is also what Solomon warns about: *My son, reject not the correction of the Lord: and do not faint when you are chastised by him: For whom the Lord loves, he chastises: and as a father in the son he pleases himself.*[66] If, therefore, we seek to be blessed, let us desire in the present life to correct our deviations [from the true and the good], thinking with a most judicious mind that which is in the book of Job: *Blessed is the man whom God corrects: refuse not therefore the chastising of the Lord, for he wounds, and he cures.*[67] This moreover, the angel told Tobias: *Because you were acceptable to God, it was necessary that temptation should prove you.*[68] Whence Scripture attests of all the elect as distinguished from other persons: *Not — as with other nations whom the Lord patiently expects, that when the day of judgment shall come, he may punish them in the fulness of their sins — does he also deal with us, so as to suffer our sins to come to their height, and then take vengeance on us. And therefore he never withdraws his mercy from us: but though he chastise his people with adversity, he forsakes them not.*[69] And with these words [the book of Maccabees] precedes that which I am often mindful of: *For it is a token of great goodness when sinners are not suffered to go on in their ways for a long time, but are presently punished.*[70]

---

62 Matt. 22:12.
63 John 1:11.
64 Rev. 3:19a.
65 Heb. 12:7b–8.
66 Prov. 3:11–12.
67 Job 5:17–18a.
68 Tob. 12:13
69 2 Macc. 6:14–16.
70 2 Macc. 6:13.

80{81}[14] *If my people had heard me: if Israel had walked in my ways:*

Si populus meus audisset me, Israel si in viis meis ambulasset,

80{81}[15] *I should perhaps for nothing have humbled their enemies and laid my hand on them that troubled them.*[71]

Pro nihilo forsitan inimicos eorum humiliassem, et super tribulantes eos misissem manum meam.

80{81}[14] Si populus meus audisset me, [Israel si in viis meis ambulasset]; *If my people had heard me: [if Israel had walked in my ways]* **80{81}[15]** pro nihilo forsitan inimicos eorum inimicos eoru humiliassem, *I should perhaps for nothing have humbled their enemies*, both visible and invisible, because I humble the proud, and I vigorously humiliate the proud demons, since I cause them to be vanquished by, and to flee from, my humble servants. And so the Apostle [Paul] states: *The God of peace crush Satan under your feet speedily.*[72] Et super tribulantes eos misissem manum meam, *and I laid my hand on them that troubled them*, overpowering them, at least after the end of the present life, and protecting the elect.

80{81}[16] *The enemies of the Lord have lied to him: and their time shall be forever.*

Inimici Domini mentiti sunt ei, et erit tempus eorum in saecula.

80{81}[16] Inimici Domini, *the enemies of the Lord*, that is, evil Christians: of which the Gospel says, *My enemies, who would not have me reign over them, bring them here, and kill them before me;*[73] mentiti sunt ei, *[they] have lied to him*, that is, they have broken those promises which they made at the Baptism font, promising to renounce Satan and his works. Also, all who return to their former vices after Confession, penance, and Holy Communion, and who do not strive *to walk solicitous* before God,[74] are enemies of Christ and are lying to him. Et... tempus eorum, *and... their time* of damnation, erit... in saecula, *shall be forever*, that is, for eternity, because they entered into the eternal fires. Now this is not to be so understood as if there will be time after the day of final judgment. For when the movement of the First Mover ceases, according

---

71 E. N. I have departed from the Douay-Rheims, exchanging "I should soon" with "perhaps for nothing" to translate *pro nihilo forsitan*. It is more literal and fits in more conveniently with Denis's *Commentary*.

72 Rom. 16:20a.

73 Luke 19:27.

74 Micah 6:8b.

to that found in Revelation, time will cease: *The angel ... lifted his hand to heaven, and he swore by him that lives for ever and ever, ... that time shall be no longer.*[75]

80{81}[17] *And he fed them with the fat of wheat, and filled them with honey out of the rock.*

Et cibavit eos ex adipe frumenti, et de petra melle saturavit eos.

80{81}[17] *Et cibavit eos,* and he fed them, namely, Christ fed the Christians, *ex adipe frumenti, with the fat of wheat,* that is, with the Sacrament of his Body under the form of bread of wheat; *et de petra melle, and with honey out of a rock:* that is, honey which designates the sweet effects of the Sacrament of the Body of Christ, namely, spiritual consolation, the infusion of sacramental grace, the fattening of the spirit: with this honey flowing out of a rock, that is Christ, or the merits of his Passion and Blood (for whatever grace in which we participate is given to us by the merits of Christ), *saturavit eos, he filled them* with an interior fulness, giving them the desires of their heart.

See we have regarded this Psalm so replete with spiritual doctrine, which brings to mind divine benefits, and briefly recalls the ingratitude of man and also the vengeance of God. And so let us work to place before our minds all these things, to exult and rejoice in God, to recall his divine benefits, to obtain the grace of the Sacrament of Christ, and let us take heed of this with great and most diligence, lest we find ourselves ungrateful for such inestimable benefits of Christ. And those things which have here [in this article] been omitted have been clearly expounded upon in what has been said before [in the preceding article].

---

75 Rev. 10:5–6.

PRAYER

CAUSE, O LORD, YOUR PEOPLE TO HEAR
your voice; open our mouths, and fill them with the praise of
your grace, so that in the tribulation of the present life you might
hear us who call upon you, and might lead us away from all the
assaults of enemies and of eternal misfortune.

---

*Fac, Domine, populum tuum vocem tuam audire; dilata os
nostrum, et imple illud laude gratiae tuae: ut in
tribulatione praesentis vitae te invocantes nos
exaudias, et ab omni impetu inimicorum
ac tempestatis aeternae subducas.*

Psalm 81

ARTICLE LV

ELUCIDATION OF THE EIGHTY-FIRST PSALM:
DEUS STETIT IN SYNAGOGA DEORUM.
GOD HAS STOOD IN THE CONGREGATION OF GODS.

81{82}[1] *A Psalm for Asaph. God has stood in the congregation of gods: and being in the midst of them he judges gods.*

Psalmus Asaph. Deus stetit in synagoga deorum; in medio autem deos diiudicat.

81{82}[2] *How long will you judge unjustly: and receive the faces of sinners?*[1]

Usquequo iudicatis iniquitatem, et facies peccatorum sumitis?

HIS SHORT PSALM IS PRE-ANNOTATED WITH a brief and easy title, which says 81{82}[1] *Psalmus Asaph, a Psalm for Asaph.* For this Psalm is said to be for Asaph, either because it was composed by him, or because the name Asaph is put forward as designating the congregation. This Psalm is literally written against unjust judges, refuting their perversity, and demanding the divine justice against their injustice.

And it therefore says: *Deus stetit in synagoga deorum, God has stood in the congregation of gods.* The incorporeal and infinite God, in whom, according to the nature of divinity, there is no fixed place or location, is said to stand and to remain in the congregation of gods (that is, in the congregation of judges) because he is everywhere, and he sees, weighs, and judges every word and deed, especially and most conspicuously does he take heed of the judgment of the heart, words, and deeds. Now judges are said to be gods, according to that said in Exodus: *Both parties shall come to the gods,*[2] that is, to the judges. Hence, Moses also said again: *You shall not speak ill of the gods.*[3] *In medio autem, and being in the midst of them,* that is, God existing in the midst of all things; or, *in the midst,* that

---

1   E. N. I have translated *facies peccatorum sumitis* as "you receive the faces of sinners," and departed from the less-literal translation of the Douay-Rheims: "accept the persons of the wicked."

2   Ex. 22:9a.

3   Ex. 22:28a.

is, according to the equality of justice; *deos, gods,* that is, judges, *diudicat, he judges,* that is, he reproves ungodly judges, and he discerns the good judges from the evil ones. Whence in the book of Wisdom is written: *Hear . . . you kings, and understand: learn, you that are judges of the ends of the earth. For power is given you by the Lord, who will examine your works, and search out your thoughts: because being ministers of his kingdom, you have not judged rightly, nor kept the law of justice. . . . Horribly and speedily will he appear to you, for a most severe judgment shall be for them that bear rule.*[4] **81{82}[2]** *Usquequo, how long,* O judges of the ungodly, *iudicatis, will you judge* with approving judgment *iniquitatem, unjustly,* excusing, praising, or hiding it, *et facies peccatorum sumitis, and receive the faces of sinners,* that is, accept the persons of evil, justifying their cause with the love of friendship, or [their dignity of] office, or because of fear of their power. This is greatly iniquitous, and it is against that example of the great king Josaphat, whose words were most fully instructive of all judgments. For of it is written: *Take heed what you do: for you exercise not the judgment of man, but of the Lord: and whatsoever you judge, it shall redound to you. Let the fear of the Lord be with you, and do all things with diligence.*[5]

> **81{82}[3]** *Judge for the needy and fatherless: do justice to the humble and the poor.*
>
> *Iudicate egeno et pupillo; humilem et pauperem iustificate.*
>
> **81{82}[4]** *Rescue the poor; and deliver the needy out of the hand of the sinner.*
>
> *Eripite pauperem, et egenum de manu peccatoris liberate.*

Therefore, the Prophet [David] admonishes the judges to amendment: **81{82}[3]** *Iudicate, judge,* that is, do justice justly, *egeno et pupillo, for the needy and fatherless,* who are unable to defend themselves against the powerful and the rich; *humilem et pauperem, to the humble and the poor* of spirit, and not the avaricious or the ungodly, *iustificate, do justice,* that is, dispose yourself to be just, in accordance with truth. **81{82}[4]** *Eripite pauperem, rescue the poor* from the violating claim of the powerful, and *egeneum de manu peccatoris liberate, and deliver the needy out of the hand of the sinner,* that is, [deliver the needy] from unjust power. Job, who testified about himself, was this kind of judge: *When I sat as a king, with his army standing about him, yet I was a comforter of them*

---

4 Wis. 6:2, 4–6.
5 2 Chr. 19:6–7a.

that mourned.[6] *I was an eye to the blind, and a foot to the lame. I was the father of the poor; and the cause which I knew not, I searched out most diligently.*[7] And this is what the Lord admonished through Isaiah: *Seek judgment, relieve the oppressed, judge for the fatherless, defend the widow.*[8]

81{82}[5] *They have not known nor understood: they walk on in darkness: all the foundations of the earth shall be moved.*

Nescierunt, neque intellexerunt; in tenebris ambulant; movebuntur omnia fundamenta terrae.

The causes of error and unjust judgment of those who are unjust are then introduced: **81{82}[5]** *Nescierunt, they have not known* the rules of right, *neque intellexerunt, nor have they understood* correctly the intention of the legislators or the law; but they understand them as it sounds good to them; *in tenebris, in darkness* of hearts and of deeds, that is, with ill-formed thoughts and by unjust deeds, *ambulant, they walk.* They *movebuntur, shall be moved,* that is, they shall be terrified at the judgment of Christ, especially in the day of judgment, *omnia fundamenta terrae, all the foundations of the earth,* that is, all the earthly princes that should have been a foundation and columns of others. Or [alternatively], all the foundations of the earth *shall be moved,* that is, the first principle of the earth will be moved:[9] because, as Wisdom states, God *will arm the creature for the revenge of his enemies, . . . and the whole world shall fight with him against the unwise.*[10]

81{82}[6] *I have said: you are gods, and all of you the sons of the most High.*

Ego dixi: dii estis, et filii Excelsi omnes.

81{82}[7] *But you like men shall die: and shall fall like one of the princes.*

Vos autem sicut homines moriemini, et sicut unus de principibus cadetis.

81{82}[8] *Arise, O God, judge you the earth: for you shall inherit among all the nations.*

Surge, Deus, iudica terram, quoniam tu haereditabis in omnibus gentibus.

---

6   Job 19:25b.
7   Job 19:15–16.
8   Is. 1:17.
9   Cf. Luke 21:26b: *For the powers of heaven shall be moved.*
10 Wis. 5:18, 21b.

However much, O evil judges, you thirst because of your abuses and malice for such unworthy things, so **81{82}[6]** *Ego dixi: dii sunt; I have said: you are gods* because I have called you gods through Moses because of the power bestowed upon you,[11] and because to you these words of God are directed. Christ asserted these words when speaking to the Jews, saying: In your law is written: *I said you are gods, to whom the word of God was spoken.*[12] But judges are called gods, not by nature, but by their participation in a divine property, namely, because they ought to provide and preside over others, which is something that corresponds properly to God. *Et filii excelsi omnes, and all of you the sons of the most High.* This can be taken in two ways, according to whether the words *most High* are received in singular sense or in a plural sense.[13] For if it is understood in a singular sense [it can be understood as follows]: You, judges, are sons *of the most High*, namely of the most sublime God, for you are created in the image of God.[14] But if it is assumed plural, the sense is this: You judges are *most high* sons, that is, you are sublime because you preside and rule over other sons of men. **81{82}[7]** *Vos autem sicut homines ceteri morietur, but you like other men shall die* in your soul when you sin and in the body when that time predetermined by God comes; for none of you has the power to deliver yourselves from death; *et sicut unus de principibus, and . . . like one of the princes*, that is, like the apostate and prideful angels, *cadetis, you shall fall*, now in pit of fault and after a time in the lake of eternal death, unless you now live justly.

And because this revenge can be inflicted by no one other than God, who alone is the *Lord of lords*,[15] and the chief and judge of kings and the judges of the earth,[16] therefore, in order that no evil remains unpunished, Asaph implores the divine judgment. **81{82}[8]** *Surge, Deus; Arise, O God*, that is, proceed, without motion or change, to the act of your justice; *iudica terram, judge you the earth*, that is, all the inhabitants of the earth, or all men, through Jesus Christ whom you appointed judge of all men;[17] *quoniam tu hereditabis in omnibus gentibus, for you shall inherit among all the nations*: that is, all peoples are your inheritance

---

11   Ex, 22L287

12   John 10:34b, 35a.

13   E. N. The word *excelsi* could be used as a plural adjective modifying sons (most high sons) or singular genitive referring to the one God ("of the most High"). Obviously, the translators of the Douay-Rheims have opted for the latter meaning.

14   Gen. 1:27.

15   Rev. 17:14;

16   Rev. 1:5; Heb. 12:23.

17   *Cf.* Acts 10:42.

to the extent that they subject themselves to you, especially in the day of judgment, because from that time the elect will be perfectly and immovably subject to the order of your mercy, but the reprobate to the order of your justice: for fault will then by rendered unto a certain just order by punishment.

ALLEGORICAL EXPOSITION

81{82}[1] ... *God has stood in the congregation of gods: and being in the midst of them he judges gods.*

... *Deus stetit in synagoga deorum; in medio autem deos diiudicat.*

Now Augustine and those who follow him expound upon this Psalm as dealing with Christ and the Jewish priests and scribes, so that it reads in this sense: **81{82}[1]** *Deus,* God, that is Christ, the Son of God become man, of whom John said, *This is the true God and life eternal;*[18] *stetit, stood,* with his bodily feet, *in synagoga deorum, in the congregation of gods:* for he frequently preached and performed miracles in the synagogues and the temple of the Jews, in the way he said to Annas: *I have always taught in the synagogue, and in the temple, where all the Jews congregate.*[19] And when he was twelve years old and he was found in the temple by his Mother, he said: *Did you not know, that I must be about my father's business?*[20] This also was so prophesied by Malachi: *And presently the Lord, whom you seek, and the angel of the testament, whom you desire, shall come to his temple.*[21] Now the priests are called gods because of reason previously given, for they were the princes and the chiefs of the people. *In medio autem,* and being in the midst of midst of the synagogue, Christ, God and man, *deos, gods,* that is, the priests and the leaders of the Jews, *diiudicat, he judges,* that is, refutes, reproves, and condemns. For often (as the Evangelists attested to) Christ rebuked the priests in the temple.[22] For this reason Malachi, speaking of Christ, said: *He like a refining fire, and like the fuller's herb... shall purify the sons of Levi, and shall refine them as gold.*[23]

---

18 1 John 5:20b.
19 John 18:20b.
20 Luke 2:49b.
21 Mal. 3:1.
22 Matt. chp. 23.
23 Mal. 3:2–3.

81{82}[2] *How long will you judge unjustly: and receive the faces of*
sinners?[24]

Usquequo iudicatis iniquitatem, et facies peccatorum sumitis?

81{82}[3] *Judge for the needy and fatherless: do justice to the humble*
and the poor.

Iudicate egeno et pupillo; humilem et pauperem iustificate.

81{82}[4] *Rescue the poor; and deliver the needy out of the hand of the*
sinner.

Eripite pauperem, et egenum de manu peccatoris liberate.

In addition, the Prophet reproves the priests and the teachers of the
temple, and says: **81{82}[2]** *Usquequo iudicatis iniquitatem, how long will you*
judge unjustly, that is, how long will you approve those who rail against the
Lord Savior with their words and assertions, calling him to be a seducer
of men,[25] *et facies peccatorum sumitis, and receive the faces of sinners*, that
is, praise and accept the false witnesses who gave false testimony against
Christ?[26] **81{82}[3]** *Iudicate egeno et pupillo, judge for the needy and*
fatherless, that is, Christ, who was needy because he did not have a place
to lay his head,[27] and [who was] fatherless because as in heaven he had a
Father without a mother, so on earth he had a Mother without a father.[28]
Humilem et pauperem, to the humble and the poor, that is to Christ, who
said, *Learn of me because I am meek and humble of heart*,[29] *iustificate, do*
justice, that is, declare him to be just, and do not allow blasphemies to
be said against him. **81{82}[4]** *Eripite pauperem, rescue the poor* Christ
from death, and not the murderer and thief Barabbas, the very contrary
of which, O chief of the priests, you did, persuading the people so that
they might plead for Barabbas, yet do away with Jesus;[30] *et egenum, and*

---

24   E. N. I have translated *facies peccatorum sumitis* as "receive the faces of sinners,"
and departed from the less-literal translation of the Douay-Rheims: "accept the
persons of the wicked."

25   Matt. 27:63.

26   Matt. 26:59–61.

27   Matt. 8:20.

28   E. N. This was a common theological couplet in the Middle Ages. For example,
Pope Innocent III (*ca.* 1160–1216) uses it in one of his Christmas sermons, PL 217,
460. St. Albert the Great (1206–1280) mentions it in his book on the praises of the
Blessed Virgin Mary, B. Alberti Magni, *De Laudibus B. Mariae Virginis*, I, 6, *Opera*
omnia (Paris:1898), Vol. 36, p. 46.

29   Matt. 11:29.

30   Matt. 27:20.

the needy Christ *de manu peccatoris, out of the hand of the sinner,* namely, the traitor Judas, and from Pilate or Caiaphas, *liberate, deliver.*

81{82}[5] *They have not known nor understood: they walk on in darkness: all the foundations of the earth shall be moved.*

Nescierunt, neque intellexerunt; in tenebris ambulant; movebuntur omnia fundamenta terrae.

81{82}[5] *Nescierunt,* they have not known, these princes of the Jews [have not known] Jesus to be the Christ, because he blinded them in their malice.[31] And if *they had known it, they would never have crucified the Lord of glory.*[32] Whence Peter speaking to the Jews said: *Brethren, I know that you did it through ignorance, as did also your rulers.*[33] *Neque intellexerunt,* they have . . . not understood his doctrine to be from God, but said: *We have found this man perverting our nation.*[34] And they also ascribed his miracles to the prince of the devils.[35] *In tenebris, in the darkness* of perfidy *ambulant,* they walk;[36] therefore, *movebuntur omnia fundamenta terra,* all the foundations of the earth shall be moved: that is, the land of the Jews will be so horribly devastated, destroyed, and their cities will be burned, and their inhabitants will be slain; and that because of the extreme disturbance the land will seem to move and to shake within itself: all of which things were done in the land and upon the people of the Jews by the Romans in vengeance of the blood of Christ, in the manner that Christ predicted.[37]

---

31 *Cf.* Wis. 2:21b.

32 1 Cor. 2:8b.

33 Acts 3:17.

34 Luke 23:2a.

35 Matt. 12:24.

36 E. N. The word "perfidy," although it may plausibly be said to have some negative connotations in English beyond the sin of disbelief, in Latin has no such similar connotation, and is merely a statement of a theological truth that the Jews do not share in the Christian faith, and so do not have the theological virtue of faith as Christians understand it: They do not say "Jesus is Lord." So, in this context, perfidy means simply disbelief of the Christian faith and its central object: Jesus Christ. See generally *Foederatio Internationalis Una Voce (FIUV),* Position Paper 28: The Good Friday Prayer for the Jews in the Extraordinary Form, https://lms.org.uk/sites/default/files/resource_documents/fiuv/pp28_good_friday_prayer.pdf

37 Luke 19:43–44: *For the days shall come upon you [Jerusalem], and your enemies shall cast a trench about you, and compass you round, and straiten you on every side, and beat you flat to the ground, and your children who are in you: and they shall not leave in you a stone upon a stone: because you have not known the time of your visitation.*

81{82}[6] *I have said: You are gods, and all of you the sons of the most High.*

Ego dixi: dii estis, et filii Excelsi omnes.

81{82}[7] *But you like men shall die: and shall fall like one of the princes.*

Vos autem sicut homines moriemini, et sicut unus de principibus cadetis.

81{82}[8] *Arise, O God, judge you the earth: for you shall inherit among*
all the nations.[38]

Surge, Deus, iudica terram, quoniam tu haereditabis in omnibus gentibus.

81{82}[8] *Surge, Deus; arise, O God,* that is, you, Only-Begotten of
God, who lay in the grave while dead, and slept in the sepulcher, rise
from the dead on the third day; *iudica terram, judge you the earth,* that
is, with just judgment condemn those lands and the carnal Jews, in the
manner that you elsewhere bore witness: *I have trampled on them in my*
indignation, and have trodden them down in my wrath.... For the day of
vengeance is in my heart, the year of my redemption is come.[39] *Quoniam tu*
hereditabis in omnibus gentibus, for you shall inherit among all the nations:
that is, for [the loss by disbelief of] the blind and forsaken Jewish people,
you shall take possession by inheritance the whole world through the
preaching of the Apostles, reigning by faith and grace in the hearts of all
people converted to the Catholic faith, in the manner that is said of you
in Scripture: *All peoples, tribes and tongues shall serve him.*[40] Augustine
asserts this verse against heretics, especially against the Donatists, proving
by it that by Christ rising again from death, [the faith was] not only
in one small corner of the earth or scanty people, so that it was only
to be found in the part of the Donatists, but that it was [to be found]
throughout the whole world, so that he might reign by faith among all
peoples.[41] And Augustine draws from the words of Christ which were

---

38   E. N. Denis skips over verse 7 in this part of *Commentary.*
39   Is. 63:3–4.
40   Dan. 7:14a.
41   E. N. This is perhaps a reference to St. Augustine's *Tractates on the Gospel*
of John (*Tractate* 9, 13). After quoting this Psalm, St. Augustine observes that this
prophecy extends to all nations, and the Donatists, localized in North Africa, have
been cast away from the wedding party for lack of an appropriate wedding garment.
The Donatists, named from their leader Donatus Magnus (died *ca.* 355), broke off
from the Catholic Church upon the election of Caecilian as bishop of Carthage.
St. Augustine wrote polemical works against the Donatists. The implication here is
that a Church localized to one area of the world (North Africa in the case of the

said to his Apostles after his Resurrection: *You shall be witnesses unto me in Jerusalem, and in all Judea, and Samaria, and even to the uttermost part of the earth.*[42] And from that which follows we see that this Psalm, according to Augustine, literally applies to Christ suffering and rising again, and of the chiefs of the priests: but especially, because (according to Augustine) an argument derived from Scripture is not valid as to the faith unless it is based upon a literal sense.[43]

Finally, the pastors of the sheep of Christ and judges of Christian people are exhorted from this present Psalm that they may be steadfastly circumspect, cautious, and just in all their judgments, weighing carefully that they have a Judge in heaven who will demand an accounting from them even up to the last farthing, of all things which they committed or omitted regarding those who were under their authority.

PRAYER

O GOD, FROM WHOM ALL JUST OPERATIONS proceed and all power stems, justify us with the spirit of justice and fortitude, so that neither judging unjustly nor receiving the faces of sinners, we might always be diligent in undertaking things that are just and pleasing to you.

Deus, a quo omnis iusta operatio procedit et fortis consistit, iustifica nos spiritu iustitiae et fortitudinis: ut non iniquitatem iudicantes, nec facies peccatorum sumentes, iusta et tibi placita semper peragere studeamus.

Donatists) could hardly justify the assertion that it possessed one of the "marks" of the Church implied by Psalm 81:8, which is catholicity. The word "catholic," of course, comes from Greek καθολικός (*katholikos*), meaning "universal."

42   Acts 1:8.

43   *E. N. See* footnote 34-54 on this Augustinian principle of exegesis.

Psalm 82

ARTICLE LVI

EXPOSITION OF THE EIGHTY-SECOND PSALM:
DEUS, QUIS SIMILIS ERIT TIBI?
O GOD, WHO SHALL BE LIKE TO YOU?

82{83}[1] *A canticle of a Psalm for Asaph.*

Canticum, Psalmi Asaph.

OW THE TITLE TO THE PSALM NOW BEING addressed is 82{83}[1] *Canticum Psalmi Asaph. A canticle of a Psalm for Asaph*: that is, the present canticle is a Psalm of Asaph, either because it was proclaimed by him, or because it is presented by the congregation of the faithful, which is designated by Asaph (which name is interpreted to mean congregation). For the present Psalm is literally written about the various enemies of the people of the Jews, and the Prophet [David] prays for the just casting down and the punishment of the adversaries of his people.

82{83}[2] *O God, who shall be like to you? Hold not your peace, neither be still, O God.*

Deus, quis similis erit tibi? Ne taceas, neque compescaris, Deus:

82{83}[3] *For lo, your enemies have made a noise: and they that hate you have lifted up the head.*

Quoniam ecce inimici tui sonuerunt, et qui oderunt te extulerunt caput.

82{83}[4] *They have taken a malicious counsel against your people, and have consulted against your saints.*

Super populum tuum malignaverunt consilium, et cogitaverunt adversus sanctos tuos.

82{83}[5] *They have said: Come and let us destroy them, so that they not be a nation: and let the name of Israel be remembered no more.*

Dixerunt: Venite, et disperdamus eos de gente, et non memoretur nomen Israel ultra.

And so it says: **82{83}[2]** *Deus,* O God eternal and omnipotent, the God of Israel, the God of our fathers, *quis similis erit tibi, who shall be like to you,* with a univocal, essential, and perfect similitude? Indeed, no one, because you alone go beyond infinity in all things, and in comparison to you the whole world is like a little dust.[1] For regarding you is written truthfully: *O Lord God, Creator of all things, dreadful and strong, just and merciful, who alone are the good king, who alone are gracious, who alone are just, and almighty, and eternal.*[2] Job also: *We cannot find him worthily: he is great in strength, and in judgment, and in justice, and he is ineffable; therefore, men shall fear him, and all that seem to themselves to be wise, shall not dare to behold him.*[3] Yet there exists a certain imitative, imperfect, and gratuitous similitude: and according to this the creature is similar to the Creator, as also an effect is similar to its cause.[4] *Whence also the Lord says: Let us make man to our image and likeness.*[5] And we are invited to [participate in] this deiform similitude in the New and Old Testament. For the Lord says: *Be holy because I am holy.*[6] And the Savior: *Be you therefore perfect, as also your heavenly Father is perfect.*[7]

Because [man] is not similar to you [in a univocal sense], therefore, *ne taceas, hold not your peace,* that is, do not disregard the injuries done to you and to your people, but vindicate them, *neque compescaris, Deus; neither be still, O God,* that is, lest by tolerating them you appear to putting up with the blasphemies of the unbelievers; but declare your omnipotence by taking vengeance. **82{83}[3]** *Quoniam ecce inimici tui; for lo, your enemies,* namely, our pagan adversaries, *sonuerunt, have made a noise,* that is, have spoken irrationally against you, and have sounded trumpets in war, and in their rage they have attacked us your servants;

---

1   *Cf.* Is. 40:15.

2   2 Macc. 1:24–25a.

3   Job 37:23–24.

4   E. N. As Denis has said earlier, there is no univocity (identity) between God and creation. Yet neither is there total equivocation (absolutely no similarity). There is similarity in dissimilarity. As opposed to both univocity and equivocity, "the faith of the Church has always insisted that between God and us, between his eternal Creator Spirit and our created reason there exists a real analogy, in which — as the Fourth Lateran Council in 1215 stated — unlikeness remains infinitely greater than likeness, yet not to the point of abolishing analogy and its language." Benedict XVI, Regensburg Lecture (South Bend, IN: St. Augustine's Press, 2010), 137–38. "[B]etween Creator and creature no similitude can be expressed without implying a greater dissimilitude." DS 806 (Fourth Lateran Council).

5   Gen. 1:26.

6   Lev. 11:44a.

7   Matt. 5:48.

et qui oderunt te, and they that hate you, namely, the aforesaid enemies, *extulerunt caput, have lifted up the head,* that is, have lifted up their necks against you, thinking presumptuously, speaking proudly, and doing things in a contumacious manner. **82{83}[4]** *Super populum tuum, against your people,* namely, the Jews, *malignaverunt, they have taken a malicious counsel,* that is, they engaged in evil *consilium, counsel,* dragging your people to complete destruction, *et cogitaverunt adversus sanctos tuos, and they have consulted against your saints,* the Prophets, those set apart for God's service, and other religious. **82{83}[5]** *Dixerunt: Venite, et disperdamus; They have said: Come and let us destroy them,* that is, let us lay waste in diverse ways, *eos de gente, so that they may not be a nation,* that is, [let us separate them] from other peoples, killing them, lest they thrive abundantly among other nations. For they did not only want to extinguish the life of your people, but they wanted truly to destroy their memory: and so it adds, *et non memoretur nomen Israel ultra, and let the name of Israel be remembered no more,* that is, let us so utterly destroy the cities and the temple of the Hebrew people, so that no one will remember them from that point on, and so that there will no longer remain any remnant of them.

82{83}[6] *For they have contrived with one consent: they have made a covenant together against you,*

   Quoniam cogitaverunt unanimiter, simul adversum te testamentum disposuerunt.

82{83}[7] *The tabernacles of the Edomites, and the Ishmaelites: Moab, and the Hagarites,*

   Tabernacula Idumaeorum et Ismahelitae, Moab et Agareni.

82{83}[8] *Gebal, and Ammon and Amalek: the foreign-born, with the inhabitants of Tyre.*

   Gebal et Ammon, et Amalec; alienigenae cum habitantibus Tyrum.

82{83}[9] *Yea, and Assur also is joined with them: they are come to the aid of the sons of Lot.*

   Etenim Assur venit cum illis, facti sunt in adiutorium filiis Lot.

82{83}[6] *Quoniam cogitaverunt unanimiter, for they have contrived with one consent,* that is, by mutual consent in evil; *simul adversum te testamentum, . . . a convenant together against you,* that is, a steadfast pact and evil purpose, *disposuerunt, they have made.* **82{83}[7]** *Tabernaculua Idumaeorum, the tabernacles of the Edomites,* that is, those who dwell in Edom, namely, those born from the seed of Esau, who was called by the other name Edom, from which the name Edomite is derived,[8] *et Ismahelitae, and the Ishmaelites,* that is, the people born of Ishmael, the son of Abraham, the brother of Isaac.[9] For in the way that Esau persecuted Jacob by wanting to kill him,[10] as is described in Genesis, so also Ishmael [did] to Isaac, as the Apostle said to the Galatians: So did the Edomites persecute the Jews who were descended from Jacob as did the Ishmaelites.[11] For this reason, Obadiah the prophet said: *For the iniquity against your brother Jacob, confusion shall cover you, and you shall perish forever. In the day when you stood against him, when strangers carried away his army captive, . . . and you also were one of them.*[12] *Moab,* that is, the Moabites born of Moab, the son of Lot, *et Agareni, and the Hagarites,* that is, the sons of Abraham from Hagar, the handmaid of Sarah. Some say that Hagar was also called by another name, namely, Ketura:[13] for we read that many sons of Abraham were born after the death of Sarah, his wife, as is clear in Genesis. **82{83}[8]** *Gebal,* so called, *et Ammon, and Ammon,* that is the Ammonites, sons of Ammon, a son of Lot,[14] *et Amalec, and Amalek,* that is, the Amalekites born of Amalek. This Amalek first fought against the sons of Israel, when they left Egypt and wandered in the desert, as is stated in Exodus,[15] where we read: *When Moses lifted up his hands, Israel overcame: but if he let them down a little, Amalek overcame.*[16] *Alienigenae, the foreign-born,* namely, the Philistines: for in the Hebrew, we have [the word] Philistine [in place of foreign-born], who were for the Jews a great annoyance; *cum habitantibus Tyrum, with the inhabitants of Tyre,* that is, with the Phoenicians. Now for a while, during the reign of Hiram their king who had a treaty with David and Solomon,[17] the Phoenicians were in a confederacy with the

---

8   Gen. 25:30. E. N. Edom is also known as Idumaea. In Hebrew, the word *edom* means red, and it was given to Esau because of his red hair. Gen. 25:25.

9   Gen. 26:15. Ishmael was actually the half-brother of Isaac, since he was born by virtue of the union of Abraham from Hagar, the handmaid of Sarah, so Denis uses the word brother loosely. Gen. 16:3.

10   Gen. 27:41

11   Cf. Gal. 4:29: *But as then he [Ishmael], that was born according to the flesh, persecuted him that was after the spirit [Isaac]; so also it is now.*

12   Ob. 10–11.

13   Gen. 25:1–2. Ketura, another wife of Abraham who some equate to Hagar, bore him Zimran, Jokshan, Medan, Midian, Ishbak, and Shuah, all of whom had children of their own.

14   Gen. 19:38.

15   Ex. 17:8.

16   Ex. 17:11.

17   2 Sam. 5:11; 1 King 5:12.

Hebrews; later, however, the peace treaty was broken. **82{83}[9]** *Etenim Assur venit cum illis; yea, and Assur also is joined with them*, that is, the Assyrians *facti sunt in adiutorium filiis Lot*, they are come to the aid of the sons of Lot, that is, the Moabites and the Ammonites, by which we see that the sons of Lot were the principal adversaries of the Israelites in the battle that is discussed here.

82{83}[10] *Do to them as you did to Midian and to Sisera: as to Jabin at the brook of Kishon.*

> *Fac illis sicut Madian et Sisarae, sicut Iabin in torrente Cisson.*

82{83}[11] *Who perished at Endor: and became as dung for the earth.*

> *Disperierunt in Endor, facti sunt ut stercus terrae.*

82{83}[10] *Fac illis*, do them them, O God of Israel, *sicut Madian et Sisarae, sicut Iabin in torrente Cison; as you did to Midian and to Sisera, at the brook of Kishon.* Because this book is written in verse, it often happens that the order of events is varied in narration, as it is in this instance. For in the book of Judges we read that Jabin, the king of Canaan, oppressed the sons of Israel; and he had a leader of the army called Sisera.[18] Now in the same book we read the sons of Israel were delivered into the hands of the Midianites.[19] The Prophet [David] therefore prays that God might destroy the previously-mentioned enemies of his people who were such during the time of the reign of Judah and Israel or afterwards, as when they fought the Midianites and Sisera. For the Midianites were miraculously vanquished by Gideon and his three hundred men.[20] Similarly, the army of Jabin, the king of Canaan, was assaulted by the hand of Barak.[21] And Jael, the wife of Heber the Kenite, drove a stake into the temple of Sisera, and killed him.[22] *Sicut Iabin in torrente Cison*, as to Jabin at the brook of Kishon: for by the torrent of Kishon the people of Jabin were defeated by the sons of Israel. Whence the prophetess Deborah said to Barak: *Go and lead an army to mount Thabor.... I will bring unto you in the place of the torrent of Kishon, Sisara ... and all his multitude.*[23] In was in this torrent where we read that also some were drowned, according to this: *The torrent of*

---

18 Judges 4:2.
19 Judges 6:1–6.
20 Judges chp. 7.
21 Judges 4:17.
22 Judges 4:21.
23 Judges 4:6–7.

Kishon dragged their carcasses.[24] **82{83}[11]** *Disperierunt in Endor, who perished at Endor,* for it was close by that place that it is said that they were killed; *facti sunt ut stercus terrae, and became as dung for the earth,* for they remained unburied, and they were regarded as worth nothing.

82{83}[12] *Make their princes like Oreb, and Zeeb, and Zebah, and Zalmunna. All their princes,*

    Pone principes eorum sicut Oreb, et Zeb, et Zebee, et Salmana; omnes principes eorum,

82{83}[13] *Who have said: Let us possess the sanctuary of God for an inheritance.*

    Qui dixerunt: Haereditate possideamus sanctuarium Dei.

82{83}[14] *O my God, make them like a wheel; and as stubble before the wind.*

    Deus meus, pone illos ut rotam, et sicut stipulam ante faciem venti.

82{83}[15] *As fire which burns the forest: and as a flame burning mountains:*

    Sicut ignis qui comburit silvam, et sicut flamma comburens montes.

82{83}[16] *So shall you pursue them with your tempest: and shall trouble them in your wrath.*

    Ita persequeris illos in tempestate tua, et in ira tua turbabis eos.

82{83}[12] *Pone principes eorum, make their princes,* namely, [the princes of] the Edomites, the Ishmaelites, the Moabites, the Hagarites, and so forth, of which we spoke about but a short time ago, *sicut Oreb et Zeb, like Oreb and Zeeb,* that is, kill them in the manner that you killed Oreb and Zeeb, *et Zebee et Salmana, and Zebah and Zalmunna,* princes of the Midianites, whom you killed through Gideon and his helpers. For Oreb and Zeeb were decapitated by the Ephramites;[25] and Gideon himself killed Zebah and Zalmuna as is written in the book of Judges.[26] **82{83}[14]**[27] *Deus meus, pone illos ut rotam; O my God make them like a wheel:* that is, cause them to be unstable, prone to run, and unaccomplished, just as a wheel moves by a circular movement, in which there is no certain end to be found; *et, and* put them *sicut stipulam ante faciem venti, as*

---

24 Judges 5:21a.
25 Judges 7:25.
26 Judges 8:21.
27 E. N. Denis skips over verse 13.

stubble before the wind, so as stubble is moved and falls with the wind, so let them succumb to your power. **82{83}[15]** *Sicut ignis qui comburit silvam, as fire which burns the forest* that is caught on fire, or the wood thrown into a forest on fire, *et sicut flamma comburens montes, and as a flame burning mountains,* that is, like a mountain place with those who dwell thereon which is set on fire, **82{83}[16]** *Ita persequeris illos, so shall you pursue them* who have been previously named, namely, Moab, the Hagarites, Gebal, and Ammon, *in tempestate tua, with your tempest,* that is, in the anger of your furor, that is, in the strict vengeance of your justice. All this has been completely fulfilled. For as the fire consumed the wood of forests, so God has frequently consumed the enemies of his people Israel, as clearly occurred in the ruin of the army of the king of the Assyrians and many others.[28] *Et in ira tua turbabis eos, and you shall trouble them in your wrath,* warning them in flight, or terrifying them, and killing them. This punishment, just as also that [punishment described in the verses] following [these], can be referred to the damnation of hell, and to the punishments of the future judgment.

82{83}[17] *Fill their faces with shame; and they shall seek your name, O Lord.*

Imple facies eorum ignominia, et quaerent nomen tuum, Domine.

82{83}[18] *Let them be ashamed and troubled for ever and ever: and let them be confounded and perish.*

Erubescant, et conturbentur in saeculum saeculi, et confundantur, et pereant.

82{83}[19] *And let them know that the Lord is your name: you alone are the most High over all the earth.*

Et cognoscant quia nomen tibi Dominus; tu solus Altissimus in omni terra.

82{83}[17] *Imple facies eorum ignominia, fill their faces with shame,* so that they may be manifestly defeated, and all know that they have been overcome; *et quaerent nomen tuum, Domine; and they shall seek your name, O Lord.* For some of the Gentiles, seeing the Jewish people prevailing in such a marvelous way and themselves unexpectedly overcome by the divine power, were converted to the God of Israel. **82{83} [18]** *Erubescant et conturbentur in saeculum saeculi, let them be ashamed*

---

28   2 King 19:35.

and troubled for ever and ever, in the day of the final judgment: as it is stated of the ungodly: *These ... shall be troubled with terrible fear;*[29] and in the book of Judges, *Let all our enemies perish, O Lord.*[30] *Et confundantur et pereant, and let them be confounded and perish.* Often [in the Scriptures] something with the same meaning is repeated to designate the zeal of justice which stirs against evildoers. For this is prayed not out of impatience or rancor, but out of the zeal of justice and for the honor of God. **82{83}[19]** *Et cognoscant, and let them know,* by the experience of their damnation in the future, or by the experience of punishment in this world, *quia nomen tibi Dominus, that the Lord is your name,* that is, that you truly and worthily are called the Lord, as you are the ruler, the provider, and the judge of the whole universe, and *all things are in your power,*[31] and who [as judge] impart to every person that which he deserves, who have declared through Isaiah: *I the Lord, this is my name: I will not give my glory to another.*[32] And let them know also, because *tu solus Alstissimus in omni terra, you alone are the most High over all the earth,* that is, that not only does Judaea subsist within your power, but that all the kingdoms of the earth and their gods are subject to your empire: as also king Hezekiah said: *You alone are the God of all the kingdoms of the earth.*[33]

ARTICLE LVII

MORAL EXPOSITION OF THE SAME EIGHTY-SECOND PSALM.

Now pursuing a moral understanding, the exposition of this present Psalm is far more exquisite and fruitful [than the literal sense]: for the subject matter of this Psalm is the second coming of Christ and the difficult and heavy persecution of the faithful by perverse men. Now the persecution of the Church has been threefold. The first was in the sword of tyrants; the second, in the words of heretics; and the third, in the evil words of false brethren. There remains a fourth, which consists of all of these, namely, the persecution of the Antichrist, by whose power

29 Wis. 5:2a.
30 Judges 5:31a.
31 Esther 13:9a.
32 Is. 42:8a.
33 Is. 37:16b.

of arms, words of disputation, and works of simulated virtues he will persecute and kill the faithful, [and by which] many will be deceived. And so that this time of most heavy persecution might be shortened,[34] Asaph therefore prays for the second coming of Christ or the acceleration of the final judgment, when, according to the Apostle, the Lord Jesus *shall kill with the spirit (spiritu) of his mouth, and shall destroy with the brightness of his coming.*[35] About this Isaiah also says, *With the breath (spiritu) of his lips he shall slay the wicked.*[36]

82{83}[2]   *O God, who shall be like to you? Hold not your peace, neither be still, O God.*

Deus, quis similis erit tibi? Ne taceas, neque compescaris, Deus:

82{83}[3]   *For lo, your enemies have made a noise: and they that hate you have lifted up the head.*

Quoniam ecce inimici tui sonuerunt, et qui oderunt te extulerunt caput.

82{83}[4]   *They have taken a malicious counsel against your people, and have consulted against your saints.*

Super populum tuum malignaverunt consilium, et cogitaverunt adversus sanctos tuos.

82{83}[5]   *They have said: Come and let us destroy them, so that they not be a nation: and let the name of Israel be remembered no more.*

Dixerunt: Venite, et disperdamus eos de gente, et non memoretur nomen Israel ultra.

And so Asaph, marveling at the power and the glory by which Christ will appear in judgment, begins by saying: 82{83}[2] *Deus, quis similis erit tibi? O God, who shall be like to you?* That is, O only Son of the eternal Father, O Lord Christ, judge of the universe, who is similar to you in the wisdom of discerning between good and evil? Indeed, no one, according to that stated in Job: *Behold, God is great, exceeding our*

---

34   Mark 13:20: *And unless the Lord had shortened the days, no flesh should be saved: but for the sake of the elect which he has chosen, he has shortened the days.*

35   2 Thess. 2:8. Denis uses the word *occidet* instead of the Sixto-Clementine's *interficiet* in his quotation of 2 Thess. 2:8; however, both may be translated by the English "kill."

36   Is. 11:4b.

knowledge.[37] Who is similar to you in equity, restoring to all things all that they are due? Indeed, no one, for of you is written: *There is no iniquity with the Lord our God, nor respect of persons, nor desire of gifts.*[38] Who is similar to you in the power of enforcing the judgment of just judgment? Indeed, no one, for of you the divine word says: *His power is an everlasting power that shall not be taken away: and his kingdom that shall not be destroyed.*[39]

Since, therefore, O Christ, you are such a kind and so great a judge, *ne taceas, hold not your peace,* now that you are reigning in heaven, or in your Second Coming and the future Judgment in the manner that you held back your judgment in the first coming, saying: *I judge not any man;*[40] and again: *God sent not his Son into the world, to judge the world, but that the world may be saved by him.*[41] *Neque compescaris, Deus; neither be still, O God,* that is, do not hold back a most just vengeance; but show yourself truly to be that which divine Scripture professes about you: *Far from God be wickedness, and iniquity from the Almighty; for he will render to a man his work, and according to the ways of every one he will reward them.*[42] **82{83}[3]** *Quoniam ecce inimici tui; for lo, your enemies,* namely, evil Christians, heretics, Jews, and pagans *sonuerunt, have made a noise,* that is, have irrationally raised iniquitous voices, uttering vain, empty, and perverse words. And so he does not say, "They have spoken," but rather "They have made a noise," because they have not in the manner of men spoken reasonably, but in the manner of wild beasts they have poured forth irrational sounds, murmuring against you and contradicting you — something which will most greatly occur at the time of the Antichrist. For at that time, Antichristians will erupt in unrestricted, but altogether irrational voice, so that it will seem more like sound rather than speech. *Et qui oderunt te, and they that hate you,* that is, they who delight in evil and love vice, *extulerunt caput, have lifted up the head,* as the proudful are accustomed to raising their head. Or *they have lifted up their head,* that is, they have exalted the Antichrist, believing him to be the Son of God, and they blasphemed the Lord Jesus: and so it does not say, "Heads," but rather "Head," because all [these who exalt the Antichrist] will unite with the one son of perdition, namely, the Antichrist.

---

37   Job 36:26a.
38   2 Chr. 19:7b.
39   Dan. 7:14b.
40   John 8:15b.
41   John 3:17.
42   Job 34:10b–11.

St. Augustine affirms that nearly no one in his conscience is able to hate God; but because Scripture frequently says that the sinners have hate for God, we ought absolutely to concede that the ungodly have the hate of God.[43] For in the way that those ruling themselves by the divine precepts are said to love God, so those who rebel against God are said to harbor hate for him. Did not he hate God who I once heard say with his mouth—when I urged him toward better things and commended to him to the beatitude of the divine majesty—"I would prefer," he said, "for God not to be, rather than that I ought to submit myself to your life, namely, the manner of the Carthusian way of life"? In what way, then, is what St. Augustine asserted true? We might respond to this question as St. Thomas responded,[44] namely, that someone may be said to hate God in two ways. The first, according to God in himself; the second, by reason of his effects. In the first way, scarcely no one hates God, since he is pure and infinite goodness; but in the second manner many hate God, namely, because of the punishment God inflicts for sin, or because he prohibits those things which please them, or commands those things which displease them.

82{83}[4] *Super populum tuum, against your people,* that is, against the Christians, tyrants and false brethren *malignaverunt consilium, have taken a malicious counsel,* since either they attract them by blandishments, or deter them by punishments, or in some other cause them to divert from, to aggrieve, or to reject God; *et cogitaverunt adversus sanctos tuos, and they have consulted against your saints:* for they have sought not only to subvert your servants who live in mediocrity, but also men who strive for perfection, in this way imitating their head, the devil, of which the Lord said to holy Job: *He will drink up a river, and not wonder: and he trusts that the Jordan may run into his mouth.*[45] In this verse, by river is meant worldly, wandering, and unstable souls, whom the devil absorbs,

---

43 Ps. 20:9; 73:4, 23; *and elsewhere;* E. N. St. Augustine clearly states this in one of his sermons of the Lord's Sermon on the Mount: *nullius enim fere conscientia Deum odisse potest,* "for scarcely no one in his conscience is able to hate God." *De Serm. Domini in Monte,* II, 14, 48. PL 34, 1290. However, though unmentioned by Denis, St. Augustine actually retracted this statement in his *Retractions,* citing the same reason as did Denis for rejecting it: "I see that this ought not to have been said, for there are many of whom it is written, 'The pride of them that hate you.'" (citing Ps. 73:23). *Retractationum* (I, 19, 8), PL 32, 617. Denis is obviously unaware of the *Retractions* on this point since he seeks to distinguish St. Augustine's statement later in the *Commentary* by the means of St. Thomas Aquinas.

44 E. N. *See* ST IIaIIae, q. 34, art. 1, co.

45 Job 40:18.

and this is not to be marveled, that is, this is not to be regarded as great; but by Jordan is understood religious and holy souls, whom he believes the devil is able to deceive. And they take pains to trip up not only the ordinary or common among the Christian people, but also those who are holy. 82{83}[5] These adversaries of you, *dixerunt, have said*, O Lord: *Venite, et disperdamus eos, come and let us destroy them*, namely, the Christians, *de gente, so that they not be a nation*: that is, let us destroy them, lest any of them from now on living among the nations; *et non memoretur nomen Israel ultra, and let the name of Israel be remembered no more*, that is, [let] the Church militant, [be remembered no more]. For many tyrants have sought completely to do away with the worship, and the faith, and the memory of the Christian people.

82{83}[6] ... *they have made a covenant together against you,*

      ... *simul adversum te testamentum disposuerunt.*

82{83}[7] *The tabernacles of the Edomites, and the Ishmaelites: Moab, and the Hagarites,*

      Tabernacula Idumaeorum et Ismahelitae, Moab et Agareni.

82{83}[8] *Gebal, and Ammon and Amalek: the foreign-born, with the inhabitants of Tyre.*

      Gebal et Ammon, et Amalec; alienigenae cum habitantibus Tyrum.

82{83}[9] *Yea, and Assur also is joined with them: they are come to the aid of the sons of Lot.*

      Etenim Assur venit cum illis, facti sunt in adiutorium filiis Lot.

82{83}[10] *Do to them as you did to Midian and to Sisera: as to Jabin at the brook of Kishon.*

      Fac illis sicut Madian et Sisarae, sicut Iabin in torrente Cisson.

82{83}[6][46] *Simul adversum te testamentum, disposuerunt, they have made a covenant together against you* 82{83}[7] *tabernacula Idumaeorum, et Ismaelitae, Moab et Agareni,* 82{83}[8] *Gebal et Ammon, etc.; the tabernacles of the Edomites, and the Ishmaelites, Moab, and the Hagarites, Gebal and Ammon, etc.* In the manner that these people were adversaries to the Synagogue of the Jews, so by them is indicated those that are adversaries to

---

46   E. N. Denis starts mid-verse, and neglects the first half of Ps. 82:6.

the Church of Christians. But we ought to think about the interpretation of these names so that we might understand who we mean by these peoples. As we read in Genesis, when Esau was born, he appeared in the manner of being hairy, with skin like the skin [of an animal] and red: for this reason, he was called Edom.[47] Edomites, therefore, is taken from the name Edom, which is interpreted as "of the blood" or "of the earth," by which is designated the avaricious or those inordinate lovers of things of the earth. Ishmaelite is interpreted to mean "disobedient": by which in this place is designated those who follow their own will, who conform to themselves alone, and not to will of God, and by this is signified the gluttonous, who do not serve Christ, but *their own belly.*[48] Moab is interpreted to mean "from the father": by whom is designated the perverse, who according to nature come forth from God, but because of their malice they are born of their father the devil, of whom Christ said, *You are of your father the devil.*[49] By these are expressed the lustful, because the eldest daughter of Lot, gave birth to Moab by means of relations with her own father.[50] By the Hagarites are understood those who are alien or foreigners, and by which are figured false brethren, who are only counted among the elect by name alone, as John asserts: They were among us, *but they were not of us, for if they had been of us, they would no doubt have remained with us.*[51] Gebal is interpreted [to mean] "empty valley": and so by it are encompassed the falsely humble and hypocrites, of whom the book of Job has the following: *Dissemblers and crafty men prove the wrath of God.*[52] And in Ecclesiasticus: *There is one that humbles himself wickedly, and his interior is full of deceit.*[53] Of such men, the Savior says: *You are they who justify yourselves before men, but God knows your hearts; for that which is high to men, is an abomination before God.*[54] By Ammon, which is interpreted to mean "disturbed people," are designated the angry, because anger disturbs reason, and it makes a man similar to a fool. For this reason, Ecclesiastes says: *Be not quickly angry: for anger rests in the bosom of a fool;*[55] and Job, *Anger indeed kills the foolish.*[56] By Amalek, whom Eliphaz the first-born

---

47 E. N. Esau is also called Edom: "And Esau dwelt in mount Seir: he is Edom." Gen. 36:8.
48 Rom. 16:18a.
49 John 8:44a.
50 Gen. 19:33, 37.
51 1 John 2:19a.
52 Job 36:13a.
53 Ecclus. 19:23b.
54 Luke 16:15.
55 Eccl. 7:10.
56 Job 5:2a.

of Esau gave birth to, and is interpreted as "licking people," are signified flatterers and those who engage in false praise. This vice the Apostle [Paul] showed himself to be free of, saying: *Neither have we used, at any time, the speech of flattery.*[57]

Alienigenae, the foreign-born, that is, the Philistine, which term is interpreted as meaning "a falling potion," and by which is designated the vice and excess of drunkenness; *cum habitationibus Tyrum, with the inhabitants of Tyre,* that is, with the envious. For Tyre is interpreted to mean narrowness: and the envious are twisted within themselves as if they were enclosed in some narrow space. These in any case oppose themselves to the lives of all forechosen people. 82{83}[9] *Etenim Assur venit cum illis; yea, and Assur also is joined with them.* By Assur, which is interpreted to mean "depressed" or "elated," signifies the devil, who has fallen into the depths by sinning and yet in the mind is inflated to the heights, and who is also the *king over the children of pride,* as is written in the book of Job.[58] *Factis sunt in adiutorium filiis Lot, they are come to the aid of the sons of Lot,* that is, those turning aside. For Lot is interpreted to mean "turning aside," which signifies the apostate angels, who with their prince, Lucifer, turned aside from God. But the previously mentioned evil men are aides to the demons, in the sense that just men are helpers of, or cooperators with, God.

Therefore, the Church prays for the destruction and just punishment of these [evil men], not in the sense of calling evil down upon them, but in the sense of predicting their future torment, or of conforming itself to the divine justice, or of praying that they may be punished in the present age, lest they be condemned eternally, or that they, by living a longer time, might more gravely transgress the common good, or that the Church might not be permitted to be persecuted any longer. 82{83}[10] *Fac illis sicut Madian et Sisarae, etc. Do to them as you did to Midian and to Sisera, etc.* Madian, who was a son of Abraham and Keturah, is interpreted to men "abandoning judgment," and he is a figure of those who do not judge themselves, nor do they fear the future judgment: for this reason, they are unable to be saved, according to that which is said of some men in the book of Job, *Can he be healed that loves not judgment?*[59] By Sisera, which is interpreted to mean "shutting out of joy," is signified those who because of their delights of the world and the flesh exclude themselves from the joy of eternal beatitude, as the

57   1 Thess. 2:5a.
58   Job 41:25b.
59   Job 34:17a.

Lord Jesus says of such persons: *Woe to you that now laugh: for you shall mourn and weep.*[60] Solomon also: *The heart of the wise is where there is mourning, and the heart of fools where there is mirth.*[61] There is, however, a certain spiritual joy that is not to be rejected, of which the Apostle [Paul] says: *Rejoice in the Lord always.*[62] By Jabin, which is interpreted as meaning "wise man," is understood those who are worldly wise, of whom Isaiah says: *Woe to you that are wise in your own eyes.*[63] By Kishon, which is interpreted as meaning "hardness," is understood obstinacy in evil or hardness of heart.

82{83}[12] *Make their princes like Oreb, and Zeeb, and Zebah, and Zalmunna. All their princes,*[64]

Pone principes eorum sicut Oreb, et Zeb, et Zebee, et Salmana; omnes principes eorum,

82{83}[13] *Who have said: Let us possess the sanctuary of God for an inheritance.*

Qui dixerunt: Haereditate possideamus sanctuarium Dei.

. . .

82{83}[17] *Fill their faces with shame; and they shall seek your name, O Lord.*

Imple facies eorum ignomnia, et quaerent nomen tuum, Domine.

The Church prays, therefore, that its persecutors be like often occurs to the sinners just now described; and these things are especially requested against the army of the Antichrist. 82{83}[12] *Pone principes eorum, make their princes,* namely, [the princes] of the persecutors of the Church, *sicut Oreb et Zeb et Zebee, etc.; like Oreb, and Zeeb, and Zebah, etc.* By Oreb, which is interpreted to mean "drought," are designated those that are arid of the grace of God: of which aridity is written, *O shepherd, and idol, that forsakes the flock, . . . his arm shall quite wither away,*[65] that is, their works will deprive them from the grace of God. By Zeeb, which is interpreted to mean "wolf," are signified the rapacious. By Zebah, which is

---

60   Luke 6:25b.
61   Eccl. 7:3.
62   Phil. 4:4.
63   Is. 5:21a.
64   E. N. Denis skips over verses 11, 14–16, and 18–19 in this part of the *Commentary*.
65   Zech. 11:17.

interpreted to mean "wolf's victim," are figured those by sinning become the prey of the devil. By Zalmunna, which is interpreted to mean "shade of commotion," or "perfect in depravity," is signified the unstable, or those who are in effect one body with the devil, who together with him are advancing toward the path of eternal fire. *Omnes principes eorum, all their princes,* that is, the captains of sin already named, on account of the devastation; 82{83}[13] *qui, who* [referring to the princes] *dixerunt: Hereditate possideamus sanctuarium Dei; have said: Let us possess the sanctuary of God for an inheritance,* that is, the lands, possessions, and the church structures of the Christians, or better yet, the Christians themselves, subjecting them to our rule, law, and cult. For the faithful people are called the sanctuary of God, according to the Apostle [Paul]: *The temple of God is holy, which you are.*[66] The rest has been expounded in the preceding article.

This Psalm inveighs in a terrible manner against evil men who are content with themselves; and in it is shown with what an inestimable confusion and punishment they will be visited with in the future judgment, if they do not in any way convert. But that which is said here — 82{83} [17] *Imple facies eorum ignominia, fill their faces with shame* — can be understood as describing the late and unfruitful penitence of the reprobate, [which is undertaken] not out of the love of justice, but from the fear of suffering the punishments of sin, of which [kind of fruitless] penance is written in the book Wisdom: *Saying within themselves, repenting, and groaning for anguish of spirit;* and [of such penance] it says the following: *Such things as these the sinners said in hell.*[67] And so this verse — *Fill their faces with shame* — can also be received in a good sense; and in such a case it will be [understood] in this sense: Grant, O Lord, that in the present, inasmuch as they are sinners, they might be repressed, and despised, and censured so they might cease from sinning as a result of such disgrace inflicted upon them. For in the manner that by adulation and most-false praise a sinner is strengthened in his fault, so by suffering shame he might withdraw from evil since he is looked upon as blameworthy by all. *Et, and* so most salubriously *quaerent nomen tuum, Domine; they shall seek your name, O Lord,* by a salutary penance and true compunction. Indeed, this seems to pertain to those about whom it is written in the Gospel: *Compel them to come in.*[68]

---

66   1 Cor. 3:17b.
67   Wis. 5:3a, 14.
68   Luke 14:23.

PRAYER

O GOD OF SUPERNAL MAJESTY, TO WHOM there is no one alike, do not cast us out from the people of the elect because of the multitude of sins; but by your merciful goodness make our name remembered in eternity in Israel.

Deus, supernae maiestatis, cui non est similis, propter multitudinem peccatorum non disperdas nos de gente electorum; sed clementi bonitate facias nomen nostrum memorari in Israel in aeternum.

Psalm 83

ARTICLE LVIII

EXPLANATION OF THE EIGHTY-THIRD PSALM: QUAM DILECTA TABERNACULA TUA! HOW LOVELY ARE YOUR TABERNACLES!

83{84}[1] *Unto the end, for the winepresses, a psalm for the sons of Korah.*

In finem, pro torcularibus filiis Core. Psalmus.

HE TITLE OF THIS PSALM NOW BEING expounded is: 83{84}[1] *In finem, pro trocularibus, filiis Core, psalmus; unto the end, for the winepresses, a Psalm for the sons of Korah:* that is, this Psalm directs us unto the end, that is, unto Christ, who is our beatitude and eternal life, fitting for the sons of Korah, that is, those who imitate Jesus Christ crucified; it is written *for the wine presses,* that is, in regard to the tribulations and the distresses of the [particular] churches, or dealing with and addressing the many tribulations of those churches. For Korah is interpreted as Calvary, and Calvary is the place in which the Lord was crucified.[1] This Psalm literally deals with the immeasurable desire of the fervent wayfarer sighing for the heavenly fatherland, and it clearly addresses the incomprehensible beatitude of those enjoying the sight of God in heaven.

83{84}[2] *How lovely are your tabernacles, O Lord of hosts!*

Quam dilecta tabernacula tua, Domine virtutum!

And therefore it says: 83{84}[2] *Quam dilecta tabernacula tua! How lovely are your tabernacles!* That is, the dwellings of the heavenly courts, places, and mansions of the blessed in the heavenly fatherland are exceedingly lovely, greatly to be loved, and incomparably desirable. And of these tabernacles, the Savior says: *Make unto you friends of the mammon of iniquity; that when you shall fail, they may receive you into everlasting dwellings;*[2]

---

1   John 19:17–18. *E. N.* For the relationship between Korah and Calvary and the crucifixion as explained by St. Augustine, *see* footnote 40-3.

2   Luke 16:9. As Denis comments on this passage in Luke in his *Commentary on Luke:* "By expending wealth and temporal goods to the poor, procure for yourselves

and again: *In my Father's house there are many mansions.*[3] It is not that in the empyreal heaven, which is the place, home, and country of the blessed, there are dwellings with walls or divided into private rooms; but the words tabernacles and mansions are said in plural form so as to designate the various grades of reward in the heavenly fatherland. For in the manner that *one is the glory of the sun, another the glory of the moon, and another the glory of the stars,*[4] so the of the glory of the blessed will be different according to the demands of their merits. For the blessed or the eternal life which they enjoy is one and the same on the part of the object, which is designated by the denarius which every one of the laborers received, as Truth teaches in the Gospel.[5] And so your heavenly tabernacles are the many with a devout heart beloved by you, *O Domine virtutum, O Lord of hosts,* that is, [Lord] of the holy angels or of all the heavenly, terrestrial, and infernal powers. For in the manner that the angelic spirits are called angels, so also they are called hosts (*virtutes*) because of the efficaciousness they have in executing all the godlike operations predetermined for them by God, according to that prince of the theologians.[6]

In respect to their bodily location, these supernal tabernacles are one tabernacle, namely the empyrean heaven, of which the Apostle [Paul] states: *We know, if our earthly house of this habitation be dissolved, that we have a building of God, a house not made with hands, eternal in heaven.*[7] And to the Hebrews: *Jesus is not entered into the holies made with hands, the patterns of the true: but into heaven itself.*[8] The tents of the children of

---

the holy friendship of the most eminently holy Trinity, and of the holy angels, and of the poor. For God and all of the elect love mercy, and they sincerely love those freely and mercifully sharing their goods." Doctoris Ecstatici D. Dionysii Cartusiani, *Opera Omnia,* Vol. 12 (Montreuil: 1901), 120.

3   John 14:2a.

4   1 Cor. 15:41a.

5   Matt. 20:9–10. E. N. In the parable of the laborers of the vineyard, all received one denarius whether hired early in the morning, mid-morning, noon, or very late in the day. The point Denis is making is that this parable shows that the beatific vision is the same in terms of object (vision of God, eternal beatitude in general, symbolized by the one denarius); however, that does not mean that the beatific vision is identical in terms of the level of beatitude and that merit and glory is identical among the blessed (which truth is indicated by the fact that there are differing mansions and tabernacles), since beatitude and glory differs as the light of the sun, moon, and stars differ from each other. Denis draws this teaching from ST IIIa (Supp.), q. 93, art. 2, co.

6   E. N. This is the epithet Denis gives to Dionysius the Areopagite (Pseudo-Denis).

7   2 Cor. 5:1.

8   Heb. 9:24.

Israel were figures of these supermundane tabernacles, of which Balaam the true prophet spoke, although he was an evil man:[9] *How beautiful are your tabernacles, O Jacob, and your tents, O Israel! As woody valleys, as watered gardens near the rivers, as tabernacles which the Lord has pitched.*[10] The soul of Christ prayed that these tabernacles would show themselves inflamed with love, saying to his spouse in the Song of Songs: *Show me, O you whom my soul loves, where you feed, where you lie in the midday.*[11] But it seems a curious thing why the Prophet did not rather commend the lovableness of the king and those who dwelt in these tabernacles, rather than the tabernacles themselves, especially since it is not for these tabernacles that the King of heaven is loved, but because of the beauty of the King that his tabernacles are loved. The response to this is that the tabernacles are commended for this reason: that we should recognize what is our fatherland upon which the affections and the gaze of our mind ought always to be raised toward and affixed. Also, the name of tabernacles insinuates the beauty, glory, and lovingkindness of their King and Creator. And these tabernacles are as beautiful and beloved as they are they are good, pleasing, and blessed. Now, how being pleasing consists in being blessed is addressed below.

83{84}[3]   *My soul longs and faints for the courts of the Lord. My heart and my flesh have rejoiced in the living God.*

> *Concupiscit, et deficit anima mea in atria Domini; cor meum et caro mea exsultaverunt in Deum vivum.*

83{84}[3] *Concupiscit et deficit anima mea,* my soul longs and faints. Sacred Scripture speaks of two kinds of desire (*concupiscentia*), of which one is holy and noble and the other fetid and vile. The holy and excellent desire is called intellectual, of which is said in the book of Wisdom, *The desire (concupiscentia) of wisdom brings to the everlasting kingdom;*[12] and Ecclesiasticus, *A good ear will hear wisdom with all desire (concupiscentia).*[13] But of the unclean and vile desire, which is called sensual, it is written in

---

9   E. N. *See* 2 Pet. 2:15 (Balaam "loved the wages of iniquity"); Jude 1:11 ("the error of Balaam") and Rev. 2:14 (disparaging the "doctrine of Balaam"). Since prophecy is a grace *gratis data*, possessing such grace does not necessarily imply sanctity or even being in a state of grace (grace *gratum faciens*). After all, even the high priest Caiaphas who conspired to put Jesus to death prophesied. John 11:51.

10   Num. 24:5–6.

11   Song 1:6a.

12   Wis. 6:21.

13   Ecclus. 3:31b.

the same [book]: *Go not after your lusts (concupiscentias), but turn away from your own will.*[14] But here [in this verse] the words refer to intellectual desire, which is a desire of the will. And so, *my souls longs,* that is, greatly desires, wishing to be with its Creator, and tending *in atria Domini, for the courts of the Lord,* that is, for the tabernacles already discussed and which are called tabernacles because they are dwelling places; and courts, because of their capaciousness or their breadth. Not only does it long, but it also *faints,* which can be understood in two ways. First thus: *Faints,* the desire for the courts is not as strong as they are desirable, for the intellect of wayfarers are not worthy or sufficient to recognize it, nor are their affections worthy or sufficient to be able to long after the joy of the blessed, according to that said by the Apostle: *Eye has not seen, nor ear heard, neither has it entered into the heart of man, what things God has prepared for them that love him.*[15] And as if we questioned him, "How do you know these things?" He responds with, *But to us God has revealed them, by his Spirit.*[16] The second [understanding the meaning of *faints*] is explained thus: *My soul faints for the courts of God,* that is, it has [in a manner of speaking] died from a vehement affection by alienation or ecstasy: because from a most vehement occupation of intellectual powers in God, the bodily nature marvelously changes, the natural harmony becomes restricted, the body stiffens and is struck senseless; and so the sensitive powers are suspended in their operations, and man appears to be separated and withdrawn from himself.[17]

Cor meum, my heart, that is, the intellectual appetite, *et caro mea, and my flesh,* that is, the sensitive appetite; or [alternatively], *My heart,* that is the soul, *and my flesh,* namely, the body; *exaltaverunt in Deum vivum, have rejoiced in the living God,* that is, with exultation they incline toward God, the principle of all life, and in him and of him they rejoice, so that God is the object, cause, and the end of their joy. But this exultation is not fittingly uniformly said of the intellective appetite or the will, or of the sensitive appetite, or of the flesh. For in the will it [this exultation]

---

14   Ecclus. 18:30.

15   1 Cor. 2:9. *Cf.* Is. 64:4.

16   1 Cor. 2:10a.

17   *E. N.* "Supernatural ecstasy may be defined as a state which, while it lasts, includes two elements: (i) the one, interior and invisible, when the mind rivets its attention on a religious subject; (ii) the other, corporeal and visible, when the activity of the senses is suspended, so that not only are external sensations incapable of influencing the soul, but considerable difficulty is experienced in awakening such sensation, and this whether the ecstatic himself desires to do so, or others attempt to quicken the organs into action." *Catholic Encyclopedia* (New York: Robert Appleton Company, 1909), Vol. 5, p. 277 (s.v. "Ecstasy").

is according to essence; in the sensitive appetite it is according to redundance [or overflowing]; but in the flesh, it is according to a certain sign of interior joy, such as a serene countenance, laughter, and the certain re-flourishing of age: for as is written, *A joyful mind makes age flourishing: a sorrowful spirit dries up the bones.*[18] But the superior appetite, which is the will, moves the sensitive appetite, which it brings along with it, in the manner that an external sphere does the inferior;[19] for this reason the great affections of the will overflow into the sensitive appetite, so that it participates in the nature of affection, which exists in the will.

83{84}[4] *For the sparrow has found herself a house, and the turtle dove a nest for herself where she may lay her young ones: Your altars, O Lord of hosts, my king and my God.*

Etenim passer invenit sibi domum, et turtur nidum sibi, ubi ponat pullos suos. Altaria tua, Domine virtutum, rex meus, et Deus meus.

83{84}[4] *Etenim passer invenit sibi domum, et turtur nidum sibi, ubi ponat pullos suos; for the sparrow has found herself a house, and the turtle dove a nest for herself where she may lay her young ones.* This verse can be explained in a variety of ways. For Jerome literally explains it so that the Prophet is trying to prove by arguing from the major[20] that the rational creature must have

---

18   Prov. 17:22. E. N. This "spiritual youth" is especially invoked in the Psalm used in the prayers at the foot of the altar in the Latin Mass, which have meaning even in mouth of the stooped, wizened, and superannuated believer: *Introibo ad altare Dei. Ad Deum qui laetificat iuventutem meam.* We might profitably turn to Dietrich von Hildebrand: "[T]his attainment of full maturity also implies eternal youth in a supernatural sense. It implies that the readiness to change, the determination to become a new man, and the unconditional willingness to crucify the old self should increase; that the impatience for Christ should not abate. As he draws nearer to the gates of eternity, such a person will direct his attention to 'the one thing necessary' with ever increasing concentration. It is this supernatural youth which is referred to in the Gradual of the Mass, by the words *qui laetificat iuventutem meam* ("who giveth joy to my youth"). Here is, paradoxically speaking, a spiritual intactness increasing with age, inasmuch as throughout the *status viae* we continually enhance our alert readiness to change towards greater proximity to God." Dietrich von Hildebrand, *Transformation in Christ* (San Francisco: Ignatius Press 2016).

19   E. N. The reference is cosmological. In the medieval view, the heavens were composed of various spheres, and the higher spheres had an influence on the lower spheres. For more on the distinctions in the appetites, *see* ST Ia, q. 80, arts. 1–2; q. 59, art. 4, and IaIIae q. 17, art. 7, co.

20   E. N. The reference is to Aristotelian syllogism, which divided argument into three terms: major premise, minor premise, and conclusion. The Prophet is therefore

a place of blessedness in which he comes upon quiet and rest, because the sparrow, which is an irrational animal, after flying and in its weariness comes upon a place where it may rest. The turtle dove also has a nest, in which it places its own chicks: therefore, also man has a place given him where he might find rest, as Christ exhorts: *Lay up to yourselves treasures in heaven.*[21] The second explanation is as follows: *For the sparrow*, that is, a penitent man — of whom a later Psalm says, *I am become as a sparrow all alone on the housetop* —[22] *has found herself a house*, that is, a place of mercy in the Church of Christ, for he that comes to her, she will in no way cast out.[23] *And the turtle dove*, that is, the perfect man keeping his eye upon heavenly things, comes upon *a nest for herself*, that is, a mansion without doubt but in heaven, *where she may lay*, that is, finally establish, *her young ones*, that is, her works, not seeking on earth mercy from men, but in heaven from God. Now a penitent man is called a *sparrow*: first, because before his conversion, he was flighty, inconstant, lustful, and petulant, similar to a sparrow; second, because after his conversion, he built [his nests] up high, again similar to a sparrow, desiring to build the tower of virtue,[24] and hiding his works from the snares of devil in Christ. Also, the perfect man is said to be a *turtle dove* because he sighs with the desire of heaven, he builds his nest in the rock that is Christ,[25] and for his song, that is, he harbors sorrow of the joys of the world, that is, a contempt for worldly things. The third [explanation is] thus: *For the sparrow*, that is, reason, which sublimely flies with the wings of contemplation and virtue like a sparrow, *has found herself a house* now in the Church militant, dwelling in it by faith and love, and afterwards in the Church triumphant, dwelling in it by sight and blessed enjoyment; *and the turtle dove*, that is, [a soul] mortified in the flesh, with a spirit promptly obedient, and sighing in works of penance, *a nest for herself where she may lay her young ones*, because [the soul] has placed her works in a secure place, namely, not in the mouth of men, but in the purity of conscience.[26]

---

arguing from the major premise by pointing to what birds do.

21   Matt. 6:20a.

22   Ps. 101:8.

23   *Cf.* John 6:37b. E. N. The verse cited refers to the mercy of the Father for those who come to him through the Word made Flesh. It is analogously applied to the Church. In this instance, I have used feminine personal pronouns to refer to the Church to emphasize her merciful embrace to the penitent sinner, when she imitates Mary, the "refuge of sinners."

24   *Cf.* Luke 14:28: *For which of you having a mind to build a tower, does not first sit down, and reckon the charges that are necessary, whether he have wherewithal to finish it.*

25   *Cf.* 1 Cor. 10:4b.

26   E. N. In interpreting 2 Cor. 1:12, and St. Paul's notion of the "testimony of conscience," St. Thomas Aquinas states the following: "I hope and trust in God

Altaria tua, Domine virtutum, Rex meus et Deus meus; Your altars, O Lord of hosts, my king and my God. This verse can be explained in one way so that it pertains to the preceding verse, and it declares what is the house and what is the nest that the sparrow and turtle dove come upon, namely *your altars,* that is, the heavenly mansions about which we have already talked about in the beginning of this Psalm. [The heavenly mansions] are therefore called altars because in them the sacrifices of praise are unceasingly offered to the Lord; indeed, our service, oblations, and devotions are displayed and offered there by the holy angels to God. These altars, therefore, O Lord, are the home and nest of the wayfarers tending towards heaven, O Lord of hosts, you who legitimately are God and king of all things because you have created and you rule all things; but you are in a special way my king by specially providing for me, preserving me from many dangers and sins, and by bestowing the grace rightly steering me to the heavenly homeland of eternal life; you are in a special way my God, for not only did you produce my natural being, but also in my spiritual being you re-formed me with divine and gratifying grace. And I before all things singularly love and worship you. Now this cannot be said of all men, but only of the perfect, and also of those fervently and efficaciously making progress, of those who daily embrace God with arms of fervor and of desire, saying: *I held him: and I will not let him go;*[27] and *It is good for me to adhere to my God.*[28] This verse can be explained in a second way, in its words, but implying under these words something else, so that it [can be understood] in this sense: *Your altars, O Lord of hosts,* are those things by which the human desires are stilled, namely, those supernal tabernacles — which are called nests because of their security; but [they are called] altars, because of the perfect oblation [there offered], especially since upon them Christ also *makes intercession for us.*[29]

'who is our glory,' that is, I glory in the testimony and purity of our conscience, from which we may securely trust in God: 'If our hearts do not condemn us,' etc. (1 Jn. 3:21)....But he [St. Paul] does not say, the conscience *of others,* but *our* conscience, because a man should always put more trust in the testimony of his own conscience about himself than in the testimony of others." *Super II Epistolam ad Corinthios,* 1–4

27 Songs 3:4a.

28 Ps. 72:28b. E. N. Jesus is both sacrifice (the perfect oblation) and the altar. Heb. 9:13–14; 13:10. "The altar is the symbol of Christ himself who is present both as sacrificial victim (the altar of the sacrifice) and as food from heaven which is given to us (the table of the Lord)." *Compendium of the Catechism of the Catholic Church,* § 288.

83{84}[5] *Blessed are they that dwell in your house, O Lord: they shall praise you for ever and ever.*

Beati qui habitant in domo tua, Domine; in saecula saeculorum laudabunt te.

83{84}[5] *Beati qui habitant in domo tua, Domine; blessed are they that dwell in your house, O Lord,* that is, in the kingdom of heaven, in the heavenly homeland of the elect, in the palace of angels, in the empyreal heaven, in the eternal *house not made by human hands,*[30] in the Church triumphant; *in saecula saeculorum, for ever and ever,* that is, without end, *laudabunt te, they shall praise you,* as is contained in Revelation: *They rested not day and night, saying Holy, holy, holy, Lord God Almighty.*[31] And elsewhere: *They who will be redeemed, shall come into Sion singing praises, and joy everlasting shall be upon their heads, they shall obtain joy and gladness, sorrow and mourning shall flee away.*[32] Indeed, such is the beatitude of the dwellers in his heavenly home, that every want, every misery, every displeasure, every insecurity, every limit is excluded; but [the state of beatitude] comprehends every sufficiency and everything pleasing. For whatever is desired is available; whatever is repelling is far away. Rightly, therefore, is it written in the Gospel: *Blessed is he that shall eat bread in the kingdom of God.*[33] And Peter: In Jesus *though you see him not, you believe: and seeing shall rejoice with joy unspeakable and glorified.*[34] And in this kingdom of beatitude, our highest and only occupation, our entire exertions, and our most delightful business will be to praise God, to glorify the superlatively most happy Trinity, to sing Alleluia to the sublime and blessed God, as is written in Isaiah: *Joy and gladness shall be found therein, thanksgiving, and the voice of praise.*[35] But who will merit to be lead to this perennial praise and heavenly mansions?

---

30   2 Cor. 5:1.

31   Rev. 4:8; Is. 6:3.

32   Is. 51:11.

33   Luke 14:15b. E. N. Our destination "is a heavenly Eucharist and marriage in which the terrifying chasms between time and eternity will be — not closed, but illuminated by God's triune life.... There will be a Eucharist; it will no longer nourish our mortal bodies (*Körper*), but those vital bodies (*Leiber*) which will simply be the 'expression' of our freedom and essentiality, what Henstenberg calls 'bodying-forth' (*Darleibung*); and for this very reason they will not be able to do without God's eternal nourishment. Eucharist, an event of love, will remain something reciprocal. Thus Ruysbroeck often spoke of God being devoured by the avid spirit and of the spirit being devoured by God." Hans Urs von Balthasar, *Theo-Drama: Theological Dramatic Theory: Volume 5: The Last Act* (San Francisco: Ignatius, 1998), 481.

34   1 Pet. 1:8. E. N. Denis replaces *credentes* with *videntes*, thus changing the verse from saying "believing shall rejoice" to "seeing shall rejoice."

35   Is. 51:3b.

None but he who now praises the Lord, now openly rejoices in him, now is glad in venerating him; he who living in the flesh, does not live according to the flesh,[36] but in the present age orders and imitates the angelic and heavenly manner of living, fulfilling zealously that which is written: *Fear the Lord, and give him honor, . . . and adore him, that made heaven and earth, the sea, and the fountains of waters.*[37]

83{84}[6]   *Blessed is the man whose help is from you: in his heart he has disposed to ascend by steps.*

             Beatus vir cuius est auxilium abs te, ascensiones in corde suo disposuit.

83{84}[7]   *In the vale of tears, in the place which he has set.*

             In valle lacrimarum, in loco quem posuit.

Moreover, the Prophet makes it clear that it is not through human and natural virtue, but with the help of the grace of God that man will be led to the heavenly home. **83{84}[6]** *Beatus vir, cuius est auxilium abs te, blessed is the man whose help is from you:* that is, happy the man now in hope, and then in reality, to whom you have bestowed, O Lord, by means of the help of your grace, that he labor and that he attain by grace (which is a supernatural gift, exceeding all natural dignity and faculties) that which he is unable sufficiently to do or to acquire by nature. In this error the Pelagians split off [from the Church],[38] as they asserted man to be able to merit and to be saved without a special and supernatural grace. For this reason, the Apostle [Paul] states: God *has quickened us together in Christ, by whose grace you are saved.*[39] And again: *By grace,* he says, *you are saved through faith, . . . and not of works. For it is a gift of God . . . that no man may glory.*[40] In addition, the Lord also says through Hosea: *Destruction is your own, O Israel; your help is only in me.*[41] Therefore, Blessed be the

---

36   Cf. 2 Cor. 10:3: *For though we walk in the flesh, we do not war according to the flesh.*

37   Rev. 14:7.

38   E. N. Pelagius (*ca.* 354–418) was a British monk who fell into heresy by denying the Church's doctrine of original sin, and in deprecating the necessity of grace for keeping the commandments and living a virtuous and supernatural life. St. Augustine wrote polemical works against him. Pelagius was ultimately condemned by the Council of Carthage (418) the Second Council of Ephesus (431). A tempered, though equally heretical Pelagianism (semi-Pelagianism) was ultimately condemned in the Second Council of Orange (529).

39   Eph. 2:5.

40   Eph. 2:8–9.

41   Hosea 13:9.

man whose help is from you, for *if God be for us, who is against us?*[42]

Ascensiones, to ascend by steps, that is, by grades of spiritual perfection, increments of virtuous progression, *in corde suo disposuit, in his heart he has disposed,* proposing [to himself] strongly to advance and by use of his free will to cooperate with the grace of God,[43] 83{84}[7] *in valle lacrimarum, in the vale of tears,* that is, in the present exile of pilgrimage in which sins always beat us down, *in loco quem posuit, in the place which has set,* that is, [in the place in] which man caused his own vale of tears, because by sinning he was cast out of paradise, and was thrown into this valley.[44] Or [alternatively], in the place where God places men is called the vale of tears since in it he bemoans his vices, and sighs crying out for the heavenly homeland. Whence the Lord said to Adam: *Cursed is the earth in your work . . . . In the sweat of your face shall you eat bread.*[45] But from this the vale of tears no one can craft for himself the gift of joy, using this world as if it were the heavenly homeland, and not as if it were but a path; as if [this world] were a paradise, and not as if an exile.[46] Scripture cries out about such men: *Whosoever therefore will be*

---

42   Rom. 8:31b.

43   E. N. Denis is pointing to what Pope John Paul II called the "law of gradualism" (*lex gradualitatis*), which is to be rigorously distinguished from any "gradualism of the law" (*gradualitas legis*). See *Familiaris Consortio,* No. 34; see also John Paul II, Homily of October 25, 1980 at the Close of the Sixth Synod of Bishops, No. 8. Under the principle of the law of gradualism, the moral norms and norms of spiritual perfection are understood to be unchanging. However, unless we are the recipient of an extraordinary grace, our understanding of them and ability to obey them is typically gradual, a mixed effort of success and of failure, with a hoped for gyral tendency upwards toward greater and greater knowledge of these norms, and greater and greater success in our ability to conform to them. Concomitantly, we might expect less and less error regarding these norms, and less and less and failure in our ability to obey them as we advance in our Christian or human pilgrimage. We are poor pilgrims, we stumble and fall, and sometimes we inadvertently take a wrong path, but our focus is on our bourne, and we get stronger and closer to our goal each day of our walk with the Lord. Thus, the law of gradualism recognizes the step-by-step process of moral and spiritual perfection, both as a part of natural virtue and spiritual virtue, as we clamber up the hillside of the moral life that strives toward perfection. But the law of gradualism does not encompass consent to the gradualism of the law. We must adapt to the natural moral law and the beatitudes; the natural law and beatitudes do not adapt to us.

44   Gen. 3:23.

45   Gen. 3:17b, 19a.

46   E. N. This seems to be a veiled reference to St. Augustine's distinction between *uti/frui,* use/enjoyment in the context of life in this world. In a nutshell, St. Augustine says that the world is to be used (*uti*) as a means to an end, and not enjoyed (*frui*) for its own sake as an end. However, with God it is the opposite: God is the end and is to be enjoyed (*frui*), and never used as a means (*uti*). Man, a spiritual

a friend of this world, becomes an enemy of God.[47] But we are to use this world as pilgrims, on the way, in exile, and in a vale and prison of tears, and we ought to dispose within ourselves to ascend the steps of spiritual advancement; but its consummation and its execution we must expect from the Lord, according to that written by Solomon: *The heart of man disposes his way: but the Lord must direct his steps.*[48] And so it adds:

83{84}[8] *For the lawgiver shall give a blessing, they shall go from virtue to virtue: the God of gods shall be seen in Sion.*

Etenim benedictionem dabit legislator; ibunt de virtute in virtutem, videbitur Deus deorum in Sion.

83{84}[8] *Etenim benedictionem, for . . . a blessing,* that is, the infusion of heavenly grace and the multiplication of divine gifts, *dabit, he shall give* in this life to his elect, [which shall be given by] *legislator, the law giver,* that is, Christ, the bearer of both Testaments, who admonishes through Isaiah: *Hearken unto me, O my people, . . . for a law shall go forth from me, and my judgment shall rest to be a light of the nations.*[49] The faithful *ibunt de virtute in virtutem, shall go from virtue to virtue,* that is, from good to better, until they are lead to the best; they shall go for the act of one virtue to the work of another, now praying, now giving aid to another, now bewailing their own evil: and so after this pilgrimage by them clearly *videbitur Deus deorum, the God of gods shall be seen,* that is, the sovereign and true God, the Lord and Creator of all things which by participation are called gods,[50] *in Sion,* that heavenly [Sion], of which the Apostle says: *You are come to mount Sion, and to the city of the living God, the heavenly Jerusalem, and to the company of many thousands of angels.*[51] Here, God separates the saints in the heavenly fatherland in the manner that is expressed in Revelation: *And they shall see his face: and his name shall be on their foreheads.*[52] See how much and what kind of

---

being "in between" material things and God, may be the object of both *uti* and *frui*. Sin reverses these relationships. *See* book I in St. Augustine's *On Christian Doctrine.*

47   James 4:4b.

48   Prov. 16:9.

49   Is. 51:4.

50   E. N. Denis appears here to interpret "of gods" (*deorum*) very loosely to refer to those things either which are *vestigia Dei* (vestiges or traces of God), i.e., brute creation, as well as those things that are *imago Dei* (image of God), i.e., man and angels, and so in some sense participate in the Creator's first cause.

51   Heb. 12:22.

52   Rev. 22:4.

joy is the reward of this spiritual ascension which has its foundation in true humility, and which is promised the vision of God. For this reason it is stated: *For the fruit of good labors is glorious,*[53] namely, the clear knowledge of God. Of which the same Scripture says: *For to know you is perfect justice: and to know . . . your power, is the root of immortality.*[54]

83{84}[9]   *O Lord God of hosts, hear my prayer: give ear, O God of Jacob.*

Domine Deus virtutum, exaudi orationem meam; auribus percipe, Deus Iacob.

83{84}[10]   *Look, O God our protector: and look on the face of your Christ.*

Protector noster, adspice, Deus, et respice in faciem Christi tui.

And so that man may deserve to obtain this help of God, he now states with devotion: **83{84}[9]** *Domine, Deus virtutum, exaudi orationem meam; O Lord, God of hosts, hear my prayer,* giving me that which I ask for; *auribus percipe, give ear,* that is, by your mercy and wisdom show yourself to have accepted my prayers, *Deus Iacob, O God of Jacob,* of the patriarch, and of the people supplanting vices who are designated by the name Jacob.[55] **83{84}[10]** *Protector noster, our protector* in adversity, *adspice, Deus; look, O God,* upon my prayers, devotions, and labors; *et respice in faciem Christi tui, and look on the face of your Christ,* of the Lord Savior, whom we have as an advocate with you,[56] and who is the *propitiation for our sins,*[57] according to John; and who according to Paul ascended into heaven *so that he may appear now* in your *presence for us.*[58] Look upon this, and through all the holiness, dignity, and all the merit which he for our salvation assumed, did, and carried out, grant to us that which our works do not merit, and whatever we beseech in his name, since that which your Christ said will prove true: *Amen, amen I say to you: if you ask the Father anything in my name, he will give it you.*[59]

---

53   Wis. 3:15a.

54   Wis. 15:3.

55   E. N. Denis identifies those who wrestle against vice as Jacobs, and so they are "supplanters" of vices: "Jacob and Israel are one and the same; and every one of the faithful in the present life is called Jacob so long as he wrestles with vice; but in the future he will truly be called Israel, when he will see God face to face." *Beatus Vir*, Volume 1, Article XXXVI (Psalm 13:7), p. 232.

56   1 John 2:1b.

57   1 John 2:2a.

58   Heb. 9:24.

59   John 16:23.

83{84}[11] *For better is one day in your courts above thousands. I have chosen to be an abject in the house of my God, rather than to dwell in the tabernacles of sinners.*

Quia melior est dies una in atriis tuis super millia; elegi abiectus esse in domo Dei mei magis quam habitare in tabernaculis peccatorum.

I pray for grace which comes before your glory, O Lord, **83{84}[11]** *Quia melior est dies una in atriis tuis,* for better is one day in your courts, that is, in your previously-mentioned beloved tabernacles and heavenly mansions, *super millia, above thousands,* that is, way more than any multitude of days of the present life. For the goods of this present life are nothing in comparison to the joys or the riches of the kingdom of heaven; and it is more noble to live so as to contemplate God by sight for one day, than to perceive him many thousands of days by faith. But it says, *better is one day, etc.* not that in heaven there is a plurality of days, for in heaven days are not interrupted by nights, nor are the vicissitudes of time suffered there; but because one of those days of the saints in the heavenly homeland, which is a participation in eternity and is called aeviternity,[60] contains and includes [in a manner of speaking] many days. Also the causal conjunction put in the beginning of this verse[61] can be said to refer to the following verse: *Elegi abiectus esse in domo Dei mei, I have chosen to be an abject in the house of my God,* that is, I prefer to appear contemptible, to be humiliated, to be below everyone, to be subject to all, to be condemned, and to be punished in the Church of Christ, or wherever there is a congregation of the faithful, *magis quam habitare in tabernaculis peccatorum, rather than to dwell in the tabernacles of sinners,* that is, than to be honored in the world, to be raised high in the present age, to preside over others, to dominate others, to mix with, to conform to, or to please impious men. For one arrives to the heights by humility, and in no other way. Thus Moses: *Depart from the tents of these wicked men,* he said, *and touch nothing of theirs, lest you be involved in their sins.*[62]

---

60 E. N. On aeviternity, *see* footnote 1-94, 38–57; *see also Dominus Illuminatio Mea,* Vol. 2, Article LXXVII (Psalm 38:5), p. 261.

61 E. N. The causal conjunction is that which signifies a preceding cause, in this case, the verse Denis is referring is "For better is one day in your courts above thousands," which is the cause of the attitude of detachment from the things of this world mentioned in the latter half of the verse.

62 Num. 16:26.

83{84}[12]   *For God loves mercy and truth: the Lord will give grace and glory.*

*Quia misericordiam et veritatem diligit Deus, gratiam et glo-
riam dabit Dominus.*

83{84}[13]   *He will not deprive of good things them that walk in innocence:
O Lord of hosts, blessed is the man that trusts in you.*

*Non privabit bonis eos qui ambulant in innocentia. Domine
virtutum, beatus homo qui sperat in te.*

83{84}[12] *Quia misericordiam et veritatem, for mercy and truth,* that
is, justice, *diligit Deus, God loves* in himself, and also in us, for by them
we please God, in the manner that Micah commemorates: *I will show
you, O man, what is good, and what the Lord requires of you: Verily, to
do judgment, and to love mercy.*[63] For also in an earlier Psalm is said, *All
the ways of the Lord are mercy and truth:*[64] which also applies to all the
works done for God. And Solomon teaches: *Let not mercy and truth leave
you ... and you shall find grace ... before God and men.*[65] *Gratiam, grace*
in the present and *gloriam, glory* in the future *dabit Dominus, the Lord
will give:* for from him descends *every best gift, and every perfect gift.*[66]
83{84}[13] *No privabit bonis, he will not deprive of good things,* namely [of
the goods] mentioned earlier, namely, the help of grace, heavenly blessing,
and the reward of glory, *eos qui ambulant in innocentia, them that walk
in innocence* of heart, that is, who live in a just manner, harming no one,
and obeying the divine commandments. Of these kinds of men, Solomon
asserts: *They that are upright shall dwell in the earth, and the simple shall
continue in it.*[67] Whence something regarding this is said by the holy
Job: *Remember, I pray you, whoever perished being innocent? ... On the
contrary, I have seen those who are iniquitous perishing by the blast of
God.*[68] And elsewhere: *The innocent shall be saved, and he shall be saved
by the cleanness of his hands.*[69] *Domine virtutum, beatus homo qui sperat
in te; O Lord of hosts, blessed is the man that trusts in you,* through a
formed hope,[70] as Isaiah foretold: *The Lord is the God of judgment:*

---

63   Micah 6:8.
64   Ps. 24:10a.
65   Prov. 3:3–4.
66   James 1:17a.
67   Prov. 2:21.
68   Job 4:7–9.
69   Job 22:30.
70   E. N. A "formed hope," *spes formata,* is a hope that is informed by charity, and
so it excludes any kind of presumption. *See* footnote 36-19.

blessed are all they that wait for him.[71] Whence also in another place is written: *My children behold the generations of men: and know you that no one has hoped in the Lord, and has been confounded.*[72]

O how glorious, how loving, and how holy is this Psalm we have heard! Now this [Psalm] is consoling to the religious or those cloistered who, spurning the world, prefer in humble and abject life to serve the Lord in a monastery than to taste the delights and flourish in the world. Let us love, therefore, and loving with an incomparable let us love before the beloved tabernacles of the Lord of hosts, transcending all transitory things and regarding them as dung. Let us desire, and so desiring let us abandon our souls upon the altars of God, knowingly and openly professing because *we have not here a lasting city, but we seek one that is to come,*[73] so that we are *as strangers and pilgrims.*[74] Above all, let us exult both inside and out in the Lord, contemplating his dignity, his goodness, and his blessedness, recalling to mind his benefits, awaiting his promises, loving him in all things, venerating, intending, and seeking him in every way. Let us endeavor also unceasingly to advance, to pass from one act of virtue in our labors unto another, and to persevere in these divine labors, so that we might be allowed to contemplate the God of gods in Sion by sight.

PRAYER

O GOD, O STRONG HELPER, WE BESEECH you, may your power be at hand for us who are in this valley of lamentation; teach us to be disposed in our hearts to ascend by steps, so that going forth from virtue to virtue, you might grant to us with great joy to see you, the God of gods, in the heavenly Sion.

*Auxiliator Deus fortis, adsit nobis, quaesumus, virtus tua hac
in valle plorationis; doce nos ascensiones in cordibus
nostris disponere: ut de virtute in virtutem
euntes, Deum deorum in caelisti Sion
nos te videre concedas laetantes.*

---

71 Is. 30:18b.
72 Ecclus. 2:11.
73 Heb. 13:14.
74 1 Pet. 2:11a.

Psalm 84

ARTICLE LIX

ELUCIDATION OF THE EIGHTY-FOURTH PSALM:
BENEDIXISTI, DOMINE, TERRAM TUAM.
LORD, YOU HAVE BLESSED YOUR LAND.

84{85}[1] *Unto the end, for the sons of Korah, a Psalm.*

In finem, filiis Core. Psalmus.

PREVIOUS PSALM HAD THE TITLE NOW BEING stated: **84{85}[1]** *In finem, filiis Core. Psalmus; unto the end, for the sons of Korah. A Psalm:* that is, this present Psalm is directing us *unto the end,* who is Christ, and it sings about and relates to the sons of Korah, and the imitators of Christ crucified, whose entire manner of living was as it were a certain continuous passion. This Psalm is literally written about the first coming of Christ, or the Incarnation, and of the combination of various benefits obtained by the human race through the Passion of Christ.

As has already been often stated, this Psalm, in whose title is stated the sons of Korah, according to St. Jerome and the Hebrews, was written by the sons of Korah, or at least one of them. But according to Augustine, all the Psalms are said to have been published by David, and the sons of Korah are explained in a spiritual way, so that by them is understood the sons of the Lord Jesus who was crucified for us,[1] because Korah is interpreted to refer to Calvary, where Christ was crucified.[2] But the Hebrews (whom Jerome follows) assert that when Korah began to rebel against Moses, in the manner that Darthan and Abiron and On of the tribe of Ruben, the sons of Korah first consented with their father, but afterwards they repented.[3] But when Moses ordered that all men back away from the tents of Korah, and Dathan, and Abiron, lest they perish together with them, the sons of Korah did not back away, but remained with their father in the tent, since they had opposed themselves in his

---

1 John 19:17–18.
2 *E. N. See, e.g.,* Vol. 2 (*Dominus Illuminatio Mea*) Article LXXXII (Psalm 41:1) and footnote 40-3.
3 *E. N. See* footnote 36-105. *See also* Num. 16:33; 26:11.

rebellion. While true that they had turned around from his defiance, the earth gave way beneath their feet, and he along with his tent was absorbed by the earth, and it descended into hell with the earth covering him up. And a great miracle occurred that while he [Korah] perished, his sons did not: for they remained suspended in the air, until after the earth had reclosed. All this is stated by Moses in the book of Numbers.[4] Given these deeds and considerations, the sons of Korah had turned back to God with all their heart: for which reason they deserved to receive the spirit of prophesy. And Jerome says: Pouring over with a wise mind over the entire Psalter, I come upon nothing in the Psalms written by the sons of Korah that is sad: for they always rejoice in all things in their Psalms, and they are agreeable and full of love; and they are contemptuous of the world, desiring heavenly and eternal things.[5]

84{85}[2]   *Lord, you have blessed your land: you have turned away the captivity of Jacob.*

Benedixisti, Domine, terram tuam; avertisti captivitatem Iacob.

And so the holy Prophet says: 84{85}[2] *Benedixisti, Domine; you have blessed Lord,* the Father or God the Trinity [has blessed], by the Incarnation of Christ, *terram tuam, your land,* that is, the Church of all the elect, giving them salvation and grace by the coming of Christ. For that which he did after the Incarnation and the Passion of Christ occurred, he did in the old times in all those who then by a formed faith believed in the Christ to come in the future, that is, all those united by the bond of charity.[6] Whence John in Revelation affirms, The Lamb which was Christ, was slain *from the beginning of the world.*[7] Now the blessing of God is that combination of the divine gifts. *Avertisti captivitatem, you have turned away the captivity,* that is, the requirement of the punishment of loss because of original sin, and the spiritual captivity by which the

---

4   E. N. Num. 26:10–11 expressly excludes the sons of Korah from punishment: "And the earth opening her mouth swallowed up Korah . . . And there was a great miracle wrought, that when Korah perished, his sons did not perish."

5   E. N. This appears to be a paraphrase of an excerpt from one of St. Jerome's homilies on Psalm 41. I was unable to find the precise source.

6   ST IIaIIae, q. 2, art. 7, ad 3: Before the coming of Christ, those Gentiles who were not privy to the revelation of Christ and yet were saved "were not saved without faith in a Mediator. For, although they did not have explicit faith (*fidem explicitam*) [in Christ], they nevertheless did have implicit faith (*fidem implicitam*) in Divine providence, believing God to be the deliverer of men in whatever way was pleasing to him."

7   Rev. 13:8b.

demons held man captive, because of the yoke of iniquity and the slavery of fault and to demons. Therefore, in this manner have you turned
away the captivity *Iacob, of Jacob*, that is, of the people of the faithful, by
supplanting vice, of those born from Jacob bodily or spiritually, delivering
them from servitude to sin and the captivity of the devil. For Christ
bound the strong man,[8] and cast out the prince of this world.[9] Zechariah
joyfully proclaimed this turning away of the captivity of Christ as being
done: *He swore to Abraham our father, that he would grant us, that being
delivered from the hand of our enemies, we may serve him without fear.*[10]
Of this future liberation, Jeremiah also said: *In those days shall Juda be
saved, and Israel shall dwell confidently.*[11] And the Lord through Isaiah
said to Christ: *I have given you for a covenant of the people, for a light of
the Gentiles . . . that you might bring forth the prisoner out of prison, and
them that sit in darkness out of the prison house.*[12] With good reason are
all the faithful literally understood by [the figure of] Jacob or the Jewish
people, because at the time that this present Psalm was written, almost
all the world had declined into idolatry, except for the sons of Jacob,
and so by [the name] Jacob is designated all those who follow his faith.

84{85}[3] *You have forgiven the iniquity of your people: you have covered
all their sins.*

> *Remisisti iniquitatem plebis tuae, operuisti omnia peccata eorum.*

84{85}[3] *Remisisti,* you have forgiven, O God, O Trinity, *iniquitatem
plebis tuae,* the iniquity of your people both faithful and elect, through the
coming and the Passion of Christ, who not only blotted out original sin,
but also removed actual sins, making satisfaction for the sins of the whole
world, in the manner that is written: *Behold the Lamb of God, behold
him who takes away the sin of the world.*[13] And the Apostle [Paul]: *God
was in Christ, reconciling the world to himself.*[14] Isaiah also: *The Lord
has laid on him the iniquity of us all.*[15] But if the virtue or merit of the
Incarnation, the manner of living, and of the Passion of Christ is to be
profitable to us, it behooves that it be applied to us: and it is applied

---

8   *Cf.* Matt. 12:29. and
9   *Cf.* John 12:31.
10 Luke 1:73–74.
11 Jer. 23:6a.
12 Is. 42:6b–7.
13 John 1:29.
14 2 Cor. 5:19a.
15 Is. 53:6b.

to us by faith and charity and the sacraments of the Church. For this reason, Paul attests: *In him every one that believes, is justified.*[16] *Operuisti omnia peccata eorum, you have covered all their sins* by Christ's death and obedience: for by dying and giving all that he had, he blotted out all sins as if they never had been. And so you, O God, have testified of Christ: *Behold, I will bring my servant the Orient, . . . and I will take away the iniquity of that land in one day,*[17] that is, in the day of his Passion.

84{85}[4]   *You have mitigated all your anger: you have turned away from the wrath of your indignation.*

Mitigasti omnem iram tuam, avertisti ab ira indignationis tuae.

84{85}[4] *Mitigasti omnem iram tuam, you have mitigated all your anger:* that is, in effect, through your mercy you have converted the vengeance of your justice, not taking vengeance any longer upon original sin: because no one is separated from the beatific vision because of it after the Passion of Christ, provided that he does not have some other sort of defect,[18] namely, [being in a state of mortal sin so] that the merits of Christ would not be applied to him; *avertisti, you have turned away* [that is, you have turned] yourself, *ab ira indignationis tuae, from the wrath of your indignation,* that is, from the great vengeance of your justice: because up to the coming of Christ, you forgave the nations of their various errors and overlooked condemning many, but once Christ came, you began to illuminate the Gentiles. For this reason, Paul said: *God indeed having winked at the times of this ignorance, now declares unto men, that all should everywhere do penance.*[19] And the Scripture says: *All we like sheep have gone astray, everyone has turned aside into his own way.*[20] But once the Lord Savior was born, *the people that walked in darkness have seen a great light;*[21] and men began to abandon their own ways, and to walk in the paths of Christ, in the manner that John taught: *He that says he abides in Christ, ought*

---

16   Acts 13:39.
17   Zech. 3:8b, 9b.
18   E. N. Denis is speaking of those baptized who have not committed actual sins that are mortal in nature which have not been forgiven by an act of perfect contrition or the Sacrament of Confession. A mortal sin committed after baptism — if unattended by reliance upon this "second plank [of salvation] after the shipwreck which is the loss of grace" — would separate a baptized person from the merits of Christ. CCC § 1446.
19   Acts 17:30.
20   Is. 53:6a.
21   Is. 9:2a.

himself also to walk, even as he walked.[22] Now this mitigation he also extended to the Jews, indeed even unto the fathers in limbo; for their guilt of original sin, by which they were delayed from glory, was forgiven by Christ. Whence the Lord said: *I will heal their breaches, I will love them freely: for my wrath is turned away from them.*[23] This also Micah brings forth, saying: *He will send his fury in no more, because he delights in mercy. He will turn again, and have mercy on us: he will put away our iniquities: and he will cast all our sins into the bottom of the sea.*[24]

84{85}[5] *Convert us, O God our Savior: and turn off your anger from us.*

Converte nos, Deus salutaris noster, et averte iram tuam a nobis.

84{85}[6] *Will you be angry with us forever: or will you extend your wrath from generation to generation?*

Numquid in aeternum irasceris nobis? Aut extendes iram tuam a generatione in generationem?

84{85}[5] *Converte nos, Deus salutaris noster; convert us, O God our Savior*, with a stable and perfect conversion, so that we may bind ourselves to you with the whole heart, the whole soul, the whole strength by sincere contemplation, fervent love, and a devout and humble worship; *et averte iram tuam a nobis, and turn off your anger from us,* by you yourself coming down to us and making satisfaction for us. But since it is said earlier [in verse 4], *You have mitigated all your anger,* why is it necessary now to pray that his anger be averted from us? The response to this is that God, inasmuch he in himself, is entirely placated by Christ with respect to us; but if we allow ourselves to become ungrateful to Christ, God is more angry with us than he was before. So let us pray that he might avert his anger: first, that he permits us not to fall; second, to the extent we might fall away, that he might immediately have mercy and come to our aid. 84{85}[6] *Numquid in aeternum irasceris nobis; will you be angry with us forever,* withdrawing your aid and grace because of our wrongdoing, *aut extendes iram tuam, or will you extend your wrath,* that is, will you continue your vengeance, *a generatione in generationem, from generation to generation,* that is, from a preceding generation unto any subsequent generation without end? Of course not, because it is your property always to have mercy and to spare: for you have spoken,

---

22 1 John 2:6.

23 Hosea 14:5.

24 Micah 7:18–19.

I know the thoughts that I think towards you, . . . thoughts of peace, and not of affliction, to give you an end and patience.[25]

84{85}[7] *You will turn, O God, and bring us to life: and your people shall rejoice in you.*

Deus, tu conversus vivificabis nos, et plebs tua laetabitur in te.

84{85}[7] *Deus, tu conversus;* you will turn, O God to us by your Incarnation and by your bodily presence, *vivificabis nos,* you will bring us life with the life of grace in the present, and the life of glory in the future. Whence Christ said: *I am come that they may have life, and may have it more abundantly.*[26] Also elsewhere: *Grace and truth came by Jesus Christ.*[27] And he said again: *I am the resurrection and the life: he that believes in me . . . shall not die forever.*[28] Now Christ vivifies us because he delivers us from the death of sin and the ruin of hell, and he fills our hearts with his saving doctrine and grace. And so it is written: *The time to seek the Lord is when he that shall teach you justice shall come;*[29] and again, *I will deliver them out of the hand of death. I will redeem them from death.*[30] *Et plebs tua,* and your people Christian, chosen, and holy, *laetabitur,* shall rejoice, not in fleshly, vain, unlawful things, but *in te, in you,* rejoicing in your goodness, perfection, and blessedness, and exulting with all their heart in your benefits and promises. To such holy joy in God we are admonished by Joel: *Be joyful in the Lord your God: because he has given you a teacher of justice.*[31] Isaiah also, speaking in the person of the Christian people, most beautifully says: *Lo, this is our God, we have waited for him, and he will save us: this is the Lord, we have patiently waited for him, we shall rejoice and be joyful in his salvation.*[32] This also Habakkuk says: *I will rejoice in the Lord: and I will joy in God my Jesus.*[33]

84{85}[8] *Show us, O Lord, your mercy; and grant us your salvation.*

Ostende nobis, Domine, misericordiam tuam, et salutare tuum da nobis.

---

25 Jer. 29:11.
26 John 10:10b.
27 John 1:17b.
28 John 11:26–26.
29 Hosea 10:12b.
30 Hosea 13:14a.
31 Joel 2:23a.
32 Is. 25:9.
33 Hab. 3:18.

84{85}[8] *Ostende nobis, Domine, misericordiam tuam; show us, O Lord, your mercy*: that is, Christ, your Son, the fountain of your mercy, by whom you most exceedingly have mercy upon us, manifest him to our eyes, since we saw him with the eyes of the mind and the body living on the earth: as was said by Baruch: *Afterwards he was seen upon earth, and conversed with men.*[34] The Prophet prays therefore that Christ, assuming human nature, might appear visibly in the world: and this a short time later was fulfilled, as John in the beginning of his first epistle makes clearly known: *That which was from the beginning, which we have heard, which we have seen with our eyes, . . . and our hands have handled, of the Word of life.*[35] And also elsewhere: *The Word was made flesh, and dwelt among us, and we saw his glory, the glory as it were of the only begotten of the Father.*[36] *Et salutare tuum, and . . . your salvation*, that is, Christ the Savior, by whom you save us, *da nobis, grant us* freely from your love and goodness, not from our justice, sending him to us in the nativity from the Virgin, in the way that was predicted by Isaiah: *For a child is born to us, and a son is given to us.*[37] And elsewhere Christ says: *For God so loved the world, as to give his only begotten Son.*[38] Now we also appropriately ought daily to pray this verse, and in this sense: *Show us, O Lord, your mercy,* that is, evidently and copiously show in us the effect of your kindness; *and . . . your salvation*, that is, your salutary salvation, *grant us,* or [grant us] even Christ, giving him to us daily in the Sacrament of the Altar and by his spiritually coming to dwell with us, as is written of him under the name of Wisdom: *Give me wisdom, O Lord, that sits by your throne.*[39]

84{85}[9] *I will hear what the Lord God will speak in me: for he will speak peace unto his people: And unto his saints: and unto them that are converted to the heart.*

Audiam quid loquatur in me Dominus Deus, quoniam loquetur pacem in plebem suam, et super sanctos suos, et in eos qui convertuntur ad cor.

84{85}[9] *Audiam, I will hear* with the ears of my mind paying great attention, *quid loquatur in me Dominus Deus, what the Lord God will speak in me* by internal inspiration, or by angelic and hidden enlightenment.

34   Baruch 3:38.
35   1 John 1:1.
36   John 1:14.
37   Is. 9:6a.
38   John 3:16a.
39   Wis. 9:4a.

And rightly will I hear, *quoniam loquetur pacem in plebem suam, for he will speak peace unto his people*, that is, he will inspire in me by an internal inspiration, those things that incline his people toward peace: for while he inspires me with the coming, Passion, and death of Christ, he speaks of those things in me by which the whole world is to obtain true and heavenly peace. For this reason, the angel said to the shepherds upon Christ's birth: *I bring you good tidings of great joy, . . . for, this day, is born to you a Savior.*[40] Now, the angel having said this, *there suddenly was . . . a multitude of the heavenly army, praising God and saying: Glory to God in the highest; and on earth peace to men of good will.*[41] *Et super sancto suos, et in eos qui convertuntur ad cor; and unto his saints: and unto them that are converted to the heart*: because this word of peace does not only touch and concern the common people, but also the perfect, and the Gentiles and sinners who — from their idolatry, which is the highest error of foolishness and irrationality, or from sensuality or perversity in judgment — return to their heart, that is, to the use of reason, obeying the divine law and right reason.[42]

We are taught in this place diligently to pay attention to that which the Lord our God says to us, especially that we acquiesce to his inspirations. And so Habakkuk says: *I will stand upon my watch, . . . and I will watch to see what will be said to me.*[43] But in order to accomplish this it is necessary to know what is the divine instinct,[44] which is angelic,

---

40   Luke 2:10.

41   Luke 2:13, 14.

42   As Cardinal Raymond Burke stated in a speech given at the closing of Human Life International's Fifth World Prayer Congress for Life on October 9, 2010: "[T]he Magisterium [of the Church] includes also the precepts of the natural law written by God upon the human heart, the requirements of conduct inherent in man's very nature and in the order of the world, God's creation. Obedience to the demands of the natural law is necessary for salvation, and, therefore, the teaching of the natural law is within the authority of the Magisterium and part of its solemn responsibility." http://lexchristianorum.blogspot.com/2010/10/compliance-with-natural-law-essential. html. The natural moral law is a divinely promulgated law based upon right reason.

43   Hab. 2:1. E. N. St. Josemaría Escrivá refers to a similar image in Isaiah 21:11 in advocating a habitual means to listen to God's promptings: *"Watchman, how goes the night?* May you acquire the habit of having a day on guard once a week, during which to increase your self-giving and loving vigilance over details, and to pray and mortify yourself a little more. Realize that the Holy Church is like a great army in battle array. And you, within that army, are defending one 'front' on which there are attacks, engagements with the enemy and counterattacks. . . . This readiness to grow closer to God will lead you to turn your days, one after the other, into days on guard." *The Furrow* No. 960 (New York: Scepter 2011), 368.

44   E. N. As explained in footnote 34-6 in Volume 2, the "divine instinct" is a

what is natural, and what is demonic. But whatever thought occurs in our mind that is according to God and the law of Christ, we can without danger ascribe to God, and we ought to implement it and preserve it. For Scripture says of this uncreated Wisdom: *Wisdom is more active than all active things: and reaches everywhere by reason of her purity.*[45] *And being but one, she can do all things,* ... and she *conveys herself into holy souls, she makes the friends of God and prophets.*[46] And the same also in John: *His unction,* John says, *teaches you of all things.* And that which Paul says is not dissonant with this: *The Lord will give you in all things understanding.*[47]

84{85}[10]   *Surely his salvation is near to them that fear him: that glory may dwell in our land.*

Verumtamen prope timentes eum salutare ipsius, ut inhabitet gloria in terra nostra.

84{85}[10] *Verumtamen prope timentes eum salutare ipsius,* surely his salvation is near to them that fear him: that is, Christ, who is the salvation of the Father, is at hand to those who fear God with an initial or filial fear. For he who fears God turns away from evil: and so Christ dwells in the heart of these kinds of people by grace. Whence it is said in an earlier Psalm: *Fear the Lord, all you his saints: for there is no want to them that fear him.*[48] Ecclesiasticus also: *They that fear the Lord, will prepare their hearts, and in his sight will sanctify their souls.*[49] *Ut inhabitet gloria,* that glory may dwell, that is, that Christ, the king of glory, *who is the image of the invisible God,*[50] *the brightness of glory, and the figure of his substance,*[51] indeed, the glory of the Father, as it is written, *A wise the Son is the glory of the Father;*[52] or [alternatively], *glory,* that is, Christ, who is our honor and glory; *in terra nostra,* in our land, that is, in Judaea, wherein

---

synonym for the prompting of the Holy Spirit which is the effect of the gifts of the Holy Spirit.

45   Wis. 7:24.
46   Wis. 7:27.
47   2 Tim. 2:7.
48   Ps. 33:10.
49   Ecclus. 2:20.
50   Col. 1:15a.
51   Heb. 1:3a.
52   Prov. 10:1a: Denis must rely upon another version, since the Sixto-Clementine Vulgate has: *Filius sapiens laetificat patrem,* "a wise son makes the father glad." Denis quotes Prov. 10:1 as *Gloria patris, filius sapiens,* "a wise son is the glory of the father."

Christ bodily lived and dwelt among men, as Zechariah testified: *Sing praise, and rejoice, O daughter of Sion: for behold I come, and I will dwell in the midst of you;*[53] and Jeremiah: *O expectation of Israel, the Savior thereof in time of trouble: why will you be a stranger in the land, and as a wayfaring man turning in to lodge?*[54]

84{85}[11]   *Mercy and truth have met each other: justice and peace have kissed.*

> *Misericordia et veritas obviaverunt sibi; iustitia et pax osculatae sunt.*

84{85}[11] *Misericordia et veritas, mercy and truth,* that is, the kindness and the justice of God, *obviaverunt sibi, have met each other,* that is, they have come together, appeared, and they have entwined together without discord in Christ. For the mercy of God appeared in the incarnation of Christ, because out of the ineffable mercy of God it was made that the only begotten Son would assume flesh. Justice also shines forth in it [the Incarnation] because God by the Incarnation of Christ fulfilled that which he had predicted and had promised through the Prophets. *Iustitia et pax osculatae sunt, justice and peace have kissed*: that is, in the just satisfaction by which Christ [in his human nature] satisfied for us by means of his way of justice, when he suffered punishment for our fault, and [effected] a peace treaty between the human race and God accompanying such satisfaction, these are lovingly united in [the man-God] Christ.[55] For Christ (according to the Apostle [Paul]) *by God is made unto us ... justice ... and redemption.*[56] *For he is our peace, who has made both one.*[57] For this reason, the Apostle said: *In him, it has well pleased the Father, that all fulness should dwell, and through him to reconcile all things unto himself, making peace through the blood of his Cross, both as to the things that are on earth, and the things that are in heaven.*[58] Also this peace and justice have kissed themselves also in us who have been redeemed by Christ, because the justification bestowed upon us by Christ, establishes immediately in us the peace by which we are made at peace with God.

---

53   Zech. 2:10.

54   Jer. 14:8.

55   E. N. That is, the justice associated with Christ's satisfaction, and the peace accord and reconciliation obtained in the New Covenant between God and man, are one and the same in Christ: justice and peace therefore have kissed.

56   1 Cor. 1:30.

57   Eph. 2:14a.

58   Col. 1:19–20.

84{85}[12] *Truth is sprung out of the earth: and justice has looked down from heaven.*

Veritas de terra orta est, et iustitia de caelo prospexit.

84{85}[13] *For the Lord will give goodness: and our earth shall yield her fruit.*

Etenim Dominus dabit benignitatem, et terra nostra dabit fructum suum.

84{85}[12] *Veritas,* truth, that is Christ, the incarnate Son of God: who said of himself, *I am the Way, the Truth, and the Life;*[59] *de terra orta est, is sprung out of the earth,* that is, he assumed flesh from the womb of the glorious Virgin, and went on to be born: regarding this earth, namely, the Holy Mary, she is most affectionately referred to by Isaiah: *Let the earth be opened, and bud forth a Savior.*[60] *Et iustitia de caelo prospexit, and justice has looked down from heaven*: that is, the equity of God, or the just God, gave approval to the springing forth of the Christ, and held him to be pleasing, and by him redeemed the human race. But morally speaking, truth sprung forth from the earth when the heart of the sinner, enveloped in the guilt of the earth, confessed fully his own faults; and then the omnipotent God immediately justified the confessing sinner, and thereupon procured for him the justice of heaven. Whence John says: *If we confess our sins, he is faithful and just, to forgive us our sins, and to cleanse us from all iniquity.*[61] Now it also is fitting to designate the Virgin Mary by earth. For as the most devout Bernard said, In the manner that a field or the earth brings forth flower without human assistance, not seeded by another, not dug by a hoe, so did the Virgin's womb blossom; thus did the inviolate, chaste, and pure flesh of Mary bring forth a flower eternally green, whose beauty and glory never withers.[62]

But lest it seem impossible to anyone that the Virgin could generate Christ, the manner of this generation should be made clear, namely, that it did not arise from human virtue, but by the divine power. **84{85}[13]** *Etenim Dominus, for the Lord,* namely, God the Trinity, whose works are indivisible,[63] *dabit benignitatem, will give goodness,* that is, the most mer-

---

59 John 15:6.
60 Is. 45:8b.
61 1 John 1:9.
62 E. N. St. Bernard of Clairvaux (1090–1153), founder of the Cistercian Order, and devotee of the Blessed Virgin. Denis paraphrases, quite closely, St. Bernard's Sermon 2 of Advent. S. Bernardi, *Opera Omnia,* (Treves 1861), Vol. 1, 12.
63 E. N. *Opera Trinitatis ad extra indivisa sint* as the theological aphorism goes: The works of the Trinity "outside" of itself are indivisible.

ciful affluence of grace, giving through the Holy Spirit to the forechosen Virgin a supernatural fruitfulness and the fullness of graces: as Gabriel declared, when he spoke thus to the Virgin: *Hail, full of grace, the Lord is with you.*[64] *Et terra nostra, and our earth,* that is, the Virgin Mary, our savioress,[65] mother, and advocate, *dabit fructum suum, shall yield her fruit,* giving birth to Christ: as it said of her in an earlier Psalm, *The earth has yielded her fruit.*[66] Of this fruit, St. Elizabeth said to her: *Blessed is the fruit of your womb.*[67] Spiritually speaking, the Lord gives his good blessings when he fills our hearts by grace and he hears our prayers, when justifies the sinner with grace, prevents the evildoer, preserves the just man, and perfects the proficient. And our earth gives its fruit when our body obeys the spirit, and when it is occupied with pious labors; when we fulfill that [exhortation] of the Apostle: *I beseech you ... that you present your bodies a living sacrifice, holy, pleasing unto God.*[68]

84{85}[14] *Justice shall walk before him: and shall set his steps in the way.*

Iustitia ante eum ambulabit, et ponet in via gressus suos.

---

64   Luke 1:28.

65   E. N. Denis uses the name *salvatrix,* a female savior, a savioress. Denis uses this title for the Blessed Virgin Mary in other of his works. It was not uncommon in the Middle Ages to apply this title, properly understood, to Mary. For example, an Anglo-Saxon litany of the 10th century invokes Mary's intercessory role under the titles *Sancta Salvatrix Mundi* and *Sancta Redemptrix Mundi. Catholic Encyclopedia* (New York: Robert Appleton 1907), Vol. 1, 510. (s.v. "Anglo-Saxon Church"). *Salvatrix mundi,* or something similar to it (*e.g., salus mundi, salus omnium, salus populi Christiani*) was used by notable authorities, including Sts. John of Damascus, Anselm, Albert the Great, Bernard, and Bonaventure. *Summa Aurea de Laudibus Beatissimae Virginis Mariae* (Migne 1862) (ed. J. J. Bourassé), Vol. 10, 240–43. Naturally, like the term *mediatrix,* Mary's role in the salvation of mankind—though in a fashion and in her way (*suo modo*) truly salvific and mediating of grace—is decisively *sub et cum,* under and with, Christ's infinitely preeminent salvific and redemptive role. It is a distinction as infinitely wide as the abyss that separates Christ's grace of union (the hypostatic union) from Mary's fullness of grace. Denis—and all others using these honorary titles—would have concurred with Vatican II's *Lumen Gentium:* Any of Mary's titular honors must be "so understood that it takes nothing away, or adds nothing to the dignity and efficaciousness of Christ.... For no creature can ever be counted as equal with the Incarnate Word and Redeemer." LG, 62. We can be sure that, in using the term *salvatrix mundi,* the orthodox and Christocentric Denis did not put Mary on the same level as our Incarnate Lord. Yet he surely would also agree with St. Bernard of Clairaux: *de Maria nunquam satis.*

66   Ps. 66:7a.

67   Luke 1:42.

68   Rom. 12:1.

84{85}[14] *Iustitia ante eum ambulabit, justice shall walk before him*:
that is, a just doctrine and holy manner of living will go before Christ in
all things, so that from his heart and mouth nothing proceeded that was
not just and holy. For Jesus *began to do and to teach* without any doubt
what was just and true. Whence Ecclesiasticus says: *In all your works
let the true word go before you, and steady counsel before every action.*[69] *Et
ponet in via gressus suos, and shall set his steps in the way*: that is, Christ
himself shall fulfill what he teaches by his works. For the teacher places
his steps in the path when the teaching, which is the way to eternal life
that he proposes to others, he openly shows to be true by himself doing
good works. Now others have expounded [this verse] in this manner:
Justice, that is, John the Baptist, *shall walk before him*, because he presented
himself as the precursor of Christ; and *he shall set his steps in the way*
because he fulfilled that which he taught. But that John the Baptist is
called justice is not something that I find in canonical Scripture: although
I do find written of Christ in Isaiah, where the eternal Father speaks
of Christ: *My salvation is near to come, and my justice to be revealed.*[70]
Now, in a moral sense [we can view this verse in this manner], *justice
shall walk before him*: that is, the justice of men subsists in confession
and the repentance of fault, and the coming of Christ to such men is
preceded by this. For the first justice of men is that of repenting of
evil: and this procures and prepares the way in the soul for the coming
of Christ. *Et, and* then Christ *ponet in via, shall set . . . in the way* thus
prepared for them *gressus suos, his steps*, giving men the grace of living
in a Christiform way. But because all our original justice was a gift of
God, true justice, namely meritorious and infused [justice], cannot be
in man unless God is prevenient to such, bestowing faith and grace:
and so, it does not appear to be properly said that the justice of man
precedes the spiritual coming of Christ;[71] indeed, the sinner is justified
by his coming. The first exposition, therefore, appears more correct.[72]

Finally, what intellect can conceive, what tongue is able to express, the
dignity and the praise of this present Psalm? In this [Psalm] first the

---

69 Ecclus. 37:20.

70 Is. 56:1b. *E. N.* Denis argues that this interpretation of Psalm 84:14 is not
well-supported by Scripture because John is nowhere referred as God's justice, and
Christ clearly is.

71 *E. N.* Such an interpretation, which Denis soundly rejects, may be said to be
semi-Pelagian, since it appears to suggest that man prepares himself for grace through
his own efforts unaided by grace.

72 *E. N.* In other words, Denis rejects the Johannine interpretation, and this moral
interpretation, preferring the one given in the beginning of the commentary on this verse.

benefits of God are most devoutly recalled, and then is a most efficacious prayer introduced, namely, *Convert us, O God our Savior*. And with good reason this verse is said at evening time before Compline against the dark snares of the demons of the night and the infinite weakness of men, since with the light of day receding, and the mind turning to God, it is imbued with the light of grace, and detached from all sensible things, and is firmly immersed in the intelligible, unchanging, and highest good. And lest such grace is denied to us because of our sins, it most conveniently adds thereto, *and turn off your anger from us*. And so we ought to say this verse, especially during Compline, with great affection and sincerity of heart. And in the verses that follow also, the hope of obtaining mercy is inflamed, and every faintheartedness and diffidence is entirely eradicated. But also this verse — *Show us, O Lord, your mercy* — does it not with wise sweetness and sweet wisdom exceed the sweetness of all carnal things?

Further, some expound literally the three first verses of this Psalm of the land of Judah and the Jewish people returning from the Babylonian captivity. But I judge it better that all this Psalm is to be expounded as pertaining to Christ and the spiritual deliverance of the Church, according to the sense introduced here, since in this way the whole sense is connected and consonant with itself. And that verse above — *Mercy and truth have met each other* — St. Bernard most profoundly and beautifully addresses in a sermon, in which he expounded upon it in this manner: that regarding the mystery of human redemption, in some way the mercy and truth of God appear to contradict each other: because mercy demands that the miserable be freed, but truth dictates that the guilty be punished. But in this encounter *justice and peace have kissed*, for the miserable has been redeemed, and fault did not go unpunished. But because it is commonly known and is quite long, I will refrain from any further exposition of it.[73]

---

73   E. N. This appears to be a reference to St. Bernard's first sermon for the Feast of the Annunciation, *Sermo I in Festa Annuntiationis Beatae Virginis*, PL 183, 387–90, where St. Bernard (probably borrowing from Hugh of St. Victor or from a Jewish *Midrash* on this verse) addresses these four attributes of God that come together in Ps. 84:11 — mercy, truth, justice, and peace — and personifies them as the "four daughters" of God fighting over man's redemption. This sets a state for a famous allegorical debate between them which explores the paradox associated with Redemption and the tension between these attributes. *See* Hope Traver, *The Four Daughters of God* (Philadelphia: John C. Winston Company, 1907). The sermon is available in English translation: *St. Bernard's Sermons for the Seasons & Principal Festivals of the Year* (Westminster, MD: The Carroll Press, 1950), Vol. III, 134–152.

PRAYER

WE HUMBLY BESEECH YOUR MERCY, O LORD God; forgive the sins of your people, turn from us the wrath of your indignation, enliven us with your kindly power and your powerful right hand, so that your people may rejoice with you in peace both in the present and for eternity.

Supplices, Domine Deus, clementiam tuam exoramus; remitte iniquitatem plebis tuae, averte a nobis iram indignationis tuae, vivifica nos pia actione, potenti dextera tua: ut plebs tua laetetur in te pace praesenti et sempiterna.

Psalm 85

ARTICLE LX

ELUCIDATION OF THE EIGHTY-FIFTH PSALM OF CHRIST:
INCLINA, DOMINE, AUREM TUAM.
INCLINE YOUR EAR, O LORD.

85{86}[1] *A prayer for David himself. Incline your ear, O Lord, and hear me: for I am needy and poor.*

Oratio ipsi David. Inclina, Domine, aurem tuam et exaudi me, quoniam inops et pauper sum ego.

HE TITLE OF THIS PSALM IS: 85{86}[1] ORA-*tio David, a prayer for David,* that is, for Christ, in whose person certainly David is here said, according to Jerome. According to others, this Psalm partly relates to Christ, and partly to his members. But according to some, it literally relates to David [alone].

And so Christ, as man, with the Passion approaching, said to God the Father, or to the entire superlatively most blessed Trinity: *Inclina, Domine, aurem tuam; incline your ear, O Lord,* that is, reach out toward me with your paternal kindness, *et exaudi me, and hear me,* giving me that which I ask for. Here, the Prophet speaks of God, as if he were a man, who, when someone is pleading with him, first inclines his ear towards the one who is pleading and then hears him. *Quoniam inops et pauper sum ego, for I am needy and poor.* Christ was poor, that is, he had recourse to no other help, especially during the Passion, according to that which is witnessed in Isaiah: *I looked about, and there was none to help.*[1] And he was poor according to that which the Apostle [Paul] said about him: *being rich, he became poor for our sakes.*[2]

85{86}[2] *Preserve my soul, for I am holy: save your servant, O my God, that trusts in you.*

Custodi animam meam, quoniam sanctus sum; salvum fac servum tuum, Deus meus, sperantem in te.

---

1 Is. 63:5a.
2 Cf. 2 Cor. 8:9.

85{86}[2] *Custodi animam meam, preserve my soul,* that is, preserve my bodily life, lest I be killed by the Jews, by Herod, or by someone else before the time ordained for my Passion. This Christ was able to pray when the Jews sought him to throw him off a cliff or to stone him.[3] Now Christ did not pray to be kept from the ruin of sin, because he was a comprehensor and he was confirmed in the good.[4] *Quoniam sanctus sum, for I am holy.* Here Christ asserts his merit and why he was worthy to be heard: *for,* he says, *I am holy.* For as God, Christ was essentially holy, and of infinite holiness; but as man, he only exceeded the holiness of all creatures. For this reason, he is called the Saint of Saints by Daniel: *The Saint of Saints may be anointed.*[5] Whence even his enemy the devil was compelled to say this: *I know who you are, the Holy One of God.*[6] *Salvum fac servum tuum, save your servant,* that is, me, Christ, who so as to redeem mankind accepted the form of a servant:[7] to whom you say: *Behold my servant, I will uphold him;*[8] and who says to you, *This says the Lord, that formed me from the womb to be his servant, that I may bring back Jacob unto him.*[9] And so, save your servant, *Deus meus,* O my God, who is the God of all things in a general sense, but is my God in a highest and special sense, as he whom I incomparably worship and love, and by whom I am incomparably chosen and beloved;[10] *sperantem in te, that hopes in you,* that is, in your power and your goodness. For Christ, inasmuch as he did not have [strictly speaking] hope (which is a theological virtue), nevertheless inasmuch as he was a passible man, he hoped [in a loose sense] in God through a certain trust or confidence,

---

3   Luke 4:29; John 10:31; 11:8.
4   *E. N.* Christ had the beatific vision of God, even while on earth (Christ was *simul viator et comprehensor*), and he was confirmed in the good, that is, he was impeccable; accordingly, he had no need to pray for these things.
5   Dan. 9:24. *E. N.* For more on this Danielic title for Christ, *see* footnote 3-26, in Volume 1.
6   Mark 1:24. *E. N.* This is what the demoniac at Capernaum exclaimed to Jesus.
7   *Cf.* Phil. 2:7: *But [he, being in the form of God] emptied himself, taking the form of a servant, being made in the likeness of men, and in habit found as a man.*
8   Is. 42:1a.
9   Is. 49:5a.
10   *E. N.* "God loves more the better things." ST Ia, q. 20, art. 4, co. It follows therefore that "God loves Christ [in his human nature], not only more than the whole human race, but also more than the whole universe of creatures, because, namely, he willed for him the greater good, for he gave to him 'a name that is above all names,' in so far as he was true God. Nor was his excellence undone from the fact that God delivered him up to death for the salvation of the human race; indeed from that he became a glorious victor; 'the government was placed upon His shoulder,' as Isaiah 9:6 says." ST Ia, q. 20, art. 4, ad 1.

and he expected to receive from him all the good that he desired. But Christ also prayed to be saved by God, not, indeed, from sin or from eternal death, since he had no sin; but from bodily passibility, from the anger of the Jews, from bodily death by the blessed Resurrection, as is brought forth about him in an earlier Psalm: *Save me from the lion's mouth, etc.*[11] Whence also he said: *Father, save me from this hour.*[12]

85{86}[3] *Have mercy on me, O Lord, for I have cried to you all the day.*

Miserere mei, Domine, quoniam ad te clamavi tota die.

85{86}[4] *Give joy to the soul of you servant, for to you, O Lord, I have lifted up my soul.*

Laetifica animam servi tui, quoniam ad te, Domine, animam meam levavi.

85{86}[3] *Miserere mei, Domine;* have mercy on me, O Lord Father, delivering me from the present life of punishment and misery, *quoniam ad te clamavi,* for I have cried out to you with an ardent heart or with sublime voice *tota die,* all the day, that is, every day which I have lived in this world. For Christ, even as man, was always in the act of divine contemplation and love: and so he unceasingly prayed, since prayer (according to the Damascene) is the ascent of the mind unto God,[13] and he who ceases not to do things in praiseworthy way ceases not to pray. The Savior, therefore, continually prayed, and especially for the salvation of humanity. 85{86}[4] *Laetifica animam servi tui, give joy to the soul of your servant,* the reward of accidental joy. For the soul of Christ was unceasingly in the joy of beatific fruition; but his soul, which was sorrowful in his Passion, so that he would say, *My soul is sorrowful even unto death,*[14] asked that he might rejoice in the Resurrection of his body of his glorification, in the leading forth from limbo of the fathers existing in limbo, and in the salvation or the justification of all the elect. For he died *for our sins, and rose again for our justification,*[15] according to the Apostle. *Quoniam ad te, Domine, animam meam levavi; for to you, O Lord, I have lifted up my soul,* by contemplating or intently praying.

---

11 Ps. 21:22.

12 John 12:27.

13 E. N. A reference to classic definition of prayer by St. John of Damascus (*ca.* 675–749) found in his *De Fide Orthodoxa* (*On the Exposition of the Orthodox Faith*), III, 24. *See* footnote 19-14.

14 Mark 14:34.

15 Rom. 4:25.

85{86}[5] *For you, O Lord, are sweet and mild: and plenteous in mercy to all that call upon you.*

Quoniam tu, Domine, suavis et mitis, et multae misericordiae omnibus invocantibus te.

85{86}[5] *Quoniam tu, Domine, for you, O Lord,* God, the Father, or the blessed Trinity, are *suavis et mitis, sweet and mild.* God truly, properly, and by nature, indeed is superessentially and unboundedly sweet;[16] and this divine essence is a fountain of sweetness, alive, simple and infinite, exceeding all senses, and, because of the immensity of his fulness, not known and not experienced by any created mind, and from it flows all sweetness, all harmony, all fragrance. But meekness or gentleness does not pertain properly to God, just like the other moral virtues employed against the passions do not, but [these are ascribed to God only] because of the similitude of effect; so meekness, which is properly called the moral virtue that checks the passion of anger, is ascribed to God transumptively,[17] namely, because he relaxes the vengeance that is just. And God is sweet and just to those contemplating him purely and lovingly, who are visited with the taste of divine sweetness which makes all the deceit of worldly delights hateful. And God is meek to the sinners that return to him with all their heart, because to such persons he immediately gives up all vengeance in the fashion of a mild-mannered man, just as he said to Jeremiah: *Return to me … and I will not turn away my face.*[18] *Et multae misericordiae omnibus invocantibus te, and plenteous mercy to all that call upon you:* that is, you are greatly merciful, and you bestow multiple effects of kindness to all who intimately plead with you: as has been stated, *God is compassionate and merciful, and will forgive sins in the day of tribulation: and he is a protector to all that seek him in truth;*[19] and in the same place, *Who has called upon him, and he despised him?*[20]

---

16 E. N. *See* footnote 35-48 on Denis's use of super-superlatives, which can mean either something most eminent within a genus (in this case sweetness) or something infinitely beyond, but analogous to, the genus (sweetness). So one could see this either as meaning eminently most sweet or beyond the most sweet.

17 E. N. Transumptively (*transumptive*), a term frequently used by Denis, means to transfer or substitute terms that are applicable to a creature and "transferring" them to God, understanding them to be used analogously or metaphorically (and not univocally, in the same sense) in reference to God.

18 Jer. 3:1b, 12b.

19 Ecclus. 2:13.

20 Ecclus. 2:12b.

85{86}[6] *Give ears,*[21] *O Lord, to my prayer: and attend to the voice of my petition.*

Auribus percipe, Domine, orationem meam, et intende voci deprecationis meae.

85{86}[7] *I have called upon you in the day of my trouble: because you have heard me.*

In die tribulationis meae clamavi ad te, quia exaudisti me.

85{86}[6] *Auribus percipe, Domine, orationem meam; give ears, O Lord, to my prayer.* Up above [in verse **85:1**] it said in singular, *Incline, O Lord, your ear:* and there by ear is understood the mercy of the Creator; but now it says in plural, *Give ears.* In what way, therefore, does it seem that the ears of God should be understood unless it means his mercy and knowledge? For God indeed hears by his mercy, but he hears all things by his knowledge. Now on occasion by [the expression] ears of God is not indicated mercy and knowledge, but knowledge and justice, as when the Lord said: *your pride came up to my ears,*[22] namely, that I might justly take vengeance upon it. But here, in this case, *give ears, O Lord, to my prayer,* [means] so that you might firmly imprint them upon yourself, not neglecting them, that is, not delaying their effects or hearing them. And so it adds: *et intende voci deprecationis meae, and attend to the voice of my petition,* that is, diligently and kindly pay heed to my vocal prayer. **85{86}[7]** *In die tribulationis meae, in the day of my trouble,* that is, during the time of persecutions suffering, *clamavi ad te, I have called upon you,* saying: *My Father, if it be possible, let this chalice pass from me;*[23] and, *Father, forgive them;*[24] and *Into your hands I commend my spirit.*[25] Now with great trust and securely I beseech you, *quia exaudisti me, because you have heard me* always and everywhere; and I myself said: *Father, I give you thanks that you have heard me. And I knew that you hear me always.*[26]

---

21   E. N. The Douay-Rheims has translated *auribus* by the singular "ear." However, the Latin is plural. Since Denis addresses this issue in his *Commentary,* I have translated as plural in the English so as to correspond with the Latin.

22   Is. 37:29a.

23   Matt. 26:39.

24   Luke 23:34a.

25   Ps. 30:6a; [Luke 23:46].

26   John 11:41b–42a.

85{86}[8] *There is none among the gods like unto you, O Lord: and there is none according to you works.*

Non est similis tui in diis, Domine, et non est secundum opera tua.

85{86}[8] *Non est similis tui in diis, Domine;* there is none among the gods like unto you, O Lord: because all gods—who are either called lying gods and truly are demons or those who excellently participate in the grace of divinity by which they are made *partakers of the divine nature*[27] and are called gods by participation—you, most high and true God, infinitely excel: as also Moses said: *Who is like to you, among the strong, O Lord? Who is like to you, glorious in holiness, terrible and praiseworthy, doing wonders?*[28] Zephaniah also declares: *The Lord shall be terrible . . . and shall consume all the gods of the earth.*[29] *Et non est secundum opera tua,* and there is none according to your works, that is, one does not find someone who is able to do things similar to you. For many works are proper to you, which pertain to no creature, such as creation, justification [of the sinner], the felicity of beatitude, the scrutinizing of hearts, the certain knowledge of future contingents, transubstantiation, and the working of miracles. Of such works Christ in particular says: *My Father works until now; and I work.*[30]

85{86}[9] *All the nations you have made shall come and adore before you, O Lord: and they shall glorify your name.*

Omnes gentes quascumque fecisti venient, et adorabunt coram te, Domine, et glorificabunt nomen tuum.

85{86}[9] *Omnes gentes quascumque fecisti, venient et adorabunt coram te, Domine;* all the nations you have made shall come and adore before you, O Lord. This is a prophecy of the enlightenment of the Gentiles and their call to the faith: and this distribution is to be as that which was told to Abraham, *In your seed shall all the families of the earth be blessed;*[31] and that [prophecy] which the Virgin Christbearer stated: *All generations*

---

27   2 Pet. 1:4.
28   Ex. 15:11.
29   Zeph. 2:11a.
30   John 5:17b.
31   Gen. 22:18. E. N. The version of Genesis Denis cites to varies from the Sixto-Clementine. His reading is: *In semine tuo benedicentur omnes familiae* (families or households) *terrae;* whereas the Sixto-Clementine reads: *et benedicentur in semine tuo omnes gentes* (peoples or nations) *terrae.*

shall call me blessed.[32] For this distribution is not to be understood as being by every individual of each kind (*pro singulis generum*), but by some individual of every kind (*pro generibus singulorum*). So [it is to be understood] in this sense: *All the nations you have made,* that is, some of each kind of men created by you, *shall come* to the faith, *and adore before you, O Lord,* who discern all things. But they will adore you God in spirit and truth, as you predicted in Zephaniah: *Because then I will restore to the people a chosen lip, that all may call upon the name of the Lord, and may serve him with one shoulder.*[33] And elsewhere: *Behold I will lift up my hand to the Gentiles, and will set up my standard to the people.*[34] All these things are clearly touched upon by Daniel in these words: *All peoples, tribes and tongues shall serve him.*[35] *Et glorificabunt nomen tuum, and they shall glorify your name,* that is, they will proclaim you to be glorious with words, and they will demonstrate it with works, as Isaiah beautifully sets forth: *Glorify the Lord in instruction: the name of the Lord God of Israel in the islands of the sea. From the ends of the earth we have heard praises, the glory of the Just One,*[36] namely, the Christ.

85{86}[10]   *For you are great and do wonderful things: you are God alone.*

  Quoniam magnus es tu, et faciens mirabilia; tu es Deus solus.

85{86}[10]   *Quoniam magnus est tu, for you are great:* which accords with this: *O Adonai, Lord, great are you, and glorious in your power.*[37]

----

32   Luke 1:48b. E. N. The Abrahamic promise is fulfilled in Mary, who might be called the "new Abraham," as she even suggests in her *Magnificat.* Consistent with the fact that Jesus did not have the theological virtue of faith (since, as Denis has many times pointed out, he enjoyed the vision of God even in his humanity), he is not properly called the "new Abraham," though he may properly be called the "new Moses," or the "New Adam." "It is quite singular," Cantalamessa says, "that Christ is never called the new Abraham in the New Testament." In her *Magnificat* it is as if Mary appropriates the Abrahamic promise and makes it her own. "Abraham actually foreshadows Mary, not Christ." Raniero Cantalamessa, O. F. M. Cap., *Mary, Mirror of the Church* (Collegeville, MN: The Liturgical Press, 1992) 125 (trans., Frances Lonergan Villa). This is what Denis appears to be implying here.

33   Zeph. 3:9.

34   Is. 49:22a.

35   Dan. 7:14a.

36   Is. 24:15–16.

37   Judith 16:16a. The Vulgate states: *Adonai Domine.* Though prominent in the Hebrew text, the Vulgate uses the Latin transliteration of the Hebrew word Adonai only twice: once here and once in Ex. 6:3. In Hebrew (אדני) it literally, "my Lords," but commonly it used as a substitute for the tetragrammaton YHWH and translated "Lord."

And indeed he is so great that *of his greatness there is no end.*[38] *Et faciens mirabilia, and doing wonderful things* in heaven and on earth. *Tu es Deus solus, you are God alone:* you who spoke: *See that I alone am, and there is no other God besides me;*[39] and again, *I am the Lord, that make all things, that alone stretch out the heavens, that establish the earth, and there is none with me.*[40] God absolutely enters upon his place, and by God we mean the Trinity. Whence the Apostle says: *One Lord, one faith, one baptism;*[41] and again: *Although there be that are called gods, ... yet to us there is but one God ... of whom are all things, ... and one Lord ... by whom are all things.*[42]

85{86}[11]   Conduct me, O Lord, in your way, and I will walk in your truth: let my heart rejoice that it may fear your name.

Deduc me, Domine, in via tua, et ingrediar in veritate tua; laetetur cor meum, ut timeat nomen tuum.

85{86}[11] *Deduc me, Domine, in via tua; conduct me, O Lord, in your way.* According to the expositors, Christ says this verse not with reference to himself, but on behalf of his Mystical Body, according to the way that is asserted by Zechariah, *He that touches you, touches the apple of my eye;*[43] and in Acts, *Saul, Saul, why do you persecute me?*[44] Yet this verse can be explained with respect to Christ in this way: *Conduct me, O Lord, in your way.* The way of God was the means whereby the soul of Christ descended into the limbo of the fathers, and after the Resurrection ascended up to heaven: and Christ prayed to God to be led in this way, just as the saints in the heavenly homeland also pray to be glorified in the body.[45] In fact, one may licitly pray for any legitimately desired future

---

38   Ps. 144:3b.
39   Deut. 32:39a.
40   Is. 44:24.
41   Eph. 4:5.
42   1 Cor. 8:5a, 6.
43   Zech. 2:8b.
44   Acts 9:4b. E. N. "Christ our Lord feels more strongly for His Mystical Body than for his natural Body. He says: *Who touches you touches the apple of My eye;* and this is no exaggeration. For he freely sacrifices the apple of His eye and every other sense of His natural Body in order to cherish and nourish us, His Mystical Body. *Saul, Saul, why dost though persecute Me? I am Jesus, Whom thou dost persecute.* Saul was only persecuting His disciples: *But so long as you did it to one of these My least brethren, you did it to Me."* Peter Gallwey, S. J., *The Watches of the Passion* (London: Art and Book Company, 1896), Vol. II, 418.
45   E. N. Presumably, this is in between the particular judgment and the final judgment, for upon death which is "the separation of the soul from the body, the

good not yet obtained.[46] *Et ingrediar, and I will walk* in the kingdom of heaven even at your right hand, *in veritate tua, in your truth,* that is, in the manner that you truthfully promised in your holy Prophets. For it is written: *I beheld therefore in the vision of the night, and lo, one like the Son of Man came with the clouds of heaven, and he came even to the Ancient of days,* that is, the eternal God; *and they presented him before him. And he gave him power, and glory, and a kingdom.*[47] *Laetetur cor meum, ut timeat nomen tuum; let my heart rejoice that it may fear your name* with a filial and chaste fear. Christ says, not praying that he be so, but wholeheartedly exulting that it is so, as the saints in the heavenly homeland say this in Revelation: *Let us be glad and rejoice and give glory to him.*[48] Now Christ as man feared God with a chaste fear, that fear which is one of the seven gifts of the Holy Spirit, according to that which is written: *He shall be filled with the spirit of the fear of the Lord.*[49]

85{86}[12] *I will praise you, O Lord my God: with my whole heart, and I will glorify your name forever:*

Confitebor tibi, Domine Deus meus, in toto corde meo, et glorificabo nomen tuum in aeternum.

85{86}[12] *Confitebor tibi, Domine Deus meus; I will praise you, O Lord my God,* that is, I will praise you, *in toto corde meo, with my whole heart,* that is, entirely, not dividedly, not with deviating affection and knowledge. This most perfectly coincides with Christ, because he unceasingly with all his soul, all his strength, all his mind was carried away by God, as also the saints in the heavenly homeland, and his heart was not divided by any deviations or by disordered loves. In this way Christ confessed to God, praising him with all of his heart, as is written of him in the Gospel: Jesus *rejoiced in the Holy Spirit, and said: I confess to you, O Father, Lord of heaven and earth, because you have hidden these things*

---

human body decays and the soul goes to meet God." Yet it remains "awaiting its reunion with its glorified body. God, in his almighty power, will definitively grant incorruptible life to our bodies by reuniting them with our souls, through the power of Jesus' Resurrection." CCC § 997. During that interval, the saints will pray to be glorified in the body.

46   E. N. The reference is to St. Augustine's Epistle 130 to Proba. It is not a direct quote, but rather is a succinct summary of a lengthy epistle. *Epist.* CXXX, PL 494–07.

47   Dan. 7:13–14a.

48   Rev. 19:7a. E. N. In other words, it is an expression of present fact, not a prayer for something in the future.

49   Is. 11:3.

from the wise and prudent, and have revealed them to little ones.[50] And elsewhere Christ confesses to the Father with the confession of praise, when he calls him just and holy,[51] and says to him: *Your word is truth.*[52] *Et glorificabo nomen tuum in aternum,* and *I will glorify your name forever* with words and deeds, by myself and through my ministers, who through my doctrine and by my grace will be lead to glorify you. Whence the Savior said: *I seek not my own glory, but I honor my Father.*[53]

85{86}[13] *For your mercy is greatly over and above me: and you have delivered my soul out of the lower hell.*

Quia misericordia tua magna est super me, et eruisti animam meam ex inferno inferiori.

85{86}[13] *Quia misericordia tua magna est super me,* for your mercy is greatly over and above me, that is, above my human nature that I assumed. The mercy of God is asserted to be over and above him who obtains mercy. Now manifold are the effects of the mercy of God, and the mercy of God is said to be greatly over and above men according to these diverse effects. For one effect of the mercy of God is to forgive sins. Another is to infuse the grace of conversion: and so the mercy of God is greatly over and above repentant and converted sinners. For this reason, Scripture says in the book of Ezra: *You, O God, are called merciful because of us sinners.*[54] Another effect of the mercy of God is to anticipate men by grace, and to preserve them in innocence without sin: and so the great mercy of God is great and in fact incomparably great in Christ, because his human nature was united to the Word of God from the beginning of his creation and was given the beatific enjoyment, confirmed in the good, and preserved from all [moral] evil only as a result of grace: and so in an earlier Psalm this was said about him to God the Father, *You have prevented him with blessings of sweetness;*[55] and

---

50   Luke 5:21; Mat. 11:25. E. N. Denis seamlessly weaves both sources together.

51   John 17:11 ("Holy Father"); 17:25 ("Just Father").

52   John 17:17b.

53   John 8:50a, 49b.

54   IV Ezra 8:31. E. N. Denis has *miseros,* pitiable, wretched, or lamentable persons; however, the Editor suggests that *peccatores,* sinners is correct.

55   Ps. 20:4. E. N. As discussed in various footnotes in the *Commentary,* the notion of "prevented" here is a translation of the Latin *praevenisti* (*prae* + *venisti*), which means to "come before," to "anticipate," to "precede." The grace of the hypostatic union was without antecedent merits (the human nature of Christ could have merited nothing for the simple reason that it was not created, but was — through no prior

in the Gospel, *For God does not give the Spirit by measure*, namely, to the man Christ. *Et eruisti, and you have delivered*, in the day of Resurrection, *animam meam ex inferno inferiori*, that is, from the limbo of hell existing beneath the earth.[56] Of this limbo, Jacob said in Genesis: *I will go down to my son into hell, mourning;*[57] Job also: *All that I have shall go down into the deepest pit: think you that there at least I shall have rest?*[58] God delivered the soul of Christ from this hell on the third day, according to that which Christ said in an earlier Psalm, *You have brought forth, O Lord, my soul from hell;* [59] and, *Because you will not leave my soul in hell.*[60]

85{86}[14] *O God, the wicked are risen up against me, and the assembly of the mighty have sought my soul: and they have not set you before their eyes.*

Deus, iniqui insurrexerunt super me, et synagoga potentium quae-sierunt animam meam, et non proposuerunt te in conspectu suo.

85{86}[14] *Deus*, O God, the Trinity, *iniqui, the wicked* Jews *insurrexerunt super me*, are risen up against me, that is, they oppose me; *et synagoga potentium*, and the assembly of the mighty, that is, the chiefs of the priests, the Scribes, the Pharisees, and the teachers of the temple, *quaesierunt*

---

merit of its own — united to the Word from the very first instant of its creation, given the full enjoyment of the beatific vision, and confirmed in the good so as to be not only sinless, but impeccable — unable (yet freely unable) to sin. See ST IIIa, q. 24, art. 3, co. So in Psalm 20:4 we are told that the human nature of Christ was visited with graces antecedent to any possible merit by that human nature. The Incarnation of Christ was — to the human nature of Christ, as well so to the elect, indeed to all of humankind — a sheer grace.

56   E. N. Denis espouses the traditional view (as ensconced in the Creed that Jesus "descended into hell") that Christ's "harrowing of hell" was limited to preaching to the souls in the limbo of the fathers and releasing them from captivity there. It did not include entry into, and release of, the captives in the hell of the damned. The orthodox and conservative Denis would decidedly side with Alyssa Lyra Pitstick, and would reject the novel theories of Hans Urs von Balthasar set forth in his work *Mysterium Paschale* that on "Holy Saturday" Christ's soul was abandoned to the hell of the damned by God the Father and that his soul suffered the spiritual torments of Hell, even a spiritual death and damnation, in a sort of "super-kenosis." See Alyssa Lyra Pitstick, *Christ's Descent Into Hell: John Paul II, Joseph Ratzinger, and Hans Urs von Balthasar on the Theology of Holy Saturday* (Grand Rapids, MI: Eerdmans, 2016) and her earlier *Light in Darkness: Hans Urs von Balthasar and the Catholic Doctrine of Christ's Descent into Hell* (Grand Rapids, MI: Eerdmans, 2007).

57   Gen. 37:35.

58   Job 17:16.

59   Ps. 29:4a.

60   Ps. 15:10a.

animam meam, have sought my soul, that is, my life, so as to extinguish it: as it is stated: *The chief priests ... sought how they might by some wile lay hold on Jesus, and kill him.*[61] And Wisdom: *The wicked have said, reasoning ... not rightly, ... let us oppress the ... just man ... for he is not for our turn, ... and he glories that he has God for his father, ... and calls himself the son of God.*[62] *Et non proposuerunt Deum in conspectus tuo, and they have not set you [God] before their eyes,* that is, they who are involved in such a crime are not frightened of the divine judgment: as is said of some of them elsewhere, *They perverted their own mind, ... that they might not ... remember just judgments.*[63]

85{86}[15]   And you, O Lord, are a God of compassion, and merciful, patient, and of much mercy, and true.

Et tu, Domine Deus, miserator et misericors; patiens, et multae misericordiae, et verax.

85{86}[16]   O look upon me and have mercy on me: give your command to your servant and save the son of your handmaid.

Respice in me, et miserere mei; da imperium tuum puero tuo, et salvum fac filium ancillae tuae.

85{86}[15] *Et tu, Domine Deus, miserator; and you, O Lord, are a God of compassion* by your works, *et misericors, and merciful* by nature, *patiens, patient,* waiting with longanimity, in accordance with this, *The most High is a patient rewarder.*[64] However, as was the case with meekness, patience is not something that is fittingly applied to God properly speaking, because patience properly speaking is the moral virtue that suppresses the passion of sorrow [and God does not suffer sorrow]. God, however, is said to be patient because of the similarity of his operations, namely, since he stands ready to forgive the sinner for long periods of time. *Et multae misericordiae, and of much mercy:* as has already been expounded upon; *et verax, and true* in words, deeds, and promises. **85{86} [16]** *Respice in me, O look upon me* with the eyes of fatherly kindness, *et miserere mei, and have mercy on me:* in the sense already explained; *da imperium tuum puero tuo, give your command to your servant,* that is, give to me, Christ, your beloved Son, the kingdom of the militant Church

---

61   Mark 14:1b.
62   Wis. 2:1a, 10a, 12a, 16b, 13b.
63   Dan. 13:9.
64   Ecclus. 5:4b.

and judicial power as was elsewhere foretold, *The Lord shall give empire to his king, and shall exalt the horn of his Christ.*[65] But because every creature is subject to [the human nature of] Christ from the beginning of his maternal conception,[66] how does he now pray that he be given the power of ruling unless it be that God the Father might make manifest to men this ruling power already bestowed upon Christ? For Christ prayed for this, saying: *Glorify your Son, that your Son may glorify you.*[67] *Et salvum fac,* and save from death by the Resurrection, *filium ancillae tuae,* the son of your handmaid, that is, me Christ born of Mary, who said, *Behold the handmaid of the Lord.*[68]

85{86}[17] *Show me a sign for good: that they who hate me may see, and be confounded, because you, O Lord, have helped me and have comforted me.*[69]

Fac mecum signum in bonum, ut videant qui oderunt me, et confundantur, quoniam tu, Domine, adiuvisti me, et consolatus es me.

85{86}[17] *Fac mecum,* show me, O Lord, Father and God, *signum in bonum,* a sign for good, that is, show in me the sign of your resurrection so that my name might be glorified throughout the world,[70] *ut videant qui oderunt me,* that they who hate me may see, that is, the Jews or the guards in the sepulcher, who, terrified by sight of the the angel, fell as if dead: let them see, I say, by certain evidence and miracles that I had risen again, *et confundantur,* and let them be confounded of their sins, now by penance, or after a while [if they do not repent], by their condemnation. For some of the Jews, who before had cried out — *Away with him, away with him; crucify him* — by these signs and evidence perceived Jesus to be the true Messiah by faith after the Resurrection. For of these persons Christ spoke: *When you shall have lifted up the Son of man,* he said, *then shall you know, that I am he.*[71] This sign that

---

65 1 Sam. 2:10b.
66 *Cf.* Heb. 2:8: *You have subjected all things under his feet. For in that he has subjected all things to him, he left nothing not subject to him. But now we see not as yet all things subject to him.*
67 John 17:1b.
68 Luke 1:38.
69 *E. N.* I have replaced the Douay Rheims's "token" as a translation of *signum* with "sign."
70 *Cf.* John 17:1.
71 John 8:28a.

Christ here asked for is the sign of Jonah the prophet, in the manner that the Lord Jesus in the Gospel tells the Jews: *An evil and adulterous generation seeks a sign: and a sign shall not be given it, but the sign of Jonah the prophet,*[72] who on the third day was vomited out of the belly of the fish.[73] The Jews were not given the sign of descending from the cross, which is what they sought, saying, *If he be the king of Israel, [let him come down from the cross, and we will believe him];*[74] but [they were given] the sign of the Resurrection from the grave. Christ spoke about this through Zephaniah, *Expect me . . . in the day of my resurrection that is to come;*[75] and of this elsewhere is stated in the divine word, *He will revive us after two days: on the third day he will raise us up.*[76] One can also understand by this sign the performance of miracles by which the holy apostles at first proved Christ to be to be resuscitated from the dead in Jerusalem. Whence Peter, healing that man who had been born lame, told the Jews: *The God of our fathers has glorified his Son Jesus.*[77] And so, *show me a sign for good,*[78] [so that they who hate me may see and be confounded,] *quoniam tu, Domine, adiuvisti me; because you, O Lord have helped me,* working in conjunction with me in all things, *et consolatus es me, and you have comforted me* in the Resurrection, delivering me from every punishment and possibility of suffering.

ARTICLE LXI

MORAL EXPLANATION OF THE SAME EIGHTY-FIFTH PSALM WITH RESPECT TO ANY TRUE MEMBER OF THE FAITHFUL.

85{86}[1] *. . . Incline your ear, O Lord, and hear me: for I am needy and poor.*

> *. . . Inclina, Domine, aurem tuam et exaudi me, quoniam inops et pauper sum ego.*

---

72   Matt. 12:39.
73   Jonah 2:11.
74   Matt. 27:42' Luke 23:35. E. N. The part in bracket replaces the "etc." of Denis.
75   Zeph. 3:8a.
76   Hosea 6:3a.
77   Acts 3:13a.
78   E. N. From being a narrator, Denis here returns to Jesus' voice, so it is a little jarring.

Now since this Psalm is potent with great excellence (for it contains the most ardent prayers of a devout man, the most beautiful praises of God, and the gratitude-inspiring recollections of the divine benefits), so it should be handled in greater depth in a manner of exhortation rather than exposition: for it does not contain difficulty in its meaning; and if there are any difficulties with it, they have already been cleared up in the previous exposition. First of all, therefore, considering what befits a man praying to God, he ought especially to lean on his mercy, saying along with the publican, *O God, be merciful to me a sinner:*[79] for it is also written elsewhere, *Justify not yourself before God;*[80] whence also holy Job asserts, *If I would justify myself, my own mouth shall condemn me.*[81] Nevertheless, on occasion a man may sometimes recall in prayer some his good works — not insolently attributing them to himself, but humbly attributing them to God — so that he might thereby engender a greater confidence of being heard. For thus Hezekiah spoke while praying: *I beseech you, O Lord, remember how I have walked before you in truth, and with a perfect heart, [and have done that which is pleasing before you].*[82] And Judith also: *O Lord God of heaven and earth, behold their pride, and look on our humility, and have regard to the face of your saints.*[83] And also the holy and venerable Esther prayed to God in this way: *O my Lord, who alone are our king, help me a desolate woman, and who have no other helper but you. You know my necessity, that I abominate the sign of my pride and glory, which is upon my head, . . . like a menstruous rag, and wear it not in the days of my silence, . . . and that your handmaid has never rejoiced since I was brought here.*[84] Oh how truly sublime a perfection! Note that the person in such a humble state was an empress, and was wife to the most potent king Ahasuerus,[85] who reigned over one hundred and twenty-seven provinces:[86] and while she was great in majesty, honor, and glory, she never stained her soul with ambition, never vainly rejoiced, never eagerly desired to bed with the uncircumcised king. What do we who are bearded say to these things?[87]

79   Luke 18:13b.
80   Ecclus. 7:5a.
81   Job 9:20a.
82   2 Kings 20:3. Is. 38:3. *E. N.* I have continued the verse in the parts in brackets since they seem particularly fitting to the point that Denis was trying to make.
83   Judith 6:15a.
84   Esther 14: 3, 16, 18a.
85   *E. N.* Also known as Xerxes I, who reigned the Achaemenid empire between 485 and 465 BC.
86   Esther 1:1.
87   This is an oblique reference to a homily by Pope St. Gregory the Great: *Quid inter haec nos barbate et debiles dicimus?* What do we who are bearded and weak say

In a similar way, this present Psalm recounts the many motives of a devout man as to why he believes it is fitting that he be heard by God, of which some are taken up on his own part, but some are taken up on the part of God. But those things are taken up on part of himself, some pertain to his confession of imperfection, yet some to his perfection. First, therefore, he asserts reasons on the part of his own behalf, of which the first is his own need and poverty, and which he acknowledges in this way: **85{86}[1]** *Inclina, Domine, aurem tuam, et exaudi me, quoniam inops et pauper sum ego; incline your ear, O Lord, and hear me: for I am needy and poor.* It is as if he were saying: You, O God, *who are rich in mercy,*[88] *whose hand . . . is not shortened,*[89] in whose hands are all things,[90] in whom are infinite riches, hear me who am destitute and poor. For it is fitting that a liberal and rich Lord should hear a poor servant, as you yourself have attested to your prophet: *I the Lord will hear the needy and the poor; I will not forsake them.*[91] It says, *Incline your ear, O Lord*: not that in the unbounded and simple God there are bodily ears or there is a bending down in the sense of movement of place, but in the sense previously pointed out.[92]

85{86}[2]   *Preserve my soul, for I am holy: save your servant, O my God, that trusts in you.*

Custodi animam meam, quoniam sanctus sum; salvum fac servum tuum, Deus meus, sperantem in te.

The second reason given on the part of men so as to be heard [by God] is a good life: and this is asserted immediately in what follows, **85{86}[2]** *Custodi animam meam, preserve my soul* from all the dangers of temptation and adversity, *quoniam sanctus sum, for I am holy,* that is, clean and innocent. For holiness (according to Dionysius) is cleanliness (*munditia*) separate and apart from any impurity (*impuritate*).[93] But what wayfarer dares to

---

to these things? *Homilia* XI, 3, PL 76, 1116. Pope St. Gregory uses it in reference to the courage displayed by St. Agnes.

88   Eph. 2:4a.

89   Is. 59:1a.

90   Cf. Ps. 94:4a: *For in his hand are all the ends of the earth.*

91   Is. 41:17.

92   E. N. *See, e.g.,* Volume 1, Article XX (Psalm 5:3), p. 100: "The ears of the Lord are his wisdom and his kindness." *See also* this Volume: Article LX (Psalm 85:6).

93   E. N. Denis's definition of holiness or sanctity is derived from Pseudo-Dionysius's *On the Divine Names,* XII, 2. "[H]oliness is freedom from all defilement. It is a purity that is total and is utterly untainted." *Pseudo-Dionysius: The Complete Works* (New York: Paulist Press, 1987), 126 (trans., Colm Luibheid). One wonders if the common expression "cleanliness is next to godliness" is derived from Pseudo-Dionysius.

say this, given that Solomon asserts: *Who can say: My heart is clean, I am pure from sin?*[94] Job also: *Although I should be simple,* he says, *even this my soul shall be ignorant of.*[95] And St. John declares: *If we say that we have no sin, we deceive ourselves, and the truth is not in us.*[96] And we see that it is extremely dangerous for a man, in whose sight *the heavens are not pure,*[97] to say before God, *I am holy:* especially since according to Isaiah *all our justices as the rag of a menstruous woman;*[98] and Scripture attests: *Man knows not whether he be worthy of love, or hatred.*[99] Up to know I have argued that it is not safe to say before God, *Preserve my soul, for I am holy.* Now, from Scripture the opposite position will be argued, since eventually by such reasonable method we come also to an appropriate solution. For we see Scripture attesting that in Confession all things are forgiven; in Baptism also all vice is washed away. An adult who is baptized, therefore, can securely and most truly say, "I am holy": indeed, he who does not say this derogates from the grace of Baptism, and he is not a Christian.[100] Similarly, in the profession of monastic life and in the suffering of martyrdom for Christ, all sins are forgiven, and man is sanctified. And he who with contrition and with the good purpose confesses [his sins] may faithfully believe himself able to free of all mortal sins. And so the Apostle Paul called his fellow apostles not only saints, but also most holy; and he showed them to be more sublime than the prophets, saying: *we ourselves have accepted the first fruits of the Spirit.*[101] For what else is it to say, *we have accepted the first fruits of the Spirit,* except we are adepts in the first fruits or the highest graces of the Holy Spirit? Jeremiah also in the beginning of his book of visions revealed himself to have been sanctified in the womb.[102]

---

94   Prov. 20:9.

95   Job 9:21a.

96   1 John 1:8.

97   Job 15:15b. As Denis clarifies in his *Commentary on Job* regarding this verse: "*And the heavens are not pure in his sight,* that is, neither the citizens [of heaven] nor the heavenly orbs of the creation bear any comparison to God, who is infinite purity, just like in comparison to him nobody is good or wise." Doctoris Ecstatici D. Dionysii Cartusiani, Opera Omnia, Vol. 4 (Montreuil: 1898), 516.

98   Is. 44:6a.

99   Eccl. 9:1b.

100   E. N. "By Baptism all sins are forgiven, original sin and all personal sins, as well as all punishment for sin. In those who have been reborn nothing remains that would impede their entry into the Kingdom of God, neither Adam's sin, nor personal sin, nor the consequences of sin, the gravest of which is separation from God." CCC § 1263.

101   Rom. 8:23a.

102   Jer. 1:5b: *Before you came forth out of the womb, I sanctified you, and made you a prophet unto the nations.*

The answer is that these [diverging statements] are making known the same thing by different opinions applying differing considerations, in the way that Christ said, *Neither me do you know, nor my Father;*[103] but also elsewhere he said this: *You both know me, and you know whence I am.*[104] Similarly, Job, as we just now mentioned, said, *Although I should be simple, even this my soul shall be ignorant of;*[105] but he himself said: *Until I die I will not depart from my innocence; my justification, which I have began to hold, I will not forsake.*[106] In these words, in any event, he confesses himself to be innocent, just, constant, and persevering. But this is not enough [justification], for he adds, *For my heart does not reprehend me in all my life.*[107] Paul was unable to say this [because before his conversion, he fought against the Christ and his Church], yet he could legitimately and truly say, *I am not conscious to myself of anything*[108] insofar as he was aggrieved over that in the past, and he purposed to abstain from sin in the future. Yet he also reproached his heart in regard to many things, for which reason he said, *I am ... not worthy to be called an apostle, because I persecuted the church of God;*[109] and again, *Christ Jesus came into this world to save sinners, of whom I am the chief.*[110] Not, however, that [in saying all this] I place holy Job in front of Paul; indeed, quite safely I place Paul before Job.

It must be said, therefore, that no one is able to say that he is simply and absolutely holy, namely, as if he is not liable to any sin: because as it is written elsewhere, *No one is free from uncleanness, not even the infant who has lived one day on the earth:*[111] for at the very least, he was found guilty of original sin. Yet nevertheless a man is also able at a particular time to be free of all sin, both as to the stain of fault and the guilt of punishment, as is clear with respect to those who fly (*evolantibus*), who without delay enter into the heavenly kingdom.[112] But man cannot last long in this life without living venially,[113] for as it is written, *A just man*

---

103   John 8:19a.

104   John 7:28a.

105   Job 9:21a.

106   Job 27:5b–6a.

107   Job 27:6b.

108   1 Cor. 4:4a.

109   1 Cor. 15.9b.

110   1 Tim. 1:15b.

111   Job 14:4–5 (according to the Greek Septuagint).

112   E. N. The *evolantes* ("those who fly") is the name give to those few, those happy few, who avoid the labors and pains of Purgatory and enter directly into the heavenly homeland.

113   E. N. That is exposing oneself to, and succumbing to, venial sins at the very least.

shall fall seven times a day;[114] and Job says, *What is man that he should be without spot, and he that is born of a woman that he should appear just?*[115] Now a wayfarer is called holy according to the demands and possibilities of the present life, because with care he may abstain from mortal sin, and ward off venial sins, and he can apply himself daily to grow in the grace of God and in love. And so, he who endeavors with a whole-hearted purpose to serve the Lord, proposing unceasingly to advance, daily to bewail evil, and in these things daily to exert himself as much as is possible, can profess himself to be holy without danger.

Therefore, to say, *Preserve my soul, for I am holy*, are not a words of self-praise, nor does it represent to be the presumption of a vain man, but rather a voice to the Lord by one who is not ungrateful, by one who wholeheartedly attributes his holiness not to his own labor or his own power, but rather to the grace and mercy of the Savior. So that which Solomon said, *man knows not whether he be worthy of love, or hatred*, is to be viewed, therefore, not in the sense that no one with a special grace knows this: indeed, many from divine revelation recognize themselves to be predestined; but many also know themselves to be in a state of grace, in whose persons the Apostle said: *The Spirit himself gives testimony to our spirit, that we are the sons of God;*[116] and again: *Now we have received not the spirit of this world, but the Spirit that is of God; that we may know the things that are given us from God.*[117] But it is also true, that man cannot know with certainty whether he is not made pleasing by sanctifying grace, without a special inspiration of the Holy Spirit or by [private] divine revelation.[118] Consequently, speaking in accord with the common rule, *man knows not whether he be worthy of love, or hatred.*[119] From this (I believe) many words of divine Scripture which at first blush appear to be dissonant, are easily able to be made concordant. For a pious man does not call himself holy out of self-praise, and this agrees that in the preceding verse he calls himself needy and poor; and presently he states himself to trust, not in himself or in his own merits, but adds: *salvum*

---

114 Prov. 24:16a.

115 Job 15:14.

116 Rom. 8:10.

117 1 Cor. 2:12.

118 "[N]o one can know with a certitude of faith that cannot be subject to error that he has obtained God's grace." DS 1534 (Council of Trent). "[N]o one, so long as he lives in this mortal condition, ought to be so presumptuous ... as to determine with certainty that he is definitely among the number of the predestined." DS 1540. *See also* DS 1565–66.

119 Eccl. 9:1b.

fac servum tuum, Deus meus, sperantem in te; save your servant, O my
God, that trusts in you.

85{86}[3]   *Have mercy on me, O Lord, for I have cried to you all the
          day.*

          Miserere mei, Domine, quoniam ad te clamavi tota die.

85{86}[4]   *Give joy to the soul of you servant, for to you, O Lord, I
          have lifted up my soul.*

          *Laetifica animam servi tui, quoniam ad te, Domine, animam
          meam levavi.*

85{86}[7]   *I have called upon you in the day of my trouble: because you
          have heard me.*[120]

          In die tribulationis meae clamavi ad te, quia exaudisti me.

The third reason which he asserts to support being heard is perseverance
in prayer. For it is fitting to pray earnestly, according to that said by the
Apostle: *Pray without ceasing.*[121] And so he adds: **85{86}[3]** *Miserere mei,
Domine; have mercy on me, O Lord* effacing faults, relaxing punishments,
multiplying graces, *quoniam ad te clamavi tota die, for I have cried to you
all the day,* [this means] the natural [day] (*which includes the time of night*),
that is, the singular hours of the day that are set off or required.[122] **85{86}**
[4] *Laetifica animam servi tui, give joy to the soul of your servant,* that is,
fill my soul with the internal consolation of the remission of sins, with
the infusion of divine gifts, with the contemplation and hope of future
goods. Give joy to the soul of your servant, so that I might serve you
with a rejoicing heart, because you love a cheerful giver.[123] Expel from
me all disordered sadness, make me rejoice with my neighbor in all his
progress,[124] to be glad of any good event. *Quoniam ad te, Domine, animam
meam levavi; for to you, O Lord, I have lifted up my soul* by faith, hope,

---

120   E. N. Denis skips verses 5 and 6 in this section of the *Commentary.*
121   1 Thess. 5:17.
122   E. N. The reference is to the set hours of prayers required by monastic discipline.
123   Cf. 2 Cor. 9:7: *Everyone as he has determined in his heart, not with sadness, or
of necessity: for God loves a cheerful giver.*
124   E. N. The prayer that one might rejoice in the boon to our neighbor and not
begrudge him of it brings to mind portions of Rafael Cardinal Merry del Val y
Zulueta's Litany of Humility: *That others may be praised and I go unnoticed, Jesus,
grant me the grace to desire it. That others may be preferred to me in everything, Jesus,
grant me the grace to desire it. That others may become holier than I, provided that I
may become as holy as I should, Jesus, grant me the grace to desire it.*

and charity, contemplating, expecting, and loving you, the highest good, and devoutly invoking you. **85{86}[7]** *In die tribulationis meae, in the day of my trouble,* when either I am aroused by the concupiscence of the flesh or I am pressed upon by a passion of the soul, or I am tempted by a demons, or I am afflicted by the world, or I am sick of body, *clamavi ad te, I have called upon you* for the help and assistance of your most kindly grace, as you yourself have elsewhere admonished: *Call upon me in the day of trouble: I will deliver you, and you shall glorify me;*[125] and again: *I am the Savior of the people; in whatever tribulation they shall cry to me, I will hear them.*[126] And so, I will call upon you, *quia exaudisti me, because you have heard me:* that is, because I have experienced being heard by you before, so also now do I trust in invoking you, and so I invoke you.

85{86}[11] Conduct me, O Lord, in your way, and I will walk in your truth: let my heart rejoice that it may fear your name [127]

Deduc me, Domine, in via tua, et ingrediar in veritate tua; laetetur cor meum, ut timeat nomen tuum.

85{86}[11] *Deduc me, Domine; conduct me, O Lord,* by your grace and by your angelic guardian, *in via tua, in your way,* that is, in the divine law, by which I travel to you, as long as I keep it without stumbling, worthily and holily traveling onward in it by your presence; *et ingrediar in veritate tua, and I will walk in your truth,* that is, I will endure in your life, and I will progress to the future life in the truth of your doctrine — believing and obeying it — and in the truth of your justice — following it: so that, O Lord Christ, that which you prayed for your elect, Father *sanctify them in truth,*[128] might be fulfilled in me. Let me not find myself in the society of those of whom Jeremiah speaks: *Surely our fathers have possessed lies, a vanity which has not profited them.*[129] *Laetetur cor meum, ut timeat nomen tuum,* let my

---

125 Ps. 49:15.

126 *Cf.* Is. 43:11: *I am, I am the Lord: and there is no Savior besides me.* E. N. The words Denis uses, *Salus populi ego sum . . . de quacumque tribulatione clamaverint ad me, exaudiam eos* stem from the Introit from the 19th Sunday after Pentecost (Extraordinary Form) and the Entrance Antiphon for the 25th Sunday in Ordinary Time (Ordinary Form). The initial letters of the first four words yield the Latin word *SPES,* HOPE.

127 E. N. Denis skips verses 8, 9, and 10.

128 John 17:17.

129 Jer. 16:19b. E. N. In his *Commentary on Jeremiah,* Denis understands this verse as referring to the Gentiles, and the lies are "the most false errors in the worship of idols," which not has not profited them, but has "greatly harmed them, namely

heart rejoice that it may fear your name, that is, with an interior delight let it fear you with a holy and chaste fear which proceeds out of love. For since fearing God is a virtuous act, it ought to be done with delight, for it is a sign of virtue that delight is attached to the operation [of a virtuous act].[130] Moreover, how necessary the fear of the Lord is toward salvation is expressed by Moses speaking to the Israelite people: *Unless . . . you fear the glorious and terrible name of the Lord, . . . he shall increase your plagues; . . . and as the Lord rejoiced upon you before doing good to you, . . . so shall he rejoice destroying you and bringing you to nothing.*[131] The Lord also stated through Malachi: *The son honors the father, and the servant his master. If then I be a father, where is my honor? And if I be a master, where is my fear?*[132] The perfect, therefore, fear God with a filial fear, lest they offend him and become separated from him. Indeed, Scripture speaks of this: *Behold the fear of the Lord, that is wisdom.*[133] For this fear truly is enjoyable, as is written in Ecclesiasticus: *There is nothing better than the fear of God.*[134] But the imperfect fear God, or better [they fear] the name of the Lord, who is called Judge, with a fear that is part servile and part servile, for regarding this fearing of the name of the Lord is written: *Behold the name of the Lord comes from afar, his wrath burns, and is heavy to bear.*[135]

85{86}[12]   *I will praise you, O Lord my God: with my whole heart, and I will glorify your name forever:*

 Confitebor tibi, Domine Deus meus, in toto corde meo, et glorificabo nomen tuum in aeternum.

85{86}[12]   *Confitebor tibi, Domine Deus meus, in toto corde meo; I will praise you, O Lord my God: with my whole heart* with a confession of your

---

through the aversion of mind to the great and true God." Doctoris Ecstatici D. Dionysii Cartusiani, *Opera Omnia*, Vol. 9 (Montreuil: 1900), 146.

130   E. N. St. Thomas, in his commentary on Aristotle's *Ethics* states: "Being happy requires a continual living and doing. It is right that the operation of the virtuous man be good and pleasurable in itself, because it is good in itself. . . . But among pleasures, a good operation is the pleasure proper to the virtuous man, for he who does not delight in virtuous operation is not virtuous." *Sententia Ethic.*, lib. 9, l. 10, n. 11.

131   Deut. 28:58a, 59a, 63a.

132   Mal. 1:6.

133   Job 28:28a.

134   Ecclus. 23:37a.

135   Is. 30:27a. E. N. Denis refers to the perfect and imperfect believers in Christ. There are those who, as St. Paul says referring to Ps. 35:2, have "no fear of God before their eyes." Rom. 3:18. Ps. 35:2: "The unjust has said within himself, that he would sin: there is no fear of God before his eyes."

praise and of my sinfulness; to your glory I will confess my sins and your proclamation [of the Gospel]. Therefore, from the most intimate part of our hearts, and with heart purely converted to God, let us confess to the Lord his goodness and his benefits and our depravity and our great unthankfulness. *Et glorificabo nomen tuum in aeternum, and I will glorify your name forever*, that is, I will acknowledge with words and I will bear witness with works your felicity and your glory, now already beginning by faith, and at last fulfilling it in heaven by vision without cessation. The creature is sanctified, magnified, and glorified by the Creator, and conversely, but in utter dissimilar ways.[136] For God sanctifies the created mind by infusing it with grace; and he magnifies it by bestowing upon it spiritual perfection; but he glorifies it by imparting beatitude. Now the created mind sanctifies, magnifies, and glorifies God not by bestowing upon him something, but through witnessing by words and deeds his holiness, dignity, and glory; that is, while he serves him in holiness and justice, and continually resounds his praises.[137] Our happiness consists in this glorification by which we glorify God, in the way the Most High says, *Whosoever shall glorify me, him will I glorify*;[138] and again, *I love them that love me.*[139]

85{86}[13] *For your mercy is greatly over and above me: and you have delivered my soul out of the lower hell.*

Quia misericordia tua magna est super me, et eruisti animam meam ex inferno inferiori.

---

136 *E. N.* In other words, the created soul is sanctified, magnified, and glorified by God, and, in a manner of speaking quite differently and distantly analogous only, God is sanctified, magnified, and glorified by the soul. God, however, does not *substantially* or *essentially* become more holy, greater, or more glorious by anything we do. "Creation can add nothing to the essential glory of God.... Hence it comes to pass that God's accidental glory seems a very slight thing to us compared with the immeasurable ocean and indefinable splendour of His essential glory. Yet God's accidental glory, and indeed the slightest measure of it, is a greater thing that we can reach even by our conceptions. It is the result of the total of creation, and is its final cause as well. Yet ... it is irreverent to suppose creation to be otherwise than of great moment even to God Himself. His accidental glory is of moment to Him; for He cannot pursue what is of no moment. It is indeed infinitely below His essential glory; but it is at the same time infinitely above our powers of measurement. It is something very intimate to Him, although it is not intrinsic. Frederick William Faber, *Bethlehem* (London: Thomas Richardson & Son, 1860), 305.

137 Cf. Luke 1:74–75: *We may serve him without fear, In holiness and justice before him, all our days.*

138 1 Sam. 2:30b.

139 Prov. 8:17a.

So for this reason will I do these things: 85{86}[**13**] *Quia misericordia tua magna est super me, for your mercy is greatly over and above me*, that is, because the multiple effects of your kindness that are given to me, sending your Son for me, and delivering me through his Passion, and with such forbearance awaiting me with your patience: so that *eruisti animam meam ex inferno inferiori, you have delivered my soul out of the lower hell*, that is, from mortal sin whose just desert is to send one to the lowest hell in which the reprobate dwell in eternal damnation. Now four are the things that are described as hell, namely: the place of Purgatory (whence in the Mass of the dead is prayed: free the souls of the faithful from the punishments of hell);[140] the second hell is the place of unbaptized infants;[141] now the third is the limbo of the fathers, to which hell Christ descended; the fourth is the place of the reprobate, of ruin without end. It is believed also that this hell is below the earth, as also Purgatory and the limbo of the fathers. But the hell of the reprobate is in the lowest place, the place where the rich man of whom Christ spoke in the Gospel is buried.[142]

85{86}[**14**]   *O God, the wicked are risen up against me, and the assembly of the mighty have sought my soul: and they have not set you before their eyes.*

Deus, iniqui insurrexerunt super me, et synagoga potentium quaesierunt animam meam, et non proposuerunt te in conspectu suo.

85{86}[**16**]   *O look upon me and have mercy on me: give your command to your servant and save the son of your handmaid.*[143]

Respice in me, et miserere mei; da imperium tuum puero tuo, et salvum fac filium ancillae tuae.

---

140   E. N. The reference is to the Offertory of the Requiem Mass: *Domine Iesu Christi, Rex gloriae, libera animas omnium fidelium defunctorum de poenis inferni,* "O Lord Jesus Christ, King of glory, deliver the souls of all the faithful departed from the punishments of hell." Denis understands this as a prayer for the suffering souls in Purgatory.

141   E. N. The so-called *limbus puerorum* or *limbus infantum* ("children's limbo"), where unbaptized children guilty of original sin alone and not personal or actual sins reside, where they do not suffer the pains of the hell of the damned, enjoy natural beatitude, but do not enjoy supernatural beatitude since the portal into the supernatural life is baptism. "It remains . . . a possible theological hypothesis," in fact one "long . . . used in traditional theological teaching." International Theological Commission, "The Hope of Salvation for Infants Who Die without Being Baptized."

142   Luke 16:22b: *And the rich man also died: and he was buried in hell.*

143   E. N. Denis skips over verse 15.

85{86}[14] *Deus, iniqui;* O God, the wicked, that is, the spiritual malignant, *insurrexerunt super me,* are risen up against me, tempting my soul; *et synagoga potentium, and the assembly of the mighty* O God, the Trinity, *iniqui,* the wicked Jews *insurrexerunt super me,* are risen up against me, that is, they oppose me; *et synagoga potentium, and the assembly of the mighty,* that is, the association of tyrants and of evil men, *quaesierunt animam meam, have sought my soul* to subvert it with evil example, to make it depart from your path, and to conform it to their perversities. **85{86}[16]** *Respice in me,* O look upon me, kindly healing the wounds of my soul, *et miserere mei, and have mercy on me,* taking away my miseries. *Da imperium tuum, give your command,* that is, give your precepts to me, *puero tuo, to your servant,* to fulfil and to keep: in the manner that is stated in the Gospel, *If you will enter into life, keep the commandments;*[144] *et salvum fac, and save me, filium ancillae tuae, the son of your handmaid,* namely, of the Church or of a Christian woman. Behold how sweet, lovely, and fair-sounding is this verse.

85{86}[17] Show me a sign for good: that they who hate me may see, and be confounded, because you, O Lord, have helped me and have comforted me.[145]

Fac mecum signum in bonum, ut videant qui oderunt me, et confundantur, quoniam tu, Domine, adiuvisti me, et consolatus es me.

85{86}[17] *Fac mecum signum in bonum, show me a sign for good:* that is, to operate such an effect in me, by which I might know myself to be beloved and predestinated by you, delivering me, namely, from every incursion of the enemy, and filling me with grace, through which I might do those things that are signs of predestination, which are: hearing the word of God cheerfully, abhorring vices because they are vices, having the good purpose to always live well;[146] *ut,* that demons and evil men

---

144   Matt. 19:17b.

145   *E. N.* I have replaced the Douay Rheims's "token" as a translation of *signum* with "sign."

146   *E. N.* Denis lists three such signs; however, there are numerous lists. Garrigou-Lagrange lists eight: (i) care to preserve oneself from mortal sin, living a good life, and keeping a clear conscience, (ii) a spirit of prayer, (iii) exhibiting humility (iv) relishing hearing the word of God, (v) suffering adversity with patience for the love of God; (vi) rendering assistance to those who are afflicted, (vii) loving one's neighbor, and (viii) a sincere devotion to our Lord and his Mother. Réginald Garrigou-Lagrange, *Life Everlasting* (Herder, 1952), 52, 261–62. Other lists include

videant, may see this sign, *qui oderunt me, that they who hate me* with an iniquitous and debased hate, envious not only over my temporal prosperity, but also of the salvation of my soul; *et confundantur, and that they may be confounded,* seeing themselves not able to obtain from me that which they desire, indeed, seeing in me the opposite of what they desire; *quoniam tu, Domine, adiuvisti me; for you, O Lord, have helped me,* so that I might not succumb to those temptations and persecutions, *et consolatus es me, and have comforted me* in all tribulations and distress, so that I might fulfill that [injunction] of St. James: *Brethren, count it all joy, when you shall fall into diverse temptations;*[147] and that of the Savior: *Be glad and rejoice* during that time, namely, when you bear insults and suffer much adversity, *for your reward is very great in heaven.*[148] Whence the Apostle [Paul] says: *We glory in the hope of the glory of the sons of God; and not only so, but we glory also in tribulations, knowing that tribulation works patience, and patience trial, [and trial hope].*[149] It was in this way that God consoled the Apostle [Paul], who attests: *As the sufferings of Christ abound in us: so also by Christ does our comfort abound.*[150]

The virtue of this verse is clearly ineffable: but also the entirety of this Psalm redounds with divine sweetness, holy fervor, spiritually joyfulness, and admirable devotion: it behooves us to chant it with mental relish, with great joy, and with particular attention.

---

suffering affliction in the name of Christ, living habitually in the grace of God, love of the Holy Eucharist, love of, and obedience to, the Church, devotion to the Saints, and zeal for souls. Other lists build upon the eight beatitudes. Of course, these signs are not signs of absolute certainty, but they give rise to moral certainty of one's predestination.

147   James 1:2.
148   Matt. 5:12a.
149   Rom. 5:2–4. E. N. The part in brackets replaces Denis's "etc."
150   2 Cor. 1:5.

PRAYER

EAD US YOUR SERVANTS TO YOU IN YOUR
way, O Lord, and let us advance in your truth: so that your
mercy greatly may flow upon us, and you may deliver our soul
from the lowest hell and enable us to participate in eternal glory.

Famulantes tibi nos, Domine, deduc in via tua, et ingrediamur
in veritate tua: ut magna super nos stillante misericordia
tua, animam nostram eruas ab inferno inferiori,
atque aeternae gloriae facias participari.

Psalm 86

ARTICLE LXII

EXPOSITION OF THE EIGHTY-SIXTH PSALM:
FUNDAMENTA EIUS.
THE FOUNDATIONS THEREOF.

86{87}[1] *For the sons of Korah, a Psalm of a canticle. Her foundations are in the holy mountains.*[1]

Filiis Core. Psalmus cantici. Fundamenta eius in montibus sanctis.

THE PSALM NOW BEING HANDLED, WHICH is small in quantity and great in power, brief in word, but great in sentiment, has this title: 86{87}[1] *Filiis Core, psalmus cantici; for the sons of Korah, a Psalm of a canticle*: that is, this Psalm containing spiritual joy was sung and written for the sons of Korah, that is, the faithful imitators of Christ. For this is what is described and praised in this Psalm: the City of God, that is, the Church, according to its dual status. For first it treats of it according to its militant state in the present: and indeed, in the title it says, *a Psalm*: by which is designated a work, for working befits the Church in its militant state. Second, namely, in the last verse, it speaks of the Church according to its triumphant state, or to the extent it is reigning in heaven with God. And so to the title is added *a canticle*: by which is signified spiritual joyfulness, which is most fitting to the Saints in the heavenly fatherland.

And it therefore says: *Fundamenta eius, her foundations.* It does not describe what it includes in the *her*: and why it does this, I suppose to be for the same reason that Mary Magdalen said to him to whom she believed to be a gardener: *Sir, if you have taken him hence, tell me [where you have laid him, and I will take him away].*[2] We may be sure that out of love's vehemence, she — whose fervid love entirely filled, occupied, and possessed her mind — believed no mind to be empty of that knowledge. Similarly here, the Prophet [David] does not explain the name *her* because

---

1 E. N. The Douay-Rheims translates *fundamenta eius* as "the foundations thereof," which is better translated here as "her foundations."
2 John 20:15b. E. N. The part in brackets replaces the "etc." of Denis.

of the most ardent love that he has for the Church in his heart:[3] and yet that he speaks about her is known from the words that follow. It hearkens back, therefore, to that which was which was earlier stated with the heart. And so he says: *Her foundations*, that is, [the foundations] of the Church, are conferred and are stable *in montibus sanctis, in the holy mountains*, that is, in Christ, the mountains of mountains,[4] and his apostles. For these founded the Church, that is, the Christian faithful, in faith and grace. For although there is one principal and supreme light, foundation, and mountain of the Holy Church, there are also other certain secondary and less principal lights, foundations, and mountains of the Church: and these are the holy Apostles, to whom Christ in the Gospel, said, *You are the light of the world.*[5] And regarding these, there is contained in Revelation: *The wall of the city had twelve foundations, and in them, the twelve names of the twelve apostles of the Lamb.*[6] We can also expound this, although in a less exquisite manner, of the mountains of the earth, in which Christ preached, confirmed, and taught the evangelical law, so that [it reads in] this sense: *Her foundations*, that is, the foundational lessons of the Church, began and were given, and by them also the apostles were instructed, *in the holy mountains*, that is: in Mount Sion, upon which was situated the temple in which Jesus often preached, and the cenacle in which he instituted the Sacrament of the Altar and sent the Holy Spirit; and in the mountain from which we read he ascended,[7] the mountain upon which he taught the eight Beatitudes and promulgated the doctrine of the evangelical law; and upon Mount Tabor, upon which, before Peter, John, and James, he was transfigured,[8] and the faith of the future resurrection was proved by such experience.

---

3   *E. N.* Denis is saying that the lover uses the personal pronoun, and not the proper or common noun, because he assumes, from the vehemence of his love, that the person he speaks with surely must now to whom he refers.

4   *E. N.* Origen referred to Jesus as the *sabbata sabbatorum, sancta sanctorum, mons montium, rex regum, opera operum, saecula saeculorum*, "sabbath of sabbaths, holy of holies, mountain of mountains, king of kings, work of works, age of ages." Henri de Lubac, *History and Spirit: The Understanding of Scripture According to Origen* (San Francisco: Ignatius Press, 2007), p. 355 (trans., Anne Englund Nash). We have seen Denis use quite frequently the name "Saint of saints" to refer to Christ. *See, e.g.,* Volume I, Article VII (Psalm 3:1), Article XXIV (Psalm 7:10), Article XXXI (Psalm 10:4), Article XXXVIII (Psalm 15:10) and *passim* in that and other volumes. *See also* footnote 3-26.

5   Matt. 5:14a.

6   Rev. 21:14.

7   Matt. chap. 5

8   Matt. chap. 17.

86{87}[2] *The Lord loves the gates of Sion above all the tabernacles of Jacob.*

Diligit Dominus portas Sion super omnia tabernacula Iacob.

86{87}[2] *Diligit Dominus portas Sion,* the Lord loves the gates of Sion, that is, he receives and approves the sacraments, powers, and the exorcisms, catechisms, and baptisms of the Church, *super omnia tabernacula Iacob, above all the tabernacles of Jacob,* that is, more than the form of worship of the Old Testament, which was displayed in various tabernacles, namely: [first] in the tabernacle of Moses;[9] second, in the tabernacle made by David;[10] third, in the temple of Solomon;[11] fourth, in the temple of Zerubbabel.[12] This is what the Apostle said: *For the law brought nothing to perfection, but a bringing in of a better hope, by which we draw nigh to God.*[13] Now by this he prefers the gates of Sion, that is, worship and the sacraments, and those things by which Christians advance the heavenly kingdom to the observances of the Old Law, and he prefers also the Church to the Hebrew people and the Synagogue. Truly, the Synagogue was a figure of the Church; and the cult of the Synagogue was a type of the cult of the Church[14] according to Dionysius. But the thing figured is preferrable to thing figuring. And so the Lord through Malachi says: *I have no pleasure in you, . . . and I will not receive a gift of your hand.*[15] See how in these words he disapproves of the Synagogue and its sacrifices. But approving the Church and its sacrifice, he adds: *For from the rising of the sun even to the going down, my name is great among the Gentiles, and in every place there is sacrifice, and there is offered to my name a clean oblation.*[16]

---

9   Num. 7:1: *And it came to pass in the day that Moses had finished the tabernacle, and set it up, and had anointed and sanctified it with all its vessels, the altar likewise and all the vessels thereof.*

10   2 Sam. 6:17: *And they brought the ark of the Lord, and set it in its place in the midst of the tabernacle, which David had pitched for it.*

11   1 Kings 8:6.

12   1 Ezra 6:15: *And they were finishing this house of God, until the third day of the month of Adar, which was in the sixth year of the reign of king Darius.*

13   Heb. 7:19.

14   E. N. The English word "cult," which comes from the Latin *cultus,* means worship or adoration (*cultus latriae*) of God or a lesser veneration (*cultus duliae*) to the saints and holy things; more broadly, *cultus* means "care" or "cultivation." As used here, it has is no derogatory, sinister, or negative sense such as when used in reference to the "cult" of the Branch Davidians.

15   Mal. 1:10b.

16   Mal. 1:11.

Viewed morally, by Sion is understood those who look upwards to heavenly things; and by Jacob, the supplanters of vices. *The Lord loves the gates of Sion more*, that is, the virtues and the good works of contemplative men than he does *the tabernacles of Jacob*, that is, the inhabitants of the land signified by Jacob: who although they live in the grace of God, yet they have not fully driven away the roots of vice, but they stand in daily need to contend against illicit movements. However much more these men labor than contemplative and perfect men, still less do the former deserve the essential reward compared to latter: because the acts of the former do not proceed from such sincere, perfect, and fervid love so they do not undertake their acts as promptly, tranquilly, and delightfully as the latter. For, absolutely speaking, to the degree any work of God is executed with more promptness, with more tranquility, and with more delight, to that degree it is more amply rewarded.

86{87}[3]   *Glorious things are said of you, O City of God!*
           Gloriosa dicta sunt de te, civitas Dei.

Thereafter he praises the Church because of the excellence of its reputation. **86{87}[3]** *Gloriosa dicta sunt de te*, glorious things are said of you, in the Old Testament, but even more in the New [Testament], *civitas Dei, O City of God*, that is, O Church of Christ. For the Prophets of old uttered many splendid things regarding the Church of the New Testament: though it is also copiously extolled in the Song of Songs. For it is written of the Church gathered from the Gentiles and founded by Christ: *Give praise, O you barren, that bear not: sing forth praise, and make a joyful noise, you that did not travail with child: for many are the children of the desolate, more than of her that has a husband.*[17] About which Isaiah again says: *The nation and the kingdom that will not serve you, shall perish;*[18] and again [Isaiah says] to God: *Behold you shall call a nation, which you knew not.*[19] Of this Church of Christ is said in Hosea: *It shall be in the place where it shall be said to them: You are not my people: it shall be said to them: You are the sons of the living God.*[20] And Amos: *In that day I will raise up the tabernacle of David, that is fallen,*[21] *that the residue of men may seek after the Lord:* by which James explains the calling of the

---

17   Is. 54:1.
18   Is. 60:12a.
19   Is. 55:5a.
20   Hosea 1:10b.
21   Amos 9:11a; Acts 15:16a.

Gentiles to the Catholic faith.[22] And elsewhere the Church of Christ is praised in this fashion: *Your hand shall be lifted up over your enemies, and all your enemies shall be cut off.*[23] Now in the Scripture of the New Testament, the Church is more splendidly praised. Whence in Revelation we have: *Come, and I will show you the bride, the wife of the Lamb;*[24] and: *I saw . . . the new Jerusalem, coming down out of heaven from God, prepared as a bride adorned for her husband.*[25]

Now the Church is called a city, for it has the unity of a city:[26] for in her are collected all nations or tribes of the earth by faith and charity, so that they are one people in Christ: in which, according to the Apostle [Paul], *there is no distinction of the Jew and the Greek.*[27] And of this union of the faithful is written, *that Jesus should die for the nation; and not only for the nation, but to gather together in one the children of God, that were dispersed.*[28] Whence Christ prayed: *Holy Father, keep them in your name whom you have given me; that they may be one, as we also are.*[29] Paul also: *I beseech you, brethren, by the name of our Lord Jesus Christ, that you all speak the same thing, and that there be no schisms among you.*[30]

86{87}[4] *I will be mindful of Rahab and of Babylon knowing me. Behold the foreigners, and Tyre, and the people of the Ethiopians, these were there.*

Memor ero Rahab et Babylonis, scientium me; ecce alienigenae, et Tyrus, et populus Aethiopum, hi fuerunt illic.

---

22   Acts 15:17a.

23   Micah 5:9.

24   Rev. 21:9b.

25   Rev. 21:2.

26   E. N. This reference is suggestive of the doctrine that the Church is a *communitas* or *societas perfecta*, a self-sufficient community or society that can attain its end by the powers and resources bestowed upon it by the Lord. "The Church," said Pope Leo XIII in his encyclical *Immortale Dei*, "no less than the State itself is a society perfect in its own nature and its own right." Moreover, the Church is a "society . . . made up of men, just as civil society is, and yet is supernatural and spiritual . . . . Hence, it is distinguished and differs from civil society, and, what is of highest moment, it is a society chartered as of right divine, perfect in its nature and in its title, to possess in itself and by itself, through the will and loving kindness of its Founder, all needful provision for its maintenance and action." Nos. 35, 10.

27   Rom. 10:12a.

28   John 11:51b–52.

29   John 17:11b.

30   1 Cor. 1:10a. The verse continues: *but that you be perfect in the same mind, and in the same judgment.*

Consequently, he declares the conversion of the Gentiles to the worship of Christ, and says: **86{87}[4]** *Memor ero Rahab et Babylonis, scientium me; I will be mindful of Rahab and Babylon knowing me*. In this place, Rahab is not a reference to the proper name of the woman, by whom Salmon bore Boaz,[31] and of whom we read that she received and hid the two messengers of Joshua;[32] but according to Jerome, Rahab is here a common noun designating pride or insolence: by which is designated pagans delivered over idolatry,[33] rebelling against God by their great self-exaltation. But Babylon is understood as those disordered by perverse vices. And so [we can understand this verse] in this sense: *I will be mindful*, impleading mercy, *Rahab and Babylon*, that is, of the pride of the Gentiles, and their living in the confusion of sins; *knowing me* by faith after I am brought to their attention. God was mindful of them, sending the holy Apostles for their conversion, by whose preaching he taught, humbled, and ordered their hearts, in the manner that is written: *Behold I will send many fishers, says the Lord, and they shall fish them*.[34] Literally also the Lord was mindful of Babylon, because through the preaching of Simon and Jude, a large part of the earth was converted to the faith by them.[35] *Ecce alienigenae, behold the foreigners*, that is, those once strangers to the faith. In Jerome's translation based upon the Hebrew text, we read, *Behold Palestine*, that is, the Philistines. *Et Tyrus, and Tyre*, that is, the people narrowed by vice and deprived of the breadth of charity: for Tyre is interpreted as meaning narrowness; *et populus Aethiopum, and the people of Ethiopians*, that is, the pagans denigrated by vice. *Hi fuerunt illic, these were there*, that is, in the city of Christ, which is the Church: for in this way sinners were made into sons of the Church. Now literally, Palestine, Tyre, and Ethiopia were converted to Christ, and the orthodox faith strongly flourished among those people; and so by the Gentile peoples dwelling around Judea is designated all infidels throughout the whole world who attained unity in the Church.

---

31   Matt. 1:5a.

32   Joshua 1:4.

33   L. *nomen appelativum*, a common name, as distinguished from a *nomen proprium*, a proper name.

34   Jer. 16:16a.

35   E. N. The Apostles Simon (sometimes called "the Zealot" or "the Cananaean") and Jude Thaddeus (the patron of impossible causes). Tradition recounts that Simon first preached in Egypt, but then joined Jude in Mesopotamia, and both proceeded to Persia (Babylon), where they eventually were martyred. *See* "Saints Simon and Jude, Apostles," in *The Golden Legend* (Princeton: Princeton University Press, 1998), 647–50.

86{87}[5] *Shall not man say to Sion? That man is born in her, and the
Highest himself has founded her?*[36]

*Numquid Sion dicet homo? Et homo natus est in ea, et ipse
fundavit eam Altissimus?*

86{87}[5] *Numquid Sion dicet homo: et homo natus est in ea, et ipse
fundavit eam Altissimus? Shall not man say to Sion: That man born in her,
and the Highest himself has founded her?* This verse can be explained in
numerous ways. For Sion in this place is in the dative case,[37] so that in
Jerome's translation according to the Hebrew we have: *It will be declared
to Sion.* And so the term "Shall" is not to be received negatively, but
affirmatively, so that [it reads] in this sense: *Shall?* As if he is saying,
"Indeed"; to *Sion* itself, that is to the Church signified by Sion, *this man
will declare* who in this Psalm refers to Christ and the Church. But we
can also understand by the word "man" here the precursor of Christ:
of whom is written in the Gospel: *There was a man sent by God.*[38] For
he was the first to preach to Sion: and of him is said in Isaiah: *Get up
upon a high mountain, you that bring good tidings to Sion.*[39] Now what
he said is added: *Et homo natus est in ea, and that man is born in her* :
that is, Christ, God and man, was begotten among the people of Sion,
because he was born of the glorious Virgin, who is the most worthy
member of the Church.[40] Whence the Apostle says to the Hebrews:
*Because the children are partakers of flesh and blood, Christ also himself in
like manner has been partaker of the same.*[41] *Et ipse Altissimus, and the
Highest,* that is, Christ born from the Virgin according to his humanity,
but *the Highest* and eternal according to his divinity, *fundavit eam, has
founded her,* that is, established the Virgin mother in all grace, to the

---

36   E. N. Since Denis understands *homo* to be the subject and *Sion* to be in the
dative case (and so the recipient of the object) and further understands the first
"homo" to be part of the first interrogative clause, I have had to depart from the
Douay-Rheims translation here, which reads: "Shall not Sion say: This man and
that man is born in her?"

37   E. N. In other words, Sion should not be the subject, but the indirect object
which receives the direct object (in this case the question).

38   John 1:6.

39   Is. 40:9a.

40   E. N. "By her complete adherence to the Father's will, to his Son's redemptive
work, and to every prompting of the Holy Spirit, the Virgin Mary is the Church's
model of faith and charity. Thus she is a 'preeminent and ... wholly unique member of
the Church' (*supereminens prorsusque singular membrum Ecclesiae*); indeed, she is the
'exemplary realization,' the 'type' of the Church." CCC § 967 (quoting VII, LG 53, 63).

41   Heb. 2:14a.

extent that she never from her very beginning fell into sin.[42] Or [an alternative interpretation], *he has founded her*, that is, the Church, which from the beginning he founded upon faith and grace, *God also bearing them witness by signs, and wonders, . . . and distributions of the Holy Spirit, according to his own will.*[43] For this reason Zechariah speaking of Christ said: *He shall build a temple to God.*[44]

And so this verse evidently reveals the dual nature and single personhood in Christ. For when it says, *that man is born in her*, it declares a temporal, created human nature to be in Christ; but when that same man is indicated by the [reflexive] pronoun *himself*, it makes clear the identity of person. Finally, since it adds, *the Highest . . . has founded her*, the divinity of Christ is manifested in two ways. First, since it says, *founded*. For no one originally founded the Church, nor made his own mother, except God.[45] Second, since it says *the Highest*. For no one is *the Highest* except for the one and true God, of whom is stated in an earlier Psalm, *You alone are the most High over all the earth.*[46] And another scripture says: *There is one most high Creator Almighty, and a powerful king, and greatly to be feared.*[47]

The second way [this verse] is expounded is thus: *Shall not man*, that is Christ, *say to Sion*, that is, to the Church? It is as if saying, "Of course." For Christ frequently said to the Jews, and to the disciples that his first coming was accomplished. The third [way to understand this verse] is

---

42   E. N. "[T]he Most Blessed Virgin Mary, at the first instant of her conception, by the singular grace and privilege of almighty God and in view of the merits of Jesus Christ, the Savior of the human race, was preserved from all stain of original sin." DS 2803 (*Ineffabilis Deus*). Mary, moreover, "was she who, [was] free of the stain of actual and original sin." DS 3915 (Pius XII). "Two special factors rendered Mary impeccable or unable to sin. The first was her constant awareness of God, living always in His presence, and the second was her reception of special and extraordinary graces. These special graces made it possible for Mary to maintain a perfect harmony in her mind, will and emotions and to recognize always what was the right thing to do and then to do it." Kenneth Baker, S. J., *Fundamentals of Catholicism* (San Francisco: Ignatius Press, 2016) Vol. 2, 332.

43   Heb. 2:4.

44   E. N. Denis's text reads *Ipse aedificabit templum Dei*, "he shall build a temple to God." The Sixto-Clementine Vulgate has *Ipse exstruet templum Domino*, "he shall construct a temple to the Lord."

45   E. N. Denis is taking both interpretations of *he founded her* (meaning Mary, the Virgin Mother, or the Church) and saying that only God can both create his own human mother and found the Church; therefore, it points to the two natures in the one divine person of Christ.

46   Ps. 82:19b.

47   Ecclus. 1:8a.

thus:[48] *Shall not Sion*, that is, the Virgin Mary, coming from Sion or from the Jewish people, or *Sion*, that is, the Church, *say* with the heart and by mouth, *man* (implying simply [a man])? It is as if saying "No." For neither the Christ-bearing Virgin nor the Church said or believed Christ to be a mere man, but both God and man. And this meaning conforms with to the words used by Chrysostom,[49] who states with respect to this verse: "Mother Sion, shall a man say."[50]

The fourth explanation is thus: *Shall not man say to Sion?* That is, shall not some mere man, persuade or suggest to the Church with human wisdom and power those things which should be held about Christ, namely, *that man is born in her, and the Highest himself has founded her?* It is as if saying, "No": for no one is persuaded of this — that Christ is both born a man and is the most high God — by human reason. Whence the Apostle says: *My preaching was not in the persuasive words of human wisdom, but in showing of the Spirit and power.*[51] Indeed, the Catholic faith is supported by divine authority, and is confirmed by God himself proving it, according to this: *But they going forth preached everywhere: the Lord working withal, and confirming the word with signs that followed.*[52] But why is it here said of Christ, *man is born in her*, and not rather, *man was conceived in her*, except to insinuate that Christ from the beginning of his conception in the Virgin was a perfect man in all virtue and knowledge?[53] And this is that new thing of which is written: *The Lord has created a new thing upon the earth: A woman shall compass a man.*[54] For this reason, the angel said to Joseph: *That which is born in her, is of the Holy Spirit.*[55]

---

48   E. N. Without warning, Denis assumes in his third explanation that Sion is the subject rather than the direct object.

49   E. N. St. John Chrysostom (347–407 AD). Patriarch of Constantinople and Doctor of the Church.

50   E. N. *Mater Sion dicet, Homo?* The reference to Chrysostom is to Homily II, I (*Cum iret in exilium*), PG 52, 435 (Μήτηρ Σιών, ἐρεῖ ἄνθρωπος). Denis is rather abstruse here, and rather assumes alot from his reader, including that this quote from Chrysostom is from the Septuagint version of Psalm 86:5. But I think Denis is simply justifying his use of Sion as a subject (and not direct object) since Chrysostom understood it that way.

51   1 Cor. 2:4.

52   Mark 16:20.

53   E. N. Since the human soul of Christ enjoyed the beatific vision from the first moment of conception in the Blessed Virgin Mary (and thus knew "all things in the Word" even before the organic human brain of Christ was developed, which is, of course what the blessed in heaven do until joined to their bodies in the final resurrection) it could be said that "man" was born in Mary from conception.

54   Jer. 31:22b.

55   Matt. 1:20b. E. N. The Latin text has *quod natum est in ea*, literally, "that which is born in her." Although it can mean "that which is conceived in her," as the translators

86{87}[6] *The Lord shall tell in the writings of peoples and of princes, of them that have been in her.*

Dominus narrabit in scripturis populorum et principum, horum qui fuerunt in ea.

Following this, evangelization and the propagation of the Christian faith and the mystery of Christ is added: 86{87}[6] *Dominus,* the Lord Christ, or God, the Holy Trinity, *narrabit,* shall tell throughout the whole world, *in scripturis populorum, in the writings of peoples,* that is, in the canonical Scriptures of the New Testament, namely, the Gospels, the Epistles, and the Acts of the Apostles. And because these were Scriptures written by the Apostles and the Evangelists, the princes of the Christians, so does it add: *et principum horum qui fuerunt in ea, and of princes of them that have been in her.* For about them is foretold: *You shall make them princes over all the earth;*[56] and, *The princes of the people are gathered together, with the God of Abraham,*[57] that is, with Christ, the true God of all.

86{87}[7] *The dwelling in you is as it were of all rejoicing.*
Sicut laetantium omnium habitatio est in te.

And then he describes the Church according to its state that is called triumphant. 86{87}[7] *Sicut laetantium omnium habitatio est in te; the dwelling in you is as it were of all rejoicing:* that is, your dwelling, O city of God, supernal Jerusalem, is *as it were of all rejoicing,* that is, of such a kind and quality is the dwelling of those who are therein that they all rejoice. This does not befit the Church militant, in which *all that will live godly in Christ Jesus, shall suffer persecution,*[58] and of which it is also said, *Blessed are they that mourn;*[59] *the world shall rejoice; and you shall be made sorrowful;*[60] and elsewhere, *with fear and trembling work out your salvation.*[61] But this most truly befits the Church triumphant, whose whole occupation is the most joyful and unceasing praise of God.

---

in the Douay-Rheims render it, I have translated it here literally since Denis adopts this verse as consistent with his argument that because of the unusual circumstances of Christ's conception (namely, enjoying the beatific vision), one can say that "a man was born in her."

56   Ps. 44:17b.
57   Ps. 46:10a.
58   2 Tim. 3:12.
59   Matt. 5:5a.
60   John 16:20.
61   Phil. 2:12b.

Of this is written in Revelation: *God shall wipe away all tears from their eyes: and death shall be no more, nor mourning, nor crying, nor sorrow shall be any more.*[62] And so in this place the statement, *as it were (sicut)* does not indicate similitude, but [the literal] truth.

See in this brief Psalm, the Church is excellently praised. It contains the mysteries of Christ, it puts trust in the joy of the heavenly fatherland: it befits us to sing it with more devotion and affection, for in it the call to the Gentiles is most clearly foreannounced. And because it is sufficiently intricate, it behooves us to endeavor to know its splendid meaning, and to look closely at its brilliance, for in no other way is it possible to recite it with perfect devotion.

PRAYER

ENLIVEN US, O LORD, FROM THE WORKS of death, and build in us the foundations of sincere faith and of good works: upon which are built the fruits of virtues; may your glorious city receive with joy our souls journeying toward you.

Vivifica nos, Domine, ab operibus mortuis, et fundamenta sincerae fidei et bonae operationis in nobis construe: quibus fructum virtutum superaedificantes, animas nostras ad te proficiscentes gloriosa civitas tua suscipiat gratulando.

---

62 Rev. 21:4.

Psalm 87

ARTICLE LXIII

LITERAL EXPOSITION OF THE EIGHTY-SEVENTH PSALM: *DOMINE, DEUS SALUTIS MEAE.* O LORD, THE GOD OF MY SALVATION.

87{88}[1] A canticle, a Psalm for the sons of Korah: unto the end, for Mahalath, to answer understanding of Heman the Israelite.

Canticum Psalmus, filiis Core, in finem, pro Maheleth ad respondendum. Intellectus Eman Israelitae.

HE TITLE OF THE PSALM NOW BEING EXPLAINED is this: 87{88}[1] *Canticum, psalmus, filiis Core, in finem, pro Maheleth ad respondendum, intellectus Eman Israelitae;*[1] *a canticle, a Psalm, for the sons of Korah: unto the end, for Mahalath, to answer understanding of Heman the Israelite*: that is, what is being handled presently is called *a canticle* because it addresses those things by which one arrives at spiritual joy, namely, the Passion of Christ, which is the gate to glory: which treatment is called also *a Psalm*, because it admonishes to the doing good works, namely, to the imitation of the Lord's Passion; and this Psalm directs us *unto the end* which is Christ. It also is put forth *for the sons of Korah*, that is, for the adherents of the Crucified One, *who have crucified their flesh with the vices and concupiscences.*[2] And this Psalm is written *for Mahalath*, that is, for the people of the faithful who, in the manner of spectators or a choir in conjunction with Christ, *to answer*, that is, imitating his lead as if responding to a song leader, so that partaking in tribulations, they may become partakers in consolation.[3] And this Psalm is the *understanding of Heman, the Israelite*, that is, by him is described what he who is a brother and co-heir of Christ should understand: namely, that the lands of delights ought to be spurned, and those hard and sparse [lands] ought to be endured willingly patiently for the love of God. *Mahalath* is understood as meaning chorus; but *Heman* [is understood] as faithful brother.

---

1 E. N. The text has *Israelite*; however, the editor in the margin notes that it should be *Ezrahitae.*

2 Gal. 5:24.

3 Cf. 2 Cor. 1:7: *That our hope for you may be steadfast: knowing that as you are partakers of the sufferings, so shall you be also of the consolation.*

Therefore, *Mahalath* are they who harmoniously and in all areas imitate Christ; also any one of these conforming himself to Christ is *Heman*, that is, a brother of Christ of whom he said in the Gospel, *Go to my brothers*.[4] He is also an *Israelite*, that is, a lookout of the Lord. According to Hugo, those Psalms upon which is placed the title, "a Psalm" deal with works; and those where the title placed upon them is "a Canticle" address spiritual joy; but in those where both are conjoined, they deal with both work and joy. And so, according to Jerome, *Heman, the Israelite* (or, as other [sources] say, *Jesraite*[5]) was the author of this present Psalm, as are the others who are placed in the titles.

87{88}[2]   *Lord, the God of my salvation: I have cried in the day, and in the night before you.*

Domine, Deus salutis meae, in die clamavi et nocte coram te.

The Prophet, speaking therefore in the person of Christ living through the Passion, says: **87{88}[2]** *Domine, Deus salutis meae; Lord, the God of my salvation.* God, the Trinity, or God the Father, is the God of the salvation (*salutis*) of Christ, speaking of the salvation of the created [human] nature of Christ, whose soul had from the beginning of its creation the view of God by sight. For the Father or the Trinity is called the God of his salvation as giver and preserver [of his human nature], and his object [of his worship as man]. But there was in Christ also an uncreated, eternal and infinite vigor (*salutis*), which is the divine essence itself. And since Christ is the Word of God, he receives this from the Father as divine essence itself; however, the Father is not called the God of this vigor of Christ, because by the name of God is designated an excellence over the one whose God he is. But the Father is not more excellent than the Son in regard to the latter's uncreated vigor (*salutem*).[6] *In die clamavi et nocte, I have cried in the day, and in the night,* that is, in prosperity

---

4   John 22:17b. Jesus had no brothers since Mary remained a virgin after his birth. Jesus may have been speaking of half-brothers, cousins, or simply his disciples (*cf.* Matt. 12:50). Since Denis speaks of "*faithful* brother" (frater *fidelis*), he would seem to be understanding this in the sense of spiritual kinship or discipleship. This is particularly confirmed by the discussion which follows.

5   E. N. The editor notes in the margin that *Ezrahite* is correct and should replace *Jesraite*.

6   E. N. Denis appears here to rely on the various meanings of the word *salus* in Latin, which can be salvation, or soundness, health, welfare, safety, flourishing, or even vigor or life. As far as I have been able to determine, this concept of a *salus increata* as an equivalent to the eternal generation of the Son by the Father is unique to Denis.

and in adversity, and I have assiduously cried out, *coram te, before you,* that is, with a heart that does not wander and is not distracted from you, but which stands before you resolved, attentive, and devoted. Or, in the day of the Passion or the Day of Preparation [before the Sabbath], and in the preceding evening, I cried out with great affection invoking you, saying, *Forgive them;* and, *If it be possible, let this chalice pass from me.*[7] Christ as man did not pray to God day and night with a vocal and exterior crying out; but it is believed that in his interior crying out he never ceased [praying]: indeed, given that he desired most ardently the salvation of the human race, so unceasingly and with greatest of all affections he mentally pleaded to God for it.

87{88}[3] *Let my prayer come in before you: incline your ear to my petition.*

Intret in conspectu tuo oratio mea, inclina aurem tuam ad precem meam.

87{88}[4] *For my soul is filled with evils: and my life has drawn nigh to hell.*

Quia repleta est malis anima mea, et vita mea inferno appropinquavit.

Now what he prayed for comes next: **87{88}[3]** *Intret in conspectus tuo oratio mea, Let my prayer come in before you,* that is, let it be accepted by you; *inclina aurem tuam ad precem meam, incline your ear to my petition,* fulfilling it. And this therefore do I pray, **87{88}[4]** *Quia repleta est malis anima mea, for my soul is filled with evil.* Evil exists in three ways, namely, evil of nature (such as a natural defect), evil of punishment, and evil of fault. But evil of nature did not exist in Christ, for according to the Damascene, he did not assume any detractible (*detrahibiles*) defect.[8] Moreover, the evil of fault (*malum culpae*) was absent from Christ, the sanctificator of all things. But his soul and flesh were full of the evil of punishment (*malis poenae*) or sufferings: namely, they were subject to injury, fear, pain, and sorrow. It is for this reason that he said: *My soul is sorrowful even unto death;*[9] and: *My God, my God, why have you*

---

7   Luke 23:34; Matt. 26:39.

8   "[A]s the Damascene points out, Christ assumed our indetractible (*indetractabiles*) defects, that is, those which are not subject to detraction (*detrahi*)." St. Thomas Aquinas, *Compendium of Theology,* I, 226 (referring to St. John Damascene, *De Fide Orthodoxa,* III, 20, PG 94, 1081; *see also* ST IIIa, q. 14, art. 4).

9   Matt. 26:38a.

forsaken me?[10] Hence in Isaiah is written: *We have seen him, ... despised, and the most abject of men, a man of sorrows, and acquainted with infirmity.*[11] Or [we can look at it this way], the soul of Christ is said to be replete with evil, that is with sin — not his own, but of those for which Christ suffered, in the manner that was said by Isaiah: *The Lord has laid on him the iniquity of us all.*[12] It is in accordance with this that the Apostle said: *Christ ... was made a curse for us, and he has redeemed us from the curse of the law, for it is written: Cursed is every one that hangs on a tree.*[13] *Et vita mea inferno appropinquavit,* and my life has drawn *nigh to hell,* that is, [my life] was exposed to death, death through which [my soul] crossed over into hell,[14] and which is thus is likened to hell.

87{88}[5]   *I am counted among them that go down to the pit: I am become as a man without help,*

   Aestimatus sum cum descendentibus in lacum, factus sum sicut homo sine adiutorio,

87{88}[6]   *Free among the dead. Like the slain sleeping in the sepulchers, whom you remember no more: and they are cast off from your hand.*

   Inter mortuos liber; sicut vulnerati dormientes in sepulchris, quorum non es memor amplius, et ipsi de manu tua repulsi sunt.

87{88}[7]   *They have laid me in the lower pit: in the dark places, and in the shadow of death.*

   Posuerunt me in lacu inferiori, in tenebrosis, et in umbra mortis.

---

10   Matt. 27:46b; Ps. 21:2.

11   Is. 53:2a, 3b.

12   Is. 53:6b.

13   Gal. 3:13; Deut. 21:23. E. N. Denis is free in rearranging Gal. 3:13 to his needs.

14   E. N. This, of course, is not the hell of the damned, but the limbo of the fathers (*limbus patrum*) also called the limbo of hell (*limbus inferni*) or the bosom of Abraham (*sinus Abrahae*). "Scripture calls the abode of the dead, to which the dead Christ went down, 'hell' — *Sheol* in Hebrew or *Hades* in Greek — because those who are there are deprived of the vision of God. Such is the case for all the dead, whether evil or righteous, while they await the Redeemer: which does not mean that their lot is identical, as Jesus shows through the parable of the poor man Lazarus who was received into 'Abraham's bosom.' 'It is precisely these holy souls, who awaited their Savior in Abraham's bosom, whom Christ the Lord delivered when he descended into hell.' Jesus did not descend into hell to deliver the damned, nor to destroy the hell of damnation, but to free the just who had gone before him." CCC § 633 (citations omitted).

87{88}[5] *Aestimatus sum, I am counted* by the perverse Jews and the unbelievers all over the world *cum descendentibus in lacum, among them that go down to the pit,* that is, among such that because of their sin descended into hell and are consigned to the grave. For since they viewed Christ as similar to other men who died, they supposed him to have shared in their similar fate of death, and by this fact supposed that his body should undergo corruption in its sepulcher, and his soul should be held in hell. And so it is said [about their thoughts]: *We have thought him as it were a leper, and as one struck by God and afflicted.*[15] And this is what the ungodly say about Christ: *Let us examine him by . . . tortures, . . . and prove what shall happen to him . . . that we may know his meekness.*[16] For *if he be the true son of God, he will . . . deliver him from the hands of his enemies,*[17] that is, God will not allow him to be killed.

Factus sum sicut homo sine adiutorio, I am become as a man without help, that is, I have been made similar to those to whom no one renders aid, those whom God does not protect, nor does man help. Christ was made similar to such men. First of all, according to exterior appearance, because God permitted him to be crucified among the ungodly, as if he belonged among them. For this reason, Christ said to the Jews: *This is your hour and the power of darkness.*[18] Indeed, it was at that time that *the Son of Man* (as he himself had predicted) was *betrayed into the hands of sinners, and they did to him whatever they wanted.*[19] Secondly, Christ is said to be as a man without help according to the reputation of the Jews, who supposed God not to be his helper, saying: *If he be the king of Israel, let him now come down from the cross, and we will believe him. He trusted in God; let him now deliver him if he will have him.*[20] And again: *He saved others; himself he cannot save.*[21] Third, because of the withdrawal of customary consolation, which filled the inferior parts of the soul of Christ, or in some degree used to participate in the fullness of the beatitude of the superior parts of his soul: and so he says, *Eloi, Eloi, lamma sabachthani? [Which is, being interpreted, My God, my God, why have you forsaken me].*[22] But in truth, absolutely speaking, Christ never was without the help of

---

15 Is. 53:4b.

16 Wis. 2:19, 17. E. N. Denis takes liberty with re-arranging these verses.

17 Wis. 2:18.

18 Luke 22:53b.

19 Matt. 26:45; 27:12.

20 Matt. 27:42–43.

21 Matt. 27:42a.

22 Mark 15:34. E. N. I have added the part in brackets. Denis only quotes the transliterated Aramaic.

God, as is attested to by Isaiah: *The Lord God is my helper, therefore am I not confounded.*[23] And also by Jeremiah: *The Lord is with me as a strong warrior.*[24] And so I, Christ,[25] who alone am **87{88}[6]** *inter mortuos liber, free among the dead,* that is, among the mortals free from fault, and not lacking a deliverer; who have no need to die, and am strong enough not to be detained in death; but by my own power I came forth from the prison of Gehenna and the pit of the sepulture. Christ,[26] who said about himself, *For the prince of this world comes, and in me he has not anything,*[27] is rightly said to be free among the dead (with the death of sin or natural death). Yet of others, the Apostle [Paul] asserts: *For all have sinned, and do need the glory of God.*[28] And again: *For God has concluded all under sin, so that he may have mercy on all.*[29]

Moreover, I am reputed by the Jews to have so perished,[30] *sicut vulnerati dormientes in sepulcris, like the slain sleeping in sepulchers,* that is, those dead from the infliction of wounds, laying quiet in the sleep of death in the tomb, *quorum non es memor amplius, whom you remember no more,* who have perished in their mortal sins, and so are were handed over to eternal oblivion as it relates to the perception of the mercy of God: and so it adds, *et ipsi de manu tua repulsi sunt, and they are cast off from your hand,* that is, they are entirely deprived from your protection and salvation. The Jews reckoned Christ to be similar to such sinners. Whence they implored Pilate: *Sir, we have remembered, that that seducer said, while he was yet alive.* They thus still maintained the opinion that he had been condemned with the deceitful.[31] **87{88}[7]** *Posuerunt me in lacu inferiori, they have laid me in the lower pit,* that is, they classified me with those who have been cast into the place in hell where those suffering the most punishment go. For in the manner that they ascribed

---

23   Is. 50:7a.
24   Jer. 20:11a.
25   E. N. As is quite common in explaining Psalms from the perspective of Christ, Denis shifts from a third-person point-of-view to a first-person point-of-view, specifically, that of our Lord.
26   E. N. Denis now slips back into a third person point-of-view.
27   John 14:30b.
28   Rom. 3:23.
29   Rom. 11:32; Gal. 3:22. Denis blends these two verses: Rom. 11:32: *For God has concluded all in unbelief, that he may have mercy on all.* Gal. 3:22: *But the scripture has concluded all under sin, that the promise, by the faith of Jesus Christ, might be given to them that believe.*
30   E. N. Denis here slips back into a first-person point-of-view, namely, Christ's.
31   Matt. 27:63. E. N. In other words, even after he was dead, the Jewish enemies of our Lord called him a seducer, showing their opinions of him had not changed.

the greatest sin to Christ while he was living, saying, *He has blasphemed,* etc., so did they judge him to be suffering the maximum torments after death. *In tenebrosis et in umbra mortis, in the dark places, and in the shadow of death.* For hell is a place of darkness and the shadow of death, according to this: *Suffer me ... before I go ... to a land that is dark and covered with the mist of death: a land of misery and darkness, where the shadow of death, and no order, but everlasting horror dwells.*[32]

87{88}[8]   *Your wrath is strong over me: and all your waves you have brought in upon me.*

Super me confirmatus est furor tuus, et omnes fluctus tuos induxisti super me.

87{88}[8] *Super me confirmatus est furor tuus; your wrath is strong over me*: that is, the rigor of your justice, which you might have displayed upon all men unless I had made satisfaction for them, you have displayed in me, not sparing your own Son,[33] but you permitted me to die in a most bitter and unseemly death: indeed you delivered me over for the sake of all men, in the manner revealed by Isaiah, *For the wickedness of my people have I struck him.*[34] *Et omnes fluctos tuos, and all your waves,* that is, all kinds of torments, *induxisti, you have brought,* that is, you have allowed to be introduced, *super me, upon me.* For the Passion of Christ was most expansive, for it reached the breadth of the entire torment of the human race, with respect to kind. For he suffered in all the powers of soul and bodily members, namely, he was taken captive, bound, buffeted, spat upon, afflicted with sorrow, rejected by all, held in contempt, derided: and all kinds of punishment which ought to have been inflicted upon the human race for sin, God the Father brought upon Christ, in a manner of speaking. Whence, in Isaiah is said: *The chastisement of our peace was upon him, and by his bruises we are healed.*[35]

87{88}[9]   *You have put away my acquaintances far from me: they have set me an abomination to themselves. I was delivered up and did not deviate.*[36]

---

32   Job 10:20–22.
33   *Cf.* Rom. 8:32a: *He that spared not even his own Son, but delivered him up for us all.*
34   Is. 53:8b.
35   Is. 53:5b.
36   E. N. I have translated the Latin *egrediabar* to "I did not deviate" from the Douay Rheims's "I came not forth."

Longe fecisti notos meos a me, posuerunt me abominationem sibi. Traditus sum, et non egrediebar.

87{88}[10] My eyes languished through poverty. All the day I cried to you, O Lord: I stretched out my hands to you.

Oculi mei languerunt prae inopia. Clamavi ad te, Domine, tota die; expandi ad te manus meas.

87{88}[9] *Longe fecisti notos meos a me, you have put away my acquaintances far from me,* that is, you have allowed my disciples to flee by reason of fear of the Jews: in the way we read in Matthew, *Then the disciples all leaving him, fled.*[37] Or [alternatively], *my acquaintances,* that is, those who knew me and approved my works and my teaching, to whom I preached and before whom I performed miracles: and of whom is written, *And all the people, when they saw it, gave praise to God.*[38] During the time of my Passion you permitted these sorts of men to depart from me. For many of the Jews who had often praised Christ and his works were seduced by the chief priests in the day of preparation before the Sabbath, and pled that Christ be put to death: of whom is said with Matthew: *And the whole people answering, said: His blood be upon us and our children.*[39] Of whom is also stated subsequently [in this Psalm]: *posuerunt me abominationem sibi, they have set me an abomination to themselves,* that is, they held me in contempt, and they reckoned me as vile: as a Psalm above states, *All they that saw me have laughed me to scorn.*[40] Whence in Luke is written: *And the people stood beholding, and the rulers with them derided him, saying: He saved others; let him save himself, if he be Christ, the elect of God.*[41]

Traditus sum; I was delivered up. We read that Christ was handed over by God the Father, according to the Apostle: *He spared not even his own Son, but delivered him up for us all.*[42] Christ also delivered himself over to death, as is said by Isaiah: *He has delivered his soul unto death.*[43] This is the reason the Gospel says: *No man takes my life away from me: but I lay it down.*[44] Jesus was also handed over by the traitor Judas. *Et non egrediebar, and I did not deviate* from the Father's will, but I was obedient to

---

37 Matt. 26:56b.
38 Luke 18:43b.
39 Matt. 27:25b.
40 Ps. 21:8a.
41 Luke 23:35.
42 Rom. 8:32a.
43 Is. 53:12a.
44 John 10:18a.

the Father even unto death, saying: *Your will be done.*[45] Or [alternatively], *I did not deviate* by fleeing from the Jews, but I fearlessly withstood them and said, *Whom do you seek?*[46] Or [another interpretation], *I did not deviate*, that is, because of my horror of the Passion and the abjection of the Cross, what I was interiorly was not recognized [by others] outwardly, because divinity was hidden under the fragility of the flesh. For this reason, it is written by Isaiah: *His look was as it were hidden and despised, whereupon we esteemed him not.*[47] **87{88}[10]** *Oculi mei*, my eyes, [my] bodily [eyes], *languerunt prae inopia*, languished through poverty of their soundness. For my exterior eyes were deprived of their soundness from their veiling and being struck by the Jews, and also from the abundance of tears, and most of all from the interior sadness of the soul of Christ,[48] because customarily the interior sorrow shows itself particularly in the eyes. Or [alternatively], *my eyes*, that is, the eyes of my Mystical Body, namely of the Apostles, who shone forth with heavenly vision and light among the rest, grew faint for lack of faith and constancy: for even their head denied me under oath.[49] For about him was said: *I will strike the shepherd, and the flock of sheep shall be scattered.*[50]

Clamavi ad te, Domine; I cried out to you, O Lord: as it plainly says in the opening verse of this Psalm; *tota die*, all the day, that is, all the days of my life, *expandi ad te manus meas*, I stretched out my hands to you, that is, I directed myself to you, and I ordered my works to the glory of your name, everywhere and always glorifying you. Or [we might see it this way]: *all the day*, that is, for the greater part of the day of preparation for the Sabbath, I stretched out my bodily arms upon the Cross, so that I might assemble and embrace all the elect for you.[51]

87{88}[11] *Will you show wonders to the dead? Or shall physicians raise to life, and confess to you?*[52]

---

45 Matt. 26:42.
46 John 18:4, 5.
47 Is. 53:3b.
48 *E. N.* For a classic meditation on Christ's sadness, see St. Thomas More's *De Tristitia Christi, The Sadness of Christ* (Princeton, NJ: Scepter Publishers, 1993) (trans., Clarence Miller).
49 Matt. 26:72, 74.
50 *Cf.* Zech. 13:7b.
51 *Cf.* Is. 65:2: *I have spread forth my hands all the day to an unbelieving people, who walk in a way that is not good after their own thoughts.*
52 *E. N.* I have translated *confitebuntur* more broadly as "shall confess," departing from "shall praise," because Denis understands the confession of Ps. 87:11 to include

> *Numquid mortuis facies mirabilia? Aut medici suscitabunt,*
> *et confitebuntur tibi?*

87{88}[12] Shall anyone in the sepulcher declare your mercy: and your
truth in destruction?

> *Numquid narrabit aliquis in sepulchro misericordiam tuam,*
> *et veritatem tuam in perditione?*

87{88}[13] Shall your wonders be known in the dark; and your justice
in the land of forgetfulness?

> *Numquid cognoscentur in tenebris mirabilia tua? Et iustitia*
> *tua in terra oblivionis?*

Then Christ expands his argument that out of the propriety of divine
justice it was becoming for him to be heard for himself and for his Mystical Body, since he would rise again in the body and the faithful would
rise again in their souls through grace. For it is befitting that God would
bestow such admirable grace to some persons; but not bestow them to
those dead [in the supernatural life]: therefore, it is given to him, that
is, to Christ and to those living [the supernatural life in grace]. Therefore, it says: **87{88}[11]** *Mortuis, to the dead* of body and soul *numquid
facies mirabilia, will you show wonders,* that is, by raising them up to their
former life and state of grace? It is as if were saying, "No":[53] like that
which was said by blessed Job, *Man when he is fallen asleep shall not rise
again;*[54] and again, *I am walking in a path by which I shall not return.*[55]
For though some of the dead, even [some of] the ungodly, are raised by
a special grace from the dead,[56] yet the dead as a matter of universal law

---

both confession of praise and confession of sins. For the difference of these confessions, *see* footnote 27-49.

53   E. N. In other words, the question in this verse is a negative rhetorical question,
which suggests a negative response.

54   Job 14:12a.

55   Job 16:23b.

56   E. N. This is a reference to the miraculous resurrections along the lines of Lazarus,
and not the final Resurrection. *See* footnote 49-94 (Volume 2) for some examples
mentioned by Pope St. Gregory the Great in his *Great Dialogue.* Denis may also have
had in mind the story of the professor at the Sorbonne and canon at Notre Dame,
Raymond Diocrès (†1084), who purportedly returned back to life briefly three times
while lying in state. When the words in the Office of the Dead *Responde mihi: quantas
habeo iniquitates* were reached, the body lifted itself out of the bier and exclaimed:
Iusto Dei iudicio iudicatus sum (I am adjudged by the just judgment of God). The same
thing occurred the following day, when the Office of the Dead was again recited. On
the third effort at reciting the Office of the Dead, the body cried out: *Iusto Dei iudicio*

do not rise again. *Aut medici suscitabunt, or shall physicians raise to life* the dead, *et confitebuntur tibi, and confess to you* of the dead raised by them by praising you for your excellence or confessing their sins? Of course not, because this transcends the natural arts and powers.[57] 87{88}[12] *Numquid narrabit aliquis in sepulcro misericordiam tuam? Shall anyone in the sepulcher declare your mercy?* It is as if he were saying, "No": for none but lifeless bodies are cast into tombs. And shall anyone declare *your truth in destruction* of eternal damnation? In no way: for truth is not declared in hell according to this, *Neither wisdom nor knowledge shall be in hell.*[58] 87{88}[13] *Numquid cognoscentur in tenebris mirabilia tua, shall your wonders be known in the dark,* that is, by those who lack faith and the light of grace? By no means. *Et, and* shall *iustitia tua in terra oblivionis, your justice in the land of forgetfulness* be known, that is, by those who are obstinate in evil, those who do not call to mind your goodness, and beseech your mercy? It is as if he were saying, "Not at all": according to that which is contained in another prophet, *The dead that are in hell, whose spirit is taken away from their bowels, shall not give glory and justice to the Lord.*[59] Since they showed themselves concerned with other things, therefore, these men are excluded from the grace of God.

Augustine and others expounded this literally in another way.[60] For because the works and the merits of Christ do not profit all men, but only with those predestined to true salvation, so does it say: *Will you show wonders* that will provide benefit *to the dead* in an inward way in the soul through mortal sin? It is as if he said, "No" because such men are hardened in fault, and they are not moved to amendment from looking

---

condemnatus sum (I have been damned by the just judgment of God). One of Diocrès's students — Bruno of Cologne (*ca.* 1030–1101) — was so affected by this event that he abandoned secular life and founded the Carthusian Order. Among other places, that event is famously depicted by the Italian painter Vicenzo Carducci (*ca.* 1630), by the French artist Eustace le Seur's paintings on the Life of St. Bruno (1645–48), and in the *Très Riches Heures du Duc de Berry* (*ca.* 1412–16).

57 The Resurrection of the Dead is beyond the powers of nature, and so involves supernatural intervention — a miracle. "For that any animal lives, sees, or moves is a work of nature: that that he should live after death, see after it is blinded, move after debilitated by lameness: this nature is not able to do." St. Thomas Aquinas, *Contra Gentiles,* lib. 3 cap. 101 n. 3. For St. Thomas — as for Denis — "[t]he resurrection of the dead is . . . paradigmatically a divine intervention in the natural order." Richard Swinburne, *The Resurrection of God Incarnate* (Oxford: Clarendon Press, 2003), 189.

58 Eccl. 9:10b.

59 Baruch 2:17.

60 E. N. *See* St. Augustine, *Commentary on the Psalms 73–98* (New York: New City Press, 2002), 266–68 (trans., Maria Boulding).

at the marvels of God. For it is told to them through Jeremiah: *If the Ethiopian can change his skin, or the leopard his spots: you may also do well, when you have learned evil.*[61] *Or shall physicians* of the spirit, that is, preachers of the word of God, who cure those who are sick of soul, *raise to life* the dead who have already been spoken about, *and [shall they] confess to you?*[62] Of course not: because unless God is within them operating by grace, the preachers labor with the tongue in vain. *Shall anyone in the sepulcher* of evil habits or with vicious body, which is the tomb of a soul already dead from sin, *declare your mercy,* praising the benefits of the divine goodness, and the restoration of human nature, *and your truth in destruction,* that is, in a desperate and lost life. No: because *Praise is not seemly in the mouth of a sinner.*[63]

87{88}[14]   *But I, O Lord, have cried to you: and in the morning my prayer shall prevent you.*

Et ego ad te, Domine, clamavi, et mane oratio mea praeveniet te?

87{88}[14] *Et ego ad te, Domine, clamavi; but I, O Lord, have cried to you.* This verse and the one that follows are expounded by teachers as dealing with the Mystical Body of Christ, which is the Church; but it seems bright and clear that the entire Psalm can be explained as relating to the Lord Savior. Christ therefore says: *But I, O Lord* Father, *have cried to you:* in the manner that the Apostle describes him to the Hebrews: Christ *with a strong cry and tears, offering up prayers ... was heard for his reverence.*[64] *Et mane, and in the morning,* that is, quickly and in the splendor of your grace, *oratio mea praeveniet te, my prayer shall prevent you,*[65] that is, before I do anything else I will direct my prayer to you. Or [another possible interpretation is], *shall prevent you,* that is, by prayer I will soften the vengeance of your justice and the horror of your judgment,[66] lest you thoroughly destroy and damn the human race.

---

61   Jer. 13:23.
62   E. N. In this exposition, the subject of those doing the confessing are those who are dead and cannot be raised to life, and not the physicians.
63   Ecclus. 15:9.
64   Heb. 5:7.
65   E. N. The word "prevent" comes from Latin and varies from its most common meaning. It means to come first, to anticipate, *pre-venire,* literally, "to pre-come."
66   *Cf.* Heb. 10:27: *But a certain dreadful expectation of judgment, and the rage of a fire which shall consume the adversaries.* Heb. 10:31: *It is a fearful thing to fall into the hands of the living God.*

87{88}[15] *Lord, why do you cast off my prayer? Why do you turn away your face from me?*

Ut quid, Domine, repellis orationem meam, avertis faciem tuam a me?

87{88}[15] *Ut quid, Domine, repellis orationem meam? Lord, why do you cast off my prayer?* With regard to Christ, this should be understood in the manner stated above [in Psalm 21:3] where it said — *O my God, I shall cry by day, and you will not hear.*[67] That the prayer of Christ is said not to be heard or is said to be repulsed does not pertain to that [prayer] made with deliberation, with reason, and with rational will. Of this kind of prayer, he said: *I know that you hear me always.*[68] But [it is said] of that prayer which flows from the natural feeling or the sensitive appetite, [such as] *Father, if it be possible, let this chalice pass from me.*[69] *Avertis faciem tuam a me? Why do you turn away your face from me?* That is, why, O Father, do you withdraw your presence of consolation and the appearance of usual kindness from my passible nature vexed upon the Cross, so that I was compelled to cry out, *O God my God, look upon me: why have you forsaken me?*[70] Yet never was the face of God, who is himself the Blessed God, in whose vision beatitude consists, turned away from the soul of Christ, but he unceasingly beheld the blessed vision, even during the time of the Passion.

---

67   Ps. 21:3a.

68   John 11:42a.

69   Matt. 26:39b. E. N. It is useful to refer to St. Thomas's treatment of this in his *Summa Theologiae:* "[W]e may be said to pray according to the sensuality (*secundum sensualitatem*) when our prayer lays before God what is in our appetite of sensuality (*appetitus sensualitatis*); and in this sense Christ prayed with his sensuality inasmuch as his prayer expressed the desire of His sensuality, as if it were the advocate of the sensuality — and this, that he might teach us three things. First, to show that he had taken a true human nature, with all its natural affections: secondly, to show that a man may wish with his natural desire what God does not wish: thirdly, to show that man should subject his own will to the Divine will. Hence Augustine says in the *Enchiridion* (Serm. 1 in Ps. 32): 'Christ acting as a man, shows the proper will of a man when he says *Let this chalice pass from me;* for this was the human will desiring something proper to itself and, so to say, private (*privatum*). But because he wishes man to be righteous and to be directed to God, he adds: *Nevertheless not as I will but as you will,* as if to say, See yourself in me, for you can desire something proper to you, even though God wishes something else.'" ST, IIIa, q. 21, art. 2, c. (Blackfriars translation).

70   Ps. 21:2a.

87{88}[16]   *I am poor, and in labors from my youth: and being exalted have been humbled and troubled.*

> *Pauper sum ego, et in laboribus a iuventute mea; exaltatus autem, humiliatus sum et conturbatus.*

87{88}[16] *Pauper sum ego,* I am poor, and the exemplar of complete poverty: I had nowhere to lay my head,[71] and I lived through the alms of devout women;[72] *et in laboribus a iuventute mea,* and in labors from my youth: for Christ was never idle either internally or externally, but he labored in praying, fasting, serving Joseph and Mary, and then preaching, travelling about, eating, sitting, suffering, and dying. For this reason, it is revealed: *You have made me to serve with your sins, you have wearied me with your iniquities.*[73] Hence it is written: *Because his soul has labored, he shall see and be filled.*[74] And elsewhere: *Jesus being wearied with his journey.*[75] *Exaltatus autem, humiliatus sum,* and being exalted have been humbled. For as the Evangelist affirms, when the Jews wanted to make Christ king, he fled from and withdrew from the crowd.[76] Also when he was praised by the people acclaiming him, and he went about doing good, and the deaf he made hear, and the mute to speak,[77] and so [they said], *never was the like seen in Israel,*[78] he attributed nothing to himself, but he referred everything to Father's glory. Also, when he was exalted by the Jews on the day of Palms, exclaiming, *Hosanna to the son of David! Blessed is he who comes in the name of the Lord;*[79] shortly thereafter he was humiliated by the same people, crying out *Away with him; away with him; crucify him.*[80] *Et conturbatus,* and troubled, not by disordered passions, but filled with vehement feelings, such as naturally fearing death or grieving for sinners. Whence we read: *Jesus weeping, groaned in the spirit, and troubled himself.*[81]

87{88}[17]   *Your wrath has come upon me: and your terrors have troubled me.*

> *In me transierunt irae tuae, et terrores tui conturbaverunt me.*

---

71   *Cf.* Luke 9:58
72   Luke 8:2–3.
73   Is. 43:24b.
74   Is. 53:11a.
75   John 4:6.
76   John 6:15.
77   Acts 10:38; Mark 7:31; Matt. 9:32.
78   Matt. 9:33.
79   Matt. 21:9.
80   John 19:15.
81   John 11:33b.

87{88}[18] *They have come round about me like water all the day: they have compassed me about together.*

Circumdederunt me sicut aqua tota die; circumdederunt me simul.

87{88}[19] *Friend and neighbor you have put far from me: and my acquaintances, because of misery.*

Elongasti a me amicum et proximum, et notos meos a miseria.

87{88}[17] *In me transierunt irae tuae, your wrath has come upon me,* that is, the vindications of your justice were inflicted on me for the sins of men which I took upon myself and whose due punishments I discharged: as is it is written, *The breath of our mouth, Christ the Lord, is taken in our sins;*[82] *et terrores tui, and your terrors,* that is, the terrible punishments which you wished me to suffer, *conturbaverunt me, have troubled me,* that is, vehemently influenced my soul, so that I would say: *Now my soul is troubled.*[83] For this reason it is written: Jesus *began to fear and to be heavy.*[84] 87{88}[18] *Circumdederunt me, they have come round about me* with the previously described anger and punishments, or the Jewish persecutors [have encircled me], *sicut aqua, like water,* that is, abundantly and copiously, *tota die, all the day* of preparation before the Sabbath; *circumdederunt me simul, they have compassed me about together,* so that *from the sole of the foot unto the top of the head, there was no soundness in me.*[85] Whence as a figure of Christ, Job said: *He has gathered together his fury against me, and threatening me he has gnashed with his teeth upon me, he has torn me with wound upon wound; he has rushed in upon me like a giant.*[86] 87{88}[19] *Elongasti a me amicum et proximum, friend and neighbor you have put far from me,* that is, my disciples, who were my friends and neighbors, you have allowed to disperse away from me, *et notos meos, and my acquaintances* you have kept aloof *a miseria mea, because of my misery,* so that they would not suffer with me in the way that was stated in an earlier Psalm, *And I looked for one that would grieve together with me, but there was none: and for one that would comfort me, and I found none.*[87] The Lord said this not of the disciples, but of the ungrateful Jews, of whom he says elsewhere: *They are*

82 Lam. 4:20a.
83 John 12:27a.
84 Mark 14:33b.
85 Is. 1:6a.
86 Job 16:10a, 15. E. N. For more on Job as a figure of Christ, *see* footnote 21-95, Volume I.
87 Ps. 68:21b.

departed from me; and I have chastised them, . . . and they have imagined evil against me.[88] Jerome's translation [of this verse from the Hebrew] is this: *And my acquaintances you have sent away,* so, namely, that they could not render me any help: in the manner that is written, *I looked about, and there was none to help;*[89] and Job also, *my acquaintances like strangers have departed from me.*[90] And this is what Christ said to his disciples: *The hour comes, and it is now come, that you shall be scattered every man to his own, and shall leave me alone.*[91]

ARTICLE LXIV

MORAL DECLARATION OF
THE SAME EIGHTY-SEVENTH PSALM.

INCE THE APOSTLE SAYS, *ALWAYS BEARING about in our body the mortification of Jesus, that the life also of Jesus... may be made manifest in our mortal flesh,*[92] we ought to follow our Head in his Passion, so that we might be glorified together with him. Whence the Apostle [Paul] says: *A faithful saying: for if we be dead with him, we shall live also with him. If we suffer, we shall also reign with him.*[93] Here therefore it ought not to be marveled at that this Psalm, which literally speaks of the Passion of Christ, can be explained spiritually as pertaining to his members.

———

87{88}[2]   *Lord, the God of my salvation: I have cried in the day, and in the night before you.*

Domine, Deus salutis meae, in die clamavi et nocte coram te.

87{88}[4]   *For my soul is filled with evils: and my life has drawn nigh to hell.*[94]

Quia repleta est malis anima mea, et vita mea inferno appropinquavit.

---

88   Hosea 7:14b–15.
89   Is. 63:5a.
90   Job 19:13b.
91   John 16:32.
92   2 Cor. 4:10a, 11b.
93   2 Tim. 2:11–12.
94   E. N. Denis skips verse three in this Article.

The Church, therefore, or any Christian enduring tribulations and surrounded by various adversities and trials, might proclaim this Psalm, saying: 87{88}[2] *Domine, Lord,* governor of all things, *Deus salutis meae, the God of my salvation,* that is, the font, origin, and cause of all of my beatitude, upon whom all my salvation depends, without whose mercy I would unceasingly perish, gravely sin, and be condemned in eternity; God of my salvation, on the way by faith and grace; and also God my salvation in the heavenly fatherland by vision and the light of glory; *in die clamavi et nocte; I have cried in the day, and in the night,* that is, certain and suitable hours of both day and night, *coram te, before you* in an attentive fashion. For it behooves one to pray *without ceasing.*[95] 87{88}[4] *Quia repleta est malis, for full of evils* of punishment and of fault is *anima mea, my soul,* namely, filled with many afflictions, various vices, and diverse passions, which are the wounds of the soul. Whence we have in Ecclesiastes: *All man's days are full of sorrows and miseries, even in the night he does not rest in mind.*[96] This deals with the evil of punishment. But of the evil of fault is elsewhere written: *In many things we all offend.*[97] *Et vita mea inferno appropinquavit, and my life has drawn nigh to hell.* For a soul which sins tends toward hell; and every time it sins it makes itself closer to hell. Now mortal sin is the gate to hell; but venial sin is a kind of preamble and a kind of disposition toward mortal sin and the punishment of Gehenna.[98] Now he who sins mortally immediately merits to be damned, although God mercifully patiently awaits, as Peter said: *The Lord deals patiently for your sake, not willing that any should perish, but that all should return to penance.*[99]

87{88}[5] *I am counted among them that go down to the pit: I am become as a man without help,*

Aestimatus sum cum descendentibus in lacum, factus sum sicut homo sine adiutorio,

---

95   1 Thess. 5:17.
96   Eccl. 2:23.
97   James 3:2a.
98   E. N. "As the Council of Trent teaches, 'the grace of justification once received is lost not only by apostasy, by which faith itself is lost, but also by any other mortal sin.'" St. John Paul II, *Veritatis splendor,* No. 68 (quoting DS 1544). "Mortal and venial sin differ infinitely as respects the aversion in the two sins. . . . Venial sins contain inordination, not with respect to the end, for the life of charity remains in the soul, but with respect to the means for that end. Such sins are reparable." John J. Elmendorf, S. T. D., *Elements of Moral Theology* (New York: James Pott & Co., 1892), 115.
99   2 Pet. 3:9.

87{88}[6] *Free among the dead. Like the slain sleeping in the sepulchers, whom you remember no more: and they are cast off from your hand.*

Inter mortuos liber; sicut vulnerati dormientes in sepulchris, quorum non es memor amplius, et ipsi de manu tua repulsi sunt.

87{88}[5] *Aestimatus sum cum descendentibus in lacum, I am counted among them that go down to the pit.* This fittingly applies to all the holy martyrs, whom tyrants, and infidels, as well as sacrilegious men put to death, killing them insofar as they think themselves as doing a service to God.[100] Also, the just who die in a state of justice yet are reputed to be unjust by perverse men are reckoned to be with them that go down to the pit. *Factus sum sicut homo sine adiutorio, I am become as a man without help.* This applies to those persons to whom the Savior in the Gospel says: *You shall be hated by all men for my name's sake.*[101] 87{88}[6] *Inter mortuos liber. Free among the dead.* Among all other people, only the Christian people truly are free. For the service of Christ is the highest freedom;[102] but the remainder of the world are servants of iniquity and demons. Whence the Apostle [Paul] says: *You have not received the spirit of bondage again in fear; but you have received the spirit of adoption of sons, whereby we cry: Abba (Father).*[103] And to the Galatians: *We are not the children of the bondwoman, but of the free: by the freedom wherewith Christ has made us free.*[104] In this manner, therefore, the Christian people, or any one who is faithful and just,[105] is regarded in comparison to unbelievers and the servants of sin, who are spiritually dead. They are also reputed, *sicut vulnerati dormientes in sepulcris, etc., like the slain sleeping in the sepulchers, etc.*

87{88}[8] *Your wrath is strong over me: and all your waves you have brought in upon me.*

Super me confirmatus est furor tuus, et omnes fluctus tuos induxisti super me.

---

100   Cf. John 16:2: *They will put you out of the synagogues: yea, the hour comes, that whosoever kills you, will think that he does a service to God.*
101   Luke 21:17.
102   L. *Christi servitus, summa libertas est.*
103   Rom. 8:15.
104   Gal. 4:31.
105   E. N. Denis treats these as synonyms: Christians and those who are faithful and just. These are not two classes of people.

87{88}[9] *You have put away my acquaintances far from me: they have
set me an abomination to themselves. I was delivered up and
did not deviate.*[106]

*Longe fecisti notos meos a me, posuerunt me abominationem
sibi. Traditus sum, et non egrediebar.*

87{88}[10] *My eyes languished through poverty. All the day I cried to
you, O Lord: I stretched out my hands to you.*

*Oculi mei languerunt prae inopia. Clamavi ad te, Domine,
tota die; expandi ad te manus meas.*

87{88}[8] *Super me confirmatus est furor tuus, your wrath is strong over
me,* that is, the rigorous effects of your justice [are strong over me]. For
that which is understood by the wrath of God follows: *Et omnes fluctus
tuos, and all your waves,* that is, all kinds of tribulations or punishments,
which are inflicted for sins, *induxisti super me, you have brought in upon
me.* This pertains to the Church of Christ and any the faithful, because,
in the manner that is written in the book of Wisdom, God in this life
in many ways and strictly chastises the just: *As gold in the furnace the
Lord has proved the elect, and as a victim of a holocaust he has received
them.*[107] And Judith: *All,* it says, *that have pleased God, passed through
many tribulations, remaining faithful.*[108] And Christ said to his disciples:
*In the world you shall have distress: but have confidence, I have overcome
the world.*[109] God also does this to the elect so that they might cleanse
themselves of their venial sins, and so that they might be disposed in
the present time to an increase in grace,[110] and also so that they might
they might be set forth as an example, and receive a greater share of
glory in the future.[111] Job experienced this powerful wrath upon him,
and he said: *His wrath is kindled against me, and he has counted me as*

---

106 E. N. I have translated the Latin *egrediabar* to "I did not deviate" from the
Douay Rheims's "I came not forth."

107 Wis. 3:6a.

108 Judith 8:23.

109 John 16:33b.

110 E. N. DS 1535 (Council of Trent): "When 'faith is active along with works' [*cf.
Jas.* 2:22], [the justified] increase in the very justice they have received through the
grace of Christ and are further justified [*cann. 24 and 32*], as it is written, 'Let he
who is just be still more justified' [*Rev.* 22:11]; and again: 'Fear not to be justified
until you die' [*Sir. 18:22*]."

111 E. N. DS 1305 (Council of Florence): "The souls of those . . . received immediately into heaven and see clearly God himself, one and three, as he is, though some
more perfectly than others, according to the diversity of merits."

his enemy;[112] Jeremiah also, and he confessed: *Of the presence of your hand: I sat alone, because you have filled me with threats.*[113] 87{88}[9] *Longe fecisti notos meo a me; posuerunt me abominationem sibi; you have put away my acquaintances far from me: they have set me an abomination to themselves.* This is what Christ in the Gospel told those he had chosen: *You shall be betrayed by your parents and brethren, . . . and friends and neighbors.*[114] And so Christ came to set at variance father from the son and brother from sister, counseling us that we should leave all those close to us, and wife, and riches.[115] Now often it happens that acquaintances flee from Christians, abhorring them because of the most violent persecutions, adversities, and punishments meted out to them, as also the holy Job admits happened to him.[116]

Traditus sum, I was delivered, either to the temptation of a demon, or to death by a tyrant, or to persecution by a depraved man; *et non egrediebar, and did not deviate,* that is, I have not fled these punishments, but I have suffered them all with equanimity, knowing that great will be my reward in heaven.[117] 87{88}[10] *Oculi mei, my eyes* of my body *languerunt prae inopia, have languished through poverty* of natural virtue, in that the interior pain shows itself more in the eyes of the body. Whence it is said by blessed Job: *My face is swollen with weeping, and my eyelids are dim.*[118] Or

---

112   Job 19:11.

113   Jer. 15:17b.

114   Luke 21:16.

115   Cf. Matt. 10:35; 19:29. E. N. Denis speaks here of the *counsels* of Christ. "The traditional distinction between God's commandments [precepts] and the evangelical counsels is drawn in relation to charity, the perfection of Christian life. The precepts are intended to remove whatever is incompatible with charity. The aim of the counsels is to remove whatever might hinder the development of charity, even if it is not contrary to it. The evangelical counsels manifest the living fullness of charity, which is never satisfied with not giving more. They attest its vitality and call forth our spiritual readiness. The perfection of the New Law consists essentially in the precepts of love of God and neighbor. The counsels point out the more direct ways, the readier means, and are to be practiced in keeping with the vocation of each: '[God] does not want each person to keep all the counsels, but only those appropriate to the diversity of persons, times, opportunities, and strengths, as charity requires; for it is charity, as queen of all virtues, all commandments, all counsels, and, in short, of all laws and all Christian actions that gives to all of them their rank, order, time, and value." CCC §§ 1973–74 (citing ST IIaIIae, q. 184, art. 3, c., and quoting St. Francis de Sales, *Love of God* VIII, 6).

116   Job 19:13–17, 19: *He has put my brethren far from me, and my acquaintance like strangers have departed from me. My kinsmen have forsaken me, and they that knew me, have forgotten me,* etc.

117   Cf. Matt. 5:12.

118   Job 16:17.

[alternatively], *my* interior and intellectual *eyes, have languished through poverty* before divine illumination and because of the abundance of my own blindness. *Tota die, all the day,* that is, during all the appropriate hours throughout the day, *expandi ad te, I stretched out to you,* O Lord, *manus meas, my hands,* that is, my desires, or the works of my bodily arms: as is written in Lamentations: *Let us lift up our hearts with our hands to the Lord in the heavens.*[119] And the Apostle says: *I will therefore that men pray in every place, lifting up pure hands, without anger and contention.*[120] Indeed, to raise one's bodily hands on high contributes greatly toward the excitement of the fervor of mind and internal devotion, since the spirit is directed to one's own Creator, who dwells in the heavens.[121]

87{88}[11]   *Will you show wonders to the dead? Or shall physicians raise to life, and confess to you?*[122]

Numquid mortuis facies mirabilia? Aut medici suscitabunt, et confitebuntur tibi?

87{88}[11] *Numquid mortuis facies mirabilia? etc. Will you show wonders to the dead? etc.* The Church or any specific member of the faithful can say this verse along with the two which follow to express how reasonable it is to be heard by the Lord, just as have been brought forth in the previous exposition about Christ [in Article LXIII], for the sense is identical.

---

119   Lam. 3:41.

120   1 Tim. 2:8.

121   E. N. St. Dominic is known for emphasizing the importance of bodily posture in prayer. Although there are various anthologies (some with as many as sixteen postures), the most popular sets forth nine basic postures, the so-called *Nine Ways of Prayer of St. Dominic.* As Pope Benedict XVI summarizes them in an audience on August 8, 2012: "There are, then, nine ways to pray, according to St Dominic, and each one—always before Jesus Crucified—expresses a deeply penetrating physical and spiritual approach that fosters recollection and zeal. The first seven ways follow an ascending order, like the steps on a path, toward intimate communion with God, with the Trinity: St Dominic prayed standing bowed to express humility, lying prostrate on the ground to ask forgiveness for his sins, kneeling in penance to share in the Lord's suffering, his arms wide open, gazing at the Crucifix to contemplate Supreme Love, looking heavenwards feeling drawn to God's world.... This Saint also reminds us of the importance of physical positions in our prayer. Kneeling, standing before the Lord, fixing our gaze on the Crucifix, silent recollection—these are not of secondary importance but help us to put our whole selves inwardly in touch with God." https://www.vatican.va/content/benedict-xvi/en/audiences/2012/documents/hf_ben-xvi_aud_20120808.html

122   E. N. I have translated *confitebuntur* more broadly as "shall confess," from "shall praise," because Denis understands the confession of Ps. 87:11 to include both confession of praise and confession of sins. For the difference of these confessions, *see* footnote 27-49 in Volume 2.

87{88}[14]   *But I, O Lord, have cried to you: and in the morning my prayer shall prevent you.*[123]

Et ego ad te, Domine, clamavi, et mane oratio mea praeveniet te?

87{88}[15]   *Lord, why do you cast off my prayer? Why do you turn away your face from me?*

Ut quid, Domine, repellis orationem meam, avertis faciem tuam a me?

87{88}[14] ... *Et mane*, *and in the morning*, that is, in the beginning of the infusion of your grace; or [alternatively], *in the morning*, that is, in the beginning of the light of the sun; *oratio mea*, *my prayer*, put forth before you, *praeveniet te*, *shall prevent you*, that is, will be offered before I do any works, in accordance with that [said in the Gospels]: *Seek first the kingdom of God and his justice.*[124] Or [yet in the further alternative], *shall prevent you*, that is, your judgment, so that now, when it is *the acceptable time*, and *the day of salvation*,[125] I will endeavor to appease your anger and please you. 87{88}[15] *Ut quid, Domine, rebellis orationem meam; Lord, why do you cast off my prayer*, by not immediately hearing it, or in delaying a long time? For it appears to the devout person, when he is not heard despite his devotion, that his prayer is being rejected. For this reason, Job said: *Behold I cry suffering violence, and no one will hear: I shall cry aloud, and there is none to judge.*[126] And Habakkuk: *How long, O Lord, shall I cry, and you will not hear?*[127] Sometimes also prayer is entirely rejected because it is not done in the name of Jesus, namely, when what is requested is not expedient to salvation. For even Paul prayed three times to the Lord, yet he was not heard.[128] And also when the prayer is offered in the name of Jesus, during those times it is rejected or delayed, as long as it is continued devoutly, and the thing prayed for is ardently longed for, it will more abundantly obtained. For we ought most certainly hold that prayer that is directed in the name of Jesus, if it is continued, and if it is done prayerfully, will always be received. *Advertis faciem tuam a me, you turn away your face from me*, suspending grace and exposing me to tribulations, and not immediately consoling me. This turning away is not a turning away strictly speaking,

---

123   E. N. For the reasons explained by Denis, versus 12 and 13 have been skipped.
124   Matt. 6:33a.
125   2 Cor. 6:2.
126   Job 19:7.
127   Hab. 1:2a.
128   2 Cor. 12:8–9.

but is similar to the turning away of a mother who turns away her face from her little child so long as he is causing offence, even if the child requests again from with tears and looks at her with greater affection.

87{88}[16]   *I am poor, and in labors from my youth: and being exalted have been humbled and troubled.*

Pauper sum ego, et in laboribus a iuventute mea; exaltatus autem, humiliatus sum et conturbatus.

87{88}[16] *Pauper sum ego, I am poor,* either with the things of this world, or with merit and grace, or with affection, assessing all earthly things as if they were dung;[129] *et in laboribus a iuventute mea, and in labors from my youth,* that is, from the beginning when there began to be among the elect in the world. For many are the labors of the saints, namely, exercises of penance, of vigils, and of abstinence, prayers, exterior works, afflictions, and punishments. For this reason, Job said: *Man is born to labor, and the bird to fly.*[130] And so of the reprobate is said in an earlier Psalm: *They are not in the labor of men: neither shall they be scourged like other men.*[131] And according to the Apostle, no one is *crowned, except he strive lawfully:*[132] for no one achieves anything without great labor. *Exaltatus autem, humiliatus sum; and being exalted, I have been humbled.* For when the good are praised and raised high by others, they are humiliated in their own hearts before God: for they know that it is not to them, but to the Lord, that all things should be attributed: and this is a sign of a good and virtuous man. For this reason, Solomon said: *As silver is tried in the fining-pot and gold in the furnace: so a man is tried by the mouth of him that praises.*[133] Or [alternatively], *and being exalted* by prosperity, *I have been humbled* straight away by adversities: for man does not remain long *in the same state,*[134] but at one time he is visited by fortune and another time by adversities. And in Ecclesiasticus is written: *In the day of good things be not unmindful of evils: and in the day of evils be not unmindful of good things.*[135] Or [a final possible

---

129   Cf. Phil. 3:8.
130   Job 5:7.
131   Ps. 72:5.
132   2 Tim. 2:5b.
133   Prov. 27:21a.
134   Job 14:1–2: *Man born of a woman, living for a short time, is filled with many miseries. Who comes forth like a flower, and is destroyed, and flees as a shadow, and never continues in the same state.*
135   Ecclus. 11:27.

interpretation]: *Being exalted* living in a prideful and disobedient way, confessing truly that *I have been humbled, et conturbatus, and I have been troubled* because of the enormity of my sins or the harshness of punishments and persecutions.

87{88}[17] *Your wrath has come upon me: and your terrors have troubled me.*

In me transierunt irae tuae, et terrores tui conturbaverunt me.

87{88}[18] *They have come round about me like water all the day: they have compassed me about together.*

Circumdederunt me sicut aqua tota die; circumdederunt me simul.

87{88}[17] *In me transierunt irae tuae, your wrath has come upon me*, that is, the effects of your justice or the painful thoughts inflicted upon me: as is contained in the book of Job: *The arrows of the Lord are in me, the rage whereof drinks up my spirit, and the terrors of the Lord war against me.*[136] And so there is added: *et terrores tui conturbaverunt me, and your terrors have troubled me*, that is, the dread of the effects of your justice, namely, of the comprehension of your future judgment, of the punishments of hell, of the expulsion from glory have made me solicitous, penitent, and troubled, just like this, *I am troubled at his presence, and when I consider him I am made pensive with fear.*[137] 87{88}[18] *Circumdederunt me, they have come round about me* the previously mentioned afflictions, *sicut aqua tota die, like water all the day*, indeed, during all the times of my life: for *the life of man upon earth is a warfare.*[138] And, according to Augustine, one must persevere even until the end, for temptation perseveres even unto the end.[139] *Circumdederunt me simul, they have compassed me about together.* For many of the elect together and at the same time are assailed and made weary by the world, the flesh, and the devil. The rest [of this Psalm] can be illuminated by the previous exposition.

See we have heard this mysterious, doctrinal, and truly devout Psalm: in it was fittingly and intently brought to our mind the Passion of Christ and that we ought to suffer intimately with him, and worthily to follow

---

136   Job 6:4.
137   Job 23:15.
138   Job 7:1a.
139   E. N. Denis summarizes the gist of St. Augustine's *On the Gift of Perseverance* (*De Dono Perseverantiae*), PL 45, 994.

his steps, so that we might be able to say that which that singularly blessed Apostle said: *From henceforth let no man be troublesome to me; for I bear the marks of the Lord Jesus in my body.*[140] And also that said by the Bride: *A bundle of myrrh is my beloved to me, he shall abide between my breasts.*[141] And we consider dispositively it to be the highest happiness, and in the present perfection and grace, to conform to the Passion of Christ, to imitate his abjections, and to assimilate at all times his charity. For this reason, the Apostle exhorts us: *Be followers of God, as most dear children; and walk in love, as Christ also has loved us.*[142] And that topmost of that apostolic order said, *If you partake of the sufferings of Christ, rejoice that when his glory shall be revealed, you may also be glad;*[143] and again, *If you be reproached for the name of Christ,* he says, *you shall be blessed.*[144] For what can be more glorious to a Christian but to be entirely similar to Christ?

PRAYER

LORD, GOD OF OUR SALVATION, KINDLY have mercy upon us; and by the abundance of your propitiation recall back our soul which is so full of evil and our life which approaches hell because of our sins, and remove us now and forever from all misery so that with the prerogative of your mercy, we might render proclamations of praise to you forever.

Domine, Deus salutis nostrae, nostri pie miserere; et repletam
malis animam nostram, et inferno peccatis appropinquantem
vitam nostram, abundantia tuae propitiationis
revoca, et ab omni miseria nunc et semper
nos elonga: ut misericordiae tuae
praerogativa, laudum tibi
praeconia persolvamus
in saecula.

---

140 Gal. 6:17.
141 Songs 1:12.
142 Eph. 5:1–2a.
143 1 Pet. 4:13.
144 1 Pet. 4:14a.

Psalm 88

ARTICLE LXV

ELUCIDATION OF THE EIGHTY-EIGHTH PSALM:
MISERICORDIAS DOMINI.
THE MERCIES OF THE LORD.

88{89}[1] *Of understanding, for Ethan the Israelite.*

Intellectus Ethan Israelitae.

THE TITLE OF THE PSALM NOW BEING explained is: **88{89}[1]** *Intellectus Ethan Israelitae;[1] of understanding, for Ethan the Israelite:* that is, in the present Psalm is contained that which a man robust with grace and contemplating God by faith ought to think of Christ. For Ethan is interpreted to mean robust. Now according to all the expositors, this Psalm treats of the stability and the perpetuity of the reign of David, which is completed in no one other than Christ. For this reason, this Psalm literally deals with Christ: and because this stability is achieved by the grace of God, therefore the holy prophet begins from the fountain of all graces, namely, from the divine mercy.

> **88{89}[2]** *The mercies of the Lord I will sing forever. I will show forth your truth with my mouth to generation and generation.*
>
> *Misericordias Domini in aeternum cantabo; in generationem et generationem annuntiabo veritatem tuam in ore meo.*

88{89}[2] *Misericordias,* the mercies, it says, *Domini in aeternum cantabo,* of the Lord I will sing forever. Clearly, a most sweet beginning, most exceedingly sweeter that all mundane, fleshly, and vain delights. It does not say, the mercy of the Lord, but *the mercies:* because according to the multitude of our miseries, multiple are the mercies of the Lord upon us. For the mercy of God is sometimes called the kindness of the divine nature which is naturally clement: and this mercy is not anything other than one, just as the divine essence [is only one]. But sometimes the mercy of God refers to the effects of divine kindness, as when [the angel]

---

1   E. N. The text has *Israelite;* however, the editor in the margin notes that it should be *Ezrahitae, Ezrahite.*

Raphael says: *Bless the God of heaven . . . because he has shown his mercy to you.*[2] And in this place, the mercy of the Lord can be understood both ways [essentially or as effect]; but if we accept the first way, then one and simple mercy of God is understood plurally because of its multiple effects. For God knows how to help mercifully in thousands of ways. And so it would be [understood] in this sense: *The mercies of the Lord*, that is, God naturally merciful, or the divine goodness in multiplicitous ways full of pity, *I will sing forever*, that is, unceasingly will I praise, now in an inchoative way, and in the future in a complete way. For in the way that, according to the Apostle [Paul], *charity never falls away*, because it begins now and is perfected in the future,[3] so the acts of charity — which are to love, contemplate, admire, and praise God, and to enjoy him, to rejoice in him — never fail; yet in the present time they have a beginning, and in the heavenly fatherland they find their completion.[4] For this reason, the Savior said regarding Mary Magdalen, who was preoccupied by charity: *Mary has chosen the best part, which shall not be taken away from her.*[5]

But if the mercies of the Lord are said with reference of the effects or the works of the most merciful Creator, the sense [of this verse] will be: *The mercies of the Lord*, that is, the gifts of grace or the benefits of God, and the multiplicitous effects of his goodness upon me as well as the entire human race are so considerable, that *I will sing forever*. This is the manner that Isaiah states: *I will remember the tender mercies of the Lord, the praise of the Lord for all the things that the Lord has bestowed upon us, . . . which he has given to us according to his kindness.*[6] Everyone of us ought to recollect here, to the extent he is able, the mercies of the Lord, that is, his benefits, both general and special. Indeed, the general benefits of God are the creation, justification, and glorification; but the special benefits of God are those which are give to every person individually. Now both of these truly transcend all reason and all speech. For who is able to conceive, declare, or number all the benefits of Christ? For us he became man, he *conversed with men*,[7] and he hung on the wood [of the Cross]. He gave himself to us in the Sacrament, he promised himself as a reward, and he wishes to dwell, to delight, and to find rest in our hearts.

2   Tob. 12:16.
3   1 Cor. 13:8
4   E. N. "Here [in the wayfaring state], charity is imperfect, but it will be perfected in heaven." ST IIaIIae, q. 23, art. 1, ad 1.
5   Luke 10:42.
6   Is. 53:7.
7   Bar. 3:38b.

In generationem et generationem annuntiabo veritatem tuam in ore meo, I will show forth your truth with my mouth to generation and generation. The prophetic author of this current Psalm brought about what he foretold. For he foretold himself showing forth the truth of God from generation to generation, that is, from one generation to another succeeding generation, because this Psalm will be sung even unto the end of the world. Now by saying generation to generation Scripture customarily seeks to designate a perpetual duration, in the manner that Mary says: *And his mercy is from generation unto generations.*[8] Since, therefore, we live but for a short time,[9] and die shortly afterwards, we ought to scrutinize how it is that any one of us in our own person is able to say this. For, to be sure, in the person of the Church it can be said by anyone.[10] The response to this issue is that any one of us is able to say this in a twofold sense. First, since he who does good and exemplary works leaves behind imitators of his good manner of life, so he unceasingly announces the divine truth through those who follow him. The second manner is explained thus: *I will show forth your truth* from a generation of a way or of wayfarers to a generation of the Saints in heaven: and so that I begin *showing forth your truth* in the generation of the holy wayfarers, but I will continue and complete it in the generation of the blessed comprehensors in heaven. Now, by the truth of God, one can understand in this place his justice, which he shows forth from the fact that he sings the mercy of God, because in all the works of God mercy and justice are mixed together. One can also understand truth to mean the fulfilling of the divine promises which God has lavished upon men through Christ, which he promised to fulfill through him. And it ought to be understood this way when he says in John, *Grace and truth came by Jesus Christ.*[11]

88{89}[3] *For you have said: Mercy shall be built up forever in the heavens: your truth shall be prepared in them.*

Quoniam dixisti: In aeternum misericordia aedificabitur in caelis; praeparabitur veritas tua in eis.

---

8 Luke 1:50.
9 Cf. Job 14:1.
10 E. N. In other words, Denis asks, when one prays the Psalm from the perspective of the Church which transcends generations, one can speak of generations upon generations; however, how can this expression mean something when someone prays this Psalm in reference to himself?
11 John 1:17b.

Then the Prophet in this verse changes person, and he says to the Lord: *in generation to generation I will show forth your truth with my mouth,* steadily turning over the divine words in my mouth, and not only pronouncing them from the mouth in passing or hastily. Now, for this reason *I will show forth your truth,* **88{89}[3]** *Quoniam dixisti, for you have said,* that is, you have decreed within yourself, and in sundry times and diverse ways you have spoken through angels, through the Prophets, through your Incarnate Son, and your Apostles,[12] this, namely: *In aeternum misericordia aedificabitur in caelis, mercy shall be built up forever in the heavens:* that is, through the effect of your mercy, the fall of the heavens may be repaired,[13] and the walls of the heavenly Jerusalem may be built from living stones,[14] when through the Incarnation and Passion of Christ, men may be transferred to the seats of the apostate angels.[15] Whence it is said in earlier Psalms, *O Lord, your mercy is in heaven;*[16] and, *Your mercy is magnified even to the heavens.*[17] Or [an alternative interpretation is] thus: *For you have said* by yourself and your holy prophets: *Mercy shall be built up forever,* that is, your mercy worked in the Apostles or by the Apostles, for through them the Catholic Church was built. For the mercy of God is said to be built forever when its effects are eternally preserved. But the Church built by the mercy of God will remain even unto the end of time. *Praeparabitur veritas tua in eis, your truth shall be prepared in them:* that is, the fulfillment of your and your prophets' promises will be fulfilled by the Apostles, so that by them it may become known to all men, since by the grace first granted to them they converted others in the way that is stated in Ecclesiasticus, *that your prophets may be found faithful.* Or [another interpretation is] thus: *Your truth shall be prepared in them,* that is, in the celestial citizens or the holy angels: because they were the first to illustrate the divine mysteries, and so by them the truth of divine illuminations is given to holy men. For the Ecclesiastical hierarchy is cleansed, illuminated, and perfected by the angelic hierarchy.[18]

---

12   *Cf.* Heb. 1:1–2.

13   *E. N.* This reference to the ruin or fall of heaven may be an oblique reference to Virgil's *Aeneid,* I, 129: *Fluctibus oppressos Troas caelique ruina.* "The Trojans oppressed by the waves and the falling heavens."

14   *Cf.* Ps. 50:20: *Deal favorably, O Lord, in your good will with Sion; that the walls of Jerusalem may be built up.*

15   *E. N.* For the theological opinion that the number of saved men will make up for the number of fallen angels, *see* footnote 16-22.

16   Ps. 35:6a.

17   Ps. 56:11a.

18   *E. N.* Denis is referring to the threefold ministries of the angels (cleansing, illuminating, and perfecting) in Pseudo-Dionysius, specifically, his *Celestial Hierarchy,*

88{89}[4] *I have made a covenant with my elect: I have sworn to David my servant:*

Disposui testamentum electis meis; iuravi David, servo meo.

88{89}[5] *Your seed will I settle forever. And I will build up your throne unto generation and generation.*

Usque in aeternum praeparabo semen tuum, et aedificabo in generationem et generationem sedem tuam.

You also said, O Lord: **88{89}[4]** *Disposui testamentum electis meis, I have made a covenant with my elect,* that is, I have given to the children of Israel the Old Testament or the Mosaic law. For the law was ordered to Christ, according to that said by the Apostle, *Wherefore the law was our pedagogue in Christ;*[19] and so it was not given to any other people except those from whom Christ chose to become incarnate, namely, the children of Israel. *Iuravi David, I have sworn to David,* the son of Jesse, *servo meo, my servant:* **88{89}[5]** *Usque in aeternum praeparabo semen tuum, your seed I will settle forever:* that is, the propagation of your children even unto Christ, out of whom he will be born, and it will be perpetuated in Christ. This was truly established in [the Gospel of] Matthew, where the genealogy from David unto Christ is traced. *Et aedificabo in generationem et generationem, and I will build up . . . unto generation and generation,* that is, through all the posterity that I will sustain and preserve, *sedem tuam, your throne,* that is, the royal power. In the first book of Chronicles and elsewhere, God promises king David that a man of his seed, seated on his throne, will not be forsaken,[20] notwithstanding whether his sons kept his divine precepts; but because they inclined towards idolatry, they frequently transgressed them;[21] and for this reason during the time of Zedekiah the reign of David sustained an interruption, as is described in the second book of Kings.[22] Though the seat or the reign of David ceased for a time, nevertheless it was restored, confirmed, and perpetuated in Christ, as the Archangel said to the Virgin: *Behold you shall conceive in your womb, and shall bring forth a son, and you shall call his name Jesus: he shall be great, and shall be called the Son of the most High, and the Lord God shall give unto him the throne of David his father, and he shall reign in*

---

iii, 2, and the parallel functions of the diaconate, priesthood, and episcopacy in *Ecclesiastical Hierarchy,* v, 3.

19 Gal. 3:24.
20 1 Chr. 17:11–14.
21 2 Kings 17:19–20.
22 2 Kings chp. 25.

the house of Jacob forever, and of his kingdom there shall be no end.[23] This is most clearly written in Isaiah: *He shall sit upon the throne of David, and upon his kingdom; to establish it and strengthen it with judgment and with justice, from henceforth and forever.*[24] Marvel at the great concordance between the evangelical narrative and the prophetic word.

Or, in greater accord with Catholic teachers, [we can think of it] thus: **88{89}[4]** *I have made,* that is, I have given and have proposed by ordinance, *a covenant,* a new one, that is, the evangelical law, where an eternal inheritance is promised: and that testament is confirmed by the death of Christ; *with my elect,* that is, with Christians in both name and reality, of which the Apostle [Paul] says: *The sure foundation of God stands firm, having this seal: the Lord knows who are his.*[25] Peter also: *You are a chosen generation, a kingly priesthood, a holy nation.*[26] Of this covenant and this disposition, Paul attests: Jesus *is the mediator of the new testament, that by means of his death, for the redemption of those transgressions, which were under the former testament, they that are called may receive the promise of eternal inheritance.*[27] *I have sworn,* that is, I have promised certainly and firmly, *to David my servant,* that is, to Christ, who as man is less than I am and is my servant: **88{89}[5]** *...forever,* that is, even unto the end of the world, indeed, even in eternal life, *your seed will I settle,* that is, I will form and govern Christians and the faithful by faith and grace. Of this seed is stated by Isaiah: *If he* (namely Christ) *shall lay down his life for sin, he shall see a long-lived seed.*[28] In the divine Scripture, frequently by David is understood Christ. Whence the Lord says through Jeremiah: *Strangers shall no more rule Jacob, but they shall serve the Lord their God and David their king,* that is, the Messiah as all expound [this verse], *whom I will raise up to them.*[29] For God did not arouse and raise the dead David, the son of Jesse, so as to reign in this world. This is also written in Hosea: *After this the children of Israel shall return, and shall seek the Lord their God, and David their king.*[30] But where has God sworn to Christ that he would settle his seed in eternity? Take a look at what he said to Abraham: *By my own self have I sworn, says the Lord, ... because you have not spared your only begotten son for my*

23   Luke 1:31–33.
24   Is. 9:7.
25   2 Tim. 2:19a.
26   1 Pet. 2:9a.
27   Heb. 9:15.
28   Is. 53:10a.
29   Jer. 30:8b–9.
30   Hos. 3:5a.

sake, I will bless you,... and in your seed shall all the nations of the earth be blessed.[31] The Apostle explains what we should understand by this seed, saying to the Galatians: *He says not, 'And to his seeds,' as of many: but as of one, 'And to your seed,' which is Christ.*[32] Daniel also says: *All peoples, tribes and tongues shall serve him.*[33] *And I will build,* that is, I will found, *unto generation and generation,* that is, in eternity, *your throne,* that is, your judiciary power and your regal dignity. Whence in Daniel is written: *He gave him power, and glory, and a kingdom.*[34] But what this power and kingdom is stated immediately thereafter: *His power is an everlasting power that shall not be taken away: and his kingdom that shall not be destroyed.*[35] Or [alternatively]: *I will build up* through charity and the gifts of the Holy Spirit, *your throne,* that is, the hearts of the faithful or the Church, in which you, O Christ, dwell through grace. Indeed, the soul of the just man is the seat of wisdom;[36] and Christ dwells in the Church in the manner that is written: *He shall... sit and rule upon his throne.*[37] Or [in the further alternative]: *I will build up your throne* not made by human hands, but a heavenly throne, so that you might sit in heaven at my right hand upon a throne, of which, you, O Christ, have spoken: *I also have overcome, and am set down with my Father in his throne.*[38]

88{89}[6] *The heavens shall confess your wonders, O Lord: and your truth in the Church of the saints.*

Confitebuntur caeli mirabilia tua, Domine; etenim veritatem tuam in Ecclesia sanctorum.

88{89}[6] *Confitebuntur caeli mirabilia tua, Domine: etenim veritatem tuam in ecclesia sanctorum. The heavens shall confess your wonders, O Lord: and your truth in the Church of the saints.* This can be explained as referring to the holy angels and all the heavenly citizens in the Church triumphant, that is, of the Saints and those blessed in the heavenly fatherland, who together confess unendingly, with the confession of unceasing

---

31   Gen. 22:16–18.
32   Gal. 3:16.
33   Dan. 7:14a.
34   *Ibid.*
35   *Ibid.*
36   Wis. 7:27. E. N. Denis cites to the book of Wisdom, but the quote is not there. It probably derives from St. Augustine. For more on this issue, *see* footnote 67-50, in Volume 3.
37   Zech. 6:13a.
38   Rev. 3:21b.

praise, the marvelous works of God and his truth, as is spoken of in Revelation: *Great and wonderful are your works, O Lord God Almighty; just and true are your ways, O King of saints:*[39] indeed, according to the divine and great Dionysius, the superior angels illumine and teach the inferior angels of some of the marvelous accomplishments of God and the truths of divine accomplishments.[40] And so these heavens confess also the marvels of God and his truth of the wayfaring saints in the Church militant, of those souls, namely, illumined by the wondrous works of God and the Sacred Scriptures. For this reason, it is written that the angel taught Joseph of the miraculous conception of Christ;[41] and we read that the angel led the Apostles out of prison, and that he told them: *Go, and standing speak in the temple to the people all the words of this life.*[42] Notwithstanding all this, by heavens in this place can be fittingly understood [to be also a reference to] the holy Apostles, and other apostolic men, having an angelic and heavenly manner of life in this earth; and so [it reads] in this sense:

The heavens, that is, the Apostles and those similar to them, *shall confess,* that is, they will fearlessly bear witness to, teach, and preach, and praise, *your wonders, O Lord,* that is, your miracles, O Christ, and all things which are written of your mysteries; *and,* that is, they will also confess and preach, *your truth,* that is, justice and the evangelical law, most fully with all truth, *in the Church of the saints,* that is, in the congregation of the faithful elect. This is clearly taught to have been fulfilled in the Acts of the Apostles, where, among other things, is written: *The chief priests, seeing the constancy of Peter and of John, . . . wondered.*[43] Their constancy was clearly apparent when they said: *We ought to obey God, rather than men;*[44] *for we cannot but speak of those things that we have heard and seen.*[45] Were not the wonders of God and his Christ confessed in this manner by the holy Apostles when through Peter's voice they said to all the Jews: *Jesus of Nazareth, a man approved by God, by miracles, and wonders, and signs . . . you have slain?*[46]

---

39   Rev. 15:3b. E. N. Denis has replaced "O King of ages," *Rex saeculorum,* with "O King of saints," *Rex sanctorum.*

40   E. N. See *Celestial Hierarchy* in Pseudo-Dionysius: *The Complete Works* (New York: Paulist Press, 1987), 143 *ff.* (trans., Colm Luibheid).

41   Matt. 1:20–21.

42   Acts 5:19, 20.

43   Acts 4:13.

44   Acts 5:29b.

45   Acts 4:20.

46   Acts 2:22–23.

88{89}[7] *For who in the clouds can be compared to the Lord: or who
           among the sons of God shall be like to God?*

           *Quoniam quis in nubibus aequabitur Domino, similis erit
           Deo in filiis Dei?*

And this is why the Apostles did these things, **88{89}[6]** *Quoniam
quis, for who* — it is as if it were implying, "no one" — *in nubibus, in the
clouds,* that is, who among the sublime creation which are the Apostles
and the Prophets, *aequabitur Domino, can be compared to the Lord,* to
God, one and three, and blessed or the Son of God, Jesus Christ? Of
him, Peter said, *He is Lord of all.* For however much a creature is able
to assimilate God,[47] he nevertheless is not able to have any power to
equal him, for he is infinitely distant from him. For this reason, it is
said: *To whom have you . . . made me equal, says the Holy One?*[48] But the
Prophets and Apostles are called clouds, as Isaiah says of the Apostles:
Who are these, that fly as clouds?[49] First, because like clouds are the
first to be illuminated by the sun and then they illuminate the earth,
so the Prophets and Apostles were first and fully taught by the Sun of
justice, Christ, and then they illuminated men. Whence the Savior says
about them: *You are the light of the world.*[50] Second, because as when
clouds pour out rain and irrigate the earth and make it fruitful, so did
the Prophets and Apostles pour out and fill the hearts of men with
the doctrine of salvation and the word of grace, and free them from a
damnable aridity and sterility. And for this reason they were told: *You
are the salt of the earth.*[51] Third, [they are referred to as clouds] because
of their height of contemplation, the elevation of their desire, and the
sublimity of their life. By clouds we can also understand the holy angels
(according to the fifteenth chapter of Dionysius's *Celestial Hierarchy*).[52]

---

47   *E. N.* It is unclear whether Denis, in using the verb *assimilari,* intends to refer
to the ontological quality of a creature (*e.g.,* a cherubim, as distinguished from a
stone, is more similar to God) or whether he is speaking of grace given to humans to
participate in the supernatural life of God by grace and become, as St. Peter says it,
"partakers of the divine nature," 2 Pet. 1:4, in what is called *theosis* or *deification,* or — as
St. Athanasius starkly put it: "God became man so that man could become God."
St. Athanasius, *De Incarnatione,* 54. Perhaps he intends to include both these senses.
48   Is. 40:25.
49   Is.
50   Matt. 5:14.
51   Matt. 5:13. *E. N.* As Denis explains this verse, "salt of the earth" means they
are the "seasoning of men living on earth." *Commentary on the Gospel of Matthew,*
Doctoris Ecstatici D. Dionysii Cartusiani, *Opera Omnia,* Vol. II (Montreuil: 1900), 59.
52   *E. N. See* footnote 88-40.

Of these is added: *similis erit Deo in filiis Dei? Who among the sons of God shall be like God?*[53] It is as if he [the Psalmist] were saying, "There is none among the angels that can be found to equal to God in any way." For all (according to the Apostle) *are ministering spirits.*[54] But the term sons of God can also be properly understood as referring to the angels, for the Lord asked Job regarding them: *Where were you when ... the morning stars praised me together, and all the sons of God made a joyful melody?*[55] Of these is also said: *On a certain day when the sons of God came to stand before the Lord, Satan was present among them.*[56]

88{89}[8]   God, who is glorified in the assembly of the saints: great and terrible above all them that are about him.

Deus, qui glorificatur in consilio sanctorum, magnus et terribilis super omnes qui in circuitu eius sunt.

88{89}[8] *Deus qui glorificatur; God, who is glorified,* that is, who is to be declared, honored, and exalted as glorious, *in consilio sanctorum, in the assembly of the saints,* that is, in the loving gaze of all the elect, of those abiding in heaven and earth: whose counsel is one and the same, so that all might glorify God with heart, mouth, and work; *magnus, great,* indeed immense, and in all excellence simply and interminably perfect, *et terribilis super omnes qui in circuitu eius sunt, and terrible above all them that are about him,* that is, venerated or feared by all the blessed and saints standing before him, and drawing near to him from all parts. Now the elect are said to be round about God, not in the sense that they have him hedged in and confined within bounds, since he exists unfixed in any one place and is entirely uncircumscribable, but because they flow towards him, attend to him, and assist him from all sides, and because they keep him within themselves or within their midst. Or [it can be explained this way], because the glorious and holy God interpenetrates all things, is most intimate, and is closer than one is to one's self,[57] or because he is the essential principle of all things with a beginning; for these reasons, they are said to be all

---

53   E. N. The text has *similis erit Domino, shall be like the Lord*; however, the editor indicates in the margin that it should be *similis erit Deo, shall be like God.*
54   Heb. 1:14.
55   Job 38:4a, 7.
56   Job 1:6; 2:1.
57   E. N. This brings to mind that beautiful observation of St. Augustine in his *Confessions*: God is closer to us that we are to ourselves: *interior intimo meo et superior summo meo,* "more inward than my innermost self and higher than my highest." *Confessions* III, 6, 11.

round about him. Even more true is it that he is round about them, as a later Psalm says: *The Lord is round about his people.*[58] Whence, in Acts, Paul attests: *He is not far from every one of us: for in him we live, and move, and have our being, as some also of your poets said: [for we are his offspring].* According to Thomas, the poet Aratus said this.[59]

88{89}[9]   *O Lord God of hosts, who is like to you? You are mighty, O Lord, and your truth is round about you.*

Domine Deus virtutum, quis similis tibi? Potens es, Domine, et veritas tua in circuitu tuo.

88{89}[9] *Domine, Deus virtutum, quis similis tibi?* O Lord, God of hosts, who is like to you?[60] Indeed, speaking in terms of natural and perfect similarity, no one. For there is no proportion that exists between the infinite and the finite, because however much of a finite thing is added to something finite, it never after such addition brings about infinity.[61] And so, to emphasize the excellent infinity of God above all things, Isaiah writes: *Who has measured the waters in the hollow of his hand, and weighed the heavens with his palm? Who has poised with three fingers the bulk of the earth, and weighed the mountains in scales, and the hills in a balance?*[62] Whence in another place is said: *The whole world before you is as the least grain of the balance, and as a drop of the morning dew, that falls down upon the earth.*[63] *Potens es, Domine; you are mighty, O Lord,* by essence, because with you to be and to have is the same thing; and since your being is infinite, so also your power — to which all

---

58   Ps. 124:2a.

59   E. N. ST Ia, q. 1, art. 8, ad 2. St. Paul's quote stems from the Greek poet Aratus of Soli (ca.315/310–240 BC), specifically, his *Phenomena*, I, 5.

60   E. N. The editor notes that Denis's text has and error, having *tui* ("of you") instead of *tibi* ("to you").

61   E. N. This appears aimed against some of the positions taken by Joachim of Fiore (ca. 1135–1202) and condemned by Lateran IV Council (1251) "When, then, he who is the Truth prays to the Father for his faithful 'that they may be one in us as we also are one' [Jn 17:22], the word 'one' as applied the disciples is to be taken in the sense of a union of charity in grace, but, in the case of the Divine Persons, in the sense of a unity of identity in nature. In the same way, on another occasion the Truth says: 'You must be perfect as your heavenly Father is perfect' [Mt 5:48] as though he were saying more explicitly: 'You must be perfect' in the perfection of grace 'as your heavenly Father is perfect' in the perfection of nature, that is, each in his own way. For between Creator and creature no similitude can be expressed without implying a greater dissimilitude." DS 806.

62   Is. 40:12.

63   Wis. 11:23.

things are easy—is boundless: as Scripture says, *Your power is at hand when you will.*[64] Yet the power of God differs from the power of other things. First, because God is powerful in and of himself or by his own power, as an earlier Psalm says of him: *He who by his power rules for ever.*[65] Second, because God is altogether powerful, according to this: *You have mercy upon all, because you can do all things.*[66] Third, because the power of God is completely infinite, there are no things so great and so sublime that are produced by God that are unable to be created or to be made infinitely more and greater, according to this: *Is the hand of the Lord unable?*[67] And elsewhere: *The Lord is the everlasting God, who has created the ends of the earth: he shall not faint.*[68] Indeed, God is designated powerful when it says in the book of Job: *God does not cast away the mighty, whereas he himself also is mighty.*[69]

Et veritas tua, and your truth divine and uncreated, results, shines forth, and appears *in circuitu tuo, round about you,* that is, in all creatures or in assisting those things which are in your midst. For in the manner that divine power in creation shines forth in things, so wisdom or truth of God shines forth in their order. For this reason, it is written: *By the greatness of the beauty, and of the creature, the creator of them may be seen, so as to be known thereby;*[70] and again: *The glory of the Lord is his work.*[71] Or [alternatively], *Your truth,* that is, your true illumination, sacred doctrine, and the wise ordering, *is round about you,* that is, is in the heart or the mind of those of which has already been said: *Great and terrible above all them that are about him.* Indeed, our truth and knowledge of things are obtained from things that are caused: but the truth and knowledge of God are the cause of things; and as the use of many mirrors by one face results in diverse images, so certainly from the one and highest truth many truths are caused in created things. For this reason, of this created truth or wisdom, we find contained in Ecclesiasticus: *God created her [that is, wisdom] in the Holy Spirit, and he poured her out upon all his works, and upon all flesh . . . and has given her to them that love him.*[72]

---

64 Wis. 12:18b.

65 Ps. 65:7a.

66 Wis. 11:24a.

67 Num. 11:23a.

68 Is. 40:28.

69 Job 36:5.

70 Wis. 13:5.

71 Ecclus. 42:16b.

72 Ecclus. 1:9–10. E. N. That truth is contained in things ("all that exists is true") is the central thesis of Josef Pieper's *Living the Truth* (San Francisco: Ignatius, 1989)

88{89}[10] *You rule the power of the sea: and appease the motion of the waves thereof.*

Tu dominaris potestati maris, motum autem fluctuum eius tu mitigas.

88{89}[10] *Tu dominaris potestati maris, you rule the power of the sea:* that is, of the sea and of all natural things, for their course, order, and power are subject to you. This is manifest in the division of the Red Sea.[73] Whence of Christ, the true and most high God, is written: *The winds and the sea obey him.*[74] Job also says: *By his power the seas are suddenly gathered together.*[75] For through the obediential potency created in conjunction with all things, all things obey their Creator.[76] *Motum autem fluctuum eius tu mitigas, and appease the motion of the waves thereof:* that is, you cause the impetuous flows of the [sea's] abyss to quiet, to come to rest, to break, in the manner that is testified to by holy Job: *I set my bounds around the sea, and made it bars and doors, and I said: Hitherto you shall come, and shall go no further, and here you shall break your swelling waves.*[77] This is also said of Christ: *He rebuked the wind, and said to the sea: Peace, be still. . . . And there was a great calm.*[78] Morally, this is explained in this fashion: *You rule the power of the sea,* that is, the powers of this age and the princes of this world, namely, tyrants and demons, not as they may want, for they rave against what is yours. And so it continues, *and . . . the motion of the waves thereof,* that is, the

---

(trans., Lothar Krauth). As Pieper himself quotes St. Anselm of Canterbury (*De veritate,* IX): "Yet few consider the truth that dwells in the essence of things." PL 158, 478. The truth in things, long abandoned by moderns, is a philosophical truth that must be recaptured.

73 Ex. chp. 14.

74 Matt. 8:27b.

75 Job 26:12a.

76 *E. N.* The notion of "obediential potency" when it comes to brute nature is of two kinds: "generic obediential potency" and "specific obediential potency." It is the capacity or openness of a created nature to receive or respond to the supernatural action of God. If the response is one within the confines or borders of its nature (*e.g.,* the winds stopping at command), then it is called specific obediential potency (since it remains within the species or its nature). If the response is beyond the confines or borders of its nature (*e.g.,* Balaam's donkey who speaks, Num. 22:28–30), then it is a generic obediential potency (since it goes beyond the species or nature and is of another genus). *See, e.g.,* Andrew Dean Swafford: *Nature and Grace: A New Approach to Thomistic Ressourcement* (Cambridge: James Clark & Co., 2015), 90–92.

77 Job 38:10–11.

78 Mark 4:39.

attacks of the devil's temptations, and the persecution of the world, *you appease*: for according to the Apostle [Paul], you do not permit us to be tempted beyond that which we are able to bear, but you make also with temptation issue [that grace] that we might be able to bear it.[79] Whence, Peter says: *The Lord knows how to deliver the godly from temptation.*[80] Does not God appease those billowing movements of which Paul asserts, *Blessed be the God . . . who comforts us in all our tribulation?*[81]

88{89}[11] *You have humbled the proud one, as one that is slain: with the arm of your strength you have scattered your enemies.*

Tu humiliasti, sicut vulneratum, superbum; in brachio virtutis tuae dispersisti inimicos tuos.

88{89}[11] *Tu humiliasti, sicut vulneratum, superbum; you have humbled the proud one, as one that is slain*: that is, you have cast down and oppressed all those that exalt themselves, and especially that first apostate angel,[82] who is the father of all the children of pride,[83] *as one that is slain is cast down* — in the manner that is written, *God resists the proud;*[84] and again, *Every one that exalts himself shall be humbled.*[85] And so the Savior says: *I saw Satan like lighting falling from heaven.*[86] And of his humiliation or fall is said: *How are you fallen from heaven, O Lucifer, who did rise in the morning?*[87] Whence elsewhere we have: *His wisdom has struck the proud one.*[88] *In brachio virtutis tuae, with the arm of your strength*, that is, through your eminent power which is yours alone, *dispersisti inimicos tuos, you have scattered your enemies*, the demons and unjust men. For God scattered them from the unity that he himself is, and so turned them toward many fleeting and vain things, cut off now from the life (*esse*) of grace, and in the future from the life (*esse*) of glory. And so it is asserted in the book of Job: *I have seen the ungodly perishing by the blast of God.*[89]

---

79   *Cf.* 1 Cor. 10:13.
80   2 Pet. 2:9a.
81   2 Cor. 1:3a, 4a.
82   Is. 14:11.
83   *Cf.* Job 41:25b: *He is king over all the children of pride.*
84   James 4:6
85   Luke 14:11.
86   Luke 10:18.
87   Is. 14:12a.
88   Job 26:12b.
89   Job 4:8a, 9a.

88{89}[12] *Yours are the heavens, and yours is the earth: the world and*
the fulness thereof you have founded:

Tui sunt caeli, et tua est terra; orbem terrae, et plenitudinem
eius tu fundasti;

88{89}[13] *The north and the sea you have created. Tabor and Hermon*
shall rejoice in your name:

Aquilonem et mare tu creasti. Thabor et Hermon in nomine
tuo exsultabunt.

    88{89}[12] *Tui sunt caeli, et tua est terra; yours are the heavens, and*
yours is the earth, that is, all things above and all things below; *orbem*
terrae, et plenitudinem eius; the world and the fulness thereof, that is, all
that is contained within it, *tu fundasti, you have founded,* that is, you have
stably placed, according to this, *The Lord by wisdom has founded the earth,*
has established the heavens by prudence.[90] **88{89}[13]** *Aquilonem, the north,*
that is, the northern part of the earth opposite of the south, or the northern wind, *et mare, and the sea,* the great [sea], the Ocean all around the
earth, *tu creasti, you created.* Whence, in the book of Job is written, *He*
stretched out the north over the empty space;[91] and in Revelation: *Fear the*
Lord, and give him honor, . . . and adore him, that made heaven and earth,
the sea, and the fountains of waters.[92] For this reason, holy Job says: *Who*
is ignorant that the hand of the Lord has made all these things?[93] Or [we
might look at it this way]: *Yours is the earth,* that is, the angelic minds,
or the holy preachers living a heavenly-fashioned life, *and yours is the*
earth, that is, the worldly men, to the degree of what they are: for they
are yours by nature.[94] *The world,* that is, the universal Church, diffused
throughout the entire world, *and the fulness thereof,* that is, its spiritual
riches, namely, the gifts of graces, the sacraments, the virtues, and all
other spiritual goods, *you have founded,* because without you they would
not be preserved, since they would not be possible except for you. *The*
north, that is, the devil, ruler over those to the north, that is, to sinners
cold because of their lack of charity, who says: *I will sit in the mountain*
of the covenant, in the sides of the north.[95] *And the sea,* that is, unstable,

---

90   Prov. 3:19.
91   Job 26:7a.
92   Rev. 14:7.
93   Job 12:9.
94   E. N. In other words, these men do not live a supernatural life of grace, but
only a natural life.
95   Is. 14:13b.

impetuous, irritable men who resemble the sea, *you created*, giving them the life (*esse*) of nature, and its natural properties, perfections, and powers: not, however, that they were created in their malice.

Thabor et Hermon in nomine tuo exsultabunt, Tabor and Hermon shall rejoice in your name: that is, these two mountains provided the occasion and matter for the faithful to exult in God because of the benefits of God exhibited upon them. For Tabor is the mountain in the Holy Land, in which the victory over Barak of Sisera and his army was pronounced.[96] And Hermon is the mountain close to the Jordan river, which the Hebrews crossed with dry feet.[97] And so because of the miraculous works of God shown on them, these mountains aroused in Jews the occasion of praising God. And they most greatly furnish to Christians the matter for exulting, for Christ was transfigured upon Mount Tabor,[98] which mountain Peter called holy, *This voice*, he said, *we heard brought from heaven, when we were with him in this holy mount*.[99] And Jesus was baptized in the Jordan, by which Mount Hermon is located.[100] Now spiritually, by the word Tabor, which is interpreted as meaning "coming light," is designated the Jews, who first were given the law and the infused grace of God. But by Hermon, which is interpreted as meaning "anathema," is signified the Gentiles, who during the time of their perfidy were anathema to God, since they were anathematized by him, as it were, because of the crime of idolatry. And so [given this understanding] it is in in this [sense that we can interpret this verse]: *Tabor and Hermon*, that is, the Jews and the Gentiles chosen to [eternal] life, *shall rejoice*, not in themselves or from their own strength, but *in your name*.

88{89}[14] *Your arm is with might. Let your hand be strengthened, and your right hand be lifted:*[101]

Tuum brachium cum potentia; firmetur manus tua, et exaltetur dextera tua.

---

96   Judges 4:6–7.
97   Joshua 3:17.
98   Mark 9:1–07
99   2 Pet. 1:18.
100   Matt. 3:13–17.
101   E. N. In translating *exaltetur*, I have replaced the Douay-Rheims's "be exalted" with "be lifted." By translating the word as "lifted" it can be applied both when the hand of God is understood in the good sense ("be lifted [in praise or in bestowal]") as well when it is understood in the bad sense ("be lifted [from the act of punishing me]").

88{89}[14] *Tuum brachium, your arm,* that is, your strength, *is cum potentia, with might,* so that nothing is difficult for it.[102] *Firmetur manus tua, let your hand be strengthened,* that is, let your strength prevail over the enemies of truth, casting them down, *et exaltetur dextera tua, and let your right hand be lifted.* One should be aware that the hand of God, which is his operative power, sometimes is to be understood in a good way, as when is said, His hand *wounds and cures: he strikes, and his hands heal;*[103] but sometimes [one understands it] in a bad sense, as when the Apostle says, *It is a fearful thing to fall into the hands of the living God;*[104] and Job, *Withdraw your hand far from me.*[105] And so when the hand of God is received in a good sense, then his right hand means eternal goods, but his left hand means temporal goods, according to what we read in Proverbs: *Length of days is in her right hand, and in her left hand riches and glory.*[106] But when the hand of God is received in a bad sense, namely, as it regards the evil of punishment, then by the left hand of God is understood a lesser punishment; but by the right hand [is understood] a power to punish more severely, through the oppression and degradation by all kinds of malicious enemies, which one pleads to be lifted. This verse can also be explained in a good sense, in this way: *Let your hand be strengthened,* that is, let your power strongly provide help to your servants, and make it be that they prevail over their enemies; *and let your right hand be lifted,* that is, let your goodness be raised up on high [in kindness], freely communicating the gifts of graces and virtues.

88{89}[15] *Justice and judgment are the preparation of your throne. Mercy and truth shall go before your face:*

> *Iustitia et iudicium praeparatio sedis tuae; misericordia et veritas praecedent faciem tuam.*

88{89}[15] *Iustitia et iudicium praeparatio sedis tuae, just and judgment are the preparation of your throne:* that is, by justice and judgment you yourself are worthy to judge; and your throne, that is, your judcial power, is ready, is fitted to give judgment, and is suited to restore things upon judgment. For by justice, every person will receive that which is his due, and the judge is worthy to adjudicate the judgment, which is an act of

---

102 *Cf.* Gen. 18:14a: *Is there anything hard to God?*
103 Job 5:18.
104 Heb. 10:31.
105 Job 13:21a.
106 Prov. 3:16.

justice. Or [alternatively, we can understand it] thus: *Justice and judgment are the preparation of your throne,* that is, a person is made worthy so that he may sit—as the Lord sits, awaits, and reposes upon his throne or inner chamber—by a just manner of living, and by the right judgment of those things which are one's own. And so to such a man the Savior says: *We will come to him, and will make our abode with him.*[107]

Misericordia, mercy by which you take away fault and bestow grace, *et veritas, and truth,* which you give as you have promised: for both mercy and truth are concurrent in all your works; *praecedent faciem tuam, shall go before your face,* that is, before your spiritual presence, by which daily you appear to your elect through contemplation: according to that said by the Apostle, *but we all beholding the glory of the Lord with open face.*[108] For God is not before someone through truthful contemplation unless he is first forgiven of his sins by his mercy and is given grace: and then, as he promised, he manifests himself formed by faith. Or [alternatively]: These two—*mercy and truth*—*shall go before your face,* that is, before your coming or the re-presentation of your face when you will appear in the final judgment. For then, indeed, will be the time of justice and of judgment; but in the interim is a time of mercy and truth.

88{89}[16]   *Blessed is the people that know jubilation. They shall walk, O Lord, in the light of your countenance:*

   Beatus populus qui scit iubilationem: Domine, in lumine vultus tui ambulabunt.

88{89}[17]   *And in your name they shall rejoice all the day, and in your justice they shall be exalted.*

   Et in nomine tuo exsultabunt tota die; et in iustitia tua exaltabuntur.

88{89}[16] *Beatus populus, blessed is the people,* now in hope, *qui scit, that know* by relish or experience, *iubilationem, jubilation,* that is, the ineffable exhilaration of the mind in God. Indeed, jubilation or joy is a certain excessive and unusual exhilaration in God, so burning and so bursting forth and vehement, that it is not possible fully to explain it, nor is it possible totally to hide it. This jubilation is caused by contemplation, and sometimes it proceeds from the contemplation of the divine goodness in himself, whose blessedness is praised; but sometimes it is

---

107   John 14:23b.
108   2 Cor. 3:18a.

from the contemplation of the divine benefits. And in a most true way, blessed in hope is he who rejoices in these considerations in so vehement a manner. For such rejoicing, to be sure, is a sweet and prodigious fore-taste of future happiness. Because of this joy, one exhilarating in God in this manner is not able to contain himself: sweet tears are shed by the eyes, and the mind is astonished that God has deigned to bestow upon him such a grace.

Domine, in lumine vultus tui; O Lord, in the light of your countenance, both natural and supernatural, *ambulabunt, they shall walk* faithfully from the good to the better, *from virtue to virtue,*[109] from wayfaring to the heavenly homeland, from consideration to good works. For there is in us a natural light, impressed upon our soul by the divine knowledge or countenance, which discerns what is good and evil, true and false. Of this an earlier Psalm says, *the light of your countenance, O Lord, is signed upon us.*[110] We are going in this way when we follow the judgment of reason. But because man is ordained towards supernatural beatitude — which is the vision of God face-to-face — the natural light [of reason] does not suffice for a meritorious life. Therefore, man is in need of a supernatural light, namely, faith and the gifts of the Holy Spirit: and so the elect walk in natural light that is informed by, and conforms to, the supernatural light, ordering all their works to the glory of God and eternal life. Whence the Savior said: *Walk while you have the light, that the darkness overtake you not.*[111] The sinners do not walk in this life, but rather in the error of sensuality and the ignorance of vice: of which way is written, The way of the wicked *shall be as a slippery way in the dark, for they shall be driven on, and fall therein.*[112] 88{89}[17] *Et in nomine tuo,* and in your name, that is, in you yourself, *exsultabunt tota die, they shall rejoice all the day,* for in their heart the light of grace produces a spiritual day; or [alternatively]: *all the day,* that is, as assiduously as is possible in the present life; *et in iustitia tua, and in your justice,*[113] that is, by the help of your grace, not in natural or personal power, *exaltabuntur, they shall be exalted,* defeating the world, the flesh, and the devil, and straining towards the heavenly kingdom.

---

109   Ps. 83:8a.
110   Ps. 4:7a.
111   John 12:35b.
112   Jer. 23:12a.
113   *E. N.* The text has *virtute,* "virtue," instead of *iustitia,* "justice" as is correct. The editor has marked the error in the margin.

88{89}[18] *For you are the glory of their strength: and in your good pleasure shall our horn be exalted.*

Quoniam gloria virtutis eorum tu es, et in beneplacito tuo exaltabitur cornu nostrum.

88{89}[19] *For our assumption is of the Lord, and of our king the holy one of Israel.*[114]

Quia Domini est assumptio nostra, et sancti Israel regis nostri.

88{89}[18] *Quoniam gloria virtutis eorum, for . . . the glory of their strength,* that is, the object, cause, and end of glorification, wherein they glory by their perfection and their good works, *tu es, you are:* because they do not rejoice in themselves, but in you, ascribing all things to you: as the Apostle says: *He that glories, let him glory in the Lord.*[115] For this reason, Isaiah asserts: *The Lord of hosts shall be a crown of glory, and a garland of joy to the residue of his people.*[116] *Et in beneplacito tuo, and in your good pleasure,* that is, your kindly will, or through the effects of your will in us which makes us pleasing to you, namely, through your grace, *exaltabitur cornu nostrum, shall our horn be exalted,*[117] that is, our strength and dignity, by which we are said to be *a chosen people, a kingly priesthood, a holy nation:*[118] for our strength perseveres, advances, and is crowned by your grace. The reason for this is **88{89}[19]** *Quia Domini est assumptio nostra, for our assumption is of the Lord,* that is, we are mercifully adopted by God, who receives us under his protection and grace, lest we be devoured by enemies; *et, and,* this assumption is *sancti Israel regis nostri, of our king the holy one of Israel,* that is, is of God as its originator, who is the Saint of Saints and the sanctifier of Israel and our king. Or [alternatively]: *of the Lord,* that is, of the Son of God, *is our assumption,* because in his most holy Incarnation, he assumed our nature.

---

114   E. N. I have departed from the Douay-Rheims which translates the Latin *assumptio* (taking, receiving, assumption, even adoption) as "protection." By staying with the more literal translation, the verse fits in better with Denis's comparison of God's assumption of us as his protectorate (his adoption of us as his people) and with the Son of God's assumption (or adoption) of our nature.

115   1 Cor. 1:31.

116   Is. 28:5.

117   E. N. For the scriptural notion of *cornu,* "horn," *see* footnote 17-141 in Volume 1.

118   1 Pet. 2:9a.

ARTICLE LXVI

CONTINUATION OF THE EXPOSITION
OF THE SAME EIGHTY-EIGHTH PSALM:

88{89}[20] *Then you spoke in a vision to your saints, and said: I have laid help upon one that is mighty, and have exalted one chosen out of my people.*

Tunc locutus es in visione sanctis tuis, et dixisti: Posui adiutorium in potente; et exaltavi electum de plebe mea.

88{89}[21] *I have found David my servant: with my holy oil I have anointed him.*

Inveni David, servum meum, oleo sancto meo unxi eum.

88{89}[20] *Tunc locutus es in visione sanctis tuis, etc. Then you spoke in a vision to your saints, etc.* Some literally expound this part of this Psalm up to that part that states, *but you have rejected and despised* as relating to David, but some to Christ.[119] Both of these expositions will be touched upon; but the first will be handled cursorily because it is less fruitful; and the second will be explained with greater diligence. It should be noted that in the feasts involving several bishop confessors, the Church sings some of the verses of this Psalm which follow.[120]

The prophet addressing the Lord, therefore, says: *Tunc, then,* that is, when these things were divinely revealed and inspired, *locutus es, you spoke* with an interior locution, namely, *in visione, in a vision,* a prophetic one, *sanctis tuis, to your saints,* [that is,] to your holy Prophets, about the anointment of David, and of the succession and progression of David's reign. These saints were Samuel, Nathan, and Gad.[121] *Et dixisti, and you said* through them: *Posui adiutorium, I have laid help,* my help, *in potente, upon one that is mighty,* that is, in David, the strong of hand, who (as we read) while still a youth, killed a lion and bear.[122] And so David, by means of my help, defended his kingdom and his people; *et*

---

119   E. N. That is, Ps. 88:20–39.
120   E. N. Some of the verses of this Psalm that follow are used in the Commons of several Confessor Bishops. Denis is implying that if the verses pertained only literally to David, they would not be used to celebrate the feasts that involve several popes or bishops who are confessors.
121   1 Sam. 16:1, 3, 12; 2 Sam. 7:12–17; 1 Sam. 22:5; 2 Sam. chp. 24.
122   1 Sam. 17:34–36.

exaltavi electum, and I have exalted one chosen, namely, David, *de plebe mea, from my people,* that is, I chose him before all others to be king: for David was revealed to be king in the second book of Samuel and the first book of Chronicles.[123] **88{89}[21]** *Inveni David servum meum, I have found David my servant,* that is, I have considered that David is my faithful and true servant: and so *oleo sancto meo unxi eum, with my holy oil I have anointed him* as king through Samuel. Indeed, three times David was anointed: first, in the house of his father by Samuel, when he was a young lad and shepherd of his father's sheep;[124] the second, after the death of Saul in Hebron, to be king over the house of Judah alone;[125] the third, over the entire kingdom of Israel.[126]

88{89}[22] *For my hand shall help him: and my arm shall strengthen him.*

Manus enim mea auxiliabitur ei, et brachium meum confortabit eum.

88{89}[23] *The enemy shall have no advantage over him: nor the son of iniquity have power to hurt him.*

Nihil proficiet inimicus in eo, et filius iniquitatis non apponet nocere ei.

88{89}[24] *And I will cut down his enemies before his face; and them that hate him I will put to flight.*

Et concidam a facie ipsius inimicos ejus, et odientes eum in fugam convertam.

88{89}[22] *Manus enim mea, for my hand,* that is, my power, *auxiliabitur ei, shall help him* against adversities; *et brachium meum, and my arm,* that is, my fortitude, *confortabit eum, shall strengthen him* in reign and prosperity. **88{89}[23]** *Nihil proficient inimicus, the enemy shall have no advantage,* the invisible [enemy], namely, the devil, *in eo, over him* at the end of the day. For although he may occasionally lead him to a great downfall, he will not finally be able to ensnare him; but also *all bad things work together unto good,*[127] for after the sin he will rise again more cautious and more humble. Or [alternatively], *the visible enemy shall have no advantage,* namely, Saul, *over him* in that he will not be

---

123 2 Sam. 6:21; 1 Chr. 28:4–7.
124 1 Sam. 16:11–13.
125 2 Sam. 2:4.
126 2 Sam. 5:3.
127 Rom. 8:28.

able to kill him.[128] *Et filius iniquitatis non apponet nocere ei, nor the son of iniquity shall have the power to hurt him*: that is, Ahithophel, Doeg, Absalom, Sheba, the son of Bichri, or any other unjust adversaries of David, shall not frequently repeat their persecution of David: for I will ward off evil from him, and I will cause that his enemies cease from their persecution, killing them, as Absalom and Sheba were killed,[129] or converting them by repentance, as Shimei repented.[130] **88{89}[24]** *Et concidam a facie ipsius, and I will cut down . . . before his face*, that is, I will separate, destroy, and repel before his face *inimicus eius, his enemies*, the Philistines, Amalekites, and the Ammonites; *et odientes eum in fugam convertam, and them that hate him I will put to flight*. According to the book of second Samuel, this frequently is narrated to have occurred.

88{89}[25]   *And my truth and my mercy shall be with him: and in my name shall his horn be exalted.*

Et veritas mea et misericordia mea cum ipso; et in nomine meo exaltabitur cornu eius.

88{89}[26]   *And I will set his hand in the sea; and his right hand in the rivers.*

Et ponam in mari manum eius, et in fluminibus dexteram eius.

88{89}[25] *Et veritas mea, and my truth*, that I will fulfill promises, *et misericordia mea, and my mercy*, that I forgive sins, *cum ipso; et in nomine meo; shall be with him, and in my name*, that is, in my power, *exaltabitur cornu eius, shall his horn be exalted*, that is, [shall] his royal dignity [be exalted]. **88{89}[26]** *Et ponam in mari manum eius, and I will set his hand in the sea*, that is, his fortitude [in the sea]. For David subjected the Philistines, whose land was situated by the Mediterranean Sea, to himself. *Et in fluminibus dexteram eius, and his right hand in the rivers*, that is, his great power I will place in Syria, in between the rivers there situated. For this reason, Syria is called Mesopotamia (from "meso" which means between and "potamos" which means river): for it lies in between both sides of these rivers.[131] For according to the book of Samuel, we read that David warred against Syria, and that Syria served him under a payment of tribute.[132]

---

128   1 Sam. chps. 18, 19, et., *passim.*
129   2 Sam. 18:14 (Absalom); 20:22 (Sheba).
130   2 Sam. 19:18–20.
131   E. N. Assyria, or Syria, lay between the rivers of the Euphrates and the Tigris.
132   2 Sam. chp. 8.

88{89}[27] *He shall cry out to me: You are my Father: my God, and the support of my salvation.*

Ipse invocabit me: Pater meus es tu, Deus meus, et susceptor salutis meae.

88{89}[28] *And I will make him my firstborn, high above the kings of the earth.*

Et ego primogenitum ponam illum, excelsum prae regibus terrae.

88{89}[29] *I will keep my mercy for him forever: and my covenant faithful to him.*

In aeternum servabo illi misericordiam meam, et testamentum meum fidele ipsi.

88{89}[30] *And I will make his seed to endure for evermore: and his throne as the days of heaven.*

Et ponam in saeculum saeculi semen eius, et thronum eius sicut dies caeli.

88{89}[27] *Ipse invocabit me: Pater meus es tu, Deus meus, et susceptor salutis meae; he shall cry out to me: you are my Father, my God, and the support of my salvation.* Often in this book, David in his prayers calls the Lord of all, his God and the support of his salvation. It is not a wonder if such a holy prophet calls God in his prayers Father, since even the presumptuous Elihu presumed also to call God that: *My Father, . . . cease not from the man of iniquity.*[133] **88{89}[28]** *Et ego primogenitum ponam illum, and I will make him my firstborn,* that is, more honored and more excellent than all others: as the firstborn is customarily more honored; *excelsum prae regibus terrae, high above the kings of the earth,* namely, of the land of Judah, for there was no one like him in that land, even though Solomon, with respect to some things, exceeded him.[134] Or [we can understand it in this way], *above the kings of the earth* reigning in his vicinity, whom he subjected to himself. **88{89}[29]** *In aeternum servabo illi misericordiam meam, I will keep my mercy for him forever:* for he will not be abandoned in the end, although for a time he will be allowed to fall into the evil of fault and punishment;[135] *et testamentum, and my*

---

133   Job 34:36. E. N. Elihu was one of Job's interlocutors, less antagonistic than the others (Bildad, Eliphaz, and Zophar).
134   *Cf.* 1 Kings 3:12.
135   2 Sam. chp. 11. E. N. A reference to his sinful actions with Bathsheba, the daughter of Eliam, and in regard to her husband, Uriah the Hittite.

covenant, that is, the promise which I made of the continuation of his kingdom, [136] *fideli ipsi*, *faithful to him*, that is, faithfully fulfilled in him. And so it adds: **88{89}[30]** *Et ponam in saeculum saeculi semen eius*, and *I will make his seed to endure for evermore*, that is, I will not permit his sons to be abandoned, but his seed shall extend out even unto Christ, and it will be perpetual in him; *et thronum eius*, and *his throne*, that is, the scepter or his regal power, I will place and will continue, *sicut*, *as* do now continue *dies caeli*, *the days of heaven*, that is, days caused by movements of the sun, for the kingdom of David is perpetual in Christ.

88{89}[31] *And if his children forsake my law, and walk not in my judgments:*

Si autem dereliquerint filii eius legem meam, et in iudiciis meis non ambulaverint.

88{89}[32] *If they profane my justices: and keep not my commandments:*

Si iustitias meas profanaverint, et mandata mea non custodierint.

88{89}[33] *I will visit their iniquities with a rod: and their sins with stripes.*

Visitabo in virga iniquitates eorum, et in verberibus peccata eorum.

88{89}[34] *But my mercy I will not take away from him: nor will I suffer my truth to fail.*

Misericordiam autem meam non dispergam ab eo, neque nocebo in veritate mea.

88{89}[35] *Neither will I profane my covenant: and the words that proceed from my mouth I will not make void.*

Neque profanabo testamentum meum, et quae procedunt de labiis meis non faciam irrita.

Then, in order that David does not imagine that this promise might be frustrated because of the sins of his posterity, therefore, the Lord adds [some words] regarding the kindly correction of the children of David: **88{89}[31]** *Si autem dereliquerint filii eius*, and *if his children forsake*, namely, the kings and the children born from them [forsake], *legem meam*, *my law*: as even many of them did, namely, Rehoboam, Ahaz,

---

136   2 Sam. 7:12–16.

Amon, and Zedekiah.[137] **88{89}[32]** *Si iustitias meas, if . . . my justices,* that is, the just laws and the ceremonies handed over by me, *profanaverint, they profane,* that is, were to be transgressed, and they would be led as it were to defilement, *et mandata mea non custodierint, and keep not my commandments:* **88{89}[33]** *Visitabo in virga, I will visit . . . with a rod,* with paternal correction, *iniquitates eorum, their iniquities,* punishing them temporarily, so that the might wish to repent: at is clear with Manasseh and Uzziah;[138] *et in verberibus, and with stripes* of eternal damnation will I visit *peccata eorum, their sins.* **88{89}[34]** *Misericordiam autem meam, but my mercy,* that is, the effect of my kindliness, namely the perpetuation of his kingdom, *non dispergam ab eo, I will not take away from him:* for the previously mentioned kings, although iniquitous, had successors that reigned even up to Zedekiah, and from that time there continued to be children of David even up to the time of Christ. **88{89} [35]** *Neque nocebo in veritate mea, neither will I profane my covenant,* that is, I will not violate my promise; *et quae procedunt de labiis meis, and the words that proceed from my mouth,* that is, the words of my mouth, *non faciam irrita, I will not make void,* that is, without effect.

88{89}[36] *Once have I sworn by my holiness: I will not lie unto David:*

   Semel iuravi in sancto meo, si David mentiar.

88{89}[37] *His seed shall endure forever.*

   Semen eius in aeternum manebit.

88{89}[38] *And his throne as the sun before me: and as the moon perfect forever, and a faithful witness in heaven.*

   Et thronus eius sicut sol in conspectu meo, et sicut luna perfecta in aeternum, et testis in caelo fidelis.

88{89}[36] *Semel iuravi in sancto meo, once have I sworn by my holiness,* that is, by myself, being essentially holy, and the Saint of Saints, as elsewhere I swore upon myself saying: *By my own self have I sworn;*[139] *si, if,* standing for not,[140] *David mentiar, I will [not] lie unto*

---

137   1 Kings 14:21–22; 2 Kings 16:2–4; 21:20–22; 24:19.
138   2 Chr. 33:11–12; 26:16–21.
139   Gen. 22:16a.
140   E. N. In Latin, in certain contexts, as in this situation, the conjunction *si*, "if," implies a negative conclusion: so here, the Latin *si David mentiar*, literally, "if I will lie unto David," implies the opposite, thus "I will not lie unto David," as the translators of the Douay-Rheims have recognized in their translation. So here *si* should stand for "not."

David: for I will fulfill that which I have said. For **88{89}[37]** *Semen eius in aeternum manebit, his seed shall endure forever*: for in Christ, the son of David is perpetuated. **88{89}[38]** *Et thronus eius sicut sol in conspectu meo, et sicut luna perfecta in aeternum; and his throne as the sun before me, and as the moon perfect forever*: that is, as the sun and moon in the natural world never fail, so the throne of David shall never fail: because Christ, his son, reigns in the Church militant by faith even until the end of time; but in the Church triumphant he reigns by glory without end. *Et, and* of this thing is *testis in caelo fidelis, a faithful witness in heaven*, namely, God, holy and blessed, who is the cause and the witness of these things: which he says through Jeremiah: *I am the judge and the witness.*[141] For these things God states elsewhere, saying: *If my covenant with the day can be made void, and my covenant with the night, that there should not be day and night in their season, also my covenant with David my servant may be made void, that he should not have a son to reign upon his throne.*[142] And again: *If I have not set my . . . laws to heaven and earth, surely I will also cast off the seed of Jacob, and of David my servant, so as not to take any of his seed to be rulers.*[143]

88{89}[39]   *But you have rejected and despised: you have been angry with your Anointed.*

Tu vero repulisti et despexisti; distulisti Christum tuum.

88{89}[40]   *You have overthrown the covenant of your servant: you have profaned his sanctuary on the earth.*

Evertisti testamentum servi tui; profanasti in terra sanctuarium eius.

88{89}[41]   *You have broken down all its walls: you have made its strength fear.*

Destruxisti omnes sepes eius; posuisti firmamentum eius formidinem.

However, because the reign of David suffered a long and great interruption, namely between the time of Zedekiah or thereabouts even unto Christ, so from this casting down of kingdom of David and of

---

141   Jer. 29:23b.
142   Jer. 33:20–21.
143   Jer. 33:25–26.

its delay or postponement until Christ's coming, in whom the kingdom of David was restored and perpetuated, the prophet complains: 88{89} [39] *Tu vero repulisti, but you have rejected* David from his kingdom, *et despexisti, and despised* him, that is, his posterity: and this most significantly occurred during the time of the Babylonian captivity, for from that time no one from the tribe Judah reigned even unto John Hyrcanus.[144] *Distulisti Christum tuum, you have been angry with your anointed,* that is, you have long delayed to send the Messiah king into the world. 88{89}[40] *Evertisti testamentum servi tui, you have overthrown the covenant of your servant,*[145] that is, you have interrupted the promises made to king David because of the sins of his children; *profanasti in terra sanctuarium eius, you have profaned his sanctuary on earth,* that is, you have allowed the Chaldeans to profane his temple in Jerusalem,[146] whose expenses and materials David had readied;[147] and by them 88{89} [41] *Destruxisti, you have broken down* permissively *omnes sepes eius, all its walls,* that is, the strongholds and walls of Jerusalem, and of the other towns of Judah;[148] *posuisti firmamentum eius formidinem, you have made its strength fear:* that is, you have allowed the strong men and the towns of the reign of David to be so devastated and destroyed so that all seeing it were terrified, and the sons of David and the people of his kingdom were full of fear. This also Jeremiah often predicted of the future time of the Babylonian captivity, God saying through him: I will place you under a curse and *a perpetual hissing,* and an *astonishment* to all the kingdoms of the earth.[149]

---

144   E. N. John Hyrcanus (164–104 BC), was the Maccabean (Hasmonean) Jewish high priest and leader of the Jews, eventually becoming ethnarch (semi-autonomous leader of the Jews under the Hellenistic Seleucid Empire). John Hyrcanus ruled between 134 BC and 104 BC.

145   E. N. Denis's text has *avertisti,* "you have averted"; however, the editor suggests in the margin the word *evertisti,* "you have overturned" or "you have overthrown." The Sixto-Clementine has *evertisti.*

146   2 Kings 25:9–17.

147   1 Chr. 22:14.

148   2 Kings 25:10.

149   Jer. 18:16; 19:8; 25:9, 8. E. N. This is a patchwork combining four similar verses of Jeremiah: Jer. 18:16 (*That their land might be given up to desolation, and to a perpetual hissing: every one that shall pass by it, shall be astonished, and wag his head*); Jer. 19:8 (*And I will make this city an astonishment, and a hissing: every one that shall pass by it, shall be astonished, and shall hiss because of all the plagues thereof*), Jer. 25:9b (*I will destroy them, and make them an astonishment and a hissing, and perpetual desolations*), and Jer. 25:18b (*to make them a desolation, and an astonishment, and a hissing, and a curse, as it is at this day*).

88{89}[42] *All that pass by the way have robbed him: he is become a reproach to his neighbors.*

Diripuerunt eum omnes transeuntes viam; factus est opprobrium vicinis suis.

88{89}[43] *You have set up the right hand of them that oppress him: you have made all his enemies to rejoice.*

Exaltasti dexteram deprimentium eum; laetificasti omnes inimicos eius.

88{89}[44] *You have turned away the help of his sword; and have not assisted him in battle.*

Avertisti adiutorium gladii eius, et non es auxiliatus ei in bello.

88{89}[45] *You destroyed it from purification: and you have cast his throne down to the ground.*[150]

Destruxisti eum ab emundatione, et sedem eius in terram collisisti.

88{89}[46] *You have shortened the days of his time: you have covered it with confusion.*

Minorasti dies temporis eius; perfudisti eum confusione.

88{89}[42] *Diripuerunt eum omnes transeuntes viam, all that pass by the way have robbed him,* that is, the Samaritans and the rest passing by Judaea and killing the Jewish people; *factus est opprobrium vicinis suis, he is become a reproach to his neighbors,* namely, the Idumeans, the Ammonites, the Moabites, the Philistines, all of whom derided the Jewish people and rejoiced in their calamity. 88{89}[43] *Exaltasti dexteram deprimentium eum, you have set up the right hand of them that oppress him,* that is, you have allowed the hand of his enemies against him to prevail; *laetificasti, you have made ... rejoice* in a permissive way *omnes inimico eius, all his enemies* which have just been named. 88{89}[44] *Avertisti adiutorium gladii eius, you have turned away the help of his sword:* that is, his arms of war were of no benefit, and the men who were warriors yielded and withdrew from them. Whence it is written that all the warriors with Zedekiah fled from him.[151] *Et non es auxiliatus ei in bello, and have not assisted him in battle,* in which Nebuchadnezzar with his army fought him. 88{89}[45]

---

150 E. N. I have translated *destruxisti eum ab emundatione* as "you have destroyed it from purification," in lieu of the Douay-Rheims's "you have made his purification cease."
151 2 Kings 25:5.

Destruxisti eum, you have destroyed it, namely, the people and the kingdom of the Jews, *ab emundatione, from purification,* that is from the purification of the temple: which [purification rites] they were unable to have, with the temple destroyed and the Jews being transferred over to Babylon; *et sedem eius, and his throne,* that is, the regal majesty *in terram collisisti, you have cast down to the ground,* that is, you have led to nothing, as when a clay vessel is thrown down [to the ground]. **88{89}[46]** *Minorasti dies temporis eius, you have shortened the days of his time:* that is, in large part you have destroyed the Jewish people from their youth; and the death of nearly all was hastened by sword, famine, or plague, in accordance with the prophecy of Jeremiah.[152] *Perfudisti eum confusio, you have covered it with confusion,* that is, filled it with contempt and derision.

Some [commentators] explain those things relating to the oppression and the casting out of the kingdom and the people of the Jews presented under the name of David, both as relating to their captivity and persecution by the Chaldeans and as pertaining to the devastation and the casting out of the Jews inflicted by the Romans.[153] And though from a literal standpoint these [verses] can be applied to this situation [involving the Romans], the earlier exposition [as it applying to the Chaldeans, rather than the Romans] is more fitting because in the beginning of the description of this devastation [in verse **88:39**], the prophet laments of the delay or postponement of the coming of Christ, saying: *But you have rejected and despised: you have been angry with your Anointed.*[154]

88{89}[47]   *How long, O Lord, do you turn away unto the end? Shall your anger burn like fire?*

Usquequo, Domine, avertis in finem: exardescet sicut ignis ira tua?

Consequently, the prophet prays for the restoration of the kingdom of David: **88{89}[47]** *Usquequo, Domine, avertis; how long, O Lord, do you turn away* your people from you, and your mercy from them, *in finem, unto the end,* namely, as long as seventy years? For from the time that they

---

152   Jer. 11:22: *Therefore thus says the Lord of hosts: Behold I will visit upon them: and their young men shall die by the sword, their sons and their daughters shall die by famine.*
153   E. N. This, of course, refers to the destruction of Jerusalem by the Romans around 70 AD.
154   E. N. Since the anointed Messiah had already appeared in Jesus Christ *before* the devastation of Jerusalem, the devastation prophesied in the Psalm would have had to occur *before* the coming of the Christ. Consequently, it could not refer to the Roman destruction of Jerusalem, and so refers necessarily to the Chaldean persecution.

had departed from Egypt, never before were the Jews repulsed by God and oppressed by their enemies as long a the time as they were during the Babylonian captivity — excepting their final rejection, of which the Lord spoke about through the prophet Amos: *For three crimes of Israel, and for four I will not convert him.*[155] *Exardescet sicut ignis ira tua? Shall your anger burn like fire?* That is, how long will the vengeance of your justice rage upon us, completely consuming us, as fire consumes dry straw.

88{89}[48]   *Remember what my substance is. For have you made all the children of men in vain?*

Memorare quae mea substantia. Numquid enim vane constituisti omnes filios hominum?

And then speaking in the person of all the people, and asserting a kind of persuasive plea so as to provoke the mercy of God, he adds: 88{89}[48] *Memorare quae mea substantia, remember what my substance is,* that is, consider how fragile, prone to fall, and imperfect human nature is. For this reason, it is written in Ezra: *What is a corruptible race, that you are so bitter against it?*[156] And in Genesis also: *The imagination and thought of man's heart are prone to evil from his youth.*[157] By this sort of reasoning, the [guilt of the] sin of man is lessened and [the hope for] forgiveness increased. And rightly, O Lord, you ought to remember this: *Numquid enim vane constituisti omnes filios hominum? For have you made all the children of men in vain?* Of course not. For that which is ordained to no due end is vainly and uselessly made. Now, since God, powerful and wise, is the highest good, he has designed all things to have some end. Whence, according to the Philosopher, God and nature do nothing in vain.[158] And Scripture says: *You being master, O Lord, judge with tranquility, and with great favor dispose of us;*[159] and again,

---

155   Amos 2:6a. E. N. In his *Commentary on Amos*, Denis observes that this verse might be understood literally as saying: "because of the sins of the ten tribes [of Israel], repeated for the third and fourth times, I will not spare them, but I will deliver them to my enemies." Doctoris Ecstatici D. Dionysii Cartusiani, *Opera Omnia*, Vol. 10 (Montreuil: 1900), 376.

156   4 Ezra 8:34: *But what is man that you angry with him, or what is a corruptible race, that you are so bitter against it?*

157   Gen. 8:24b.

158   E. N. The reference is to Aristotle's principle that nature does nothing in vain. This principle is the centerpiece of Aristotle's "teleological" understanding of nature (that nature has an "end," a *telos*, a purpose, and so intimates a design and a Designer). This teleology also is a source of natural moral law, for the end informs proper use. *See, e.g., De anima*, III, 12 (434a 30–31).

159   Wis. 12:18a.

So much then as you are just, you order all things justly.[160] For God rules all things in the manner that is written: *What other has he appointed over the earth? Or whom has he set over the world which he made?*[161] Whence holy Job again says, *The end of all things he considers;*[162] and yet again, *He beholds the ends of the world: and looks on all things that are under heaven.*[163] For this reason, it is elsewhere said: *You have ordered all things in measure, and number, and weight.*[164]

And so, O Lord, because you have made man not in vain, but with a certain end in mind, namely supernatural and eternal beatitude — which end man is unable to attain without your grace and great mercy — so it behooves you to have mercy, and to kindly hear me who am praying, because otherwise we are unable to be saved or to obtain this end. However, they who do not obtain this end, but are eternally condemned are not made in vain, because God with his antecedent will wants all men to be saved, according to the Damascene.[165] For this reason, the Savior said: *It is not the will of your Father, who is in heaven, that one of these little ones should perish.*[166] And the Apostle [Paul] said: God *will have all men to be saved, and to come to the knowledge of the truth.*[167] And so Ezechiel says: *Return and live,* says the Lord, for I desire not the death of the sinner, but that he be converted and live.[168] The ungodly are therefore created for eternal life, and for their last end who is God. This Solomon also proclaims, saying: *The Lord has made all things for himself.*[169] Although the unjust are deprived of this end, they are not for all that created vainly, for their damnation increases the glory of the elect, commends divine justice, and provides increase to the glory of God.

---

160   Wis. 12:15a.
161   Job 34:13.
162   Job 28:3a.
163   Job 28:24.
164   Wis. 11:21b.
165   E. N. The reference is probably to *On the Orthodox Faith*, II, 29, which is cited by St. Thomas in his *Summa Theologiae* Ia, q. 19, art. 6, s.c., and which article discusses the question of whether God's will is always fulfilled and 1 Tim 2:4's statement that God wills all men to be saved and to come to the knowledge of the truth. St. Thomas explains that in a similar manner, a just judge antecedently wants all men to live, but consequently wills a convicted murderer to be hanged, so does God antecedently will all men to be saved, but, consequent to the sins of some men and their free rejection of grace, he wills them consequently to be damned. ST Ia, q. 19, art. 6, co.
166   Matt. 18:14.
167   1 Tim. 2:4.
168   Cf. Ez. 18:32, 23.
169   Prov. 16:4a.

Whence the Apostle says: *In a great house there are not only vessels of gold and silver, but also of wood and earth.*[170]

88{89}[49]   *Who is the man that shall live, and not see death: that shall deliver his soul from the hand of hell?*

Quis est homo qui vivet et non videbit mortem? Eruet animam suam de manu inferi?

Now the fragility of our substance is declared, when he adds: **88{89} [49]** *Quis est homo qui vivet, et non videbit mortem? Who is the man that shall live and not see death?* It is as if he were saying, "There is no such man this living in this world who does not die." For all men die, both by the necessity of their natural condition and by reason of original sin — except for Christ, who, according to the teachers, died by willing it freely. For Christ as man alone was not able to die because of his union with the Word, but also because of the beatitude of his soul, which was so great that it redounded so fully into the body of Christ and its inferior powers that — unless there had been a divine dispensation suspending it — Christ's body would have been impassible and Christ as man would have been completely immortal. [This is so] according to Augustine in his epistle to Dioscorus.[171] And what man living *eruet animam suam de manu inferi, shall deliver his soul from the hand of hell,* that is, from infernal damnation, by mere natural virtue and without the help of Christ? It is as if he were saying, "None other than Christ." First, because before his coming all saints regardless [of

---

170   2 Tim. 2:20. *E. N.* The verse continues: *and some indeed unto honor, but some unto dishonor.*

171   *E. N.* The principle is fleshed out in St. Augustine's Letter 118, 14 to Dioscorus: "God made the soul with such a powerful nature that in its full beatitude, which at the end of time is promised to the saints, there will also overflow into the inferior nature, which is the body, ... the vigor of incorruptibility." *Epistolae,* 118, 3, 14, PL 33, 439. It follows that since Christ enjoyed the fulness of the beatific vision even while in this life, this would have redounded to his body, making it incapable of suffering without his willing otherwise, which he did for the sake of our salvation, as St. Thomas observes. ST IIIa, q. 14, arg. 2, co., & ad 2. We might also look at the *De Fide Orthodoxa,* III, 27, of St. John of Damascus: "Since our Lord Jesus Christ was without sin, ... He was not subject to death, even though death had by sin entered into the world. And so for our sake He submits to death and dies and offers Himself to the Father as a sacrifice for us." This was voluntary: "For with him nothing is found to be one under compulsion; on the contrary, everything was done freely. Thus, it was by willing that ... that he died." St. John of Damascus, *Writings* (New York: Fathers of the Church, Inc. 1958), 324, 332. (trans., Frederic H. Chase, Jr.)

the circumstances] descended into hell.[172] It was to these that Christ by his own accord ultimately descended so that he might deliver them, as he said through Hosea: *I will deliver them out of the hand of death. I will redeem them from death: O death, I will be your death; O hell, I will be your bite.*[173] Second, because without the grace of God no adult is able to avoid mortal sin, specially since without faith and grace one does not know to what end he ought to direct his work.

88{89}[50] *Lord, where are your ancient mercies, according to what you did swear to David in your truth?*

Ubi sunt misericordiae tuae antiquae, Domine, sicut iurasti David in veritate tua?

Since this is the case, therefore the prophet prays for the grace of God and the coming of Christ. **88{89}[50]** *Ubi sunt misericordiae tuae antiquae, Domine; Lord, where are your ancient mercies,* that is, the great effects of your goodness promised from the beginning of the world to your elect, in which you promised that Christ would be sent? It is as if he said: "You, who from the most ancient times showed your mercy, now show it." *Sicut iurasti David in veritate tua, according to what you did swear to David in your truth,* that is, in yourself, who are the highest and unchangeable truth: you who promised to David that Christ would be born from his seed.

88{89}[51] *Be mindful, O Lord, of the reproach of your servants (which I have held in my bosom) of many nations:*

Memor esto, Domine, opprobrii servorum tuorum, quod continui in sinu meo, multarum gentium:

88{89}[52] *By which your enemies have reproached, O Lord; by which they have reproached the change of your Anointed.*

Quod exprobraverunt inimici tui, Domine, quod exprobraverunt commutationem Christi tui.

88{89}[53] *Blessed be the Lord in eternity. So be it! So be it!*

Benedictus Dominus in aeternum. Fiat! Fiat!

---

172   E. N. Those dying in a state of grace did not go to the hell of the damned, but the limbo of the Fathers (*limbus partum*), also known as Sheol or Abraham's bosom (*sinus Abrahae*).

173   Hosea 13:14.

88{89}[51] *Memor esto, Domine, opprobrii servorum tuorum; be mindful,*
O Lord, of the reproach of your servants, that is, take heed of how many
adversities your people are suffering as a result of their enemies, from which
they need to be delivered by Christ: *of the reproach,* I say, *quod continui*
in sinu meo, which I have held in my bosom, that is, which I have suffered
with equanimity in the middle of my heart; and of the reproach *multarum*
gentium, of many nations, inflicted upon your people by diverse nations.
This the prophet speaks in the person of the people suffering tribulations.
Jeremiah also prays that such reproach be removed from the faithful: *Give*
us not to be a reproach, he says, *for your name's sake, and do not cause in us*
disgrace.[174] **88{89}[52]** *Quod, by which* reproach *exprobraverunt, they have*
reproached, that is, by reproaching your people they have caused, *inimici*
tui, your enemies, the perverse and the unbeliever; *quod exprobraverunt*
commutationem Christi tui, by which they have reproached the change of your
Anointed, that is, by which reproach of your faithful they have objected the
change of your Christ, that is, his new doctrine, his marvelous manner of
living, and his ignominious passion. For the Jews who were perverse, laid
upon the early Church the charge that Christ taught in a manner that
contradicted the Prophets,[175] and that he ate with publicans and with
sinners.[176] Whence they said to Stephen: *For we have heard him say, that*
this Jesus of Nazareth shall destroy this place, and shall change the traditions
which Moses delivered unto us.[177] But the Pagans opposed themselves to
Christians by the fact that they believed in a man crucified and suspended
between two thieves. In Jerome's translation [from the Hebrew], we have
this: *By which they have reproached the paths of your Christ.* For the leaders
of the Jews along with their followers censured the words and the works
of Christ, and they afflicted the early Church because of its imitation of
the paths of Christ, and, after this, tyrants and false brethren and heretics
greatly persecuted [the early Church].

But because Christ accepted this change on our behalf, and God
bestowed upon us the grace of patience, so **88{89}[53]** *Benedictus Domi-*
nus in aeternum, blessed be the Lord in eternity, that is, let him be praised
by all without end, and blessed may he who knows him and glorifies
him be. *Fiat! Fiat! So be it! So be it!* That is, so may it be! So may it be!
This is repeated to suggest a zeal of ardent desire and to provoke the
affection in others.

---

174 Jer. 14:21a.
175 Mark 7:5.
176 Matt. 9:11.
177 Acts 6:14.

ARTICLE LXVII

EXPLANATION OF THE SAME WORDS
OF CHRIST AND HIS MEMBERS.

88{89}[20] *Then you spoke in a vision to your saints, and said: I have laid help upon one that is mighty, and have exalted one chosen out of my people.*

> *Tunc locutus es in visione sanctis tuis, et dixisti: Posui adiutorium in potente; et exaltavi electum de plebe mea.*

88{89}[20] *Tunc locutus es in visione sanctis tuis,* then you spoke in a vision to your saints. Then, it says, when you revealed to me from heaven those things just spoken, you spoke in a vision of your holy Prophets, to whom you customarily revealed yourself as if a member of the family or a friend, in the manner that Amos said, *The Lord God does nothing without revealing his secret to his servants the prophets.*[178] This is spoken in vision; it is not only an imaginary vision, but also an intellectual one: *for there is need of understanding in a vision,* as is stated in the tenth chapter of Daniel.[179] Indeed, sometimes [these occur] through dreams, according to this: *By a dream in a vision by night, . . .* God *opens the ears of men.*[180] But sometimes also when one is awake, as is clearly the case with Daniel:[181] and so did the divine mysteries appear to Moses, whom the Lord (that is, the angel of the Lord) spoke face to face, *as a man might customarily speak to his friend.*[182] *Et dixisti, and you said,* in the hearts of the Prophets by an internal inspiration; this this sort of speech is also the ministry of the angels, according to that which Zechariah revealed about himself: *And behold the angel that spoke in me went forth, and another angel went out to meet him, and he said to him: Run, speak to this young man.*[183] Or [alternatively], *you said* manifestly to some *by the mouth of your holy prophets, who are from the beginning.*[184] *Posuisti adiutorium, I have laid help,* my [help], namely, the redemption of the human race, *in potente, upon one that is mighty,* that is, in Christ, who

---

178   Amos 3:7.
179   Dan. 10:1.
180   Job 33:15a, 16b.
181   Dan. 10:4 *ff.*
182   Ex. 33:11.
183   Zech. 2:3–4a.
184   Luke 1:70.

is *the power of God and the wisdom* of the Father,[185] who (according to the Apostle [Paul]) upholds *all things by the word of his power, making purgation of sins.*[186] *Et exaltavit electum, and he exalted one chosen* and forechosen, as is foretold of him in the Song of Songs: *My beloved is white and ruddy, chosen out of thousands.*[187] Hence, according to the Apostle, *the Son of God was predestinated . . . in power, according to the spirit of sanctification.*[188] *De plebe mea, out of my people,* that is from the Jewish people, from whom Christ [was chosen]; or [alternatively], *out of my people,* for Christ is exalted above and beyond all other men.

88{89}[21] *I have found David my servant: with my holy oil I have anointed him.*

Inveni David, servum meum, oleo sancto meo unxi eum.

88{89}[21] *Inveni David, I have found David,* that is, Christ, strong of hand and with desirable aspect, *servum meum, my servant:* because as man, he was less than God and was his servant, as the Lord says of him through Isaiah: *Behold my servant, I will uphold him.*[189] And also with Ezechiel, Christ is both called David and the servant of God: *I will save my flock,* says the Lord, *and I will set up one shepherd over them, and he shall feed them, even my servant David.*[190] *Oleo sancto meo, with my holy oil,* that is the unction of the Holy Spirit, the plenitude of grace, and all the gifts of the Holy Spirit, *unxi eum, I have anointed him*: as has been previously stated in an earlier Psalm, *God, your God, has anointed you with the oil of gladness.*[191] For this reason, Christ asserts in another place: *The spirit of the Lord is upon me, because the Lord has anointed me.*[192] And the Evangelist says: *For God does not give the Spirit by measure,*[193] namely, to Christ as man. For the entire capacity of created nature in Christ was full of the grace of God.[194]

---

185   1 Cor. 1:24b.

186   Heb. 1:3b.

187   Songs 5:10.

188   Rom. 1:4a.

189   Is. 42:1a.

190   Ez. 34:22b–23a.

191   E. N. The editor notes in the margin that Denis's text say *oleo exsultationis,* "with the oil of exulation," but that *oleo letitiae,* "with the oil of gladness," as is contained in the Sixto-Clementine Vulgate is proper.

192   Is. 61:1a.

193   John 3:34: *For he whom God has sent, speaks the words of God: for God does not give the Spirit by measure.*

194   E. N. This grace derived from the anointing of the Holy Spirit is in addition to the grace of the hypostatic union and the beatific vision.

88{89}[22] *For my hand shall help him: and my arm shall strengthen him.*

> *Manus enim mea auxiliabitur ei, et brachium meum confortabit eum.*

88{89}[22] *Manus enim mea, for my hand,* that is, my divinity united to it, *auxiliabitur ei, shall help him* in all things. For the humanity of Christ was the animated instrument conjoined and proper to the power of divinity with which it was united and through which it worked, according to the Damascene, just as our body is a conjoined animated and proper instrument of our soul.[195] Whence Christ says through Isaiah: *The Lord God is my helper;*[196] and in the Gospel, *I cannot of myself do anything.*[197] *Et brachium meum confortabit eum, and my arm shall strengthen him.* In the way that the Holy Spirit is the finger of God[198] — for by him all truth is revealed to us, according to this, *When he, the Spirit of truth, is come, he will teach you all truth*[199] — so the arm of God is his only begotten Son, for through him all things are done. Of this arm is written in Isaiah: *The Lord has prepared his holy arm in the sight of all the Gentiles.*[200] And in another place: *He has showed might in his arm.*[201] And so it is [to be understood in this sense: *My arm,* that is, the Word or my Son, *shall strengthen him,* namely, Christ as man, assuming his humanity to himself in a personal union, and confirming him in the beatific enjoyment, and working together with him through singular grace.

---

195   E. N. This is the teaching of St. Thomas Aquinas, *e.g.,* SCG, lib. 4, cap. 41, n. 11: "The teachings of the ancient doctors are in accord that the human nature in Christ was a kind of instrument (*organum*) of the divinity, as the body is held to be an instrument (*organum*) of the soul." *See also Super Sent.,* lib. 3, d. 18, q. 1, a. 6, qc. 1, co. This teaching is derived from St. John of Damascus's teaching that Christ's humanity (his flesh, σάρξ, *sarx*) was an instrument of Christ's divinity (*instrumentum* or *organum divinitatis,* ὄργανον θεότητος, *organon theotētos*) in the *De Fide Orthodoxa,* III, 15, PG 94,1059–60.

196   Is. 50:7a.

197   John 5:30a.

198   E. N. The Holy Spirit is referred to as the "finger of God," the *digitus Dei,* due to such the combination of Luke 11:20 ("it is by the finger of God that I cast out devils") and Matt. 12:28 ("it is by the Spirit of God that I expel demons"). In the hymn *Veni Creator Spiritus,* the Holy Spirit is called the *digitus paternae dexterae,* the "finger of the Father's right hand."

199   John 16:13a.

200   Is. 52:10a.

201   Luke 1:51a.

88{89}[23]   *The enemy shall have no advantage over him: nor the son of
iniquity have power to hurt him.*

*Nihil proficiet inimicus in eo, et filius iniquitatis non apponet
nocere ei.*

88{89}[24]   *And I will cut down his enemies before his face; and them
that hate him I will put to flight.*

*Et concidam a facie ipsius inimicos ejus, et odientes eum in
fugam convertam.*

88{89}[23] *Nihil proficient inimicus in eo, the enemy shall have no
advantage over him,* namely, the devil, for the defeated and confounded
tempter departed from Christ who said to him, *Get behind me, Satan.*[202]
Et filius iniquitatis, nor the son of iniquity, that is, Judas, whom Christ in
the Gospel named a devil and the son of perdition;[203] or [alternatively],
the son of iniquity, that is the Hebrew people to whom Christ said, *You
are of your father the devil;*[204] *non apponet nocere ei, have power to hurt
him,* that is, he will not repeat the harm they inflicted upon Christ. For
although before the Resurrection they could kill him, yet afterwards they
were unfit to harm him in effect, for neither were they able to hold his
body in the sepulcher nor to impede the glory of the risen one. Indeed,
Christ rising again from the dead, dies now no more.[205] Or [alternatively],
he *shall have no power over him* in the soul, because they were not able to
cause spiritual injury to Christ: and that injury that they inflicted upon
his body, added to the glory of Christ and did so forever. Whence it is
said by Isaiah: *Who will contend with me? Let us stand together. Who is my
adversary? Let him come near to me.... Lo, they shall all be destroyed as a
garment.*[206] 88{89}[24] *Et concidam a facie ipsius inimicos eius, and I will
cut down his enemies before his face,* namely, the Jews, who were massacred,
sold into slavery, and dispersed throughout the world by the Roman army
because of their murder of Christ, in the manner that is written: *The Lord
my God will cast them away, because they hearkened not to him: and they
shall be wanderers among the nations.*[207] *Et odientes eum in fugam convertam,
and them that hate him I will put to flight:* for the aforementioned Jews
in Jerusalem fled from the face of the Romans, but they were unable to

202   Matt. 4:10.
203   John 6:71–72; 17:12.
204   John 8:44a.
205   Rom 6:9.
206   Is. 50:8, 9b.
207   Hosea 9:17.

escape. The demons also frequently fled from Christ and his ministers. And finally, in the day of judgment, all the adversaries of the Savior will desire to flee, according to this: *The kings of the earth, and the princes, and tribunes, and the rich, and the strong, . . . hid themselves in the dens and in the rocks of mountains, saying to the mountains and the rocks: Fall upon us, and hide us from the face of him that sits upon the throne.*[208]

88{89}[25]   And my truth and my mercy shall be with him: and in my name shall his horn be exalted.

Et veritas mea et misericordia mea cum ipso; et in nomine meo exaltabitur cornu eius.

88{89}[26]   And I will set his hand in the sea; and his right hand in the rivers.

Et ponam in mari manum eius, et in fluminibus dexteram eius.

88{89}[25] *Et veritas mea et misericordia mea cum ipso, and my truth and my mercy shall be with him.* For Christ was full of truth, as is written: *We saw his glory, the glory as it were of the only begotten of the Father, full of grace and truth.*[209] For the truth of God was with Christ since all things that had been predicted of Christ by the Prophets were fulfilled in him. And the children of falsity truly spoke: *Master, we know that you are a true speaker, and teach the way of God in truth, neither do you care for [what] any man [may think].*[210] With Christ, as there is with any just and infallible judge, there is also the truth of God. But the mercy of God also was with Christ: because by the mercy of God alone was his human nature assumed by the Word of God, preserved from all fault, and filled with the grace of all divine gifts; and Christ is ready to communicate to us his ample mercy. *Et in nomine meo exaltabitur cornu eius, and in my name shall his horn be exalted,* that is, the regal dignity, *so that all peoples, tribes and tongues shall minister to him.*[211] Hence, the Father or the Trinity says by Isaiah about the Christ: *Behold my servant shall understand, he shall be exalted, and extolled, and shall be exceeding high.*[212] 88{89}[26] *Et ponam in mari manum eius, and I will set his hand in the sea,* that is, Christ will dominate in the lands and with the peoples surrounding the sea. This we see fulfilled in Cyprus, Portugal, and other

---

208   Rev. 6:15–16.
209   John 1:14b.
210   Matt. 22:16.
211   Dan. 7:14.
212   Is. 52:13.

kingdoms. *Et in fluminibus dexteram eius, and his right hand in the rivers:* that is, I will place the strength of Christ in islands, so that the people dwelling in islands might obey Christ. Whence the Lord says through Isaiah: *I will send of them that shall be saved, to the Gentiles into the sea, into Africa, and Lydia.*[213] Elsewhere we also have: *They shall give glory to the Lord, and shall declare his praise in the islands.*[214]

88{89}[27]   He shall cry out to me: *You are my Father: my God, and the support of my salvation.*

     Ipse invocabit me: Pater meus es tu, Deus meus, et susceptor salutis meae.

88{89}[27] *Ipse invocabit me: Pater meus es tu, Deus meus, et susceptor salutis meae; he shall cry out to me: You are my Father, my God, and the support of my salvation.* For Christ said: *Father, forgive them;*[215] and *Father, into your hands I commend my spirit.*[216] Do you see how often Christ called upon God calling him Father? He called him his God, saying: *My God, my God, why have you forsaken me?*[217] And he also called him the undertaker of his salvation (that is, he who undertook his salvation), saying: *All my things are from you.*[218]

88{89}[28]   And I will make him my firstborn, high above the kings of the earth.

     Et ego primogenitum ponam illum, excelsum prae regibus terrae.

88{89}[29]   I will keep my mercy for him forever: and my covenant faithful to him.

     In aeternum servabo illi misericordiam meam, et testamentum meum fidele ipsi.

88{89}[30]   And I will make his seed to endure for evermore: and his throne as the days of heaven.

     Et ponam in saeculum saeculi semen eius, et thronum eius sicut dies caeli.

---

213   Is. 66:19a.
214   Is. 42:12.
215   Luke 23:34a.
216   Luke 23:46a.
217   Matt. 27:46; Ps. 21:2b.
218   *Cf.* John 17:7b: *All things which you have given me, are from you.*

88{89}[28] *Et ego primogenitum ponam illum, and I will make him my firstborn.* Christ as God is the only begotten of God; but as man, he is firstborn in the areas of predestination and dignity, though not in time. Whence the Apostle [Paul] said: *Whom he foreknew, he also pre-destinated to be made conformable to the image of his Son; that he might be the firstborn amongst many brethren;*[219] and again: *Who is the image of the invisible God, the firstborn of every creature.*[220] Christ is also said to be the firstborn because he was [eternally] begotten before all cre-ation. And so God set up Christ as the firstborn, making him the most excellent among all the elect, and [making him] the head of the Church. I will place him *excelsum prae regibus terrae, high above the kings of the earth*: because he is the *King of kings, and Lord of Lords,*[221] and he is *the prince of the kings of the earth.*[222] And so in an earlier Psalm is said about him: *All the kings of the earth shall adore him.*[223] 88{89}[29] *In aeternum servabo illi misericordiam meam, I will keep my mercy for him forever,* that is, whatever I have mercifully given to his humanity I will preserve it without cessation; *et testamentum meum fidele ipsi, and my covenant is faithful to him,* that is, I will faithfully fulfill the promises made to him by me; as he also said, *All things must needs be fulfilled, which are written in the Law of Moses, and in the Prophets, and in the Psalms, concerning me.*[224] 88{89}[30] *Et ponam in saeculum saeculi semen eius, and I will make his seed to endure for evermore,* that is, I will con-tinue in existence the Christian people reborn in Christ by water and the Holy Spirit even unto the end of the world.[225] For the Church will last until the end of the world, especially since Christ promised: *Behold I am with you all days, even to the consummation of the world.*[226] Of the perpetuation of this seed of Christ is written: *If he shall lay down his life . . . he shall see a long-lived seed.*[227] I will place *thronum eius, his throne,* that is, his regal seat or power, *sicut dies caeli, as the days of heaven,* so that they will never cease; and *he will reign in the house of Jacob forever, and of his kingdom there shall be no end.*[228]

---

219   Rom. 8:29.
220   Col. 1:15.
221   Rev. 19:16b.
222   Rev. 1:5a.
223   Ps. 71:11a.
224   Luke 24:44b.
225   Cf. John 3:5.
226   Matt. 28:20b.
227   Is. 53:10a.
228   Luke 1:32b–33.

88{89}[31] *And if his children forsake my law, and walk not in my judgments:*

Si autem dereliquerint filii eius legem meam, et in iudiciis meis non ambulaverint.

88{89}[33] *I will visit their iniquities with a rod: and their sins with stripes.*[229]

Visitabo in virga iniquitates eorum, et in verberibus peccata eorum.

88{89}[34] *But my mercy I will not take away from him: nor will I suffer my truth to fail.*

Misericordiam autem meam non dispergam ab eo, neque nocebo in veritate mea.[230]

88{89}[31] *Si autem dereliquerint filii eius, and if his children forsake,* [that is, his children] by faith and baptismal grace, namely, Christians, *legem meam, my law,* [my] evangelical [law], not observing it: as Hosea has written of some, *They have forsaken the Lord in not observing [his law].*[231] 88{89}[33] *Visitabo in virga iniquitates eorum, I will visit their iniquities with a rod,* paternally correcting them, not completely expelling them: because *such as I love, I rebuke and chastise.*[232] 88{89}[34] *Misericordiam autem meam non dispergam ab eo, but my mercy I will not take away from him,* that is, I will not completely withdraw my grace from the Christian people. And this marks the greatness of the mercy of God during the time of the evangelical law, for which reason it is call the time of grace. Hence it is written: *He that has offended among them in that day shall be as David: and the house of David,*[233] to whom, of course, God showed great mercy. 88{89}[35] *Neque profanabo testamentum meum, neither will I profane my covenant,* that is, my promises that I made to Christ and his seed. 88{89}[36] *Semel iuravi in sancto meo, once I have sworn by my holiness,* that is, by my own self; *si David mentiar, I will not lie unto David,* that is, I will not lie to Christ: 88{89} [37] *Semen eius, his seed,* that is, the Christian people, *in aeternum manebit,*

---

229   E. N. Denis skips verse 32.

230   E. N. Because only excerpts of verses 35, 36, 37, and 39 are used in this section or because the verses are so short, I will not repeat the entire verse here. Denis skips over verse 38.

231   Hosea 4:10b.

232   Rev. 3:19a.

233   Zech. 12:8a.

shall endure forever, now in the way by faith and grace, and then in the heavenly fatherland by the enjoyment [of the beatific vision] and glory.

88{89}[39] *Tu vero repulisti et despexisti, but you have rejected and despised.* The Catholic doctors expound this and the following [verses] as dealing with the degradation of the reign and people of David, as is apparent in the preceding exposition [in Article LXVI]. These also in a certain way can be understood as pertaining to the state of the Church, because the Christian people have often suffered from pagans and heretics those things that the Jews had to withstand from the Chaldeans and other nations: and literally it can be applied to this.

Finally, in feasts involving confessors who are bishops, the Church sings some contents of this Psalm, namely: 88{89}[20] *Posui adiutorium in potente, I have laid help upon one that is mighty*: for God placed the help of his grace in them. *Et exaltavi electum de plebe mea, and I have exalted one chosen out of my people*: that is, whichever holy bishop I have raised to the episcopal state, grace, and order. For no one assumes this *honor to himself, but he that is called by God, as Aaron was.*[234] 88{89} [21] *Inveni David servum meum, I have found David my servant*, that is, any holy confessor bishop, struggling mightily against the world, the flesh, and the devil; *oleo sancto meo unxi eum, with my holy oil I have anointed him*: for bishops are anointed with holy oil; and holy bishops are spiritually anointed by the infusion of the grace of the Holy Spirit, whose anointing instructs them. But how the rest [of the verses] that are sung applies to them is most clearly set forth in what was said before.

See we have heard this Psalm, great with words and meaning, full of mysteries, worthy of all praise, in which first of all, the mercy of God is sweetly entrusted, and his promises are touched upon, while his most high Divinity is most beautifully proclaimed, Christ according to both natures is marvelously described, his mysteries are most fully recounted; then it recalls of the fragility of his human nature imploring the goodness of the divine majesty; and finally God is praised with that happy verse which says: *Benedictus Dominus in aeternum. Fiat! Fiat! Blessed be the Lord in eternity. So be it! So be it!* Let us endeavor carefully, therefore, with proper devotion and holy gaiety and special purity, to utter forth this Psalm appropriately, seeing that it behooves us to sing that which is in it, 88{89}[16] *Beatus, populos qui scit iubilationem, blessed is the people that know jubilation*; and, *Domine in lumine vultus tui ambulabunt; they shall walk, O Lord, in the light of your countenance*, 88{89}[17] *et*

---

234   Heb. 5:4.

in nomine tuo exsultabunt tota die, etc. and in your name they shall rejoice all the day, etc. Truly every day it befits us sincerely to exult and most highly to rejoice in the praise of God, our Creator and Savior, as in our highest good, the abounding stream and most superlatively merciful fountain of all our good.

PRAYER

O GOD, GLORY OF THE POWER OF THE Saints, grant us always to walk in the light of your countenance, and to exult in your name, so that with your mercy before our faces, and, having completed the course of justice, we might be found worthy to come before you.

Deus, gloria virtutis Sanctorum, da nobis semper in lumine vultus tui ambulare, et in nomine tuo exsultare: ut misericordia tua faciem nostrum praeeunte, perfecto cursu iustitiae ad te valeamus pervenire.

Psalm 89

ARTICLE LXVIII

ELUCIDATION OF THE EIGHTY-NINTH PSALM:
DOMINE, REFUGIUM FACTUS ES NOBIS.
LORD, YOU HAVE BEEN OUR REFUGE.

89{90}[1]   *A prayer of Moses the man of God. Lord, you have been our*
refuge from generation to generation.

Oratio Moysi, hominis Dei. Domine, refugium factus es nobis
a generatione in generationem.

THE TITLE OF THE PSALM NOW BEING
expounded upon is this: **89{90}[1]** *Oratio Moysis, hominis Dei; a*
prayer of Moses, the man of God. According to the Hebrew scholars as
well as Jerome, Moses is the author of this present Psalm. But according
to Augustine and those who follow him, David composed it, but it is
entitled with the name of Moses because certain parts of it touch upon
aspects of the Old Testament, while other parts pertain to the New
Testament; and so it is appropriately entitled to Moses, who was the
legislator of the Old Testament and the prophet of the New Testament.
And so the author of this present Psalm, whoever he may have been, in
asking God so as to acquire his benefits, first gives thanks for the benefits already conceded: because the most optimal way to pray for future
gifts is to be thankful for past and received gifts. For he who has, that
is, he who is thankful, will be given; but he who do not have, that is, he
who is an ingrate, that which he seems to have will be taken from him.[1]

And so he says: *Domine, refugium factus es nobis; Lord, you have been our*
refuge: that is, you have given us the trust, through the benefits bestowed
upon us, to find refuge in you with complete faith and in all necessities
and situations. For from the beginning, you made heaven and all the stars,
the sun, and the moon,[2] for you *created for the service of all the nations that*
are under heaven, as is stated in Deuteronomy.[3] And so you made man in
your image and likeness, and you made him to rule over the fish of the sea

---

1   Cf. Matt. 25:29.
2   Gen. 1:1, 16.
3   Deut. 4:19b.

and the beasts of the earth.[4] You have had from the beginning a special providence over the human race, inasmuch as the Apostle said: *Does God take care for oxen?*[5] Because of this and for similar reasons, you have been our refuge *a generatione in generationem, from generation to generation*, that is, unceasingly, through the successions of all generations. But how much more of a refuge you are for us, O Lord, through your benefit of the most blessed Incarnation, by the merits of your most holy manner of living, by the effusion of your most precious Blood, by the sending of the Holy Spirit, and by the Sacrament of your Body and Blood. And so you say: *Come to me all you that labor and are burdened, and I will refresh you;*[6] and again: *He that thirsts, let him come: and he that will, let him take the water of life, freely.*[7] But God is said to be our refuge not through some sort of change or newness in him, but by a new conversion of our mind toward him: as a fixed column standing still is to my right or to my left without itself moving according to how I am differently situated towards it.[8]

89{90}[2]   *Before the mountains were made, or the earth and the world was formed; from age and to age you are God.*[9]

Priusquam montes fierent, aut formaretur terra et orbis, a saeculo et usque in saeculum tu es Deus.

---

4   Cf. Gen. 1: 27, 28.

5   1 Cor. 9:9b. E. N. In his *Commentary on First Corinthians*, Denis regards this question as a negative rhetorical question, *i.e.*, it suggests a negative answer. However, Denis sees that as seemingly repugnant to other scriptures (Ps. 146:9, Job. 38:41, and Wis. 12:13), all of which indicate God's Providence extends itself to all creatures. But Denis notes that God's Providence extends in a particular way to his intellectual creation, those of his creatures who are capable of beatitude (*felicitatis capaces*). This singular Providence for intellectual creatures is insinuated by St. Paul through the use of the word "cure" (*cura*), by which God is particularly solicitous towards man (as distinguished from oxen) as is testified to in Psalm 32:18: *The Lord is careful* (*sollicitus est*) *for me* and 1 Pet. 5:7: *For he has care* (*cura*) *of you.* See Doctoris Ecstatici D. Dionysii Cartusiani, *Opera Omnia*, Vol. 13 (Montreuil: 1901), 163–64.

6   Matt. 11:28.

7   Rev. 22:17b.

8   E. N. Denis is describing what philosophers describe as a "Cambridge change," where the object (a column, God) does not change, but the subject's relationship or intention to that fixed object changes (Denis moving visa vis-à-vis a fixed column, he who seeks refuge from God).

9   E. N. I have departed from the Douay Rheims here in translating *a saeculo et in saeculum* as "from age to age," rather than from "eternity to eternity." The Latin term *saeculum* is rather flexible, and can mean age, generation, a lifetime, and indefinitely long period (and hence, by extension, eternity). However, since Denis is making a point that God's eternity is outside time, it demanded a change in the underlying translation.

89{90}[2] *Priusquam montes fierent, et formaretur terra et orbis ; before the mountains were made, or the earth and the world was formed,* that is, the entire world, namely, before all creatures or the entirety of the universe, *a saeculo et in saeculum, from age to age,* that is, eternally, *tu es Deus, you are God:* not that before the creation of the world there were ages and ages, but because then he was eternity itself, containing immovably the duration of all eternity. By the word mountains we can also understand the angels, or the parts of the earth that are sublime. Before all these things God existed, indeed: he was their Creator, and the Creator outdoes the creature by nature, dignity, and time. Whence he says through Isaiah: *I am the Lord, that make all things, that alone stretch out the heavens, that establish the earth, and there is none with me.*[10] Fittingly, it also says, *you are,* and not *you were,* God: for being in God is always stable and invariable, in which [being] there is neither past nor future, but an eternal present, and an always present and pure eternity which is the simultaneous, total, and perfect possession of unceasing life.[11] Also Christ used this way of speaking: *Before Abraham was made, I am.*[12]

89{90}[3] *Turn not man away to be brought low: and you have said: Be converted, O sons of men.*

Ne avertas hominem in humilitatem; et dixisti: Convertimini, filii hominum.

89{90}[3] *Ne avertas hominem, turn not man away,* that is, do not permit men to turn away from you, the supreme good, and from spiritual goods and virtues, *in humilitatem, to be brought low,* that is, in vicious living, so that they turn to temporal and fleeting goods and the desires of the flesh. Do this because *dixisti: Convertimini filii hominum; you have said: Be converted, O sons of men:* that is, you have exhorted men to repentance by angels and holy men. Therefore, give [what is needed] to fulfill what you command.[13]

---

10   Is. 44:24.
11   E. N. The definition of eternity given by Denis — *interminabilis vitae tota simul perfecta possessio* — is the classic definition given by Boethius in his *On the Consolation of Philosophy*, V, 6.
12   John 8:58b.
13   E. N. This is a great aspiratory prayer: *Da implere quod mones,* give us [the grace] to fulfill what you command.

89{90}[4] *For a thousand years in your sight are as yesterday, which is*
           past. And as a watch in the night,

> *Quoniam mille anni ante oculos tuos tamquam dies hesterna*
> *quae praeteriit, et custodia in nocte.*

And so man is exhorted to a saving conversion, **89{90}[4]** *Quoniam*
mille anni ante oculos tuos, for a thousand years in your sight, that is, for any
duration of time or the length of human life, however long it might be,
or may be regarded by you, it is brief before you or brief in comparison
to your eternity, *tanquam dies hesterna quae praeteriit, are as yesterday,*
which is past, that is, it is of utterly no moment, and it is as if it had
not existed: for there is no proportion to be found between finite and
the infinite. And so in the manner stated in Isaiah: *All nations are before*
him as if they had no being at all, and are counted to him as nothing, and
vanity[14] (for this reason it is said in an earlier Psalm, *my substance is as*
nothing before you);[15] and so the duration of the entirety of this present
life is as if it were nothing in comparison to the duration of the future
life or eternal happiness.[16] For this reason, God admonishes we should
despise present, transitory, and worldly things, and seek after future, eternal,
and heavenly goods. For this reason, the Apostle says: *We have not here*
a lasting city, but we seek one that is to come;[17] and again, *Let us hasten*
therefore to enter into that rest.[18] Regarding this Solomon also spoke: *If*
a man live many years, and have rejoiced in them all, he must remember
the darksome time, and the many days: which when they shall come, the
things past shall be accused of vanity.[19] And this verse also accords with
that which is written: *One day with the Lord is as a thousand years, and*
a thousand years as one day.[20]

Et custodia in nocte, and as a watch in the night. The meaning of this
concerns the prior part of this verse, so that it reads in this sense: A

---

14   Is. 40:17.
15   Ps. 38:6a.
16   E. N. This is suggestive of "Pascal's Wager," *Le Pari de Pascal,* an argument in
Pascal's (1623–1662) *Pensées* that weighs the finite goods of this life with the infinite
goods of the next life (or infinite losses, *i.e.,* hell). "Let us weigh up the gain and the
loss involved in calling heads that God exists. Let us assess the two cases: if you
win you win everything, if you lose, you lose nothing. Do not hesitate then; wager
that he does exist." *Pensées,* B.233, L.418. Blaise Pascal, *Pensées* (London: Penguin
Books, 1995), 122–23 (trans. A. J. Krailsheimer).
17   Heb. 13:14.
18   Heb. 4:11a.
19   Eccl. 11:8.
20   2 Pet. 3:8b.

thousand years in your sight are as yesterday, which is past, and as a watch in the night, that is, as a watch of the night, which is shorter than the day because it contains three hours. And so it says: The duration of human life is not only compared to a day which is past, which has twenty four hours, but even to a watch of the night containing three hours.[21] And it fittingly joins the similarity of a watch in the night containing three hours because the duration of the life of men after the flood is so far from, and falls so sort of, the duration of the lives of those who lived before the flood,[22] as the full twenty-four day exceeds a watch in night: and so men ought now especially to weigh little this life, and seek after the future one. The word watch is used for vigil because the night is divided into four vigils, which in antiquity those keeping watch undertook to guard the army, and which the military did by turns in four successive changes, according to the four vigils of the night. Moreover, most aptly is human life compared to the watch in the night, which all things are under darkness and laden with fear: because all our life is in ignorance and is exceedingly dangerous.

89{90}[5]   *Things that are counted nothing, shall their years be.*

Quae pro nihilo habentur eorum anni erunt.

89{90}[6]   *In the morning man shall grow up like grass; in the morning he shall flourish and pass away: in the evening he shall fall, grow dry, and wither.*

Mane sicut herba transeat; mane floreat, et transeat; vespere decidat, induret, et arescat.

89{90}[5]   *Quae pro nihilo habentur, eorum anni erunt; things that are counted nothing, shall their years be:* that is, the years or the time of life of men are numbered among those things that are regarded as nothing, because exceedingly brief is their life. For this reason James says: *For what*

---

21   E. N. The term "watch of night" is a military term equivalent to vigil. The first watch or vigil was between 6 p.m. and 9 p.m. The second vigil was between 9 p.m. and midnight. The third between midnight and 3:00 a.m. And the fourth vigil or watch was between 3:00 a.m. and 6:00 a.m.

22   E. N. The Scriptures report the ages of the pre-diluvian fathers as very long. Adam, for example, lived to 930 years, Gen. 5:4, and Noah lived to 960, Gen. 9:29. The longest living man recorded in the Scriptures was Methuselah, who is said to have lived to 969 years, Gen. 5:27. The lives of the patriarchs post-diluvium are notably shorter. For example, Abraham lived 175 years, Gen. 25:7, and Isaac 180 years, Gen. 35:28–29. By the time the Psalms were written, "the days of our years in them are threescore and ten [70] years. But in the strong they may be fourscore [80]." Ps. 89:10.

is your life? It is a vapor which appears for a little while, and afterwards shall vanish away.[23] And consequently, this is made more expressly clear. **89{90}[6]** *Mane sicut herba transeat, in the morning man shall grow up like grass:* that is, the first age or the childhood of man runs through, changes, and vanishes so quickly, as quickly the grass dies; *mane, in the morning,* that is, the [during the childhood] stated before *floreat, he flourishes:* for in the beginning of his time man is like a flower, and is similar to fresh hay; *et transeat, and he passes away,* not long remaining in that state; in the way that Job says, *Man . . . who comes forth like a flower and is destroyed . . . and flees like a shadow, and never continues in the same state;*[24] *vespere, in the evening,* that is, in old age or the last age of man, *decidat, he shall fall* from his earlier strength, *induret, grow dry,* that is, he will dry up because of the consumption of radical moisture,[25] *et arescat, and he withers,* because of the lack of natural heat,[26] not having the power to restore that which he has lost. Whence the elderly are naturally dry and cold.

89{90}[7] *For in your wrath we have fainted away: and are troubled in your indignation.*

Quia defecimus in ira tua, et in furore tuo turbati sumus.

Now why this befalls us is subjoined [in the verse that follows]: **89{90} [7]** *Quia defecimus, for . . . we have fainted away* from the primordial institution of the human condition, and the usual span of the age of the fathers, or our fathers who preceded the flood (and they lived a long time, around nine-hundred years, as we read in Genesis);[27] *in ira tua, in your wrath,* that is, in your vengeance or because of the vindication of your justice: for because of original sin we — who would otherwise have been born in original justice, would have been placed in a terrestrial paradise, and would have been immortal by being obedient[28] — come into this state

---

23   James 4:15a.
24   Job 14:1a, 2.
25   E. N. According to the state of medical science at the time radical moisture (*humiditas radicalis*), also known as substantial, natural, or radical moisture or humidity was considered a property of youth which was lost over the years resulting in the desiccated appearance and qualities of old age.
26   Again, according to the contemporary medical science, natural heat (*calor naturalis*) was what allowed food to be metabolized and serve as nutrient. This capacity also diminished at old age.
27   Gen. 5:5 *et seq.*
28   E. N. Had the head of mankind — Adam — not sinned, each one of us would

of mortality and the valley of tears. Or we can understand this wrath as the flood, which God brought upon the world of the ungodly, and from that time our days are much less and exceedingly abbreviated and the human condition weakened. For this reason, the Lord said: *My spirit shall not remain in man forever, because he is flesh, and his days shall be a hundred and twenty years.*[29] *Et in furore tuo, for in your wrath,* that is, in the punishments which you set upon us because of original sin and by the flood, *turbati sumus, we are troubled,* that is, we are greatly afflicted, made unstable, and prone to fear, and full of misery. For we were created with great mental tranquility, because by original justice the flesh in man was subject to the spirit, his sensuality [was subject] to reason, and his reason [was subject] to God. But once man fell, various and weighty punishments were inflicted upon us: for with the flesh there follows weakness, the ability to suffer, and death; and the life of passions, fear, pain, and sorrow; but in the mind, ignorance, instability, and difficulty in accomplishing the good: and so there has come upon us that which was said to the first of our parents: *Cursed is the earth in your work.... In the sweat of your face shall you eat bread until you return to the earth, out of which you were taken: for dust you are, and into dust you shall return.*[30]

89{90}[8] *You have set our iniquities before your eyes: our life in the light of your countenance.*

Posuisti iniquitates nostras in conspectu tuo, saeculum nostrum in illuminatione vultus tui.

89{90}[8] *Posuisti iniquitates nostras in conspectu tuo, you have set our iniquities before your eyes,* that is, you have not been indulgent towards them, but you have carefully regarded them, since you have inflicted a just punishment for them, in the manner that you stated through Amos: *I know your manifold crimes, and your grievous sins;*[31] and elsewhere, *Their own devices... have been done before my face.*[32] You have put also *saeculum nostrum, our life,* that is, the words of the time within which we live, *in illuminatione vultus tui, in the light of your countenance,* that

---

have been conceived in original justice and would have enjoyed the preternatural gifts of infused knowledge, the absence of concupiscence, and bodily immortality which could have been lost only for each individual through actual or personal mortal sin.

29 Gen. 6:3.
30 Gen. 3:17b, 19.
31 Amos 5:12.
32 Hosea 7:2b.

is, in the clear inspection of your intellect, since you will reward every person that which he merits: according to that stated by Jeremiah: *O most mighty, great, and powerful, the Lord of hosts is your name, ... whose eyes are open upon all the ways of the children of Adam, to render unto every one according to his ways.*[33] And Ecclesiasticus: *The eyes of the Lord, it says, are far brighter than the sun, beholding round about all the ways of men.*[34]

89{90}[9]   *For all our days are spent; and in your wrath we have fainted away. Our years shall be considered as a spider:*

Quoniam omnes dies nostri defecerunt; et in ira tua defecimus. Anni nostri sicut aranea meditabuntur.

89{90}[10]   *The days of our years in them are seventy years. But if in the strong they be eighty years: and what is more of them is labor and sorrow. For mildness is come upon us: and we shall be corrected.*[35]

Dies annorum nostrorum in ipsis septuaginta anni. Si autem in potentatibus octoginta anni, et amplius eorum labor et dolor; quoniam supervenit mansuetudo, et corripiemur.

89{90}[9] *Quoniam omnes dies nostri, for all our days,* that is, the duration or the labors of our life, *defecerunt, are spent,* that is, are brief and quickly exhausted: as Job says: *My days have been swifter than a running courier.... They have passed by as ships carrying fruits.*[36] And it is written: *Our days upon earth are as a shadow, and there is no stay.*[37] *Et in ira tua defecimus, and in your wrath we have fainted:* as has already been stated and has also explained [in verse 7]. *Anni nostri sicut aranea meditabuntur, our years shall be considered as a spider,* that is, to be judged similar to that of a spider, because a spider dissipates and exhausts itself in fashioning webs so as to catch flies, and yet its work is quickly destroyed, that is to say, but a light breeze and its labor is destroyed and is lost. So men are similarly occupied for a time in so many ways gathering up transitory

---

33   Jer. 32:18b–19.
34   Ecclus. 23:28a.
35   E. N. I have replaced the Douay-Rheims's "threescore and ten" with "seventy," and "fourscore" with "eighty."
36   Job 9:25a, 26a. E. N. I have departed from the Douay Rheims by replacing "post" with "running courier" for *cursore,* which can mean both a runner or a courier or a messenger.
37   1 Chr. 29:15b.

things, seeking honor and glory in this age, and oppressing others; and yet they soon die, which makes their labors useless, indeed, they tend unceasingly to this condition, in the manner that holy Job asserts: *I am to be consumed as rottenness, and as a garment that is moth-eaten.*[38] Whence also elsewhere it is said: *We all die, and like waters that return no more.*[39] **89{90}[10]** *Dies annorum nostrorum, the days of our years,* according to the common course, are *in ipsis in them,* [that is,] in men, *septuaginta anni, seventy years,* which corresponds with what a man who is healthy is able to live. *Si autem in potentatibus, but if they are strong,* that is, strong and well constituted men, we find *octaginta anni, et amplius eorum, eighty years, and what is more of them,* that is, times of greater age, will be *labor et dolor, labor and sorrow*: because the old man is full of complaints, and old age is akin to continual labor. This is understood as a common course or law. For there are also many before seventy years of age who incur sickness and weakness of old age; and some after eighty years of age live quite strongly and happily.

St. Thomas relies upon these two verses to show that the life of men before the flood was lengthened chiefly because of divine or miraculous power rather than from natural causes: and he is led to this [assertion] by that which is written about Barzillai: *Barzillai the Gileadite was of a great age, that is to say, eighty years old.*[40] And this was also confirmed by what was stated of David: *King David was old, and advanced in years:*[41] yet David died in his seventies. And so Thomas asserts David wrote these verses in reference to his own time. And so, according to Thomas, David was the author of this present Psalm:[42] from which it seems to follow that Thomas feels all the Psalms were written by David.

But you have brought upon us the brevity of life and temporal punishment, *quoniam supervenit mansuetudo, for mildness is come upon us,* that is, because you have attached mercy to your judgment by which you have tempered the rigor of your justice. For men deserved to be entirely destroyed or condemned: but, in lieu of total destruction, a shortening of life was placed upon us; and in lieu of eternal damnation, [we obtained] temporal affliction. *Et corripiemur, and we shall be corrected* by these your chastisements mildly inflicted upon us, being wary from that point of sin, lest we suffer more heavy scourging.

---

38 Job 13:28.
39 2 Sam. 14:14a.
40 2 Sam. 19:
41 1 Kings 1:1.
42 *E. N.* Perhaps a reference to St. Thomas Aquinas's *De malo,* q. 4, a. 3, ad 11.

89{90}[**11**] *Who knows the power of your anger, and before your fear,*

Quis novit potestatem irae tuae, et prae timore tuo,

89{90}[**12**] *to number your wrath? So make your right hand known: and men learned in heart, in wisdom.*

iram tuam dinumerare? Dexteram tuam sic notam fac, et eruditos corde in sapientia.

89{90}[**13**] *Turn back, O Lord, how long? And be entreated in favor of your servants.*

Convertere, Domine; usquequo? Et deprecabilis esto super servos tuos,

89{90}[**11**] *Quis novit, who knows*, without your special enlightenment, *potestatem irae tuae, the power of your anger*, that is, the force of your justice and the rigor of your vengeance? *Et, and* who knows *prae timore tuo, before your fear*, that is, the fear of your justice or the fear in one's own heart at the realization of your majesty, 89{90}[**12**] *iram tuam dinumerare, to number your wrath*, that is, to measure and to explain all the punishments prepared for sinners by your justice? It is as if he is saying, "No one." For the works of the divine justice which operate upon the sinner are incomprehensible.[43] For some punishment begins now and is continued in the future; other [punishment] starts now and desists in the future; yet other punishment differs in manner, since in will be continued in eternity.[44] But who has the power to discern this, and to consider why particular things happen to particular people, unless God supernaturally and miraculously shows him? In considering this, it is apparent that some holy men may be disheartened by the contemplation of the divine justice because of their excessive fear of the divine majesty.[45] For a vehement fear interferes with the act of reason and speaking. For this reason, the book of Job has this: *Let not his fear terrify me; for I cannot answer while I am in fear.*[46] But suffering a moderate of fear or sorrow serves sometimes to arrive at the knowledge of truth, since it

---

43   Cf. Rom. 11:33: *O the depth of the riches of the wisdom and of the knowledge of God! How incomprehensible are his judgments, and how unsearchable his ways!*

44   E. N. Denis is distinguishing between temporal punishments on earth (which do not continue after death), temporal punishments suffered in Purgatory (those which start at death and continue for a time in the future) and those temporal punishments suffered in Hell (which last for eternity).

45   Cf. Job 6:4: *For the arrows of the Lord are in me, the rage whereof drinks up my spirit, and the terrors of the Lord war against me.*

46   Job 9:34b, 35b.

excludes dissolute living and excessive lack of restraint and merriment. Hence, Isaiah says: *Lord, they have sought after you in distress, in the tribulation of murmuring your instruction was with them.*[47] In addition, he prays for divine illumination, saying: *Dexteram tuam, your right hand*, that is the divine power and its terrible correction, *sic notam fac, so make... known* to us now by a sincere contemplation of faith, infused by the Holy Spirit, so that we might respect it, and we might fear God's anger or punishment, saying with the spirit in Revelation: *Just and true are your ways, O King of ages. Who shall not fear you, ... and magnify your name?*[48] Make it also be that we men be *eruditos corde in saptientiae, learned in heart in the wisdom* of the divine law: because, *All wisdom is from the Lord God;*[49] and *Blessed is the man whom you shall instruct, O Lord.*[50] **89{90}[13]** *Convertere, Domine; Turn back, O Lord*, turning me toward you without you being changed, and mercifully looking upon me, *usquequo, how long*, that is, without ceasing from this conversion until I attain the ultimate end. Or [alternatively], *A little* — as other translations have it[51] — that is, in due measure, reduce and diminish my tribulations; do not take them away entirely, because tribulation is necessary for the elect. *Et deprecabilis esto super servos tuos, and be entreated in favor of your servants*, not dispersing them or being indignant with them because of their sins, but quickly and sweetly saving them in accordance with your mercy. This verse is most efficacious, and it contains a most affectionate and most devout prayer, which we ought to say — both more ardently and more frequently — with an attentive heart and a meaningful affection of speech.

89{90}[14] *We are filled in the morning with your mercy: and we have rejoiced, and are delighted all our days.*

> *Repleti sumus mane misericordia tua; et exsultavimus, et delectati sumus omnibus diebus nostris.*

89{90}[14] *Repleti sumus mane, we are filled in the morning*, that is, quickly, *misericordia tua, with your mercy*: for the more quickly we invoke you with a sincere heart, the more we worthy we are to receive. Or [we

---

47   Is. 26:16.
48   Rev. 15:3b–4a.
49   Ecclus. 1:1a.
50   Ps. 93:12. E. N. The Psalm verse continues: *and shall teach him out of your law.*
51   E. N. The Sixto-Clementine Vulgate has *Convertere, Domine, usquequo* — *Turn back, O Lord, how long.* Other translations of this verse have *Convertere, Domine, aliquantulum* — *Turn bank, O Lord, a little.*

can look at it thus], *In the morning,* that is, in the spiritual sunrise or the beginning of the spiritual day, namely, when the Sun of Justice, Christ the Lord, imprints upon our mind the light of grace into our minds. Or [yet another way of looking at it], *In the morning,* that is, in the hour of the Lord's Resurrection, and in the hour of the sending of the Holy Spirit: for Christ rose again in the morning,[52] and the Holy Spirit visibly came upon the disciples in the morning of the day of Pentecost;[53] and so we are then filled with the mercy of God because Christ (according to the Apostle [Paul]) *rose for our justification;*[54] and the mission of the Paraclete was the illumination of the entire world. *Et exaltavimus, and we have rejoiced,* that is, we have displayed forth an external sign of joy, *et delectati sumus, and we are delighted* interiorly. Or [alternatively], *we have rejoiced* according to our intellectual appetite, and *we are delighted* according to our sensitive appetite by the overflowing of the intellectual joy in it, as it says in an earlier Psalm: *My heart and my flesh have rejoiced in the living God,*[55] that is, both the superior and the inferior appetite. *In omnibus diebus nostris, all our days,* that is, in those certain hours of the entire days in which we live in a state of grace: in the way that the Apostle says, *Always rejoice;* and, *In all things give thanks;*[56] and, sing and make melody *in your hearts to the Lord.*[57] For virtuous men do not only rejoice in prosperity, but also in adversity, in the manner that Christ exhorts: Rejoice and exult in that hour.[58] *Blessed is the man that endures temptations;*[59] and,

---

89{90}[15]   *We have rejoiced for the days in which you have humbled us: for the years in which we have seen evils.*

Laetati sumus pro diebus quibus nos humiliasti, annis quibus vidimus mala.

89{90}[15] *Laetati sumus pro diebus quibus nos humiliasti, we have rejoiced for the days in which you have humbled us,* that is, you have permitted us to be humbled, tempted, and oppressed, namely for *annis quibus vidimus, for the years in which we have seen,* that is, we have

---

52   Mark 16:9.
53   Acts 2:3, 4, 15.
54   Rom. 4:25b.
55   Ps. 83:3b.
56   1 Thess. 5:16, 18a.
57   Eph. 5:19b.
58   *E. N. Cf.* Luke 6:23.
59   James 1:12a.

experienced, *mala, evils* of punishment. Indeed, to have endured adversities and calamities patiently is a great reason for rejoicing in God: because this is a sign of eternal predestination, for Scripture says, *Blessed is the man whom God corrects;*[60] and, *Blessed are they that suffer persecution for justice's sake;*[61] and, *Such as I love, I rebuke and chastise.*[62] Some expound these verses of the Church triumphant, explaining the past for the future, and by [the words] *In the morning,* understanding [them to refer to] the hour of future Resurrection: there is no doubt, that this verse understood in this way fully agrees with the blessed in the heavenly fatherland, rather than with the elect on the way. For mercy is consummated in the blessed, and with it comes unceasing joy and the joyful memory of past tribulations.

89{90}[16] *Look upon your servants and upon their works: and direct their children.*

Respice in servos tuos et in opera tua, et dirige filios eorum.

89{90}[17] *And let the brightness of the Lord our God be upon us: and direct the works of our hands over us; yea, the work of our hands do direct.*

Et sit splendor Domini Dei nostri super nos; et opera manuum nostrarum dirige super nos, et opus manuum nostrarum dirige.

89{90}[16] *Respice, look* with the eyes of fatherly kindness *in servos tuos et in opera tua,* upon your servants and upon their works, that is, in your servants who are the works of your hands. Or [understood another way], *in your works,* that is, in your operations by which you cause grace to be in them, in the way we find in Isaiah, *You have wrought all our works for us.*[63] The Apostle also states: *It is God who works in you, both to will and to accomplish, according to his good will.*[64] These works are both yours and ours. They are yours, because they come forth from you principally; and ours, because they are done by us. Take heed, conserving and perfecting them unto eternal life; *et dirige, and direct,* by guiding grace, unto eternal life, *filios eorum, their children,* namely, [the children] of your servants. So that this may be done, I pray: **89{90}[17]** *Et sit*

---

60 Job 5:17a.
61 Matt. 5:10a.
62 Rev. 3:19a.
63 Is. 26:12b.
64 Phil 2:13.

splendor Domini Dei nostri super nos, and let the brightness of the Lord
our God be upon us, that is, may your grace always shine forth from
our hearts, as Ecclesiasticus says, *Have mercy upon us, O God of all,
and behold us, and show us the light of your mercies.*[65] *Et opera manuum
nostrarum, and the works of our hands,* that is, our internal and exterior
operations, which are caused by operative virtues that are designated
by the word "hands," *dirige super nos, direct . . . over us,* that is, unto a
supernatural end, unto eternal life, to your own honor and glory, so that
we might choose to please in everything not men, but you, and that
we might take care and intend to receive by our labors the reward that
is above the heavens. *Et opus manuum nostrarum dirige, yeah, the work
of our hands do direct.* [One might ask,] why is it necessary for one to
pray more than once that one's works may be directed when one has
already once exhorted that one's work might be directed, except that
one especially and greatly desires that God direct an act of charity?
Because so long as the act of charity remains subsisting, the works of
other virtues continue [in charity]; but all meritorious acts cease when
the act of charity ceases, because without an act of charity, no act of
virtue merits eternal life.[66]

See how we have heard a powerful Psalm, whose first verse is a verse
of great trust and of special love. For we ought to seek refuge from the
Lord our God, as to from a Father and Savior, with all confidence and
love. Whence the Savior said: *If you who are evil, know how to give good
gifts to your children, how much more will your Father from heaven give
the good Spirit to them that ask him?*[67] Let us strive, therefore, following
the teachings of this present Psalm, to ponder on the brevity of our
life, to strive unfailingly for the days of eternal felicity, and to cleanse
our hearts from all worldly loves, carnal affections, vain concerns, and
restless passions, so that we might render ourselves always more capa-
cious to receive the brightness of the grace of God, and immediately
at the completion of this exiled dwelling, we might brought into the
light of glory.

---

65   Ecclus. 36:1.
66   E. N. "Prayer that is undertaken without being in a state of sanctifying grace
is not meritorious, just like other acts of virtue are not" meritorious if undertaken
outside of a state of sanctifying grace, that is, in faith formed by charity. ST IIaI-
Iae, q. 83, art. 15, ad 1. Acts of natural virtue, while naturally good, have utterly no
supernatural worth. "If I should distribute all my good to feed the poor, . . . and have
not charity [sanctifying grace], it profits me nothing." 1 Cor. 13:3.
67   Luke 11:13.

PRAYER

BE OUR REFUGE IN ALL THINGS, O LORD, who are God from eternity even unto eternity; look mercifully upon us your servants, and may the splendor of your divinity be upon us, so that our works may always be directed by you, and, once having begun by you, they might be completed by you.

*Sis, Domine, nostrum ubique refugium, qui es Deus a saeculo
et usque in saeculum; respice clementer in nos servos
tuos, et sit splendor divinitatis tuae super nos:
ut opera nostra a te semper dirigantur,
et coepta per te finiantur.*

Psalm 90

ARTICLE LXIX

EXPOSITION OF THE NINETIETH PSALM:
QUI HABITAT IN ADIUTORIO ALTISSIMI.
HE THAT DWELLS IN THE AID OF THE MOST HIGH.

90{91}[1] *The praise of a canticle for David. He that dwells in the aid of the most High, shall abide under the protection of the God of heaven.* [1]

Laus cantici David. Qui habitat in adiutorio Altissimi, in protectione Dei caeli commorabitur.

TO THIS PSALM BEING NOW ADDRESSED IS given this title: 90{91}[1] *Laus cantici, ipsi David; The praise of a canticle for David*: that is, in this Psalm is contained praise of spiritual joy, relating to David himself, and to any member of the faithful signified by David. For this Psalm deals with the various temptations of the human race: the victory over which is praised in this Psalm, and of the eternal joy that is certainly effected by the promise of God. Nicholas of Lyra[2] recounts that this Psalm along with the following one and even unto the hundredth Psalm, which begins, *Mercy and judgment, etc.*[3] lacks a title in the Hebrew, and that this title was placed by some other expositor according to his own inclination. He also asserts that, according to the Hebrews, this Psalm along with the following even up to the hundredth Psalm, was written by Moses. But the Catholic teachers disagree with this. For it is believed that the titles of the Psalms were formed by others under the inspiration of the Holy Spirit: and also nearly all the holy teachers, point to the words of the Psalms, which frequently memorialize the holy David as their author.

Therefore, it says: *Qui habitat in adiutorio Altissimi, he that dwells in the aid of the most High*, that is, a man firmly founding his mind upon God, leaning upon the help of his grace, in the manner that Isaiah says:

---

1 E. N. The Douay-Rheims has "God of Jacob," which has no support in the text of the Sixto-Clementine Vulgate. I have translated it to conform to the Latin.
2 E. N. Nicolas of Lyra (*ca.* 1270–1349 AD) was a Franciscan friar noted for his biblical studies from Lyre, Normandy.
3 Ps. 100:1a.

Who . . . walks *in darkness and has no light? Let him hope in the name of the Lord, and lean upon his God.*[4] And Solomon: *Have confidence in the Lord with all you heart, and lean not upon your own prudence.*[5] Such men as these *in protectione Dei caeli commorabitur,* shall abide under the protection of the God of heaven, that is, they are firmly protected by God. For just as he who dwells in the aid of God is hoping to be helped by him, so he who remains in the protection of the God of heaven shall abide in the effect of hope, because God is *the protector of all who trust in him,*[6] according to this: *My children behold the generations of men, and know that no one has hoped in the Lord and has been confounded.*[7] And so, in order that we might be worthy to be defended by the God of heaven, it does not suffice to lean upon his assistance cursorily or without constancy; rather, we must *dwell* in the aid of the most High, that is, we must remain with fixed soul, thinking ourselves unceasingly needful of his help, in the manner that the Son of God said: *Without me you can do nothing.*[8] For none of us is permitted to trust in ourselves or in our own merits and powers if we truly want to acknowledge that which the Apostle said, *By the grace of God, I am what I am;*[9] and again, *We are not sufficient* to *think any thing of ourselves, as of ourselves, but our sufficiency is from God.*[10] And Christ said, *He that abides in me, and I in him, the same bears much fruit.*[11] But it is known that some men do not hope in God, and others despair of God, and yet others vainly hope in God. For they who trust in their own vanity, in their own strength, merits, or riches hope in themselves and not in God. And he who hopes in God without good works, hopes vainly. However much we may have progressed [in the spiritual life], let us dwell, therefore, always in the aid of the most High, ascribing, with a most complete devotion, all our progress and perfection to his most merciful goodness, and say with Isaiah, *In your presence, O Lord, we have conceived, and been as it were in labor, and have brought forth wind;*[12] and again, *Only in you let us remember your name.* For God most plainly guides us to this through Hosea, saying: *Destruction is your own, O Israel: your help is only in me.*[13]

---

4   Is. 50:10.
5   Prov. 3:5.
6   Ps. 17:31b.
7   Ecclus. 2:11.
8   John 15:5b.
9   1 Cor. 15:10a.
10   2 Cor. 3:5.
11   John 15:5a.
12   Is. 26:17b–18a.
13   Hosea 13:9.

90{91}[2] *He shall say to the Lord: You are my protector, and my refuge: my God, in him will I trust.*

Dicet Domino: Susceptor meus es tu et refugium meum; Deus meus, sperabo in eum.

90{91}[2] *Dicet Domino, he shall say to the Lord,* [that is,] a man who dwells in this fashion in the aid of the most High in this way [shall say]: *Susceptor meus es tu, you are my protector,* that is, you are the hearer of my pious prayers, the merciful curer of my weakness, the embracer with your most clement arms of mercy of me when I am penitent and return to you, for I surely seek refuge from you in all danger, necessity, and weakness as I would from a father or deliverer. *Deus meus, my God.* In truth, generally speaking God is [the God] of all, just like he is the Creator and the Provider of all, but in a particular sense, my God: first—on your part—due to the special kindness and graces which you have bestowed upon me; second—on my part—because of the special love and devotion by which I adhere to you, I honor you, and I worship you completely and you alone. *Sperabo in eum, in him will I trust:* not in in mere man, because *cursed be the man who trusts in man;*[14] nor in any other mere creature: but in you, trusting to avoid all evil by your aid and grace and to acquire all good. For it is written: *Blessed be the man that trusts in the Lord, and the Lord shall be his confidence.*[15]

90{91}[3] *For he has delivered me from the snare of the hunters: and from the sharp word.*

Quoniam ipse liberavit me de laqueo venantium, et a verbo aspero.

And so I will trust in him **90{91}[3]** *Quoniam ipse, for he* by grace *liberabit me de laqueo, has delivered me from the snare,* that is, from the deception and the pestiferous infection, *venantium, of the hunters,* that is, of the iniquitous, from the sins by which the soul is led to be captured and killed. For here, they, who run[16] and busy themselves with deceiving souls—to divert them from God, and by this to deprive them of grace in the present and glory in the future—are called hunters. But here, the hunters are not only demons, but also those who are their imitators, namely, reprobate men: of whom it is written, *By the envy of the*

---

14   Jer. 17:5.
15   Jer. 17:7.
16   E. N. The editor notes that an alternative reading to *current* (run) is *curant* (attend to).

devil, death came into the world. And they follow him that are of his side.[17]
Whence we read: *Everyone hunts his brother to death.*[18] Now a snare is
here said to be that which subjects a soul to the servitude of the devil,
through which its salvation is captured by its enemies, and by which it
is bound in the fetters of eternal death. But this is nothing other than
mortal sin. For this reason, the Apostle [Paul] on occasion describes
this snare (in its singular form) as avarice:[19] *They that will become rich,*
he says, *fall into temptation, and into the snare of the devil.*[20] But sometimes he expresses it (in its plural form), understanding any mortal sins
by the name of snares, such as when he says: *If peradventure God may
give them repentance, . . . and they may recover themselves from the snares
of the devil, by whom they are held captive at his will.*[21] Whence, of this
snare — by which the soul is miserably ensnared and is spiritually put to
death — the Gospel asserts: *The cares of the world, and the deceitfulness
of riches, and the lusts after other things entering in choke the word, and it
is made fruitless.*[22] Therefore, what else does *he has delivered me from the
snare of the hunters* mean except "he by his mercy has delivered me, and
will save me from the traps of visible and invisible enemies"? Precisely
according to this: *The Almighty shall be against your enemies.*[23]

He will deliver me also *a verbo aspero, from the sharp word,* that is, from
all noxious words spoken against me, so that I do not become impatient
when others laugh, calumniate, and reproach me.[24] For the simplicity of
the just man is derided, and perverse men censure the life of just men
with impious words. But with the grace of God providing aid, I will not
be disturbed by this; indeed, I will rejoice, thinking about that which the
Savior said: *Blessed* will you be *when they shall revile you, and persecute
you, and speak all that is evil against you, untruly, for my sake.*[25] For we

---

17 Wis. 2:24–25.

18 Micah 7:2b.

19 E. N. *Cf.* Rom. 1:29; Eph. 4:19, Eph. 5:3; Col. 3:5; Heb. 13:5 (recall, Denis
attributes the epistle to the Hebrews to Paul). Avarice is considered one of the seven
deadly or capital sins — the others being pride, lust, gluttony, sloth, anger. CCC §
1866. In this instance, Denis argues that St. Paul is using avarice as a synonym for
mortal sin, and so what is true for avarice (that it lands us in the snare of the devil)
is true for all mortal sins, and not just those arising from avarice. Thus, "snare of
the devil" = "avarice" = "mortal sin."

20 1 Tim. 6:9.

21 2 Tim. 2:25b–26.

22 Mark 4:19.

23 Job 22:25.

24 *Cf.* Job 12:4: *He that is mocked by his friends as I, shall call upon God and he
will hear him: for the simplicity of the just man is laughed to scorn.*

25 Matt. 5:11.

ought to glory when the abusive talk of ignorant men is raised against us, because we can thereby conform ourselves in some way to our Lord Jesus Christ, who says: *The reproaches of them that reproached you are fallen upon me;*[26] and *All they that saw me have laughed me to scorn.*[27] The Jews frequently told him: *He has a devil, and he is mad;*[28] and *he is a glutton, . . . and a friend of sinners;*[29] and, *by the prince of devils he casts out devils.*[30] Or [alternatively], *from the sharp word,* that is, from the sentence of the judge, who will say in the day of judgment to the ungodly that most harsh word: *Go, you cursed . . . into everlasting fire.*[31]

90{91}[4] *He will overshadow you with his shoulders: and under his wings you shall trust.*

Scapulis suis obumbrabit tibi, et sub pennis eius sperabis.

90{91}[4] *Scapulis suis obumbrabit tibi; he will overshadow you with his shoulders.* By the shoulders of God is understood the divine power protecting the elect. Therefore, this is the meaning [of this verse]: *he will overshadow* you, that is, from the heat of temptation and the fire of persecutions he will refresh you and will relieve you with *his shoulders,* that is, with his benignant power: just as it is said in a later Psalm: *You have overshadowed my head in the day of battle.*[32] Hence, the Apostle [Paul] says: *As the sufferings of Christ abound in us: so also by Christ does our comfort abound.*[33] *Et sub pennis eius, and under his wings,* that is, under the pinions of the mercy and the power of God, *sperabis, you shall trust* that by the mercy and the power of God you will be saved.

90{91}[5] *His truth shall compass you with a shield: you shall not be afraid of the terror of the night.*

Scuto circumdabit te veritas eius: non timebis a timore nocturno.

90{91}[5] *Veritas eius, his truth,* that is, the knowledge of sacred Scripture, or the enlightenment of the Holy Spirit, *circumdabit, shall compass you,* that is, defend you all about, *scuto, with a shield,* a spiritual [shield]

---

26   Ps. 68:10.
27   Ps. 22:8a.
28   John 10:20a.
29   Matt. 11:19.
30   Matt. 9:34.
31   Matt. 25:41.
32   Ps. 139:8b.
33   2 Cor. 1:5.

in the soul. Whence the Savior said: *If you continue in my word, you shall be my disciples indeed. And you shall know the truth, and the truth shall make you free.*[34] And the Apostle [Paul]: *All Scripture inspired of God,* he said, *is profitable to teach, to reprove, to correct, and to instruct in justice, that the man of God may be perfect, furnished to every good work.*[35] For in the way that a material shield defends the body from injury by the enemy, so by the consideration of sacred Scripture and the recollection of divine doctrine the soul is protected by the assaults of the tempter, and it drives away from its consent whatever its perceives to be dissonant with the divine law. For this reason, the book of Wisdom says: *Your word preserves them that believe in you.*[36] For he who applies the testimony of sacred Scripture in all that he does or all he relinquishes leans upon an impregnable shield which cannot err.[37]

Non timebis a timore nocturno, you shall not be afraid of the terror of the night, that is, you will not be terrified to run up against the dread of night, nor will you tremble at those things which customarily excite fear during the nighttime hours. For many weak and of little hope, who are petrified during the night, fear even during the day. And some a little stronger in spirit do not fear [during the day], yet in the night they easily become terrified from some noise, or from the imagination, or from a dream. This fear is an indication of a great imperfection; and the truth of sacred Scripture or of supernal illumination which says, *Be not afraid of sudden fear,*[38] frees one from it. Whence Solomon said: *The wicked man flees, when no man pursues: but the just, bold as a lion, shall be without dread.*[39] And so against this foolish fear—by which we fear the night because of the absence of men, or because of dreams, or because of the appearance of phantasms, as if God and the holy angels were not with us during the night as they are during the day, or as if demons are able to do something within us without the permission of God—is written:

---

34   John 8:31b–32.

35   2 Tim. 3:16–17.

36   Wis. 16:26b.

37   E. N. "[S]o far is it from being possible that any error can co-exist with inspiration, that inspiration not only is essentially incompatible with error, but excludes and rejects it as absolutely and necessarily as it is impossible that God Himself, the supreme Truth, can utter that which is not true. This is the ancient and unchanging faith of the Church." DS 3292 (Leo XIII, *Providentissimus Deus*, 20). "For as the substantial Word of God became like to men in all things, 'except sin,' so the words of God, expressed in human language, are made like to human speech in every respect, except error." Pius XII, *Divino afflante Spiritu*, 37.

38   Prov. 3:25a.

39   Prov 28:1.

He that fears the Lord shall tremble at nothing;[40] and again: *The vision of dreams is like him that catches at a shadow and follows after the wind.*[41] He who considers these words of eternal Truth will be free of the nighttime fear, in the manner that is declared by Wisdom: *He that shall hear me, shall rest without terror.*[42] But if the imaginations of things stir up the fear of harmful things for us, for example, thoughts of those already dead, *etc.* it is very profitable immediately to picture in the heart the image of Christ hanging on the Cross, and those things which he endured for us.[43]

90{91}[6] *Of the arrow that flies in the day, of the business that walks about in the dark: of invasion, or of the noonday devil.*

A sagitta volante in die, a negotio perambulante in tenebris, ab incursu, et daemonio meridiano.

You will not therefore fear **90{91}[6]** *A sagitta volante in die,* of the *arrow that flies in the day,* that is, from the unpleasant adversities which are openly occasioned, such as being reproached, plundered, and suffering any other manifest affliction: indeed, such adversities should be received as a sort of gift of God, and should be suffered with joy, in accordance with that stated by the Apostle [Paul]: *For unto you it is given for Christ, not only to believe in him, but also to suffer for him.*[44] And to the Hebrews: *You have received with joy being stripped of your own goods.*[45] You will not have fear *a negotio,* of the *business,* that is, of the devil,[46] *perambulante in*

---

40   Ecclus. 34:16a.

41   Ecclus. 34:3a, 2b.

42   Prov. 1:33a.

43   E. N. "The best remedy against your fear of death," St. Francis de Sales wrote to a correspondent, "is mediation on Him Who is our life: never think of one without going on to think of the other." St. Francis de Sales, *The Spiritual Letters of St. Francis de Sales* (London: Rivingtons, 1871), Letter XXXIII (Jan. 20, 1609), 116–17.

44   Phil. 1:29.

45   Heb. 10:34a.

46   E. N. The Latin word *negotio* translates the Hebrew מדבר, which is translated in the Septuagint by the Greek word πράγματος (*pragmatos*). The Latin work *negotium*, which is translated by the Douay Rheims as "business," ("busy-ness") is actually a negative of its opposite, *non otium*, which might be translated as a negation of peace or of leisure, the devil being one who disrupts one's peace. The Hebrew word דבר, might be alternatively translated as "plague" or "pestilence" (*deber*) or "matter" or "thing" (*dabar*) (with the implication of it being evil). The Septuagint used the word πράγματος (*pragmatos*), which means "thing" or "deed," to translate the Hebrew, but there is an implication of evil, as indicated by Brenton's English translation of the Septuagint, where he translates πράγματος here as "the evil thing," There is therefore a basis for understanding this as a reference to the devil. As St. Thomas More wrote:

tenebris, that walks about in the dark, that is, who is permitted during the nighttime hours to disquiet men; nor will you fear *ab incursu et daemonio meridiano; of invasion, or of the noonday devil*, that is, the devil who is permitted to rage during the day.[47]

He who dwells in the aid of the most High is freed from four temptations, therefore, namely, from the terror of the night, from the arrow that flies by day, from the business that walks about in the dark, and from the invasion or of the noonday devil. And saying with the Apostle, *I can do all things in him who strengthens me*, and with Jeremiah, *O Lord, my might, and my strength, and my refuge in the day of tribulation*,[48] one ought not to dread any temptation, however great it is or from wherever it comes. Hence, it is stated in an earlier Psalm: *The Lord is my light and my salvation, whom shall I fear? [The Lord is the protector of my life: of whom shall I be afraid?]*[49] For this reason, Peter declares: *Who is he that can hurt you, if you be zealous of good?*[50] Indeed, *If God be for us, who is against us?*[51] Therefore you will not fear either the devil that walks about in the dark nor the noonday devil.

90{91}[7]   *A thousand shall fall at your side, and ten thousand at your right hand: but it shall not come nigh you.*

Cadent a latere tuo mille, et decem millia a dextris tuis; ad te autem non appropinquabit.

90{91}[7]   *Cadent a latere tuo, at your side shall fall*, [that is,] at your left side [shall fall], *mille, a thousand* of the demons, *et decem millia, and ten thousand* of the demons shall fall *a dextris tuis, at your right hand*: for whatever kind or however many [demons] approach to tempt you, they will be overwhelmed and shall flee through the divine power, in the manner that the Apostle [Paul] states: *The God of peace crush Satan under your feet*

Negotium is here . . . the name of a devil that is ever full of busyness, in tempting folk to much evil business." *The Dialogue of Comfort Against Tribulation*, II, 17 (*The Essential Works of Thomas More* (New Haven: Yale University Press, 2020), p. 1182 (eds. Gerard B. Wegemer and Stephen W. Smith).

47   E. N. Traditionally, the "noonday devil" is identified with depression, melancholy, or acedia. *See* Jean-Charles Nault, O. S. B., *The Noonday Devil: Acedia, the Unnamed Evil of our Times* (San Francisco: Ignatius Press, 2015) and R. J. Snell, *Acedia and Its Discontents: Metaphysical Boredom in an Empire of Desire* (Angelico Press, 2015).

48   Jer. 16:19a.

49   Ps. 26:1. E. N. I have placed the whole verse. That part in brackets replaces the "etc." in the text.

50   1 Pet. 3:13.

51   Rom. 8:31b.

speedily.[52] And so Elisha spoke: *Fear not: for there are more with us than with them.*[53] Now by the left side, where it is asserted that a thousand fall, is understood the state of the soul in adversity; but by the right, [is understood] its state in prosperity. It states, therefore, that a thousand are fallen at your left side, because no adversity will defeat you if you dwell in the aid of the most High; indeed, however much your spirit might be afflicted, it will not complain, nor will it withdraw from God, nor will it succumb to the tempter by being overcome with faintheartedness. Also, ten thousand fall at your right hand because no prosperity makes you grow proud; and however much you succeed in prospering, never will you rejoice in yourself, nor will you ascribe any good to yourself, nor will you consent to the flattery of the tempter. But why is it asserted that a thousand will fall on the left side, but ten thousand at the right hand? First, it ought to be known that here a determinate number is placed for an indeterminate number, in the manner that Daniel states: *Thousands of thousands ministered to him, and ten thousand times a hundred thousand stood before him.*[54] And in Revelation: *The number of the angels was thousands of thousands ... saying ... The Lamb that was slain is worthy to receive power.*[55] So it is [to be understood] in this sense: that at your sight will fall a multitude of demons, however many numerous or many they might be. For as we have in Scripture, *it is easy for the Lord to save either by many, or by few;*[56] for undoubtedly, the holy angels are many more in number and stronger than the evil angels that are against us. Now more are said to fall at one's right than at one's left because more men are seduced by the blandishments and enticements of prosperity than they are by the annoyances of adversity. For all men naturally and strongly long for pleasure.

Ad te autem, but ... to you, the temptation of the devil, *non appropinquabit, shall not come nigh to you* by consent, that is, a multitude of demons will be overcome by you through the help of the grace of God. For having been defeated, the demons cease from temptation and they flee, in the manner that is written: *Resist the devil, and he will fly from you.*[57] And some assert that a devil once he has been defeated by someone never returns to tempt the same person. Others say that once he has been defeated he will never return and tempt the same person of that sin [the temptation of which] came forth from him. But I think

52   Rom. 16:20a.
53   2 Kings 6:16.
54   Dan. 7:10.
55   Rev. 5:11b–12a.
56   1 Sam. 14:6b.
57   James 4:7b.

more probable that which also St. Thomas thinks more likely, namely, that however much the demons are defeated and retreat for a time and cease from temptation, they still return again to tempt the same person of any manner of sin. And in confirmation of this, Thomas refers to that which is written in Luke regarding Christ: *All the temptation being ended, the devil departed from him for a time.*[58]

90{91}[8]   *But you shall consider with your eyes: and shall see the reward of the wicked.*

Verumtamen oculis tuis considerabis et retributionem peccatorum videbis.

90{91}[8]   *Verumtamen oculis tuis,* but . . . *with your eyes,* with [your] interior [eyes], *considerabis, you shall consider,* this, your victory performed for you by God, lest you be ungrateful to God, and, in order for this to be considered, an infusion of the Holy Spirit is required according to that stated by the Apostle [Paul]: *We have received not the spirit of this world, but the Spirit that is of God; that we may know the things that are given us from God.*[59] *Et retributionem peccatorum videbis, and you shall see the reward of the wicked:* that is, you will weigh and discern the just punishment of the reprobate, now indeed by the contemplation of faith, bringing to mind the strictness of the future judgment and the punishments of hell; and in the future age and at the final judgment you will see it by a most certain manifestation. And so that you might seek to avoid it, you say to God:

90{91}[9]   *Because you, O Lord, are my hope: you have made the most High your refuge.*

Quoniam tu es, Domine, spes mea; Altissimum posuisti refugium tuum.

90{91}[10]   *There shall no evil come to you: nor shall the scourge come near your dwelling.*

Non accedet ad te malum, et flagellum non appropinquabit tabernaculo tuo.

---

58   Luke 4:13. E. N. The reference is to ST Ia, q. 114, art. 5, co. St. Thomas also cites to Matt. 12:44, where Jesus speaks of the evil spirit who leaves a man and states, "I will return *into my house from whence I came out,*" which suggests that a demon will return to tempt the same man he had previous tempted.
59   1 Cor. 2:12.

90{91}[9] *Quoniam tu es, Domine, spes mea; because you, O Lord, are my hope,* that is, the object, cause, and end of my hope; or *my hope,* that is, the good that is principally and finally awaited by me, for I do not desire any other good, nor do I seek any other reward, nor do I expect any other end, but you yourself. *Altissimum posuisti refugium tuum, you have made the most High your refuge:* that is, you have placed the end of our refuge in you yourself, namely that we will not find rest unless we abide by and below you; but let us raise the mind in the contemplation of your goodness, and so let us find refuge in your ineffable and superlatively most high clemency. **90{91}[10]** *Non accedet ad te malum, there shall no evil come to you,* that is, the sinner will not be admitted to your fellowship and glory. Or [alternatively], *evil,* that is, sin, shall not *come to you* by approbation, for it will not please you, as has been said in an earlier Psalm: *You are not a God that wills iniquity.*[60] *Et flagellum non appropinquabit tabernaculo tuo, nor shall the scourge come near your dwelling,* that is, [the scourge shall not come into] the triumphant Church or the empyrean heaven: for in the heavenly homeland one will not come upon any sadness, affliction, or misery, but *joy and gladness, . . . thanksgiving and the voice of praise.*[61]

Or [we can understand it] thus: A just man says: *Because you, O Lord, are my hope* — and if you truly say this to God, O man, whoever you might be, then assuredly — *you have made the most High your refuge,* that is, you have placed yourself in a place of refuge in Christ, the Creator of all things, not in created and lowly things. And so *there shall no evil,* either of punishment or of fault, *come to you* in this age, where you will receive the mercy [which is the object] of your hope; *nor shall the scourge come near your dwelling,* that is, your body, which you will take up again in the future resurrection, because you will have an impassible, glorified, agile, and subtle body. For it is proper (according to the Apostle [Paul]) that *this mortal must put on immortality.*[62] Hence the Lord says by Isaiah: *There shall be . . . security forever; and my people shall sit in the beauty of peace, and in the tabernacles of confidence, and in wealthy rest.*[63] Or [we can see it this way]: *There shall no evil come to you,* [the evil] of mortal fault in the present through consent [to mortal sin] in the present, because, according to that stated in the second epistle of Peter — *labor . . . that by good works you may make sure your calling and election; for by doing these*

---

60   Ps. 5:5b.
61   Is. 51:3b.
62   1 Cor. 15:53b.
63   Is. 32:17–18.

things, you shall not sin at any time[64]—the Lord preserves from ruin those who hope in him. *Nor shall the scourge come near your dwelling,* that is, your body to its detriment or its harm: indeed, such scourge should be considered rather as a sweet and profitable purification and a great merit than as a difficult torment or some kind of harm: for, as the Apostle says, *The sufferings of this time are not worthy to be compared with the glory to come, that shall be revealed in us.*[65] And again he says: *That which is at present momentary and light of our tribulation, works for us above measure exceedingly an eternal weight of glory.*[66]

90{91}[11]   *For he has given his angels charge over you; to keep you in all your ways.*

Quoniam angelis suis mandavit de te, ut custodiant te in omnibus viis tuis.

90{91}[11] *Quoniam angelis suis mandavit de te, ut custodiant te in omnibus viis tuis; for he has given his angels charge over you; to keep you in all your ways.* For all [angels] *are ministering spirits* (according to the Apostle) *sent to minister to them who shall receive the inheritance of salvation.*[67] For that the angels are appointed to keep custody of men is insinuated by Christ in Matthew: *Their angels,* he says, *in heaven always see the face of my Father who is in heaven.*[68] Whereby Jerome says: Great is the dignity of souls in that every one of them has a holy angel from the time of their birth to appointed to keep guard over it.[69] But since all men have their own angel set over them, why does it not say [in this verse], "he has given his *angel* charge over you *(te),*" or "he has given his angels charge of *all of you (vobis)?* The response to this is that although man, insofar as he is one person, has an angel especially assigned to him, yet as many devils tempt one and the same man, so also many angels are able to be present and render aid to the same man. Now the angels keep guard over us to the extent they can, in all our ways, that is, in all our works. For they keep guard over us in our good works, so that we do not cease doing good, but that we always persevere to the end. In evil acts they also keep guard over us, lest we remain in the clutches of the

---

64   2 Pet. 1:10.
65   Rom. 8:18.
66   2 Cor. 4:17.
67   Heb. 1:14.
68   Matt. 18:10.
69   E. N. The reference is to St. Jerome's *Commentary on Matthew,* III, 28 (interpreting Matt. 18:10), PL 26, 130. It is quoted by St. Thomas: ST Ia, q. 113, art. 2, s.c.

devil, and so that we do not persist in vice. They also protect us from the temptations of demons, so that they cannot molest us as much as they might desire, and [they therefore protect us] from many dangers of soul and body. Hence, according to Thomas [Aquinas], infants in the womb of their mothers receive a special angel to keep them, lest some harm befall the infant in the womb.[70]

90{91}[12]   *In their hands they shall bear you up: lest you dash your foot against a stone.*

In manibus portabunt te, ne forte offendas ad lapidem pedem tuum.

90{91}[12] *In manibus suis, in their hands,* that is, in their power and wisdom, *portabunt, they shall bear you up,* that is, they shall direct *te, you* during this exile in the path to the heavenly fatherland of the elect. For they give aid to our weakness with their power and they enlighten the darkness of our hearts with their wisdom: and so they walk along with us, carrying us with them, cooperating with us in all our good works. They shall therefore bear you up, *ne forte offendas ad lapidem pedem tuam, lest you dash your foot against a stone,* that is, lest something obstruct you in the way, so that you might remain directed toward the heavenly homeland by unhindered steps and by a secure road. Or [we can understand it thus], *lest you dash your foot against a stone,* that is, lest you offend by sin Christ who is the cornerstone.[71] Or [alternatively], *lest you dash . . . against a stone,* that is, [lest you incur] a mortal fault, prohibiting you ingress into the heavenly fatherland, in the manner that a rock obstructs the way and prohibits ingress; *your foot,* that is, your affections, or the path of your works, serving and attaching to the creature more than to the Creator.

The devil proposed these two verses to Christ as being predictive of Christ;[72] but because he is a liar, and since he speaks lies,[73] he speaks

---

70   E. N. This seems a misstatement of St. Thomas's opinion, at least as it is contained in the *Summa Theologiae.* In the *Summa,* St. Thomas's position is that guardian angel of the mother is responsible for both mother and child so long as the child is in the womb, and the child is allotted its own guardian angel at birth. *See* ST Ia, q. 113, art. 5, ad 3.

71   1 Pet. 2:6; Is. 28:16: *Behold I will lay a stone in the foundations of Sion, a tried stone, a corner stone, a precious stone, founded in the foundation.* Acts 4:11: *This is the stone which was rejected by you the builders, which is become the head of the corner.*

72   Matt. 4:6.

73   *Cf.* John 8:44.

on his own behalf, and so he asserts this mendaciously. For, according to Jerome, these [verses] are not said of Christ, but of his members:[74] for Christ did not need the custody of angels at all—indeed, he was unable to err; and though the angels ministered unto him, this was not because of any necessity, but on the grounds of reverence and decency.[75]

90{91}[13]   *You shall walk upon the asp and the basilisk: and you shall trample underfoot the lion and the dragon.*

Super aspidem et basiliscum ambulabis, et conculcabis leonem et draconem.

90{91}[13] *Super aspidem et basiliscum ambulabis, et conculcabis leonem et draconem; you shall walk upon the asp and the basilisk: and you shall trample underfoot the lion and the dragon.* This is similar to that which Christ said to his disciples: *Behold, I have given you power to tread upon serpents and scorpions, and upon all the power of the enemy: and nothing shall hurt you.*[76] It is fitting to understand these in a literal way as dealing with irrational and venomous brute animals, upon which many of the Saints, especially those in the New Law, have trampled upon without injury, just as when they drank poison without harm, as Christ said to them in Mark: *If they shall drink any deadly thing, it shall not hurt them.*[77] (This also in part relates to the children of Israel proceeding out of Egypt through the vast and horrible wilderness, full of venomous animals, which did not bring harm to the children of Israel, as Moses wrote: *The Lord was your leader in the great and terrible wilderness, wherein there was the serpent burning with his breath, and the scorpion and the dipsas.*[78]) By these animals we may also fittingly understand demons, those having the properties of animals, or the same demon with diverse properties,

---

74   *Cf.* St. Thomas Aquinas's *Catena Aurea, In Matt.*, cap. 4, l. 3; however, though Jerome notes that the devil interprets the Scriptures badly and that this verse does not pertain to Christ, he suggests that it is a prophecy that relates to a holy man. He does not appear to attribute it to the Church, the members of Christ's body. See St. Jerome's *Commentary on Matthew*, I, 32, PL 26, 32 (*Male ergo interpretatur Scripturas diabolus*, "the devil badly interprets the Scriptures, therefore.") See also *Breviarium in Psalmos*, PL 26, 1090–1100.

75   Matt. 4:11.

76   Luke 10:19.

77   Mark 16:18a.

78   Deut. 8:15. E. N. Dipsas are small, venomous snakes. The word comes from Greek διψάς (*dipsas*). The Vulgate draws from the Septuagint here, rather than from the Hebrew text.

or more likely, informed with evil, or with such harmful a vice, that he causes injury just like these animals.

And so the devil is described as an asp inasmuch as he inserts into the heart the venom of envy, and he infects and kills the soul with occult temptations. And so by the asp can be understood envy, which by its venom poisons, and completely demolishes and destroys, the love of God and of neighbor, and indeed all the virtues of men: because as John says, *He that loves not, abides in death*; and again, *Whosoever hates his brother is a murderer.*[79] The devil is also called a basilisk since he tempts and kills the soul with fraudulent suggestions, proposing to it evil under the guise of good, since he *transforms himself into an angel of light*, according to the Apostle.[80] For the basilisk destroys by its sight alone, not all men, but those (as it is said) who do not see him first. For if a man sees him from the first, he is not harmed by the eyes of the most poisonous basilisk: indeed (as we read) if anyone places a mirror before the basilisk, the venom is reflected, returning to him from whom it came, and it destroys the very one who poured it forth, namely, the basilisk himself.[81] Clearly, the devil, who is signified by the basilisk, is like this; and, since he also transforms himself into an angel of light, he is not seen by the one who is destroyed; but if a man is first able to espy this devil and to perceive his cunning, he will not be harmed, but will cast back the evil intent of the devil upon his head. And so by basilisk is also designated vainglory, which destroys the incautious and those who are mentally blind, yet it does not have the power to harm those who see and are spiritually enlightened. The devil is also called a lion, since he persecutes men contumaciously, violently, and impetuously. For this reason the prince of the Apostles admonishes: *Be sober and watch, because your adversary the devil, a roaring lion, goes about seeking whom he may devour. Whom you, strong in faith, resist.*[82] Whence by a lion is

---

79   1 John 3:14, 15.

80   2 Cor. 11:14.

81   E. N. Denis is drawing from popular descriptions of the basilisk like Pliny the Elder's (1st cent. AD), *Natural* History, VIII, 33, and Isidore of Seville (7th cent. AD), *Etymologies*, XII, 4:6–9, and the Franciscan Bartholomaeus Anglicus (13th cent. AD), *De proprietatibus rerum*, XVIII. The basilisk is called the "king of serpents," as the word itself (which comes from Greek βασιλίσκος (*basiliskos*) meaning "little king"). "The basilisk," says St. Augustine, "is the king of serpents, as the devil is the king of wicked spirits." *Rex est serpentium basiliscus, sicut diabolus rex est daemoniorum. Enar. In Psalmos*, 90.2, 9, PL 37 1168. In iconography, St. Michael the Archangel is depicted as killing a basilisk, precisely as a symbol of the Devil.

82   1 Pet. 5:8–9a.

signified a ferocious animal, or all sin that has a relation to violence. Now the devil is also called a dragon, since he thoroughly devours men by the abundance of his pestiferous exactions, as is written about him: *He will drink up a river, and not wonder.*[83]

We might also by this brute animal understand ungodly men because of their similarity [to these animals] in the imitation of evil. For John the Baptist said to the perverse and unbelieving Jews: *You brood of vipers, who has showed you to flee from the wrath to come?*[84] Pharoah is also called by Ezechiel: *You great dragon.*[85]

If, therefore, you entrust yourself to God with all your soul, you shall walk upon all these asps and basilisks, and you shall trample underfoot all these lions and dragons: for you will be immune from sin against all temptation, persecution, and the impulses of vice, according to that which the Apostle said: *In all these things we overcome, because of him that has loved us.*[86]

90{91}[14]   *Because he hoped in me, I will deliver him: I will protect him because he has known my name.*

Quoniam in me speravit, liberabo eum; protegam eum, quoniam cognovit nomen meum.

Thereafter follows the most beneficent consolation of the God of promises to those who place hope in him for many graces in the present life, and the fullness of beatitude in the future. 90{91}[14] *Quoniam in me speravit*, because he hoped in me, not with an empty or void hope, but a working and a formed hope, doing all that which was possible to him, and yet neither attributing anything to his own power nor trusting in his own perfection, but placing hope foremost in me, *liberabo eum*, *I will deliver him*, now from vice, and in the future resurrection from all punishment and imperfection of mind and body when I will reform the body of its lowness, and make it *like to the body of his glory.*[87] *Protegam eum, I will protect him* from all danger, *quoniam cognovit nomen meum*, *because he has known my name*, that is, because he knew me, and he

---

83   Job 40:18a. E. N. As Denis states in his *Commentary on Job*, these verses point to an animal that drinks great quantities in a singular manner since he is dry and hot in nature. Doctoris Ecstatici D. Dionysii Cartusiani, Opera Omnia, Vol. 5 (Montreuil: 1897), 24.
84   Matt. 3:7; Luke 3:7.
85   Ez. 29:3a.
86   Rom. 8:37.
87   Cf. Phil. 3:21.

acknowledged me with faith and works, to be merciful in forgetting, faithful in rendering aid, and truthful in promising. For there is a certain knowledge of God, which is called unformed, that is, without decorum or adornment, because it is not joined to charity or a good manner of living: of which knowledge, the Apostle [Paul] says [to Titus], *They profess that they know God: but in their works they deny him;*[88] and to the Romans, *When they knew God, they have not glorified him as God, or given thanks.*[89] The other knowledge of God is called formed, that is, it is united with love, and of which is written in another place, *He who says that he knows God, and keeps not his commandments, is a liar.*[90] Here, therefore, the Prophet speaks of the formed knowledge of God, which indeed is worthy of the divine protection, since it is more acceptable to God than holocausts, in the way that the Lord said through the prophet Hosea: *For I desired . . . the knowledge of God more than holocausts.*[91] Take heed how great a good this knowledge of God is. Truly, it is so great that it is said to be the end of the coming of Christ and eternal life. For it is written: *We know that the Son of God is come: and he has given us understanding that we may know the true God.*[92] And again: *Now this is eternal life: That they may know you, the only true God.*[93]

90{91}[15] *He shall cry to me, and I will hear him: I am with him in tribulation, I will deliver him, and I will glorify him.*

Clamabit ad me, et ego exaudiam eum; cum ipso sum in tribulatione; eripiam eum, et glorificabo eum.

90{91}[16] *I will fill him with length of days; and I will show him my salvation.*

Longitudine dierum replebo eum, et ostendam illi salutare meum.

90{91}[15] *Clamabit ad me,* he shall cry to me, fervently praying, *et exaudiam eum,* and I will hear him, giving that which he reasonably and steadfastly requests; *cum ipso sum in tribulatione,* I am with him in tribulation: as is stated in a Psalm above: *The Lord is nigh unto them that are of a contrite heart.*[94] If we desire God to be unceasingly at hand

---

88   Titus 1:16a.
89   Rom. 1:21a.
90   1 John 2:4.
91   Hosea 6:6.
92   1 John 5:20.
93   John 17:3a.
94   Ps. 33:19a.

with us, therefore, let us not fear, and let us not refuse happily to endure tribulations. *Eripiam eum, I will deliver him* from adversity, *et glorificabo, and I will glorify,* that is, I will make *eum, him* glorious and blessed in the heavenly homeland, saying to him: *Well done, good and faithful servant, because you have been been faithful over a few things, I will place you over many things: enter into the joy of your Lord.*[95] **90{91}[16]** *Longitudine dierum, with the length of days,* that is, with the unceasing duration of blessed life or aeviternally, which is a participation in eternity.[96] This is the measure of action which the blessed in the heavenly homeland blessedly enjoy, in which the enjoyment is without any interruption, vicissitude, or alteration; *replebo eum, I will fill him,* giving to him eternally [the prize] of remaining with me eternally, as his desires strive for, so that he will neither will, nor will he be able to will, nor will he fear [to be able to will] to be separated from me; *et ostendam illi, and I will show him* clearly by sight, *my salvation,* that is, my beloved Son, the Savior of all, the eternal Word, in whom the blessed in the heavenly homeland see all things, he whom with me, his Father, and the Holy Spirit, is one and the same object and cause of the blessedness of all the elect. In this showing or vision of the divinity of Christ consists the entirety of our happiness, our highest joy, and our essential reward. Whence also Christ, intimates that our happiness consists in this showing of himself, saying: *He that loves me, shall be loved of my Father; and I will love him and will manifest myself to him.*[97]

See, we have heard this concise, moral, doctrinal, and consolatory Psalm. In it we are taught how spiritually wholesome it is to hope in God. It ought to be said to God in great confidence so that we might obtain that which we hope for. How many are the temptations in this life; yet how great is manifold help of the holy angels against them that God will grant to us; and how great the happy effects of those who have steadfast hope in the Lord. For good reason, we recite this Psalm at Compline[98] against the snares of nighttime, and the many temptations of the devil. For it is then that we especially need divine protection, and grace, and angelic protection. And each of us ought to honor his angel with special veneration, especially invoking him in the morning, so that he might protect us and guide us the entire day, and late in the day, so that he might take care of our heart and body throughout the entire

---

95   Matt. 25:21, 23b.

96   E. N. On the *aevum* or aeviternity, *see* footnote 38-57.

97   John 14:21b.

98   E. N. In the Divine Office, Compline is the last prayer of the day.

night, and, unceasingly standing by us, he might repel tormenting dreams, enlighten our mind, and kindly go before us when we wake. And so that we might be found worthy to be given the divine promises described at the end of this Psalm, let us preoccupy ourselves with singing this song at Compline with a most devout mind. If we do this, we will often taste with the interior palate the virtue and sweetness of this present Psalm, which overflows with truly marvelous sweetness.

PRAYER

O GOD MOST HIGH, WE BESEECH YOU, GRANT us to dwell in your aid and to abide in your protection, so that, averted by your right hand, evil might not draw near us or the scourge of sin touch us; but we might be guarded by the angels, under your command, in all of our ways.

Deus altissime, concede nos, quaesumus, in adiutorio tuo habitare,
et in tua commorari protectione: ut dextera tua avertente,
non accedat ad nos malus, nec tangat nos
peccatoris flagellum; sed te mandante,
ab angelis in omnibus custodiamur
viis nostris.

Psalm 91

ARTICLE LXX

EXPLANATION OF THE NINETY-FIRST PSALM:
BONUM EST CONFITERI DOMINO.
IT IS GOOD TO GIVE PRAISE TO THE LORD.

91{92}[1] *A Psalm of a canticle on the Sabbath day.*

Psalmus cantici, in die sabbati.

HE PSALM BEING NOW EXPOUNDED HAS this title: **91{92}[1]** *Psalmus cantici, in die sabbati; a Psalm of a canticle on the Sabbath day*, that is, a Psalm of spiritual joy sung in the day of the Sabbath, that is, in the Sabbath of the mind, namely, in the tranquility of conscience, so that we might be found worthy to be led to the Sabbath of eternity. Literally, this Psalm relates to the Sabbath in particular, and it was sung by the Jews during it, because it deals with the works of creation: the commemoration of which the Lord commanded that such be celebrated on the day of the Sabbath, and that all servile acts cease during that time,[1] because God on the seventh day or the Sabbath rested from all the works that he had accomplished.[2] For the Lord desired to introduce men to the knowledge of his eternity and to recognize all things to be created. Now given this purpose (according to Rabbi Moses), the most evident and easiest way to achieve this was the celebration of the Sabbath, during which the world was recalled to have been newly begun, or to be have been produced in time, from which it was most clearly established the Creator of the world to be eternal.[3]

91{92}[2] *It is good to confess to the Lord: and to sing to your name, O most High.*

Bonum est confiteri Domino, et psallere nomini tuo, Altissime.

---

1 Ex. 20:8–11.
2 Gen. 2:2.
3 E. N. The reference to "Rabbi Moses" is to Moses Maimonides (1138-1204). Born in Córdoba during the time that Andalusian Spain was ruled by the Almoravids, Maimonides wrote a number of Jewish, philosophical, logical, and medical works. His best-known work is his *Guide for the Perplexed*. His works were informed by his Jewish faith and the philosophical works of Aristotle.

And so the holy Prophet says: **91{92}[2]** *Bonum est confiteri Domino*, *it is good to confess to the Lord*. As it has abundantly been stated before, confession is of a two-fold nature, namely: there is the confession of divine praise, of which the Savior said, *I confess to you, O Father, Lord of heaven and earth;*[4] and the confession of our fault, of which elsewhere is written, *Confess therefore your sins one to another.*[5] Now both kinds of confession are good and salubrious; but the first kind is better, more noble, and more divine, since it is an angelic act. But because *praise is not seemly in the mouth of the sinner,*[6] for this reason the confession of fault is more necessary and salubrious for the sinner, since when one's vices have been blotted out by this confession, he is rendered worthy to confess or to praise the Lord. But here the Psalm speaks of the confession of praise. It is also good to *psallere, to sing*, that is, publicly and by the sublime Psalms and divine praises to sing, *nomini tuo, to your name*, that is, to the honor of your name, O God *altissime, most High*. Whence the angel Raphael said to Tobias: *Bless the God of heaven, give glory to him in the sight of all that live, because he has shown his mercy to you.*[7] And so it now continues:

91{92}[3] *To show forth your mercy in the morning, and your truth in the night:*

> *Ad annuntiandum mane misericordiam tuam, et veritatem tuam per noctem.*

91{92}[3] *Ad annuntiandum mane, to show forth . . . in the morning*, that is, at the beginning of the day: of which Isaiah says, *In the morning early I will keep watch for you;*[8] or [we can understand it thus], *in the morning*, that is, in the spiritual sunrise, when, namely, we sense the infusion of supernal brightness in the heart from the change and newness of holy devotion; or [in this manner], *in the morning*, that is, during the time of prosperity and happiness; *misericordiam tuam, your mercy*, that is, praising and proclaiming the gracious benefits of your most kind bounty, or the goodness that is connatural to you. In whatever manner *in the morning* is said, we ought to show forth the mercy of God, most devoutly ascribing all our goods to the divine goodness. It is moreover a good and excellent thing to begin the day with divine praise, so that

---

4   Luke 10:21a.
5   James 16:1.
6   Ecclus. 15:9.
7   Tob. 12:6a. The Latin word for to "give glory" is *confitemini*, "confess" in the sense of "give praise."
8   Is. 26:9a.

we might spend all the day in the proclamation of God, in the way that it is stated in a Psalm above, *Let my mouth be filled with praise, that I may sing your glory; your greatness all the day long.*[9]

But one ought also to show forth *veritatem tuam, your truth,* that is, sacred Scripture, the doctrine of Christ, or the divine justice, *per noctem, in the night,* that is, during certain hours of nighttime: as Jeremiah exhorted, *Arise, give praise in the night, in the beginning of the watches.*[10] Or [alternatively], *in the night,* that is, during the time of adversity, so that in the time of our chastisement we might praise your justice, and we might acknowledge our malice by reason of which we deserve to be scourged, saying that which Tobias said: *I bless you, O Lord God of Israel, because you have chastised me;*[11] and also that [stated] by Job, *I have sinned, and indeed I have offended, and I have not received what I have deserved.*[12] Or [viewed another way], *in the night,* the spiritual [night] of the soul, when, namely, spiritual consolation is taken away, the grace of God is suspended, and one's own soul endures weakness. For at such times we ought to praise divine justice; and we should not be faint of heart, nor desire counterfeit consolations, but we ought most affectionately to pray for the return of the first grace, and patiently to suffer the absence or, better said, the concealment of the beloved (for truly, he is present, his presence is just not then being felt), saying with Isaiah, *My soul has desired you in the night;*[13] and wholeheartedly thinking that which the Lord asserted through the same Prophet: *For a small moment have I forsaken you, but with great mercies will I gather you. In a moment of indignation have I hid my face a little while from you, but with everlasting kindness have I had mercy on you.*[14]

91{92}[4] *Upon an instrument of ten strings, upon the psaltery, with a canticle, upon the harp.*

In decachordo, psalterio, cum cantico, in cithara.

And because the Hebrews were accustomed to praise God with instruments, as the Church now does using the organ,[15] so it adds: **91{92}**

---

9   Ps. 70:8.

10   Lam. 2:19a.

11   Tob. 11:17a.

12   Job. 33:27. *E. N.* He should have been punished worse.

13   Is. 26:9a.

14   Is. 54:7–8.

15   *E. N.* "In the Latin Church the pipe organ is to be held in high esteem, for it is the traditional musical instrument which adds a wonderful splendor to the Church's

[4] *In decachordo, psalterio, cum cantico, in cithara; upon an instrument of ten strings, upon the [seven-stringed] psaltery, upon the harp.* Now the way that the ten-stringed psaltery (that is, the instrument of ten strings) and the [seven-stringed] psaltery can be explained in a spiritual sense is stated above in the elucidation of the eightieth Psalm, whose beginning is, *Rejoice to God our helper*.[16] But briefly touching upon this matter, he who keeps the ten commandments praises God with the ten-stringed psaltery; and he who does not omit the works of mercy also praises with the [seven-stringed] psaltery. The life and the praise of him who observes such things effects a sweet melody in the ears of God, so that he says this: *Let your voice sound in my ears: for your voice is sweet.*[17]

91{92}[5] *For you have given me, O Lord, a delight in your doings: and in the works of your hands I shall rejoice.*

Quia delectasti me, Domine, in factura tua; et in operibus manuum tuarum exsultabo.

And so it is good for me to sing your name, O most high God: 91{92} [5] *Quia delectasti me, Domine; for you have given me, O Lord, a delight,* a spiritual, internal, and pure delight, *in factura tua, in your doings,* that is, in the consideration and use of your creatures; *et in operibus manuum tuarum, and in the works of your hands,* that is, in your omnipotence, namely, in the order of the universe, in the splendor of things, in the beauty of the world, in the works of creation, re-creation, and glorification, in the contemplation of visible and invisible things, *exsultabo, I shall rejoice.* Whence, it is written: *O how desirable are all his works! And who shall be filled with beholding his glory?*[18] But in the creatures of God, there are two kinds of delight which one can have: the first, referring all of their perfections to the Creator, so that man rejoices in the wisdom and the power of God rather than in the created things; and this sort of delight is holy. And the first kind [of delight] is not evil in itself unless it dwells upon it finally[19] or is immoderately preoccupied with, distracted by, or weakened by it.

---

ceremonies and powerfully lifts up man's mind to God and to higher things." VII, *Sacrosanctum Concilium,* 120.

16   *E. N. See* Article LIV (Psalm 80:3).

17   Songs 2:14b.

18   Ecclus. 42:23a, 26b.

19   *E. N.* In other words, one views a created good, not as a means to God, but as an end in itself.

But because in this life we do not have the ability to perceive God in himself or by sight, we are compelled rise upwards from created things to the knowledge of him. For as is written in Proverbs, *The Lord has made all things for himself*: namely, to a certain extent the perfections of divine nature are reflected in that which exists, just as the perfection of a cause shines forth in its effect. To the degree, therefore, the order of all species is as a ladder extending upwards to knowledge of the Creator, we ought to take delight in and to exult in the works of God.[20] From the consideration of those things above, namely, from the most rapid and superlatively most velocious movement of the heavens and stars, of the sun, and of the planets, from the magnitude of the celestial orb, from the order, purity, and ministerial office of the angels, we are taught how sublime God is, how reverently he ought to be served, how promptly he ought to be obeyed. But in the lower things, for example, in the bee, the ant, the young hare, and the like, one knows the ineffable wisdom of God. For all beauty, adornment, sweetness, goodness, harmony, and amiability of the creatures bespeak to us the desire and love of the Creator. Whence, to this kind of contemplation and delight we are invited by Isaiah: *Lift up your eyes on high*, he says, *and see who has created these things*.[21] Man ought therefore to exult in the works of God, because all things are made for us, and almighty God created the fish of the sea, the birds of the air, the beasts of the earth, the fruit-bearing trees, and diverse kinds of plants so as to support us in our weakness.

91{92}[6] *O Lord, how great are your works! Your thoughts are exceeding deep.*

Quam magnificata sunt opera tua, Domine! Nimis profundae factae sunt cogitationes tuae.

---

20   E. N. This is a reference to the "great chain of being," or the *scala naturae*, the "ladder of nature," a cosmological model intrinsic to traditional Christian thought (though it has Platonic and Aristotelian roots also) that viewed the world as one vast graduated, hierarchical series of contingent beings, extending from minerals, through plants, to brute animals, and man (who straddles the world of matter and the world of spirit), to the heavenly bodies, through the nine choirs of angels, even — through the abyssal "line of one-way indeterminacy," as Steven A. Long calls it, or "the Christian distinction," as Robert Sokolowski calls it, unto God, the necessary Being, the Being, infinitely more unlike all created being than created being is like him, whose essence is existence. As St. Thomas Aquinas describes "the distinction": "Since God is totally outside the order of creatures, and all creatures are ordered to him, but not conversely, it is manifest that creatures are really related to God himself, but in God there is not any real relation to his creatures, but one according to reason (*i.e.*, conceptual), inasmuch as the creatures are related to him." ST Ia, q. 13, art. 7, c.
21   Is. 40:26a.

91{92}[6] *Quam magnificata sunt opera tua, Domine! How great are your works, O Lord!* That is, greatly magnificent, wise, powerful, and inscrutable are the things that are instituted, distinguished, and embellished. For it is befitting (in the manner that Plato affirms) that the most beautiful, the most resplendent, and the most excellent work — which is how the mechanism of the universe, which consists of incomparable beauty, is constituted — be produced by a most wise, a most beautiful, and a most excellent Maker.[22] Now greater and more incomprehensible than creation are the works of re-creation and glorification.[23] Whence, those things which the only begotten Son of God assumed, did, and endured for our salvation transcend all magnificence, inquiry, and description in words. For this reason, it states in Revelation: *Great and wonderful are your works, O Lord God Almighty.*[24] And in Ecclesiastes: *All things are difficult: man cannot explain them by word.*[25] Wisdom also: *With difficulty do we guess aright at things that are upon earth: and with labor do we find the things that are before us. But the things that are in heaven, who shall search out?*[26]

And so, if we desire to contemplate more precisely how magnificent are the works of the Creator, we ought deeply to think that which the Lord said to holy Job:

Where were you when I laid up the foundations of the earth? Tell me if you have understanding. Who has laid the measures thereof, if you know? Or who has stretched the line upon it? Upon what are its bases grounded? Who shut up the sea with doors, when it broke forth as issuing out of the womb? When I made a cloud the garment thereof, and wrapped it in a mist as in swaddling bands? I set my bounds around it, and made it bars and doors, and I said: Hitherto you shall come, and shall go no further, and here you shall break your swelling waves. Who has put wisdom in the

---

22   E. N. The reference is likely to Plato's *Timaeus*, 29a2–6. "for the world is the fairest of creations," Plato concludes, "and he is the best of causes." *Plato: Collected Dialogues* (Princeton, NJ: Princeton University Press, 1961), p. 1162. (eds., Edith Hamilton and Huntington Cairns).

23   "Justification is the most excellent work of God's love made manifest in Christ Jesus and granted by the Holy Spirit. It is the opinion of St. Augustine that 'the justification of the wicked is a greater work than the creation of heaven and earth,' because 'heaven and earth will pass away but the salvation and justification of the elect . . . will not pass away.' He holds also that the justification of sinners surpasses the creation of the angels in justice, in that it bears witness to a greater mercy." CCC § 1994 (quoting St. Augustine, *Tractates the Gospel of John*, 72, 3, PL 35, 1823).

24   Rev. 15:3b.

25   Eccl. 1:8a.

26   Wis. 9:16.

*heart of man? Or who gave the cock understanding? Who can declare the
order of the heavens, or who can make the harmony of heaven to sleep?*[27]

But truly, whatever we have the ability to know or to say of the works
of the most superlatively glorious Creator, it is nearly of no significance
to that which in reality he himself is. For this reason we have again in
Job: *Lo, these things are said in part of his ways: and seeing we have heard
scarce a little drop of his word, who shall be able to behold the thunder of
his greatness?*[28] For this reason also Plato attests that those things we
know are little and are close to nothing with respect to those things of
which we are ignorant.[29] Aristotle also explains this: For as the eyes of
the bat are at the brightness of the sun, so is the human intellect with
respect to the knowledge of the manifestations of nature, that is, in the
knowledge of separate substances.[30]

And so, if the works of God are so great and so incomprehensible,
how incomprehensible is their Creator! (For he infinitely transcends all
things in every excellence.) And so it adds: *nimis profundae factae sunt
cogitationes tuae, your thoughts are exceeding deep,* that is, the counsel, reason,
and order of your wisdom, by which you have ordered all things and
*have made all things to exist within certain limits, in measure, and number,
and weight,*[31] is powerful and entirely inscrutable and ineffable. For most
certainly we know, nothing is permitted by you to occur without a legitimate reason. But to assign the reason of your works in each particular

---

27   Job 38:4–6a, 8–11, 36–37.
28   Job 26:14.
29   E. N. Denis attributes this statement — *ea quae scimus, minima et prope nulla
sunt respectu eorum quae ignoramus* — to Plato, but it appears to be a reference to
Aristotle's *De anima* III, 427b1–3, though it is more a paraphrase of Aristotle's thought
than a true quotation.
30   E. N. This is a reference to Aristotle's *Metaphysics* II.1, 993b9–11, though it is
modified by scholastic concepts: "Just as it is with bats' eyes in respect of daylight,
so it is with our mental intelligence in respect of those things which are by nature
most obvious." *Aristotle in 23 Volumes,* Vol.17 (Cambridge, MA: Harvard University
Press, 1989) (trans., Hugh Tredennick). By "separate substances," Denis means essences
or substances separate from their individual instantiations (we don't know "dogness"
separate from what we abstract from the "dogness" instantiated in individual dogs, and
even here we really never perfectly know "dogness"). In fact, St. Thomas rejects both
Plato's and Aristotle's opinions that we can know separate substances. The reasons
for his rejection are given in ST Ia, q. 88, arts. 1, 2. St. Thomas famously said in
his exposition on the Creed: "[O]ur knowledge is so weak that no philosopher was
able ever perfectly to investigate the nature of a single fly. Hence, we read that one
philosopher spent thirty years in solitude so that he might know the nature of the
bee." *Expositio in Symbolum Apostolorum* (prologue).
31   Wis. 11:21b.

instance we profess to be entirely impossible.[32] For who is able to think why in the very beginning of the institution or creation of things, when there were no preceding entitlements (*merita*), you bestowed to one thing [one sort of perfection] rather than another greater perfection? Who knows why you did not create world from eternity, or why you created it in the instant that you did, and not before or after? Who moreover can comprehend why from eternity you preferred to elect one angel and one man to eternal life rather than another? Since, therefore, all these things are so incomprehensible, it is clear that your thoughts — that is, the wisdom underlying your disposition and weighing the end, the reason, and order of all things — are exceedingly deep: and so *he that is a searcher of majesty, shall be overwhelmed by glory.*[33] And truly is it written: *Who shall know your thought, O Lord, except you give wisdom, and send your Holy Spirit from above?*[34] Isaiah also addresses the profundity of the thoughts of the divine mind, and from that declares that no one observed the form of the activity prior to God, but he, from out of the superlatively most splendid and most certain fountain of his own wisdom, planned all things. For he says: *Who has forwarded the spirit of the Lord? Or who has been his counsellor, and has taught him? With whom has he consulted, and who has instructed him, and taught him the path of justice, and taught him knowledge, and showed him the way of understanding?*[35] And these prophetic words are consistent with the Apostolic words: *O the depth of the riches of the wisdom and of the knowledge of God! [How incomprehensible are his judgments, and how unsearchable his ways!]*[36] Now the thoughts of God are said to be plural, not that there are in God distinct and many thoughts, for the thought of God is his essence, understanding, and wisdom, but as there are said to be many and distinct ideas in God with reference to the relation of created things existing ideally in God, so there are said to be many thoughts in God according to the diversity of operations which are known to God.

---

32   E. N. "All Thy acts of Providence are acts of love. If Thou sendest evil upon us, it is in love. All the evils of the physical world are intended for the good of Thy creatures, or are the unavoidable attendants on that good. And Thou turnest that evil into good.... I acknowledge with a full and firm faith, O Lord, the wisdom and goodness of Thy Providence, even in Thy inscrutable judgments and Thy incomprehensible decrees." St. John Henry Newman, *Mediations and Devotions*, "The Providence of God" (New York: Longmans, Green, and Co. 1903), 421.

33   Prov. 25:27b.

34   Wis. 9:17.

35   Is. 40:13–14.

36   Rom. 11:33. E. N. The part of the verse in brackets replaces the "etc." of Denis.

91{92}[7] *The senseless man shall not know: nor will the fool understand these things.*

Vir insipiens non cognoscet, et stultus non intelliget haec.

91{92}[7] *Vir insipiens,* the senseless man, that is, [the man] lacking that wisdom which is the gift of the Holy Spirit, and which does not enter into an evil soul:[37] by which wisdom, of course, man judges rightly about God, not by unformed knowledge, but by formed and wise knowledge; *non cognoscet,* shall not know in what way God the Creator ought to be honored and loved from creatures, and about which is written, God has made works *that he may be feared.*[38] For this reason, the Apostle [Paul] said about the philosophers of this world: *They became vain in their thoughts, and their foolish heart was darkened.*[39] *Et stultus,* and the fool, that is, either he that is deprived of the true knowledge of the divine law, that is, of that [knowledge] by which he knows what is to be done and not to be done, *non intelligent haec,* will not understand these things said and which will be said through a saving and laborious knowledge. For this reason, the Lord said through Jeremiah: *Hear, O foolish people, who have not understanding. You will not fear me, . . . who have set the sand bound for the sea?*[40] And the Apostle [Paul] said: *But the sensual man perceives not these things that are of the Spirit of God; for it is foolishness to him, and he cannot understand,*[41] namely, the mysteries of God, the reward of the good, and the punishments of the evil.

91{92}[8] *When the wicked shall spring up as grass: and all the workers of iniquity shall appear: That they may perish for ever and ever:*

Cum exorti fuerint peccatores sicut foenum, et apparuerint omnes qui operantur iniquitatem, ut intereant in saeculum saeculi.

91{92}[9] *But you, O Lord, are most high for evermore:*

Tu autem Altissimus in aeternum, Domine.

---

37 *Cf.* Wis. 1:4a.

38 Eccl. 3:14b.

39 Rom. 1:21b. *E. N.* In other words, the fear of the Lord, in particular the *filial fear* of the Lord, which is a gift of the Holy Spirit will not be learned by a purely natural theology. Nor will natural theology inform us how the Creator wants to be worshipped. Revelation and supernatural grace are required for this.

40 Jer. 5:21a. *E. N.* In his *Commentary on Jeremiah,* Denis points to this verse as a metaphor of God's overwhelming power, since God is able to curb such great and powerful elements found in the immense abyss of waters and the might of the battering seas. *See Doctoris Ecstatici D. Dionysii Cartusiani, Opera Omnia,* Vol. 9 (Montreuil: 1900), 69.

41 1 Cor. 2:14.

91{92}[10] *For behold your enemies, O Lord, for behold your enemies shall perish: and all the workers of iniquity shall be scattered:*

Quoniam ecce inimici tui, Domine, quoniam ecce inimici tui peribunt; et dispergentur omnes qui operantur iniquitatem.

91{92}[8] *Cum exorti fuerint peccatores sicut foenum,* when the wicked shall spring up as grass, that is, when the iniquitous begin to rise, prosper, and to flourish like the grass which today flourishes and exists, but *tomorrow is cast into the oven* and ceases to exist:[42] because as has just now been said above, the prosperity of the ungodly is momentary, and soon thereafter their flourishing fades away, in the manner that the green grass quickly dies. Whence we read in Isaiah: *All flesh is grass, and all the glory thereof as the flower of the field;*[43] and again: *Indeed the people is grass; and the grass is withered, and the flower is fallen.*[44] *Et apparuerint,* and they shall appear to be otherwise, or for a short while they will prevail and glory in themselves, *omnes qui operantur iniquitates,* all the workers of iniquity: those whom God permits during their hour to walk according to their desires, since they will suffer just punishment eternally, in the manner that [is stated] as follows: *Ut intereant, that they may perish,* that is, that they might spiritually die and be condemned, *in saeculum saeculi, for ever and ever,* that is, without end, as one separated from the fountain of all life and glory. Whence Solomon said: *The Lord has made ... the wicked ... for the evil day.*[45] Of this day of the damnation of the ungodly is written in the book of Job: *The wicked man is reserved to the day of destruction; and he shall drink of the wrath of the Almighty.*[46] **91{92}[9]** *Tu autem Altissimus in aeternum; but you, O Lord, are most high for evermore:* for you incomparably surpass all things in power, in wisdom, in equity, in goodness, and in happiness. And it is apparent from this, **91{92}[10]** *Quoniam ecce inimici tui, for behold your enemies,* that is, those rebelling against you, those ungrateful, those who are reprobate, *Domine, quoniam ecce inimici tui peribunt, O Lord, for behold your enemies shall perish,* losing grace in the present, and sent away from the glory of the heavenly kingdom a while thereafter, and receiving the fires of eternal death in hell. How exceedingly horrible is it to be an enemy of God! Indeed, horrible is it merely to hear it: and so it is repeated, so that you might begin to

---

42   Matt. 6:30a.
43   Is. 40:6b.
44   Is. 40:7b–8a.
45   Prov. 16:4.
46   Job 21:30a, 20b.

begin to fear more. *Et dispergentur, and shall be scattered,* that is, they will be expelled from the flock of the elect in the day of judgment, *omnes qui operantur, all the workers* without ceasing and repentance, *iniquitatem, of iniquity.* For he will say to them at that time: *Depart from me, you cursed, into everlasting fire.*[47] For this reason, Scripture says: *The ungodly shall meet with ruin, and I will destroy men from the face of the earth, says the Lord;*[48] and again, *I will destroy, them that turn away from following after the Lord, says the Lord, and that have not sought the Lord, nor searched after him.*[49]

91{92}[11] *But my horn shall be exalted like that of the unicorn: and my old age in plentiful mercy.*

Et exaltabitur sicut unicornis cornu meum, et senectus mea in misericordia uberi.

Thereafter the elect are distinguished from this damnation, and it continues with their tribulation and glory: **91{92}[11]** *Et exaltabitur sicut unicornis cornu meu, but my horn shall be exalted like that of a unicorn*: that is, the empire of my reason, ruling over my sensuality and inclinations, is raised up by the confirmation of the grace of God, as a unicorn is raised up by his horn: for this animal is most strong,[50] and it protects itself with one horn from the attacks of others. So my horn, that is, my fortitude or the dominion of my reason, is strengthened against all assaulting passions, temptations, and persecutions. For in the day of judgment, the horn of the soul will be so exalted in the elect that the flesh never will desire against the spirit, nor will anything hinder the act of reason.[51] Nay, indeed, the corruptible body at the present time aggravates souls,[52] but then it will be spiritual, immortal, an ornament and exhilaration to souls. *Et senectus mea, and my old age,* that is, my last age, will be *in misericordia uberi, in plentiful mercy*: for when my strength

---

47   Matt. 25:41a.
48   Zeph. 1:3b.
49   Zeph. 1:6a.
50   E. N. The unicorn (rhinoceros) is a symbol of strength: "God has brought him out of Egypt, whose strength is like to the rhinoceros (unicorn)." Num. 23:22; *see also* Num. 24:8. On the "unicorn" itself as a rhinoceros, *see* footnote 28-40.
51   *Cf.* Gal. 5:17: E. N. Until such confirmation of the elect, they elect have to contend with the rebel passions: *For the flesh lusts against the spirit: and the spirit against the flesh; for these are contrary one to another: so that you do not the things that you would.*
52   *Cf.* Wis. 9:15: *For the corruptible body is a load upon the soul, and the earthly habitation presses down the mind that muses upon many things.*

is deficient, you will not abandon me.[53] And *though our outward man is corrupted, yet the inward man is renewed day by day* by the grace of God, according to the Apostle [Paul].[54] These things are the words of good hope, and not of unfounded presumption: because these things are said by the Church and by any just man out of the mind's ardent charity and a great trust in God.

91{92}[12]   *My eye also has looked down upon my enemies: and my ear shall hear [of the downfall] of the malignant that rise up against me.*

Et despexit oculus meus inimicos meos, et in insurgentibus in me malignantibus audiet auris mea.

91{92}[12] *Et despexit oculus meus,* my eye also has looked upon [speaking] in an intellectual sense *inimicos meos, my enemies,* that is, demons and perverse men: because of the hope that I have in the Lord my God, I do not fear that I will be overcome by them: as it says in a later Psalm, *The Lord is my helper, I will not fear what man can do unto me.*[55] And again it is written: *Be not afraid of their fear, and be not troubled.*[56] Our visible enemies, namely, evil men, insofar as they are men with the capacity of grace and glory, are to be loved, according to this: *Love your enemies.*[57] But insofar as they are ungodly, and adversaries of truth, they are to be held in contempt, hated, and despised. Whence in a Psalm above it has been stated of a just man: *In his sight the malignant is brought to nothing.*[58] *Et insurgentibus in me,* and [they] *that rise up against me* (unjustly, that is) *malignantibus, audiet auris mea, my ear shall hear* [of the downfall] of the malignant, since I will hear their threats with a certain derision and without fear. Or [alternatively], [with respect to] the malignant *that rise up against me,* that is, to their own confusion, *my ear shall hear* the just judgment of the just Judge, who will condemn them, and will save me.

91{92}[13]   *The just shall flourish like the palm tree: he shall grow up like the cedar of Lebanon.*

Iustus ut palma florebit; sicut cedrus Libani multiplicabitur.

---

53   Cf. Ps. 70:9b: *When my strength (virtue) shall fail, do not forsake me.*
54   2 Cor. 4:16.
55   Ps. 117:6.
56   1 Pet. 3:14b.
57   Matt. 5:44a.
58   Ps. 14:4a.

91{92}[13] *Iustus, the just,* that is, those observing the divine commandments, *ut palma, like the palm tree,* which is a fruitful tree, *florebit, shall flourish* with the flower of charity and with the strength of virtue and of good works. For they will not flower as the grass, which soon dries up and fades away, but like a palm, which daily grows green and flourishes. *Sicut cedrus Libani multiplicabitur, he shall grow up like the cedar of Lebanon,* with the procreation of spiritual children and in the amount of merit. For in the manner that the cedar growing in mount Lebanon is a graceful tree not liable to decay, and grows higher than other trees, so the just man is illustrious by grace, by interior justice does not grow old, and, profiting much more in doing good, he passes swiftly above others, and does not rest until he arrives to the throne of grace.

91{92}[14] *They that are planted in the house of the Lord shall flourish in the courts of the house of our God.*

> *Plantati in domo Domini, in atriis domus Dei nostri florebunt.*

91{92}[14] *Plantati, they that are planted,* that is, the faithful rooted in faith and obedience, *in domo Domini, in the house of the Lord,* that is, in the Church of Christ, *in atriis domus Dei nostri, in the courts of the house of our God,* that is, in their own hearts which are the courts of the divine mansions, in the manner that the Apostle says, *Christ may dwell by faith in our hearts,*[59] *florebant, shall flourish,* advancing in the grace of God, fulfilling the [words] of the Apostle: *Present yourselves holy and unspotted and blameless before him;*[60] and elsewhere, *Be renewed in the spirit of your mind.*[61] Moreover, there is a concordance when this is compared to that which the Lord said through the prophet Hosea: *I will be as the dew, Israel shall spring as the lily, and his root shall shoot forth as that of Lebanon. His branches shall spread, and his glory shall be as the olive tree: and his smell as that of Lebanon.*[62] This is also similar [to what is stated] in Ecclesiasticus: *Hear me, you divine offspring, and bud forth as the rose planted by the brooks of waters; send forth flowers, as the lily, and yield a smell, and bring forth leaves in grace.*[63]

----

59   Eph. 3:17a.
60   Col. 1:22b.
61   Eph. 3:17.
62   Hosea 14:6–7.
63   Ecclus. 39:17, 19a.

91{92}[15] *They shall still increase in a fruitful old age: and shall be well treated,*

  Adhuc multiplicabuntur in senecta uberi, et bene patientes erunt:

91{92}[16] *That they may show, that the Lord our God is righteous, and there is no iniquity in him.*

  Ut annuntient quoniam rectus Dominus Deus noster, et non est iniquitas in eo.

 91{92}[15] *Adhuc multiplicabuntur, they shall still increase,* that is, they will continuously persevere in the good, and will accumulate the many gifts of the Holy Spirit and merit, *in senecta uberi, in a fruitful old age,* that is, in a fertile, mature, and eminent agedness, filled with good works. This is written about in the book of Wisdom: *Venerable old age is not that of long time, nor counted by the number of years: but the understanding of a man is grey hairs; and a spotless life is old age.*[64] *Et bene patientes erunt, and [they] shall be well treated,* that is, cheerfully and happily they will suffer the infusion of the divine enlightenment. Whence, according to the Philosopher [Aristotle], a beneficiary is said to have suffered well.[65] For this is a perfective, not destructive, suffering. **91{92}[16]** *Ut annuntient, that they might show* the praise of God which follows: *quoniam rectus Dominus Deus noster, et non est iniquitas in eo; that the Lord our God is righteous, and there is no iniquity in him:* in the manner that is elsewhere stated: *There is no iniquity with the Lord our God, nor respect of persons, nor desire of gifts.*[66] And in the book of Job: *Far from God be wickedness, and iniquity from the Almighty. For he will render to a man his work, and according to the ways of every one he will reward them.*[67] For God, sublime and blessed, is the fountain-like cause of all holiness, truth, and justice, an unerring judge, the unmoving preserver. For this reason it is stated by Wisdom: *Your power is the beginning of justice.*[68]

---

64 Wis. 4:8–9.

65 *E. N. Beneficiatus dicitur bene passus.* Since the beneficiary means one who is made well (*bene* = well + *facere* = to make), the notion expressed here is that the beneficiary passively receives, endures, undergoes, or suffers good from the benefactor. "The beneficiary is the work of the benefactor." Aristotle, *Nicomachean Ethics*, IX.7.4, 1168a4. (The translation is Leon R. Kass's, found in Amy A. Kass, ed., *Giving Well, Doing Good* (Bloomington, IN: Indiana University Press, 2008), 76). A perfective passion (suffering) is distinguished from a destructive or corrupting passion. For example, when wood is burnt, it suffers a destructive passion. On the other hand, when a man is taught a new language, he suffers a perfective passion.

66 2 Chr. 19:7b.

67 Job 34:10b–11.

68 Wis. 12:16a.

See we have heard this Psalm replete with a melody of heavenly sound and sweetness, in which the praise of God is commended, the benefits of the Creator are recalled, God is glorified in his effects, and in distinguishing between the elect and the reprobate, and finally God is blessed. If therefore we love the Lord our God, let us apply ourselves to utter this Psalm with a happy, devout, guarded, and fearful heart if we are thankful for his benefits, if we strive to contemplate him in his works, if we desire to evade the torments of the ungodly, if we endeavor to receive the rewards of the elect.

PRAYER

Y YOUR POWER, PLANT US IN YOUR HOUSE, O Lord, and as good seed make it be that we bear fruit in all religious beauty: by which, rising as a palm with the flower of justice, and perfected in it by you, we might, rejoicing, perennially flower before you.

Virtutibus planta nos in domo tua, Domine, et ut bonum semen
fac nos in omni speciosa religione fructificare: in
quo ut palma flore iustitiae surgentes, in eo
per te consummati, perenniter ante te
floreamus exsultantes.

Psalm 92

ARTICLE LXXI

EXPLANATION OF THE NINETY-SECOND PSALM:
DOMINUS REGNAVIT, DECORUM INDUTUS EST.
THE LORD HAS REIGNED, HE IS CLOTHED WITH BEAUTY.

HIS TITLE IS ASSIGNED TO THE PRESENT Psalm: *Laus cantici ipsi David, in die ante sabbatum, quando fundata est terra. Praise in the way of a canticle, for David himself, on the day before the Sabbath, when the earth was founded.* Now some say that this title is not to be found in the [original] Hebrew, but was placed before it by some expositor on his own will and fancy: and consequently the same is frequently stated in other Psalms. But given the fact that it may have been added by some expositor, yet it does not sound right to say that this title was appended according to his will and fancy: indeed, firmly is it to be believed, that the titles of the Psalms and placed in front of them are fashioned by the inspiration of the Holy Spirit, because all Catholic teachers commonly accept and expound on these titles. Therefore, the sense of this title is this: This present Psalm is *laus cantici, praise in the way of a canticle*, fittingly to be sung *ipsi David, for David himself*, that is, Christ, of whom this Psalm is literally written. A sung praise, I say, to Christ *in die ante sabbatum, on the day before the Sabbath*, that is, because of those things which he did and suffered on the sixth day, namely, on the Day of Preparation before the Sabbath, *quando fundata est terra, when the earth was founded*, that is, when the Church was formed by the blood pouring forth from his side.[1] According to all Catholic expositors, this Psalm literally treats of Christ and his kingdom. For it describes the beginning of, the assault upon, and the confirmation of the kingdom of Christ, which is the Church.[2]

---

1 John 19:34.
2 "The mission of the Church is 'to proclaim and establish among all peoples the kingdom of Christ and of God, and she is on earth, the seed and the beginning of that kingdom.' On the one hand, the Church is 'a sacrament — that is, sign and instrument of intimate union with God and of unity of the entire human race.' She is therefore the sign and instrument of the kingdom; she is called to announce and to establish the kingdom. On the other hand, the Church is the 'people gathered by the unity of the Father, the Son and the Holy Spirit'; she is therefore 'the kingdom of Christ already present in mystery' and constitutes its seed and beginning. The kingdom of God, in fact, has an eschatological dimension: it is a reality present in time,

92{93}[1] *The Lord has reigned, he is clothed with beauty: the Lord is clothed with strength, and has girded himself. For he has established the world which shall not be moved.*

Dominus regnavit, decorem indutus est: indutus est Dominus fortitudinem, et praecinxit se. Etenim firmavit orbem terrae, qui non commovebitur.

Whence, it begins with the inception of this reign: **92{93}[1]** *Dominus, the Lord,* namely, Christ: of whom Peter said, *He is Lord of all;*[3] and he in the Gospel asserted regarding himself, *You call me Master, and Lord, and you say well, for so I am;*[4] *regnavit, has reigned,* by faith in the heart of the believers, or in the Church militant. For Christ as God reigned from the beginning of the world in the hearts of the elect, bringing them under by humble service to the divine will by grace; but [Christ] as man had the power of reigning throughout the world from the beginning of his conception. For in that very instant where his humanity was united with the Word, power of dominion over every creature was given to him. For this reason, before the Passion of Christ, it was asserted [by John the Baptist]: *The Father loves the Son: and he has given all things into his hand.*[5] But when he began to preach,[6] to perform miracles, and to gather disciples together, then he began to reign in the house of Jacob, and to sit upon the throne of David.[7] But after the Passion, Christ reigned both openly and latently by sending the Holy Spirit and by the public preaching of the Apostles and the conversion of many thousands, until the faith was spread throughout the whole world, and the Church built up, and Christ was known and honored by all peoples, tribes, and tongues. And then was fulfilled that in Isaiah: *Your Redeemer, the Holy One of Israel, shall be called the God of all the earth.*[8]

Decorem indutus est, indutus est Dominus fortitudinem. He is clothed with beauty: the Lord is clothed with strength. Why is it not better said the Lord Christ, the only-begotten Son of God, as beautiful and powerful as the Father, was clothed with baseness and weakness or frailty?[9]

---

but its full realization will arrive only with the completion or fulfilment of history." Congregation of the Doctrine of the Faith, *Dominus Iesus,* no. 18 (Aug. 6, 2000).

3   Acts 10:36b.

4   John 13:13.

5   John 3:35.

6   Matt. 4:17 *et seq.*

7   Luke 1:32; Is. 9:7.

8   Is. 54:5b.

9   E. N. Why, Denis asks, is the Incarnation, and the assumption of human nature by the Word, described in this verse as being "clothed with beauty" and "clothed

Now the response to this is twofold. First, the God Christ, in assuming human nature, is said to be clothed with beauty and with strength because—granted that his humanity considered in itself, and, compared to his divinity, can be said to been base and weak—in light of the fact that it was conjoined in a personal union with the divine nature, and made his instrument, he truly may be called with the names beauty and strength. For it was full with the plenitude of all grace, the beatific enjoyment of divinity, and all the gifts of the Holy Spirit from the beginning of its creation. And so also by it were performed all the miracles, the vanquishing of the powers of the air, and the restoration of the human race. The second response is that Christ is said to be clothed in beauty, not in the Incarnation when *the Word became flesh*,[10] nor in the Passion when there was *no beauty in him, nor comeliness, but he was as it were a leper, and as one struck by God*; but [he is said to be clothed in beauty] in the Resurrection, because then he resumed his body, not with that quality that it had before, but glorious, splendid, agile, subtile, and immortal. And he was then clothed also with strength, that is, with an impassible body. Or [alternatively], *he is clothed with beauty*, because then he began to exhibit his power, saying this, *All power is given to me in heaven and in earth:*[11] this power he also had (as I said) before the Passion, because at the instance of his Passion he said about himself when speaking to the Father, *You have given him power over all flesh, that he may give eternal life to all whom you have given him.*[12] This also was observed to be done when by a word alone he made his enemies fall prostrate. For when he told the Jews, *I am he, they went backward, and fell to the ground.*[13] Also, at the time that he led the Saints out of the limbo of hell and when he sent the Holy Spirit to his apostles. And so in this was the human nature clothed with beauty and power. And regarding this clothing it is written: *Why then is your apparel red?*[14]

---

with strength," when it would appear to be better described by its opposite, namely that he "emptied himself, taking the form of a servant, being made in the likeness of men, and in habit found as a man," (Phil 2:7) and so was "clothed in meanness" and "clothed with weakness"?

10 John 1:14.

11 Matt. 28:18b.

12 John 17:2.

13 John 18:6.

14 Is. 53:2a. In his *Commentary on Isaiah*, Denis explains the meaning of this verse: "We have already become acquainted with who you [Jesus] are, but since you are the teacher of justice and a just judge, and the author of human redemption, we are amazed and want to know *why then is your apparel red*, that is, why was your flesh drenched with blood during the time of your Passion, as your scars demonstrate (for the flesh

Et praecinxit se, and Christ *has girded himself*: that is, he prepared himself so as to redeem the human race and to vanquish the demonic hosts, saying to the Father: *My Father, if this chalice may not pass away, but I must drink it, your will be done.*[15] For he was made *obedient unto death, even to the death [on the Cross],* according to the Apostle.[16] And *he has rejoiced as a giant to run the way:*[17] which St. Ambrose elegantly expressed as beyond human knowledge in a hymn, saying:

> *Proceeding from his chamber free*
> *That royal home of purity*
> *A giant in twofold substance one,*
> *Rejoicing now his course to run.*[18]

Whence, in a Psalm above it is stated regarding Christ: *Gird your sword upon your thigh, O you most mighty.*[19]

Etenim firmavit orbem terrae, qui non commovebitur; for he has established the world which shall not be moved. Although this can be understood as referring to the creation and the firm placement of the earth in the center of the world, which Christ as God created and established, in accordance with this, *I am the Lord, that make all things, that alone stretch out the heavens, that establish the earth*[20] (and which earth is not moved with respect to the whole, since it is the immobile center of the world: for this reason Scripture says, *One generation passes away, and another generation comes: but the earth stands forever*);[21] this verse can also fittingly be explained

---

of Christ, and similarly his humanity, was a temple, vestment, robe, garment, and mantle of divinity), and *your apparel,* namely, *the seamless tunic, woven from the top throughout* [John 19:23], and the *white garment* by which Herod mocked you [Luke 23:11], or rather, your body and soul assumed by the Word in the manner of a garment, were red, that is, bloodied or reddened with the fire of the Passion." Doctoris Ecstatici D. Dionysii Cartusiani, *Opera Omnia,* Vol. 8 (Montreuil: 1899), 735–36.

15   Matt. 26:42b.

16   Phil. 2:8b.

17   Ps. 18:6b.

18   *E. N.* This is taken from the hymn *Veni, Redemptor gentium,* "Come Redeemer of the Nations," by St. Ambrose (340–397 AD). The translation is that of J. M. Neale (1818–1866).

19   Ps. 44:4.

20   Is. 44:24.

21   Eccl. 1:4. *E. N.* Clearly, Denis, writing in the 1430s, assumes a Ptolemaic model of the universe. The "Copernican Revolution" had not yet occurred. The Polish astronomer Nicolaus Copernicus (1473–1543) was to write his *Commentariolus,* which proposed the heliocentric model against the geocentric, Ptolemaic model, somewhere before 1514, and his *De Revolutionibus* in 1543.

as applying to the confirmation of the Church; [in which case] it will be [understood] in this sense: *for he*, the Lord Christ, *has established* through the help or the grace of the Holy Spirit, *the world*, that is, the militant Church, which is spread throughout all four parts of the earth. Christ confirmed in a special way the early Church on the day of Pentecost by sending the Paraclete. For at that time he fulfilled that which he promised before the Passion: *I will give you a mouth and wisdom, which all your adversaries shall not be able to resist and gainsay.*[22] Elsewhere also he said to Peter: *You are Peter; and upon this rock I will build my church, and the gates of hell shall not prevail against it.*[23] For in such a manner did Christ confirm the Church that the Apostle could say: *The Church of the living God is the pillar and ground of truth.*[24] Hence, in the Acts of the Apostles, Luke testifies: *Now the Church had peace throughout all Judea, and Galilee, and Samaria; and was edified, walking in the fear of the Lord, and was filled with the consolation of the Holy Spirit.*[25] And so now [the Psalm here] adds, *which shall not be moved.* For the Church will remain steadfast even until the end of the world in the faith and service of Christ, who *shall reign in the house of Jacob forever, and of his kingdom there shall be no end,* according to the testimony of [the angel] Gabriel.[26]

92{93}[2] *Your throne is prepared from of old: you are from everlasting.*

Parata sedes tua ex tunc; a saeculo tu es.

92{93}[2] *Parata sedes tua, your throne is prepared,* O Christ, that is, the throne by which you sit at the right hand of the Father, of which you said: *I have overcome, and am set down with my Father in his throne;*[27] *ex tunc, from of old,* that is, from the beginning of the world. For if the kingdom of God was prepared for all saintly men from the foundation of the world,[28] how much more was your heavenly throne prepared at the beginning of time? Or [alternatively, we can look at it thus], *your throne is prepared,* that is, the empyreal heaven, which is your throne, according to this, *Heaven is my throne, and the earth my footstool;*[29] now your throne is also said to be also of all the elect, of which you have

---

22   Luke 21:15.
23   Matt. 16:18.
24   1 Tim. 3:15b.
25   Acts 9:31.
26   Luke 1:32b.
27   Rev. 3:21b.
28   *Cf.* Matt. 25:34b.
29   Is. 66:1a.

witnessed: *To him that shall overcome, I will give to sit with me in my throne,*[30] that is, in the empyreal heaven in which all the blessed happily reside. Or [yet another alternative interpretation is], *Your throne is prepared,* that is, the Church, or the soul of the just man, which is the seat of wisdom, *from of old,* that is, from the time already stated, at which time you strengthened it by the grace of the Holy Spirit. For *from of old* it was prepared by your dwelling, obedience, and coming, fulfilling that which you told them: *Watch, therefore, praying at all times, that you may be accounted worthy . . . to stand before the Son of man.*[31]

A saeculo, from everlasting, that is, from eternity, *tu es,* you are unchangeably as God. Whence the Apostle [Paul] says: *Jesus Christ, yesterday, and today, and the same forever.*[32] And fittingly, the Psalm says, *from everlasting you are,* and not, "you were": because Christ as God, is immutable by way of eternal presence, in which there is no before or after. For this reason, he said: *Before I Abraham was, I am.*[33] Indeed, to be (*esse*) is most truly, most fully, and most essentially proper to God, because in him is being (*essendi*) with infinite fullness, immense nobility, unbounded perfection, and perfect simplicity. Now any creature, in comparison to the divine being, is rather nothing or not being (*nihil seu non esse*), than it is something (*aliquid*). For this reason, the Lord said to Moses: *I am who am. Thus shall you say to the children of Israel: He who is has sent me to you.*[34] This also Hilary [of Poitiers] asserts in his seventh book on the Trinity:[35] Being (*esse*) is no accident in God, but subsisting truth, abiding cause, and an inherent natural property.

92{93}[3]   *The floods have lifted up, O Lord: the floods have lifted up their voice. The floods have lifted up their waves,*

Elevaverunt flumina, Domine, elevaverunt flumina vocem suam, elevaverunt flumina fluctus suos,

92{93}[4]   *With the noise of many waters. Wonderful are the surges of the sea: wonderful is the Lord on high.*

A vocibus aquarum multarum. Mirabiles elationes maris; mirabilis in altis Dominus.

---

30   Rev. 3:21a.
31   Luke 21:36.
32   Heb. 8:8.
33   John 8:58.
34   Ex. 3:14.
35   E. N. *De Trinitate,* VII, 11, PL 10, 208.

92{93}[3] *Elevaverunt flumina, Domine, elevaverunt flumina vocem suam. Elevaverunt flumina fluctos suos. The floods have lifted up, O Lord: the floods have lifted up their voice. The floods have lifted up their waves.* By the floods that have lifted up their voice, some [commentators] understand the first and principal proclaimers of the Christian faith, who are called floods because they pour into the hearts of men the *water of wholesome wisdom,*[36] and here, as faithful, they *have lifted up their voice,* speaking rationally and preaching publicly of the faith of Christ. But by *floods which have lifted up their waves* is understood the persecutors of the Church, namely, the [Jewish] chiefs of the priests, the Roman rulers, and other tyrants who disapproved of the Christian teaching and endeavored to extirpate it. For here, as the perverse and the reprobate, they do not lift up rational voice, but rather their waves, that is, weighty threats, words of blasphemy, the impetuosity of passion, and unyielding persecution against the Church of Christ and the floods of God. But some [commentators] explain both floods that are lifted up as being the adversaries of Christ and the persecutors of the sacrosanct Church. But floods, that is, tyrants, lift up their waves **92{93}[4]** *a vocibus aquarium multarum, with the noise of many waters,* that is, by the statements or the words of many of the people, who were led to act by the edicts of tyrants. For they were administrators and executors of the judgments which the tyrants dictated against the Church.

Mirabile elationes maris; wonderful are the surges of the sea, that is, surprisingly great and atrocious were the persecutions or the ungodly men against the Church of Christ of that time. But also *mirabilis in altis Dominus, wonderful is the Lord on high,* that is, Christ, who strengthened the holy martyrs, protected the Church, and miraculously showed himself and exhibited his omnipotence during the time of the persecution of the Church from *on high,* that is, in great miracles, in sublime signs, and in unheard-of prodigies: these things God did through his faithful, in that even amidst the most cruel persecutions, the Church not only did not fear, nor did it diminish, but it marvelously expanded, increased, strengthened, and with remarkable alacrity endured the universal torments until such time that the tyrants gave up, and the very Roman empire itself subjected its neck to the faith of Christ.

92{93}[5] *Your testimonies are become exceedingly credible: holiness becomes your house, O Lord, unto length of days.*

---

36 Ecclus. 15:3a.

> *Testimonia tua credibilia facta sunt nimis; domum tuam decet*
> *sanctitudo, Domine, in longitudinem dierum.*

Hence, **92{93}[5]** *Testimonia tua, your testimonies,* O Christ, that is, whatever the sacred Scriptures attest about you, namely, the predictions of the Prophets, the words of the Evangelists, the articles of faith, *credibilia facta sunt nimis, are become exceedingly credible,* because of the miracles by which you confirmed the faith. For the parts of the divine law are two, namely testimony and precepts. Testimony pertains as to what is to be believed (*credenda*): precepts as to what is to be done (*operanda*). There are also two ways to establish the truth,[37] namely, by the arguments of natural reason,[38] and by the operation of divine miracles.[39] Now, to prove the testimony of the Christian faith by natural reason is not possible, because *faith is the substance of things to be hoped for, the evidence of things that appear not,* according to the Apostle. They are proved, therefore, by divine miracles, that is, by such manner of works that no one else is able to do other than God: such as the resurrection of the dead;[40] or changes in the movement of the sun or moon such as Christ performed while hanging on the Cross, in that he supernaturally eclipsed the sun by the moon;[41] or the certain foretelling of pure future contingents, or the revelation of the secrets of the heart, which in the name of Christ and from Christ were most abundantly performed under the Christian law and

---

37 "The perpetual common belief of the Catholic Church has held and holds also this: there is a twofold order of knowledge, distinct not only in its principle but also in its object; in its principle, because in the one we know by natural reason, in the other by divine faith; in its object, because apart from what natural reason can attain, there are proposed to our belief mysteries that are hidden in God and can never be known unless they are revealed by God." DS 3015 (Vatican I).

38 "If anyone says that human reason is so independent that faith cannot be enjoined upon it by God, let him be anathema." DS 3031 (Vatican I).

39 "Miracles ... hold a very prominent place in the evidence of the Jewish and Christian Revelations. They are the most striking and conclusive evidence; because, the laws of matter being better understood than those to which mind is conformed, the transgression of them is more easily recognised. They are the most simple and obvious; because, whereas the freedom of the human will resists the imposition of undeviating laws, the material creation, on the contrary, being strictly subjected to the regulation of its Maker, looks to Him alone for a change in its constitution." St. John Henry Newman, *Two Essays on Scripture Miracles and on Ecclesiastical* (London: Basil Montagu Pickering, 1870), 7–8 (2nd ed.). "If anyone says that no miracles are possible ... or that miracles can never be recognized with certainty and that the divine origin of the Christian religion cannot be legitimately proved by them, let him be anathema." DS 3034 (Vatican I).

40 Matt. 27:52.

41 Luke 23:45.

among [the Christian] people. And from these it is most certainly clear
that either the faith of the Church is true and divine, or (just to hear it
mentioned is horrible) God is the confirmer of falsity and the deceiver
of men. And so John: *He that believes not the Son,* he says, *makes him a
liar: because he believes not in the testimony which God has testified of his
Son.*[42] And again: *The Spirit . . . testifies that Christ is the truth.*[43] This also
Christ said: *The works which the Father has given me to perfect; the works
themselves, which I do, give testimony of me.*[44] And again when speaking
to the Jews: *If I do not the works of my Father,* he said, *believe me not. But
if I do, and if you will not believe me, believe the works.*[45]

Our faith is also ineffably strengthened by this: that not only Christ,
but his ministers just mentioned performed signs, as Christ also promised
before his Passion: *He that believes in me, the works that I do, he also shall
do; and greater than these shall he do, because I go to the Father.*[46] Moreover,
we most obviously know who are those through whom Christ performs
miracles: because they are men perfect in all virtue who have expelled
completely their own private love,[47] and they are continuously absorbed
entirely in the love of God, steadfast in faith, patient in hope, humble,
meek, most innocent, most fearful in their divine service, and fervent.

Look, and ponder well those things that are for us powerfully credible
and firm testimonies of the faith for those who believe, because it would
be more possible for heaven and earth to perish,[48] than for one tittle
of the Christian law to be rendered false. For this reason, the Apostle
[Paul] admonishes: *We ought more diligently to observe the things which we
have heard. How shall we escape if we neglect so great a salvation, which is
confirmed unto us, . . . God also bearing them witness with sign and diverse
miracles and distributions of the Holy Spirit?*[49]

Domum tuam, your house, that is, the Church or the Christian people,
according to that stated by the Apostle: *You may know how you ought to
behave yourself in the house of God, which is the Church of the living God;*[50]

---

42 1 John 5:10b.
43 1 John 5:6.
44 John 5:36.
45 John 5:37–38a.
46 John 14:12–13a.
47 E. N. Denis characterizes "private love" as a disordered love of self, what St.
Augustine called *improbus amor sui* (a bad self-love), as distinguished from a *probus
amor sui,* a good self-love. See footnote 33-43 for more on this notion of "private love."
48 Cf. Luke 16:17.
49 Heb. 2:1a, 3a, 4.
50 1 Tim. 3:15.

decet sanctitudo, holiness becomes, that is, [is becoming of] a holy manner of living and cleanliness of heart, *Domine, in longitudinem dierum; unto length of days,* that is, perseveringly, so long as a man lives, so that he may serve you in holiness and justice all the days of his life,[51] in the way that Peter says: *According to him that has called you, who is holy, be you also in all manner of conversation holy.*[52]

See we have heard this Psalm brief in word, but abounding in meaning, illustrious with truth, full of mystery, most sweet and pleasing in the proclamation of God, in which the holy soul engages in a sweet, trusting, and loving colloquy with God. We ought not therefore to sing this Psalm unless it be with devotion. And so that we might be worthy to sing it as it deserves, let us purge *ourselves from all defilement of the flesh and of the spirit,*[53] so that our body might be the temple of the Holy Spirit,[54] and our soul the seat of eternal Wisdom,[55] namely, of Christ: and so that holiness adorns our soul and our flesh is obedient to the spirit, so that it might fulfill in us that which Moses teaches: *You shall be perfect and without spot before the Lord your God.*[56] Whence Christ also said: *Be you therefore perfect, as also your heavenly father is perfect.*[57] For it is becoming to every person that he conform and accommodate himself to his house. If, therefore, we choose to be the house of Christ, it is necessary that we follow his manner of living, and that we assimilate his holiness.

---

51   *Cf.* Luke 1:75.
52   1 Pet. 1:15.
53   2 Cor. 7:1a.
54   *Cf.* 2 Cor. 6:16; 1 Cor. 3:16, 6:19.
55   *Cf.* Wis. 7:27.
56   Deut. 18:13.
57   Matt. 5:48.

PRAYER

O LORD, RULER OF HEAVEN AND EARTH, clothe us with the beauty of good works and with the strength of your grace, and gird us with the virtue of chastity; and grant that we might go forth to meet you with these bright wedding garments, and that, adorned with such splendor, we might enter into the eternal wedding banquet with you, who live and reign with God the Father forever and ever.

Domine, regnator caeli et terrae, indue nos bonorum operum decore
et fortitudine gratiae tuae, ac praecinge castimoniae virtute;
daque his nitidis et nuptialibus vestibus tibi venienti
obviare, et ornatis lampadibus ad aeternitatis
nuptias tecum intrare: qui cum Deo Patre
vivis et regnas Deus per omnia
saecula saeculorum.

Psalm 93

ARTICLE LXXII

ELUCIDATION OF THE NINETY-THIRD PSALM:
DEUS ULTIONUM DOMINUS.
THE LORD IS THE GOD TO WHOM REVENGE BELONGS.

HIS TITLE IS ASSIGNED TO THE PRESENT Psalm: *Psalmus David, quarta sabbati; a psalm for David on the fourth day of the week*: that is, this Psalm, which has the Prophet David as its author, addresses those things that are signified by works of the fourth day from the Sabbath or [the fourth day] of the week. For in the manner that is written in Genesis, the stars of heaven and the two great lights, namely the sun and moon, were created on the fourth day:[1] these, in accordance with the divine precept, traverse the heavens with great speed, serve their Creator most promptly, just as is written about the sun: *Great is the Lord who made it, and at his words he has hastened its course.*[2] Now, by the stars and lights of heaven are signified the elect and the just, of which the Apostle says: *Do all things without murmurings and hesitations, that you might be...without reproof in the midst of a crooked and perverse generation, among whom you shine as lights in the world.*[3] This Psalm deals with the patience, obedience, and the zeal of justice of these men, particularly showing the error and just damnation of those men who deny divine providence, and so it says:

93{94}[1] *The Lord is the God to whom revenge belongs: the God of revenge has acted freely.*

Deus ultionum libere egit; Deus ultionum libere egit.

93{94}[1] *Deus ultionum,* the God to whom revenge belongs, that is, of just vengeance is *Dominus,* the Lord: because from his own power and equity he avenges himself upon the ungodly, when, where, in whatever manner, and however much he wills. And there is none who is able to impede him or to argue against him: and so it adds, *Deus ultionum libere*

---

1 Gen. 1:16–19.
2 Ecclus. 43:5.
3 Phil. 2:14–15.

391

egit, the God of revenge has acted freely, that is, according to that which pleases him. For there is no other superior law to which he is subject, but his will is the cause of the law of all created things. Whence, the Apostle [Paul] says: *he works all things according to the counsel of his will;*[4] and again, *He has mercy on whom he will; and whom he will, he hardens.*[5] And this is not dissonant with that which he said through Moses: *I will have mercy on whom I will, and I will be merciful to whom it shall please me.*[6] But in Deuteronomy is also written about the just, sudden, and untrammeled vengeance of God: *The Lord God is strong, repaying forthwith those that hate him, so as to destroy them, without further delay immediately rendering to them what they deserve.*[7] And the prophet Nahum said: *The Lord is a jealous God, and a revenger . . . and has wrath, . . . taking vengeance on his adversaries.*[8]

93{94}[2] *Lift up yourself, you that judge the earth: render a reward to the proud.*

Exaltare, qui iudicas terram, redde retributionem superbis.

Conforming his affection with the divine justice, the Prophet next prays: **93{94}[2]** *Exaltare, lift up yourself,* that is, declare your justice, and show yourself to be the most high judge of the whole universe, *qui iudicas terram, you that judge the earth,* that is, all the inhabitants of the earth; *redde retributionem, render a reward,* that is, a just punishment, *superbis, to the proud* rebelling against you, punishing them now with temporal punishments so that they might not eternally perish. For we ought to pray for the good of all men, and we ought not to desire the eternal damnation of anyone, since we are commanded to love our enemies,[9] and to despair of no one.[10] But we are able to exhort, in a

---

4   Eph. 1:11b.
5   Rom. 9:18.
6   Ex. 33:19b.
7   Deut. 7:10.
8   Nahum 1:2.
9   Luke 6:27.
10   "But so long someone lives in this flesh, this impenitence, or this impenitent heart, may not be judged upon. For, so long as the patience of God leads to repentance and he — who does not wish the death of the ungodly, but rather than he might live — does not snatch the ungodly out of this life, we are to despair of no one. He is a pagan today; but how do you know whether tomorrow he may not be a Christian? The Jew is an infidel today, what if tomorrow he were to believe in Christ? He is a heretic today; but what if he were to follow the Catholic truth tomorrow? He is a schismatic today, yet what if tomorrow he were to embrace Catholic peace tomorrow? What if

conditional way, for the perpetual damnation of the ungodly, namely in this sense: that if they disdain their conversion, and if they remain obstinate, and then it befalls them that they quickly die and perish and not live a long time, they will store for themselves *wrath, in the day...* *of the just judgment of God.*[11] For of such men is stated in the prophet Amos: *They have not known to do the right thing, ... storing up iniquity.*[12]

93{94}[3] *How long shall sinners, O Lord: how long shall sinners glory?*

Usquequo peccatores, Domine, usquequo peccatores gloriabuntur?

93{94}[4] *Shall they utter, and speak iniquity: shall all speak who work injustice?*

Effabuntur et loquentur iniquitatem, loquentur omnes qui operantur injustitiam?

93{94}[3] *Usquequo, how long,* that is, how much more time, *peccatores, Domine;* shall sinners, O Lord who are a just judge, *usquequo peccatores gloriabuntur,* how long shall sinners glory, not with a true, but with a false and deformed glory, namely since *when they have done evil,* and rejoiced *in most wicked things?*[13] Of these, James says: *Now you rejoice in your arrogancies. All such rejoicing is wicked.*[14] And how long, O Lord, **93{94}** **[4]** *Effabuntur et loquentur,* shall they utter and speak that is, shall they say with in their heart and with their mouth, *iniquitatem,* iniquity, that is, iniquitous words: *loquentur,* shall they speak, I say, *omnes qui operantur iniustitiam,* all those who work injustice, that is, [how long shall those who do] works contrary to the divine precepts, say such things?

93{94}[5] *Your people, O Lord, they have brought low: and they have afflicted your inheritance.*

Populum tuum, Domine, humiliaverunt; et haereditatem tuam vexaverunt.

---

these — whom you now see in whatever kind of error, and whom you damn as most desperate cases — what if they repent before the end of this life and find the true life? For this reason, brothers, what the Apostle says also admonishes you: 'Judge nothing before its time.' [1 Cor. 4:5] For this blasphemy of the Spirit, of which there is no forgiveness ... cannot be found in anyone ... as long as he is still found in this life." St. Augustine, *Sermon* 71, 13, 22, PL 38, 456.

11   Rom. 2:5.
12   Amos 3:10.
13   Prov. 2:14.
14   James 4:16.

93{94}[6] *They have slain the widow and the stranger: and they have murdered the fatherless.*

Viduam et advenam interfecerunt, et pupillos occiderunt.

93{94}[5] *Populum tuum, Domine; your people, O Lord,* obedient to, chosen by, and pious towards you, *humiliaverunt, have been brought low,* that is, they have been held in contempt and oppressed; *et hereditatem tuam, and your inheritance,* namely, the people just mentioned whom you possess as your inheritance, taking care of them, making them fruitful, and preserving them until you elevate them into eternal life, *vexaverunt, have been afflicted.* For **93{94}[6]** *Viduam, the widow* deprived of the solace of her husband, *et advenam, and the stranger,* namely, the foreigner bereft of the help of his fellow countrymen, *interfecerunt, ut pupilos occiderunt, they have slain, and they have murdered the fatherless.* These especially are the people and the inheritance of God, and God in a special way vindicates their injuries, according to this: *God, great, and mighty, and terrible . . . does judgment to the fatherless and the widow, and he loves the stranger.*[15]

But because it is written truly, *The sinner will add sin to sin,*[16] and so for these evil men it is not sufficient to sin in this way against their neighbor, but they also sin against God; and as the apostle Jude in his epistle says, *They deny the Lord who bought them, they hold dominion in contempt, and blaspheme majesty.*[17] Whence, is added:

93{94}[7] *And they have said: The Lord shall not see: neither shall the God of Jacob understand.*

Et dixerunt : Non videbit Dominus, nec intelliget Deus Iacob.

93{94}[7] *Et dixerunt: Non videbit Dominus; and they have said, the Lord shall not see* us, *nec intelligent Deus Iacob, neither shall the God of Jacob understand,* [that is, neither shall the God] of the patriarch Jacob or of the people born of him, [understand] our works. It is as if they were saying: God does not have particularized knowledge of the individual human species, nor does he distinctly perceive human acts; consequently, the divine judgment is not to be feared, nor is retribution in another age to be expected. This is the most pernicious error of denying the providence of God. Of these persons, the book of Job says: *Do you think that God . . . walks about the poles of heaven . . . and does not consider our*

---

15   Deut. 10:17a, 18a.
16   Ecclus. 3:29b.
17   2 Pet. 2:1; Jude 4, 8.

things?[18] Of these the Lord also says through the prophet Malachi: *Your words have been unsufferable to me; and you have said . . . he labors in vain that serves God, and what profit is it that we have kept his ordinances?*[19] And the Lord denounces against these through Jeremiah, saying: *Shall a man be hid in secret places, and I not see him, says the Lord?*[20]

93{94}[8] *Understand, you senseless among the people: and, you fools, be wise at last.*

Intelligite, insipientes in populo; et stulti, aliquando sapite.

93{94}[9] *He that planted the ear, shall he not hear? Or he that formed the eye, does he not consider?*

Qui plantavit aurem non audiet? Aut qui finxit oculum non considerat?

93{94}[10] *He that chastises nations, shall he not rebuke: he that teaches man knowledge?*

Qui corripit gentes non arguet, qui docet hominem scientiam?

But now the prophet more fully argues against them. **93{94}[8]** *Intelligite,* understand [he says to] those who follow, *insipientes in populo, et stulti; you senseless among the people, and you fools,* that is, those deprived of the true faith and knowledge of divine things, *aliquando sapite, be wise at last,* that is, with intellectual fervor pay heed to this: **93{94}[9]** *Qui plantavit aurem non audiet? He that planted the ear, shall he not hear?* That is, God—who gave men the sense of hearing, and instituted the means, way, and order by which others hear from the fountain of his own wisdom, foreseeing, namely, what was required to be heard, and bestowing those things necessary to be able to hear—can he not hear? It is as if he were saying, "Indeed." For unless he knew beforehand all things, namely, the nature of words and of sound, and also those other things previously stated, he would not have been able to have planted the organ of hearing. And in a similar way he argues of the eye: *Or he that formed the eye* both external and internal, *non considerat, does he not consider?* It is as if he were saying, "Of course." For whatever of perfection is found in creatures exists in a much more excellent and much more perfect way in the Creator. **93{94}[10]** *Qui corripit gentes,*

---

18   Job 22:12, 14. E. N. Denis re-arranges the words in his quotation.
19   Malachi 3:13–14a.
20   Jer. 23:24a.

he that chastises nations, that is, he who scourges sinners in this life on account of their fault, as is clearly shown in Pharaoh and in his people whom he drowned,[21] and the Canaanites, whom he destroyed by the sons of Israel;[22] or *he that chastises nations*, that is, refutes their sins by the Prophets and other Saints; *non arguet, shall he not rebuke* even you? It is as if he were saying, "Indeed he shall rebuke and condemn you," as he frequently attested by Jeremiah: *Shall I not visit for these things, . . . and shall not my soul take revenge on such a nation?*[23] *Qui docet hominem scientiam, he that teaches man knowledge* giving him the written and evangelical law, shall he not have knowledge and providence of human life? He who would consider carefully and follow these things is able to ascertain from them incontestable reasons establishing the providence of God and the distinct intellectual knowledge of God of all created things.

93{94}[11] *The Lord knows the thoughts of men, that they are vain.*

   Dominus scit cogitationes hominum, quoniam vanae sunt.

93{94}[11] *Dominus scit cogitationes hominum, the Lord knows the thoughts of men*: for all things are open and naked to his eyes; *quoniam vanae sunt, that they are vain*, that is, he knows this about them, that they are empty and foolish. This the Lord also demonstrates in Revelation, rebuking the nefarious woman Jezebel, threatening her with a most heavy punishment: whence he concludes, *All the churches shall know that I am he that searches the reins and hearts, and I will give to every one of you according to your works.*[24] The Apostle mentions this verse in this manner: *The Lord knows the thoughts of the wise, that they are vain.*[25]

93{94}[12] *Blessed is the man whom you shall instruct, O Lord: and shall teach him out of your law,*

   Beatus homo quem tu erudieris, Domine, et de lege tua docueris eum,

93{94}[13] *That you may give him rest from the evil days: till a pit be dug for the wicked.*

   Ut mitiges ei a diebus malis, donec fodiatur peccatori fovea.

---

21   Ex. 14:27–28.
22   E. N. Joshua 11:20–23.
23   Jer. 10:9.
24   Rev. 2:23.
25   1 Cor. 3:20.

93{94}[12] *Beatus homo quem tu erudieris, Domine; blessed is the man whom you shall instruct, O Lord,* by internal inspirations, by hidden, special, and continual illuminations, *et de lege tua, and out of your law* given by Moses and by Christ, *docueris eum, you shall teach him,* giving him grace so that he may soundly and lucidly understand and observe it. For this reason, in the beginning of his letter to the Colossians, the Apostle prays: We beg *that you may be filled with the knowledge of the will of God in all wisdom and spiritual understanding, that you may walk worthy of God, and increasing in all things in the knowledge of God.*[26] And to the Ephesians: *The Father of Glory may give unto you the spirit of wisdom, . . . that you may know what the hope is of your calling.*[27] Whence the divine word says: *The people that do not understand shall be beaten.*[28] But because according to Scripture, *wisdom does not enter into a malicious soul, nor dwell in a body subject to sins,* therefore he who desires to obtain this knowledge of divine beatitude should remove obstacles, that is, he should abhor, repent of, and confess sins and correct himself; and then he must beg for the illumination of divine grace, and he will experience to be true that which is written: *If any of you want wisdom, let him ask of God, . . . and it shall be given him.*[29] And so, O Lord, blessed is he whom you have so instructed, namely in this: **93{94}[13]** *Ut mitiges ei, that you may give him rest* during the time of this exile, *a diebus malis, from the evil days,* in which the malignant and ungodly glory and flourish, but he suffers tribulations and tears: that is, that you might kindly and sweetly provide for him, so that he might patiently suffer the tribulations which may befall him, and that he may not sorrow at the prosperity of the ungodly, judging them to be something [to be envied] or as being desirable. *Give him rest,* I say, only as long *donec fodiatur peccatori fovea, till a pit be dug for the wicked,* he might stand before [the pit] of a tomb, and the lake of hell, that is, until the sinner dies, and his body is in the grave, but his soul is placed in hell: when this is done, you will finally lead to glory him who has been taught by you.

93{94}[14] *For the Lord will not cast off his people: neither will he forsake his own inheritance.*

Quia non repellet Dominus plebem suam, et haereditatem suam non derelinquet.

---

26 Col. 1:9–10.
27 Eph. 1:7, 18b.
28 Hosea 4:14b.
29 James 1:5.

93{94}[15] *Until justice be turned into judgment: and who are they that are near it? All that are upright in heart.*

Quoadusque iustitia convertatur in iudicium, et qui iuxta illam omnes? Qui recto sunt corde.

Now God gives these benefits to those who ask him, **93{94}[14]** *Quia non repellet Dominus plebem suam, for the Lord will not cast off his people* who are faithful to him, that is, he will not spurn their prayers, he will fulfill their desires, and he will accept their homage; *et hereditatem suam, and his own inheritance,* that is, the flock of his elect, *non derelinquet, he will not forsake* in the final consummation. Because of this, the Apostle [Paul] says: *The Lord has not cast away his people*[30] whom he has foreknown. And the Savior: *Fear not, little flock, for it has pleased your Father to give you a kingdom.*[31] And so he will not abandon them, **93{94}[15]** *Quoadusque iustitia, until justice,* his [justice] *convertatur, be turned,* that is, proceeds, *in iudicium, into judgment,* that is, in the act or the execution of justice, giving to the good and to the evil their suitable deserts, which will be accomplished in the day of judgment. Until then, therefore, God takes care of his own by grace, lest they be ensnared and completely overwhelmed by the ungodly; but after the judgment he takes care of them by glory, so that they will suffer no more evil things from those who are evil. *Et qui iuxta illam? And who are they that are near it?* That is, [who are the] men that now acquiesce to the divine justice, and in the future judgment harmoniously adhere to it? He responds: *Omnes qui recto sunt corde, all who are upright in heart,* that is, all of the just. Truly their intention, affection, and manner of life pleases, adheres to, and eternally joins itself with the divine justice. For since likeness is the cause of love and of union,[32] the just God joins himself to the just and loves them. Whence Moses says: *The Lord will make known who belong to him, and the holy he will join to himself; and whom he shall choose, they shall approach him.*[33]

93{94}[16] *Who shall rise up for me against the evildoers? Or who shall stand with me against the workers of iniquity?*

Quis consurget mihi adversus malignantes? Aut quis stabit mecum adversus operantes iniquitatem?

---

30   Rom. 11:2a.
31   Luke 12:32.
32   E. N. ST IaIIae, q. 27, art. 3, c.
33   Num. 16:5a.

And then the Prophet speaking in the person of the just man, lit with the love of God and neighbor, with zealous zeal *for the Lord God of hosts,*[34] and for the preservation of the servants of God in the good also says, **93{94}[16]** *Quis consurget mihi, who shall rise up for me,* that is, to my salvation, *adversus malignantes, against the evil doers?* That is, who will help me so that I might resist the evildoers, and I might hamper their ungodly achievements, lest their evil example corrupt others, and they lead many to be irreverent to God? *Aut quis stabit mecum, or who shall stand with me,* that is, who will constantly assist me, *adversus operantes iniquitatem, against the workers of iniquity* so that those things that they wish to practice they are unable to follow, but rather are punished with just punishment. The heart of Moses was inflamed with this holy zeal, when he said upon the sons of Israel making for themselves a molten and golden calf: *If any man be on the Lord's side, let him join himself to me, . . . and put every man his sword upon his thigh, . . . and let every man kill his brother, and friend, and neighbor.*[35]

93{94}[17] *Unless the Lord had been my helper, in short time my soul might have dwelt in hell.*[36]

Nisi quia Dominus adiuvit me, paulo minus habitasset in inferno anima mea.

93{94}[17] *Nisi quia Dominus adiuvit me, unless the Lord had been my helper,* that is, if the Lord had not helped me against the evildoers, *paulo minus, in a short time,* that is, absolutely, *habitasset in inferno anima mea, my soul might have dwelt in hell* after the end of this present life; and also in this life I would have dwelt in hell in doing works by which I would arrive to hell,[37] in way [analogously] that holy wayfarers are said to dwell and have a manner of life in heaven because they do the works which strive toward the kingdom of heaven.[38] Or [we can view it thus], *in hell,* that is, in mortal sin, which is the reason of one heading to the punishments of hell. Indeed, truly one is able to say of all those who mortally offend God, though they are not yet cast into hell; *unless the Lord*

---

34   1 Kings 19:10a.

35   Ex. 32:26–27.

36   E. N. I have departed from the Douay-Rheims, which reads "my soul had almost dwelt in hell."

37   E. N. There is a theological commonplace that "grace is glory inchoate, and grace is glory consummated." Denis suggests a corollary to this: "mortal sin is hell (or damnation) inchoate, and hell (or damnation) is mortal sin consummated."

38   Phil. 3:20.

had been my helper, that is, unless the goodness of God had mercifully led me, *my soul might have dwelt in hell* by being eternally damned. For when man sins mortally, he deserves to be deprived of all the benefits of the grace of God and come upon eternal punishment. Whence it is necessary to summon the mercy of God so that man might rid himself of the punishment of hell. And so it is said by Jeremiah: *The mercies of the Lord* [must be sought so] *that we are not consumed.*[39]

93{94}[18] *If I said: My foot is moved: your mercy, O Lord, assisted me.*

Si dicebam: Motus est pes meus, misericordia tua, Domine, adiuvabat me.

93{94}[19] *According to the multitude of my sorrows in my heart, your comforts have given joy to my soul.*

Secundum multitudinem dolorum meorum in corde meo, consolationes tuae laetificaverunt animam meam.

But because the humble confession of one's own weakness is followed with the kindly help of God, there is added: **93{94}[18]** *Si dicebam, if I said* with my mind before you, or with my heart in humble confession: *Motus est pes meus, my foot is moved*, that is, the affection of my heart or the path of my manner of living is moved by the rightness of life and toward the observation of the divine law, *misericordia tua, Domine, adiuvabat me, your mercy, O Lord, assisted me:*[40] that is, at that instant of time your mercy will immediately come to my aid, pardon will be bestowed, and grace will be infused. Whence Job: *My ways*, he said, *in his sight I will reprove; and he shall be my Savior.*[41] And this is more clearly manifested in what follows. **93{94}[19]** *Secundum multitudinem dolorum meorum in corde meo, according to the multitude of my sorrows in my heart*, that is, in accordance with the fact many are the afflictions in the heart by reason of justice, namely, for one's own sin, or for another's, because of the delay of eternal happiness, because of injuries to the divine majesty, *consolationes tuae laetificaverunt animam meam, your comforts have given joy to my soul*, that is, in many ways I am consoled

---

39   Lam. 3:22.
40   E. N. Denis departs slightly from the Sixto-Clementine Vulgate by using *adiuvit* (perfect indicative active = assisted), rather than *adiuvabat* (imperfect indicative active = was assisted). The editor notes in the margin that other authorities have *adiuvabat*.
41   Job 13:15b–16a.

by spiritual, hidden, and angelic consolations. This is what the Apostle says: *As the sufferings of Christ abound in us: so also by Christ does our comfort abound.*[42] And again: *Blessed be God . . . who comforts us in all our tribulation.*[43] This is also written elsewhere: *After a storm you make a calm, and after tears and weeping you pour in joyfulness.*[44] Indeed, anyone who is afflicted because of a just cause (provided he endures his affliction with equanimity) and who despises all carnal and vile delights is worthy to be consoled by the Lord, the more exuberantly, the more abundantly he is afflicted. If, therefore, we endeavor to obtain the relish of divine consolations which are true and most sweet, let us not disdain, but rather rejoice, in suffering tribulation and affliction: for if we were *partakers of the sufferings,* we will be also *of the consolation,* according to the Apostle [Paul].[45]

93{94}[20] *Does the seat of iniquity stick to you, who frame labor in commandment?*

Numquid adhaeret tibi sedes iniquitatis, qui fingis laborem in praecepto?

93{94}[20] *Numquid adhaeret tibi sedes iniquitatis, does the seat of iniquity stick to you,* that is, the unjust soul (which is the seat of sin, just as the righteous soul is the seat of wisdom and virtue):[46] that is, will a sinner be with you or please you, *qui fingis laborem in praecepto, who frame labor in commandment,* that is, who find certain difficulties to arise in the observation of your precepts? For we are not able to fulfill the divine commandments without labor. Now according to the Philosopher, the things that are difficult involve both art and virtue.[47] For this reason, it is stated in a Psalm above: *For the sake of the words of your lips, I have kept hard ways.*[48] And so it asks: *Does the seat of iniquity stick to you, etc.?* It as though it is saying, "No," because as is elsewhere found, *God is faithful and without any iniquity, he is just and right.*[49] And so the unjust can in no fashion adhere to the sinner, especially since Solomon says: *The*

---

42 2 Cor. 1:5.
43 2 Cor. 1:3a, 4a.
44 Tob. 3:22b.
45 2 Cor. 1:7b.
46 *Cf.* Wis. 7:27.
47 E. N. Aristotle, *Nicomachean Ethics,* II, 3, 1105a10.
48 Ps. 16:4b.
49 Deut. 32:4b.

Lord is far from the wicked.[50] For sins are what cause a division between God and us, as Isaiah asserts.[51] Or [we can understand it thus], *who frame labor in commandment,* that is, who form, undertake, and fashion from this labor and suffering the precepts, for you command us in this life to labor and to suffer, saying, *Blessed are they that mourn, for they shall be comforted;*[52] and again, *The kingdom of heaven suffers violence, and the violent bear it away.*[53] For this reason Paul says, *Labor as a good soldier of Christ Jesus;* [54]and James, *Let your laughter be turned into mourning, and your joy into sorrow.*[55]

One can also direct this verse as applying to men, and expound it to be about the sinner; and so it would be [understood] in this sense: *Does, O man, the seat of iniquity stick to you,* that is, does iniquity inseparably stick to you, or are you habituated in sin, which is the *chair of pestilence,*[56] *who frame labor in commandment,* that is, who lyingly say that you are unable to fulfill the commandments of God? It is as if he were saying, "No." For man is able to correct himself while he is on the way [that is, while he is a wayfarer on earth]. This is said against those, who when admonished to cease from sin, respond: I am unable to abandon my habit, I am not able to leave the world or to curb concupiscence; and so: I am not able to fast, to pray much, to engage in vigils constantly, or to remain in solitude. The damnation of these kinds of men is just, because they are lying, and they affirm God to be rash, as if God would command the impossible; they also acknowledge their affection to be contrary altogether to the divine will.

93{94}[21]   *They will hunt after the soul of the just, and will condemn innocent blood.*

Captabunt in animam iusti, et sanguinem innocentem condemnabunt.

93{94}[22]   *But the Lord is my refuge: and my God the help of my hope.*

Et factus est mihi Dominus in refugium, et Deus meus in adiutorium spei meae.

---

50   Prov. 15:29a.
51   Is. 49:2a: *But your iniquities have divided between you and your God.*
52   Matt. 5:5.
53   Matt. 11:12b.
54   2 Tim. 2:3.
55   James 4:9.
56   Ps. 1:1a.

93{94}[23] *And he will render them their iniquity: and in their malice he will destroy them: the Lord our God will destroy them.*

Et reddet illis iniquitatem ipsorum, et in malitia eorum disperdet eos; disperdet illos Dominus Deus noster.

93{94}[21] *Captabunt, they will hunt,* that is, frequently they will perform acts of violence, *in animam iusti, after the souls of the just,* since they seek to separate, oppress, and hinder the virtues by their false convictions, by their perverse works, by their smooth flattery. Hence the Lord says of these kinds of persons: *With lies you have made the heart of the just to mourn, whom I have not made sorrowful: and have strengthened the hands of the wicked.*[57] And the just man says to the ungodly: *How long will you afflict my soul, and break me in pieces with words? Behold, these ten times you confound me, and are not ashamed to oppress me.*[58] *Et sanguinem innocentem, and innocent blood,* that is, the man who is just and single-minded, *condemnabunt, they will condemn,* disapproving of his life or asserting him to be worthy of death. And so it is written: *They killed which should not die,* and they allowed to live *souls which should not live.*[59] **93{94}[22]** *Et factus est mihi Dominus in refugium, but the Lord is my refuge:* because he gave me charity and hope by which I confidently seek refuge in him in all necessity; *et Deus meus, and my God* is become for me *in adiutorium spei meae, the help of my hope,* that is, God leads my hope to its effect, working in me with his grace, so that my hope may not be frustrated, but that I may be able to do all things *in him who strengthens me.*[60] **93{94}[23]** *Et reddet illis, and he will render them,* namely, the ungodly, *iniquitatem ipsorum, their iniquity,* that is, just torments, which their sins deserve, as is asserted in Joel: *I will very soon return you a recompense upon your own head.*[61] *Et in malitia eorum, and in their malice,* that is, because of their evil life, *disperdet eos, he will destroy them,* that is, he will ruin them in various ways as they individually in various ways deserve. For he will give to each person as much punishment as that person had gloried in fault, according to that said by John in Revelation: *As much as she has glorified herself, . . . so much torment and sorrow give to her.*[62] *Disperdet illos Dominus Deus noster, the Lord our God will destroy them,* that is, Christ the judge of all will say to them in the day of judgment: Go, *you cursed, into everlasting fire.*

---

57 Ez. 13:22.
58 Job 19:2–3.
59 Ez. 13:19b.
60 Phil. 4:13.
61 Joel 3:4b.
62 Rev. 18:7a.

We are taught by this present Psalm to fear the divine vengeance, and wholeheartedly to abhor all sins, lest, while we recite this Psalm, our mouths may condemn us. For as we read in Ecclesiasticus: *While the ungodly curse the devil, he curses his own soul;*[63] and so while the sinner utters imprecations against vices, he condemns himself. For this reason, the Apostle [Paul] states: *For wherein you judge another, you condemn yourself.*[64] Let us attend to Christ the judge in such a fashion, let us conform our affections to the divine will in such a manner, so that with sincere and untroubled mind we might speak with him against the perverse, and unceasingly let us think about his providence and most rigorous judgment, saying with holy Job: *Does he not consider my ways, and number all my steps?*[65] And again: *I feared all my works, knowing that you did not spare the offender.*[66]

Finally, because the mention of the Sabbath in this Psalm has be often explained, we know that the Sabbath is three-fold, namely, the temporal Sabbath, which is the day of the week, or the week itself; the second is the Sabbath of the soul, that is the quiet of a stainless conscience; but the third is the Sabbath of eternity, of which this present Psalm deals with.

PRAYER

GOD, HELP OF OUR HOPE, BE THE REFUGE of your servants in all necessity; provide us ease from evil days, and let the consolations of your goodness always gladden our soul.

Deus, auxilium spei nostrae, in omni necessitate esto refugium familiae tuae; mitiga nobis a diebus malis, et semper laetificent animam nostram consolationes tuae pietatis.

---

63   Ecclus. 21:30.
64   Rom. 2:1b.
65   Job 31:4.
66   Job 9:28.

Psalm 94

ARTICLE LXXIII

EXPOSITION OF THE NINETY-FOURTH PSALM:
VENITE, EXSULTEMUS DOMINO.
COME, LET US EXULT IN THE LORD.

94{95}[0] *Praise of a canticle for David himself.*[1]

Laus cantci ipsi David.

HE TITLE TO THIS PSALM IS: *LAUS CANTICI ipsi David, praise of a canticle for David himself*: that is, this present Psalm, which is the spiritual praise of exultation, of [the mental] conception of the contemplation of the Godhead, is sung for David himself, that is, Christ. For while it says *David himself* in the title, commonly by David is understood Christ. For this Psalm addresses the time of grace, by which we are led to the mysteries of Christ and unto eternal rest. And so this Psalm speaks of Christ and his coming, and of the entry into the celestial quiet or the kingdom of heaven. For the apostle Paul refers to this Psalm to the Hebrews by this verse, *Today if you hear his voice,*[2] even unto the end of that verse, as speaking of Christ or of the entry into the kingdom of heaven which was laid open for us by Christ. Whereby he also asserts this Psalm to be composed by David, among other places saying this: For this reason, *he determined a certain day... saying in David: Today, if you shall hear his voice, etc.*[3]

From this it can be absolutely concluded by any Christian that what is said by the Hebrews — who say that eleven of the Psalms, namely, *Lord, you have been our refuge,* and those which follow, even unto the Psalm which begins, *Mercy and judgment will I sing to you, O Lord,*[4] within which Psalms are contained the words "written by Moses" — is false. But he who, following the Hebrews, affirms these Psalms to be written by Moses, must [certainly] except this one, since the foundation

---

1 E. N. Psalm 94 in the Sixto-Clementine Vulgate (and hence also the Douay Rheims translation) bears no title; hence the first verse begins below. I have therefore numbered this verse 94{95}:0.

2 Heb. 3:7b.

3 Heb. 4:7.

4 Ps. 89(90)–100(101) inclusive

it leans on is ruinous.[5] Briefly, wherever in the canonical Scriptures of
the New Testament there are asserted words of the Psalms, either no one
is stated to be the author or David is expressed [to be the author]. And
so the probability is great that all the Psalms were written by David.[6]
It is not valid for someone to argue that, since in some places [in the
New Testament] the name David is not asserted [as being the author of
the Psalms], therefore he did not compose all the Psalms. [This is so]
because even in those Psalms that assert [Davidic authorship] and which
all say in agreement were authored by David, the Scriptures of the New
Testament do not always state that they were written by David himself,
as it becomes clear to those carefully examining this issue.[7]

94{95}[1] *Come let us exult in the Lord with joy: let us joyfully sing to
God our Savior.[8]*

Venite, exsultemus Domino; iubilemus Deo salutari nostro.

And so, the holy Prophet, inviting us all to a heartfelt praising of the
most high Trinity, of the one true and simple God, or of Christ, which in
the unity of Person is both God and man, says: **94{95}[1]** *Venite*, come,
with affection of mind, and if there be a work involved, also with a body
in keeping [with the mind's affection], since mind and body are as one,
let us do that which follows. *Come*, all you distant from God by an evil
life: *come*, I say, that is, to those things that follow, prepare yourself by
humble confession and through making satisfaction for your sins. *Come*,
all you devout and religious men and women, that is, pull your minds
away from various and many things which are not necessary and draw

---

5   E. N. In other words, the notion that Psalm 94 is one of the Psalms written
by Moses is contradicted by the inspired and inerrant statements in the epistle to
the Hebrews which provide for a Davidic authorship; accordingly, the argument is
founded upon the ruinous assumption that the New Testament scripture contains error.
6   E. N. The assumption being that if it had been another author, the writer would
have mentioned it. By silence, the authorship of David is implied.
7   E. N. In other words, the New Testament expressly ascribes Davidic authorship
to some Psalms. However, it is silent with respect to Davidic authorship as to other
Psalms where the Psalms themselves attribute authorship to David. Therefore, the
New Testament silence as to Davidic authorship cannot imply that any particular
Psalm does not enjoy Davidic authorship.
8   E. N. I have modified the Douay-Rheims from "let us praise" to "let us exult in."
This is necessary since the *Commentary* distinguishes between the similar notions
of exultation and jubilation (which the Douay-Rheims translates as joyfully singing),
and the much broader disparity between "praise" and "joyfully sing" simply does not
allow for a proper fit with the point of the commentary.

near to that one thing which alone is necessary. *Come*, by the contemplation of faith, by the most certain expectation of hope, by the fervor of charity. *Come*, by mental purity, by vocal praise, by a laudable manner of life. *Come*, understanding, loving, and doing good works. *Exsultemus Domino, let us exult in the Lord*, that is, let us so strongly interiorly rejoice in God, let us take delight in his glory, so that an outward sign of interior joy might appear. Let us therefore praise the Lord, that is, for his immense goodness, and let us glory in his benefits, in the manner that Habakkuk says: *I will rejoice in the Lord: and I will joy in God my Jesus.*[9] *Iubilemus Deo salutari nostro, let us joyfully sing to God our Savior*: that is, to Christ our Savior, or to the triune God, our Savior and our Salvation, that is, the object and the cause of our salvation; let us so exuberantly rejoice in the soul that this gladness through its excess is not able to be completely restrained or hidden, nor it is able to be fully explained. For exultation is the exhilaration of the mind exhibited externally by sensible signs, because "to exult" is to jump outside one's self. And jubilation [or joyfully singing] is such a copious rejoicing in God with the mind that it is not able to be fully contained, nor is it able to be completely expressed.

94{95}[2]   *Let us come before his presence with thanksgiving; and make a joyful noise to him with Psalms.*

Praeoccupemus faciem eius in confessione, et in psalmis iubilemus ei.

94{95}[2] *Praeocupemus faciem eius, let us come before his presence*, that is, let us set ourselves before the sight of our God or his presence, so that we seek him before anything else, in the manner that is written: *Seek first the kingdom of God and his justice.*[10] Let us come before him, I say, *in confessione, with thanksgiving* joyful of his great goodness, and also in the painful confession of our depravity. Or [alternatively]: *Let us come before his presence*, that is, let us at the outset cast out of our hearts all impediments to the veneration of the Godhead, and before we admit in any extraneous thoughts or vain mental representations, let us come before him, let us contemplate him, let us honor the presence of God. *Et in psalmis, and with Psalms*, that is, spiritual canticles and devout verses, *iubilemus ei, let make a joyful noise to him*, praising him with our mouth in the manner that the Apostle [Paul] teaches: *Be filled with the Holy*

---

9   Hab. 3:18.
10   Matt. 6:33a.

Spirit . . . singing and making melody in your hearts to the Lord always.[11]

We offer this Psalm in the beginning of the office of Matins, so that our heart might be enflamed with the heat of divine love, and that it might begin the divine service with a prompt and fervent mind, and not with a reluctant, wandering, cold, and insincere one. But also when we are alone, we can say, *Come, let us exult in the Lord,* etc., that is, O all the powers of my soul, all my substance, O all things that are within me, and especially, O reason, will, and memory, *come*: so that the reason may consider the divine reason, and the will may desire it, and the memory might be firmly established in it; let us exult with all our heart in the Lord: as has already been said.

94{95}[3]   *For the Lord is a great God, and a great King above all gods.*

Quoniam Deus magnus Dominus, et rex magnus super omnes deos.

Following this various reasons are put forth why we ought to do these things: **94{95}[3]** *Quoniam Deus, for . . . God* the Trinity, or Christ, God incarnate, is *magnus Dominus, a great Lord:*[12] for all things are placed under his jurisdiction, and there is nothing that is able to resist his will, as is written in the book of Esther.[13] He also is *rex magnus, a great King,* indeed boundless and omnipotent, *super omnes deos, above all gods,* who by grace are made *partakers of the divine nature,*[14] namely, above all the Saints living in heaven and on earth. For all these gods are creatures of the most high God, and infinitely fall short of his excellence; and God alone is the universal Lord and the King of all things. Yet the creatures are allotted by him a certain dominion, and a special reign, and they are relationally ordered to God as servants to a lord, as instruments to a principal agent, as secondary causes to a primary and independent cause. Whence the Apostle [Paul] says: *There is no power but from God;*[15] and: *He that resists the power, resists the ordinance of God;*[16] *for he,* namely, the earthly prince, *is God's minister.*[17] This also Jethro, the kinsman of Moses, hearing about the wonders of God, said: *Now I know that the Lord is great above all gods.*[18]

---

11   Eph. 5:18b, 19b.

12   *E. N.* The translator of the Douay-Rheims attributes the adjective *great* to the noun *God*, whereas Denis sees it as referring to *Lord*.

13   *Cf.* Esther 8:9: *O Lord, Lord, almighty king, for all things are in your power, and there is none that can resist your will, if you determine to save Israel.*

14   2 Pet. 1:4a.

15   Rom. 13:1. *E. N.* And the verse continues: *and those that are, are ordained of God.*

16   Rom. 13:2a.

17   Rom. 13:4a.

18   Ex. 18:11a.

Quoniam non repellet Dominus plebem suam, for the Lord does not repel his people.[19] This can refer to the Jews whom God did not totally destroy, for *there is a remnant saved according to the election of grace*,[20] according to the Apostle, and at the end of the world they will convert to Christ. For this reason, the Apostle says of them: *Has God cast away his people? God forbid.*[21] Yet this verse is better expounded as referring to the Christian people, delivered by the most sacred Blood of Christ, whom Christ does not repel, as he attested: *Him that comes to me, I will not cast out.*[22] These words which were stated and were expounded upon in the preceding Psalm,[23] do not pertain to this Psalm, even though they are annexed to the daily Office.[24]

94{95}[4] *For in his hand are all the ends of the earth: and the heights of the mountains are his.*

Quia in manu eius sunt omnes fines terrae, et altitudines montium ipsius sunt.

94{95}[5] *For the sea is his, and he made it: and his hands formed the dry land.*

Quoniam ipsius est mare, et ipse fecit illud, et siccam manus eius formaverunt.

And so *God is the great king above all gods.* **94{95}[4]** *Quia in manu eius sunt omnes fines terrae, for in his hand are all the ends of the earth*, that is, within his power are all the regions of the world and their inhabitants, namely, all people. For he created, he preserves, and he is able to destroy all things; and he mercifully saves those from the nations that he wills, and those he wills he justly abandons and damns. *Et altitudines montium, and the heights of the mountains*, that is, the powers, perfections, and graces of the holy angels and of good men or of those who preach [the Gospel],

---

19   E. N. This interpolation found in the Roman Psalter (*Versio Romana*), probably borrowed from Ps. 93:14a, is not part of the original Psalm, and is therefore not in the Sixto-Clementine Vulgate, though it made it into the liturgy of Matins. In any event, Denis includes it in his *Commentary*, though he later states that it is not part of the original Psalm, but includes it in the *Commentary* because it is attached to the Office of Matins. Unsurprisingly, the verse has been excised from the Invitatory following the reforms of Vatican II. It is no longer found in the Invitatory of the Liturgy of the Hours.

20   Rom. 11:5b.

21   Rom. 11:1a.

22   John 6:37b.

23   Ps. 93:14a. Psalm 93:14a is identical.

24   E. N. In other words, they are recited daily in the *Invitatory* at the hour of Matins, when this Psalm is recited even though they do not properly belong to the Psalm.

ipsius sunt, are his, that is, they are Christ's, because all good things flow out from his as origin. Whence the Apostle: *By the grace of God,* he says, *I am what I am.*[25] **94{95}[5]** *Quoniam ipsius est mare, for the sea is his,* that is, the oceans encircling the earth, from which the various seas are derived, *et ipse fecit illud, and he made it,* as he also did all other elements. For this reason, Jonah said: *I fear... the God of heaven, who made both the sea and the dry land.*[26] *Et siccam, and the dry land,* that is, the earth which by its nature is dry and cold, *manus eius fundaverunt, his hands formed,* that is, the omnipotent powers of God or his wisdom and strength [formed], in accordance to this: *The Lord by wisdom founded the earth.*[27]

94{95}[6] *Come let us adore and fall down: and weep before the Lord that made us.*

Venite, adoremus, et procidamus, et ploremus ante Dominum qui fecit nos.

94{95}[7] *For he is the Lord our God: and we are the people of his pasture and the sheep of his hand.*

Quia ipse est Dominus Deus noster, et nos populus pascuae eius, et oves manus eius.

And so **94{95}[6]** *Venite, come:* in accordance with the ways already addressed; *adoremus, let us adore* with the adoration of latria which is exhibited to God alone, *et procidamus, and let us fall down,* that is, let us humbly prostrate ourselves, *et ploremus, and let us weep* because of our great desire of living with God, and because of our and others' sins, *ante Dominum qui fecit nos, before the Lord that made us,* placing ourselves in his presence by faithful contemplation: saying with Elijah, *As the Lord lives... in whose sight we stand,*[28] having no improper intention, but in all things seeking the honor of God and fulfilling that [exhortation] of the Apostle: *With one mind, and with one mouth, may you glorify God and the Father.*[29] **94{95}[7]** *Quia ipse est Dominus Deus noster, for he is the Lord our God,* who created us and governs, shepherds, preserves, and perfects us. *Et nos, and we are populus pascuae eius, the people of his pasture,* that is, we feed both soul and body in his pastures, namely, with bodily food and drink, with the Sacrament of the Altar, and with

---

25   1 Cor. 15:10a.
26   Jonah 1:9b.
27   Prov. 3:19a.
28   1 Kings 17:11a.
29   Rom. 15:6.

the grace of self-sacrifice, which is the highest nourishment of the soul, *it is best* to establish *the heart with grace*, according to the Apostle.[30] We are also *oves manus eius, the sheep of his hand*, that is, the sheep by divine power, or constituted in the power of God, because in his hands is our entire salvation.

94{95}[8]   *Today if you shall hear his voice, harden not your hearts.*

Hodie si vocem eius audieritis, nolite obdurare corda vestra.

94{95}[9]   *As in the provocation, according to the day of temptation in the wilderness: where your fathers tempted me, they proved me, and saw my works.*

Sicut in irritatione, secundum diem tentationis in deserto, ubi tentaverunt me patres vestri, probaverunt me, et viderunt opera mea.

94{95}[8] *Hodie si vocem eius audieritis, [nolite obdurare corda vestra]; today, if you shall hear his voice, [harden not your hearts].* According to the most certain exposition of the holy Apostle [Paul], these words are said in a special way of the Jews who lived during the time of the preaching of the Gospel,[31] whom the Prophet here exhorts, so that at the time of grace they might receive the evangelical law, and not be rebellious towards the Son of God, in the manner that their fathers were rebellious against God the Father. And so he says: *Hodie, today,* that is, during the time of grace, which is called a day as Zechariah says, *And many nations shall be joined to the Lord in that day;*[32] and Isaiah, *In that day the bud of the Lord shall be in magnificence and glory;*[33] *si vocem eius, if . . . his voice,* that is, if the preaching of Christ or of his disciples, *audieritis, you shall hear,* O Jews, *nolite obdurare corda vestra, harden not your hearts,* that is, do not be incredulous or perverse, **94{95}[9]** *sicut in irritatione, as in the provocation* where it occurred, *secundum diem tentationis in deserto, according to the day of temptation in the wilderness,* that is, in the day when because of disbelief they wanted to test my power and the truth of my words. *Ubi tentaverunt me patres vestri, where your fathers tempted me,* in the wilderness, saying: *Is the Lord amongst us or not?*[34] Here the Prophet speaks in the person of God: *Probaverunt, they tempted me* by a test to see what I might be able

-----

30   Heb. 13:9.

31   Heb. 3:3–4:11. *Whereas, as the Holy Spirit says, 'Today if you shall hear his voice, harden not your hearts, as in the provocation, etc.*

32   Zech. 2:11a.

33   Is. 4:2a.

34   Ex. 17:7b.

to do, *et viderunt, and they saw* with their own eyes *opera mea, my works,* [namely,] the marvels in Egypt, in the Red Sea, and in the wilderness. In this place, one is to understand, *if (si)* as meaning *because (quia)*: so that it has the sense, *If you shall hear his voice,* that is, *because you will hear his voice.* This is also in accordance with the manner that Christ speaks to the Jews of the Antichrist: *I am come in the name of my Father, and you receive me not: if (si) another shall come in his own name, him you will receive.*[35]

The Holy Spirit exhorts us, therefore, that we not harden our hearts, repelling from outselves the evangelical lessons when we hear the voice or the teaching of the Savior from ourselves, as the Hebrew people hardened their heart, inciting God, that is, leading him to a just vengeance. Any one of us is able to say these words with respect to our interior in this way: *Today,* namely, in the present day, *if you shall hear his voice,* O intellect, memory, and will of my soul, *harden not your hearts,* that is, your resolution; but pay heed diligently, hold tightly in the memory, and fulfill manly whatever things are said to you.

94{95}[10]   *Forty years long was I offended with that generation, and I said: These always err in heart.*

Quadraginta annis offensus fui generationi illi; et dix: Semper hi errant corde.

94{95}[10] *Quadraginta annis offensus fui generationi illi, forty years long was I offended with that generation*: that is, by tempting me the Jewish people enraged me, and I justly punished them the entire time that I led them through the desert, for (as we read in Deuteronomy) they were always rebellious against me.[36] Other versions [of the Scriptures] have, *Proximus fui generationi huic, I was close to that generation*: because God did not abandon them completely; indeed he unceasingly rained down manna upon them, and he led them in the day by a column of cloud, and during the night with a column of fire. For this reason Moses said: *Neither is there any other nation so great, that has gods so nigh them, as our Lord God is present to all our petitions.*[37] *Et dixi, and I said* to Moses through the angel, and by Moses also to the people, reproving them: *Semper hi, these always,* these ungrateful to me and unbelieving murmurers, *errant corde, always err in heart,* believing falsities and desiring illicit things.

---

35   John 5:43b.
36   *Cf.* Deut. 31:27.
37   Deut. 4:7.

94{95}[11] *And these men have not known my ways: so I swore in my wrath that they shall not enter into my rest.*

Et isti non cognoverunt vias meas: ut iuravi in ira me: Si introibunt in requiem meam.

94{95}[11] *Et isti non cognoverunt vias meas, and these men have not known my ways,* that is, they have not acknowledged my commandments by approbation of the mind and by obedience of the will: they also have known by unformed knowledge,[38] because Moses manifestly promulgated the law to all of them. Or [alternatively]: *these men have not known my ways,* that is, they have not understood all the wondrous works that the Lord did before them, and the Lord did not give them an understanding heart, lasting even unto the present day. Their children also acted in this manner, namely, the Jews that lived during the time of Christ and of the Apostles. For this reason Christ said to them: *Blind guides of the blind, fill up then the measure of your fathers.*[39] And Augustine: Murmurers, he said, children of murmurers.[40] *Quibus iuravi, to whom I swore,*[41] that is, I firmly informed through Moses: *Si introibunt in requiem mea, that they shall not enter into my rest,* that is, they will not be admitted entry into the land of promise, in which I would have given them a quiet dwelling had they not be disobedient, as is written: *All you that... have murmured against me, shall not enter into the land, over which I lifted up my hand to make you dwell therein.*[42] Here the word "if" (*si*) as meaning "not" (*non*) in conformity with the manner that is understood that which is said by Amos, *There shall not be (si erit) evil in a city, which the Lord has not done.*[43]

And so, because the land of promise was a figure of the heavenly kingdom or the heavenly fatherland, and because its quiet was a figure of the

---

38 E. N. By "unformed knowledge" Denis means knowledge of the Law without any charity, without any supernatural love of God or neighbor for love of God.

39 Matt. 23:24a, 32.

40 E. N. The reference is to St. Augustine's Tractates on the Gospel of John, specifically Tractate XXVI, 11, PL 35, 1611.

41 E. N. The editor in the margin suggests the proper reading should be *ut* (so) and not *quibus* (to whom) as in Denis's text.

42 Num. 14:29b–30a. E. N. Caleb, the son of Jephunneh, and Joshua, the son of Nun, were alone excepted.

43 E. N. In Latin, the verse in Amos is in the form of a negative rhetorical question—*numquid... si erit malum in civitate,* translated in the Douay-Rheims as "shall there be evil in a city" (implying the answer "no, there shall not be evil in a city.")—which Denis restructures into a declarative sentence—*si erit malum in civitate,* "there shall not be evil in a city." I have followed Denis's reading.

quiet of the blessed in heaven; and so David intended by these words to admonish the faithful, and especially the Hebrew people, that they might not—because of their rebellion against the Christ—be impeded from entrance into the heavenly homeland, which is the land of the living, in which there is the perfect quiet of all the blessed. For this reason, the Apostle admonishes: *Take heed, brethren, lest perhaps there be in any of you an evil heart of unbelief, to depart from the living God; but exhort one another every day, . . . that none of you be hardened through the deceitfulness of sin.*[44] And elsewhere: *Let us hasten into that rest.*[45]

See, we have heard a Psalm full of all sorts of rejoicing: indeed, a Psalm totally igniting the pious soul with the fire of the Holy Spirit, which it behooves us to sing, to hear, or to read with complete attention and fervor in the beginning of the office of Matins, since by beginning the work of God (*opus Dei*) ardently we may spend the entire day in a wholesome way. Let us do, therefore, what we are invited to do by the present Psalm; and when we arise from the matutinal Office, let us strenuously begin, let us banish far away from the heart all vain thoughts and useless images, let us solicitously occupy our heart with God alone, saying to our own interiors, or to others who may be at hand: *Come, let us exult in the Lord,* etc., and let us accomplish all those acts to which this Psalm excites in us, with a recollected and a love-filled mind. And these are the acts: the Lord to exult, to rejoice, to come before his presence in confession, and to adore, fall prostrate, and weep before him.

PRAYER

BY THE GIFT OF YOUR BOUNTY AND THE received good of continuous peace, let us exult and rejoice in you, God our Savior: grant us to know your way, which walking therein, by the strength of your promise, we may enter into your rest.

Tuae largitatis dono, accepto continuae pacis bono, exsultemus
et iubilemus tibi, Deo salutari nostro: praesta nos
cognoscere viam tuam, quam perambulantes,
te iurante, intremus in requiem tuam.

---

44   Heb. 3:12–13.
45   Heb. 4:11a.

Psalm 95

ARTICLE LXXIV

ELUCIDATION OF THE NINETY-FIFTH PSALM:
CANTATE DOMINO CANTICUM NOVUM,
CANTATE DOMINO, ETC.
SING TO THE LORD A NEW CANTICLE,
SING TO THE LORD, ETC.

95{96}[1] *A Psalm for David himself, when the house was built after
the captivity. Sing to the Lord a new canticle: sing to the
Lord, all the earth.*[1]

*Psalmum ipsi David, quando domus aedificabatur post capti-
vitatem. Cantate Domino canticum novum, cantate Domino
omnis terra.*

HE TITLE OF THE PSALM NOW BEING
addressed is: **95{96}[1]** *Psalmus David, quando domus aedificabatur
post captivitatem; a Psalm for David himself, when the house was built after the
captivity.* This title must explained in a spiritual sense because this present
Psalm in no way speaks of the building of the temple of Jerusalem after
the return [of the Jews] from the Babylonian captivity, but [it deals with]
the thing signified by the building of that temple. For the general captivity
of the human race—which by unbelief and an ungodly life had become
captive to the devil—is figured by the captivity under which the Jews were
held captive by the Chaldeans; so the construction of the Church—which
is the house of God, not built with insensible rocks, but by living stones,[2]
mainly the Christian faithful gathered as one, and built by Christ, and
founded upon him—is signified by the building of the temple of Jerusalem
after that captivity. For this reason, the Apostle [Paul] says: In Christ *all
the building, being framed together, grows up into a holy temple in the Lord, in
whom you also are built together into a habitation of God in the* Holy Spirit.[3]
This Psalm speaks, therefore, literally about Christ and his two-fold coming
and of the construction as well as the sacrifice of the Church.

---

1 The Douay-Rheims, drawing from the Sixto-Clementine Vulgate, has "a canticle,"
and not "a Psalm." I have followed Denis in this verse.
2 *Cf.* 1 Pet. 2:5.
3 Eph. 2:21–22.

And so the sense of the title is this: *a Psalm of David,* that is, this Psalm is of the prophet David as its author, written for that time, *when the house was built*: that is, when the Church of Christ began to be built by the preaching of Christ and of his Apostles, *after the captivity,* that is, after the liberation of the human race, which was done through the Incarnation and the Passion of the Son of God, who redeemed the human race from the power of the devil and the servitude of sin, in the manner he asserted: *Now shall the prince of this world be cast out; and I, if I be lifted up from the earth, will draw all things to myself.*[4] Whence John: *For this purpose, he said, the Son of God appeared, that he might destroy the works of the devil.*[5]

The holy Prophet [David], inviting us to the public worship of Christ and thereby of the most high Trinity, begins this way: *Cantate Domino canticum novum, sing to the Lord a new song,* that is, the Scriptures of the New Testament, the evangelical law, and the highest hymn composed from the counsel of Christ, whose counsel some were ignorant of prior to his coming. For Christ the Lord is the new teacher, the heavenly doctor, and the *fountain of wisdom*[6] who has come and brought with him a new doctrine and a new song proposed to the whole world. This is the new song: that henceforth *one thing is necessary;*[7] and, *If you will be perfect, go sell what you have, and give to the poor.*[8] And also, *Unless your justice abounds more than that of the scribes and Pharisees, you shall not enter into the kingdom of heaven;*[9] and, *Call none your father upon earth, for one is your Father, who is in heaven.*[10] And in this way, the Scripture of the New Testament is new and full of songs which we ought to sing to Christ and to the most high Trinity, by devotion of mind, by the praise of the mouth, by the reverent pronouncement of the divine word, and by the execution of good works or holy obedience. *But to the sinner God has said: Why do you declare my justices, and take my covenant in your mouth?*[11] And Christ in the Gospel: *Why do you call me, Lord, Lord, and not do the things which I say?*[12] It suffices not, therefore, that I sing with my mouth, unless it agrees with the exhibition

---

4   John 12:31b–32.
5   1 John 3:8.
6   Ecclus. 1:5a.
7   Luke 10:42a.
8   Matt. 19:21a.
9   Matt. 5:20.
10   Matt. 23:9.
11   Ps. 49:16.
12   Luke 6:46.

of an honest manner of living.[13] Nor does a merely external honesty suffice: it must exist together with an interior sincerity of mind, as the Lord says through Isaiah of the people who do not please him: *This people draw near me with their mouth, and with their lips glorify me, but their heart is far from me.*[14] *Cantate Domino, omnis terra; sing to the Lord, all the earth,* that is, all the inhabitants of the earth, for you know you are pilgrims in this world and you will be brought quickly to the heavenly homeland in the future age, proclaiming to the Lord that sweet and new song that the Apostle sounded beforehand to you: *For his exceeding charity wherewith* God the Father *loved us,*[15] God has *sent his only begotten Son into the world.*[16]

95{96}[2] *Sing to the Lord and bless his name: show forth his salvation from day to day.*

Cantate Domino, et benedicite nomini eius; annuntiate de die in diem salutare eius.

95{96}[3] *Declare his glory among the Gentiles: his wonders among all people.*

Annuntiate inter gentes gloriam eius, in omnibus populis mirabilia eius.

95{96}[2] *Cantate Domino, et benedicite nomini eius; sing to the Lord, and bless his name,* that is, praise him, recall his benefits, saying with great rejoicing: *Behold what manner of charity the* God the *Father has bestowed upon us, that we should be called, and should be, sons of God.*[17] This is also said to be a new song, not only because of its newness in terms of time, but also because of the newness in the devotion of the soul: and so we ought from our fervent love of the Savior, always to find the song to be new according to the illumination of our own heart, in the fashion that worldly lovers contrive and sing of him or of her whom they carnally love. *Annuntiate de die in diem, show forth . . . from day to day,* that is,

---

13 E. N. The *conversatio honesta*, the honest manner of life, is described by St. Thomas Aquinas as a thing of beauty in his Commentary on Psalm 44. In living a morally honest manner of life, we participate in one of Christ's beauties, the *pulchritude conversationis honestae*, the beauty of an honest manner of living, that is a life without sin. *Super Psalmo 44, n. 2*

14 Is. 29:13.

15 Eph. 2:4b.

16 1 John 4:9b.

17 1 John 3:1a.

every day, *salutare eius, his salvation,* that is, unceasingly proclaim, praise, and preach Christ by whom and in whom God the Father saves us. Of this salvation, the patriarch Jacob speaks: *I will look for your salvation.*[18]

95{96}[3] *Annuntiate, declare,* O preachers and all others having zeal for the divine honor and the salvation of their brothers, *inter gentes, among the Gentiles,* converting them to the faith, so that they might believe, or [rather] you might convert them, and that they might love Christ and praise *gloriam eius, in omnibus populis mirabilia eius; his wonders among all people,* that is, all the glorious things which are written about him: how from the beginning of his Incarnation even until the Ascension the holy angels ministered to him,[19] and how all creation was obedient to him;[20] and that on the third day he rose from the dead,[21] on the fortieth day, he ascended into heaven,[22] and on the fiftieth, he sent the Paraclete.[23]

95{96}[4]   *For the Lord is great, and exceedingly to be praised: he is to be feared above all gods.*

Quoniam magnus Dominus, et laudabilis nimis; terribilis est super omnes deos.

95{96}[5]   *For all the gods of the Gentiles are devils: but the Lord made the heavens.*

Quoniam omnes dii gentium daemonia; Dominus autem caelos fecit.

95{96}[4] *Quoniam magnus Dominus et laudabilis nimis, for the Lord is great and exceedingly to be praised,* indeed he is as worthy to be praised as he is good. Since, therefore, his goodness is without measure, he is also infinitely worthy to be praised, and he is not able fully able to be praised by any creature. For this reason, the book of Judith states: *O Adonai, Lord, great are you, and glorious in your power.*[24] And also in the book of Job: *We cannot find him worthily... and he is ineffable.*[25] *Terribilis est super omnes deos, he is to be feared above all gods,* that is, more than other gods. Or [alternatively], *above all other gods* because he will most

---

18   Gen. 49:18.
19   Matt. 4:11.
20   Matt. 8:27.
21   Matt. chp. 28.
22   Acts 1:9.
23   Acts 2:1–4.
24   Judith 16:16a.
25   Job 37:23.

terribly condemn and torment all gods. Now, in the preceding Psalm they who in an excellent way participate in the grace of divine perfection are called gods,[26] as the Lord said to Moses, *Behold, I have appointed you the god of Pharaoh, and Aaron your brother shall be your prophet;* but in this place gods means those who are mendaciously believed in by the Pagans and are worshipped in vain by them. But God is also said to be terrible before all of his creatures and gods for two reasons: first, because nothing is so evil as to separate oneself from as is God; second, because no one can inflict such dreadful torments as can God. Whence it is written: *God, whose wrath no man can resist, and under whom they stoop that bear up the world.*[27] Regarding these false gods, there is added: **95{96}[5]** *Quoniam omnes dii gentium, for all the gods of the Gentiles,* that is, of the infidels, are *daemonia, are devils.*

A certain difficulty occurs to me here, one which I have not seen addressed by others, and which I hesitate to address, since perhaps am I not able adequately able to answer it. In this regard, note that many of the Gentiles worshipped some men as if they were gods, namely, Saturn, Jove, Mercury, Hercules, Priapus, *etc.*[28] Others worshipped the sun, the moon, and the stars of heaven; others fire; others water; others the beasts of the earth, as the Apostle states to the Romans.[29] How, then, can all the gods of the Gentiles be devils? In answer to this question, one can say that the ungodly men whom they worship as gods are called devils because of their imitation of diabolical depravity, in manner that some men are called angels because of their participation in angelic dignity — such as John calls the pastors or the seven bishops of the churches in Asia,[30] and elsewhere the priest is called an angel of the Lord of hosts.[31] It seems that this can also be said of others, though they are in no way devils, because their worshippers by the very fact that they worship them, serve devils, and so all the gods of the Gentiles are asserted to be devils.[32] For the Apostle states to the Corinthians: *The*

---

26   Ps. 94:3.
27   Job 9:13.
28   E. N. This is the theory of Euhemerism, which theorizes that the Greek gods were historical men, generally great kings or warriors, apotheosized. *See* footnote 41-28.
29   Rom. 1:23.
30   Rev. chps. 1–3.
31   Mal. 2:7.
32   E. N. Denis argues that some of the gods of the Gentiles are devils (*e.g.,* Ba'al or Anubis), others are men who were evil who are worshipped as devils (*e.g.,* Heracles), and yet others because worship of the inanimate object (*e.g.,* the Sun) engenders slavery to the devil. Therefore, all these "gods" of the Gentiles can be called "devils."

things which the heathens sacrifice, they sacrifice to devils, and not to God.[33]

Dominus autem caelos fecit, but *the Lord made the heavens*, that is, he created, distinguished, and adorned all celestial bodies, holy angels, and men on earth living in a heavenly manner. For in the beginning, God created heaven and earth, as it states in Genesis.[34] And again it is written: *You perhaps have made the heavens with him, which are most strong, as if they were of molten brass?*[35]

95{96}[6]   *Confession and beauty are before him: sanctimony and magnificence in his sanctification.*[36]

Confessio et pulchritudo in conspectu eius; sanctimonia et magnificentia in sanctificatione eius.

95{96}[6]   *Confessio et pulchritudo in conspectu eius; sanctimonia et magnificentia in sanctificatione eius; Confession and beauty are before him: sanctimony and magnificence in his sanctification.* This verse is extremely decorous if its brilliance is understood. One is said to be or to come before the sight of God or before God—not because one is [physically] present before him, but because he is in his favor and is pleasing to him, as when it is stated in the book of Ruth: *Jesse begot David*, who walked before the Lord.[37] And the Lord said to Abraham: *Walk before*

---

33   1 Cor. 10:20a.

34   Gen. 1:1.

35   Job. 37:18. E. N. This is a rhetorical question by Elihu to Job suggesting a negative response; therefore, it suggests that God alone made the heavens.

36   E. N. I have departed significantly from the Douay-Rheims here, translating the Latin with the English derivatives. I felt this was required better to follow Denis's *Commentary*. Therefore, I have translated the Latin *confessio* with the more generic "confession," replacing the Douay-Rheims's translation narrower "praise." I have also translated *sanctimonia* with "sanctimony," replacing the Douay-Rheims's "holiness," and *sanctificatione* with the word "sanctification" to replace the word "sanctuary" in the Douay-Rheims. The Latin word *sanctimonia* translates the Greek word ἁγιασμός [*hagiasmos*], and beyond the notion of holiness it carries also the notion of chastity or purity. For example: 1 Thess. 4:3: "For this is the will of God, your sanctification (*sanctificatio*/ἁγιασμός/*hagiasmos*); that you should abstain from fornication (*fornicatione*/πορνείας/*porneias*)." See Jean Danielou, *The Origins of Latin Christianity* (Philadelphia: Westminster, 1977), 83–84, 89 (trans., David Smith and John Austin Baker). Finally, I replaced "majesty" with "magnificence" to translate *magnificentia*. I have also followed these conventions in translating this part of Denis's *Commentary*.

37   *Cf.* Ruth 4:22. E. N. It is difficult to understand what precisely Denis intended by relying on this verse, since it does not readily appear to support his argument, and the part that does is not in the book of Ruth (though it may have been a gloss in the Bible he was using). In his *Commentary on Ruth*, Denis notes that upon the

me. And as if you were asking,[38] "What is it, O Lord, to walk before you?" he adds: *And be perfect.*[39] And it is in this sense that it is written: *No hypocrite shall come before his presence.*[40] Finally, confession is of two kinds, namely the confession of the divine praise and the confession of one's own fault. Also, some beauty is interior and some is exterior. But if it were because of exterior beauty by which one pleases God, the most beautiful Absalom would not have displeased him so,[41] nor would that unconventional Martin have pleased him so.[42] We should strive, therefore, not for the beauty of the body, but for the beauty of the soul. It is also certain that there is no place for confession of fault in the heavenly homeland. But in the wayfaring state both confessions are met with; and the confession of praise while in the wayfaring state is greatly imperfect.

And so we intend first of all to explain how this present verse should be expounded as having to do with God and the triumphant Church. For it is most fittingly proper to understand it in this way. *Confession,* that is, divine praise, *and beauty,* that is, interior decorousness, or the splendor of internal purity, *are before him,* that is, before God in the heavenly fatherland, so that the saints in heaven unceasingly offer to God the confession or praise of his infinite goodness, as it states in an earlier Psalm: *Blessed are they that dwell in your house, O Lord: they shall praise you for ever and ever.*[43] Now this confession pleases God greatly, because there is interior beauty, that is, pure holiness, unadulterated purity, and consummated grace in his ministers who so praise him in heaven. For one does not come upon any culpable imperfection in heaven. And so, because the confession of the blessed in heaven is so beautiful, it is especially gratifying to God. But our confession [as wayfarers] is

---

birth of David, the prophecy of Jacob that the regal dignity would be given to the tribe of Judah first took effect. God tells Solomon that David walked before him "in simplicity of heart, and in uprightness." 1 Kings 19:4.

38   E. N. The phrase is in the second person in the original Latin, though it seems jarring.

39   Gen. 17:1b.

40   Job 13:16b.

41   2 Sam. 14:25.

42   St. Martin (368–397), the third bishop of Tours, was an extraordinary miracle worker, a thaumaturge; however, as the *Life of Martin* of Sulpitius Severus puts it, he was initially opposed as bishop of Tours because he appeared unworthy of the episcopate in that "he was a man despicable in countenance (*vultu despicabilem*)," his "clothing was mean, and his hair disgusting." Life of St. Martin, *Nicene and Post-Nicene Fathers* (2nd Series) (New York: The Christian Literature Co., 1894), Vol. II, p. 8 (eds., Philip Schaff and Henry Wace).

43   Ps. 83:5.

imperfect in many ways, because *all our justices* are *as the rag of a menstruous woman.*[44] Our interior beauty is also mixed with, and hampered by, many deformities, at least those associated with venial sin, especially since *the just man shall fall seven times a day.*[45] And so before the sight of God in heaven there is the confession of unceasing praise, by which the most superlatively blessed Trinity is continually praised, and the beauty of the most pure holiness, for nothing of impurity or fault is possible in the ministers praising God in this way. For this reason, it is written: *There shall not enter in it,* namely, the homeland of the blessed, *anything defiled.*[46] Moreover, it also states this confession and beauty are before the sight of God because it is pleasing to him. *Sanctimonia et magnificentia in sanctificatione eius, sanctimony and magnificence in his sanctification:* that is, in the worship, praise, or veneration by which God is addressed as holy by the blessed in heaven, is sanctimony, that is, holiness, namely the exclusion of all impurity, and magnificence, that is, the greatest excellence, or the greatest power and sublime honor. Now this sanctification of the Godhead is especially eminent. And hence the worship by which God is recognized to be holy and is praised and honored by the blessed [in heaven] as holy is called the sanctification of God. But in this sanctification is holiness or sanctimony, for God is more ample or more perfect than he can be sanctified by his ministers, because that sanctification is more true, more pure, and more immune from all fault, for the praise of God has no excess;[47] but inasmuch as he is greater, so is he more holy. Whence in Ecclesiasticus is said: *Glorify the Lord as much as ever you can, for he will yet far exceed . . . for he is above all praise.*[48] But this [confession and beauty] does not befit the creature. Now insomuch as these [creatures] can be sanctified by us, that is, to be believed so holy and so great, and to be so magnificently honored, such sanctification is not sanctimony, but idolatry; not sanctity, but falsity; not true honor, but the most wicked error: as when someone applies to a mere creature the cult of latria or ascribes to it infinite perfections. Here it is clear how it is that in the sanctification of God is magnificence. For in it is the highest excellence, because God, the Creator and Savior of all things, is to be

---

44   Is. 64:6a.

45   Prov. 24:16a.

46   Rev. 21:27a.

47   E. N. With regard to absolute quantity, *non potest esse superfluum in divino cultu, quia nihil potest homo facere quod non sit minus eo quod Deo debet,* "there cannot be excess in the worship of God, because whatever man does is less than he owes God." ST IIaIIae, q. 93, art. 2, c.

48   Ecclus. 43:32–33.

extolled infinitely above everything, and he is addressed as the Lord of unbounded majesty. There is in it also a certain great power, because no effect or act of man is more dignified than to sanctify God: for which reason in this sanctification the sublime honor, namely, adoration or the cult of latria, is to be exhibited only to God.

Further, this verse is also fittingly applied to God also in the Church militant, although in a manner less perfect or proper [than to the Church triumphant]. Therefore, in the Church militant there is the confession of one's own fault as well as the divine praises before God, because such confession is reverently offered to God by the faithful, who accuse themselves together with praising God, and it is mercifully received by God. But along with this confession comes the interior beauty of the soul, because in confession all things are scrubbed clean, according to the Scriptures.[49] The faithful are also diligent to stand with God in beauty of the soul, that is, in holiness and purity of heart to adhere to, to attend to, and to serve [God], so that they are before God in beauty, that is, pleasing and welcome before him, keeping in mind the words of their Savior, saying: *Blessed are the clean of heart, for they shall see God.*[50] In the sanctification also which sanctifies God by the obedience to the divine precepts as they daily pray, *Hallowed be thy name,*[51] is found the sanctimony or holiness according to the manner and possibilities of this present life, namely, pure and pious in intention, and devout and prompt in subjection; and so they arrive through it to a certain magnificence which exalts God with mind, and mouth, and in deed above everything else, saying that which Daniel said: *Blessed are you, O Lord the God of our fathers: and worthy to be praised . . . and exalted above all forever: and blessed is the holy name of your glory: and worthy to be praised, and exalted above all in all ages.*[52]

95{96}[7]   *Bring to the Lord, O you kindreds of the Gentiles, bring to the Lord glory and honor.*

Afferte Domino, patriae gentium; afferte Domino gloriam et honorem.

---

49   Ps. 31:5: *I have acknowledged my sin to you, and my injustice I have not concealed. I said I will confess against myself my injustice to the Lord: and you have forgiven the wickedness of my sin.* Rom. 10:10: *For, with the heart, we believe unto justice; but, with the mouth, confession is made unto salvation.*
50   Matt. 5:8.
51   Matt. 6:9.
52   Dan. 3:52.

95{96}[8]   *Bring to the Lord glory unto his name. Bring up sacrifices, and come into his courts.*

Afferte Domino gloriam nomini eius. Tollite hostias, et introite in atria eius.

95{96}[9]   *Adore the Lord in his holy court. Let all the earth be moved at his presence.*

Adorate Dominum in atrio sancto eius. Commoveatur a facie eius universa terra.

95{96}[10]   *Say among the Gentiles, the Lord has reigned. For he has corrected the world, which shall not be moved: he will judge the people with justice.*

Dicite in gentibus, quia Dominus regnavit. Etenim correxit orbem terrae, qui non commovebitur; iudicabit populos in aequitate.

95{96}[7] *Afferte, bring,* that is, show, *Domino, to the Lord,* the Savior, *patriae gentium, O you homelands of the Gentiles,* that is, O men dwelling in the Gentile countries who have received the faith of Christ. Or [alternatively]: O men, *bring to the Lord O you homelands of the Gentiles,* that is, to Christ who is the God of all regions, countries, and nations. *Afferte, bring,* I say, *Domino, to the Lord,* that is, devote to God alone, *gloriam et honorem, glory and honor,* in the manner that we find held by the Apostle: *To the King of ages, immortal, invisible, the only God, be honor and glory.*[53] Glory is brilliant knowledge with praise, according to Ambrose.[54] What is it to bring glory to God, therefore, other than to make his name illustrious before others, or to introduce others to such brilliant and conjoined knowledge with praise, so that they truly know God and praise him in a worthy manner? Now honor is the showing of reverence at the display of virtue.[55] What is it to bring honor to God other than to humbly obey God, to attribute to him all good, and to order toward him all reverence? 95{96}[8] *Afferte Domino, bring to the Lord* not only external gifts, but *gloriam nomini eius, glory unto his name,*

---

53   1 Tim. 1:17.

54   *E. N.* This definition of glory — *clara cum laude notitia* — is actually from St. Augustine and is misattributed by St. Thomas Aquinas to Ambrose, from where Denis probably took it. *See* footnote 8-22 in Volume I.

55   *E. N.* This definition is derived from Aristotle (*Nich. Ethic.*, I, 5, 4–6, 1095b20), and is mentioned by St. Thomas Aquinas in ST IIaIIae, q. 103, art. 1, arg. 2 (*Honor enim est exhibitio reverentiae in testimonium virtutis*).

saying: *Not to us, O Lord, not to us, but to your name give glory.*[56] In the beginning of this Psalm it was stated three times, *Sing*; but now, three times it is stated *Bring*, in order that the mystery of the holy Trinity may be shown in both places. It is as if it were saying: *Sing to the Father, sing to the Son, sing to the Holy Spirit.* And again, *Bring to the Father, bring to the Son, bring to the Holy Spirit* glory and honor.

Tollite hostias, bring up sacrifices, that is, carry with you gifts and sacrifices to be offered unto the Lord, namely: an afflicted spirit, because *a sacrifice to God is an afflicted spirit;*[57] a disposition to the ready obedience to God, because *it is a wholesome sacrifice to take heed to the commandments,* as it states in Ecclesiasticus;[58] and also devout prayers which penetrate the heavens,[59] or any other gifts offered to the Lord. *Et introite, and come* with a devout mind and a body subject to reason, *in atria eius, into his courts,* that is, into the Church of God, or a sacred space that is set apart for divine worship, and most of all in one's own heart, turning back toward your own interior, so that God might honor God within you, contemplating, loving, and with all care avoiding vices. *For the temple of God is holy, which you are.*[60] **95{96}[9]** *Adorate Dominum in atrio sancto, adore the Lord in his holy court,* that is, in his material temple, which is the house of prayer;[61] but more significantly in his interior temple, which is the soul or the spirit itself, where God dwells by grace, where it is fitting to adore him, in the manner that the Savior said: *God is a spirit, and they that adore him, must adore him in spirit and truth.*[62] And elsewhere: *But you when you shall pray, enter into your chamber, and having shut the door, pray to your Father in secret,*[63] namely, with a recollected, steadfast, and unwandering heart.

Commoveatur a facie eius universa terra; let all the earth be moved at his presence. That is, from the consideration of the presence and majesty of Christ, let all of the inhabitants of the earth be moved with chaste fear, and wonder, and in obedience let them be converted from iniquity to God. **95{96}[10]** *Dicite, say* O holy Apostles and their successors and imitators, *in Gentibus, among the Gentiles,* to whose conversion or informing you are sent, *quia Dominus, that the Lord* Christ *regnavit, has reigned* in the

---

56 Ps. 113:9. E. N. Curiously, Denis cites to the Hebrew numbering (Ps. 115:1).

57 Ps. 50:19a.

58 Ecclus. 35:2.

59 *Cf.* Ecclus. 35:21a: *The prayer of him that humbles himself, shall pierce the clouds.*

60 1 Cor. 3:17b.

61 *Cf.* Is. 56:7b: *My house shall be called the house of prayer, for all nations.*

62 John 4:24.

63 Matt. 6:6.

whole world, especially in the hearts of his faithful through charity and faith. Christ as God has reigned from the beginning of the world; but as man, he began to reign (that is, he began to exercise and to exhibit his power) especially after his Resurrection and the sending of the Holy Spirit: for, according to the Apostle, by death he vanquished him *who had the empire of death, that is to say, the devil.*[64] Whence, after the Resurrection he despoiled hell, and converted the world to his service. And that these things were done by merit of the Passion of Christ is according to that stated by the Apostle, *becoming obedient unto death, even to death of the Cross, for which cause God has also exalted him;*[65] and there is added [to the Psalm], *from the tree,* that is, from the gibbet of the Cross, upon which he redeemed the world, that which the the Apostle said: *Christ has redeemed us from the curse of the law, being made a curse for us, for it is written: Cursed is every one that hangs on a tree.*[66] Note that this has been added — the words *on the tree* are not part of the [received] text, nor are they contained in the Hebrew, but they are supposed to have been placed by some translator.[67] From this it comes to light that the present Psalm was written by David, as we sing in the hymn of the Church:

> *Fulfilled is all that David told*
> *In true prophetic song, of old*
> *Unto the nations, Lo! Says he,*
> *Our God has reigned from the Tree.*[68]

And they who say otherwise do not seem united adequately with the Church, when singing generally and solemnly this hymn.[69]

Etenim, for Christ *correxit orbem terrae,* has corrected the world, that is, he has turned all men, or the whole Church dispersed throughout the whole world, from vices and idolatry, by the reproof and the preaching

---

64   Heb. 2:14.

65   Phil. 2:8–9a.

66   Gal. 3:12; Deut. 21:23.

67   E. N. This clause is a "well-known Christian addition," a Christian gloss, per Jean Danielou, S. J., *The Origins of Latin Christianity* (London Westminster, 1977), 41 (trans., David Smith and John Austin Baker).

68   E. N. This is taken from the hymn *Vexilla Regis* written by Venantius Fortunatus (530–609)

69   E. N. In other words, the absence of the words "from the tree" in the received Latin text or Hebrew Scriptures do not detract from the Messianic interpretation of this verse or the Davidic authorship, inasmuch as the Church has understood it in this manner as is reflected in the ancient and solemn hymn that is used in the Church's liturgy.

of his servants. Whence, it is written: *The Lord shall be exalted in that day, and idols shall be utterly destroyed.*[70] And Zechariah: *In that day, says the Lord of hosts, I will destroy the names of idols out of the earth.*[71] This also is said about Christ: *He shall strike the earth with the rod of his mouth.*[72] And so he has corrected the world, *qui non commovebitur, which shall not be moved,* from the truth of the faith in its entirety, for the Church even unto the end of time will remain firm in the faith, with respect to some men, regardless how troubled with tribulations. *Iudicabit populos in aequitate, he will judge the people with justice.* Christ in his first coming judged the people with justice (speaking of the judgment of discretion),[73] as he himself said: *Now is the judgment of the world.*[74] And elsewhere: *For judgment I am come into this world; that they who see not, may see; and they who see, may become blind.*[75] By this, therefore, Christ judges the people with justice in the judgment of discretion: by which he calls some in his great kindness to faith and grace, and other justly he abandons, which discrimination is entirely just, though it may be incomprehensible and unknowable to us. Christ does not, however, judge the people in his first coming with the judgment of remuneration. For this reason, he says: *For God sent not his Son into the world to judge the world.*[76] But this judgment [of remuneration] Christ will act upon in the last day.

95{96}[11]   *Let the heavens rejoice, and let the earth be glad, let the sea be moved, and the fullness thereof.*

Laetentur caeli, et exsultet terra: commoveatur mare et plenitudo eius.

95{96}[12]   *The fields and all things that are in them shall be joyful. Then shall all the trees of the woods rejoice.*

Gaudebunt campi, et omnia quae in eis sunt. Tunc exsultabunt omnia ligna silvarum.

---

70   Is. 2:17b–18a.
71   Zech. 13:2a.
72   Is. 11:4b.
73   E. N. The judgment of discretion is distinguished from the final judgment, the former being one of mercy and hidden, and the latter being one of strict scrutiny and retribution and public. *See* footnote 34-101 in Volume 2 and Article XXXVIII (Psalm 9:1) in Volume 1.
74   John 12:31a.
75   John 9:39.
76   John 3:17.

95{96}[13] *Before the face of the Lord, because he comes: because he comes to judge the earth. He shall judge the world with justice, and the people with his truth.*

A facie Domini, quia venit, quoniam venit iudicare terram. Iudicabit orbem terrae in aequitate, et populos in veritate sua.

And so creatures are invited to spiritual joy from the consideration of this first coming of Christ, which was and is a great reason for this world to rejoice, in the manner that the angel told the shepherds: *I bring you good tiding of great joy, that shall be to all the people, for this day is born to you a Savior, who is Christ the Lord.*[77] And therefore it says: **95{96}[11]** *Laetentur caeli,* let the heavens rejoice, that is, the citizens of heaven, or the holy angels: for accompanying the angel at the birth of Christ was *a multitude of the heavenly army praising God.*[78] Indeed, the Incarnation of Christ was a matter of joy for the angels, for by it was repaired their ruin.[79] *Et exsultet terra, and let the earth be glad,* that is, the human race on earth being led in their exile. *Commoveatur, let be moved,* to repentance and by the action of grace, *mare, the sea,* that is, the turbulent, bitter, and sharp vices of the Gentiles, *et plenitude eius, and the fullness thereof,* that is, their most interior inner parts, namely, the reason and will and other powers of the soul. **95{96}[12]** *Gaudebunt campi, the fields . . . shall be joyful,* that is, men flowering with good works, and fruitful with grace, will spiritually rejoice in Christ's first coming and thereafter, *et omnia quae in eis sunt, and all things that are in them,* that is, with their interiors they will rejoice in the Lord. *Tunc exsultabunt omnia ligna silvarum, then shall all the trees of the wood rejoice,* that is, the people of those nations converted to the faith [shall rejoice], **95{96}[13]** *a facie Domini, before the face of the Lord,* that is, from the consideration of the presence of Christ, *quia venit, because he comes* into the world by the Incarnation. Hence in the Acts of the Apostles is stated: *The Gentiles hearing it, were glad, and glorified the word of the Lord.*[80]

---

77 Luke 2:10–11.

78 Luke 2:13.

79 Ps. 109:6a: *He shall fill ruins.* E. N. As discussed in footnote 16-22 in Volume 1, it was a common belief that the number of the predestined humans would equal to the number of the angels that fell; accordingly, the angels would rejoice that the loss of their number would be restored by the number of men who would be saved as a result of Christ's Incarnation. In his commentary on this verse, Denis says: "In the future judgment, [Christ] will fill the ruin of the angels from those men who are saved, restoring the heavenly mansions evacuated by the fall of the angels."

80 Acts 13:48a.

These two verses accord with that which is read in Isaiah: *Give praise, O you heavens; and rejoice, O earth; you mountains, give praise with jubilation: because the Lord has comforted his people.*[81] And because not only is the first and hidden coming of Christ in which he came to be judged to be rejoiced in, but also the second coming of his, when he returns to judge.[82] This accords with that which he stated, *When these things begin to come to pass, look up, and lift up your heads,* that is, let your hearts rejoice (according to Gregory), for *your redemption is at hand;*[83] and so is added: *quoniam venit iudicare terram, because he comes to judge the earth,* that is, because Christ will come again to judge the living and the dead with the judgment of remuneration. For in accordance with prophetic custom, he states in past tense meaning the future tense because of the certainty of the prophecy.[84] It is for this reason, therefore, that he says twice, "he comes," intimating at the dual coming of Christ: of which the first was in humility and hidden; but the second will be in majesty and openly, as it written in the Gospel: *Then shall they see the Son of man coming in the clouds, with great power and glory.*[85] *Iudicabit, he shall judge* in the day of the final judgment *orbem terrae, the world,* that is, men, *in aequitate, with justice,* giving to each person that which he merited; *et populos in veritate sua, and the people with his truth,* that is, he will so judge them as is foretold in holy Scripture. This is what of is written of Christ in Isaiah: *He shall not judge according to the sight of the eyes, . . . but he shall judge the poor with justice, and shall reprove with equity for the meek of the earth.*[86] And in the book of Job says this sort of thing: *The Almighty will look into the causes of everyone.*[87]

See how we have heard this Psalm adorned with heavenly beauty, in which the conversion of the Gentiles is foreannounced, the divine majesty

---

81   Is. 49:13.

82   E. N. "At His first coming 'He humbled Himself, taking the form of a servant'; His Divinity was hidden; He came to be judged, to suffer, and to die; but at His return He will come with great power and majesty; His Divinity shill shine forth in His humanity; He will come to judge the living and dead." Joseph Wilhelm and Thomas B. Scannell, *A Manual of Catholic Theology Based on Scheeben's "Dogmatik"* (Londong: Kegal Paul, Trench Trübner & Co., Ltd, 1901) (2nd ed.), Vol. 2, 544.

83   Luke 21:28. E. N. The reference to Gregory is, of course, to Pope St. Gregory the Great, specifically, his Homilies on the Gospels, Book I, Sermon 1, 3, PL 76, 1079.

84   E. N. The Douay-Rheims translators translated the Latin *venit* in the present tense, rather than the perfect tense, both of which would be possible translations. Denis obviously understands it in the past sense, and so he reads *because he came to judge the earth.*

85   Mark 13:26; Luke 21:27.

86   Is. 11:3b, 4a.

87   Job 35:13b.

is commended with sonorous prophetic utterance, the faithful are invited to praise and oblation, the double coming of Christ is intimated, and the justice of the divine judgment is praised. Because, therefore, this present Psalm is full of the praise and mysteries of Christ, we ought to sing it with singular devotion, and to so keep guard over our manner of living with great fear of the future judgment, so that find ourselves suitable praisers of the Lord Savior.

PRAYER

LORD WHO MADE THE HEAVENS, AND who are terrible above all other gods, through your prevenient mercy make us pleasing to your countenance with the beauty of confession, so that cleansed of the filth of sins, we might with a sincere mind and voice sing continually to you O Lord.

Domine, qui fecisti caelos, et terribilis es super omnes deos,
misericordia tua praeveniente fac nos confessionis
pulchritudine faciem tuam placare: ut expurgati
peccatorum colluvionibus, sincera mente
et voce tibi Domine iugiter cantemus.

Psalm 96

ARTICLE LXXV

EXPLANATION OF THE NINETY-SIXTH PSALM:
DOMINUS REGNAVIT, EXSULTET TERRA.
THE LORD HAS REIGNED, LET THE EARTH REJOICE.

96{97}[1] *For the same David, when his land was restored again to him.
The Lord has reigned, let the earth rejoice: let many islands
be glad.*

*Psalmus ipsi David, quando terra eius restituta est. Dominus
regnavit; exsultet terra; laetentur insulae multae.*

HE TITLE OF THE PSALM NOW BEING HAN-
dled is as follows: **96{97}[1]** *Psalmus ipsi David, quando terra eius
restituta est ei; for the same David, when his land was restored again to him:*
that is, this present Psalm applies to Christ strong of hand and desirable in
aspect; it deals with that which occurred, *when his land,* that is, the human
race or the Church of the elect, which, having fallen through the sin of the
first parents, was restored by the price of his Blood. For this Psalm speaks
literally of Christ and his second coming, and of his judicial power which
Christ as man merited by his Passion. For Christ both restored his land just
referred to and was conferred the judicial power at the same time, namely,
immediately upon the departure of his soul from his body. For then he most
fully rendered satisfaction for the human race, and at that time the Father
gave him the Gentiles as his inheritance, as it states in a Psalm above: *Ask
of me and I will give you the Gentiles for your inheritance:*[1] although (as has
often been made clear) Christ as man from the beginning of his conception
in the Virgin was given *all power in heaven and on earth.*[2] And that this
Psalm speaks of Christ is certain from this, that Paul introduces the words
of this Psalm to the Hebrews as foreannouncing Christ, saying: *And let
all the angels of God adore him.*[3] Indeed, this is expressed as such [in this
Psalm in a verse below]: *Adore him, all you his angels.*[4]

---

1   Ps. 2:8a.
2   Matt. 28:18b.
3   Heb. 1:6b. *E. N.* For Denis's belief that St. Paul was the author of Hebrews, *see*
footnote 8-34 in Volume I.
4   *E. N.* Ps. 96:7b.

And therefore it states: *Dominus, the Lord,* namely, Christ, *having on his garment and on his thigh written: King of kings and Lord of lords;*[5] *regnavit, has reigned* in the Church militant, or in the hearts of the elect: as Obadiah the prophet said of him, *And the kingdom shall be for the Lord.*[6] Of which the saints joyfully sing in Revelation: *The Lord our God the Almighty has reigned; let us be glad and rejoice, and give glory to him.*[7] *Exultet terra, let the earth rejoice,* that is, let the inhabitants of the earth rejoice in their ruler, Christ the Lord, and let them piously be glad of his reign in themselves. *Laetentur, let . . . be glad* in the Lord in this manner *insulae multae, the many islands* converted to the faith, such as England, Ireland, Cyprus, Sicily, of which has been predicted, *They shall give glory to the Lord, and shall declare his praise in the islands.*[8] For islands are said to be lands located atop the sea. Whence in Isaiah we have: *Glorify the Lord . . . in the islands of the sea.*

96{97}[2]   *Clouds and darkness are round about him: justice and judgment are the establishment of his throne.*

Nubes et caligo in circuitu eius; iustitia et iudicium correctio sedis eius.

96{97}[2] *Nubes et caligo in circuitu eius, clouds and darkness are round about him:* that is, in the day of judgment there will be material clouds and they will appear around Christ in judgment, for he will come *in a cloud.*[9] For, according to this, Christ ascended in a cloud: *he was raised up: and a cloud received him out of their sight;*[10] he will return, therefore, in a cloud, because as the holy angels that were there testified to the holy Apostles, he *shall so come, as you have seen him going into heaven.*[11] *Et caligo, and darkness,* that is, in obscurity of air, because, *The day of the Lord shall so come as a thief in the night,*[12] and *At midnight there was a cry made: behold the bridegroom comes:*[13] just as the Spouse and the Judge himself testified. For it is believed that Christ will return to judge during the nighttime. But the question is, how will it be dark at that time, especially since the

---

5   Rev. 19:16.
6   Ob. 21.
7   Rev. 19:6b–7a.
8   Is. 42:12.
9   Luke 21:27a.
10   Acts 1:9.
11   Acts 1:11b.
12   1 Thess. 5:2b; *cf.* 2 Pet. 3:10a.
13   Matt. 25:6.

whole world will be in the state of the fire of conflagration, which, it would appear, would illuminate the air. One perhaps can respond to this in this way, that this fire will be smokey, and so it will not expel all the darkness, such as the fires of hell do not [dispel the darkness]. But we are compelled by necessity to concede that he, namely Christ, the Judge, will be able to observe with his bodily eyes all men, as also Job said, *in the last day, I shall rise out of the earth, . . . and in my flesh I will see God,* my Savior.[14] And indeed, according to Gregory, all angels will at that time be seen with bodily eyes, how much more shall men? Therefore, I do not think that in the day of judgment there will be a darkness round about the judge, so that the entire air will be dark; but because of the smokiness of that fire it is possible that there be some darkness remaining in the air. But one is also able to understand by darkness that horrible tempest that will exist in that day of final judgment, of which is said in a Psalm above, *a mighty tempest shall be around him.*[15] Whence also Nahum: *The Lord's ways are in a tempest, and a whirlwind.*[16]

96{97}[3]   *A fire shall go before him, and shall burn his enemies round about.*

Ignis ante ipsum praecedet, et inflammabit in circuitu inimicos eius.

96{97}[4]   *His lightnings have shone forth to the world: the earth saw and trembled.*

Illuxerunt fulgura eius orbi terrae; vidit, et commota est terra.

96{97}[3] *Ignis, a fire* of conflagration, which will consume and will purify the elements, and will ascend to such heights as the waters of the flood,[17] *ante ipsum praecedet, shall go before him,* that is, they shall go before Christ's second coming: for in the way that the first world perished by the water of the flood,[18] so at its end it will perish with the fire of conflagration which will put to death all those who are then

---

14   Job 19:25b–26.
15   Ps. 49:3b.
16   Nahum 1:3b.
17   E. N. *See* ST III (Supp.) q. 74, art. 4, s.c. St. Thomas notes that a gloss on 2 Thess. 1:8 states "Preceding his [Christ's] coming, there will a fire in the world, and shall occupy so much of the air as did the waters in the [Noahide] flood." Referring to Gen. 7:20, Thomas observes that the flood waters during the time of Noah rose to 15 cubits higher than the mountain summits, and so rejects the opinion that the fires of the conflagration will reach the heavens. This would appear to be the most likely source of Denis's statement.
18   Gen. 7:21, 23.

living in the world. *Et inflammabit in circuitu inimicos eius*, and *he shall burn his enemies round about*, namely, the reprobate, because during the time of judgment the fire of conflagration will set afire the evil among all those then remaining, but the elect it will not touch, nor cause sorrow to, nor bring with it any distress. A figure of this is seen in the three young men, whom the king of Babylon sent to the furnace of fire, and whom the fire did not touch, but it caused the Chaldeans to burst into flames, as Daniel has stated.[19] 96{97}[4] *Illuxerunt fulgura eius orbi terrae, his lightings have shone forth to the world*: that is, great and terrible flashes of light will appear around the time of the hour of judgment, of which men will be terrified, as Luke describes it, *Men [will be] withering away for fear and expectation of what shall come upon the whole world.*[20] And so it adds: *vidit et commota est terra, the earth saw and trembled*, that is, the inhabitants of the earth shall perceive such lighting, and they will be moved unto great fear. For this reason, it is written elsewhere: *Let all the inhabitants of the land tremble, because the day of the Lord comes, . . . a day of darkness and of gloominess . . . the like to it has not been seen from the beginning nor shall be after it . . . Before the face thereof a devouring fire, and behind it a burning flame. At their presence, the earth has trembled.*[21]

96{97}[5] *The mountains melted like wax, at the presence of the Lord: at the presence of the Lord of all the earth.*

Montes sicut cera fluxerunt a facie Domini; a facie Domini omnis terra.

96{97}[5] *Montes sicut cera fluxerunt a facie Domini*, *the mountains melted like wax at the presence of the Lord*: for in the day of judgment, or shortly thereafter after it is over, the earth will be made level: but also before the judgment there will be great earthquakes in places.[22] But better yet, by mountains in this place may be understood the proud, who climb up not the mountain of the Lord, but rather the mountain of pride, following him who said: *I will sit in the mountain of the covenant, . . . I will ascend above the height of the clouds.*[23] In the day of judgment, these persons will melt like wax, that is, their hearts will melt and they will

---

19   Dan. 3:40, 22.

20   Luke 21:26.

21   Joel 2:1b–3a, 10a.

22   Matt. 24:7b.

23   Is. 14:13b–14a. E. N. The verse, which reveals the thoughts of Satan which led to his fall, continues: *I will be like the most High.*

be terrified, *a facie Domini, at the presence of the Lord,* that is, at the sight of the Judge; and not only this, but *a facie Domini, at the presence of the Lord,* that is, at the dreaded presence of the Judge, *omnis terra, all the earth* shall flow in this way, that is, every man who is worldly and a sinner. And so this is predicted by another [prophet]: *The mountains tremble at him, and the hills are made desolate: and the earth has quaked at his presence, and the world, and all that dwell therein.*[24] And elsewhere: *Behold the whirlwind of the Lord's indignation shall come forth, and a tempest shall break out and come upon the head of the wicked.*[25]

96{97}[6] *The heavens declared his justice: and all people saw his glory.*

Annuntiaverunt caeli iustitiam eius; et viderunt omnes populi gloriam eius.

96{97}[6] *Anuntiaverunt caeli iustitiam eius, the heavens declared his justice,* that is, the just vengeance of Christ against the ungodly will be made manifest by signs appearing in the heavens. For *there will be signs in the sun and the moon and the stars.*[26] Whence the Savior said: *Immediately after the tribulation of those days, the sun shall be darkened and the moon shall not give her light.*[27] By this means it will be clear how great is the justice of Christ in avenging sins. *Et viderunt omnes populi gloriam eius, and all people saw his glory,* that is, all then existing in the world shall perceive the mightiness of this divine work. This verse is perhaps better explained as referring to the holy apostles, for, lest one not believe in this judgment without being forewarned and threatened of the future, it adds: *The heavens declared,* that is, the apostles, *iustitiam eius, his justice:* for throughout the whole world they preached Christ to be the most just judge who without respect of persons will irreproachably render judgment; *and they saw,* that is, *all people* who converted to Christ by the proclamation of these heavenly things acknowledged by faith *his glory,* that is, the majesty and the excellence of Christ, which is most copiously described in the Gospels. Whence also the Lord says through Isaiah: *I will send of them that shall be saved . . . to the islands afar off . . . and they shall declare my glory to the Gentiles.*[28]

---

24 Nahum 1:5.
25 Jer. 23:19.
26 Luke 21:25.
27 Matt. 24:29a. E. N. The remainder of the verse pertinently continues: *and the stars shall fall from heaven, and the powers of heaven shall be moved.*
28 Is. 66:19.

96{97}[7] *Let them be all confounded that adore graven things, and that glory in their idols. Adore him, all you his angels.*

> *Confundantur omnes qui adorant sculptilia, et qui gloriantur in simulacris suis. Adorate eum omnes angeli eius.*

96{97}[8] *Sion heard, and was glad. And the daughters of Juda rejoiced, because of your judgments, O Lord.*

> *Audivit, et laetata est Sion; et exsultaverunt filiae Iudae, propter iudicia tua, Domine.*

96{97}[9] *For you are the most high Lord over all the earth: you are exalted exceedingly above all gods.*

> *Quoniam tu Dominus altissimus super omnem terram; nimis exaltatus es super omnes deos.*

Since, therefore, the glory of Christ is so great, **96{97}[7]** *Confundantur,* let them all be confounded, either by means of salutary repentance or, if not by means of repentance, let them be eternally shamed, *omnes qui adorant sculptilia, et qui gloriantur in simulacris;* all that adore graven things and that glory in their idols or their false gods, who worship *the creature rather than the Creator.*[29] For how grave is this sin is declared by Wisdom: *The beginning of fornication is the devising of idols. For the worship of abominable idols is the cause, and the beginning, and the end of all evil.*[30]

Adorate eum, adore him, namely, Christ, or God, three and simple, *omnes angeli eius,* all you his angels. For regarding these angels, the Lord spoke to Job: *Where were you . . . when the morning stars praised me together, and all the sons of God made a joyful melody?*[31] **96{97}[8]** *Audivit, et laetata est Sion; Sion heard and was glad:* that is, the Church militant, which is called Sion, the watcher of heavenly goods, heard of the two-fold coming of Christ and the just judgment with the ears of both the mind and the body through the proclamation or the preaching of the Apostles, or their doctrine, and so was gladdened with spiritual joy inasmuch as she conforms herself to, promotes, and unites herself to the will of the Savior and its Judge.[32] *Et exsultaverunt*

---

29 Rom. 1:25b.

30 Wis. 14:12a, 27.

31 Job 38:4a, 7. E. N. As Denis observes in his *Commentary on Job* this verse may be understood as a reference to "spiritual creatures, namely, the angels, created before the material world." Doctoris Estatici D. Dionysii Cartusiani, *Opera Omnia,* Vol. 5 (Montreuil: 1898), 3.

32 E. N. Denis uses the word "speculatrix," a female spy or watcher to refer to the Church; consequently, I have translated the pronouns that refer to the Church in this instance with feminine personal pronouns.

filiae Iudae, and the daughters of Judah rejoiced, that is the souls truly placing their trust in God. For Judah is interpreted as confession. Whence, when Leah, the wife of Jacob the patriarch, gave birth to Judah her son, she said: *Now will I praise the Lord: and for this she called him Judah.*[33] And so these daughter rejoiced, *propter iudicia tua, Domine; because of your judgments, O Lord,* that is, from the consideration of your just judgments, wherein you leave nothing out of order, you cause no one injury, and you leave no violence unavenged, but you will exalt in eternity those who in this world are disregarded, oppressed, regarded as nothing, and suffer for justice's sake;[34] yet those who only flourish and prosper in, and are allured by, this world, you will condemn without end. **96{97}[9]** *Quoniam tu Dominus, for you Lord* are *latissimus super omnem terram, the most high Lord over all the earth.* For you created all things, and you infinitely excel all things, and you are the omnipotent Judge of all: and so *nimis, exceedingly,* that is incomparably, incomprehensibly, and without measure *exaltatus es super omnes deos, are exalted . . . above all gods* (of which we have already spoken about): for you stand as their Creator and Judge.[35] For this reason Scripture declares regarding you: *Blessed are you, O Lord, . . . in the temple of your glory, and exceedingly to be praised and exalted above all forever.*[36]

96{97}[10] *You that love the Lord, hate evil: the Lord preserves the souls of his saints, he will deliver them out of the hand of the sinner.*

Qui diligitis Dominum, odite malum; custodit Dominus animas sanctorum suorum, de manu peccatoris liberabit eos.

96{97}[10] *Qui diligitis Dominum, odite malum; you that love the Lord, hate evil,* that is, abhor all sin, not because it merits punishment, but because sin is displeasing to God. For he who loves the Lord ought to have the desire to conform himself to the divine will; and so, in the way that God hates sin, insofar as it is sin, so he who loves God ought to hate sin, insofar as it is sin or contrary to the divine will. To have such hatred of sin, therefore, is an evident sign of the love and the grace of God in man: indeed, in this way we obtain the fellowship and intimacy with God. Whence John says: *Our fellowship may be with the Father, and*

---

33 Gen. 29:35. E. N. In this case, the confession is not of sin, but of praise.
34 Matt. 5:10–12.
35 E. N. The "gods" referred to here are humans who wield power over others, such as judges and priests, and who are ultimately answerable to God, their Creator and Judge for the use or abuse of their power. *See* in particular Article LV (Psalm 81:1, 81:6).
36 Daniel 3:52a, 53.

with his Son, Jesus Christ;[37] and again, *God is light, and in him there is no darkness. If we say that we have fellowship with him and walk in darkness, we lie.*[38] *Custodit Dominus animas sanctorum suorum, the Lord preserves the souls of his saints,* in the present life by grace and angelic custody, but in the future judgment he will preserve them from all damnation and danger; *de manu peccatoris, from the hand of the sinner,* that is from the power of all the ungodly, *liberabit eos, he will deliver them,* namely, [he will deliver] his saints. For now he delivers them from temptations and persecutions, lest they be harmed, by giving them patience in adversity or by a complete rescue from them; and also in the day of judgment he will perfectly redeem them. For here it is written: *Whosoever is born of God, commits not sin: for his seed abides in him, . . . and the wicked one touches him not.*[39]

96{97}[11]   *Light is risen to the just, and joy to the right of heart.*

   Lux orta est iusto, et rectis corde laetitia.

96{97}[12]   *Rejoice, you just, in the Lord: and confess to the remembrance of his holiness.*[40]

   Laetamini, iusti, in Domino, et confitemini memoriae sanctificationis eius.

96{97}[11] *Lux, light,* that is, the splendor of the grace of God or Christ the sun of justice, *orta est iusto, is risen to the just,* who obey God out of charity: something which no one is able to do unless the light of the grace of Christ—who declared *without me you can do nothing*—is risen in him;[41] *et rectis corde, and to the right of heart,* that is, to all the just, *laetitia, joy* is risen, that is, an abundant reason and matter of spiritual joy [arising] from the Incarnation and the other benefits and promises of Christ. For this reason, **96{97}[12]** *Laetamini, iusti, in Domino; rejoice, you just, in the Lord* in your most high Creator, most kindly Redeemer, and most generous Benefactor, *et confitemini, and confess* with the confession of praise, *memoriae sanctificationis eius, to the remembrance of his holiness,* that is, to the recollection of the divine mind, or to the divine

---

37   1 John 1:3b.
38   1 John 1:5b–6a.
39   1 John 3:9a, 5:18b.
40   E. N. I have changed "give praise" to the more generic "confess," as in the *Commentary* Denis clarifies that this is not the confession of sin, but the confession of praise.
41   John 15:5b.

mind, which mercifully is mindful of you, namely, sanctifying you freely by the gifts of the Holy Spirit, for which reason you ought unceasingly to give thanks, lest you be forgetful of him who is not forgetful of you.

Let us be mindful from this present Psalm to reflect upon the horror of the future judgment and its strictness, thinking and holding in one's heart how *fearful* it will then be *to fall into the hands of the living God;*[42] to witness the anger of the most high God and judge; to see the armed minions assisting Christ the judge against the ungodly; to see the assessment of all thoughts, words, and deeds before heaven and earth published; to hear those hopeless words uttered before all men, angels, and demons to be confounded and condemned, *Depart . . . you cursed into everlasting fire;*[43] to expect the uncertain, or rather certain, judgment of the Judge; and to gaze at the gaping chaos of the infernal prison beneath oneself; and finally, to be separated from the fellowship of the elect, and to obtain the sentence of eternal damnation, to fall into infernal depths, and to burn with unextinguishable flames without any hope whatsoever of evading them. For regarding this day is suitably received that which is elsewhere written: *That day is a day of wrath, a day of tribulation and distress, a day of calamity and misery, a day of darkness and obscurity, . . . a day of the trumpet and alarm.*[44] And again: *Behold, the day of the Lord shall come, a cruel day, and full of indignation, . . . to destroy the sinners from the earth. For the stars of heaven, and their brightness shall not display their light: the sun shall be darkened in his rising, and the moon shall not shine with her light.*[45] Whence, that most high arch-apostle: *The day of the Lord,* he said, *shall come as a thief, in which the heavens shall pass away with great violence, and the elements shall be melted with heat, and the earth and the words which are in it, shall be burnt up.*[46] And so, while Christ might have spoken many horrible things, yet concluding the sermon, he exhorted us thus: *Watch you, therefore, praying at all times, that you may be accounted worthy to escape all these things that are to come, and to stand before the Son of man.*[47]

---

42 Heb. 10:31.
43 Matt. 25:41.
44 Zeph. 1:15–16a.
45 Is. 13:9–10.
46 2 Pet. 3:10.
47 Luke 2:36.

PRAYER

OST HIGH LORD AND GOD WHO ARE above all the earth, teach us to love you with total devotion and to hate evil: protect our souls during this life, and when these depart from here, deliver them from the place of perpetual punishment.

Super omnem terram, altissime Domine Deus, doce nos te tota
devotione diligere, et malum odire: custodi in hac vita
animas nostras, et hinc migrantes eas, de locis
perpetuarum poenarum eripias.

Psalm 97

ARTICLE LXXVI

DECLARATION OF THE NINETY-SEVENTH PSALM:
CANTATE DOMINO CANTICUM NOVUM,
QUIA MIRABILIA FECIT.
SING TO THE LORD A NEW SONG,
BECAUSE HE HAS DONE WONDERFUL THINGS.

97{98}[1] *A psalm for David himself. Sing to the Lord a new song: because he has done wonderful things. His right hand has wrought for him salvation, and his arm is holy.*

Psalmus ipsi David. Cantate Domino canticum novum, quia mirabilia fecit. Salvavit sibi dextera eius, et brachium sanctum eius.

THE TITLE OF THIS PRESENT PSALM IS: 97{98}[1] *Psalmus ipsi David, a Psalm for David himself.* This Palm literally deals with Christ, for it is written about him and his two-fold coming; in a special way, it evidently speaks of Christ's first coming, or his Incarnation, and it says:

Cantate Domino, sing to the Lord, to Christ, *canticum novum, a new song,* namely, the proclamation of the evangelical law, just like a short while before was fully explained in the ninety-fifth Psalm, which in great part follows both with its words and meaning this Psalm. And so sing to the Lord a new song, *quia mirabilia fecit, because he has done wonderful things:* indeed, he has done superlatively incomprehensible things,[1] assuming human nature in a supposital unity,[2] coming forth from the enclosure of the womb of the Virgin Mary, rising again also from the enclosure of the tomb and leaving it, ascending into heaven, and sending the Holy Spirit. What wondrous works, moreover, did Christ undertake by his preaching and Passion is unfolded for us in the Gospel; it is a most great

---

1   E. N. This is an instance of Denis's use of superlatives, in this instance, *superincomprehensibilia. See* footnote 17-128 in Volume 1 for more on this topic.

2   E. N. The words "supposital unity" (*unitate suppositali*), means that the human nature of Christ was joined to the divine nature of Christ (without any confusion or mixture of the two natures) by means of unity in a *suppositum,* or *hypostasis,* or *person,* namely the second Person of the most Holy Trinity.

marvel that God the Father sent his own Son into the world,[3] so that by his Passion and death, he might save the human race.

Salvavit sibi dextera eius, et brachium sanctum eius; his right hand has wrought for him salvation, and his arm is holy: that is, the right hand of Christ and his arm, namely, the great virtue of Christ and his surpassing fortitude, wrought salvation, that is, redeemed the human race from eternal death, *for him*, that is, to the honor of his own name. For Christ freed men by his own power. Whence he said through Isaiah: *My own arm has saved for me.*[4] Others explain it this way: *his right hand, and his arm is holy*, that is, Christ: who is the power or the right hand of God, according to that said by the Apostle [Paul]: *We preach Christ . . . the power of God and the wisdom of God.*[5] He also is said to be the arm of the Father because he has done all things through him. And so by arm is understood Christ, about whom we read in Isaiah: *To whom is the arm of the Lord revealed?*[6] *Has wrought . . . salvation* for the human race, *for him*, that is, for God the Father, or to his glory. For this salvation was the work which the Father gave to the Son so that it might be accomplished, of which Christ, suspended on the Cross, said, *It is finished;*[7] and before the Passion, Father, *I have glorified you on the earth, I have finished the work which you gave me to do.*[8]

97{98}[2]   *The Lord has made known his salvation: he has revealed his justice in the sight of the Gentiles.*

Notum fecit Dominus salutare suum; in conspectu gentium revelavit iustitiam suam.

And then the Prophet speaking of the future by means of the past, of that which we have already come to see completed, adds: **97{98}[2]** *Notum fecit Dominus*, the Lord has made known, namely, God the Father [has made known], *salutare suum, his salvation*, that is, Christ his Son, the Savior of the world: first in Judea, for the Father declared Jesus of Nazareth to be his Son and the Messiah King by means of the miracles which Christ performed in the name of the Father. For this reason, Christ said, *The works which the Father has given me . . . give testimony of*

---

3   *Cf.* Gal. 4:4.
4   Is. 63:5b.
5   1 Cor. 1:23a, 24b.
6   Is. 53:1b.
7   John 19:30.
8   John 17:4.

me.[9] The Father also made known his Son to the shepherds through the angel, and to Zechariah and Elizabeth by the Holy Spirit, and similarly to Anna and Simeon.[10] Moreover, at the baptism of Christ and after his Transfiguration, the Father thundered from heaven saying, *This is my beloved Son*.[11] Whence it continues: *in conspectu gentium revelavit, he has revealed . . . in the sight of the Gentiles* by the preaching of the Apostles, *iustitiam suam, his justice*, that is, Christ, who is in his essence both just and justice, and who is called the justice of God, for the Father redeemed the world by him, and not by sheer power, but rather by the means and the way of justice.[12] Or [alternatively], *His justice*, that is, the precepts and the counsels of the Evangelical law, in which is contained the fullness of justice. The sense and words of these beautiful and sweet verses Isaiah frequently brings forth in the book of his visions. For he says: *The glory of the Lord shall be revealed, and all flesh together shall see . . . the salvation of our God*.[13] And: *I have brought my justice near, it shall not be afar off: and my salvation shall not tarry*.[14]

97{98}[3]   *He has remembered his mercy and his truth toward the house of Israel. All the ends of the earth have seen the salvation of our God.*

Recordatus est misericordiae suae, et veritatis suae domui Israel. Viderunt omnes termini terrae salutare Dei nostri.

97{98}[3] *Recordatus est, he has remembered*, God the Father [has remembered], *misericordiae suae, his mercy*, whereby he mercifully promised to send his Son into the world, *et veritatis suae, and his truth*, whereby he truly fulfilled the promise, sending Christ. God is also said to have remembered his mercy and his truth by bestowing the effects of his mercy and truth. And because he especially promised to the Patriarchs and the Prophets and their children regarding Christ's coming, so now it is said to have remembered his mercy and his truth *domui Israel, toward the house of Israel*, that is, to the Jewish people, namely, toward

---

9   John 5:36
10   Luke 2:9–12; 1:67–79, 41–45; 2:25–38.
11   Matt. 3:17; 17:5.
12   E. N. God could have redeemed the human race by sheer power—by *fiat*—but it was more fitting and consonant with justice to do so through the Incarnation and Passion of Christ. *See* ST IIIa, q. 46, arts. 1–4.
13   Is. 40:5a, 52:10b.
14   Is. 46:12.

their salvation. Whence also Christ in the Gospel says: *I was not sent but to the sheep that are lost of the house of Israel.*[15] And the Virgin, the bearer of Christ, said: *He has received Israel his servant, being mindful of his mercy, as he spoke to our fathers, etc.*[16] *Viderunt omnes termini terrae salutare Dei nostri,* all the ends of the earth have seen the salvation of our God: that is, all the ends of the world, or all men (as a distribution of the genus of each individual),[17] by faith shall know the salvation of our God, namely, Christ. Therefore, Simeon justly said: *My eyes have seen your salvation, which you have prepared before the face of all peoples.*[18] And Christ said to his Apostles: *Go into the whole world and preach the Gospel to every creature.*[19]

97{98}[4]   *Sing joyfully to God, all the earth; make melody, rejoice and sing.*

   Iubilate Deo, omnis terra; cantate et exsultate, et psallite.

97{98}[5]   *Sing praise to the Lord on the harp, on the harp, and with the voice of a psalm.*

   Psallite Domino in cithara; in cithara et voce psalmi.

97{98}[6]   *With long trumpets, and sound of cornet. Make a joyful noise before the Lord our King.*

   In tubis ductilibus, et voce tubae corneae. Iubilate in conspectu regis Domini.

97{98}[7]   *Let the sea be moved and the fulness thereof: the world and they that dwell therein.*

   Moveatur mare, et plenitudo eius; orbis terrarum, et qui habitant in eo.

97{98}[8]   *The rivers shall clap their hands, the mountains shall rejoice together.*

   Flumina plaudent manu, simul montes exsultabunt.

---

15   Matt. 15:24.

16   Luke 1:54–55a.

17   E. N. Denis means that the words should be understood that at least some of all kinds of men will have seen the salvation of God, not all men absolutely (which would a distribution of the individual of each genus). See footnote 21-54 and 21-130 in Volume 1.

18   Luke 2:30–31.

19   Mark 16:15.

97{98}[9] *At the presence of the Lord: because he comes to judge the earth. He shall judge the world with justice, and the people with equity.*

A conspectu Domini, quoniam venit iudicare terram. Iudicabit orbem terrarum in iustitia, et populos in aequitate.

Because of the magnitude of such benefits, all men are invited to give thanks: **97{98}[4]** *Iubilate, sing joyfully*, that is, with an overabounding and indescribable joy of the mind, declare praises to the Lord Christ or *Deo, to God*, the triune [God], *omnis terra, all the earth*, that is, all the inhabitants of the earth; *cantate, make melody*, praising with voice, *et exsultate, and rejoice*, being jubilant at heart, *et psallite, and sing*, by living well. **97{98}[5]** *Psallite, sing*, that is, offer devoutly psalms, *Domino, to the Lord*, and this, *in cithara, in cithara et voce psalmi; on the harp, on the harp, and with the voice of a psalm*, **97{98}[6]** *in tubis ductilibus, with long trumpets*. The Hebrew tribes literally used these musical instruments in the praise of God, singing with their mouth and [playing] these musical organs. But spiritually speaking, by harp is understood the works of mercy or the mortification of the flesh, as has frequently been stated. By long trumpets, which are shaped by being pounded [by the craftsman] are designated the tribulations and adversities of the present life, which pound upon the elect so that they might be suitable stones for the edifice of the heavenly kingdom. By *tubam corneae, cornet*, that is, of a horn made from leather, which covered with skin and is distinguished [in sound], is signified the contemplation of God, by which temporal things are transcended. And so [it should be understood] in this sense: *Sing praise to the Lord on the harp*, that is, with mortification of the flesh and with works of mercy, lest a carnal life and your cruel songs be found unacceptable; *on the harp, I say, and with the voice of a psalm*, so that the life conforms to the voice. *Sing* also to the Lord *with long trumpets*, that is, in your adversities and tribulations, giving thanks to Christ in the manner that James admonishes, *Count it all joy, my brothers, when you fall into diverse temptations.*[20] Sing also to the Lord in *the sound of cornet*, that is, in vocal praise which follows from the contemplation of God.

Iubilate in conspectu regis Domini, make a joyful noise before the Lord our King, that is, before Christ, the King and the Lord of all, praising him with a recollected heart and gathered together in his presence; **97{98}[7]** *moveatur mare, let the sea be moved*, that is, [let] this present world [be moved], *et plenitude eius, and the fulness thereof*, that is, the inhabitants

---

20 James 1:2.

in it, to faith and reverence in the Savior. This is more clearly expressed in what follows: *orbis terrarum et qui habitant in eo, the world and they that dwell therein.* Or by *the sea . . . and the fullness thereof* is understood those who negotiate the sea, and those who dwell by it. **97{98}[8]** *Flumina, the rivers,* that is the faithful who are regenerated by the waters of Baptism, and full with streams of grace, *plaudent manu simul, shall clap their hands . . . together,* that is, shall concordantly praise God together, with exultation of heart and good works; *montes, the mountains,* that is, the contemplatives and those sublime in all virtues, *exsultabunt, shall rejoice together,* **97{98}[9]** *a conspectu Domini, at the presence of the Lord,* that is, from the consideration of the coming and the presence of Christ, which can be understood as referring the presence associated with both of his comings. For either [of these comings] is joyful to the just, *quoniam venit iudicare terram, because he comes to judge the earth,* in his first coming with the judgment of discretion, inveighing against their vices; but in the second coming he will come to judge the world with the final judgment of retribution, as it states in what follows: *Iudicabit orbem terrarum in iustitia, he shall judge the world with justice;* and what this is, he explains by adjoining, *et, and,* meaning "that is," *populus in aequitate, the people with equity. For we must all be manifested before the judgment seat of Christ, that everyone may receive . . . according as he has done,*[21] according to the Apostle. But there is also a twofold judgment of examination or of retribution, namely, the particular, by which single souls are judged at the time they exit their body; and the universal, which will be at the end of the world. And what is written may be understood as referring to both these judgments: *Be you . . . also patient, and strengthen your hearts, for the coming of the Lord is at hand. . . . Behold, the judge stands at the door.*[22] I quickly pass over these matters because I have dwelt upon these things greatly in the exposition of the preceding two Psalms.

And so it befits us to sing this sweetly-flowing and pleasant Psalm with greater affection and devotion, and to rejoice in the Lord by singing it with great rejoicing inasmuch that it most clearly refers to Christ, and his first coming, and other mysteries, and the calling of the Gentiles to the faith and the grace of the Savior; and by it we are more frequently invited to acclaim God. For nothing ought to taste sweeter to a Christian than divine words in which the Incarnation of Christ and the redemption of the world are addressed; and so the things spoken of in this Psalm are to be most devoutly sung.

---

21   2 Cor. 5:10.
22   James 5:8, 9b.

PRAYER

LMIGHTY AND ETERNAL GOD, WHO ALONE
are able to do marvels, remember your mercy and correct
us who lose our way, and makes us to adhere to you perseveringly
and faithfully, so that we might be found worthy to sing pleasing
songs to you Lord forever.

Omnipotens, aeterne Deus, qui facis mirabilia solus, recordare
misericordiae tuae, nosque aberrantes corrige, atque
tibi perseveranter atque fideliter fac adhaerere:
ut digni efficiamur tibi Domino cantica
placita perpetim decantare.

Psalm 98

ARTICLE LXXVII

EXPOSITION OF THE NINETY-EIGHTH PSALM:
DOMINUS REGNAVIT, IRASCANTUR POPULI.
THE LORD HAS REIGNED, LET THE PEOPLE BE ANGRY.

98{99}[1] *A psalm for David himself. The Lord has reigned, let the people be angry: he that sits on the Cherubims: let the earth be moved.*

Psalmus ipsi David. Dominus regnavit: irascantur populi; qui sedet super Cherubim: moveatur terra.

NOW, THE TITLE OF THE PSALM HERE BEING expounded upon is in both words and sense the same with the title of the Psalm immediately preceding. For this Psalm speaks literally of Christ and his magnificent reign and manifold praiseworthiness. And they who expound it as literally applying to David and his reign are not only more superficial than the holy Catholic teachers, but also [more superficial than] some of the Hebrew teachers who expound it as literally dealing with the reign of the Messiah.

Therefore, the Prophet David, speaking of God, says: **98{99}[1]** *Dominus,* the Lord Christ, who in his first coming *did not come to be ministered to, but to minister,*[1] *regnavit, has reigned* in the Church militant after the Resurrection and Ascension; and he will reign in it even unto the end of the world. *Irascantur populi, let the people be angry,* let the unbelievers, that is, however many of these may have been angry, indignant, resistant to the reign of Christ, for they will not be able to impede it. Or [alternative], *let be angry,* that is, they will be angry: for perverse men tried to destroy the reign of Christ and to extirpate his renown and glory. For this reason, Paul says: *For a great door and evident is opened unto me: and many adversaries.*[2] Or [yet another interpretation], *let be angry,* that is, let wholesome anger rise up and conquer their vices. *Qui sedet super Cherubim, he that sits on the Cherubims,* that is, Christ—who as God superlatively exceeds all the fullness of created knowledge (about which is

---

1   Matt. 20:28a.
2   1 Cor. 16:9.

stated in the book of Job, *All that seem to themselves to be wise, shall not dare to behold him*),[3] and who also as man is raised above all the orders of the angels — reigned; *moveatur terra, let the earth be moved*, that is, let all the people of the entire earth be moved to convert by submission and faith to the Lord Savior. Or [alternatively], let howsoever many he wishes be moved to impatience, envying the glory of Christ, but to no avail. Now this is asserted neither wishing for it nor praying for it, but as suggesting the insuperable power of Christ. Or [yet another alternative], *let be moved*, that is, [the world] will be moved toward resisting Christ: this ought to be understood not as desiring it, but as foreannouncing it. Whence the Apostle says: *As Jannes and Jambres resisted Moses, so these also resist truth;... but they shall proceed no farther, for their folly shall be manifest to all men.*[4]

98{99}[2] *The Lord is great in Sion, and high above all people.*

Dominus in Sion magnus, et excelsus super omnes populos.

98{99}[2] *Dominus*, the Lord Christ *in Sion*, that is, in the Church, which faithfully contemplates him, is *magnus*, great: in the way Gabriel foretold the Virgin Mother, *He shall be great, and shall be called the Son of the most High.*[5] Now there is in Christ a two-fold greatness. For as God he is great with the infinite and uncreated magnitude of the one and indivisible three Persons, and this is identical with the divine essence. Whence the Apostle states: *We should live soberly, and justly, and godly in this world, looking for the blessed hope and coming of the glory of the great God [and our Savior Jesus Christ].*[6] But there is also in Christ a great and finite created magnitude, not bodily, but spiritual, that is, perfect in all grace, wisdom, and virtue, according to this: *The child (Jesus) grew and waxed strong, full of wisdom; and the grace of God was in him.*[7] This great magnitude began from the beginning of his conception in the Virgin; and from it he is said to be a man, though

---

3   Job 37:24.

4   2 Tim. 3:8–9. E. N. Jannes and Jambres (or Mambres) are the names of two magicians or sorcerers mentioned (though not by name) in the book of Exodus. See Ex. 7:10–12. The names mentioned by Paul come from some non-scriptural or apocryphal source.

5   Luke 1:32a.

6   Tit. 2:12–13. E. N. I have added the rest of verse 13 though not in Denis's text for the purpose of better context, in that what is being dealt with here is the divinity of Christ.

7   Luke 2:40.

still in the womb of his mother, according to that which is written about it in Jeremiah: *The Lord has created a new thing upon the earth, A woman shall compass a man.*[8] And this Lord is *excelsus, high* in both place and dignity *super omnes populos, above all people.* For he sits at the right hand of the Father,[9] and as God he exceeds all things infinitely in all dignity and perfection; but as man, he is more perfect in all graces than all the elect both in heaven and on earth put together. For this reason, Isaiah says: *Behold the Gentiles are as a drop of a bucket, and are counted as the smallest grain of a balance.*[10]

98{99}[3] *Let them confess your great name: for it is terrible and holy:*[11]

Confiteantur nomini tuo magno, quoniam terribile et sanctum est,

98{99}[4] *And the king's honor loves judgment. You have prepared directions: you have done judgment and justice in Jacob.*

Et honor regis iudicium diligit. Tu parasti directiones; iudicium et iustitiam in Iacob tu fecisti.

98{99}[3] *Confiteantur, let them confess,* O Christ, all men *nomini tuo magno, your great name:* of which the Apostle [Paul] says, *He has given him* (namely, the Father to Christ) *a name which is above all other names.*[12] This let all men confess to you, that is, with a two-fold confession, namely, praising you and accusing themselves, *quoniam terribile et sanctum est, for it is terrible and holy.* For [your name] is terrible because you most strictly judge all men; and it is holy because it is pure and good, and the fountain-like principle of all purity. **98{99}[4]** *Et honor regis, and the king's honor,* that is, the regal dignity of Christ, *iudicium diligit, loves judgment,* that is, [loves] the act of justice. For in both the Old and the New Testaments,

---

8 Jer. 31:22b. *E. N.* As Denis expounds on this verse in his *Commentary on Jeremiah,* this is stated in a supernatural sense which is incomprehensible to us mere wayfarers, for "from the beginning of the first instant of the Incarnation, [Jesus] was a man (*vir*), not in the measure of his body, but [in his soul] with the perfection of all wisdom and all virtue." *Doctoris Estatici D. Dionysii Cartusiani, Opera Omnia,* Vol. 9 (Montreuil: 1900), 225. In other words, his soul was fully operative *in utero beatae Mariae virginis,* though his body (including the organic brain), developed naturally; thus, it "lagged behind" the soul which enjoyed the beatific vision and infused knowledge from the first instant of conception.

9 Mark 16:19.

10 Is. 40:15.

11 *E. N.* I have rendered the Latin *confiteantur* to "let them confess," departing from the Douay-Rheims, "let them praise," because Denis understands the Latin word in both its sense of confession of sins and confession of praise.

12 Phil. 2:9.

Christ our King[13] renders judgment, ordaining prelates and the leaders in the Church militant, whose duty it is to render judgment upon those below them. He wishes, moreover, that these prelates and judges scrutinize, distinguish, and judge their own deeds; indeed, he requires this from any one of us, so that one might judge himself against [the demands of] reason, condemning, avenging, and forsaking one's own vices.[14] For this reason, the Apostle [Paul] states: *If we would judge ourselves, we should not be judged.*[15] And elsewhere we have: *Seek judgment, relieve the oppressed.*[16]

Tu, you O Christ, our lawgiver,[17] *parasti directiones, you have prepared directions,* that is, you indicated to us commandments for our lives, and by which man is directed to his ultimate end or eternal life; *iudicium, you have done judgment,* that is, you have discriminated between good and evil and true and false, *et iustitiam, and justice,* that is, [you have engaged in] the execution of justice or in the doing of good and the avoiding of evil, *in Iacob, in Jacob,* in the patriarch and in the Jewish people, or in the Christian people, which means the supplanting of vice,[18] which *tu fecisti, you have done* by grace, giving to them the power of judging rightly and acting justly. For *you have wrought all our works for us,* according to Isaiah;[19] and God is he who *works* in us *both to will and to accomplish,* according to the Apostle [Paul].[20]

98{99}[5] *Exalt the Lord our God, and adore his footstool, for it is holy.*

Exaltate Dominum Deum nostrum et adorate scabellum pedum eius, quoniam sanctum est.

And so in regard of such great benefits, O faithful, **98{99}[5]** *Exaltate, exalt,* that is, worship sublimely, honor most excellently, and proclaim

---

13   Is. 33:22: *For the Lord is our judge, the Lord is our lawgiver, the Lord is our king: he will save us.*

14   E. N. "Sin is an offense against reason, truth, and right conscience." CCC § 1849.

15   1 Cor. 11:31.

16   Is. 1:17a. E. N. As Denis states in his *Commentary of Isaiah*: "Seek judgment of discretion, that is, pray to God that he might confer upon you the grace and prudence to judge justly yourself or others over which you preside: in the manner that is stated in Zechariah: *Judge true judgment* [Zech. 7:9]." Doctoris Estatici D. Dionysii Cartusiani, *Opera Omnia,* Vol. 8 (Montreuil: 1899), 327.

17   Is. 33:22.

18   E. N. On the name Jacob being equivalent to the supplanting of vice (based upon its Hebrew etymology), *see* footnote 43-103, where other references to Denis's texts may be found on this topic.

19   Is. 26:12.

20   Phil 2:13.

before all with splendid praise, *Dominum Deum nostrum, the Lord our God,* who alone is the true God, proclaiming that which is said by Daniel: *I lift my eyes to heaven, . . and I bless the most High, and I . . . glorify him that lives forever, . . . and I praise and magnify . . . the King of heaven.*[21] *Et adorate scabellum pedum eius, and adore his footstool,* that is, the human nature of Christ, in which the divinity of the Word stands as upon a footstool.[22] This humanity, insofar as it is united to God in the unity of person, is adored with the adoration of latria, not in itself (*per se*), nor separately; but since Christ, both God and man, is adored, his humanity is also adored.

But thinking that this present material, which raises for many difficulties and troubling perplexity, that according to blessed Thomas in the third part [of the *Summa Theologiae*], question **25**, two points might be considered about that which is honored, namely, we might consider the subsistent thing in its entirety, and those things which are in it.[23] Now the honor [to any part of the subsistent thing in its entirety] is not aimed at it exclusively and in itself (*per se*), but to the whole subsistent thing. For if any part is honored, for example, the hand or the foot, this is not because of them, but insofar as they are part of the whole: and so the whole is honored through the part.[24] Now the cause of [a part] being honored is the excellence of the one being honored: because honor is the exhibition of reverence exhibited to another as a sign or a testimony of his perfection or virtue. When, therefore, there are many excellences in one subject — for example, privilege, wisdom, holiness of life — the

---

21   Dan. 4:31a, 34a.

22   *E. N.* In his commentary on this Psalm, St. Augustine waxes eloquently showing how the adoration of latria is due both the humanity of Christ and the Holy Eucharist: "What ought we adore? His footstool. . . . In doubt [about its meaning] I turn to Christ, for I seek him here, and I discover . . . the manner how such a footstool may be worshipped without impiety. For he took upon himself earth from earth (*de terra terram*), for flesh is from earth, and he received flesh from the flesh of Mary. And because he walked here in this very flesh, and gave that same flesh to us to eat for our salvation, and no one eats that flesh unless he first adores it, we have discovered how such a footstool of the Lord may be adored: and not only do we not sin by adoring it, we sin by not adoring it (*non solum non peccemus adorando, sed peccemus non adorando*)" *Enarr. in Ps.* 98, 9, PL 37, 1264.

23   *E. N.* ST IIIa, q. 25, arts. 1–2.

24   *E. N.* As St. Thomas states: "Now properly speaking honor is shown to a subsistent thing in its totality: for we do not say that a man's hand is honored, but that the man is honored. And if it ever happens that we speak of honoring the hand or the foot of some man, this is not said by reason of these members being honored in this manner of themselves (*secundum se*): but because the whole is honored in these parts." ST IIIa, q. 25, art. 1, c.

many and distinct honors are one according to the order and the cause of honor, but are many according to the fact that the causes are many and distinct; but out of the part of the person which is being honored, the honor will be one.[25] And so adoration (*adoratio*) in sacred Scripture is not always understood as an act of latria, namely, as the worship that is shown to God alone, but on the contrary it is understood as the veneration paid to another for some excellence. Whence it is written: King Solomon *arose to meet* his mother, *and he bowed* (*adoravit*) *to her*.[26] And in the same book we read that Bathsheba with an inclined head worshipped (*adoravit*) King David.[27] Similarly, in the book of Joshua it is written how Joshua worshipped (*adoravit*) an angel.[28]

Therefore, when we ask whether the divinity and humanity of Christ is to be adored with one and the same adoration, the answer is certainly yes according to its relation or ordering to the total subsistent, because the adoration by which the whole Christ is adored is one because of the unity of his person. But one can say that there are many adorations, understanding adoration as commonly understood according to the diverse reasons of honor on account of which Christ is adored. For he is adored with the adoration of latria strictly speaking because of his uncreated wisdom; but because of his created wisdom and holiness and grace, he is adored with adoration as commonly understood, which is called the adoration of dulia, or rather hyperdulia, that is, with the most excellent honor of dulia. For just as latria is the virtue by which the worship and religious rite are offered to God, so dulia is called the virtue by which the excellences of the creature are given their due honor.[29]

Since it was asked above whether the adoration of latria is to be offered to the humanity of Christ, the response, as has now been touched upon, is that such adoration properly is not fitting except to the whole subsistence or supposit;[30] and so the humanity of Christ is not strictly

---

25   E. N. "And so, if in one man there are several causes of honor, for example, privilege, knowledge, and virtue, there will be one honor given to him with respect to the person being honored, but many according to the causes which are honored, for it is the man that is honored." ST IIIa, q. 25, art. 1, c.

26   1 Kings 2:19a.

27   1 Kings 1:16a.

28   Joshua 5:15. *Joshua fell on his face to the ground and worshipping* (*adorans*) *said: What says my lord to his servant?*

29   E. N. ST IIIa, q. 25, arts. 1–2.

30   E. N. In other words, *through* the humanity *to* the Person of the Word, or the second Person of the Holy Trinity, which is *the hypostasis, supposit, subsistent thing,* or *subsistence.* Subsistence is "that mode of existence which is self-contained and independent of any subject, and also a being that exists in this manner, synonym

speaking or directly to be adored for itself or in itself [apart from any reference to the divine person], but yet in a certain way it is able to be adored. In response to this, it should be noted that the adoration of the humanity of Christ can be understood in two ways. First, as that adoration of it understood to be as that whose it is, namely of the Word: and as such the humanity of Christ is owed the adoration of latria. For to adore the humanity of Christ in this way is nothing other than to adore the Incarnate Word, just as to adore the purple robe of the king is to adore the king robed in purple.[31] Second, the adoration of the humanity of Christ can be understood so that it is in reference to itself, namely as given to it for its own reason, or because of the plenitude of its grace;[32] and thus, the adoration of latria is neither due or owed to it, but rather the veneration of dulia.

And so Christ is adored with a twofold honor, namely, with the adoration of latria because of his divine and uncreated nature, and the adoration of dulia because of the human nature. Speaking, therefore, of adoration in a strict sense, it is to be given to nothing properly and in itself, except to an uncreated Suppositum.[33] Whence, the Damascene in his third book says: The flesh of Christ is adored in the Incarnate Word of God, not on account of its own sake, but because of its union with the second Hypostasis, the Word.[34] Something similar to this is said of the purple robe of the king that is honored — though the king alone is

---

of *hypostasis, res subsistens, persona*, i.e., both that which exists for itself and not in another and also the manner of existence and the relations of being belonging to it." *A Lexicon of St. Thomas Aquinas based on the Summa* (Washington, DC: Catholic University Press, 1948) 1063 (s.v. "*subsistentia*") (eds., Roy Deferrari, Inviolata Barry, Ignatius McGuiness); *see also* s.v. "*suppositum*," p. 1079: Suppositum is "that which is the subject of existence and all accidental modifications which constitute the individual, synonym of *hypostasis, subiectum*, and *substantia*."

31   E. N. This example is taken from ST IIIa, q. 25, art. 2 c.

32   E. N. In other words, in reference only to the created good (grace) that is found in the human nature of Christ, without direct reference to, and therefore abstracted from, the person of the Word.

33   E. N. That is to say, the Holy Trinity, which is three uncreated *supposita* (persons) in one substance or essence or nature; hence, any one or more of the *supposita* may be worshipped with the adoration of latria.

34   E. N. Denis erroneously refers to the third book of St. John of Damascus's *An Exposition of the Orthodox Faith*. The reference is in fact to the fourth book (IV, 3): "Along with the Father and the Holy Spirit, we worship the Son of God . . . . so also the flesh, in its own nature, is not to be worshipped, but is worshipped in the incarnate God Word, not because of itself, but because of its union in subsistence with God the Word. And we do not say that we worship mere flesh, but God's flesh, that is, God incarnate." *Nicene and Post-Nicene Fathers* (2nd Series) (Buffalo, NY: Christian Literature Publishing Co., 1899, Vol. 9, 74–75 (eds. Philip Schaff and Henry Wace).

due honor—not on account of itself or because of itself, but as being the vesture of the king: and as the purple-robed king is venerated with the regal honor, and indeed the king properly and for himself, yet the purple robe, since it is something that is conjoined to the king, [is also honored]; so the Incarnate Word is adored with the adoration of latria for itself properly and directly, but his flesh or humanity [is honored with latria], as something that is united to him.

98{99}[6]   *Moses and Aaron among his priests: and Samuel among them that call upon his name. They called upon the Lord, and he heard them:*

Moyses et Aaron in sacerdotibus eius, et Samuel inter eos qui invocant nomen eius; invocabant Dominum, et ipse exaudiebat eos :

98{99}[7]   *He spoke to them in the pillar of the cloud. They kept his testimonies, and the commandment which he gave them.*

In columna nubis loquebatur ad eos. Custodiebant testimonia eius, et praeceptum quod dedit illis.

98{99}[6] *Moyses et Aaron in sacerdotibus eius, Moses and Aaron among his priests*, that is, from among the number of priests of God that were in the Old Testament. For Aaron was the pontifex and the high priest, offering to the Lord the prayers and sacrifices of the people. But Moses functioned in the office of the priest by consecrating or ordaining Aaron in his high priesthood and his children as priests, as we read in Leviticus. *Et Samuel inter eos qui invocant nomen eius, and Samuel among them that call upon his name*, that is, he was from the number of those who intimately prayed to God in the Old Testament. For he even prayed for his adversaries, saying: *Far from me be this sin against the Lord, that I should cease to pray for you.*[35] *Invocabant, they called upon*, Moses, Aaron, and Samuel [called upon] *Dominum, the Lord* because of the ignorance of the people, *et ipse, and he*, the Lord, *exaudiebat eos, heard them*: this clearly refers to Moses and Aaron in the book of Exodus and Numbers, and elsewhere.[36] Also this refers to what is written of Samuel in the first book of Samuel.[37] **98{99}[7]** *In columna nubis, in the pillar of cloud*, that is, in the cloud which appeared as a column, the Lord *loquebatur*

---

35   1 Sam. 12:23a.
36   Ex. 32:1–14; 33:11 *et seq.*; Num. 16:48; 21:7–9.
37   1 Sam. 12:17–18.

ad eos, spoke to them, [though the Lord did so], not in his own person, but through a ministering angel, about which the Lord said to Moses: *Behold I will send my angel, who shall go before you.*[38] The Lord also spoke in this way to Moses and Aaron in the column of the cloud, as we read in Exodus;[39] but with Samuel we do not read about this clearly in any canonical Scripture except in the present Psalm; and for this reason [alone], it is certain to be so. Nevertheless, in the first book of Samuel it is clearly described how the Lord gave thunder and rain to Samuel when he prayed for it, which would not have existed without a cloud.[40] And perhaps it was then that the Lord spoke to Samuel in the pillar of the cloud, since others did not hear that speech. This (as some assert) is just like others did not hear the voice of the Father saying about Christ, *This is my beloved Son,*[41] which, however, John the Baptist heard when baptizing and entreating Christ, as Luke says.[42]

98{99}[8] *You did hear them, O Lord our God: you were a merciful God to them, and taking vengeance on all their inventions.*

Domine Deus noster, tu exaudiebas eos; Deus, tu propitius fuisti eis, et ulciscens in omnes adinventiones eorum.

98{99}[8] *Domine Deus noster, O Lord our God,* adorable and most highly blessed Trinity, *tu exaudiebas eos, you did hear them* in their just petitions. *Deus, tu propitius fuisti eius, you were a merciful God to them,* that is, you kindly forbore both their own sins and the sins of others. This is most clearly seen in Aaron, who sinned in an exceedingly grave way in fashioning the golden calf and in grumbling against Moses.[43] *Et ulciscens, and taking vengeance,* that is, paternally punishing in the present life, *in omnes adinventiones eorum, on all their inventions,* that is, in all their sins; these did not proceed from divine inspiration, but from human invention. For in this world God mercifully and for a time avenged their sins, lest they be punished in the future age more grievously. Whence, because of their disbelief, when Moses and Aaron wavered in faith at the waters of contradiction, they were prohibited from entering the land of promise.[44] It is manifest, therefore, that Lord permits some

---

38   Ex. 23:20a.
39   Ex. 33:9.
40   1 Sam. 12:17–18.
41   Matt. 3:17.
42   Luke 3:21–22.
43   Ex. 32:2–6; Num. 12:1–2.
44   Num. 20:12.

of his holy ones to fall in their human weakness; and then he mercifully applies the remedy of temporal punishment, so that both from their own fault and from the divine punishment they may be warned of their weakness, and they might rise more humble and more cautious.[45] But the inventions of him whom God hates[46] are not completely or always punished in this age, but in the future: sometimes, however, they are avenged in the present incipiently, as is clear with the reprobate whose punishment begin here, and which perdure in hell without end.

98{99}[9] *Exalt the Lord our God, and adore at his holy mountain: for the Lord our God is holy.*

Exaltate Dominum Deum nostrum, et adorate in monte sancto eius, quoniam sanctus Dominus Deus noster.

98{99}[9] *Exaltate,* exalt with reverence of mind, with the proclamation of the mouth, with the service of works, *Dominum Deum nostrum, the Lord our God,* Christ, the Son of God, who is true God and eternal life; *et adorate, and adore him in monte sancto eius, at his holy mountain,* that is the Church militant, founded upon Christ the high mountain; and not only upon mount Sion, which was in Jerusalem, or the mountain located next to Sychar at which the Savior said to the Samaritan woman: *Believe me, that the hour comes, when you shall neither on this mountain, nor in Jerusalem, adore the Father.*[47] *Quoniam sanctus Dominus*

---

45   E. N. On this topic, see the excellent anthology of St. Francis de Sales's works by Joseph Tissot: *How to Profit from Your Faults* (London: Scepter 2017), 48. "Quoting St. Paul, St. Augustine sums up this advantage in three words: *Omnia in bonum* (*All things work for the good of those who love God*). Yes, everything, even our failures. Because one then gets up and is more *humble* and more *careful,* and more *fervent."*

46   E. N. *Quem Deus odit,* whom God hates. While moderns wince at the notion that God hates sinners, the notion of the hatred of God of some sinners — namely, the reprobate — is undeniably Biblical. E.g., "You hate (*odisti*) all the workers of iniquity." Ps. 5:7. St. Paul refers to some sinners as "hateful to God," *Deo odibiles,* θεοστυγής (*theostygēs*) (Rom. 1:30). The Christian Cicero, Lactantius (ca. 250-ca. 325), insisted that God's hatred was the necessary negative concomitant of his mercy: "If he is able to pardon (*ignoscere*), he is therefore able also to be angry (*irasci*)." *De Ira Dei,* 20, PL 7, 137. "The divine election is called the love of God; the hatred of God is reprobation: *I have loved Jacob, but Esau have I hated.* [Mal. 1:2–3; Rom. 9:13]." Hugh of St. Victor, *Summa Sentiarum,* IV, 8, PL 176, 126. It also has a hearing in natural theology, as Socrates observed: "The thing and the person that are dear to the gods (θεοφιλές τε καὶ θεοφιλὴς) are holy (ὅσιος), and the thing and the person that are hateful to the gods (θεομισὲς καὶ ὁ θεομισὴς) are unholy (ἀνόσιος); and the two are not the same, but the holy and the unholy are the exact opposites of each other." Plato, *Euthyphro,* 7a7–8 (trans., H. N. Fowler).

47   John 4:21.

Deus noster, for the Lord our God is holy. For he is substantially holy, and is pure, separate, and infinite holiness. He also is the prime origin, measure, and cause of all holiness, virtue, and pureness. For this reason, our heavenly Father, wanting us to be similar to him, and in order that we might be called truly and worthily his adoptive sons, says: *Do not defile your soul.*[48] *Be holy because I am holy.*[49] But those stained, unclean, or vicious he abominates, hates, and damns, in the manner that Joshua said: *He is a holy God, and mighty and jealous, and will not forgive your wickedness and sins.*[50] But also Christ calls God the Father holy, and entreats from him that his faithful be made holy, saying in the Gospel: *Holy Father, . . . sanctify them in truth.*[51] Let us do this, therefore, because Christ comes to us. For *he swore* that he would *grant* himself to us, that *we may serve him . . . in holiness and justice all our days.*[52]

See how it does not become us to sing this present Psalm — which is sweet with the praise of God, and which recalls the benefits of Christ and exhorts us in repeated succession to the veneration of God — without internal joyfulness and special devotion. And we ought to exalt God, not only by words, but also with humble and diligent obedience.

PRAYER

OD, HIGH ABOVE ALL PEOPLE, BE MERCIFUL to your servants; grant us the means, we beseech you, to keep the testimonies and the holy commandments that you gave us, so that observing them even unto the end with devotion, we might receive our reward from you in blessed eternity.

Excelsus super omnes populos Deus, famulis tuis esto propitius;
da nobis, quaesumus, custodire testimonia et sancta
quae dedisti nobis praecepta: ut ea in finem
usque observantes devote, mercedem a
te in beata sortiamur aeternitate.

---

48 Lev. 11:43a.
49 Lev. 11:44a.
50 Joshua 24:19.
51 John 17:11a, 17.
52 Luke 1:73a, 75.

Psalm 99

ARTICLE LXXVIII

ELUCIDATION OF THE NINETY-NINTH PSALM:
IUBILATE DOMINO, OMNIS TERRA.
SING JOYFULLY TO GOD, ALL THE EARTH.

99{100}[1]   *A Psalm of confession.*[1]

Psalmus in confessione.

HE TITLE OF THE PSALM NOW BEING DIS-
cussed is: **99{100}[1]** *Psalmus in confessione, A Psalm of confession:*
that is, this Psalm has to do with the confession of divine praise, and
also of the confession of one's own indictment. Principally, however, it
treats with the confession of divine praise, for it intends to set us afire
and induce us to praising, giving thanks, and blessing God, our Creator.

99{100}[2]   *Sing joyfully to God, all the earth: serve the Lord with gladness.*
Come in before his presence with exceeding great joy.

Iubilate Deo, omnis terra; servite Domino in laetitia. Introite
in conspectu eius in exsultatione.

Therefore, it states: **99{100}[2]** *Iubilate Deo,*[2] *sing joyfully to God,* that
is, so exuberantly and inexpressibly rejoice and sing hymns to God that
the joy of holy devotion is unable to be contained and restrained, but
rather that it may break forth externally by sensible signs, even though
it is not able fully to be expressed. So sing joyfully to the Lord, *omnis*
terra, all the earth, that is, the entirety of the inhabitants of the earth.
So completely does it teach us to sing joyfully to the Lord because as
his majesty infinitely exceeds our smallness, so ought our capacity at
enjoyment transcend our own weakness and speech. Now we ought to
sing joyfully to the Lord [for three reasons]. First and principally, because

---

1   E. N. Since Denis interprets this Psalm as dealing with both the confession of
praise and the confession of sin, I have translated *confessione* with "confession," rather
than "praise," as in the Douay-Rheims.
2   E. N. The text has *Iubilate Domino,* but the editor in the margin notes that *Deo*
is an alternative reading. I have followed the Sixto-Clementine Vulgate and the
Douay-Rheims.

of his own goodness and blessedness, which makes it becoming for us to rejoice ineffably if we likewise love him, as Christ said to his Apostles: *If you loved me, you would indeed be glad, because I go to the Father,* that is, you would rejoice in my exultation and glorification. Second, because of the manifold benefits of God exhibited towards us, namely, because of the gifts of nature and the bestowal of grace. For he gave to us being, sense, understanding, the body and soul, powers and members, and also the multiform gifts of grace and his immense mercy. Third, because of the great goods promised us and that are prepared for us in the heavens.

For this reason, therefore, O all you men, *servite Domino in laetitia, serve the Lord with gladness,* that is, promptly and with great joy, not, by any means, dissolutely and irreverently, but in a joy conjoined with fear, as it states in a Psalm above, *Serve the Lord with fear, and rejoice unto him with trembling.*[3] Now, what does this mean — to serve the Lord with gladness — unless it be to obey the divine commandments with true and fervid charity? Indeed, there is no quality that so easily, promptly, and delightfully operates as does charity; in all its doings, fervid charity has attached to it heartfelt joy. For *it does not rejoice in iniquity, but rejoices with the truth,* according to the Apostle [Paul].[4] And so we ought to minister to the Lord in joy, for forced service is not pleasing to him. For this reason, the Apostle says: *God has not given us the spirit of fear: but of power, and of love, and of sobriety.*[5] And also to the Colossians: *Whatsoever you do,* he says, *do it from the heart.*[6] Now the more we serve the Lord from a more prompt and joyful affection, the more fully we will receive mercy from him — namely a more expansive grace in the present, and a greater glory in heaven.

Introite, come in the temple of the Lord *in conspectu eius, before his presence:* for the Lord's eyes of mercy are wide open upon his temple, in the manner that Solomon prayed: *Hear the hymn and the prayer, which your servant prays . . . that your eyes may be open upon this house day and night.*[7] It is possible for this also to be understood as referring to the material temple, which is the *house of prayer*[8] in which God is beheld; and in which also men are beheld by God, that is, they are known by him with the knowledge of approbation and are mercifully attended to.[9]

---

3   Ps. 11:11a.
4   1 Cor. 13:6.
5   2 Tim. 1:7.
6   Col. 3:23a.
7   1 Kings 8:28b–29a.
8   Is. 66:7b.
9   E. N. The knowledge of approbation is a "knowledge" that is ascribed to God when he approves a man. *See* footnote 5-11 in Volume 1.

It also can be aptly understood as referring to the immaterial temple, which is the rational soul, since the soul is the room, bedchamber, throne, seat, house, and temple of its Creator and Savior. We ought therefore to enter into our souls, that is, *return . . . to the heart,*[10] consider divine things, and scrutinize our interiors, *in conspectu eius, before his presence,* that is, before God, thinking in the presence of God, and placing ourselves before him, and uttering that which is stated in Genesis: God is *a witness who is present and beholds.*[11] And so enter *in exsultatione, with exceeding great joy:* that is, by entering you confess to God of his praises and your misdeeds in order that you might rejoice in the contemplation of the divine goodness and you might sorrow in the consideration of your depravity, so that to being saddened you might be consoled and might be found worthy of eternal consolation.

99{100}[3] *Know because the Lord he is God: he made us, and not we ourselves. We are his people and the sheep of his pasture.*[12]

Scitote quoniam Dominus ipse est Deus; ipse fecit nos, et non ipsi nos; populus eius, et oves pascuae eius.

99{100}[4] *Go into his gates with confession, into his courts with hymns: and confess to him. Praise his name.*[13]

Introite portas eius in confessione, atria eius in hymnis; confitemini illi. Laudate nomen eius.

99{100}[5] *For the Lord is sweet, his mercy endures forever, and his truth to generation and generation.*

Quoniam suavis est Dominus; in aeternum misericordia eius, et usque in generationem et generationem veritas eius.

99{100}[3] *Scitote, know,* not only by faith, but also by natural reason, and taste, and experience, *quoniam, because,* that is, that, *Dominus, the Lord* of all things, *ipse est Deus, he is God,* your Creator and Governor; *ipse fecit nos, he made us* by creation, he restored us by his Incarnation and

---

10   Is. 46:8b.

11   Gen. 31:50b.

12   E. N. I have departed from the Douay-Rheims and translated *quoniam* as because, so that the English reads "Know that the Lord he is God" to "Know because the Lord he is God." This is required so as to fit within the Commentary.

13   E. N. Again, I have departed from the Douay-Rheims by changing "praise" and "give glory" to the more generic "confession," since Denis understands it as being a confession of both praise and fault.

through the infusion of grace, *et non ipsi nos, and not we ourselves.* Now all things bear witness to and proclaim, the order of all things manifests, reason dictates, Scripture affirms,[14] the philosophers all acknowledge, and the theologians all preach that God made all things by creating them. For we perceive a most befitting order to exist in all the species of the universe, because any one nature comes after, is connected, is inferior, or is dependent upon another. It is necessary, therefore, to come to one simple and first nature, extremely simple, highest in dignity, and entirely independent, and needful of nothing: and this nature is God. But the first and most noble of every kind of thing is the cause of those of its kind which come after it, in the manner that the first heat is the cause of heat in other things.[15] Therefore God—who is the first, highest, perfect, simple, and independent Being—is the cause of all being, truth, and perfection in all other things. Aristotle demonstrated this in in the second book of his *Metaphysics.*[16] For this reason, he says elsewhere: *From this Being is communicated the being and life of all other things,* indeed to some more manifestly, and to others more obscurely.[17]

And so in the manner that we receive from God all that we have and that we are, so we must offer to God ourselves and all our exterior and interior things, and we are obliged to expend them in the praise and in the service of God. And so the Psalmist adds: *Populus eius et oves pascuae eius, we are his people and the sheep of his pasture,* that is, O all you faithful, whom God possesses by faith and grace, who are the sheep of his pasture, that is, who are restored by his sacraments, and are sustained and nourished in both mind and body by the gifts of God, 99{100}[4] *introite, go into,* not with bodily steps, but rather forward with a mental movement, *portas eius, into his gates,* that is, into the virtues or virtuous works which lead towards the heavenly kingdom, *in confessione, with confession* of your sins. For it is fitting that the confession of one's own fault precede the doing of other virtuous works. For by confession fault is blotted out, grace is given, and a man is made suitable to be a praiser [of God]. Whence the Lord states about those who do not confess through Isaiah: *When you stretch forth your hands, I will turn away my eyes from you . . . for your hands are full of blood.*[18] Go into also *atria eius, into his courts,* that is, the breadth of his charity, fulfilling that which the

---

14   Gen. chp. 1.
15   E. N. ST Ia, q. 2, art. 2, co.
16   E. N. Aristotle, *Metaphysics,* II, 2, 994a–b.
17   E. N. A reference to Aristotle's *On the Heavens (De Caelo),* I, 9.
18   Is. 1:15.

most blessed prince of the Apostles said: *Before all things have a constant mutual charity among yourselves: for charity covers a multitude of sins.*[19] Hence also Paul: *Walk in love,* he says, *as Christ has also loved us. For love is the fulfilling of the law;*[20] and *he that loves his neighbor has fulfilled the law.*[21] Or [we can understand it this way]: *Go into his courts,* that is, by contemplation and hope enter into the amplitude of the heavenly palace, and with the eyes of faith behold the broad streets of the heavenly kingdom, and the ranks of the blessed having conversation in heaven.[22] And this verse can be understood as applying to the material gates and courts of the church made of stones: so that it admonishes us to visit and enter the church of God, where divine things are done, Masses are celebrated, and the preaching of the heavenly word is heard. *In hymnis,* with hymns, that is, with spiritual praises, *confitemini illi, confess to him,* that is, praise God, as one is admonished in Revelation: *Give praise to our God, all you his servants; and you that fear him, little and great.*[23]

Laudate nomen eius, praise his name, with a devout, recollected, and loving soul, **99{100}[5]** *quoniam suavis est Dominus, for the Lord is sweet.* For the blessed and holy God is essentially sweet; and his infinite essence is nothing other than precisely immeasurable sweetness, from whose infinite fragrance, sweetness, and delightfulness drops down all created sweetness. However, in some way, one who diligently persists in his continual praise deserves to taste this sweetness of God, saying and fulfilling that which is said in a Psalm above: *I will bless the Lord at all times, his praise shall be always in my mouth.*[24] And in Ecclesiasticus: *I will glory to you O Lord, O King,* it says, *and I will praise you, O God, my Savior. I will praise your name continually.*[25] *In aeternum misericordia eius, his mercy endures forever.* For the mercy of God is the merciful God himself: and so it is eternal, as is God. Or [alternatively], *his mercy endures forever,* that is, the effects of the divine goodness remain eternally in the elect, who are *the vessels of mercy.*[26] *Et usque in generationem et generationem, and ... to generation and generation,* that is, unto all generations without end, *veritas eius, his truth* shall remain, that is the truth of sacred Scripture, in the way that Christ attested: *Heaven and earth shall pass*

---

19   1 Pet. 4:8.
20   Rom. 13:10b.
21   Rom. 13:8b.
22   Phil 3:20.
23   Rev. 19:5.
24   Ps. 33:2.
25   Ecclus. 51:1, 15a.
26   Rom. 9:23b.

away, but my words shall not pass away.[27] For this reason we also have in Isaiah: *The word of our Lord endures forever.*[28] Or the truth of God can be understood to be the truthful God himself, or true fulfillment of his promises which will never cease, because the reprobate will go to eternal fire, but the elect unto eternal life.[29]

See we have heard this mellifluous Psalm, full of angelic gaiety, fragrant with the proclamations of God, whom we ought to make known with great attention in the person of the Church, and whose exhortations we ought efficaciously to obey, singing joyfully to God, gladly serving him, thinking unceasingly of his presence, and praising him outwardly to be our God with faith and works, in no way ever wandering off by sluggish praise. This we can in no way do unless we daily abhor grave vices with an irreproachable heart, and also avoid, correct, and deplore venial ones as diligently as possible, confessing frequently and fervently making amendment, thinking that which Solomon said: *He that hides his sins, shall not prosper: but he that shall confess, and forsake them, shall obtain mercy.*[30] These things are required to undertake the acts which this present Psalm invites us to undertake, because these acts are all Godlike, heavenly, and angelic, most salutary and of incomparable merit.

PRAYER

O GOD, ETERNAL GLORY OF HEAVEN, GRANT us entry into your gates in confession and into your courts with hymns, so that declaring your majesty, we might, by your gift, receive the crown of life which you have promised to those who love you.

Aeterna caeli gloria, Deus, fac nos portas tuas in confessione, et atria tua in hymnis introire: ut confitentes maiestati tuae, coronam vitae quam repromisisti te diligentibus, te donante, accipiamus.

---

27   Luke 21:33.
28   Is. 40:8b.
29   Matt. 25:46.
30   Prov. 23:13.

Psalm 100

ARTICLE LXXIX

EXPOSITION OF THE HUNDREDTH PSALM:
MISERICORDIAM ET IUDICIUM CANTABO TIBI, DOMINE.
MERCY AND JUDGMENT I WILL SING TO YOU, O LORD.

100{101}[1] *A Psalm for David himself. Mercy and judgment I will sing to you, O Lord: I will sing,*

Psalmus ipsi David. Misericordiam et iudicium cantabo tibi, Domine; psallam,

THE TITLE OF THE LAST OF THIS SECOND set of fifty Psalms is this: **100{101}[1]** *Psalmus [ipsi] David, a Psalm for David himself.*[1] For this Psalm is of the prophet David as its author, but it sings to Christ as the dispenser of all perfections, virtues, or graces of which this Psalm treats. But it is fittingly applied to any virtuous man whose life can be proposed as an example for others. For in this Psalm the perfect man acknowledges his virtues, not presumptuously or to his own glory, but to the honor of God and the edification of his neighbors, in the manner that Job, Tobias, Jeremiah, and many other of the saints carefully describe their own good. This also Paul often did in his epistles, inasmuch as he said several times: *I am become foolish: you have compelled me,*[2] that is, the charity by which I desire your salvation, compelled me to praise myself; this is similar to foolishness, and it would seem contrary to the divine Scriptures, because Solomon says: *Let another praise you, and not your own mouth: a stranger, and not your own lips.*[3] But this is asserted so that one does not praise himself without legitimate reason or from vainglory. For we are not prohibited by this [general prohibition] from recounting our own virtues to the glory of the Creator, to the edification of the hearer, and especially of those subject to us, particularly because Christ says in the Gospel: *So let your light shine before men that they may see your good works, and glorify your*

---

1   E. N. Denis's title does not contain the word *ipsi*, himself; however, it is of not great moment, so I have stayed with the Sixto-Clementine text.
2   2 Cor. 12:11a.
3   Prov. 27:2.

Father who is in heaven.[4] Whence also Peter says: *Having your manner of living good among the Gentiles that whereas they speak against you as evildoers, they may, by the good works, which they shall behold in you, glorify God in the day of visitation.*[5] And Paul to his beloved disciple: *Your profiting may be manifest to all.*[6]

David, therefore, speaking in the person of the Church or any perfect man, thus begins: *Misericordiam et iudicium cantabo tibi, Domine; mercy and judgment will I sing to you, O Lord*: that is, I will ascribe to you, kindness and equitableness, O God, with joyful praise, that is, I will not only praise you as merciful, mercifully indulgent, and a bestower of great mercies to sinners, but also as just, scrutinizing and rendering just judgment with terrible vengeance, and leaving no evil unpunished, indeed leaving utterly nothing unexamined, undecided, and unrecompensed.[7] For by now it has been frequently stated [in this Commentary] in what way *all the ways of the Lord are mercy and truth,*[8] understanding by truth, justice or judgment. We therefore sing to the Lord of a multiple judgment: namely, the particular, which he does separately, to every single person, when they die; and the universal, which is effected at the end of the world. We sing of his judgment of discretion, which he does within us every day, dividing in this life by grace, promise, and merit the elect from the reprobate; the judgment also of final retribution, when the good are separated from the evil by both place and reward.[9] Or [we can understand it] thus: *Mercy* in prosperity, *and judgment* in adversity, *I will sing to you*, that is, to your praise, O Lord, so that I might attribute entirely to you whatever good or consolation of yours that you might cause to bestow upon me, and whatever merit there might be in me, and I will ascribe it all to your most merciful goodness. Finally, whatever adversity, imperfection, or fault befalls me, this I will figure to be as a result of my sins and your just judgment, singing to you that which is in read in Daniel: *You are just, O Lord, in all that you have done to us, and all your works are true, and everything that you have done to us, you have done in true judgment, for we have sinned against you, and we have not obeyed your commandments.*[10]

---

4   Matt. 5:16.

5   1 Pet. 2:12.

6   1 Tim. 4:15.

7   Cf. Prov. 19:5: *A false witness shall not be unpunished: and he that speaks lies shall not escape.*

8   Ps. 24:10a.

9   Matt. 13:49.

10   Daniel 3:27, 31b, 29a.

As God, therefore, in a singular way enjoins upon us mercy — in regard
to our neighbors — and judgment — in regard to ourselves — (according
to that in Zechariah: *Judge you true judgment, and show you mercy and
compassion every man to his brother;*[11] and Micah: *I will show you, O man,
what is good, and what the Lord requires of you: Verily, to do judgment,
and to love mercy*[12]); so God in all his works mixes mercy and judgment.
For this reason, these two things we especially sing about to him, lest the
judgment of God incite us to despair, or lest the mercy makes us to lose
any fear; but thinking of both of these things, we should hope fearing
and we should fear hoping, and we should solicitously walk with our
God,[13] and with fear and dread and trembling work out our salvation,
according to the admonition of the divine apostle.[14]

100{101}[2] *And I will understand in the unspotted way. When shall you
come to me? I walked in the innocence of my heart, in the
midst of my house.*

*Et intelligam in via immaculata: quando venies ad me? Peram-
bulabam in innocentia cordis mei, in medio domus meae.*

100{101}[3] *I did not set before my eyes any unjust thing: I hated the
workers of iniquities.*

*Non proponebam ante oculos meos rem iniustam; facientes
praevaricationes odivi.*

Psallam, I will sing, offering spiritual canticles, **100{101}[2]** *et intelligam,*
and I will understand, that is, I will read internally, or intently pay attention
to what I sing, lest I do so with a wandering and empty mind, and I will
fulfill that stated by the Apostle: *I will sing also with the understanding.*[15]
Whence it is said in a Psalm above, *Sing wisely.*[16] And so will I sing and
understand *in via immaculata, in the unspotted way,* that is, with sincere
intention, with pure desire, in the observation of the divine law, so that life
might accord with voice. For these things are the unspotted way by which
the soul attends to God, and of which we read in Proverbs, *Her ways are
beautiful ways, and all her paths are peaceable.*[17] And it in the way of holy

---

11 Zech. 7:9.
12 Micah 6:8.
13 Cf. *ibid.*
14 Cf. Phil. 2:12.
15 1 Cor. 14:15b.
16 Ps. 46:8b.
17 Prov. 3:17.

desires, in which my soul thirsts for you, I declared, vehemently desiring your presence: *Quando venies ad me, when shall you come to me?* That is, would that you would come quickly—indeed daily—by the accumulation of grace, and—in a short while—taking me from this exile to the heavenly homeland: *for I desire to be dissolved and to be with you, for this is far better.*[18]

Appropriately, it continues in detail how I had sung in the unspotted way, saying: *Perambulabam, I walked,* that is, I maintained myself in this valley of tears *in innocentia cordis mei, in the innocence of my heart,* so that I did not do anything to others that I did not want done to me, but I lived in simplicity and purity of conscience in the manner that the Apostle [Paul] said: *We have injured no man, we have corrupted no man,*[19] *neither have we used at any time the speech of flattery;*[20] *in medio domus meae, in the midst of my house,* that is, in the midst of the Church or my brothers, poisoning no one with evil example. 100{101}[3] *Non proponebam ante oculos meos, I did not set before my eyes,* [my] bodily or interior [eyes], *rem iniustam, any unjust thing,* that is, anything unlawful that I might have otherwise sought for: as is had in Job, *I made a covenant with my eyes, that I would not so much as think upon a virgin.*[21] Whence it is again written: *Let every man cast away the scandals of his eyes,* says the Lord.[22] For eyes that are not taken custody of harm greatly, according to what is said in Ecclesiasticus: *What is created more wicked than an eye?*[23] We must always check, therefore, the eyes of both the heart and body if we desire to please God with a pure heart.[24] Had David taken custody of his eyes in this way, he would not have lapsed into adultery and murder.[25] *Facientes praevaricationes, the workers of iniquities,* that is, those transgressing the divine commandments, *odivi, I hated,* insofar as they remain in this way, though I love them inasmuch as they are men and have the capacity of grace and salvation, for I desire their conversion because I am enjoined

---

18   Phil. 1:23b.
19   2 Cor. 7:2.
20   1 Thess. 2:5a.
21   Job 31:1.
22   Ez. 20:7a.
23   Ecclus. 31:15a.
24   E. N. This custody of the eyes, *custodia oculorum,* is an essential discipline in the spiritual life: "Without control over the eyes it is impossible to stay on the road of virtue or even in the state of grace. The soul that aspires seriously to sanctification will flee from every dangerous occasion of this sort. One will keep a custody over the eyes, and, without going to ridiculous extremes, one will always be vigilant and alert lest he be taken by surprise." Antonio Royo Marín, O. P., *The Theology of Christian Perfection* (Eugene, OR: Wipf & Stock 2011), 286–87 (trans., Jordan Aumann, O. P.).
25   2 Sam. chp. 11.

to pray for enemies and ungodly men.[26] And by doing this one shows himself to be in conformity with the divine will, because, as Wisdom says, *To God the wicked and his wickedness are hateful alike.*[27] And of the ungodly, the Lord says to Jeremiah: *My soul is not towards this people.*[28]

100{101}[4] *The perverse heart did not cleave to me: and the malignant that turned aside from me, I would not know.*

Non adhaesit mihi cor pravum declinantem a me malignum non cognoscebam.

100{101}[4] *Non adhaesit mihi cor pravum,* the perverse heart did not cleave to me, that is, an evil affection of the heart did not please me. Indeed, the affections and acts of a perverse man are heavy punishments to a just man, in the manner that Peter attests of Lot: *In sight and hearing he was just: dwelling among them, who from day to day vexed the just soul with unjust works.*[29] But in such circumstances or cases patience is to be preserved, immoderate and impetuous displeasure is to be set aside, and kind compassion is to be applied, as the Apostle [Paul] teaches: *Brethren, and if a man be overtaken in any fault, you, who are spiritual, instruct such a one in the spirit of meekness.*[30] And again: *Bear,* he says, *one another's burdens.*[31] *Declinantem a me malignum,* and the malignant that turned aside from me, that is, set afire with the fire of vices, adverse to my rightly-ordered will, and dissimilar to me in manner of life, *non cognoscebam, I would not know* by approval, because his works have not pleased me. And God—who will say to the ungodly in the day of judgment, *I do not know you*—conforms himself to this.[32] Of these is also elsewhere said: *I have no pleasure in you.*[33]

100{101}[5] *The man that in private detracted his neighbor, him did I persecute. With him that had a proud eye, and an unsatiable heart, I would not eat.*

Detrahentem secreto proximo suo, hunc persequebar, superbo oculo, et insatiabili corde, cum hoc non edebam.

---

26 Matt. 5:44.
27 Wis. 14:9.
28 Jer. 15:1.
29 2 Pet. 2:8.
30 Gal. 6:1.
31 Gal. 6:2a.
32 Luke 13:25. E. N. That is, God adapts to the evildoer's will who did not want to know God and turned aside from, by not knowing the evildoer and turning him aside.
33 Mal. 1:10b.

100{101}[5] *Detrahentem secreto proximo suo,* the man that in private detracted his neighbor, denigrating his reputation in my presence or upon me learning about it, *hunc persequebar,* him did I persecute by afflicting, censuring, or avoiding him. For detraction is an exceedingly great sin, and it is more grave than theft, which also because of its genus is a mortal sin. Whence it is written: *If a serpent bite in silence, he is nothing better than he that backbites secretly.*[34] Therefore, the prelate ought truly and diligently to pursue the detractor and, if there is hope of his amendment, any one of us ought to censure him; but if he does not receive the correction of words, one ought to show him a sad countenance, or one ought entirely to turn his face from him, or to state something good [of the person being detracted], so that he might be embarrassed and make amendment. For this Solomon said: *By the sadness of the countenance the mind of the offender is corrected.*[35] And elsewhere we have: *Hedge in your ears with thorns, hear not a wicked tongue.*[36] And so the persecutor of the detractor is good and pious, and is not cruel; and whoever desires to make progress [in the virtuous life] truly ought first of all completely to abhor and radically extirpate this vice, and he ought not to believe every spirit, or easily assent to furthering any stories of others, especially of the imperfect. For he who is quick to believe everything and begins to lightly to hold onto obloquious words greatly troubles his soul, and he takes away and impedes his stability and seriousness of mind. And these [sorts of words] generate frequent discords and unjust hatreds, so that sometimes enemies are made from the greatest of friends, who indeed were once of one mind, but whom excessively credulous souls cleave by an evil-speaking tongue. But greatly at rest is the soul, and greatly serious in manner of life, who wants neither rashly nor easily to receive or to hear something unfavorable of another. And this ought the innocent and the simple most strongly to think because they so easily believe all things, supposing others to be [as innocent and simple] as they are themselves. For this reason, Solomon says: *The innocent believes every word.*[37]

Superbo oculo et insatiabili corde, with him that had a proud eye and an unsatiable heart, that is, the avaricious man who is not satiated with money, *cum hoc non edebam, with him I would not eat* with an interior consent. Literally applied, if one can do so without loss, the tables of the proud and the avaricious ought to be avoided, according to this: *Let just men be*

---

34   Eccl. 10:11.
35   Eccl. 7:4b.
36   Ecclus. 28:28a.
37   Prov. 14:15a.

your guests.[38] And the Apostle says: *If any man obey not our word by this epistle, note that man, and do not keep company with him, that he may be ashamed.*[39] Also elsewhere: With such kind, he says, *do not so much as eat.*[40] Yet nevertheless, we can eat with such persons so as to correct and inform them or for some other reasonable cause, especially since Christ got together to eat with publicans and sinners so that he might convert them.

100{101}[6] *My eyes were upon the faithful of the earth, to sit with me: the man that walked in the perfect way, he served me.*

Oculi mei ad fideles terrae, ut sedeant mecum; ambulans in via immaculata, hic mihi ministrabat.

100{101}[7] *He that works pride shall not dwell in the midst of my house: he that speaks unjust things did not prosper before my eyes.*

Non habitabit in medio domus meae qui facit superbiam; qui loquitur iniqua non direxit in conspectu oculorum meorum.

100{101}[6] *Oculi mei,* my eyes, both interior and also exterior, *ad fideles terrae,* were upon the faithful of the earth, that is, were upon the men faithfully serving God, *ut sedeant mecum,* to sit with me in counsel, table, and judgment, because with great affection I look for such persons and desire to have communion with them. *Ambulans in via immaculata, the man that walked in the perfect way,* that is, one that is not conversant with the stain of sin and is serving God with purity of heart, *hic mihi ministrabat, he served me.* For it is fitting for such persons to be ministers of prelates and princes; it especially befits religious to have devout servants, not worldly, light-minded, and vain servants who are overly attentive to dress, and inconstant in work. **100{101}[7]** *Non habitabit in medio domus meae qui facit superbiam, he that works pride shall not dwell in the midst of my house:* that is, I will not dwell with the proud, lest I be perverted by the perverse;[41] and if I dwell with them bodily, nevertheless I will distance myself far away from them with my mind, because it is written: *He that touches pitch, shall be defiled with it: and he that has fellowship with the proud, shall put on pride.*[42] Whence Wisdom asserts: *I hate arrogance, and pride, and every wicked way, and a mouth with a double tongue.*[43] *Qui loquitur iniqua, non direxit in conspectus*

---

38   Ecclus. 9:22a.
39   2 Thess. 3:14.
40   1 Cor. 5:11b.
41   *Cf.* Ps. 17:27b.
42   Ecclus. 13:1.
43   Prov. 8:13.

oculorum meorum, he that speaks unjust things did not prosper before my eyes: that is, he has not done good in my judgment, nor has he walked directly towards God; indeed I have rejected him.

100{101}[8]   *In the morning I put to death all the wicked of the land: that I might cut off all the workers of iniquity from the city of the Lord.*

In matutino interficiebam omnes peccatores terrae, ut disperderem de civitate Domini omnes operantes iniquitatem.

100{101}[8] *In matutino, in the morning,* that is, as soon as conveniently and justly was possible, *interficiebam, I put to death* with a material or spiritual sword *omnes peccatores terrae, all the wicked of the land,* that is, all seriously criminal persons adjudged of crimes worthy of death, *ut disperderem de civitate Domini, that I might cut off . . . from the city of the Lord,* that is, from the Church or the congregation of the just, *omnes operantes iniquitatem, all the workers of iniquity* which is grievous, as has been stated. For the secular princes with a material sword and the prelates also with a spiritual sword should kill the iniquitous, or declare them interiorly dead, so that they might cleanse the Church from commingling with the depraved, according to the Decretals.[44] Or [alternatively], *in the morning,* that is, at the beginning of a temptation, *I put to death,* that is, I caused to fall or to fail, by devout prayer and the help of the grace of Christ, *all the wicked of the land,* that is, the devils tempting me, and the worldly desires making suggestions to me; *that I might cut off . . . from the city of the Lord,* that is, from the consent of my soul, which is the city of God, *all the workers of iniquity,* that is, all the diabolical temptations seeking to lead me into evil works.

Now how this Psalm befits Christ is certain and easy to see. For he sang mercy and judgment to God the Father and to the whole Trinity most perfectly, for in the entirety of the Gospel he teaches God to be both kindly and just. He sang also and understood in the unspotted way, that is, in the whole of his most holy manner of living: *When shall you come to me?* That is, when, O Father God, will I come to you? For he desired to return to the Father in the manner that he testified: *O incredulous generation, how long shall I be with you?*[45] A perverse heart did not cleave to Christ, as is clear from the traitor Judas.[46] All the rest [of this Psalm, and how it applies to Christ] is clearly apparent.

---

44   24, q. 1. *Audivimus. E. N.* This is a reference to a canon regarding excommunication.
45   Mark 9:18a.
46   John 15:1–8.

Finally, according to teachers, the states of the Christian religion are three in number. The first is the state of the beginners, of those who are occupied with sorrow and with acts of penitence; and here the first group of fifty of the Psalter, which ends with the penitential Psalm, namely, [that Psalm which begins with] *Have mercy upon me, O God,*[47] is appropriate. The second is the state of the proficient, of those who *walk in the spirit,*[48] who exercise acts of justice, going *from virtue to virtue.*[49] And here these second fifty, which end with the present Psalm that deals with the rigors of justice, are appropriate. But the third is the state of the perfect, who have ascended to the active and contemplative life, who adhere to the praise of God unceasingly; and to these is appropriate the third fifty, which end in the divine praise.[50]

And so every person is taught to reach higher by this present Psalm, that he may hold himself devoutly toward God, justly to his neighbor, and spotless and holy as to himself. Indeed, this is incumbent upon each of us, so that we may live in this deceitful world and with this weak body so that our life may be rendered as an example to others; and let us sing the words of this Psalm in our own person to the glory of the Savior, who is above all things God, sublime and blessed. Amen.

PRAYER

ITH YOUR MERCY INTERVENING, O LORD, grant to us, we beseech you, not to adhere to a depraved heart; but make us always to walk innocently in the courts of your house, and so by us pleasing you, you might find us worthy to share in your eternal glory.

Misericordia tua, Domine, interveniente, praesta nobis, quaesumus,
cordi pravo non adhaerere; sed fac nos domus tuae
innocenter semper perambulare atria, quo tibi
placentes, aeternae gloriae tuae nos
digneris associare.

---

47 Ps. 50(51).
48 Gal. 5:16.
49 Ps. 83:b.
50 Ps. 150. E. N. *Praise the Lord in his holy places; praise him in the firmament of his power,* etc.

End of the Commentary
of the
Second Fifty Psalms

ABOUT THE TRANSLATOR

ANDREW M. GREENWELL IS A MARRIED Catholic layman, with three children and nine grand-children. He is a civil trial and appellate lawyer based in Corpus Christi, Texas, who has written articles for Catholic Online and for a number of years wrote a blog on the natural moral law called *Lex Christianorum*. He has translated works from German, Latin, French, and Italian into English. He is a member of the Latin Mass Community at St. John the Baptist Church in Corpus Christi, Texas. Angelico Press is publishing his translations of all of Denis the Carthusian's works on the Mass and the Eucharist.

Printed in the USA
CPSIA information can be obtained
at www.ICGtesting.com
LVHW092120141023
760910LV00033B/388/J